T3-BFD-873

MODERN WORKING CAPITAL MANAGEMENT

Text and Cases

Frederick C. Scherr
Department of Finance
West Virginia University

Prentice Hall
Englewood Cliffs, NJ 07632

LIBRARY OF CONGRESS
Library of Congress Cataloging-in-Publication Data

Scherr, Frederick C.
    Modern working capital management : text and cases / Frederick C.
Scherr.
    Bibliography.
    Includes index.
    ISBN 0-13-599317-2 : $35.00
    1. Working capital. 2. Business enterprises—Finance. 3. Working
capital—Case studies. 4. Business enterprises—Finance—Case
studies. I. Title.
HG4028.W65S34 1989   88-23814
658.1'5244—dc19   CIP

Editorial/production supervision and
   interior design: Fred Dahl
Cover design: Wanda Lubelska
Manufacturing buyer: Edward O'Dougherty

© 1989 by Prentice-Hall, Inc.
A Division of Simon & Schuster
Englewood Cliffs, New Jersey 07632

All rights reserved. No part of this book may be
reproduced, in any form or by any means,
without permission in writing from the publisher.

Printed in the United States of America

10 9 8 7 6 5 4 3

ISBN   0-13-599317-2

Prentice-Hall International (UK) Limited, *London*
Prentice-Hall of Australia Pty. Limited, *Sydney*
Prentice-Hall Canada Inc., *Toronto*
Prentice-Hall Hispanoamericana, S.A., *Mexico*
Prentice-Hall of India Private Limited, *New Delhi*
Prentice-Hall of Japan, Inc., *Tokyo*
Prentice-Hall of Southeast Asia Pte. Ltd., *Singapore*
Editora Prentice-Hall do Brasil, Ltda., *Rio de Janeiro*

To Sue, Tom, and Ellen

Contents

Preface

Working capital management is the management of the firm's short-term assets and liabilities, individually and in aggregate. Of all the functional areas of business financial decision making, the one that occupies the largest amount of the time and effort for practicing financial managers is the management of current assets and liabilities. Survey evidence shows that 60 percent of a financial manager's time is spent on decisions related to working capital management.[1] Credit management, cash management, inventory management, and accounts payable management are all part of the management of working capital. There are many more people employed in these endeavors than in other occupations concerned with the financial management of firms. Despite this prevalence in the workplace, however, the management of working capital has traditionally been neglected in academic programs and in academic research. This text is an attempt to partially remedy this neglect by providing a reference from which complete courses in the management of current assets and liabilities can be taught.

INTENDED AUDIENCE

This text is intended for senior undergraduates majoring in finance and for M.B.A. students concentrating in finance. It can be used as a primary text in a one-semester course in working capital management, or selected portions of it can be used as supplementary material for a course in corporate finance.[2]

---

[1]See Lawrence J. Gitman and Charles E. Maxwell, "Financial Activities of Major U. S. Firms: Survey and Analysis of Fortune's 1000," *Financial Management*, (Winter 1985), p. 60.

[2]Suggestions for tailoring this text to various audiences and uses may be found in the instructor's manual.

It can also be profitably used by finance practitioners wishing to update their knowledge of working capital management. Readers should possess a basic knowledge of business finance, algebra, basic calculus, probability and statistics, and common mathematical techniques such as integer programming. We assume that students have access to and can utilize a microcomputer, a spreadsheet package, and an integer programming package.[3] Access to and facility with a simulation package is useful but not necessary.

ORIENTATION AND FEATURES

This text is an improvement over other texts in working capital management in several respects. First, this text presents a balanced coverage of the various aspects of the topic. The management of cash, accounts receivable, inventory, and short-term liabilities all receive significant and approximately equal attention. Other texts have a more uneven coverage of the important topics in working capital management.

Second, we have strongly emphasized analysis and decision-making techniques that are in keeping with the principles of modern corporate finance. We have opted for emphasis on the state of the art as we see it; cash flows and shareholder wealth maximization are the benchmarks of our discussion. Students and instructors who are comfortable with such concepts as net present value and risk-adjusted discount rates will find this text to their liking. We avoid becoming involved with the minutiae of accounting techniques wherever possible.

Third, the analysis of risk is emphasized as an integral part of decision making. We will see that the very existence of working capital accounts is made necessary, in part, by risk. Consequently, risk considerations are a major part of working capital decisions. Discussions of numerous risk-pricing and hedging strategies are included in this text. For example, we present mechanisms for hedging the risk of cash shortages, the use of interest rate futures and options in hedging interest rate risk, and the use of currency futures and forwards to hedge exchange rate risk.

Fourth, while extensive examples of calculation methodologies occur frequently throughout, we have included cases as well as problem sets for each chapter within the text.[4] This is in keeping with the level of expected

---

[3]Within this text we have tried to keep the discussion of these packages as generic as possible. At West Virginia University we use the popular Lotus® 1-2-3® and LINDO® packages; we anticipate that many other universities are similarly equipped. However, for students who are fortunate enough to have access to a spreadsheet package with integer programming capacity, or to a spreadsheet package and an add-on program which utilizes spreadsheet files as integer programming inputs, familiarity with a separate integer programming package is not necessary.

[4]The cases within this text may be addressed at various levels; suggestions for use are given in the instructor's manual.

knowledge and expertise that we assume of our audience. Cases require not only a facility for the mathematical analysis techniques associated with a particular situation, but also the ability to identify problems, to make decisions based on incomplete data, and to deal with nonquantified considerations. These are important skills for the practicing business manager. All the cases in this volume have been extensively class tested.

Fifth, the text is heavily oriented toward the microcomputer. We believe that the use of a computer is vital to the student's understanding of financial techniques and prepares him or her for the conditions under which he or she will function in the business world. Examples of spreadsheet analysis occur in virtually every chapter, and data for the student's use in solving the cases are presented in spreadsheet format on a diskette.

Sixth, we have put extensive effort into the development of the instructor's manual and the instructor's diskette. We recognize that these aids are critical to the effective teaching of a nonintroductory course. It is useful for instructors to examine these aids before making decisions regarding text adoption.

Seventh, we have included a chapter on the management of working capital in an international setting. The increasingly worldwide nature of business relationships makes discussion of the special risks and issues in such dealings an important topic. Chapter 13, "Working Capital Management in International Settings," introduces the student to these risks and issues in the management of short-term international assets and liabilities.

Finally, we have included a review of survey evidence on the current practice of working capital management for each of the major topics in the text. There is a substantial amount of survey evidence on some of these topics, and a review of survey findings helps put the material presented in the text into perspective.

With these features and orientation, we have created a text that can be used on a stand-alone basis for courses in the management of working capital. Our aim was to eliminate the necessity for instructors to assign extensive lists of outside readings or additional case problems. By providing a course package consisting of an up-to-date text, challenging cases, a student diskette, an instructor's diskette, and an extensive instructor's manual, we hope to facilitate the teaching of working capital management.

ACKNOWLEDGMENTS

We express our gratitude to the financial researchers whose efforts have contributed to our thinking on various topics, to Scott Barr, the Finance Editor at Prentice Hall, and to those who reviewed parts of this text prior to publication or in other ways contributed directly to its development. Included among those making contributions were Scott Besley (University of South Florida), Ali Mansour (West Virginia University), Ike Mathur (Southern

Illinois University, Carbondale), Ed Roberts (Union Carbide Corporation), Venkat Srinivasan (Northeastern University), Timothy Sugrue (George Mason University), and Tirlochan Walia (Indiana University of Pennsylvania). Our thanks also goes to Susan Scherr, who provided extensive editorial advice. Finally, we thank the students at West Virginia University, who gave valuable feedback on earlier versions of the chapters and cases. All errors, of course, remain the author's own.

FCS

chapter 1

Introduction to the Management of Working Capital

This chapter sets forth the themes and concepts which form the basis for the discussion and analysis in this text. We first define working capital, then show why it exists and why it is important in the financial management of firms. We then present three sets of ideas that we will use extensively later: the principles of modern finance (shareholder wealth maximization and cash flow decision making), the importance of risk, and the role of the computer in its relationship to financial analysis. The organization of the rest of the book is also outlined, followed by a summary that concludes this chapter. As with the introductory chapters of most advanced texts, it is assumed that students are familiar with many of the concepts and ideas presented. However, the principles outlined in this chapter are so important that a thorough review and grounding is worthwhile.

WHAT IS WORKING CAPITAL MANAGEMENT?

The financial management of business firms involves three functions: the management of long-term assets, the management of long-term capital, and the management of short-term assets and liabilities. The first of these is *capital budgeting*, the second is the management of *capital structure*, and the last is *working capital management*. The management of working capital, which is the topic of this book, is concerned with the managment of the assets and liabilities in the *top half* of the balance sheet (see Figure 1-1). Included here are assets such as cash, marketable securities, accounts receivable, inventory, prepaid expenses, and other current assets; also, liabilities such as accounts payable, wages payable, and accruals. We will analyze decisions such as:

☐ How should the firm manage its cash?
☐ To whom should the firm grant credit?

1

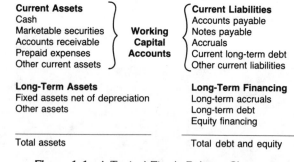

Figure 1-1. A Typical Firm's Balance Sheet.

☐ How much inventory should the firm keep?

☐ What should be the composition of the firm's current debt?

In any finance text, the authors must make a decision regarding what should be presented. Specifically, should the text concentrate on the current financial practices and procedures of existing firms or should it present the best that finance has to offer (the state of the art)? In this text, while some recognition of current procedure is included, we will concentrate on the *best* methods currently available. In this sense, the text is *prescriptive*: it recommends the most advantageous ways of addressing the problems of working capital management.

WHY IS WORKING CAPITAL NECESSARY?

To produce the best possible returns, firms should keep no unproductive assets and should finance with the cheapest available sources of funds. In this section, we discuss why, in general, it is often advantageous for the firm to invest in short-term assets and to finance with short-term liabilities. More detailed explanations for the existence of specific working capital accounts are provided later in the text.

In a "perfect" world, there would be no necessity for working capital assets and liabilities. In such a world, there would be no uncertainty, no transaction costs, information search costs, scheduling costs, or production and technology constraints. The unit cost of producing goods would not vary with the amount produced. Firms would borrow and lend at the same interest rate. Capital, labor, and product markets would reflect all available information and would be perfectly competitive. In such a world, it can be shown that there would be no advantage for firms to invest or finance in the short term.[1]

---

[1]See W. Beranek, "Towards a Positive Theory of Working Capital," available from W. Beranek at the University of Georgia.

But the world in which real firms function is not perfect. It is characterized by the firm's considerable uncertainty regarding the demand, market price, quality, and availability of its own products and those of suppliers. There are transactions costs for purchasing or selling goods or securities. Information is costly to obtain, and the firm is faced with limits on the production capacity and technology that it can employ. There are fixed as well as variable costs associated with producing goods for sale, and there are spreads between the borrowing and lending rates for investments and financings of equal risk. Information is not equally distributed and may not be fully reflected in the prices in product and labor markets, and these markets may not be perfectly competitive.

These real-world circumstances introduce problems with which the firm must deal. While the firm has many strategies available to address these circumstances, *strategies that utilize investment or financing with working capital accounts often offer a substantial advantage* over other techniques. For example, assume that the firm is faced with uncertainty regarding the level of its future cash flows and will incur substantial costs if it has insufficient cash on hand to meet expenses. Several strategies may be formulated to address this uncertainty and the costs that it may engender. Among these strategies are some that involve working capital investment or financing such as holding additional cash balances beyond expected needs, holding a reserve of short-term marketable securities, or arranging for the availability of additional short-term borrowing capacity.[2] One of these strategies (or a combination of them) may well be the least costly approach to the problem. Similarly, the existence of fixed set-up costs in the production of goods or of uncertainty regarding the future price or availability of goods may be addressed in several ways, but one possible alternative is to hold inventory.

By these examples, we see that strategies using working capital accounts are some of the possible ways firms can respond to many of the problems engendered by the imperfect and constrained world in which they deal. One of the major features of this world is uncertainty (risk), and it is this feature that gives rise to many of the strategies involving working capital accounts.

THE IMPORTANCE OF WORKING CAPITAL MANAGEMENT

In addition to its use as a means of handling uncertainty, the management of working capital plays an important role in maintaining the financial health of the firm during the normal course of business. This critical role can be seen by examining Figure 1-2, which loosely portrays the flow of resources through the firm. By far the major flow, in terms of its yearly magnitude, is

---

[2]These and other strategies for dealing with the uncertainty in the firm's cash flows will be discussed in Chapter 3.

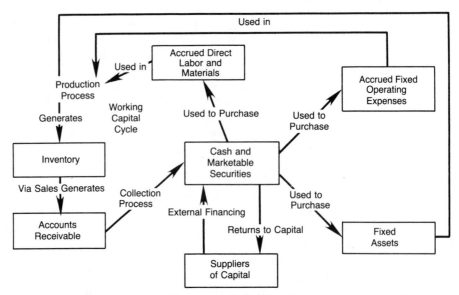

A square is a balance sheet account. An arrow indicates a flow. Note that, for a service firm, there is little or no inventory, so the inventory generation step is deleted. All the other parts of the resource flow cycle are unaffected.

Figure 1-2. *Resource Flows for a Manufacturing Firm.*

the *working capital cycle*. This is the loop which starts at the cash and marketable securities account, goes through the current accruals accounts as direct labor and materials are purchased and used to produce inventory, which is in turn sold and generates accounts receivable, which are finally collected to replenish cash. The major point to notice about this cycle is that *the turnover (or velocity) of resources through this loop is very high* relative to the other inflows and outflows of the cash account.

To see why this cycle is critically important to the firm's survival, visualize the cash account as a bathtub with both the drain and the faucet open. While there are other inflows and outflows, the *major* flow is the working capital cycle. As long as the firm has cash or marketable securities on hand, it can pay bills and thus survive. But if for some reason the resources stop flowing in, as when one of the working capital accounts slows in turnover and starts draining off resources, the level of the tub starts to fall. Unless the firm takes relatively costly action, such as raising new external funds, reducing dividend outflows, or postponing capital expenditures, the resources will all drain out, the firm will be unable to pay bills, and financial embarrassment will occur. It is clear that *the working capital cycle is the lifeblood of the firm.*

It would seem a practical solution to this problem to keep a very high balance in the cash and marketable securities account (analogous to a very high level of water in the bathtub). In this way, when flow problems occur, hasty and painful remedial actions will not be necessary since the large reserve provides some safety; the leaks can be plugged before the water is exhausted. However, as we will see in later chapters, such a strategy can depress the level of a firm's profitability, since cash and marketable securities are two of the firm's least profitable assets. Too little water (liquidity), and the firm is subject to bankruptcy risk if the inflow slows even slightly. Too much liquidity, and profits are lower than necessary. A major function of decision making for working capital is the management of the various working capital accounts with regard to the firm's level of liquidity: not too much liquidity and not too little liquidity.

Besides this basic and continuing reason for the importance of working capital management to the firm, several developments in the late 1970s and early 1980s led to increasing concern for the management of these accounts. One of these developments was a level of interest rates that climbed extremely high by historic standards. Working capital accounts, particularly accounts receivable and inventory, are major investments of the firm; the rise in interest rates caused the financing of investments to become more costly. A second development was the rapid evolution of deregulated money markets. This evolution provided financial managers with access to many new instruments for short-term financing and investment. Together, these developments kept corporate treasurers seeking new and better ways of managing individual working capital accounts to balance the firm's overall liquidity position.

PRINCIPLES OF MODERN FINANCE

To be most effective, management should be guided by a set of principles that can be applied to decision making in diverse situations. Over the last 30 years, financial researchers, including theoreticians and empiricists, have developed very significant insights about how financial markets work and how financial decisions should be made. The principles for financial decision making that were developed during this period form the basis for the management of working capital as discussed in this text. Two of the most important of these principles are *shareholder wealth maximization* and *cash flow decision making*.

Shareholder Wealth Maximization Let us first address the question of the appropriate goal of management in a publicly held firm. Shareholders, who own the firm, hire managers to act in such a way as to maximize their wealth. The only part of the shareholder's wealth that the manager can influence is the *market value of the firm's shares* held by the shareholder. We therefore say that *to maximize the wealth of shareholders, the firm should maximize the price of its shares*. In the finance literature, this is called the principle of *shareholder wealth maximization*.[3] The methodologies for the management of working capital presented in this text follow this principle.

Cash Flow Decision Making The principle of shareholder wealth maximization must be put into operation. Just what actions should managers take to maximize the trading price of the firm's shares? Since shares are valued in the capital market, specifying these actions requires an understanding of how such markets value shares. Until a few years ago, it was thought that the market valued (looked at in determining price) the accounting earnings of the firm. However, there has been considerable recent evidence that the market reflects, instead, the public information regarding the firm's *cash flows*. Accounting earnings appear to be valuable information only when they reflect cash flow.[4] Therefore, in order to maximize shareholder wealth, the firm should *maximize the value of the firm's cash flows*.

The principle of maximizing the value of the firm's cash flows raises two additional questions. First, what types of cash flows are we talking about? Second, how is the value of a cash flow to the firm determined? Referring to the first question, if markets allow for *existing* cash flows, then only *changes in cash flows* result in changes in the market price of shares. Thus changes in cash flows are relevant considerations in making financial decisions. We call these changes in cash flows the *marginal cash flow* associated with a financial decision.[5] For example, if the firm's cash flow is expected to be $100,000 in a particular period, and a given decision will increase the expected flow to $110,000, the marginal cash flow associated with this decision in that period is $10,000.

Turning now to the question of valuation, shareholders are assumed to be risk averse and (because of the time value of money) are assumed to value cash flows further in the future less than flows closer to the present. Thus,

---

[3]Note that it is assumed here that shareholders prefer more wealth to less. Note also that it is not implied that all real-world managers follow this principle; in fact, the structuring of compensation for managers so that they follow the principle of shareholder wealth maximation is a major concern in the business literature.

[4]Important articles in the area include S. Sunder, "Relationship between Accounting Changes and Stock Prices: Problems of Measurement and Some Empirical Evidence," in *Empirical Research in Accounting: Selected Studies*, 1973, pp. 1–45, and R. S. Kaplan and R. Roll, "Investor Evaluation of Accounting Information: Some Empirical Evidence," *Journal of Business* (April 1972), pp. 225–257. A review of the major literature is presented in T. E. Copeland and J. F. Weston, *Financial Theory and Corporate Policy*, Second Edition (Reading, Mass.: Addison-Wesley, 1983), pp. 319–327.

[5]For a relevant marginal cash flow to occur, the cash flows for the firm taken as a whole must change. Note that some financial decisions will change the cost allocation pattern of cash flows among the firm's units without changing the overall cash flows of the firm; such variations in allocation among units are irrelevant from a financial standpoint.

the riskier the cash flow and the further in the future it occurs, the less its contribution to the value of the firm's stock and thus to shareholder wealth. This risk and time pattern can be addressed via the use of *net present value with risk-adjusted discount rates*. In the risk-adjusted discount rate, net present-value procedure, the value of the cash flow is computed as:

$$\text{Net Present Value} = E(NCF_t)/(1+k)^t \tag{1-1}$$

where $E(NCF_t)$ is the expected net cash flow, k is the per-period risk-adjusted discount rate, and t is the number of periods in the future at which the cash flow is expected to occur. The risk-adjusted discount rate is determined as:

$$k = R_f + \text{risk premium} \tag{1-2}$$

where R_f is the risk-free rate and accounts for the time value of money, and the risk premium accounts for the risk of the cash flow.

For example, suppose that a marginal cash flow of $10,000 is expected to occur two periods in the future, the risk-free rate is 6 percent per period, and the risk premium for a flow of this level of riskiness is 9 percent per year. The risk-adjusted discount rate would be 15 percent and the net present value of the flow would be:

$$\text{Net Present Value} = \$10,000/(1.15)^2 = \$7,561 \tag{1-3}$$

The risk-free rate is usually estimated as the per-period interest rate on short-term federal government debt obligations. Methods of estimating the risk premium are discussed in the next section of this chapter.

The principles of modern finance may be summarized as follows: In making their decisions, the firm's managers should act so as to maximize the wealth of shareholders, which means to maximize the market price of their shares. This market price is maximized by making decisions based on the net present value of the marginal cash flows associated with the firm's decisions; higher net present values are preferred. While this sounds like a relatively simple procedure, a few caveats are in order. Many complications arise in the execution of this rule, and management consequently must be very careful in its application. Decisions regarding the firm's policies do not affect only shareholders; there are other stakeholders in the firm besides shareholders, including bondholders, employees, customers, and so forth. The reactions of these stakeholders to management decisions can affect shareholder wealth via the firm's cost of funds, labor expense, and sales revenue.[6] Also, because the market prices of shares reflect only public information, differences in

---

[6]See B. Cornell and A. Shapiro, "Corporate Stakeholders and Corporate Finance," *Financial Management* (Spring 1987), pp. 5–14.

information on the expected future cash flows of projects and their risk must be communicated to capital markets. This communication is a costly and difficult process.[7] While such difficulties pose a considerable challenge to management, they do not negate the basic principles of shareholder wealth maximization.

RISK AND FINANCIAL DECISION-MAKING

Because risk management is a major part of many working capital strategies, a substantial portion of this text will deal with risk in relation to working capital management. In finance, risk is dealt with in two steps. First, the amount and types of risk are *assessed* (measured or estimated in some way). Second, the assessed risk is *addressed* (accounted for in the decision-making process). Addressing risk takes two forms: either the risk may be *priced* within the financial decision process and/or a *hedging strategy* may be formulated to remove all or part of the risk. In this section, we review methods of assessing and addressing risk.

Assessing Risk   For the purposes of this text, we use two concepts of risk: *total risk* and *systematic risk*. "Total risk" is the total variability of returns from a decision, while "systematic risk" is the degree of comovement between the decision's returns and the returns on a large group of assets. The amounts of these risks are assessed in quite different ways. Total risk is assessed by *sensitivity analysis* and *simulation analysis*, and systematic risk is assessed by estimating the *beta* of the decision or project.

Sensitivity analysis is a method of estimating the effect of variation in *individual output variables* on important outcome variables.[8] Sensitivity anal-

---

[7]Providing accounting information (annual reports, and so forth) to the market does not solve this problem, since such accounting data deals with past cash flows, and is not primarily concerned with the future cash flows of the firm (which are used by the market to value shares). Research has shown that markets react to publicly available information, and not any information known to the firm's managers but not to the public (for a literature review, see Copeland and Weston, *Financial Theory*, pp. 285–307 and 327–346). Consequently, management must signal its estimates of future cash flows to the market in order to affect shareholder wealth. It may do this through public announcements, dividend policy, capital structure policy, management's holdings of the firm's shares, or in various other ways, though the resulting signals are subject to misinterpretation. See, for example, S. Ross, "The Determination of Financial Structure: The Incentive-Signalling Approach," *Bell Journal of Economics* (Spring 1977), pp. 23–40.

[8]An excellent discussion of sensitivity analysis is presented in K. L. Hastie, "One Businessman's View of Capital Budgeting," *Financial Management* (Winter 1974), pp. 36–44. Simulation analysis is discussed in B. D. Hertz, "Risk Analysis in Capital Investments," *Harvard Business Review* (January–February 1964), pp. 95–106 and in most major corporate finance texts.

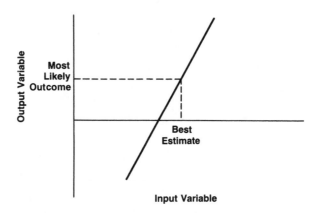

Figure 1-3. A Possible Sensitivity Analysis Plot.

ysis involves asking "what if" questions regarding the effect of one variable in a financial situation on another. For example, in a cash forecasting situation, the analyst might make estimates of the likely future levels of sales, fixed expenses, material and labor expenses, and so forth. The result of the analysis procedure, as we will see later in this text, is a forecast of future cash needs and surpluses that is very useful for planning purposes. But this forecast is subject to various uncertainties. What if sales are more or less than estimated? What if fixed expenses are higher than estimated? Sensitivity analysis addresses questions such as these, which occur frequently in the management of working capital and in other financial decisions.

To use sensitivity analysis to assess the relationship between an input variable and an important output variable of a financial analysis algorithm, the estimate of the input variable is changed, the algorithm is recomputed, and the effect on the outcome variable observed. After several such changes and recalculations, the results are graphed, with a result similar to that shown in Figure 1-3. A steeply sloped function indicates that the outcome variable is very sensitive to changes in the input variable; a relatively flat function indicates that the output variable is not very sensitive to changes in the input variable. Hence the name, "sensitivity analysis."

Sensitivity analysis is a very useful tool for the assessment of the risk associated with input variables. Using it, the analyst can decide which input variables are critical to a particular decision and which are not. Sensitivity analysis does not require the specification of probability distributions of the input variables. It can provide important information in many decision situations. Sensitivity analysis is, however, restricted to the assessment of *individual variable effects*. Firms, on the other hand, are often more concerned with the *total variability* of critical outcome variables. One method of estimating this total variability is simulation analysis.

Simulation analysis is an attempt to assess the total risk (variability) of outcomes based on variation in *all* the uncertain input variables taken si-

Table 1-1. Some Possible Probability Distributions Used as Part of the Simulation Analysis of a Cash Forecast.

Direct Labor as a Percent of Sales		Sales for January	
Percent	Probability	Dollars	Probability
61	.20	10,000	.10
62	.60	12,000	.25
63	.20	14,000	.30
		16,000	.25
		18,000	.10

multaneously. To do simulation analysis, the analyst starts by making estimates of the probability distributions of the variables which serve as inputs to the analysis process. For a cash forecast, the analyst would have to obtain estimates not only of the *most likely levels* of each uncertain variable (sales, fixed expenses, direct labor as a percent of sales, and so forth) but also of the *probabilities of other levels*. The estimated probability distributions may be continuous or discrete, but as a practical matter, businessmen are generally more comfortable estimating discrete distributions. Some probability distributions that might result are shown in Table 1-1.

Once every input variable that has any reasonable degree of uncertainty has been quantified in this way, analysis can begin. First, using a random number table or random number generator, an outcome for each uncertain variable for the first trial is determined. For example, consider the probability distribution of direct labor as a percent of sales in Table 1-1. If a two-digit random number was being used, there are 100 possible random numbers from 00 to 99. The analyst might assign the numbers 00–19 to 61 percent, 20–79 to 62 percent, and 80–99 to 63 percent. This way, the probabilities of occurrence of the three outcomes in the simulation procedure for this variable match those estimated by the analyst (for example, there is a 20 percent chance that direct labor will be 61 percent of sales, since this outcome is represented by the 20 numbers—00 through 19—of the possible 100). A random number would then be drawn; assume it is 82. This falls in the range for direct labor to be 63 percent of sales, which would then be the estimate of direct labor for the first trial. All the other uncertain variables would be determined for the trial in the same fashion. The analysis algorithm (in this example, the cash forecasting procedure) would then be executed using these trial variable values and the critical outcome variables (cash needs and surpluses by period in the case of a cash forecast) would be calculated. Several hundred trials would be run and a frequency histogram of the results generated. A typical histogram for a cash forecasting example is presented in Figure 1-4.

It should be obvious that a histogram of this sort gives a lot of useful information about the ranges of critical outcome variables and the probabilities of these ranges. The simulation analysis method is, however, not without

Figure 1-4. *A Possible Frequency Histogram Generated from the Results of a Simulation Analysis of a Cash Forecast.*

its difficulties. It requires estimates of the probability distributions of many variables. It is difficult to execute when there are significant covariances among the uncertain variables (that is, when drawings for input variables are not independent). Finally, it is computationally cumbersome.

In addition to total risk, which is assessed by sensitivity and simulation analysis, our other concept of the relevant risk for a decision is *systematic risk*, which is measured by beta. In this concept, total risk is divided into two components: *diversifiable risk* and *nondiversifiable risk* (also called systematic risk). Diversifiable risk is the risk particular to an individual asset, that is, the fluctuation in the asset's returns that is due to peculiarities of that asset. Nondiversifiable risk is the inherent economic risk common to all assets to varying degrees. Nondiversifiable risk can also be thought of as *market* or *general economic risk*. The total risk of any asset or security is the sum of its diversifiable and nondiversifiable risks. Diversifiable risk can, however, be avoided if the investor holds a sufficiently large number of assets (10 or 15 will do). Since investors do not like risk, they diversify away the diversifiable risk of their individual security holdings. Thus, in this concept only the non-diversifiable risk of the projects undertaken by the firms is said to matter to investors; only nondiversifiable risk then affects security prices.

Beta is a measure of nondiversifiable risk; it is the relative comovement of the project's returns with the returns on all assets and securities. Mathematically, beta is measured as:

$$b_i = COV(R_i, R_m)/VAR(R_m) \tag{1-4}$$

where b_i is the beta of project i, $COV(R_i, R_m)$ is the covariance of the return on the project with the market portfolio (a completely diversified portfolio of assets), and $VAR(R_m)$ is the variance of the return on the market portfolio. Betas of a firm's common shares are measured by regressing the returns on these shares with those of the market as a whole. Firms whose projects' returns do not vary as much as market returns (such as utility firms) tend to have common share betas less than one; firms whose projects' returns vary much more with market returns (such as manufacturers of recreational vehicles) tend to have common share betas greater than one. The beta of a firm's common shares can be used in evaluating new projects if these projects are expected to have the same beta as the firm's current average project.

However, when new projects are expected to differ in their response to nondiversifiable risk relative to existing projects, estimation of the appropriate beta is a bit more difficult. The finance literature suggests two methods of estimating a beta of such an individual project. The first, called the *pure-play technique*, involves finding a firm engaged solely in the line of business represented by the project and then using that firm's beta as an estimate of the nondiversifiable risk of the project. The other method involves finding several firms with divisions engaged in the line of business of the project and using *mathematical programming* to assess the betas of the relevant divisions. This divisional beta would then be used as the project's beta.[9]

Addressing Risk Once the amount of risk in a working capital or other financial decision has been assessed, the risk must be *priced* to reflect shareholders' risk aversion and/or a *hedging strategy* must be formulated to remove the risk. The firm may consider using either or both of these techniques relative to any financial decision. When risk is priced but not hedged, the cash flows are less valuable (because of shareholder risk aversion), but the firm does not bear the cost of a hedging strategy. Conversely, when a hedging strategy is employed, the expected cash flows are lower (because of the cost of the hedge), but are less risky.

Pricing risk when using net present value procedures involves the determination of the appropriate risk premium to use in discounting risky cash flows [see equation (1-2)]. There are two commonly used approaches to determining this risk premium: benchmark risk-adjusted discount rates and the Capital Asset Pricing Model (CAPM).[10]

Benchmark risk-adjusted discount rates can be used to reflect either total risk or systematic risk. In the benchmark risk-adjusted discount rate method, the analyst determines the appropriate risk premium by comparing the risk of the marginal cash flow with that of traded assets and employing

[9]For more extensive discussion of these methodologies, see R. J. Fuller and H. S. Kerr, "Estimating the Divisional Cost of Capital: An Analysis of the Pure-Play Technique," *Journal of Finance* (December 1981), pp. 997–1009, and J. A. Boquist and W. T. Moore, "Estimating the Systematic Risk of an Industry Segment: A Mathematical Programming Approach," *Financial Management* (Winter 1983), pp. 11–18.

[10]A third approach to the pricing of risk is the Arbitrage Pricing Theory (APT), originally presented in S. Ross, "The Arbitrage Theory of Capital Asset Pricing," *Journal of Economic Theory* (1976), pp. 341–360. In the APT, other factors besides the risk-free rate of interest and nondiversifiable risk (which are priced in the CAPM) may affect required return. However, more development is required before the APT can be widely used as a risk-pricing mechanism; see D. Bower, R. Bower, and D. Logue, "A Primer on Arbitrage Pricing Theory," *Midland Corporate Finance Journal*, Vol. 2, No. 3 (Fall 1984), pp. 31–40, particularly page 40.

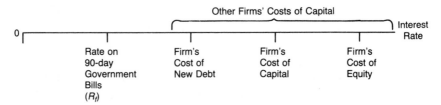

Figure 1-5. *Some Benchmark Market Interest Rates.*

the market's required returns for traded assets of comparable risk. Sometimes, a traded asset of similar risk to the cash flow being evaluated cannot be found, and the analyst must start with a market-required return and adjust upward or downward based on the relative risk of the cash flow being evaluated. This is called the "benchmark" procedure because the analyst starts with the market's required return on assets of known risk—the "benchmarks." These benchmarks may include the risk-free rate of interest, the firm's cost of debt, the firm's cost of capital, the firm's cost of equity, and other firms' costs of capital. Figure 1-5 presents some of these rates.

Let us replicate the logic of an analyst in deciding on a risk-adjusted discount rate using the benchmark method. He or she knows the current risk-free rate; this represents the time value of money with no risk. No risky cash flow can be discounted at a rate less than this. The analyst also knows the firm's marginal cost of capital, which represents the appropriate market-determined discount rate on projects that are as risky as the average project within the firm's current portfolio of projects. Assume that the cash flow being considered is perceived by the analyst to be slightly more risky than the firm's current cash flows from projects. (This risk estimate might be based on any of the risk assessment methodologies discussed previously, or it might be made in a more informal manner.) At this point, the analyst might judgmentally adjust the firm's cost of capital upward to a discount rate that is appropriate for this higher risk. Alternatively, he or she might compute the costs of capital of firms with similar financial structures (financial risk) where these firms are of business risk similar to that of the cash flow to be analyzed. In this way, a discount rate reflecting the time value of money and the appropriate level of business and financial risk would be estimated. It is obvious that this is in part a subjective process since adjustments are often made judgmentally from the benchmarks.

The capital asset pricing model (CAPM), like the risk-adjusted discount rate method, is used to determine the appropriate discount rate to apply to the expected value of a risky future cash flow.[11] The CAPM implies that the risk premium used in obtaining the appropriate discount rate should be based only on the nondiversifiable risk, not on the total risk, of a particular project.

---

[11]An extensive treatment of the capital asset pricing model can be found in Copeland and Weston, *Financial Theory*, pp. 185–211.

In the CAPM, only systematic risk is the relevant measure of the project's business risk. Unlike the benchmark method, the CAPM enables the analyst to directly compute the risk-adjusted discount rate associated with the risk of such a cash flow. Once the project's beta has been estimated, this statistic is used in the CAPM formula to obtain the required rate of return of shareholders for the equity investment in the project. The CAPM formula is:

$$R_i = R_f + b_i(R_m - R_f) \qquad (1\text{-}5)$$

where R_i is the required return on the equity investment in project i, R_m is the expected return on the market portfolio, and the other symbols are as before. This required return on equity investment is used in conjunction with the costs of the other sources of the firm's long-term capital and its target capital structure weights to estimate a required return for that particular project. For example, assume that a firm is trying to decide on an appropriate required rate of return for a particular project via the CAPM method. Based on the business line of the project, its beta is estimated as 1.4. The risk-free rate of interest is 6 percent per year and the expected return on a fully diversified portfolio of assets is 13 percent. The firm's capital structure includes 40 percent interest-bearing debt; new issues of debt are expected to yield 9 percent. The remaining 60 percent of the firm's capital structure is equity. The firm is in the 33 percent marginal tax bracket. To find the required return, we first use equation (1-5) to obtain the required return on equity for projects with a beta of 1.4 and the assumed market conditions:

$$R_i = 0.06 + 1.4(0.13 - 0.06) = 0.158 \qquad (1\text{-}6)$$

so the appropriate required return on equity is 15.8 percent per year. We then compute the required return for the project:

$$\text{Required Return} = 0.6(0.158) + 0.4(1 - 0.33)(0.09) = 11.9\% \qquad (1\text{-}7)$$

A comment on the benchmark risk-adjusted discount rate and CAPM methods is appropriate. Both are methods for determining the market's required returns for projects of a particular risk. These returns are then used in the net present value methodology to evaluate projects and other decisions. This project/decision evaluation procedure for physical assets is essentially a search for *excess returns*—projects/decisions whose net present value is greater than their market required returns.[12] A great deal is sometimes made about the fact that these two approaches do not necessarily produce exactly the same discount rate. There are several reasons for this: the judgmental nature

[12]Note that the search for excess returns is restricted to *physical assets*. In an arbitrage-free capital market, all traded securities are priced such that their net present values are zero; there are no excess returns to be made without insider information. See R. Roll, "A Critique of the Asset Pricing Theory's Tests," *Journal of Financial Economics* (March 1977), pp. 129–176.

of the benchmark process, statistical difficulties in the estimation of a project's beta, and so forth. However, there are about equal difficulties associated with the application of *either* method; neither method completely dominates. Thus, sophisticated firms should be familiar with each method and should make an informed choice based on their view of the situation. We will use both methods in determining risk-adjusted market rates of return at various points in this text.

Hedging Hedging means to adopt a strategy that negates, in whole or in part, the risk associated with a decision. Hedging strategies are used every day by financial managers and by the man on the street. "Saving for a rainy day" is a hedging strategy. The "Principle of Conservancy" in accounting is a hedging strategy. *The very act of carrying cash* is partly a hedging strategy. Hedging is quite different from risk pricing; risk pricing is a way of *allowing for risk that is not hedged*. Hedging as a method of controlling risk is very important in working capital management. In no other area of finance are there so many means for dealing with risk by hedging, though each of these means is costly. It is useful to think of hedging strategies as being of two types: *hedging strategies that do not use financial instruments* and *hedging strategies that use financial instruments*.

Hedging strategies that do not involve financial instruments may take several forms, but the most common involves the arrangement of additional available financing or the investment in additional assets beyond what is expected to be needed. Keeping a reserve of cash or of marketable securities to hedge cash flow risk is an example of this type of hedging. The best level for this type of hedge depends on several factors: the riskiness of the variable being hedged, the potential costs of going unhedged, and the costs of the hedge. One method of weighing these factors to produce an optimum strategy is *separate risk modeling*.

In separate risk modeling, two parameters of an uncertain variable—its expected value and its variability—are handled separately, using different modeling procedures. One strategy deals with the expected value of the variable under the assumption of certainty, and a second strategy hedges the uncertainty inherent in the variable. For example, in a popular approach to inventory management, optimal ordering strategies are generated based on expected sales levels, assuming that these levels are certain. Then, in a separate procedure, the uncertainty with regard to the sales level, the potential costs of events relative to this uncertainty, and the cost of hedges for this uncertainty are recognized (after the fact, so to speak) and a second methodology (determination of the safety stock level) is used to deal with these factors.

Another example of separate risk modeling and hedging can occur in cash forecasting. Here, a cash forecast can be generated using the expected values of all variables and an investment and financing plan formulated as if the cash flows are certain. As a hedge against uncertainty, the firm can keep a mix of cash, marketable securities, and a reserve line of credit. The amount of these reserves can be determined by the cost of carrying them, the degree of uncertainty in the cash forecast (determined by simulation), and the cost of running out of funds. We will use these separate risk modeling strategies to formulate hedges in inventory and cash forecasting situations later in the text.

Another hedging strategy is to use *financial instruments* to hedge risk. When these are available, they can provide effective and low-cost hedges to the uncertainties facing the firm. Financial hedging instruments include *futures contracts*, *forward contracts*, *options*, and *options on futures contracts*. Currently available instruments can be used to hedge changes in interest rates, changes in exchange rates among currencies, changes in the price of purchased inventory, and other risks. Options can be valued via the Option Pricing Model (OPM). We will discuss these instruments at length later in the text.

Risk analysis and risk hedging are relatively new aspects of financial analysis and financial management. Sophisticated strategies of this sort are, to a great extent, the outgrowth of the improved calculation and data analysis capacity available to financial managers. We discuss this new calculation capacity in the next section.

THE COMPUTER IN FINANCE

By far the most important technological innovation affecting financial analysis in recent years has been the advent of inexpensive and readily available computing capacity. A microcomputer is on the desk of virtually every financial analyst at progressive and innovative firms. The primary impact of this cheap computing capacity and user-friendly software has been the ease with which previously laborious financial analysis can now be performed and, in particular, the heightened ability of firms to assess risk. Previously, if the firm was going to perform a particularly tedious procedure, such as a forecast for the next year's cash flows for each month, it was quite costly in time and effort to go through the procedure even once. Thus, analysis was often limited to one pass through the algorithm, utilizing the best estimates of the input variables. Sensitivity and simulation analysis procedures could be justified only for the most critical decisions. But the microcomputer revolution has changed all that. Now, the changing of input variables and the observation of the effects on output variables takes seconds, not hours. Procedures to assess risk, which in the past were too expensive, can now be performed routinely.

Three types of microcomputer software are currently available and are useful for the analysis of working capital decisions: the *spreadsheet*, the *mathematical programming package*, and the *simulation package*. Spreadsheets are now a commodity item; dozens are on the market. Spreadsheets consist of rows and columns, and are useful in the analysis of many types of finance problems. The power of the spreadsheet stems from its *copying feature* and its *quick execution of recalculations*. The former is useful if the financial analysis procedure requires more than a few similar calculations; it makes model building in such circumstances much easier and faster than manual methods. If the analyst wants to see the effect of a deviation from the original estimate on important outcome variables, the quick recalculation feature of the spreadsheet makes substantial analysis feasible; the analyst merely changes the data or formula, and the spreadsheet automatically recalculates all the other cells. However, one note of warning is appropriate. Spreadsheets are a financial modeling tool, not an end in themselves. The data outputs they provide are only as good as the estimated input data and the financial algorithms used.[13]

While spreadsheets are very useful in a number of respects, they are tools of *analysis*, not *optimization*. Some of the problems we study in the management of working capital are such that an *optimum* solution can be found by the proper application of *mathematical programming techniques*. These techniques should be familiar to all students of finance; among them are *linear programming* (where all the variables may assume noninteger values) and *integer programming* (where only one or several variables may assume integer values). Mathematical programming packages, like spreadsheets, are now available from numerous software houses. In this text, we will be using an integer programming approach to several working capital decisions. However, because of the complexity of the theory and calculation procedures necessary to solve this mathematical algorithm, it is not our purpose in this text to discuss solution procedures. Instead, our emphasis will be on describing the formulation of the objective function and constraint equations necessary to execute this algorithm. Students interested in the mathematics of solving integer programming problems may consult any good operations research text.

Simulation programs are less common and less well developed than spreadsheets and mathematical programming software. Consequently, simulation is often a very time-consuming analysis methodology for the student to execute, though its results are quite useful. While several opportunities for simulation analysis occur in this text, our discussion of it will focus mainly on the use of simulation results rather than on the actual programming of simulation models.

ORGANIZATION OF THIS TEXT

The reader should now have some feeling for what working capital is, why its management is critical to the firm's survival and prosperity, and the concepts and methodologies used in its analysis. It is appropriate at this point

---

[13]For a good discussion of these problems, see R. M. Freeman, "A Slip of the Chip on Computer Spread Sheets Can Cost Millions," *The Wall Street Journal*, August 20, 1984, p. 11.

to discuss the organization of the remainder of this text. Chapters 2 through 4 discuss the management of cash and marketable securities, addressing decisions regarding how much cash the firm should keep and how investments in marketable securities can best be made. The next part of the text, consisting of Chapters 5 through 7, concerns the management of accounts receivable. Here, we discuss decisions regarding the monitoring of accounts receivable balances, the firm's terms of sale, and the granting of credit to the firm's customers. Inventory management is discussed in Chapters 8 and 9. These chapters address the firm's inventory strategy: how much of various types of goods to keep, when and how much to order, and so forth. Chapter 10 discusses the firm's aggregate liquidity decision, which involves the firm's overall structure of current assets and liabilities. The measurement of total liquidity is investigated, and the risk-return tradeoffs involved are discussed. Chapters 11 and 12 involve the structuring of the firm's current liabilities accounts such that the costs of these liabilities are minimized. The final chapter, Chapter 13, discusses the management of international working capital.

SUMMARY

In this chapter, several important concepts that form the basis for the remainder of the text were introduced. Working capital was defined as the firm's short-term assets and liabilities. Working capital is made necessary by the imperfect nature of the real market and production situations faced by firms. Working capital management is a critical concern of management, since the working capital cycle is the major cash flow through the firm. Basic principles of modern finance were reviewed, including the idea that the appropriate goal of managers is maximizing the market price of their firm's common shares. This requires that managers act so as to maximize the net present value of marginal cash flows. Also reviewed were the methods by which risk will be assessed and addressed in this text. Sensitivity analysis, simulation, and beta estimation will be used for assessing risk. The risk estimated via these techniques may be addressed via pricing or hedging. We will use benchmark risk-adjusted discount rates and the CAPM for pricing; hedging procedures will include separate risk modeling (in which nonfinancial instruments provide the hedge) and the use of futures, forwards, options, and options on futures as hedging vehicles. The chapter included a discussion of the importance of the microcomputer to modern financial management, recounting the types of programs of primary use in the management of working capital and their advantages over manual procedures.

Working capital management, and finance as a whole, is a rapidly changing specialization. We trust that serious students will be challenged and enlightened by the remainder of this text as we put the principles outlined in this chapter to work.

Problems

1-1. Lane Toys, a small toy manufacturer, has experienced modest growth and reasonable profitability over the last three years. Purchases of property, plant, and equipment have been carefully controlled, as have dividend payouts and debts. Despite this, the firm has run out of cash:

	Lane Toys		
	Financial Statements		
	(rounded thousands)		
Date	*12/31/85*	*12/31/86*	*12/31/87*
Statements of Income and Retained Earnings			
Sales	$13,000	$13,650	$14,060
Cost of Goods Sold	9,100	9,555	9,842
Selling and Admin. Expenses	1,950	2,048	2,109
Earnings Before Taxes	$ 1,950	$ 2,048	$ 2,109
Taxes	683	717	738
Earnings After Taxes	$ 1,268	$ 1,331	$ 1,371
Common Dividends	$ 507	$ 532	$ 548
Changes in Retained Earnings	$ 761	$ 799	$ 822
Balance Sheets			
Cash	$ 150	$ 118	$ −6
Accounts Receivable	1,561	1,852	2,228
Inventories	2,090	2,551	3,076
Other Current Assets	100	105	108
Total Current Assets	$ 3,901	$ 4,627	$ 5,406
Net Fixed Assets	$ 7,000	$ 7,350	$ 7,570
Total Assets	$10,901	$11,977	$12,977
Accounts Payable	$ 379	$ 398	$ 410
Accrued Wages	455	478	492
Other Current Liabilities	100	110	120
Total Current Liabilities	$ 934	$ 986	$ 1,022
Long-Term Debt	4,500	4,725	4,867
Common Equity	5,467	6,266	7,088
Total Liabilities and Equity	$10,901	$11,977	$12,977

Compute the following ratios as of the end of each of the last three fiscal years (12/31/8X) for Lane Toys:

a. Earnings After Taxes/Total Assets

b. Sales/Net Fixed Assets

c. Year-to-Year Sales Growth

d. Total Debt/Total Assets

e. Current Ratio

f. Sales/Accounts Receivable

g. Cost of Goods Sold/Inventory

Discuss these results relative to the working capital cycle. Indicate why the firm has run out of cash despite its continuing profitability.

Selected Readings

Beranek, W., "Towards a Positive Theory of Working Capital," available from the author at the University of Georgia.

Copeland, T. E., and J. F. Weston, *Financial Theory and Corporate Policy*, Second Edition (Reading, Mass.: Addison-Wesley, 1983) Chapters 2, 4, 7, 9, 10, 11, and 12.

Freeman, R. M., "A Slip of the Chip on Computer Spread Sheets Can Cost Millions," *Wall Street Journal*, August 20, 1984, p. 11.

Hastie, K. L., "One Businessman's View of Capital Budgeting," *Financial Management* (Winter 1974), pp. 36–44.

Hertz, B. D., "Risk Analysis in Capital Investments," *Harvard Business Review*, 42 (January–February 1964), pp. 95–106.

Citizens' Band Antenna Company
The Working Capital Cycle

The Citizens' Band (CB) is a set of radio frequencies near 27 megahertz of the radio spectrum that has been set aside in the United States for personal, low-power communication. This type of communication underwent an upsurge in popularity in the mid-1970s. Communication on any radio frequency requires certain equipment comprised principally of a transmitter and receiver (or, more commonly, a combination of the two, called a transceiver) and an antenna. The main beneficiaries of the CB boom were manufacturers of transceivers (mostly Japanese electronics firms) and manufacturers of antennas. The Citizens' Band Antenna Company was one of the latter.

The Citizens' Band Antenna Company was a family-owned firm. Prior to the upsurge in the popularity of CB radio, the firm had sold a mix of antennas for industrial, military, and amateur ("ham") radio applications as well as antennas for CB frequencies. Antennas are generally frequency-specific. For example, those made for the frequencies used in amateur radio do not work well in other applications. When CB radio became popular, executives of the Citizens' Band Antenna Company decided to devote the firm's full manufacturing capability to this marketplace, and had changed the firm's name to the current one to reflect this new emphasis.

The various types of CB antennas (called "beam antennas," "vertical antennas," and so forth) were all manufactured from tubing, wire, plastic parts, and other components. The firm did some fabrication in-house, including all final assembly work, while some of the manufacturing steps (including the molding of all plastic parts) were subcontracted. Labor and materials accounted for approximately equal portions of the firm's cost of goods sold.

As of the end of fiscal 1974, the firm was financed by long-term loans from a local bank and by equity. The bank loans were secured by the firm's fixed assets, and new term loans were taken out as needed when such assets were purchased. The original contribution of equity capital by family members had grown substantially over the years, and as of December 31, 1974, the book net worth of the firm stood at $1,178,000. Many of the family members were retired and living in part on the dividends paid by the firm. Several younger family members were employed there.

While some of the firm's sales were directly to the public, the majority were made

Exhibit 1

Financial Statements
Citizens' Band Antenna Company
Fiscal Years 1974 to 1976
(thousands of dollars)

Statements of Income and Retained Earnings

Fiscal Year Ending	*12/31/74*	*12/31/75*	*12/31/76*
Sales	$2,896	$3,695	$4,878
Cost of Goods Sold	2,062	2,712	3,464
Depr., Int., and Admin. Exp.	356	484	590
Earnings Before Taxes	$ 478	$ 499	$ 824
Taxes	220	230	379
Earnings After Taxes	$ 258	$ 269	$ 445
Common Dividends	129	134	156
Changes in Retained Earnings	$ 129	$ 135	$ 289

Balance Sheets

	12/31/74	*12/31/75*	*12/31/76*
Cash	$ 145	$ 185	$ 73
Marketable Securities	174	0	0
Accounts Receivable	278	409	588
Inventory	255	401	572
Other Current Assets	28	36	49
Total Current Assets	$ 880	$1,031	$1,282
Gross Fixed Assets	$2,172	$2,571	$3,258
Less: Accumulated Depreciation	1,086	1,125	1,194
Net Fixed Assets	$1,086	$1,446	$2,064
Total Assets	$1,966	$2,477	$3,346
Accounts Payable	$ 82	$ 108	$ 337
Accrued Wages	82	108	139
Other Accruals	74	98	118
Short-Term Notes Due	0	150	300
Current Portion—L.T.D.	50	60	70
Total Current Liabilities	$ 288	$ 524	$ 964
Long-Term Debt	$ 500	$ 640	$ 780
Common Stock	$ 100	$ 100	$ 100
Retained Earnings	1,078	1,213	1,502
Total Common Equity	$1,178	$1,313	$1,602
Total Liabilities and Equity	$1,966	$2,477	$3,346

to jobbers and electronics supply houses. Fiscal 1974 had been a banner year for the firm in terms of sales and profits, but things were actually just starting to move. Demand for the firm's products was even higher in 1975. In response to this, the firm added extra workers, scheduled a second production shift, purchased some new equipment, and increased inventories.

Despite this seemingly rosy picture, the firm started to have cash flow problems in fiscal 1975. Executives of the firm were forced to liquidate the firm's portfolio of marketable securities, which had been used as temporary investments during periods of the year when the firm had surplus funds, and instead funded seasonal variations in asset needs by borrowing on a new short-term credit line from the firm's bank. Because of funding shortages, the firm was forced to curtail some fixed asset acquisition plans.

The firm's financial executives initially blamed the firm's problems on lower-than-expected profitability; although sales had increased by 27.6 percent from fiscal 1974 to fiscal 1975, earnings after taxes had increased by only 4.3 percent. (Exhibit 1 shows the firm's balance sheets and income statements for the fiscal years 1974 through 1976.) Their initial

effort in 1976 was therefore directed at cost cutting. Overtime work and administrative expenses were controlled closely, even as sales kept expanding. Still, the firm seemed continually short of cash. More long-term debt was borrowed. Fixed asset purchases were postponed again. More short-term borrowings were utilized. The firm's cash account was allowed to decline to what the firm's treasurer believed was a dangerously low level.

As the fiscal year 1976 progressed, the situation grew desperate. The firm's management took two further steps which they had been loathe to do previously: they cut the firm's dividend payout rate and then implemented a policy of delaying payments to trade suppliers beyond the suppliers' stated terms of sale.

In summary, the firm's two-year record involved an increase in sales of 68.4 percent and an increase in profits of 72.5 percent. Despite these seemingly magnificent results, the executives of the firm had the strong suspicion that if the firm had one more year of this sort of success, it would end up in bankruptcy court. They wondered what had happened and what they could do about it (although their exact sentiments were almost always expressed in much stronger language).

chapter 2

Managing Cash Inflows
And Outflows

This is the first of three chapters dealing with *cash management*. The term "cash management" refers to the management of cash from the time it starts its transit to the firm until it leaves the firm in payments. Cash management encompasses the design of collection and disbursement systems for cash and the temporary investment of cash while it resides with the firm.[1] In this chapter, systems for efficiently gathering, investing, and disbursing cash are discussed. But first, it is useful to consider why it is advantageous for firms to hold cash and similar assets at all.

WHY HOLD CASH AND MARKETABLE SECURITIES?

Cash and short-term, interest-bearing investments (marketable securities) are the firm's least productive assets. They are not required in producing goods or services, unlike the firm's fixed assets. They are not part of the process of selling as are inventory and accounts receivable. When firms hold cash in currency or in noninterest-bearing checking accounts, they obtain no direct return on their investment. Even if the cash is temporarily invested in marketable securities, its return is much less than the return on other assets held by the firm. So why hold cash or marketable securities at all? Couldn't the firm's resources be better deployed elsewhere?

Despite the seemingly low returns, there are several good reasons why firms hold cash and marketable securities. It is useful to think of the firm's portfolio of cash and marketable securities as comprised of three parts with each part addressing a particular reason for holding these assets.

[1]For a critical review of the techniques available to address these tasks, see V. Srinivasan and Y. Kim, "Deterministic Cash Flow Management: State of the Art and Research Directions," *Omega*, Vol. 14 No. 2 (1986), pp. 145–166.

Cash for Transactions One very important reason for holding cash in the form of noninterest-bearing currency and checking deposits is *transactions demand*. Since debts are settled via the exchange of cash, the firm must hold some cash in the bank to pay suppliers and some currency to make change if it makes sales for cash.

Cash and Near-Cash Assets as Hedges Unfortunately, the firm's future cash needs for transactions purposes are often quite uncertain; emergencies may arise for which the firm needs immediate cash. The firm must hedge against the possibility of these unexpected needs. Several types of hedges are possible. For example, the firm can arrange to be able to borrow from its bank on short notice should funds suddenly be needed. Another approach is to hold extra cash and near-cash assets beyond what would be needed for transactions purposes. By "near-cash assets," we mean interest-earning marketable assets that have *very* short maturities (a few days or less), and thus can be liquidated to provide funds on short notice with very little risk of loss.

Clearly, the more of this total hedging reserve held in near-cash assets and the less held in cash, the greater the interest earned. However, there is a trade-off between this interest revenue and the transactions costs involved in purchasing and selling such near-cash assets. These transactions costs have a fixed cost component; the firm bears these fixed costs when it buys or sells these assets regardless of the size of investment. Thus, whether it is economical to invest part or all of the hedging reserve in near-cash assets depends on the dollar amount of the reserve. Firms that keep smaller reserves (because their transactions needs are either smaller or more certain) are more likely to hold these reserves in cash, while firms with larger reserves keep them in near-cash assets.

Temporary Investments Many firms experience some seasonality in sales. Often, there will be times during the year when such firms have excess cash that will be needed later in the year. Firms in this situation have several choices. One alternative is to pay out the excess cash to its security holders when this cash is available, and then issue new securities later in the year when funding is needed. However, the costs of issuing new securities usually make this a disadvantageous strategy. More commonly, firms will temporarily invest the cash in interest-earning marketable securities from the time the cash is available until the time it is needed. Proper planning and investment selection for this strategy can yield a reasonable return on such temporary investments; we will discuss this planning and strategy in Chapter 3.

All of these are valid reasons for holding cash and marketable securities in response to the needs and uncertainties faced by the firm. In fact, firms generally hold a surprisingly large portion of their assets in these forms, despite the disadvantage of low returns. Between 1978 and 1982, large firms held, on average, 7.7 percent of their assets in cash and marketable securities.[2]

Those readers who are familiar with the requirements of some firm's relations with banks will want to know why *compensating balances* have not been listed as a reason for holding cash. "Compensating balances" are non-interest-bearing deposits made by firms with their banks as part of their banking arrangements. Historically, banks have required firms to make such deposits (which the banks then loaned out at interest) as repayment for the availability of reserve credit lines and other functions that banks perform for their clients. However, recent developments in the banking industry have rendered this approach increasingly less common relative to fee-based systems of bank compensation. Since the orientation of this text is toward *modern* working capital management, we will concentrate on these fee-based systems.[3] If the firm uses fee-based banking, it does not need to hold cash for the purposes of compensating balances.

THE MONEY MARKET

In the above discussion of the reasons for holding cash and near-cash assets, it was suggested that near-cash, interest-earning assets could be substituted for cash when the motivation for holding these assets is the hedging of cash flow uncertainties or is the temporary investment of surplus funds. In either case, a primary concern of the cash manager is the *safety and liquidity* of the investment instrument used, since the money will eventually be needed for the operations of the firm. Near-cash assets of high safety and liquidity are traded in the *money market*. For larger corporations with strong financial positions, the money market also provides a source of short-term borrowings. It is important for the student of working capital management to be familiar with the basic instruments of the money market that are used by many firms as investment alternatives to cash and by larger firms as financing vehicles. While all the instruments traded in this market are quite safe relative to other investments (such as common stock), they differ somewhat in risk and return. One difference in per-period investment return is the *yield curve effect*, also known as the *term structure of interest rates*.

[2]See James Vander Weide and Steven Maier, *Managing Corporate Liquidity: An Introduction to Working Capital Management* (New York: John Wiley, 1985), p. 4.

[3]See Jarl Kallberg and Kenneth Parkinson, *Current Asset Management: Case, Credit, and Inventory* (New York: Wiley, 1984), pp. 76–8. Further, if firms choose to use one or more banks that require compensating balances rather than fees, it is possible to convert required compensating balances into equivalent fees; see Kallberg and Parkinson, *Current Asset Management*, pp. 67–75.

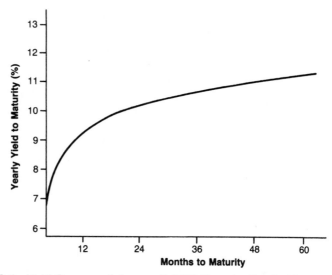

Figure 2-1. *Yield Curve as of January 7, 1985 Treasury Bonds, Notes, and Bills.*

Term Structure of Interest Rates The term structure of interest rates relates the market's required return on an asset to the time to maturity of that asset. The market relationship between time to maturity and required return can be observed in the plot of the yield to maturity of securities versus their time to maturity; this plot is called the *yield curve*. An example is shown in Figure 2-1.

This curve represents the required returns on securities of a given default risk for various times to maturity. That is, it plots the supply/demand intersections for securities of various maturities. These required returns may be influenced by various factors, such as the level of inflationary expectations, the relative levels of supply and demand for securities of different maturities, and differences in investors' perceptions of the interest rate risk of securities of different maturities. The three most common theories of the determination of term structure of interest rates are based on these differences in inflation, relative demand, and risk among securities of various maturities.[4] *Expectations theory* holds that the differences in per-period required returns among securities of various maturity dates reflect expectations that inflation will change over time. If the near-term inflation is expected to be high, for example, that expectation will raise interest rates on the short-maturity end of

[4]More complete discussions of theories of interest rate determination and yield curve level and shape can be found in T. E. Copeland and J. F. Weston, *Financial Theory and Corporate Policy*, Second Edition (Reading, Mass.: Addison-Wesley, 1983) pp. 65–70 and in E. F. Brigham and L. C. Gapenski, *Intermediate Financial Management* (Chicago: Dryden, 1985) pp. 584–92.

the yield curve more than on the long-maturity end. *Market segmentation theory* holds that investors have preferences for securities of different maturities, and the yield curve's level and shape reflect the availability of various maturities relative to these preferences. For example, if there is a large supply of securities with a particular maturity relative to demand for that maturity, the price of securities with that maturity declines and the yield to maturity rises. Upsloping yield curves in this theory are present when there are relatively larger supplies of longer maturities, and downsloping yield curves are present when there are relatively larger supplies of shorter maturities. *Maturity preference theory* holds that the shape of the yield curve is merely a reflection of the differences in interest rate risk among maturities. In particular, longer maturities are said to contain more interest rate risk, and therefore have higher required rates of return than do shorter maturity issues. Interest rate risk is the relationship between the interest rate prevailing at the time and the trading price of the security. Because the repayment of principal is further in the future, the prices of longer-term securities fluctuate much more with changes in interest rate levels than do the prices of shorter-term securities. They are, therefore, riskier, and investors require a higher return on them.

Maturity preference theory has substantial appeal because it explains one of the important *empirical* observations about the yield curve: *it is usually positively sloped*. Yield curves are upsloping most of the time, although they can sometimes be flat or even negatively sloped. One implication of this empirical phenomena is that, on average, the longer the maturity of the security, the higher the per-period rate of return.

One important aspect of the yield curve with respect to the firm's investments in cash and near-cash assets is the risk-return trade-off that is caused by its (usually) positive slope. The longer the term to maturity of the investment, the higher the per-period yield. Therefore, there is an incentive for firms to invest in longer-term securities. Offsetting this is the greater interest rate risk for longer maturities; if the investing firm chooses a security with a longer maturity and is forced to sell that security before maturity and if interest rates have risen, the return achieved may be less than had the firm invested in shorter-term securities. This interest rate risk can be reduced by hedging with interest rate futures, a technique that will be discussed in Chapter 3.

In addition to yield curve effects, risks and returns among near-cash assets differ because of the *default risk* characteristics of their issuers. Some securities are extremely safe while others entail a nonzero probability of default, and carry higher interest rates to compensate buyers for this risk. At this point it is useful to present a list of typical money market instruments that are used by firms as investment alternatives to cash with discussion of their relative returns and default risks. We call this a list of "typical" money market instruments because of the fluid and consumer-oriented nature of this market. The money market is relatively unregulated and is very competitive.

Consequently, there is quite a large amount of continuing product innovation; issuers and dealers continually seek instruments that draw investment funds, generating commissions for dealers and lowering financing costs for the firms issuing the securities. With this diversity of products, many strategies are used, and firms will rapidly change strategy in response to new instruments and conditions. Thus, any list of currently popular money market instruments is subject to rapid obsolescence.[5]

Treasury Bills These are securities sold by the U.S. government, generally with maturities of 91, 182, or 365 days. They are considered to be free of default risk, although interest rate risk occurs, particularly in the longer maturities. They are sold at a discount and redeemed at their principal value at maturity. They can be bought through banks, dealers in government securities, or directly from the government.

Treasury bills (called T-bills) are quite popular as investment alternatives to cash. There are several reasons for this. First, they can be purchased in very low denominations (as little as $10,000), although when investments are made in small amounts the costs of purchase and sale are relatively higher and will lower the net yield. Second, they are extremely liquid. There is a very active secondary market for T-bills, and the firm's position can be liquidated at any time. This is a very valuable feature if the firm holds securities as a hedge against cash flow uncertainties, since the money may be needed quickly. This active secondary market also means that the firm's investments in T-bills need not be limited to the maturities of new issues. For example, if the firm needs a three-day investment, it need only purchase, in the secondary market, a T-bill with three days to maturity.

Treasury bills are issued directly by the U.S. government. The federal government also issues debt instruments through its federal agencies, such as the Federal National Mortgage Association and the Federal Home Loan Bank Board. These debt instruments are issued in various maturities, many under one year, and in various denominations. While there is a slight chance that the federal government might let these quasi-public agencies default, the probability is so small that these investments are generally considered to be almost free of default risk. They are traded through securities dealers. The traded volume of these securities is less than that of T-bills and other securities issued directly by the federal government.

The default-free nature of T-bills is both a positive and a negative feature in cash management. While it means that the principal is safe (except for

---

[5]For a more complete discussion of short-term investment vehicles, see Timothy Cook and Bruce Summers, eds., *Instruments of the Money Market*, Fifth Edition (Richmond: Federal Reserve Bank of Richmond, 1981) or James Vander Weide and Steven Maier, *Managing Corporate Liquidity: An Introduction to Working Capital Management* (New York: John Wiley, 1985), pp. 169–90.

interest rate risk), it also means that T-bills earn a lower return than do instruments with a bit more default risk. To earn extra return, many firms are willing to invest in slightly riskier instruments, such as commercial paper.

Commercial Paper Commercial paper is large-denomination, unsecured debt, generally in maturities of about 30 days. It is issued by firms, finance companies, and bank holding companies, and provides financing for such companies as well as an investment vehicle for the surplus funds of firms. Some larger issuers sell a portion of their commercial paper directly to investors, but the majority is sold through commercial paper dealers.

Since there is some default risk involved, the yields on commercial paper are often quite a bit higher than the yields on T-bills of the same maturity. This risk is somewhat lessened by the general requirement that issuers of commercial paper obtain backup lines of credit from commercial banks in the amount of their commercial paper borrowings to refund the paper if the firm is unable to sell new debt when the paper comes due. Default risk on commercial paper can be estimated by the ratings of this paper; these ratings are issued by ratings services. Fitch Investor Service, Moody's Investor Service, and Standard & Poors Corporation all issue ratings on commercial paper.

Certificates of Deposit These are very large-denomination debt instruments issued by banks. They are of various maturities, sometimes longer than one year. Shorter maturities carry a prespecified interest rate, but some variable-rate certificates are sold among the longer maturities. Because the Federal Deposit Insurance Corporation insures bank debts only up to $100,000, and principal on the certificates of deposit used as investments for large firms' surplus cash are commonly over $1 million, these securities are subject to the risk of failure of the issuing bank, and yields are consequently above those of U.S. government issues. Certificates of deposit are placed directly with investors; some are also traded in the secondary market by dealers. In addition to the standard certificates, firms with a substantial amount of funds to lend may also negotiate private purchases of certificates or time deposits with major banks; these private deals can be tailored to the firm's specific needs.

Banker's Acceptances Like certificates of deposit, these are issued by banks, but are slightly safer because of the security arrangements entailed. Banker's acceptances are generated in the course of international trade, and the holder of a banker's acceptance has recourse to both the issuing bank and the purchaser of the goods. Given the very small likelihood of *both* the purchaser and the bank defaulting, banker's acceptances are relatively safe investments. Banker's acceptances are traded through dealers and are quite liquid.

Repurchase Agreements Repurchase agreements (repos) are used for very short-term investments and financing. In a repo, the seller agrees to sell a security (usually a T-bill) to the buyer, and the seller also agrees to repurchase the security a few days later at a higher price. The return on the investment is the difference between the sale price and the agreed-upon buy-back price, and represents the appreciation, over the period, of the discounted security that serves as collateral. Since the loan of the funds to the seller of the repo is collateralized, the transaction is substantially safer than an unsecured loan. Aside from the security provided by the collateral, the repo transaction is a loan and can also be used for financing purchases (by selling the contract rather than purchasing it). Government agencies (both federal and state), banks, and firms make extensive use of repos for short-maturity (often overnight) borrowing and lending.

The danger in repos is fraud. In purchasing a repo from a dealer, the investor trusts the dealer to, in fact, possess the security used as collateral; the security itself is not exchanged. If, however, the dealer does not possess the collateral, investors can sustain substantial losses.[6]

Eurodollars These are dollar-denominated loans and certificates of deposit in non-U.S. banks. (This is called the "Eurodollar Market," although the funds may be located anywhere in the world.) Because of their international character, we will defer detailed discussion of Eurodollar investments and financing until Chapter 13. Suffice to say that these must be made in large denominations, are commonly of one-week or six-month maturities, entail modest default risk, and carry slightly higher interest rates than domestic securities.

Hedged Dividend Capture Strategies The securities previously described constitute only a partial list of the more popular short-term investment vehicles used by firms. Dozens of other investments are used less frequently. Cash managers are constantly searching for short-term, low-risk investment strategies that yield higher returns, and this search has led to very innovative strategies, some involving instruments outside of the type usually considered for temporary investment purposes. One set of strategies revolves around the relative tax rates on interest income and on intercorporate dividends. While interest income from investments is taxed at the firm's corporate tax rate (which is 33 percent for large firms, based on tax legislation passed in 1986), the effective rate for dividend income is only 20 percent of this (or 6.6 percent) for dividends on stock held sufficiently long to qualify for the 80 percent dividend exclusion (46 days under the same law). Thus, there is a substantial

---

[6]For discussion, see Daniel Hertzberg and Martha Brannigan, "Dealer Losses in Collapse of ESM Unit Are Manageable, New York Fed Says," *Wall Street Journal*, March 7, 1985, p. 5, and "Former ESM Chief Nicholas Wallace Gets 30-Year Prison Term," *Wall Street Journal*, October 20, 1986, p. 14.

incentive to structure short-term investments to obtain dividend income. However, the use of dividend-paying securities as temporary investments requires special strategies—holding the stock alone would be far too risky, given the short-term nature of the investment and the eventual need of the firm for the invested cash. In particular, when some of these instruments are purchased for dividend income, a hedging strategy must also be employed to lessen the risk from price fluctuations. Some possible strategies are:

1. Holding adjustable rate preferred stock. Since the rate on this stock floats with general interest rates, the interest rate risk inherent in the typical perpetual preferred stock is lessened considerably.[7]

2. Holding common shares of firms and hedging with call options. In this strategy, the firm buys the shares of a firm that is expected to pay a dividend and at the same time sells an option to sell the stock at a specific price (a call option). In this way, the risk of stock price movement is lessened, since any swings in the price of the stock are partially offset by changes in the price of the call. When the stock is sold, the call is rebought; since the gains and losses on the call and the stock tend to offset, the firm is left with the dividend income.[8]

3. Holding shares of an index fund and hedging with index fund call options. This is the same as holding shares in individual firms, except that the investing firm benefits from the wide diversification of the index fund.[9]

All these strategies yield higher after-tax returns than does the strategy of holding money market instruments. Unfortunately, none of these three strategies reduces risk to the levels inherent in holding T-bills, repos, banker's acceptances, or commercial paper. Regarding the first strategy, the prices of adjustable rate preferred stock are somewhat volatile; although the adjustable nature of the preferred returns lessens interest rate risk, it does not remove it entirely. The second and third strategies are also risky, since it is very difficult to construct the perfect hedge required to completely eliminate the price risk in shares of common stock or in index funds, although the hedging strategy does reduce this price risk significantly. Consequently, these strat-

---

[7]See Bernard Winger and others, "Adjustable Rate Preferred Stock," *Financial Management* (Spring 1986), pp. 48–57.

[8]See Keith Brown and Scott Lummer, "The Cash Management Implications of a Hedged Dividend Capture Strategy," *Financial Management* (Winter 1984), pp. 7–17, and Keith Brown and Scott Lummer, "A Reexamination of the Covered All-Option Strategy for Corporate Cash Management," *Financial Management* (Summer 1986), pp. 13–17.

[9]See Terry Zivney and Michael J. Alderson, "Hedged Dividend Capture Strategy with Stock Index Options," *Financial Management* (Summer 1986), pp. 5–12.

egies remain less popular than those based on standard money market investments.

Summary To summarize this discussion of the money market, the normally positive slope of the yield curve gives incentives for the firm to invest cash in instruments with longer maturities. This adds interest rate risk to investments unless the firm hedges this risk with interest rate futures. In the rapidly evolving money market, several vehicles are popular: Treasury bills, commercial paper, certificates of deposit, banker's acceptances, repurchase agreements, and Eurodollar investments. New and innovative strategies, such as hedged dividend capture, are being developed continuously. In order to select the most advantageous investment strategies for their circumstances, firms must consider the amount involved, the purpose for the investment of cash (hedging of cash flow uncertainty or the investment of a temporary surplus of funds), the size of the firm, and the amount of risk that the firm is willing to take. Very short-term investments (as alternatives to holding cash in hedging the firm's cash flow risk) are commonly made by purchasing nearly matured Treasury bills, commercial paper, or repurchase agreements. All but the very smallest firms can purchase Treasury bills; larger investments are required for the other vehicles. Treasury bills are the safest of these in terms of default risk. Longer-term investments (as necessary for the higher-return investment of temporary surplus funds when the yield curve is upsloping) can be made in longer-maturity Treasury bills, in banker's acceptances, in Eurodollar securities, and in certificates of deposit. Because of the required minimum investments, smaller firms will tend to use Treasury bills here also. With regard to default risk, Treasury bills are the safest, followed by banker's acceptances, commercial paper, and Eurodollar investments. Interest rate risk depends on maturity. Some of these instruments can also be used for financing; larger firms sell commercial paper, Eurodollar securities, and repurchase agreements ("reverse repos"). Firms may also use banker's acceptances to finance foreign trade.

FLOTATION AND CHECK CLEARING

To this point, this chapter has recounted the reasons and mechanisms for holding cash and near-cash assets. The management of these holdings by the firm is an important part of the cash management function. But another important function in this area of finance is the management of cash *when it is not in the firm's hands*, that is, when it is in transit to and from the firm. To understand this transit process, let us track the flow of cash and documents in a typical passage from one firm to another in payment of a debt. Since the most common method of remittance is by check, we will use a check remittance as an example. We will also assume that the firm receiving the cash has

Figure 2-2. Transit Times for a Typical Check.

not taken any steps to accelerate this transit. Later in this chapter, we will discuss possible steps to achieve this acceleration.

The check starts its passage to the receiving firm when the firm making the remittance mails the check.[10] The check then winds its way through the mail service to the receiving firm. This usually takes between one and five days, depending on the distance the check must travel and the efficiency of the parts of the postal system through which the check passes. When the check is received by the firm, the documents enclosed with the check (that indicate what the check is intended to pay) are removed; the check is then forwarded to the firm's bank. Depending on the receiving firm's procedures, the check may spend a few hours or even a day at the firm before it is forwarded to the bank. The bank then sends the check to the Federal Reserve Bank (the "Fed") or the Fed's Regional Check Processing Center, which undertakes to present the check for payment to the bank on which it was written.[11] The Fed guarantees that this clearing process will take at most two days; it if takes longer, the Fed credits the deposit in two days anyway. *Only after this entire process is completed* does the receiving firm receive credit for the cash so that it is able to use the money. This transit process, with estimated delays, is depicted in Figure 2-2.

Why should the firm care about this process? The answer is that every delay in the receipt of money by the firm lowers the firm's returns, and therefore its shareholders' wealth. To see this, suppose that a firm receives $2 million per day via this transit system. Assume that checks were in the mail an average of 4 days, that the firm takes 0.5 days to process checks and get them to the bank, and that the firm's bank takes 1.3 days to obtain funds for the checks. The total delay is then 5.8 days. Since the firm receives $2 million per day, at any time there is $11.6 million in incoming funds that the firm cannot access, and thus cannot use to produce increases in shareholder

[10]We assume here that the check is *truly* in the mail, not that the remitting firm merely says that it is (truly or less truly). In most firms, it is the task of the firm's credit department to get the check put in the mail; the task of cash management starts where that of credit management ends.

[11]There are some special cases here in which the receiving firm is credited with the funds at the time of deposit or almost immediately thereafter. Any cash deposits are immediately credited to the receiving firm's account. Also, checks received by the firm that are drawn on the bank at which the firm makes the deposit (that is, cases where the paying and receiving firms use the same bank) are cleared simply by the bank's reducing one firm's account and increasing the other's.

Table 2-1. Opportunity Cost of Float for Text Example.

Float Type	*Float Time (days)*	*Receipts (per day)*	*Float in Dollars*
Mail Float	4.0	$2 mil.	$8.0 mil.
At-Firm Float	0.5	$2 mil.	$1.0 mil.
Clearing Float	1.3	$2 mil.	$2.6 mil.
Total Transit Time	5.8	Total Float	$11.6 mil.
		Required Return	0.10 per year
		Opportunity Cost of Float	$1.16 mil. per year

wealth. If the firm could accelerate the transit process such that it had these funds in hand, and could invest them at the firm's cost of capital (10 percent, for example), it could earn an additional $1.16 million, and shareholders' wealth would increase because of these increased earnings. This lost opportunity for investment is called the *opportunity cost of float*. Calculation of the opportunity cost for this example is presented in Table 2-1.

There are several strategies that firms can use to reduce the delay in receiving funds. Each of these strategies addresses one or more of the three float times (mail float time, at-firm float time, and clearing float time) that make up the total transit time of funds from one firm to another. In the following paragraphs, several such strategies are discussed.

Selection of Banks with Accelerated Clearing Capabilities There is no requirement that the bank must clear all checks through the Fed. Banks have several alternative routes for check clearing, some of which can significantly reduce clearing float. One route is the *clearinghouse*. Clearinghouses are places where banks meet to exchange checks drawn on each other. Clearinghouses may involve only local banks or may involve both local banks and banks outside the local area, as many clearinghouses do. Banks that are members of clearinghouses can clear checks against other clearinghouse banks more rapidly than through the Fed; often, checks processed through clearinghouses can be cleared in one-half day or less. Another method by which a bank may clear checks is through the use of its *correspondent banks*. Correspondent banks in other parts of the country have agreements with the clearing bank. Often, they are participants in local clearinghouses in their own areas. In this system, the clearing bank sends the check to the correspondent bank nearest the bank on which the check was drawn. The correspondent bank then proceeds with the check clearing process. Well-connected banks can often accelerate check clearing in this way.

Acceleration of Check Processing at the Firm A surprising number of firms are not very careful about the delay between when the checks are received at their various locations and the eventual deposit of these items. While good cash management requires that the firm adopt processing procedures that speed checks into the clearing process, they are sometimes left to sit at the firm for several days (or longer!). Government agencies are particularly prone to this practice, as several studies have shown.

Use of Electronic Collection Procedures It should be clear from the prior discussion that the time necessary for transmittal of cash from one firm to another revolves largely around the passing from one hand to another of a piece of paper—the remitting firm's check. One alternative to this process is to substitute an electronic message of payment for the check. This eliminates the need for the paper and thus the various floats associated with taking the paper from one place to another. Efforts to convert to electronic remittance systems began in the 1970s, but they have met with little success and are currently used only for an insignificant proportion of transactions. Further, the outlook for more widespread adoption is not very bright. Given the appeal (in terms of reduced flotation) of electronic remittances, it is useful to briefly review the history of the proposed electronic payment systems and the problems in adopting these systems.[12]

The major experiment in the development of a system for electronic remittances was the corporate trade payments (CTP) system developed by the National Automated Clearing House Association. This system was tested in 1983 and introduced in 1984, but has not attracted a significant volume of transactions. Several causes of this failure are commonly cited, such as the costs of converting to electronic payments, the absence of adequate marketing efforts, and the difficulty in sending proper advice as to what the remittance is supposed to pay.[13] The *major* problem with electronic payments, however, does not relate to these factors, but to the relative benefits and costs of the system to the paying and receiving firms. To see this, it is first necessary to recognize that the elimination of float on checks benefits the receiving firm *but extracts the same costs from the paying firm*, and that paying firms *must agree to remit electronically*. While outgoing checks in nonelectronic systems remain uncollected, the paying firm retains the cash which it can then use. But in electronic systems, this float is eliminated, to the advantage of the receiving firm but to the disadvantage of the paying firm. This disparity in

---

[12]Required reading for those interested in electronic trade payments systems are the March and April 1986 issues of *Economic Review*, published by the Federal Reserve Bank of Atlanta. These two issues present nine articles summarizing the history and problems of electronic trade payments systems.

[13]In response to the latter problem, another service has been developed (the corporate trade exchange, or CTX) to ease the transmittal of remittance advice information.

benefits has led to considerable reluctance by paying firms to participate in electronic payment systems. The remaining advantages of electronic payments, such as the reduction in printing costs for checks and the reduction in charges to the receiving firm by its bank for processing these checks, are not large enough to offset the initial costs of instituting an electronic payments system. Unless these economics change, electronic trade payments will continue to be unattractive to remitting firms.

Use of Lockboxes A "lockbox" is a post office box number to which some or all of the firm's customers are instructed to send their checks. The firm grants permission to its bank to take these checks and immediately start them in the clearing process. In fact, the mail addressed to this "post office box" is actually delivered directly to the firm's lockbox bank. In this way, at-firm float is eliminated. Judicious placement of lockboxes and instructions to customers on where to send their checks can also serve to reduce mail and clearing float substantially.

While lockboxes are very useful, not all firms will find them of advantage. Their use entails giving customers two mailing addresses for the firm: the lockbox (for checks) and the firm's usual business address (for all other documents). This inevitably leads to the misrouting of some documents to the lockbox that the firm would prefer to go directly to its business. A consequent delay in the delivery of these documents to the firm occurs, since banks often do not forward items received at the lockbox until the next day. This entails costs to the firm. For example, misrouted purchase orders from customers, which the firm would like to process as soon as possible, are delayed. Further, lockbox check processing systems at banks are oriented toward the rapid processing of routine checks, not extraordinary items (such as postdated checks, unsigned checks, and promissory notes). While lockbox personnel are instructed to look for these items and not to send them on through the banking system, errors occur rather frequently, with consequent inconvenience for the firm.

While lockboxes are not a problem-free panacea for flotation problems, *their proper use can reduce all the types of flotation* on incoming checks. The important decisions in the formulation of a lockbox strategy are:

☐ Where should the firm locate its lockboxes?
☐ To which lockboxes should each of the firm's customers send their checks?

The best solutions to the lockbox problem require that these questions be answered simultaneously. The next section, in which the general solution to this lockbox strategy problem is presented, provides the major analytic thrust of this chapter.

THE LOCKBOX LOCATION PROBLEM

The *lockbox location problem* involves answering the two questions just posed. A note on the mathematical and programming procedures presented here for solving this problem is appropriate. While we present the mathematics of a general solution to the lockbox problem, firms designing lockbox systems do not directly use these mathematics. Computer programs to determine lockbox location are sufficiently complex and the lockbox location decisions to be made by various firms are sufficiently similar that the development of this software by individual firms is not cost effective. Instead, the firm usually undertakes the study of this problem in conjunction with a commercial bank that has developed or purchased lockbox location software and that sells the use of this software to corporate clients. The intent of this section is to make the reader able to understand in a specific way *how the software works*: the inputs it requires, the mathematical techniques it uses, and how its outputs are to be interpreted. With this knowledge, the reader should be able to use an appropriate microcomputer package to solve a small example lockbox location problem and interpret the results (full-size lockbox location problems require a mainframe because of the number of computations necessary to solve them). More importantly, the reader should *understand the lockbox solution procedure* sufficiently to be able to work intelligently with a commercial bank in the formulation of a lockbox strategy for a firm.

The lockbox location problem is a cost minimization problem. The firm seeks to minimize the sum of (1) the opportunity cost of the float on incoming cash, and (2) the costs of the lockbox system. The opportunity cost of the incoming cash is the total float in dollars times the firm's required return (as in Table 2-1). The costs of the lockbox system include the fixed costs that banks charge to provide lockbox service (regardless of the number of checks processed), the per-check processing charges, and any charges necessary to gather up the cash from the lockbox banks after it is collected. There is a trade-off between these two sets of costs. As the firm increases the number of lockboxes (properly placed), the opportunity cost of float will be reduced.[14] However, each additional lockbox adds another fixed charge to the costs of the lockbox system. Eventually, the addition of another lockbox increases rather than decreases total costs. This relationship is portrayed in Figure 2-3.

To solve the lockbox location problem, the firm must collect four sets of data:

1. The mail and clearing times for sending checks from each part of the

[14]Note that, for a multiple-lockbox system to be considered by the firm, there must be gains from reduced opportunity costs in adding lockboxes in several locations. This is true only for firms whose receipts come from several different areas. Unless receipts are widely dispersed, multiple lockboxes will not reduce mail and clearing float; one lockbox, near the origin of the receipts, is sufficient.

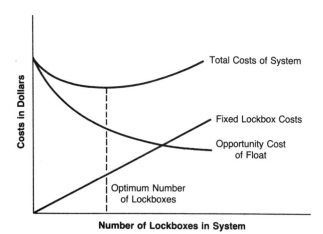

Figure 2-3. *Costs in Lockbox Systems Versus Number of Lockboxes.*

firm's geographic sales area to each possible lockbox. Mail times are usually obtained from Phoenix-Hecht, Inc., a firm that supplies mail data on a commercial basis from one three-digit zip code location to another. Clearing times (called "availability schedules") are generally obtained from the banks which are potential lockbox sites.

2. The total amount of daily funds and number of checks received by the firm from each part of the sales area. This is usually collected by an examination of the postmarks on a sample of the firm's incoming checks. A stratified sample of high-value checks may be used to reduce collection costs for these data.

3. The required rate of return (for computing opportunity costs).

4. The variable and fixed costs of each proposed lockbox site. To speed clearing times, lockboxes are usually located in cities where the Fed has a major district or branch bank, plus a few other major locations; there are about 50 possible lockbox cities. There are often several banks which offer lockbox services in each of these cities, so the total potential lockbox sites is over 100.[15]

With these data in hand, it is relatively simple to calculate the *one best lockbox* if the firm is constrained to have only one. This optimal solution to the *one-*

[15]See Steven Maier and James Vander Weide, "What Lockbox and Disbursement Models Really Do," *Journal of Finance* (May 1983), p. 364. To keep the following discussion as simple as possible, we will hereafter assume that the firm has examined the banks providing lockbox services in each location and has selected the most advantageous of these; there will then be only one candidate lockbox bank per lockbox city. The mathematical procedures described do not, however, require this assumption.

lockbox problem is simply the lockbox which has the lowest total cost, defined again as the sum of the opportunity cost of float and the costs of the lockbox. Beyond this, it is rarely clear whether a *group* of lockboxes would do a better job (in the sense of lower total costs) than this single best lockbox. For example, suppose that the firm sells over the continental United States, with about equal receipts from the various parts of the country. In this case, a centrally located lockbox (perhaps in Kansas City) might be the best one-box solution. But would two lockboxes, perhaps one in the East and one in the West, be better? If so, to which lockbox should customers from each part of the country be instructed to send their checks? To answer these questions, some sort of optimization technique (an optimization algorithm) is necessary.

A Lockbox Location Problem Algorithm There are several lockbox location and customer assignment routines in the cash management literature. Some of these will always find the optimum (least cost) combination of lockboxes and assignments while others will not. In general, the routines that always lead to optimum solutions are more difficult to calculate (particularly by hand) than those which may not lead to optimums. The trade-off has been between ease of computation versus the guarantee of an optimum solution. However, one of the mathematical approaches that will always lead to an optimum solution—*integer programming*—is now commonly available as a user-friendly microcomputer software package. Thus, there no longer seems any need to compromise on technique in illustrating lockbox location decisions because of computational difficulty considerations. The solution to the lockbox location problem presented here is based on the integer programming approach.

Integer programming can be conceived as linear programming in which some of the variables are constrained to take on only integer values. In the formulation presented here, the variables that must be integers are those that represent whether a lockbox is in use ("open") or whether it is not ("closed") and whether the customers from a particular region are assigned to a particular lockbox or not.[16] Let j designate the prospective lockbox bank location and i designate the zone (area) from which the customer's check originates. Let the number of possible lockboxes be n and number of zones be m. To evaluate a lockbox at location j we need to know the charges that the firm will bear from opening and using that lockbox. These will be composed of the fixed charges from the bank for opening the lockbox, the check processing charges for checks received there, and the opportunity cost of float on checks from customers who send their remittances to that lockbox. Let d_j be the fixed charges for lockbox j. The check processing charges will be the product of

[16]The notation and procedure here follows Robert M. Nauss and Robert E. Markland, "Solving Lock Box Location Problems," *Financial Management* (Spring 1979), pp. 21–31.

the bank's processing charge per check and the number of incoming checks. Let s_j be the processing charge per check at lockbox j and let h_i be the expected number of checks originating from customers in zone i.

The opportunity cost of float from the checks of customers originating in zone i and going to lockbox j is designated as c_{ij}. This is the product of the total float in days on these checks times the dollar amount of checks originating daily in zone i times the firm's required return (a risk-adjusted discount rate). For example, suppose that $5 million in customers' checks originate in a particular zone, that these customers are assigned to a lockbox where the total float time on these checks will be 4 days, and that the required return on checks is 10 percent. The c_{ij} term for this assignment would be ($5 million) (4) (0.10) = $200,000 per year. The total float time, in turn, is the sum of the mail and clearing times for checks originating in zone i and directed to lockbox j.

To complete the integer programming formulation, a few more variables must first be defined. Let K be the maximum number of lockboxes allowed by the analyst in the solution. For the solution involving the lowest possible cost, K would be set equal to n, the total number of possible lockbox sites. Let y_j be a zero-one integer variable indicating whether the lockbox at location j is open (1.0 if it is, zero if it is not) and x_{ij} be a zero-one integer variable indicating whether customers originating checks in zone i are assigned to lockbox j (1.0 if they are, zero if they are not). Of course, since the intent of the lockbox location problem is to determine which lockboxes should be open and which customers should be assigned to which lockboxes, the solution algorithm determines the optimum y_j and x_{ij} terms based on the minimization of total cost. The objective function is:

$$\text{Minimize} \sum_{\text{all } j} d_j y_j + \sum_{\text{all } i} \sum_{\text{all } j} (c_{ij} + h_i s_j) x_{ij} \tag{2-1}$$

which says that the objective is to minimize the sum of the total fixed costs of opening lockboxes (the sum of $d_j y_j$), the opportunity costs of flotation ($c_{ij} x_{ij}$), and the check processing costs ($h_i s_j x_{ij}$).

The solution to this problem is subject to some very logical constraints. The checks from each customer zone must be received at a lockbox somewhere. Also, a lockbox must be open for receipts from a customer zone to be received there. There should be one and only one lockbox open at location j and customers from zone i may send their checks to one and only one lockbox. Finally, it is often useful to constrain the solution to the problem to the best solution for a maximum of K lockboxes (in part, to limit the computer's required computational time in the initial stages of examining the problem). The following equations model these constraints:

$$\sum_{\text{all } j} x_{ij} = 1 \tag{2-2}$$

$$\sum_{\text{all } i} x_{ij} \leq my_j \tag{2-3}$$

$$\text{All } x_{ij} \text{ and } y_j \geq 0, \leq 1 \tag{2-4}$$

$$\text{All } x_{ij} \text{ and } y_j \text{ integer} \tag{2-5}$$

$$\sum_{\text{all } j} y_j \leq K \tag{2-6}$$

The meaning of these constraints is fairly straightforward. Equation (2-2) says that one of the x_{ij} variables for each origin zone (each i) must be 1.0 and the others zero, so that the checks from zone i are assigned to one and only one lockbox. Equation (2-3) bounds the solution to assign customers only to open lockboxes. In this equation, if y_j is zero, all the x_{ij} terms representing checks to be received at location j must also be zero; if y_j is 1.0, any of the x_{ij} terms may be 1.0 (up to a maximum of m, the number of zones and therefore the number of x_{ij} terms for a given j). Equation (2-4) bounds the x_{ij} and y_j terms to zero or 1.0 and equation (2-5) bounds these variables to be integers, since customers from a zone can send checks to only one lockbox and lockboxes may be either open or closed. Equation (2-6) limits the maximum number of lockboxes in the solution; the integer programming algorithm will compute the least-cost lockbox strategy for this maximum number.

AN EXAMPLE LOCKBOX LOCATION PROBLEM

The application of lockbox location analysis to a small problem is illustrative. Assume that the firm receives checks from four customer zones (zones A, B, C, and D), and has solicited lockbox proposals from banks in three of the zones (zones B, C, and D). It has also collected the other data necessary to analyze costs from various lockbox strategies. Data from lockbox proposals, the mail times from zone to zone, the dollar amount of checks originating in each zone, and the clearing times for the proposed lockboxes are presented in Table 2-2. The firm's required rate of return is 9 percent and the average size of an incoming check is $2,500. This average size does not vary among the origin zones.

It is instructive to first address this example by solving the one-lockbox problem: if the firm is constrained to having only one lockbox, and all checks are sent to that lockbox, where should that lockbox be located? To answer this question, a spreadsheet to calculate the opportunity cost of float, the check processing cost, and the total cost for each of the three potential lockboxes can be generated. One such spreadsheet is presented in Table 2-3.

Table 2-2. *Data for the Example Lockbox Location Problem.*

Data on Lockbox Proposals from Banks:

		1	2	3
Proposal Number:		1	2	3
Lockbox Location		B	C	D
Fixed Cost per Year		$3,000	$10,000	$4,000
Processing Charge per Check		$0.10	$0.15	$0.13

Mail Time Data (days):

			Destination	
	Origin	B	C	D
	A	2.6	2.8	3.0
	B	2.5	3.1	3.3
	C	2.7	2.8	3.5
	D	3.3	3.5	1.8

Clearing Time Data (days):

			Destination	
	Origin	B	C	D
	A	1.2	1.8	1.7
	B	0.8	1.3	1.5
	C	1.3	1.1	1.3
	D	1.5	1.3	1.0

Check Origination Data (per day):

	Origin	Dollars
	A	$3,500,000
	B	$4,500,000
	C	$3,000,000
	D	$2,500,000
	Total	$13,500,000

After setting up the necessary headings, the data on mail float times and clearing float times from Table 2-2 were entered into columns B and C for the first lockbox. The entries in column D, cells 8 through 11, are the sum of the corresponding cells in B and C. The dollar origins appear in column E; column F, cells F8 through F11, is E times D (for example, cell F8 contains "D8*E8"). Summing these gives the total dollar float for this one-lockbox strategy.

The remainder of the calculations takes place in column F. The total dollar float (cell F13) times the required return (F14) gives the opportunity cost of float (F16). The fixed cost of this lockbox is contained as data in cell F18. The number of checks processed per year is calculated in cell F20. Here, the total dollars received per day ($13.5 million) is divided by the average check size ($2,500) and multiplied by 360 to get the number of checks processed yearly. This times the cost per check for this lockbox (cell F21) gives the yearly cost of check processing (F23). The total cost of this lockbox

Table 2-3. Spreadsheet Analysis of One-Lockbox Solution to Example Problem.

	A	B	C	D	E	F
1	Origination	Mail	Clearing	Total	Dollar	Total
2	Zone	Float	Float	Float	Originations	Float
3		Time	Time	Time	per Day	Dollars
4					(thousands)	(thousands)
5						
6	Proposal 1 (Lockbox Located in Zone B)					
7						
8	A	2.6	1.2	3.8	$3,500	$13,300
9	B	2.5	0.8	3.3	$4,500	$14,850
10	C	2.7	1.3	4	$3,000	$12,000
11	D	3.3	1.5	4.8	$2,500	$12,000
12						
13	Total Dollar Float for This Lockbox					$52,150
14	Required Return					0.09
15						
16	Opportunity Cost of Float—One Lockbox Solution					$4,694
17						
18	Fixed Cost of Lockbox for This Location					$4
19						
20	Number of Checks Processed per Year					1,944
21	Processing Cost per Check					$0.10
22						
23	Cost of Check Processing—One Lockbox Solution					$194
24						
25	Total Cost (Op. Cost of Float + Fixed + Proc.)					$4,892
26						
27						
28	Proposal 2 (Lockbox Located in Zone C)					
29						
30	A	2.8	1.8	4.6	$3,500	$16,100
31	B	3.1	1.3	4.4	$4,500	$19,800
32	C	2.8	1.1	3.9	$3,000	$11,700
33	D	3.5	1.3	4.8	$2,500	$12,000
34						
35	Total Dollar Float for This Lockbox					$59,600
36	Required Return					0.09
37						
38	Opportunity Cost of Float—One Lockbox Solution					$5,364
39						
40	Fixed Cost of Lockbox for This Location					$10
41						
42	Number of Checks Processed per Year					1,944
43	Processing Cost per Check					$0.15
44						
45	Cost of Check Processing—One Lockbox Solution					$292

46						
47	Total Cost (Op. Cost of Float + Fixed + Proc.)					$5,666
48						
49						
50	Proposal 3 (Lockbox Located in Zone D)					
51						
52	A	3.0	1.7	4.7	$3,500	$16,450
53	B	3.3	1.5	4.8	$4,500	$21,600
54	C	3.5	1.3	4.8	$3,000	$14,400
55	D	1.8	1.0	2.8	$2,500	$7,000
56						
57	Total Dollar Float for This Lockbox					$59,450
58	Required Return					0.09
59						
60	Opportunity Cost of Float—One Lockbox Solution					$5,351
61						
62	Fixed Cost of Lockbox for This Location					$4
63						
64	Number of Checks Processed per Year					1,944
65	Processing Cost per Check					$0.13
66						
67	Cost of Check Processing—One Lockbox Solution					$253
68						
69	Total Cost (Op. Cost of Float + Fixed + Proc.)					$5,607

strategy is presented in cell F25 (the contents of this cell are "F16+F18+F23"). This part of the spreadsheet was then copied (replicated) into rows 28 through 47 and 50 through 69, and modifications made to reflect the characteristics of the other two possible lockbox locations.

Comparison of the three total costs shows that proposal 1, entailing a lockbox in zone B, is the least costly, with a yearly total cost of $4.892 million. But would some combination of lockboxes do a better job? Can costs be reduced further? These questions can be answered by executing the integer programming approach previously described. To execute this approach, the coefficients of the x_{ij} and y_j variables in the objective function [the d_j, c_{ij}, h_i, and s_j terms in equation (2-1)] must first be calculated. The resulting objective function and the problem's constraint equations are then input into an integer programming package and the optimum solution is found via the software.

For the example lockbox problem, there are three possible lockboxes and thus three y_j variables (y_B, y_C, and y_D). There are four origin zones and thus twelve x_{ij} variables (since customers in each zone could be assigned to send checks to any of the lockboxes, the number of possible assignments of customers to lockboxes is the number of lockboxes times the number of zones). There are thus 15 terms in the objective function. The coefficients

Table 2-4. *Spreadsheet Computation of Coefficients of x_{ij} for Example Problem.*

	A	B	C	D	E	F	G	H	I	J	K	L
	Origination Zone	Mail Float Time	Clearing Float Time	Total Float Time	Dollar Originations per Day (thousands)	Total Float Dollars (thousands)	Required Return	c_{ij}	h_i	s_i	$h_i s_i$	$c_{ij} + h_i s_i$
1												
2												
3												
4												
5												
6	Proposal 1 (Lockbox Located in Zone B)											
7												
8	A	2.6	1.2	3.8	$3,500	$13,300	0.09	1197.0	504	$0.10	50.4	1247.4
9	B	2.5	0.8	3.3	$4,500	$14,850	0.09	1336.5	648	$0.10	64.8	1401.3
10	C	2.7	1.3	4	$3,000	$12,000	0.09	1080.0	432	$0.10	43.2	1123.2
11	D	3.3	1.5	4.8	$2,500	$12,000	0.09	1080.0	360	$0.10	36.0	1116.0
12												
13												
14												
15	Proposal 2 (Lockbox Located in Zone C)											
16												
17	A	2.8	1.8	4.6	$3,500	$16,100	0.09	1449.0	504	$0.15	75.6	1524.6
18	B	3.1	1.3	4.4	$4,500	$19,800	0.09	1782.0	648	$0.15	97.2	1879.2
19	C	2.8	1.1	3.9	$3,000	$11,700	0.09	1053.0	432	$0.15	64.8	1117.8
20	D	3.5	1.3	4.8	$2,500	$12,000	0.09	1080.0	360	$0.15	54.0	1134.0
21												
22	Proposal 3 (Lockbox Located in Zone D)											
23												
24	A	3.0	1.7	4.7	$3,500	$16,450	0.09	1480.5	504	$0.13	65.5	1546.0
25	B	3.3	1.5	4.8	$4,500	$21,600	0.09	1944.0	648	$0.13	84.2	2028.2
26	C	3.5	1.3	4.8	$3,000	$14,400	0.09	1296.0	432	$0.13	56.2	1352.2
27	D	1.8	1.0	2.8	$2,500	$7,000	0.09	630.0	360	$0.13	46.8	676.8

of the y_j variables in this function (the d_j terms) are simply the fixed costs of the lockboxes in these locations. The major analytic problem in specification of the objective function is therefore the calculation of the coefficients of the x_{ij} terms (equal to $c_{ij} + h_i s_j$ for each x_{ij}). A spreadsheet approach to calculating these coefficients is presented in Table 2-4.

In this table, cells A1 through F11 are the same as those in Table 2-3. Cells F8 through F11 are multiplied by the required return in column G to obtain the c_{ij} terms in column H. The number of checks originating yearly from each zone is calculated in column I by dividing the dollar origins in column E by the average check size (to get daily check numbers) and multiplying by 360 (thus, cell I8 contains "(E8/2500*360)". Column K (which contains $h_i s_j$) is column j (which contains the processing charge per check for this lockbox, s_j) times column I. Column L, the coefficient of the respective x_{ij} term, is column H plus column K. For example, the number 1247.4 in cell L8 is $c_{AB} + h_A s_B$, since for this cell checks originate in zone A and the lockbox is in zone B. This will be the coefficient of x_{AB} in the objective function.

Once the coefficients of the x_{ij} and y_j are calculated, objective function and the constraint equations are input into an integer programming package. The appropriate formulation for the example problem is presented in Table 2-5. We have used the popular LINDO mathematical programming package here (from LINDO Systems, Inc.). Other popular integer programming packages use similar input and output formats. The objective function is equation (2-1) with the appropriate coefficients of the three y_j and the 12 x_{ij} variables. Lines 2 through 5 represent equation (2-2), which says that the checks from each origin zone must be sent to one of the lockbox locations. There is one such equation for each origin zone. Here, since there are three possible lockboxes, there are three x_{ij} variables in each equation, and since there are four origin zones, there are four equations. Line 6 represents equation (2-6), which constrains the maximum number of lockboxes in the solution. We have not constrained the solution to any number of lockboxes less than the maximum; there are three possible lockboxes, any of which we allow to be open. If we wished to constrain the solution to a lesser number of lockboxes, this would be reflected on the right-hand side of this line. Lines 7 through 30 and 34 through 36, along with the integer constraints (which do not print in the LINDO package), constrain values of the y_j and x_{ij} variables to be zero-one integers, representing equations (2-4) and (2-5). Lines 31, 32, and 33 represent equation (2-3), and allow the assignment of the customer's checks from a zone to a lockbox location only if that lockbox is open. Since there are three lockboxes, there are three such constraints.[17]

The results of the integer programming solution to this lockbox problem

---

[17]Some of these constraints are redundant. We include them only to follow the problem format as given in equations (2-1) through (2-6).

Table 2-5. *LINDO Formulation for Example Problem (any number of lockboxes up to* n *allowed).*

MIN   3 YB + 10 YC + 4 YD + 1401.3 XBB + 1247.4 XAB
       + 1524.6 XAC + 1546 XAD + 1879.2 XBC + 2028.2 XBD + 1123.2 XCB
       + 1117.3 XCC + 1352.2 XCD + 1116 XDB + 1134 XDC + 676.8 XDD

SUBJECT TO

2)	XAB + XAC + XAD = 1
3)	XBB + XBC + XBD = 1
4)	XCB + XCC + XCD = 1
5)	XDB + XDC + XDD = 1
6)	YB + YC + YD <= 3
7)	XAB <= 1
8)	XAC <= 1
9)	XAD <= 1
10)	XBB <= 1
11)	XBC <= 1
12)	XBD <= 1
13)	XCB <= 1
14)	XCC <= 1
15)	XCD <= 1
16)	XDB <= 1
17)	XDC <= 1
18)	XDD <= 1
19)	XAB >= 0
20)	XAC >= 0
21)	XAD >= 0
22)	XBB >= 0
23)	XBC >= 0
24)	XBD >= 0
25)	XCB >= 0
26)	XCC >= 0
27)	XCD >= 0
28)	XDB >= 0
29)	XDC >= 0
30)	XDD >= 0
31)	- 4 YB + XBB + XAB + XCB + XDB <= 0
32)	- 4 YC + XAC + XBC + XCC + XDC <= 0
33)	- 4 YD + XAD + XBD + XCD + XDD <= 0
34)	YB <= 1
35)	YC <= 1
36)	YD <= 1

END

INTEGER-VARIABLES =   15

Table 2-6. *LINDO Solution for Example Problem (any number of lockboxes up to n allowed).*

OBJECTIVE FUNCTION VALUE

1)   4455.70000

VARIABLE	VALUE	REDUCED COST
YB	1.000000	3.000000
YC	.000000	10.000000
YD	1.000000	4.000000
XBB	1.000000	1401.300000
XAB	1.000000	1247.400000
XAC	.000000	1524.600000
XAD	.000000	1546.000000
XBC	.000000	1879.200000
XBD	.000000	2028.200000
XCB	1.000000	1123.200000
XCC	.000000	1117.800000
XCD	.000000	1352.200000
XDB	.000000	439.200000
XDC	.000000	457.200000
XDD	1.000000	.000000

are presented in Table 2-6.[18] Only two of the possible lockboxes appear in the optimal formulation: proposal number 1 (with a lockbox in zone B) and proposal number 3 (with a lockbox in zone D). Proposal number 2, with a lockbox in zone C, does not appear since it does not reduce the total cost of the system. The cost with these two lockboxes, given an optimal assignment of customers to these lockboxes, is $4.456 million per year, which is $336,000 a year less expensive than the best one-box solution. In the optimal strategy, customers' checks originating in zones A, B, and C are sent to the lockbox in zone B (since x_{AB}, x_{BB}, and x_{CB} are all 1.0), while checks originating in zone D are sent to the lockbox in zone D (since x_{DD} is 1.0). All the remaining assignment variables are, of course, zero.

One of the substantial advantages of approaching the lockbox location problem in this way is *flexibility*. While Table 2-5 presents the formulation for the *optimal* (lowest total cost) solution, judicious changes in the constraint equations can provide very interesting information to the firm performing the analysis. For example, changing the constraints on the y_j terms in lines 34 through 36 to force one of these terms to 1.0 and the others to zero will produce the one-lockbox solution for that lockbox. The formulation and

[18]In the interest of space, and because of the difficulty in interpreting slack values and dual prices in the solution to an integer programming problem, the slacks and duals are not presented here or for any of the other integer programming solutions in this text.

Table 2-7. LINDO Formulation for Example Problem (one-lockbox problem; lockbox at location B).

MIN   3 YB + 10 YC + 4 YD + 1401.3 XBB + 1247.4 XAB + 1524.6 XAC
          +1546 XAD + 1879.2 XBC + 2028.2 XBD + 1123.2 XCB + 1117.8 XCC
          +1352.2 XCD + 1116 XDB + 1134 XDC + 676.8 XDD

SUBJECT TO

2)	XAB + XAC + XAD =	1
3)	XBB + XBC + XBD =	1
4)	XCB + XCC + XCD =	1
5)	XDB + XDC + XDD =	1
6)	YB + YC + YD <=	3
7)	XAB <=	1
8)	XAC <=	1
9)	XAD <=	1
10)	XBB <=	1
11)	XBC <=	1
12)	XBD <=	1
13)	XCB <=	1
14)	XCC <=	1
15)	XCD <=	1
16)	XDB <=	1
17)	XDC <=	1
18)	XDD <=	1
19)	XAB >=	0
20)	XAC >=	0
21)	XAD >=	0
22)	XBB >=	0
23)	XBC >=	0
24)	XBD >=	0
25)	XCB >=	0
26)	XCC >=	0
27)	XCD >=	0
28)	XDB >=	0
29)	XDC >=	0
30)	XDD >=	0
31)	− 4 YB + XBB + XAB + XCB + XDB <=	0
32)	− 4 YC + XAC + XBC + XCC + XDC <=	0
33)	− 4 YD + XAD + XBD + XCD + XDD <=	0
34)	YB =	1
35)	YC =	0
36)	YD =	0

END

INTEGER-VARIABLES =   15

Table 2-8. LINDO Solution for Example Problem (one-lockbox problem; lockbox at location B).

OBJECTIVE FUNCTION VALUE

1)   4890.900000

VARIABLE	VALUE	REDUCED COST
YB	1.000000	3.000000
YC	.000000	10.000000
YD	.000000	−1752.800000
XBB	1.000000	1401.300000
XAB	1.000000	1247.400000
XAC	.000000	1524.600000
XAD	.000000	1985.200000
XBC	.000000	1879.200000
XBD	.000000	2467.400000
XCB	1.000000	1123.200000
XCC	.000000	1117.300000
XCD	.000000	1791.400000
XDB	1.000000	.000000
XDC	.000000	18.000000
XDD	.000000	.000000

output for this alteration is presented in Tables 2-7 and 2-8 for lockbox y_B. Note that the value of total cost in the objective function is the same as that calculated via the spreadsheet approach in Table 2-3, allowing for rounding.

The integer programming approach can also be used to optimally schedule other configurations of lockbox locations so that the firm might contrast the cost of these strategies with the lowest-cost solution. For example, suppose that the firm wants to assess the cost of including the lockbox bank represented by proposal 2 (lockbox location C) in the firm's lockbox system. Perhaps the firm desires to have borrowing capacity available from this bank and believes that having a lockbox location at the bank would help in negotiations, or perhaps there is an existing lockbox at location C which the firm does not wish to close. In the lowest-cost solution, there is no lockbox at this location; y_C, as determined by the algorithm, is zero. To be sure that this lockbox is included in the system, we can change a constraint on y_C in line 35 from "YC ≤ 1.0" to "YC = 1.0". This requires the algorithm to give the minimum-cost solution which includes an open lockbox at location C. This formulation and solution is presented in Tables 2-9 and 2-10. With this constraint on y_C, the optimal solution is to open all the lockboxes. Checks for zones A and B are assigned to the lockbox at B, those from C to C, and those from D to D. The total cost is $4.460 million per year, which is $4,000 more expensive than the lowest-cost solution. With this information, the firm could decide

Table 2-9. *LINDO Formulation for Example Problem (solution constrained to include lockbox at location C).*

MIN   3 YB + 10 YC + 4 YD + 1401.3 XBB + 1247.4 XAB + 1524.6 XAC
    +1546 XAD + 1879.2 XBC + 2028.2 XBD + 1123.2 XCB + 1117.8 XCC
    +1352.2 XCD + 1116 XDB + 1134 XDC + 676.8 XDD

SUBJECT TO

2)	XAB + XAC + XAD =	1
3)	XBB + XBC + XBD =	1
4)	XCB + XCC + XCD =	1
5)	XDB + XDC + XDD =	1
6)	YB + YC + YD <=	3
7)	XAB <=	1
8)	XAC <=	1
9)	XAD <=	1
10)	XBB <=	1
11)	XBC <=	1
12)	XBD <=	1
13)	XCB <=	1
14)	XCC <=	1
15)	XCD <=	1
16)	XDB <=	1
17)	XDC <=	1
18)	XDD <=	1
19)	XAB >=	0
20)	XAC >=	0
21)	XAD >=	0
22)	XBB >=	0
23)	XBC >=	0
24)	XBD >=	0
25)	XCB >=	0
26)	XCC >=	0
27)	XCD >=	0
28)	XDB >=	0
29)	XDC >=	0
30)	XDD >=	0
31)	− 4 YB + XBB + XAB + XCB + XDB <=	0
32)	− 4 YC + XAC + XBC + XCC + XDC <=	0
33)	− 4 YD + XAD + XBD + XCD + XDD <=	0
34)	YB ≤	1
35)	YC =	1
36)	YD ≤	1

END
INTEGER-VARIABLES =   15

Table 2-10. *LINDO Solution for Example Problem (solution constrained to include lockbox at location C).*

OBJECTIVE FUNCTION VALUE

1)   4860.30000

VARIABLE	VALUE	REDUCED COST
YB	1.000000	3.000000
YC	1.000000	.000000
YD	1.000000	4.000000
XBB	1.000000	.000000
XAB	1.000000	.000000
XAC	.000000	277.200000
XAD	.000000	298.600000
XBC	.000000	477.899900
XBD	.000000	626.899900
XCB	.000000	.000000
XCC	1.000000	− 5.399902
XCD	.000000	229.000000
XDB	.000000	439.200000
XDC	.000000	457.200000
XDD	1.000000	.000000

whether having a lockbox relationship with the bank at location C is worth this additional yearly cost.

SOME WARNINGS ABOUT LOCKBOX LOCATION DECISIONS

This integer programming approach to lockbox location analysis should seem a relatively straightforward approach to a rather complex problem. However, there are difficulties associated with both the collection of the necessary data and with the lockbox location algorithm. These difficulties do not invalidate this approach to the lockbox location problem, but they do limit its accuracy. They should be kept in mind when the firm is considering, analyzing, and implementing a lockbox strategy.[19]

Determining Customer Zones Because the opportunity cost of float is computed as the sum of the mail and clearing floats, the customer zones must be defined such that these should be as homogeneous as possible within the zone. Otherwise, nonoptimal strategies may result. For example, suppose we define one zone as "checks originating in Chicago" and one of the possible

[19]Many of these problems are discussed in Maier and Vander Weide, "What Lockbox and Disbursement Models Really Do."

lockboxes is located in Chicago. If this lockbox is opened, all the customers from Chicago might be assigned to this lockbox. But suppose that there are, within this customer group, some customers who pay with checks written on Chicago banks and some who pay with checks written on West Coast banks. Depending on the disadvantage in mail time and the advantage in clearing time, it might be better to have the customers issuing checks drawn on West Coast banks send their checks to a West Coast lockbox. This possibility would be allowed if the customers with checks originating in Chicago were broken up into two zones: "customers with checks originating in Chicago drawn on Chicago banks" and "customers with checks originating in Chicago drawn on West Coast banks." Greater accuracy in defining zones leads to more nearly optimal solutions, but increases the cost of data collection and the cost of computation.

Obtaining Bank Cost Data   Estimating the least-cost placement of lockboxes requires data on the fixed costs of opening a lockbox at a particular location and the variable cost of processing checks at that location. The logical approach to collecting this data is to conduct a telephone or mail survey of potential bank lockbox sites, inquiring as to these costs. However, such surveys do not necessarily produce accurate results. Banks seem prone to offer their services in packages, with the costs of individual services tied to the size of the package. For example, a firm requesting only a lockbox service might pay more for that service than would a firm requesting a package of a lockbox service and a borrowing arrangement. Thus, the cost of a lockbox service might depend on the amount of other services that the firm is willing to purchase from the lockbox bank.

The criticality of this bank cost data depends on the average size of the checks received by the firm. If the firm receives many checks for relatively small amounts, data on bank charges (particularly processing costs) are very important, as these will be an important fraction of the total costs associated with the lockbox. If the average size of the checks received by the firm is relatively large, bank cost data will be a good deal less important, as the dominant cost will be the opportunity cost of float and not check processing cost.[20]

Obtaining a Representative Sample of Check Volume and Origination   Since a one-month sample of the receiving firm's incoming checks is usually used for this purpose, the firm must be very careful that this sample is representative of the entire year's check patterns. If the firm has seasonality in its sales, or if receipts are concentrated from a few remitting firms that pay infrequently, a small sample may not adequately represent the total pattern of receipts.

[20]See Kallberg and Parkinson, *Current Asset Management*, pp. 21–23.

Further, *the very redesign* of the firm's cash receipt system may cause changes in this pattern of receipts if some of the firm's customers practice "disbursement management." Disbursement management, we will see later in this chapter, can entail an attempt by the disbursing firm to stretch the clearing float on outgoing checks. This strategy may negate the receiving firm's attempts to speed float via lockbox strategy. For example, suppose that a major customer of a firm currently pays from Cleveland with checks drawn on a bank in Cleveland. Based on this data, the firm locates a lockbox in Cleveland to reduce clearing float and instructs the major customer to send remittances to this box. The disbursing firm may counter this by paying to the Cleveland lockbox with checks drawn on a bank in Los Angeles, increasing clearing float to counter the receiving firm's acceleration strategy.

The Costing of Float In most lockbox location analysis systems, the opportunity cost of float is determined by multiplying the total float in dollars times the required rate of return. This approach is intended to account for the time value of money, but it is exactly equivalent to net present value only when the future cash flow stream is a perpetuity.[21] When there is growth in the future cash flows, the opportunity cost approach will misstate the time cost of funds relative to their proper discounted value. In the analysis of lockbox strategies, an understatement occurs; the amount of this bias is a nonlinear function of the rate of growth, the float time, and the required return.[22] Because of problems such as this, in this text we try to avoid using the opportunity cost approach to the time value of money, calculating instead the net present values whenever possible. However, it does not appear that a reasonably simple solution to the lockbox location problem can be achieved unless the opportunity cost system is adopted.

Interaction with the Availability of Borrowing Capacity As noted previously, banks are prone to provide services in packages. Thus, the location of a lockbox at a bank may make the bank more likely to lend to the firm, possibly at favorable rates.[23] This borrowing availability and lower cost have a value to the firm. In such a case, the cash cost of the lockbox overstates the disadvantage to the firm of having a lockbox at a particular bank.

To restate, these difficulties do not negate the analysis methodologies presented in this text as a valid approach to the lockbox location problem. However, managers should be aware of these difficulties and their implications for lockbox analysis.

[21]We will prove this in Chapter 5.

[22]See Howard Lanser and John Halloran, "Evaluating Cash Flow Systems Under Growth," *Financial Review* (May 1986), pp. 309–18.

[23]See C. A. Batlin and Susan Hinko, "Lockbox Management and Value Maximization," *Financial Management* (Winter 1981), pp. 39–44.

CASH CONCENTRATION STRATEGIES

Once the remittances from the firm's customers have been received and cleared, the resulting cash balances are available in the firm's lockbox (depository) banks. It is useful for the firm to gather these balances from the lockbox banks into a central bank account. The process of collecting funds is called *cash concentration*. There are two reasons why cash concentration is advantageous. First, the collection process results in a larger pool of funds. The larger pool makes any temporary interest-earning investments more economical because it reduces the transaction costs per dollar invested. For example, if the firm gathers $10,000 from each of 10 accounts, the firm will have $100,000 to invest, resulting in one purchase of securities rather than 10. Also, the larger amount of funds may enable the firm to take advantage of higher-interest investments that require a larger minimum purchase. Second, with all the cash in a central location, keeping track of the cash (controlling the cash) is considerably simplified.[24]

In concentrating cash, firms channel collected funds from the depository banks to the central concentration bank, sometimes through regional concentration banks (see Figure 2-4). The main questions in the generation of a cash concentration system revolve around the design of the system and the scheduling of transfers. Typical questions include:

☐ What banks should be the firm's concentration banks?

☐ What mechanism should the firm use to concentrate funds?

☐ How frequently should transfers to the concentration banks be made?[25]

Concentration Banks The choice of concentration banks is not a simple one and is not easily quantified. For best clearing availabilities, these banks are usually located in major Fed cities, and firms often have a regional concentration bank located in each of the Federal Reserve districts in which it does a major amount of business. Cost is one consideration in choosing con-

[24]Another function of the cash concentration system, according to some authors, is to generate *dual balances*. Dual balances are caused by the Fed's policy of crediting cash to the firm on a fixed schedule even when the cash has not actually been collected, with the Fed funding the difference. Moving funds from one account to another sometimes creates dual balances. However, since 1979 the Fed has greatly reduced the amount of these dual balances, and is striving to reduce them further. Also, the Fed is certainly not in support of cash management strategies aimed at creating dual balances. For these reasons, the author does not consider the creation of dual balances to be a valid consideration in the design of a cash concentration system.

[25]In the interests of tractability, it will be assumed that the firm formulates separate strategies to address each of these questions. Simultaneous approaches to more than one of these questions tend to be extremely complex. For a critique of this approach, see Srinivasan and Kim, "Deterministic Cash Flow Management," pp. 154–156.

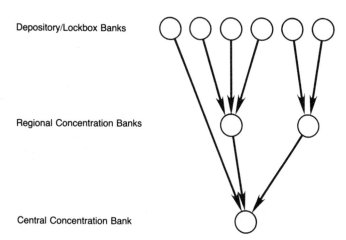

Depository/Lockbox Banks

Regional Concentration Banks

Central Concentration Bank

Figure 2-4. *A Typical Cash Concentration System (arrows indicate transfers of collected funds).*

centration banks, but more important is the array of other services that concentration banks can provide, particularly by assisting with the firm's credit needs and arrangements.

Concentration Mechanisms Several mechanisms are available for the firm to use in transferring funds from its collection banks to regional concentration banks, and from there to the central concentration bank. These mechanisms differ in cost and in the availability of funds that they provide. The cheapest transfer mechanism is the *depository transfer check*. This document instructs one bank to send funds to another, and is treated the same as any other check. A depository transfer check typically costs less than $1.00 and provides availability of the funds at the depositing bank in one or two days. A second alternative is the *automated clearinghouse (ACH) electronic transfer*. This vehicle is essentially an electronic version of the depository transfer check, and can be used between banks that participate in the automated clearinghouse system. Depending on the expense of preparation, these typically cost less than $5.00 and provide one-day availability. The most expensive vehicle is the *wire transfer*. These are electronic messages between banks; they cost about $10.00 and provide same-day availability.

Decisions regarding concentration mechanisms *usually hinge on the size and spread of the firm's deposits*. Firms with small deposits spread over a substantial number of banks will tend to have more extensive concentration systems and will transfer among accounts using low-cost transfer vehicles that offer only delayed availability (such as depository transfer checks). These characteristics are made necessary by the small individual amounts involved in the firm's deposits; concentration systems for supermarket chains and fast-food restaurants have these characteristics. Firms with larger deposits will have fewer accounts (since a local deposit for transfer to an upstream bank is not needed) and will use more expensive and more rapid transfer mechanisms (such as wire transfers). The concentration systems of major chemical companies, for example, tend to be structured in this way.

The choice among alternative mechanisms for the transfer of cash in concentration systems can be analyzed based on their relative cost. Comparison of the opportunity cost of float during transfer and the transfer costs gives the optimum. For example, assume that a particular lockbox of a firm receives an average of $75,000 per day in receipts. The firm follows a policy of transferring the collected cash from this lockbox bank to a regional or central concentration bank at the end of each business day. For this particular situation, a depository transfer check would cost $1.50 and provide two-day availability; an ACH electronic transfer would cost $3.00 and provide one-day availability; and a wire transfer would cost $16.00 and provide one-half-day availability. The required return is 8 percent per year.

The alternatives are compared in Table 2-11. In this table, the transfer cost per year is the number of transfers times the cost per transfer. For example, for the alternative of depository transfer checks, there are 250 transfers per year (the assumed number of business days) and each costs $1.50, so the transfer cost per year is $375. The float resulting from the transfer policy is the daily deposit amount times the availability from the transfer mechanism (for depository transfer checks, $75,000 per day times the two-day availability gives a $150,000 float). Costing this float at the required return produces its opportunity cost, and the total transfer cost of each alternative is that alternative's transfer cost plus its opportunity cost of float. For this

Table 2-11. Costing of Transfer Mechanisms for Example Problem.			
Daily Deposit	$75,000		
Transfers/Year	250		
Transfer Mechanism	*Depository Transfer Check*	*ACH Electronic Transfer*	*Wire Transfer*
Cost per Transfer	$ 1.50	$ 3.00	$ 16.00
Availability (Days)	2.00	1.00	0.50
Transfer Cost per Year	$ 375	$ 750	$ 4,000
Float	$150,000	$75,000	$37,500
Required Return	0.08%	0.08%	0.08%
Opportunity Cost of Float	$ 12,000	$ 6,000	$ 3,000
Total Transfer Cost	$ 12,375	$ 6,750	$ 7,000

problem, the lowest cost solution is to use the ACH electronic transfer mechanism.[26]

Frequency of Transfer Similar to the decision of what transfer vehicle to use is the decision on how frequently to make transfers. Frequent transfers to the concentration banks are costly but result in funds being available more quickly for use. Less frequent transfers reduce the out-of-pocket cost of these transfers but slow the availability of funds. While most large firms make daily transfers, other policies may be more economical.[27] Three of these policies are *scheduled transfers, trigger points*, and *anticipation transfers*.

Daily transfers are one variant of the *scheduled transfers* system. In this system, the firm decides on a predetermined time pattern of transfers from the depository bank to the concentration bank. These transfers are made regardless of the actual amounts of money received at the depository banks. For example, the firm might transfer every third business day or might set up a more complex schedule to reflect its historic pattern of cash receipts. Thus, a firm with heavy receipts early in each week and lighter receipts later in the week might choose to make transfers each Tuesday and Friday. The advantage of the scheduled transfers system is simplicity. The disadvantage is that transfers of uneconomically small amounts of funds may be made if receipts for a particular period happen to be less than expected.

The *trigger point* system avoids the transfer of small amounts by basing the transfer decision on account balance rather than on timing. In this system, the firm transfers all or part of the balance once the balance of collected funds in the depository bank reaches some predetermined level. This eliminates the transfer of small amounts, but results in a more complex decision process; balances at depository accounts must be monitored by the firm, or the depository bank must be given instructions to execute the trigger point transfers.

Anticipation transfers are a method of reducing the float within the transfer process. Here, the transfer is initiated based on anticipated (not actual) balances in the depository bank. For example, a firm with $100,000 in a depository account and expecting receipts of $900,000 over the next two days might initiate a depository transfer check for $1 million with a two-day availability. If receipts are as planned, the depository transfer check will reach the depository bank just as the funds are available for transfer. If the firm's daily cash forecasts are very accurate, this is an effective mechanism. How-

---

[26]The student may verify that for an average daily deposit of $100,000 the lowest cost solution is to use the wire transfer mechanism.

[27]The following discussion draws heavily from Berell Stone and Ned Hill, "Cash Transfer Scheduling for Efficient Cash Concentration," *Financial Management* (Autumn 1980), pp. 35–43.

ever, if there is uncertainty in these forecasts, the firm must hedge against the possibility that the depository transfer check will arrive but that there will not be sufficient funds to cover it (because collections over the two-day period were lower than expected). One such hedge is to keep a reserve of funds at the depository bank; the cost of this hedge offsets against the gains from the reduction of float in the transfer system.

Alternative frequency-of-transfer policies may be evaluated based on the cost of the transfers and the float resulting from various policies in a fashion similar to the evaluation of transfer mechanisms. However, advances in information technology may soon make all preplanned frequency-of-transfer systems a good deal less useful, particularly for larger firms. These preplanned systems are partly a result of the costliness of monitoring the balances in the various depository accounts maintained by the firm. The usual procedure for monitoring these balances used to require that a clerk (or a team of clerks) telephone all the firm's lockbox banks early in the morning to assess collected balances. This was an expensive procedure, and was prohibitively costly and complex if the firm had more than a few depository accounts; prespecified frequency-of-transfer systems avoid this data collection cost. However, software is now available to transfer balance information to the cash manager's computer before the opening of the work day. Investments and transfers based on actual account balances can then be initiated from the manager's computer work station. The Treasury Management System from BYAD Inc. (Arlington Heights, Illinois) is one software product with these capabilities. Systems such as this reduce the need for predetermined, inflexible transfer policies.

DISBURSEMENT MANAGEMENT

Lockbox systems address the collection of cash from the point at which the customer mails the check until the money is collected. Concentration systems address the gathering of this collected cash so that it may be used. *Disbursement management* addresses the efficient paying out of this cash once it is concentrated.

The firm's objective in disbursement management is to retain the cash for as long as possible. In this way, the firm will have the maximum amount of funds available for investment and transactional purposes. Obviously, this management entails making disbursements only when they are due and not before. Beyond this, the firm has several available sets of techniques for disbursement management. Included among these are the management of *disbursement float*, the use of *zero-balance accounts*, and the use of *controlled disbursing*.

Management of Disbursement Float   In this set of techniques, the disbursing firm tries to defeat the receiving firm's attempts to reduce the float on incoming checks. It does this by attempting to increase the length of time between the mailing of its checks and the eventual withdrawal of funds from its banks. This involves strategies for *increasing* mail float, at-firm float, and clearing float on its *outgoing* checks. For example, the disbursing firm may intentionally address checks to the firm's office address rather than its lockbox, creating at-firm float. Mathematical methodologies are available to maximize the expected mail and clearing float on outgoing checks.[28] These methods are mirror images of lockbox location routines, which *minimize* float on *incoming* checks.

This text does not present analysis techniques for the maximization of disbursement float nor does it recommend their use. There are four reasons for this position. First, in maximizing mail float, these techniques assume that a receiving firm calculates the receipt date for checks based on the check's postmark. Many firms, particularly larger ones, do not use this practice, but instead use the date of receipt at the firm's lockbox. When the receiving firm uses the lockbox receipt date, attempts to increase mail float by disbursing firms are irrelevant. Second, in maximizing clearing float, these algorithms often recommend disbursement locations in remote cities, cities where the disbursing firm does relatively little business. Having bank accounts with the small banks in these cities is of little advantage to the firm in negotiating other banking requirements (such as credit lines; remember, banks like to offer services in packages). Third, the maximization of disbursement float will not go unnoticed by sophisticated creditors for very long. When it is noticed, it will negatively affect relations with these creditors, reducing the firm's bargaining power with them. This may eventually cost the disbursing firm dearly when future prices and delivery schedules for goods and services purchased from trade creditors are negotiated. Finally, our experience with businesspersons indicates that the practice of lengthening disbursement float is regarded as being somewhat unethical, rather than as a legitimate business strategy. Firms that use this strategy will find their reputations with potential suppliers and others damaged.

Zero-Balance Accounts The remaining two methods of managing disbursements, zero-balance accounts and controlled disbursements, do not entail significant extensions of disbursement float to trade suppliers and other creditors. Instead, they are methods of synchronizing the arrival of funds at the disbursement bank accounts with the presentation of checks for disbursement at these accounts. That is, the firm holds the cash until the checks arrive (or are expected to arrive) at the disbursing bank. This coordination of funds inflows to disbursement banks with the presentation of checks does not work

---

[28]See Lawrence Gitman, D. Keith Forrester, and John R. Forrester, "Maximizing Cash Disbursement Float," *Financial Management* (Summer 1976), pp. 15–24.

to the detriment of creditors since the disbursing firm's checks to them are honored as presented, and these strategies do not affect float in any major way.

Zero-balance accounts are a very common strategy for funding disbursements as the checks are presented. In this strategy, an account for disbursement is first established at a bank. For the zero-balance system to be effective, the participating bank *must* be one on which most disbursements are made via the Fed's clearance system (which presents disbursements to banks early in the morning), and not a bank where disbursements occur throughout the day (as with a major money-center bank). Consequently, the banks used in zero-balance strategies are usually branches of major banks and not their main locations.

The once-a-morning disbursement requirement is *critical* to the zero-balance system. As implied by the name, the disbursing firm does not keep any permanent stock of cash in the disbursing account. Instead, the participating bank agrees that when the morning disbursements for the firm are presented to it, the bank will advise the firm of the amount of the cash required to cover these disbursements. The money will then be wire-transferred into the zero-balance account and the checks honored. In this way, the disbursing firms' checks are honored as presented, but the firm does not tie up cash while the checks are in the mail and while they are clearing.

Controlled Disbursing. If the zero-balance system is not feasible, another (though less attractive) is the use of *controlled disbursing*, which is often used when the firm's disbursing bank receives checks throughout the day. In this system, the firm projects the dollar amount of checks to arrive each day at the disbursement bank (based on the checks written in previous days and historic statistics on disbursement float) and transfers the amount of the expected checks to the account on that day or just before.[29] Of course, the firm does not know exactly what outstanding checks will be presented on any particular day; the forecasting procedure is subject to error because the disbursement float figures are uncertain. To hedge this uncertainty, firms keep a *safety stock of cash* in the disbursement account. The amount of this safety stock may be calculated if the probability distribution of disbursements is known.[30] For example, suppose that the probability distribution of disbursements is normal, that the firm wishes to have only a 1.0 percent chance that the initial cash will be insufficient to cover the presented checks, and that for a particular day the expected presentments are $500,000 with a standard deviation of $50,000. Since the Z-score for 1.0 percent of the normal distribution is 2.72, the firm will need to start with an additional $136,000 (2.72

[29]See Vander Weide and Maier, *Managing Corporate Liquidity*, pp. 142–65, for methods of projecting disbursement float times.

[30]We will extensively discuss this approach to the hedging of the risk of cash flows in the next chapter.

times $50,000) in its disbursement account, above the expected requirement of $500,000, to have only a 1.0 percent chance of having insufficient funds. Thus, the firm should arrange to have $636,000 in its account to cover disbursements for that day. The additional $136,000 is a hedge, and its carrying cost is the result of uncertainty regarding the firm's disbursement figure for that day.

SUMMARY

This chapter concerns the management of cash inflows and outflows. The management of these flows is a major task of the cash management group within the firm. This task starts when checks are in the mail to the firm and includes the management of these checks while they are in the postal system and while they are in the process of being cleared against the banks on which they are drawn. The major technique for the management of cash during this time is *lockbox location strategy*. Once the incoming checks have been cleared, the firm must gather the cash together so it can be efficiently used. The firm's system for the management of this gathering process is *cash concentration strategy*. When the firm is required to disburse the cash, it must also manage this process so the firm may retain the cash for the longest possible time. The management of outgoing cash is done via the firm's *disbursement management strategy*. All three strategies are discussed in this chapter.

This chapter also gives three reasons for holding cash and near-cash assets: for transactions needs, as a hedge against uncertainties in the firm's cash flow, and as a temporary investment of surplus funds. The popular near-cash assets used as alternatives to cash in hedging and as temporary investments for surpluses are discussed. Included in this discussion is an assessment of the relative risks (based on default and interest rate risks) and returns of these assets. What is not discussed (except in a very general way) is how firms develop strategies for the timing and amount of their investments in these assets. The following chapter, Chapter 3, discusses cash forecasting. The formulation of strategy for the temporary investment of surplus funds is a major outcome of cash forecasting procedures. Strategy for investment in the near-cash assets that are used as alternatives to cash in the hedging of the firm's cash flow uncertainty will be discussed in Chapter 4.

Looking to the future, one factor which may substantially impact lockbox location analysis and cash concentration strategies is the trend toward the deregulation of banks. A primary response by the financial sector to deregulation has been the geographic expansion of well-managed banks. Should true interstate banking come to pass, banks with interstate branches may be able to offer additional lockboxes to their customers at costs substantially less than the current costs of opening lockboxes at remote locations. Firms would then have additional incentives to locate lockboxes so as to reduce flotation on incoming checks. Also, the costs of transferring funds to and from depository, concentration, and disbursement accounts at branch locations of multistate banks is likely to be much lower than the current costs of transfer mechanisms among banks, and more frequent transfers of funds will result. It is clear that interstate banking would be likely to increase the amount of firms' activity in the collection, concentration, and disbursement of cash flows while decreasing the cost of these systems. Firms' relationships with their banks would also become less complex since larger interstate banks would be able to provide a wider range of services, and firms would then be able to reduce the number of banks with which they deal.[31]

Problems

2-1. A firm is trying to decide where to locate its lockbox(es). Checks come to the firm from three different locations, and the firm has received proposals for lockboxes in two of these locations. Data on the lockbox proposals are:

Lockbox Location	A	B
Yearly Fixed Lockbox Charge	$10,000	$15,000
Processing Charge per Check	$0.10	$0.15
Clearing and Processing Float	1.5 days	1.0 day

The mail float matrix (in days) is:

		Origin Location		
		A	B	C
Destination	A	2.3	3.0	3.5
Location	B	3.0	2.2	3.2
	C	3.5	3.2	2.0

The check origination data is:

Origin Location	Daily Receipts from This Origin Location	Yearly Number of Checks from This Origin Location
A	$10,000,000	2,500,000
B	$15,000,000	3,500,000
C	$12,000,000	4,500,000

The firm's required return is 8.5 percent per year. Use a 360-day year. Based on the above data, calculate the yearly cost of: (a)

---

[31]For additional discussion, see Srinivasan and Kim, "Deterministic Cash Flow Management," p. 159.

using only one lockbox, with that lockbox located at A, and (b) using only one lockbox, with that lockbox located at B.

2-2. Develop the objective function and the necessary constraint equations for the lockbox location problem given in Problem 1. Use the following variable definitions:

YA = a 0–1 integer variable indicating whether there is a lockbox open at location A (1 if there is, 0 if there is not).

YB = a 0–1 integer variable indicating whether there is a lockbox open at location B (1 if there is, 0 if there is not).

XAA = a 0–1 integer variable indicating whether checks originating at location A are sent to the lockbox at location A (1 if they are, 0 if they are not).

XAB = a 0–1 integer variable indicating whether checks originating at location A are sent to the lockbox at location B (1 if they are, 0 if they are not).

XBA = a 0–1 integer variable indicating whether checks originating at location B are sent to the lockbox at location A (1 if they are, 0 if they are not).

XBB = a 0–1 integer variable indicating whether checks originating at location B are sent to the lockbox at location B (1 if they are, 0 if they are not).

XCA = a 0–1 integer variable indicating whether checks originating at location C are sent to the lockbox at location A (1 if they are, 0 if they are not).

XCB = a 0–1 integer variable indicating whether checks originating at location C are sent to the lockbox at location B (1 if they are, 0 if they are not).

2-3. Assume that the firm described in Problem 1 has solved its lockbox location problem via integer programming, with the following result:

$$YA = 1.0$$
$$YB = 1.0$$
$$XAA = 1.0$$
$$XAB = 0.0$$
$$XBA = 0.0$$
$$XBB = 1.0$$
$$XCA = 0.0$$
$$XCB = 1.0$$

Calculate the yearly cost of this solution to the lockbox location problem.

Selected Readings

Brown, Keith, and Scott Lummer, "The Cash Management Implications of a Hedged Dividend Capture Strategy," *Financial Management* (Winter 1984), pp. 7–17.

Cook, Timothy, and Bruce Summers, eds., *Instruments of the Money Market*, Fifth Edition (Richmond: Federal Reserve Bank of Richmond, 1981).

Copeland, T. E., and J. F. Weston, *Financial Theory and Corporate Policy*, Second Edition (Reading, Mass.: Addison-Wesley, 1983) pp. 65–70.

Economic Review, March and April 1986 issues, published by the Federal Reserve Bank of Atlanta.

Maier, Steven, and James Vander Weide, "What Lockbox and Disbursement Models Really Do," *Journal of Finance* (May 1983), p. 364.

Nauss, Robert M., and Robert E. Markland, "Solving Lock Box Location Problems," *Financial Management* (Spring 1979), pp. 21–31.

Srinivasan, V., and Y. Kim, "Deterministic Cash Flow Management: State of the Art and Research Directions," *Omega*, Vol. 14, No. 2 (1986), pp. 145–166.

Stone, Berell, and Ned Hill, "Cash Transfer Scheduling for Efficient Cash Concentration," *Financial Management* (Autumn 1980).

Butler Manufacturing[1]
Lockbox Location

The Butler Manufacturing Company was started in the mid-1950s, and was a subsidiary of a large German firm. By 1983, annual sales had reached the half-billion dollar level. The company was organized into five divisions of unequal size. This organization resulted, in part, from the piecemeal fashion in which the company had grown through acquisitions and, in part, from attempts to parallel the parent organization's structure with respect to product lines. Each division had, until recently, been operated quite autonomously; in fact, the divisions had been separately incorporated subsidiary operations until 1970.

In 1982, the firm had decided to centralize certain operations. Operating separately, each division had developed (or had inherited from its predecessor) different methods for handling various operations. Top management felt that some of these operations could be better addressed on a centralized basis. The corporate offices in New York City were closed and the company's top management was moved to recently constructed

[1]This case has been adapted from Iqbal Mathur and Frederick C. Scherr, *Cases in Financial Management* (New York: Macmillan, 1979), pp. 37–44.

corporate headquarters in Philadelphia. The site was adjacent to the headquarters of Butler's largest division in terms of sales volume.

An example of how differently the five divisions were operated was provided by their respective accounts receivable management and cash application systems. The largest division of the firm had annual sales of $325 million. Its cash application system was a manual-computer hybrid, wherein the cash application clerk identified the items being paid from alphabetical listings and manually removed a computer card from a deck of such cards signifying the outstanding items. The computer then compared the cards pulled against the tape record of the division's accounts receivable to determine which items were to be removed. The firm's second-largest division, headquartered in St. Louis (with sales of $100 million per year), used an entirely computer-based system. As checks came in, data were encoded; a computer program then scanned the tape of outstanding accounts receivable items to determine which had been paid. The cash application clerk audited this cash application program by examining the check and invoice information presented on a CRT. A slightly smaller division, head-

67

Exhibit 1

Butler Manufacturing
Some Characteristics of Five Divisions

Headquarters Location	*Plant Locations*	*Annual Sales (Millions)*	*Number of Checks Received per Year*
Philadelphia	Virginia Texas	$325	67,000
St. Louis	Missouri	$100	25,000
Charlottesville	Virginia New Jersey	$80	53,000
Los Angeles	California	$40	81,000
New York	None—Products imported from Germany	$10	20,000

quartered in Charlottesville, Virginia (annual sales of $80 million), used a totally manual system; copies of invoices generated by this division were physically filed in alphabetical order as they were generated. When paid, they were removed from the file and stored by date of payment. The firm's smallest division, headquartered in New York (with annual sales of $10 million), used a similar system. The remaining division was headquartered in Los Angeles and had annual sales of $40 million. Its cash application and accounts receivable system was similar to that of the Philadelphia division except that no manual cards were used. The cash application clerk worked from computer printouts; after he had determined what item had been paid, this data was encoded and the paid item removed from the accounts receivable data tape. A chart of the divisions and some of their characteristics is presented in Exhibit 1.

Like the divisions' cash application and accounts receivable systems, their cash management policies also differed substantially, though top management had recently made some attempts at coordination and rationalization. Each division kept a central receiving

and disbursing bank account for cash receipts and trade payments. Each division also had a payroll account at a local bank for each plant and/or headquarters location. Money was wire transferred into these payroll accounts on the day that paychecks were written, and drawn out by employees shortly thereafter. Sales offices (which were scattered about the United States) were not allowed to have local bank accounts; emergency needs were met from petty cash. Other disbursements were made from the divisional receipts and disbursements accounts. Paychecks for field salesmen were mailed to their homes, and were drawn on payroll accounts at their division's headquarters locations. The corporate headquarters used the accounts of the Philadelphia division. It was the company's policy to pay for all bank services on a straight fee (rather than compensating balance) basis.

In addition to the receipts and disbursements and the payroll accounts, the Philadelphia division had several small accounts with international banks. This division did a sizable export business, and it was felt that having these accounts was necessary to facilitate receipts from export sales. A chart of

Exhibit 2

Butler Manufacturing
Current Location and Number of Bank Accounts

Headquarters Location	Rec.-Disb. Account Locations	Payroll Account Locations	International Account Locations	Total Account Locations
Philadelphia	Philadelphia	Virginia Texas Pennsylvania	New York (5)	9
St. Louis	St. Louis	Missouri	None	2
Charlottesville	Char.	Virginia New Jersey	None	3
Los Angeles	Los Angeles	California	None	2
New York	New York	None— Products Imported from Germany	None	1
				17

the bank accounts of the firm is presented in Exhibit 2.

To facilitate the deposit of checks, most of the divisions kept lockboxes at the bank handling their receipts and disbursements account. The exception was the Los Angeles division. The credit manager of this division was opposed to using a lockbox because he felt that too large a portion of the checks for his division were nonroutine items: they were restrictively endorsed, postdated, and so on. Lockboxes do not handle these items well. It had not been determined if this contention was valid, but the Los Angeles division did deal (on average) with smaller customers than the other divisions.

Centralization of Butler's cash management functions had already resulted in several changes. The division had been required to submit weekly and monthly cash forecasts showing expected future bank balances. The cash management staff at the corporate headquarters then combined these forecasts and planned the firm's borrowing and investment strategies. However, with five divisions and thus five receipts and disbursements accounts, coordination was a problem. After the cash managers at headquarters had stripped off excess cash, unexpectedly low receipts at any division could cause a cash stockout at that division's disbursements account. This was handled by transferring cash from the accounts of one or more other divisions that had experienced greater-than-expected receipts. This transfer procedure led to substantial additional transfer costs and had necessitated significant time and effort on the part of the corporate cash management group to make and record such transactions.

Also, it was clear that the rather arbitrary location of the firm's lockboxes needed to be reconsidered. It was obvious that the divisionalized character of the lockbox locations did not lead to the quickest receipt of funds. For example, the Philadelphia division did substantial business with customers in Virginia and in the Carolinas. However, under the current system all the checks from these customers were sent to the division's lockbox in Philadelphia even though the firm had a much closer lockbox in Charlottesville serving the division based there.

To address these problems, the firm's treasurer decided to rationalize the firm's cash collection system. The divisions would no longer operate their own collections systems. Instead, a series of lockboxes would be set up across the country; a customer of any division would be instructed to send remittances to the lockbox that would result in the shortest flotation. Concentration bank accounts would be set up at the firm's Philadelphia bank, and the receipts to these lockboxes would be transferred to the concentration account at the end of each day. Needed funds would be transferred to the disbursement accounts at the divisions as needed, similar to the procedure currently used for payroll disbursements at plant locations. It was felt that this concentration system would eliminate the transfers between divisions and result in the minimum economical flotations on incoming funds. The main question was where to put the lockboxes.

To address this problem, the firm divided the originating zip codes of incoming checks into six regions and solicited bids from one bank in each of these regions that could provide lockbox services.[2] The details of these bids are presented in Exhibit 3.

Prior to soliciting these bids, Butler had to decide what level of lockbox service was

[2]The situation here has been considerably simplified to aid in calculation. Typically, two-digit zip code designations are used to designate regions (resulting in 100 regions) and many more offers are solicited, including some from several banks in the same region.

Exhibit 3

Butler Manufacturing
Details of Lockbox Bids

Lockbox Location	Processing Cost per Check	Yearly Fixed Fee
Northeast	$0.145	$2,500
Southeast	$0.130	$2,000
North Central	$0.160	$1,500
South Central	$0.140	$2,500
Northwest	$0.175	$4,000
Southwest	$0.180	$3,500

---

acceptable for the firm. These levels related to how much time and attention the bank providing the lockbox service would give to each check, how much information would be forwarded to Butler regarding each check, and how this information would be forwarded. The most expensive service involved the manual handling of each check, and the forwarding of the envelope in which the check was received, any remittance advice on how the check was to be applied, and a photocopy of the check itself. This careful handling and complete forwarding gave Butler the most information about each received check but was relatively costly (about $0.25 per check). The least expensive service provided only minimal data about each check (usually a computer printout listing only the payer and the check amount), and generally cost about $0.11 per check. Butler decided that an intermediate level of information (and thus processing charges) would be sufficient to identify the items paid by each check received, and had specified this level of service in soliciting lockbox bids from each of the banks.

A few more details on these bids are useful. The bid from the bank in the Northeast region was from the concentration bank in Philadelphia. Thus, no daily wire transfers

Exhibit 4

Butler Manufacturing Company
Average Mail Times between Parts of the Country in Days

| | Destination | | | | | |
Origin	Northeast	Southeast	N. Central	S. Central	Northwest	Southwest
Northeast	2.2	2.3	2.8	3.0	3.5	4.2
Southeast	2.3	2.1	3.2	2.9	4.2	3.6
North Central	2.8	3.2	2.5	3.0	2.9	3.0
South Central	3.0	2.9	3.0	2.3	3.1	3.2
Northwest	3.5	4.2	2.9	3.1	2.5	2.6
Southwest	4.2	3.6	3.0	3.2	2.6	2.5

Exhibit 5

Butler Manufacturing Company
Analysis of Customer Pay—from Location by Division
(percent of total receipts)

| | Division | | | | |
	Philadelphia	St. Louis	Charlottesville	Los Angeles	New York
Northeast	31	12	30	0	76
Southeast	21	32	61	0	20
North Central	20	2	0	0	0
South Central	9	27	9	0	0
Northwest	2	10	0	26	0
Southwest	17	17	0	74	4

would be required with respect to this bid. For the other location proposals, daily wire transfers of collections would add $6,000 per year to the lockbox costs. Average mail times between regions are given in Exhibit 4. Butler's management decided to add one day to these mail times to account for clearing and processing float for all checks received from within a region and 1.5 days for all checks received from outside a region.[3] Butler's required rate of return on any funds freed due to decreased float was 8 percent. Remittance origin locations (pay-from locations) for Butler's customers are given in Exhibit 5.

[3]This structure of clearing times is assumed for simplicity. Clearing times usually vary from bank to bank, and thus from lockbox location to lockbox location.

chapter 3

Cash Forecasting

In this chapter, methods for generating the firm's *cash forecast* (sometimes known as the firm's *cash budget*) are discussed. The cash forecast is an estimation of the flows in and out of the firm's cash account over a particular period of time, usually a quarter, month, week, or day. The cash forecast is primarily intended to produce a very useful piece of information: an *estimation of the firm's borrowing and lending needs* and the uncertainties regarding these needs during various future periods.

Cash forecasting is extremely important to most firms. It enables them to *anticipate* periods of surplus cash and periods where financing will be necessary. This anticipation is the reason that cash forecasts are generated. Anticipation enables the firm to *plan* much more effectively for investment and financing, and via this planning, produce superior returns.

WHY FORECAST CASH FLOWS?

To see why the cash forecasting process produces additional returns, let us consider the situation where the firm *does not* use cash forecasting.[1] Unanticipated cash shortages could occur. During these periods, the firm would have to slow down its cash outflows, dip into reserves, or get emergency financing. A typical method of slowing outflows in such a situation would be to delay payments to trade suppliers.[2] Because of these late payments, sup-

---

[1]For an excellent discussion of the need for cash forecasting, see E. M. Lerner, "Simulating a Cash Budget," *California Management Review* (Winter 1968), pp. 79–86, particularly pages 79–80.

[2]We refer here to an *unanticipated* delay in paying suppliers *beyond* their stated terms of sale. The *planned* use of delaying suppliers as a financing tool is discussed in Chapters 11 and 12, where we cover short-term financing.

72

pliers might delay delivery of critical materials, causing expensive production delays. The firm's slowness in payment might become known to customers and shareholders, who would question the firm's financial soundness. Alternatively, if the firm tried to get an emergency bank loan to provide the needed funds under these circumstances, the firm's bank might be reluctant to grant such a loan on reasonable terms, since their confidence in the ability of the firm's management would be lessened. Higher interest rates or onerous constraints on management actions would likely be the result.

Now let us consider the situation where the firm has an unanticipated, unplanned *surplus* of cash. This happy surprise causes almost as many problems as an unplanned deficit. Without a cash forecast, the firm has no way of knowing how long the surplus will persist, that is, if and when the cash will be needed for expenses. Without such knowledge, the firm cannot make an investment plan that will maximize interest income on the surplus funds. To see this, assume that the yield curve (discussed in Chapter 2) is upsloping. The longer the maturity of the investment, the higher the interest yield per period. But without a cash forecast, the firm cannot take advantage of this effect *because it does not know how long it will have the surplus funds*. If the money is going to be available for only a few days, it would be a mistake to buy a 90-day instrument; the firm would have to sell it prior to maturity, and subject itself to unnecessary interest rate risk. On the other hand, if the money is going to be available for six months, putting it in a relatively low-interest but highly liquid near-cash instrument would not produce the highest interest income. Thus we see that the cash forecast is a critical tool for effective financing of temporary deficits and investment of temporary surpluses.

While the firm's cash forecast is an important document, it is not generated nor does it function in isolation. The cash forecast is an important part of the firm's *cash control system* and is one of the forecasts that is part of the firm's *financial plan*. The firm's cash control system includes its lockboxes, its marketable securities portfolio, its short-term borrowing structure, and its cash management and transfer system. (All of these topics are discussed in other chapters.)[3]

Besides the cash forecast, the firm also makes numerous other forecasts as part of its financial planning process. In fact, these other documents are *critical inputs* to the cash forecast.[4] The firm's *capital budget* details planned outflows for capital expenditures. The firm's *production plan* provides significant information on expected manufacturing expenses. The firm's *sales forecast* is important in determining many other expected cash inflows and outflows. In fact, the firm's other financial plans and estimates are usually

[3]For more discussion of the relationship between the firm's cash budget and the other aspects of its cash management system, see F. W. Searby, "Use Your Hidden Cash Resources," *Harvard Business Review* (March-April 1968), pp. 71–80.

[4]For a discussion of the relationship between the firm's cash forecast and its other financial planning documents, see K. V. Smith, *Guide to Working Capital Management* (New York: McGraw-Hill, 1979), pp. 39–61.

generated *before* the cash forecast is made because so many of the estimates used in the cash forecast are dependent on these other plans.

TYPES OF CASH FORECASTS

The types of cash forecasts generated by firms can be differentiated along two dimensions: the *length of the periods* included within the cash forecast and the *approach to cash flows* used in the cash forecast.

The *length of the periods* refers to the units of time into which the cash forecast is divided. Firms may make cash flow forecasts over periods of various lengths: yearly flows, quarterly flows, monthly flows, weekly flows, or even daily flows. The most popular forecast involves monthly flows, but most firms do not confine themselves to a single forecast. Instead they use several forecasts with periods of various lengths.[5] The important question is what the length of the *shortest* period to be forecast should be. This depends critically on the volume of the firm's cash inflows and outflows because of the transaction costs involved in short-term investments. If the firm is sufficiently large that the investment of a day's surplus is profitable, it will probably pay the firm to forecast on a daily basis (as well as on periods of longer lengths). Small firms with lesser amounts to lend are probably better off using a week or even a month as the length of their shortest period (assuming that any temporary shortages of funds within these periods can be covered without undue cost).

Another question that arises when the firm makes forecasts involving multiple and overlapping period lengths is how one forecast relates to another. To see how this question arises, assume that a firm is practicing multiple period-length forecasting and is generating forecasts for the next quarter, months within this quarter, and weeks within these months. Does the forecaster start with quarterly data and break this down into months, then break the months down into weeks, or does the forecaster start with weekly data and aggregate this into months and quarters? Starting with data on relatively long periods and breaking it down into smaller periods is called *distribution*; starting with data on relatively short periods and aggregating into longer periods is called *scheduling*.[6] Both methodologies have advantages and disadvantages. Scheduling requires more data manipulation, but distribution requires more sophisticated statistical techniques. The cash forecasting systems of most sophisticated firms involve a combination of the two methods.[7]

---

[5]See D. I. Fisher, *Cash Management* (New York: The Conference Board, 1973), page 5.

[6]See B. K. Stone and R. W. Wood, "Daily Cash Forecasting: A Simple Method for Implementing the Distribution Approach," *Financial Management* (Fall 1977), pp. 40–50.

[7]See Stone and Wood, "Daily Cash Forecasting," page 41.

Table 3-1. *A Typical Spreadsheet Cash Forecast by the Receipts and Disbursements Method.*

!	A	!!	B	!!	C	!!	D !
1	Cash Forecast						
2							
3	Month:		Jan.		Feb.		. . .
4							
5	Receipts:						
6	Collections on Receivables		2,500		3,000		. . .
7							
8	Disbursements:						
9	Labor Expenses		1,000		1,200		. . .
10	Materials Expenses		900		1,300		. . .
11	Other Expenses		300		600		. . .
12							
13	Net Cash Flow (Rec − Disb)		300		−100		. . .
14							
15	Beginning Cash		100		400		. . .
16	Net Cash Position		400		300		. . .
17	Required Cash Level		300		450		. . .
18	Surplus Cash		100				. . .
19	Deficit Cash				−150		. . .

Firms use two common *approaches to cash flows* in generating the cash forecast: the *receipts and disbursements approach* and the *adjusted net income* approach. The receipts and disbursements approach uses the amounts of cash expected to be received and disbursed by the firm over the periods chosen for the forecast. This method minutely traces the movement of cash and is preferred by firms that exercise very close cash control. It is usually used for cash forecasts with relatively short period lengths (daily, weekly, or monthly) and short time horizons (up to a year or so in the future). The format of a typical spreadsheet cash forecast using the receipts and disbursements method is illustrated in Table 3-1; we will discuss the possible types of entries in such a spreadsheet forecast later in this chapter.

The adjusted income statement approach is sometimes called the sources and uses approach. Here, the forecaster starts with projected net income on an accrual basis and adjusts to a cash basis. The format of a typical spreadsheet cash forecast using the adjusted net income method is provided in Table 3-2. This method provides a representation of changes in asset and liability accounts; since the levels of these accounts are of interest to the firm, this aspect of the adjusted income statement approach is an advantage over the receipts and disbursements method. However, the adjusted net income method does not permit the tracing of the individual types of cash inflows and outflows for any given period, which is often useful information for the firm. The adjusted net income method is usually used by firms for longer-

Table 3-2. A Typical Spreadsheet Cash Forecast by the Adjusted Net Income Method.

!	A	!!	B	!!	C	!!	D !
1	Cash Forecast						
2							
3	Month:		Jan.		Feb.		. . .
4							
5	Sources:						
6	Earnings After Taxes		100		150		. . .
7	Depreciation Addback		150		150		. . .
8	Increases in Liabilities		200		50		. . .
9	Decreases in Assets		50		300		. . .
10	Total Sources		500		650		. . .
11							
12	Uses:						
13	Dividends		25		25		. . .
14	Decreases in Liabilities		125		225		. . .
15	Increases in Assets		50		500		. . .
16	Total Uses		200		750		
17							
18	Net Cash Flow (Sour − Use)		300		− 100		. . .
19	Beginning Cash		100		400		. . .
20	Net Cash Position		400		300		. . .
21	Required Cash Level		300		450		. . .
22	Surplus Cash		100				. . .
23	Deficit Cash				− 150		. . .

term forecasts of surpluses and deficits (a year or more in the future). Since our concern in this text is with the management of short-term assets and liabilities, we will concentrate on the receipts and disbursements approach to forecasting. In our examples, we will center on monthly forecasts because of the popularity of this period length.

ITEMS TO BE FORECAST

In the receipts and disbursements cash forecasting method, estimates need to be made of the numerous major and minor items that the firm collects (receipts) and that it pays (disbursements). The more individual categories of items the firm includes in its forecast procedure, the more accurate the forecast may be, but the more costly in terms of time and effort it will be to generate.

Most firms find that the receipts portion of the cash forecast contains far fewer potential individual categories of items than does the disbursements forecast. Most firms' primary source of receipts is the collection of monies

Table 3-3. *Some Possible Types of Cash Receipts.*

Accounts Receivable Collections—Domestic Customers
Accounts Receivable Collections—Foreign Customers
Notes Receivable
Rental Income
Interest Income
Principal on Maturing Investments
Dividends from Subsidiaries
Miscellaneous Receipts

from sales: either via direct inflows from cash sales or via inflows resulting from the collection of accounts receivable, which are the results of prior sales. However, inflows from other sources not related to sales are sometimes non-trivial. In deciding what categories of inflows to include in the receipts portion of its cash forecast, management should first list all the firm's major types of inflows. A list of some possible types of inflows is provided in Table 3-3. Whether relatively minor categories of inflows should be examined in detail or merely aggregated and approximated depends on their size relative to other inflows *and their seasonality*. A type of inflow that contributes relatively little to total flow during one month may be quite important in another.

Table 3-4. *Some Possible Types of Cash Disbursements.*

Cash Purchases of Materials
Payroll—Executive
Payroll—Nonexecutive
Taxes—Local
Taxes—State
Taxes—Federal Income
Taxes—FICA Withheld
Maturing Accounts Payable
Mortgage Payments
Maturing Notes Payable—Interest and Principal
Capital Expenditures
Utility Payments
Dividends—Preferred Stock
Dividends—Common Stock
Sinking Fund Payments—Outstanding Bonds
Interest Payments—Outstanding Bonds
Maturing Bonds—Principal Repayments
Payments to Pension Fund
Market Repurchase of Outstanding Stock or Bonds
Miscellaneous Disbursements

The types of disbursements that a firm makes are usually more diverse than the types of receipts. The firm's major outflows are often for payroll, payments to suppliers, capital expenditures, and interest and principal payments. However, as with receipts, types and patterns of disbursements vary considerably with the firm's line of business, business style, and business strategy. Rent and lease payments, for example, are often a substantial portion of outflows for firms that do not own their facilities, but are less important to firms following other ownership policies. A list of potential outflow categories in the disbursements portion of the firm's cash forecast is provided in Table 3-4.

A primary question, after the firm has determined what types of receipts and disbursements are important in its overall cash flow, is how to forecast the future levels of these types of inflows and outflows. A brief review of the procedures most commonly used for financial forecasting is in order.

METHODS OF FINANCIAL FORECASTING

Financial forecasting is the estimation of the future level of a financial variable, often a cash flow, asset level, or liability level. It is usually assumed that the relationship between the financial variable and other variables is linear. The *general linear model* can then be used:

$$Y_t = a_o + a_1X_1 + a_2X_2 \ldots a_nX_n \qquad (3\text{-}1)$$

Here, Y_t is the financial variable (Y) to be forecast in period t. The X's are the *explanatory variables*; they are assumed to cause the level of Y in period t. The a_o term represents a constant unaffected by the X's. The other a terms are the estimated coefficients of the explanatory X variables. There are n terms with X's in them. This general methodology will be clearer as examples are presented. It is understood that any forecast made in this way is subject to some prediction error because of uncertainty about both the future levels of the X's and uncertainty about the exact relationship between the explanatory variables (the X's) and the outcome variable (the Y; that is, uncertainty about the a coefficients). There are four common approaches to forecasting financial variables, but they are all special cases of the general linear model. These four methods are discussed below.

Spot Method Here it is assumed that the variable to be forecast is independent of all other variables, or alternatively, is predetermined. The variable is forecast by using its expected or predetermined level. All other explanatory variables are presumed to be irrelevant and the formula used is

$$Y_t = a_o \qquad (3\text{-}2)$$

were a_o is the expected or predetermined level of Y_t. For example, if we are doing a cash forecast and we know that the level of a particular type of disbursement (such as rental payments) will be $12,000 in every month because of the firm's lease agreement, it would be reasonable to use the spot method to estimate rental payments as $12,000 per month.

Proportion of Another Account This technique is used to project financial variables that are expected to vary directly with the level of another variable. The formula used is:

$$Y_t = a_1 X_1 \qquad (3\text{-}3)$$

where X_1 is the other variable to which Y is related and a_1 is the constant of proportionality between the two. The "percent of sales" method is a variation of this technique, wherein X_1 is sales for a particular period and a_1 is the percent. The "proportion of another account" method is widely used when there is a causal link from the explanatory variable to the variable to be forecast. For example, if sales volume (units sold) increases, it is natural that more units will have to be produced to replenish inventory. It is then reasonable to project certain direct costs of production, such as direct materials, as a percent of sales. In this circumstance, if costs of direct materials have historically been 50 percent of sales, and sales for a particular period have been forecast as $100,000, the firm would normally project direct material purchases at $50,000 for that period.

Compounded Growth This method is used when a particular financial variable is expected to grow at a steady growth rate over time. The formula is the same as equation (3-3), but the explanatory variable X_1 is the *prior period's* level of Y, and a_1 is one plus the expected growth rate. That is:

$$Y_t = (1 + g) Y_{t-1} \qquad (3\text{-}4)$$

where g is the period's growth rate. For example, if it is expected that a firm's level of selling expenses will grow at 10 percent per year, and this year's selling expenses are $1 million, we would project next year's selling expenses as $1.1 million.

Multiple Dependencies Here the variable is thought to depend on more than one factor; not just sales or some other variable but a combination of several variables. The general linear model as expressed in equation (3-1) is used, and the statistical technique of *linear regression* is often employed with historic data to estimate which explanatory variables are significant in determining Y_t and to estimate the coefficients of these variables. A classic example of multiple dependency is inventory level. Firms often keep a "base level" or "safety stock" of inventory to hedge uncertainty and vary the remaining portion of inventory in response to demand. In such a system, there are two appropriate variables associated with inventory level:

$$Y_t = a_o + a_1X_1 \qquad (3\text{-}5)$$

The a_o term represents the base inventory level, the X_1 the square root of the sales level, and a_1 the proportionality constant.[8] If the firm's base level of inventory is $50,000, the proportionality constant is 15 and sales are expected to be $500,000, we could estimate inventory as:

$$Y_t = 50,000 + (15) ((500,000)^{1/2}) = \$60,607 \qquad (3\text{-}6)$$

All these forecasting methods will be used at times in the course of this text.

In deciding which of these methods to use to forecast a particular variable, a primary consideration is the *term of the forecast*: how far into the future are we projecting? To see this, the concepts of *the short run* and *the long run* from economics can be employed. In the short run, most things are predetermined or preplanned; very little can be changed. In the long run, almost everything is variable. In terms of financial forecasting, this means that in short-term forecasts, many things will result from plans and events that are already in place (contracts, capital budgets, long-range financing plans, and so forth). But in the long run, most things can vary and are dependent on outside influences such as the firm's long-term growth rate. Since cash forecasts deal mostly with the near future, *many of the items on the cash forecast are estimated by some variation of the spot method*. The bases for these spot estimates are usually the firm's other financial plans. Remaining estimates are mostly on a "proportion of another account" basis, with this "other account" often being a particular period's sales; the other two methods are employed less frequently. This is quite unlike longer-term forecasting, where compounded growth and multiple dependency methodologies play a more important role.

FORECASTING COLLECTIONS FROM ACCOUNTS RECEIVABLE

The firm's *cash disbursements* are generally forecast in a straightforward fashion using the firm's other plans and a combination of the forecasting methods described previously. However, a major challenge for the analyst comes in estimating the *receipts from the collection of the firm's receivables*. There are two major decisions to be made: the *forecasting methodology* to

---

[8]The rationale for this approach to inventory management strategy will be discussed in Chapters 8 and 9.

be used and the *degree of aggregation* of the forecast across the firm's lines of business.[9]

One forecasting methodology used by firms is the *turnover method*. This is a variation of the percent of sales method in which it is assumed that receivables will all be collected based on the average turnover of the receivables of the firm. For example, if the firm's average receivables' turnover is 30 days, it is projected that all sales for one month will be collected in the following month. The problem with this system is that it does not do a very good job of capturing the actual process of receivables collection, and therefore it does not produce accurate forecasts except in special cases. This problem stems from the turnover statistic as a *weighted average* of the payment patterns of various customers paying at different times. A better receipt forecasting method is the *payment patterns approach* (also known as payment fractions or payment proportions approach). In this method, the analyst determines (using historical data) the proportion of customers that pay at various times after the date of sale and from this information projects future receipts.

The payment patterns method gives forecasts quite different from the turnover method. To see this, let us develop an example. Assume that last month's sales were $20,000, that this month's sales are expected to be $30,000, and that next month's sales are expected to be $20,000. Assume that 30 percent of the customers purchased products for cash, 40 percent paid in 30 days, and the remaining 30 percent paid in 60 days. These payment patterns would produce a 30-day turnover in periods of constant sales. Forecasts of cash receipts for next month by the turnover and payment patterns methods are presented in Table 3-5. The forecast of collections made by the turnover method of $30,000 is quite different from the forecast of $24,000 made by the payment proportions method. Since the payment patterns method is a better representation of the underlying customer remittance habits, the cash receipt forecast associated with this method is likely to be more accurate.[10]

The second issue that must be addressed in forecasting receivables collections is the *level of aggregation* of these forecasts across lines of business for multibusiness firms. Firms selling various types of products often employ different terms of sale for their product lines and often sell these different products to customers with quite different payment habits. For example, it would not be expected that a unit of a firm selling on terms of 3 percent 10 days, net 30 days, to a group of very well-financed customers would have the same receipt patterns as a unit selling to less well-financed firms on net 60-

---

[9]The following discussion draws from B. K. Stone, "The Payment-Patterns Approach to the Forecasting and Control of Accounts Receivable," *Financial Management* (Autumn 1976), pp. 65–82.

[10]Note that, when the firm has bad debts, the payment pattern coefficients will not sum to 1.0. Note also that it is possible to use statistical techniques to adjust the payment pattern coefficients for seasonality and other effects. See Stone, "The Payment-Patterns Approach," for discussion of both issues.

Table 3-5. *Collections Forecasts by the Turnover and Payment Patterns Methods.*

Month:	Last Month	This Month	Next Month
Sales:	$20,000	$30,000	$20,000
Receipts Forecast Based on 30 Days Turnover (Last Month's Sales Figure)			30,000
Receipts Forecast Based on Payment Patterns:			
Collections from Cash Sales (30 Percent of the Month's Sales)			6,000
Collections from Last Month's Sales (40 Percent of Last Month's Sales)			12,000
Collections from Sales Two Months Ago (30 Percent of That Month's Sales)			6,000
Total Collections Forecast by Payment Patterns			$24,000

day terms. In a situation where the firm is in multiple business lines, the use of *overall* payment patterns to forecast receipts will be accurate *only when the proportions of total sales made in each business line are constant*—an unlikely situation, particularly since the different lines usually have different seasonal variations. In such a multiline situation, the most accurate forecasting result is achieved by forecasting receipts for the *different units of the firm individually* based on their own receipt patterns, then summing these receipt forecasts to obtain total cash receipts for the firm.[11]

AN EXAMPLE SPREADSHEET CASH FORECAST

To see how cash forecasting works, let us generate a hypothetical cash forecast. An analyst for a firm is charged with creating a monthly cash forecast for the next six months. Consultation with the firm's credit manager indicates that, historically, 10 percent of the firm's sales have been for cash, 60 percent

[11]See Stone, "The Payment Patterns Approach," page 79.

of sales have been collected in the month following sale, and 29 percent of sales have been collected in the second month following sale; the remaining 1 percent of sales are bad debts and are never collected. A check of accounting records shows that sales for the prior two months (May and June) were $500,000 and $550,000, respectively. The analyst then meets with the firm's sales manager and is advised that the current sales forecast calls for sales of $600,000 in July, $700,000 in August, $800,000 in September, $750,000 in October, $650,000 in November, and $500,000 in December. The firm's production manager has made a production plan based on this sales forecast; the analyst is informed that direct materials will be 42 percent of sales. Direct labor will be 34 percent of sales for July, August, and September based on the production plan, but will rise to 35 percent for the remainder of the year because of a new wage scale to take effect in October. Consultation with the payables manager reveals that direct labor is generally paid for in the month incurred, but that trade suppliers grant terms of sale of net 60 days, which are fully utilized. Also, the payables manager advises that monthly fixed expenses such as rents, executive payroll, and so forth will total $40,000 per month, and that tax payments of $220,000 per month are due in July and October. No repayments on the firm's outstanding debt are due during the next six months. A conference with the firm's capital planners yields the information that the progress payments on the firm's new construction in the amount of $90,000 will be due in August, October, and December. The firm has a starting cash balance of $25,000, no temporary investment of surplus cash in marketable securities or temporary short-term borrowings to cover deficits, and wishes to keep cash on hand at a level of 5 percent of monthly sales.

A few notes on the structure of this particular cash forecast are appropriate. In it, we will ignore the effect of interest income from the investment of surplus funds and interest expense from the financing of deficits on cash flow. This is the standard procedure; the amounts involved are usually small relative to other flows. Where these inflows and outflows are a significant part of total flow, the appropriate procedure is to first calculate the net cash flow for a period; from this, calculate the amount of interest income or expense; and finally, include this income or expense in the cash flow of the appropriate future periods. If this income or expense is sufficient to affect the firm's tax payments, pro forma income statements for tax purposes are also required. We will also ignore the disbursement flotation between the time when checks are written for outflows and the time when these checks are actually cashed. Because it is a few days, this disbursement flotation effect is not important in monthly forecasts, though it must be accounted for in cash forecasts of shorter period lengths.[12] Note that the payment proportions method

[12]See J. H. Vander Weide and S. F. Maier, *Managing Corporate Liquidity: An Introduction to Working Capital Management* (New York: Wiley, 1984), pp. 142–56, for discussion.

Table 3-6. *An Example of Spreadsheet Cash Forecast.*

	A	B	C	D	E	F	G	H	I
1	Cash Forecast								
2									
3	Month	May	June	July	Aug.	Sept.	Oct.	Nov.	Dec.
4		(act.)	(act.)	(est.)	(est.)	(est.)	(est.)	(est.)	(est.)
5	Sales	550	550	600	700	800	750	650	500
6									
7	Cash Receipts Forecast								
8	Cash Sales			60	70	80	75	65	50
9	Collections: 1st Prior Mo.			330	360	420	480	450	390
10	Collections: 2nd Prior Mo.			145	159.5	174	203	232	217.5
11									
12	Total Receipts			535	589.5	674	758	747	657.5
13									
14	Cash Disbursements Forc.								
15	Direct Labor Payments			204	238	272	262.5	227.5	175
16	Direct Materials Payments			210	231	252	294	336	315
17	Monthly Fixed Expenses			40	40	40	40	40	40
18	Tax Payments					220			220
19	New Construction				90		90		90
20									
21	Total Disbursements			454	599	784	686.5	603.5	840
22									
23	Net Cash Flow			81	−9.5	−110	71.5	143.5	−182.5
24	Beginning Cash			25	106	96.5	−13.5	58	201.5
25									
26	Total Cash			106	96.5	−13.5	58	201.5	19
27	Desired Cash			30	35	40	37.5	32.5	25
28									
29	Surplus or (Borrowings)			76	61.5	−53.5	20.5	169	−6

used in our forecast of receipts by its very nature accounts for the flotation on incoming checks, assuming that the payment proportions are calculated using cleared items. Later in this chapter, we will discuss the implications of the firm's strategy regarding the level of desired cash, which is in part a hedge against the uncertainties inherent in the cash forecast.

The resulting forecast, in rounded thousands of dollars, is presented in Table 3-6.[13] This spreadsheet was started by expanding column A to allow for longer titles. The necessary titles were then entered in column A and the month abbreviations in line 4. The "act." and "est." notations under the month abbreviations indicate which sales data are actuals and which are projections. The actual and projected sales data are entered in line 5. The formula "D5*.1" was entered in cell D8 and replicated (copied) into E8 through I8 to get receipts from cash sales. The formula "C5*.60" was inserted into cell D9 and replicated, and the formula "B5*.29" placed into cell D10 and replicated, giving projections of collections from last month's sales and from the sales of two months ago, respectively. Cells D8 through D10 were summed in cell D12 to obtain total receipts.

The disbursements section contains both formulas and data. The cells in columns D, E, and F of line 15 (Direct Labor Payments) contain 34 percent of the corresponding month's sales (sales appear on line 5) while the cells in columns G, H, and I contain 35 percent of the corresponding sales figures. The direct materials payments are made with a two-month lag, so ".42*B5" was entered into cell D16 and replicated for the other months. The remaining cells in this section are data.

Net cash flow (line 23) was computed as the contents of the cell in lines 12 (Total Receipts) minus the contents of the cell in line 21 (Total Disbursements) for each column. The initial cash balance was entered as data; after the first month, formulas were inserted in this line such that the contents would be the same as the cell one column to the left and two rows down (for example, cell E24 contains "D26"). Total cash is net cash flow plus beginning cash (cell D26 contains "D23+D24"). In cell D27, "0.05*D5" was entered to make the desired level of cash equal to 5 percent of the month's sales and replicated this across the line. Total cash less desired cash determines the firm's cumulative surpluses or required borrowings.

USING THE CASH FORECAST

Line 29, the cumulative surpluses and required borrowings for the firm, is the important result of a cash forecast. This estimate of available funds for investment and needed financing enables the firm to plan so as to obtain the

---

[13]In this example, we have generated a spreadsheet of a level of sophistication similar to that which a small firm might employ.

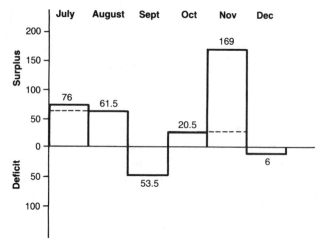

Figure 3-1. *Bar Chart of Cash Surpluses and Deficits from Table 3-6 (rounded thousands of dollars).*

most advantageous borrowing terms for deficits and achieve the greatest interest income on surplus. A useful chart for these planning purposes is a bar chart of this line. A bar chart of the surpluses and deficits from Table 3-6 is presented in Figure 3-1.

Let us assume that the yield curve is upsloping. The firm starts the forecast with no surplus or deficit. During July, a surplus of $76,000 is accumulated. For maximum interest income, these funds should be invested in temporary instruments with the longest possible maturity. In examining the forecast for August we see that the surplus for *this* month is only $61,500; of July's $76,000 surplus, $14,500 will be needed to cover cash outflows and increases in the desired level of cash. Further, there is a deficit in September. Therefore, of the $76,000 surplus in July, $61,500 can be invested until these funds are needed in September; the remaining $14,500 will be needed in August and must be invested in shorter maturity instruments. The firm will need to borrow $53,500 in September to cover the deficit in this month. They should make arrangements to have these funds available at that time. The entire $20,500 surplus in October can be invested until December, since the surplus of $169,000 in November is larger than the surplus in October (November being a month of large anticipated cash inflows). The additional $148,500 surplus in November can be invested at that time until it is needed in December. The firm's maximum borrowing needs over this six-month period are $53,500, reached in September.[14]

[14]For many firms this simple strategy regarding borrowing and lending is insufficiently descriptive. One possible approach to planning more complex strategies is to add a section to the cash forecast detailing the intended remedies to the projected shortfalls and surpluses. This methodology is suggested in M. A. Nunes, *Operational Cash Management and Control* (Englewood Cliffs, N.J.: Prentice-Hall, 1982), pp. 57–61.

Some firms that borrow on short-term credit lines are required to be out of debt for a specific period during the year (often 60 to 90 consecutive days) under these credit agreements. For such firms, the cash forecast has an additional significant benefit: it can help determine whether the firm will fulfill this out-of-debt requirement, given the firm's current plans. For example, examination of Table 3-6 reveals that the firm in the example will not be out of debt for 90 consecutive days during the July through December period.

DISTRIBUTION TO A DAILY CASH FORECAST

The monthly cash forecast thus can be used to enhance the firm's planning process. In addition, a monthly forecast can be *scheduled* to a quarterly or yearly forecast or *distributed* to a daily forecast. Scheduling to longer periods is simply a matter of summing the forecast monthly cash inflows and outflows over the longer period. Distribution requires a bit more analysis, but the results can be useful for planning over the very short term.[15]

Distributing the monthly cash forecast to a daily basis requires that the pattern of cash flows within the month be estimated for each type of cash inflow and outflow. The estimated pattern is then applied to the month's forecast for each cash flow type to generate the daily forecast. One formula which can be used is:

$$Forecast_{nw} = (P_{nw}) \text{ (forecast of monthly cash flow)} \qquad (3\text{-}7)$$

where $Forecast_{nw}$ is the daily forecast for a particular type of cash flow on day n of week w and P_{nw} is the proportion of the month's total that is expected to occur on day n of week w for this type of cash flow. The P_{nw} terms reflect two important cash flow effects within months: the *week-of-the-month effect* and the *day-of-the-week effect*. Due to numerous circumstances, a firm's various types of cash inflows and outflows do not tend to be the same over the weeks within the month of the days within these weeks. They tend to exhibit time patterns that must be reflected in daily cash forecasts. One way to reflect these patterns is to estimate separate coefficients representing the week-of-the-month and day-of-the-week effects and then use these coefficients in a multiplicative fashion to estimate the proportion of the month's total flow that will occur as a result:

$$P_{nw} = A_n B_w \qquad (3\text{-}8)$$

[15]The discussion in this section draws from T. W. Miller and B. K. Stone, "Daily Cash Forecasting and Seasonal Resolution: Alternative Models and Techniques for Implementing the Distribution Approach," *Journal of Financial and Quantitative Analysis*, Vol. 20, No. 3 (September 1985), pp. 335–51.

Table 3-7. Distribution of July's Monthly Forecast to Daily Cash Flows.

! A	B	C	D	E	F	G	H	I	J
1 Week	1	1	1	1	1	2	2	2	2
2 Week Coefficient (An)	.30	.30	.30	.30	.30	.20	.20	.20	.20
3 Day of Week	1	2	3	4	5	1	2	3	4
4 Day Coefficient (Bw)	.30	.25	.20	.10	.15	.30	.25	.20	.10
5 Proportion of Month (Pnw)	.09	.075	.06	.03	.045	.06	.05	.04	.02
6									
7 Total Receipts	48	40	32	16	24	32	27	21	11
8									
9 Direct Labor Payments					51				
10 Direct Materials Payments				53				53	
11 Monthly Fixed Expenses				10				10	
12 Tax Payments									
13 New Construction									
14									
15 Total Disbursements	0	0	0	63	51	0	0	0	63
16									
17 Net Cash Flow	48	40	32	−46	−27	32	27	21 .	−52
18 Beginning Cash	25	73	113	145	99	72	104	131	152
19									
20 Total Cash	73	113	145	99	72	104	131	152	100
21 Desired Cash	30	30	30	30	30	30	30	30	30
22									
23 Surplus or (Borrowings)	43	83	115	69	42	74	101	122	70

where A_n and B_w represent coefficients for the week-of-the-month and day-of-the-week effects.[16]

Let us apply this technique to the prior example cash forecasting problem. Suppose that the firm generating our example monthly cash forecast wants to distribute the monthly forecast for July to a daily basis. Ignore any holidays and assume that there are 21 working days in this month: five in each of the first four weeks (designate these weeks as numbered 1 through 4) and one in the final week (week number 5). Number Monday as 1, Tuesday as 2, and so forth. The firm must estimate patterns within this month (the A_n and B_w) for all the types of cash flows on its cash forecast.

For the six-month period of the original month-by-month forecast, re-

---

[16]This particular approach to the estimation of P_{nw} assumes that the day-of-the-week and week-of-the-month effects are independent. See Miller and Stone, "Daily Cash Forecasting and Seasonal Resolution," for statistical estimation techniques, alternate approaches, and methods for handling seasonality, month-endings, and holidays.

Table 3-7. Continued.

! K !!	L !!	M !!	N !!	O !!	P !!	Q !!	R !!	S !!	T !!	U !!	V !!	W !
2	3	3	3	3	3	4	4	4	4	4	5	
.20	.25	.25	.25	.25	.25	.2	.2	.2	.2	.2	.05	
5	1	2	3	4	5	1	2	3	4	5	1	
.15	.30	.25	.20	.10	.15	.30	.25	.20	.10	.15	1	
												Monthly
.03	.075	.063	.05	.025	.038	.06	.05	.04	.02	.03	.05	Totals
16	40	33	27	13	20	32	27	21	11	16	27	535
51					51					51		204
			53						53			210
			10						10			40
												0
												0
51	0	0	0	63	51	0	0	0	63	51	0	454
-35	40	33	27	-49	-31	32	27	21	-52	-35	27	81
100	66	106	139	166	117	86	118	145	166	114	79	25
66	106	139	166	117	86	118	145	166	114	79	106	106
30	30	30	30	30	30	30	30	30	30	30	30	30
36	76	109	136	87	56	88	115	136	84	49	76	76

ceipts are from sales, and disbursements in various months are for direct labor payments, direct materials payments, monthly fixed expenses, tax payments, and payments for new construction. However, since there are no forecast payments for taxes or for new construction to be made in July, these categories can be ignored for purposes of this distribution example. Turning first to the cash receipts, assume that the firm has found, from research on prior patterns, that for months with the structure of July, 30 percent of cash receipts occur in the first week of the month (week number 1), 20 percent occur in week number 2, 25 percent occur in week 3, 20 percent occur in week 4, and 5 percent occur in week 5. A_1 would then be 0.30, A_2 would be 0.20, and so forth. Assume also that, within each week, 30 percent of receipts occur on Monday (day number 1), 25 percent on Tuesday, 20 percent on Wednesday, 10 percent on Thursday, and 15 percent on Friday (except for week 5, which has only one day—all that week's receipts will occur on day number 1). The B_w coefficients would reflect this pattern; B_1 would be 0.30, B_2 would be 0.25, and so forth.

Assume that payments for direct labor clear the firm's bank on Friday, and that each payment is to be for one-fourth of the month's wage bill.[17] Finally, assume that checks representing one-fourth of the monthly direct material payments and fixed monthly expenses are expected to clear the firm's bank on Thursday of weeks 1 through 4.[18]

The resulting distributed daily cash forecast is presented in Table 3-7 in rounded thousands of dollars. As the distribution of the cash disbursements in this example is obvious, the main point of this table is to illustrate the distribution method as applied to the daily forecast of the cash receipts. The week numbers and their associated A_n coefficients appear in rows 1 and 2. The days of the week and their associated B_w coefficients appear in rows 3 and 4. In this distribution method, the product of A_n and B_w is P_{nw}; this proportion appears in row 5. For example, cell B5 contains "B2*B4"; the result of 0.09 indicates that 9 percent of the month's expected cash receipts (of $535 thousand; see Table 3-6) are expected to occur on the first day of week number 1. The remaining cells in row 5 are similarly interpreted. Multiplying these cells times $535 thousand gives the expected daily receipts in row 7.

Once the various receipts and disbursement types are distributed among the days of the month, the remainder of the cash forecast proceeds as with any other forecast of this sort. For illustrative purposes, monthly totals (across columns B through V) have been included in column W; note that these totals are exactly the same as July's monthly forecast in column D of Table 3-6. However, the distributed daily forecast enables the firm to plan not only on a month-to-month but also on a day-to-day basis. This is a useful addition if the firm's cash flows are sufficiently large to make day-to-day planning of investment and borrowing strategy worthwhile. In the case of the example for July, while there is an overall surplus of $76,000 for the month, there are several times during the month when the surplus is considerably larger than this, though the funds are needed shortly thereafter. These temporarily higher surpluses offer opportunities during the month for short-term, temporary investments having maturities of a few days.

Up until now, we have discussed cash forecasting as if the future cash flows were known with certainty. In practice, the estimated inflows and out-flows (and thus the computed surpluses and deficits) are often subject to substantial *uncertainty*. Because of the costs that this uncertainty introduces, *it must be addressed within the firm's planning process*. Uncertainty assessment techniques and strategies for the management of this uncertainty in the cash

---

[17]While the disbursements in this example will not be dealt with in as much detail as the receipts, this is equivalent to assuming that for direct labor A_1 through A_4 are 0.25 while A_5 is zero and that B_5 is 1.00 while all the other B_w are zero.

[18]Therefore, for these types of expenses, the A_n terms are the same as for direct labor, B_4 is 1.0, and the other B_w are zero.

forecast are addressed in the remainder of this chapter.[19] In discussing these uncertainties and their assessment, we will use, as a primary illustration, the example monthly cash forecast previously developed.

SOURCES OF UNCERTAINTY IN CASH FORECASTING

Given the short-run nature of the cash forecast, with most things occurring in the near future and the forecast period typically being a year, one would tend to think that most financial transactions over this period could be forecast very accurately. Unfortunately, this is far from true. Even with this short period, there are numerous sources of risk. Among the sources are *sales uncertainty, collection rate uncertainty, production cost uncertainty*, and *capital outflow uncertainty*. Let us look at each one of these in turn.

Sales uncertainty refers to the risk regarding the firm's future levels of sales. Most firms try to forecast accurately enough to hold errors in short-run sales forecasts to less than 10 percent, but are often unsuccessful in these efforts.[20] Sales-dollar projections are a product of two other projections, units to be sold and price per unit. Both are often quite uncertain and depend on economic and competitive conditions. Note that *any errors in sales forecasts have multiple impacts* on the firm's cash flows; they impact on receivable levels (and therefore collections) and also on production expenses (and therefore disbursements).

Collection rate uncertainty is the uncertainty regarding the firm's actual future collection patterns of receivables. The firm may historically have collected an average of a certain percent of its outstanding receivables from a particular period in another particular period, but this average contains considerable variability. Further, changing market and economic conditions may make for chancy extrapolation of past historic data into future periods. Because of this and the uncertainties in forecasting sales, forecasts of the collection of future receivables contain at least three sources of uncertainty: uncertainty regarding the number of units that will be sold, uncertainty regarding the price at which these units will be sold, and uncertainty regarding the patterns with which the receivables generated by these sales will be collected.

Production cost uncertainty has to do with the risk of the actual labor and material costs that go into the making of a product or service.[21] Labor productivity may be more or less than expected, making labor costs uncertain.

[19]It is assumed in the forthcoming discussion that sources of uncertainty are uncorrelated.

[20]See J. Pan, D. R. Nichols, and O. M. Joy, "Sales Forecasting Practices of Large U.S. Industrial Firms." *Financial Management* (Fall 1977), pp. 72–77.

[21]See Lerner, "Simulating a Cash Budget," page 79, for discussion.

The cost of materials used may vary due to unexpected changes in price or in the amount of materials necessary to produce products and services.

Capital outflow uncertainty is one of the biggest sources of surprises in cash flow forecasting. This is the uncertainty regarding the timing of cash disbursements related to the firm's major capital expenditure and construction programs.[22] The uncertainty arises from the nature of payments made for new construction. When the firm undertakes to build a new plant or other project of this sort, the total price (subject to specified revisions) is generally agreed upon in advance. The construction firm then starts the project. After a certain percent of the project is done, the construction firm submits a "progress report" to the firm and is paid for what has been completed, less a retainage. For example, assume that the firm has contracted to have built a $10 million building with a 10 percent retainage. Once the construction firm completes the first 20 percent of the project, a payment of $1.8 million will be due ($10 million times 20 percent times 90 percent). Such payments are subject to at least two uncertainties. First, the weather, a very risky variable, plays a significant part in the rate of construction completion. Second, construction firms are notorious for filing late progress reports and then expecting immediate payment. While only a small percent of the firm's total bills are from capital construction programs, the amounts involved are usually very large. One unexpected item of this sort can destroy a carefully planned cash flow management strategy.

PROBLEMS WITH THE CERTAINTY APPROACH

These sources of uncertainty cause risk in the individual items of the cash forecast, and therefore risk in the net cash flow and the resultant surpluses and required borrowings. To see the difficulties this uncertainty causes, think about a manager looking at a cash forecast based on the assumption of certainty and who is attempting to develop a cash management plan. He or she knows the expected flows and knows that these are subject to considerable risk, but he or she has no estimate of this risk. Going back to the cash forecasting example previously done in this chapter, the maximum financing needed occurred in September in the expected amount of $53,500 (see Table 3-6). This is the *expected value of a probability distribution of borrowings*. Assume this probability distribution is symmetric; if the manager arranges to borrow *exactly* $53,500, then *this amount will be insufficient 50 percent of the time*, since for a symmetric distribution the observed value will be greater than the mean 50 percent of the time. Yet arranging to borrow more funds than needed is costly; for example, banks often charge a commitment fee

[22]See Fisher, *Cash Management*, p. 8, for discussion.

based on the *maximum* amount of the firm's line of credit.[23] What maximum amount of financing should the firm arrange to have available in order to be safe? Answering this question *requires an estimate of the uncertainty present* in the estimation procedure. If it is low, a maximum amount of $60,000 may be adequate; if there is very substantial uncertainty, a maximum of $125,000 may be necessary.

Uncertainty as to the amount and length of cash surpluses causes other, equivalent problems. Returning again to the example forecast, the firm is expected to have a $76,000 surplus in July and a $61,500 surplus in August. We previously argued that in a period of upsloping yield curves, the highest-yield strategy involved investing $61,500 of the initial $76,000 for 60 days and the balance for 30 days. However, the cash flows are uncertain. The surplus in August may be less than $61,500; in this case, the firm might have to liquidate part of the 60-day investment before maturity. If interest rates have risen since the investment was purchased, a capital loss may result. To avoid this, the manager may elect to put part of the $61,500 in a more liquid but lower-yielding instrument, sacrificing interest yield for some hedging against interest rate risks. As with the borrowing case, uncertainty regarding the expected cash flows is costly.[24] Therefore, an estimation of the amount of the uncertainty would greatly assist the manager in generating an investment policy as well as a financing policy.

ESTIMATING UNCERTAINTY IN CASH FORECASTS

There are two basic approaches to the assessment of risk in cash forecasting. First, we could assess the effects of *individual sources* of uncertainty on important *individual outcome variables*. Second, we could assess the effects of *all the uncertainties* in all the risky estimated variables on *all the important outcome variables* with all the uncertainties allowed to vary simultaneously. Both of these methodologies are very useful. The first requires sensitivity anal-

---

[23]When the firm finances deficits of this sort in other ways, the cost arguments are more complicated, but the conclusion that the uncertainty is costly remains valid. For example, if the firm finances deficits with commercial paper and must issue more of this paper than they may eventually need due to lack of an estimation of the uncertainty, additional interest expenses will be incurred.

[24]As with borrowing, other strategies to deal with uncertainty in investments are also costly. Note that at this point in the chapter we are discussing uncertainties in the cash forecast that may cause a cash shortage and the costs that these uncertainties may engender. We will later discuss another source of uncertainty related to the cash forecast: the interest rates on the borrowing and lending necessary to finance temporary deficits. The uncertainty in this case arises not from the uncertain cash flows, but entirely from the possibility of changing interest rates.

ysis; the second requires simulation. To illustrate these, let us return to our cash forecasting example problem, whose solution is contained in Table 3-6.

Sensitivity Analysis of the Cash Forecast We know that there are uncertainties in the estimation of sales, collection rates, production and other cost amounts, and the timing and amount of capital disbursements, at the least. Using sensitivity analysis, we can assess some of the effects of these individual sources of uncertainty. For example, recall that the direct labor payments were estimated as 34 percent of sales for the first three months of the forecast, but that this was expected to rise to 35 percent of sales for the last three months because of a new wage scale. If this new wage scale was the result of a new labor contract that is yet to be negotiated when the forecast is made, the actual wage rate would be subject to uncertainty. Let us assess the effects of variation in the direct labor payments as a percent of sales on the projected surpluses and deficits in October, November, and December. As discussed in Chapter 1, this is done by changing the input variable and observing changes in the output variable. The first step might be to estimate the surpluses and deficits with direct labor at 36 percent of sales. Cell G15 presently contains "G5*.35". We change this to "G5*.36" and replicate this into H15 and I15. The results are presented in Table 3-8. The projected surplus in October drops from $20,500 to $13,000, the surplus in November drops from $169,000 to $155,000, and the projected deficit in December increases from $6,000 to $25,000. Trying various values of direct labor as a percent of sales—from 32 to 38 percent—produces the graphs of deficits and surpluses for the three months that are presented in Figure 3-2. The slopes of the functions in this table indicate the relative sensitivities of the three months' balances to changes in the wage cost.

Another uncertain variable is the timing of payments for new construction. As was discussed previously, the weather plays a significant part in the rate of progress of construction. It is possible that the weather may be good and that the firm's construction company may progress ahead of schedule; instead of $90,000 being due in August, October, and December, this could result in $135,000 being due in August and October and nothing due in December. To model this, the "90" in cells E19 and G19 is replaced with "135," and cell I19 is erased. The results are presented in Table 3-9. Other variations in the timing of construction payments could also be investigated.

This kind of analysis provides very useful information about the amounts of possible surpluses and deficits in various future periods. With regard to the construction payments example, the expected amounts of surpluses and borrowings in the beginning and ending months are unaffected, but the pattern from September to November is significantly altered. The maximum amount of the firm's necessary borrowings are now $98,500, not $53,500 as in the original calculation. If there is a significant chance that this speedup of con-

Table 3-8. Sensitivity Analysis of Example Cash Forecast, Direct Labor for October through December Changed to 36 Percent of Sales.

!	A	!!	B	!!	C	!!	D	!!	E	!!	F	!!	G	!!	H	!!	I	!
1	Cash Forecast																	
2																		
3	Month		May		June		July		Aug.		Sept.		Oct.		Nov.		Dec.	
4			(act.)		(act.)		(est.)		(est.)		(est.)		(est.)		(est.)		(est.)	
5	Sales		500		550		600		700		800		750		650		500	
6																		
7	Cash Receipts Forecast																	
8	Cash Sales						60		70		80		75		65		50	
9	Collections: 1st Prior Mo.						330		360		420		480		450		390	
10	Collections: 2nd Prior Mo.						145		159.5		174		203		232		217.5	
11																		
12	Total Receipts						535		589.5		674		758		747		657.5	
13																		
14	Cash Disbursements Forc.																	
15	Direct Labor Payments						204		238		272		270		234		180	
16	Direct Materials Payments						210		231		252		294		336		315	
17	Monthly Fixed Expenses						40		40		40		40		40		40	
18	Tax Payments										220						220	
19	New Construction								90				90					
20																		
21	Total Disbursements						454		599		784		694		610		845	
22																		
23	Net Cash Flow						81		−9.5		−110		64		137		−187.5	
24	Beginning Cash						25		106		96.5		−13.5		50.5		187.5	
25																		
26	Total Cash						106		96.5		−13.5		50.5		187.5		0	
27	Desired Cash						30		35		40		37.5		32.5		25	
28																		
29	Surplus or (Borrowings)						76		61.5		−53.5		13		155		−25	

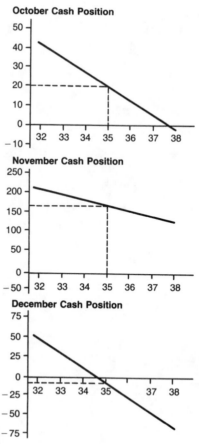

Figure 3-2. *Sensitivity Analysis Graphs of October, November, and December Cash Position in Example Cash Forecast for Variations in Direct Labor as a Percent of Sales for These Months.*

struction may occur, the firm should make far different financing arrangements than were originally anticipated.

Simulation Analysis of the Cash Forecast While sensitivity analysis methodologies give useful information, it is generally the *overall variation* from the means of the monthly cash deficits and surpluses that concerns management for planning purposes. This information on the probability distributions of cash surpluses and deficits is necessary to plan advantageous strategies. To estimate these probability distributions, a simulation of the overall uncertainty in the ending cash balances for each of the periods within the forecast is needed. To get these, the methods of simulation analysis described in Chapter 1 are used. First, probability distributions for each of the major uncertain variables are developed. For a cash forecast, the variables

Table 3-9. *Sensitivity Analysis of Example Cash Forecast, New Construction Payments Accelerated.*

	A	B	C	D	E	F	G	H	I
1	Cash Forecast								
2									
3	Month	May	June	July	Aug.	Sept.	Oct.	Nov.	Dec.
4		(act.)	(act.)	(est.)	(est.)	(est.)	(est.)	(est.)	(est.)
5	Sales	550	550	600	700	800	750	650	500
6									
7	Cash Receipts Forecast								
8	Cash Sales			60	70	80	75	65	50
9	Collections: 1st Prior Mo.			330	360	420	480	450	390
10	Collections: 2nd Prior Mo.			145	159.5	174	203	232	217.5
11									
12	Total Receipts			535	589.5	674	758	747	657.5
13									
14	Cash Disbursements Forc.								
15	Direct Labor Payments			204	238	272	262.5	227.5	175
16	Direct Materials Payments			210	231	252	294	336	315
17	Monthly Fixed Expenses			40	40	40	40	40	40
18	Tax Payments					220			220
19	New Construction				135		135		
20									
21	Total Disbursements			454	644	784	731.5	603.5	750
22									
23	Net Cash Flow			81	−54.5	−110	26.5	143.5	−92.5
24	Beginning Cash			25	106	51.5	−58.5	−32	111.5
25									
26	Total Cash			106	51.5	−58.5	−32	111.5	19
27	Desired Cash			30	35	40	37.5	32.5	25
28									
29	Surplus or (Borrowings)			76	16.5	−98.5	−69.5	79	−6

involved would include sales, collection rates, production costs, and capital expenditures. Statistical estimation procedures or management estimates could be used; discrete or continuous distributions are possible. Then, a large number of trials are run. From these trial results, frequency histograms of the important outcome variables would be developed and these compared to known probability distributions via goodness-of-fit methods.[25]

To apply simulation analysis in estimating the total uncertainty in a cash forecast, one of the uncertainties that must be quantified is that of the *collection rates on accounts receivable*. Uncertainty in the collection rates of receivables is an important component in the overall uncertainty of the cash forecast. The usual method of estimating these rates is to compute individual collection rates on various period's sales using historic data. Another approach to the problem aids in quantifying the multivariate uncertainty in these rates. This approach estimates all the collection rates simultaneously by regressing past sales figures against past collections.[26] The estimated coefficients of the sales figures in the regression can be interpreted as the collection proportions, and the standard errors of the estimated regression coefficients as the uncertainty inherent in the estimation of these collection proportions.[27] For example, assume that the firm has regressed its monthly collections for past months against the appropriate past monthly sales figures and has obtained the following results:

$$C_t = \underset{(0.250)}{0.754} \; S_{t-1} + \underset{(0.087)}{0.241} \; S_{t-2} \qquad (3\text{-}9)$$

In this equation, C_t is the collection from receivables in period t, S_{t-1} is the sales in period $t-1$, and S_{t-2} is the sales in period $t-2$. Assume also that these were the only statistically significant explanatory variables, and that the overall estimated equation was highly significant. The estimated collection rates are 75.4 percent of the previous month's sales and 24.1 percent of the sales from two months previously. The implied bad debt rate is 0.5 percent, equal to one minus the sum of the collection rates. The figures in

---

[25]The primary concern of this text is not with the methodologies of simulation analysis; rather, simulation is one of the methodologies used herein to assess risk. A good reference on simulation analysis is J. C. T. Mao, *Quantitative Analysis for Financial Decisions* (New York: Macmillan, 1969), pp. 553–77.

[26]See J. K. Shim, "Estimating Cash Collection Rates from Credit Sales: A Lagged Regression Approach," *Financial Management* (Winter 1981), pp. 28–30. Additional discussion of such time series approaches to cash forecasting can be found in Vander Weide and Maier, *Managing Corporate Liquidity*, pp. 125–38.

[27]See Shim, "Estimating Cash Collection Rates," pp. 29–30. Shim uses a correction factor applied to the standard error in obtaining confidence intervals of collections. We shall omit this adjustment, interpreting the standard error of the estimate as the estimated standard deviation.

Table 3-10. *Hypothetical Simulation Results for the Example Cash Forecasting Problem.*

Month:	July	Aug.	Sept.	Oct.	Nov.	Dec.
Mean Ending Cash Position (Rounded Thousands):	76.0	61.5	−53.5	20.5	169.0	−6.0
Standard Deviation of Ending Cash Position (Rounded Thousands):	20.0	25.0	30.0	20.0	60.0	30.0

Goodness-of-fit tests on histograms produced by the simulation showed no significant deviation from the normal distribution.

parentheses below the estimated collection rates are the standard errors of these collection rates. These standard errors of these estimated proportions are interpreted as the standard deviations of these estimates. If the number of observations in the sample used to estimate this regression was over 30, it is assumed that these estimated collection rates are normally distributed.[28]

Assume that the simulation analysis methodology has been applied for the example cash forecasting problem, and that all the uncertain variables have been simulated as part of this procedure. Hypothetical results are presented in Table 3-10.

With data of this type in hand, we can now address the formulation of appropriate investment, financing, and hedging strategies, taking into consideration the uncertainties of the projected cash surpluses and deficits. The usefulness of these data stems from the ability to convert the summary statistics regarding the probability distributions of the cash surpluses and deficits into *probabilities that outcomes will fall into various ranges*. Since the probability distributions and estimates of the means and standard deviations of the borrowings and surpluses are now known, it is relatively simple to compute the probability that the actual outcome in any of the periods will lie in any particular range.[29] For the normal distribution, the probability is computed from the Z statistic, which is calculated as:

$$Z = (X - E(X))/SD(X) \tag{3-10}$$

[28]An underlying normal distribution is, of course, implied by the linear regression technique used to estimate the equation.

[29]See Lerner, "Simulating a Cash Budget," pp. 82–92, for discussion of these procedures and for extensions to questions involving more than one period's cash flows.

where X is the test value, $E(X)$ is the mean of X, and $SD(X)$ is the standard deviation of X.

Let us proceed with some example calculations under the assumption that the surpluses and deficits in Table 3-10 are normally distributed. For example, assume that the costs of having insufficient cash and the costs of hedges are such that the firm wishes to incur, at maximum, a 5 percent chance of having insufficient cash to cover expenses. What is the maximum amount the firm should arrange to borrow so that they will have only a 5 percent chance of having insufficient borrowing capacity to cover deficits while keeping cash at the desired level? The maximum expected borrowing is in September, with a mean of $53,500 and a standard deviation of $30,000. Let us assume, for purposes of this particular analysis, that September is the month when the probability of having insufficient cash is greatest. The Z statistic for 5 percent is 1.645, and 1.645 times $30,000 is $49,350. The amount that the firm should arrange to have available is $49,350 plus $53,500, or $102,850. There is a 5 percent chance that the actual requirements in September will be greater than this and a 95 percent chance that the requirements will be less than this. Another example: the firm is trying to decide how much of the estimated July surplus of $76,000 to invest in a 60-day investment. The estimated August surplus is $61,500 and the standard deviation in August is $25,000. How much can the firm invest and have only a 10 percent chance of having to resell the investment in August? The Z statistic for 10 percent is 1.28; 1.28 times $25,000 is $32,000; $61,500 less $32,000 is $29,500. There is a 10 percent chance that the cash surplus in August will be less than $29,500 and a 90 percent chance that it will be greater than $29,500. Thus, the firm can invest $29,500 in the 60-day investment and have a 10 percent chance that they will have to liquidate these bills prior to maturity.

These examples highlight the costs that the firm bears as a result of the cash flow uncertainty and hedging strategies that the firm must pursue to address these uncertainties. In the first example, the firm must arrange for an additional $49,350 in available borrowing to cover the potential shortfall; in the second, the firm can invest only $29,500 of $61,500 in longer-term, higher-yield investments. But these examples are intended to illustrate the mechanics of manipulating means, standard deviations, and probabilities of cash balances rather than to present realistic hedging strategies. In practice, the array of possible hedging strategies is quite a bit more complicated. In the second example, the firm could elect to invest more than $29,500 in the longer-term investment and plan to reduce its cash balance rather than liquidate the securities if the cash surplus in August turned out to be less than expected. That is, the firm has hedging strategies other than the very simple and obvious ones. The costs, alternatives, and risks in hedging strategies are described in the following section.

HEDGING CASH BALANCE UNCERTAINTIES

To understand the mechanics and alternatives in hedging, it is first necessary to understand a bit better why it is of advantage to the firm to hedge. At the end of each period of the cash forecast, the firm expects to be in either a surplus or a deficit position. Let us examine the risks and costs that the firm would face if it did not hedge in each of these cases. That is, assume that the firm keeps no cash, near-cash marketable securities, additional borrowing arrangements, or any other possible hedge.

If the firm is in a period of borrowing, is at its maximum available borrowing limits (as determined by its credit line arrangements), and cash flows turn out to be less than expected (so that borrowing needs would be greater than expected), the firm would be faced with a substantial problem. All the solutions to this problem are costly. For example, the firm could raise cash to cover the deficit by obtaining an emergency loan from its bank. However, bankers are not very receptive to emergency requests of this type, and this solution could endanger the firm's relationship with its bank. Alternatively, the firm could delay one or more types of outflows, such as payments to trade suppliers. This would, of course, endanger relationships with these suppliers. Another strategy the firm might consider would be to sell an asset quickly to generate cash; but the rushed sale might net the firm less for the asset than if it sold the asset in a more considered fashion. In a time of surplus, where the firm has invested the extra funds in longer-maturity securities (to take advantage of yield curve effects), the firm has another alternative: it may sell the investment prior to maturity. But by purchasing longer-term securities, the firm has subjected itself to interest rate risk; if interest rates have increased, the return on the investment will be reduced.

The point is that, without some kind of hedge against the uncertainties of future cash flows, *the firm incurs costs that could be avoided by the use of a hedging strategy.* Of course, there is a trade-off between the cost of the hedge and the expected costs that it avoids. It would not be cost-effective to hedge against all possible future costs if their probability of occurrence was very small. Because of this trade-off, it is necessary to understand the relative costs and other characteristics of the various methods commonly used to hedge the uncertainty of the firm's cash flows. The following pages contain descriptions of some of the possible hedging methods and their costs.

Holding a Stock of Extra Cash We refer here to a stock of cash kept by the firm beyond that needed for transactions.[30] Cash is the most flexible but the most costly hedge available to the firm. It is the most flexible in that

---

[30]Recall that keeping extra cash or near-cash assets for hedging purposes was one of the reasons for holding cash given in Chapter 2.

it can hedge a shortage in any circumstances, at any time, with no transaction costs. If the firm holds a stock of extra cash as a hedge and experiences a shortage during a period of borrowing or a period of lending, it can cover the deficit simply by drawing funds from its cash account. There are no significant transaction costs involved, since the firm simply writes checks.

The problem with holding a stock of extra cash as a hedge is the high cost of this hedging strategy. When we say that the firm holds a stock of cash, we mean cash held in a noninterest-earning checking account. If the firm, instead, invested this cash in its operations, it would earn a return of at least the firm's cost of capital. If the firm's after-tax cost of capital is 9 percent, this entire return is lost to the firm, since the cash hedge earns no interest.

Holding a Stock of Near-Cash Assets One strategy that is nearly as flexible as holding a stock of cash and that reduces the cost disadvantage of cash is holding a stock of near-cash assets. Near-cash assets are securities such as repurchase agreements or nearly matured Treasury bills. Since maturity is very near, these assets carry almost no interest rate risk and thus are almost as safe as cash. However, their use to cover deficits requires that they be sold, with attendant transactions costs. Like keeping extra cash, holding near-cash assets can be used to cover deficits whether the firm is in a period of temporary borrowing or lending. The cost of near-cash assets as a hedge depends on the return of these investments relative to the firm's cost of capital. If these instruments yield 6 percent per year, and the firm's income is taxed at 33 percent, the after-tax yield is 4 percent. If the firm's cost of capital is 9 percent, the 5 percent difference is the cost of this hedge. By using this method of hedging, the firm cuts the cost of the hedge relative to holding cash, but experiences some transactions costs in investing and reinvesting the near-cash assets as they mature and in liquidating these assets when funds are needed. For large firms, these expected transactions costs are small relative to the interest that accrues from the use of near-cash assets as a hedge. Consequently, larger firms commonly invest a substantial portion of their hedging funds in these assets.

Extra Borrowing Capacity One common strategy for funding the firm's expected financing needs is the establishment of a reserve credit line with a bank or group of banks. In doing this, the firm arranges for the maximum credit line with the bank(s) to exceed the *expected* amount of borrowing. This *extra* credit line, beyond that which the firm is expected to need, is a *hedge against cash flow uncertainty*.[31] For example, suppose that a firm expects to

---

[31]For simplicity, at this point in the text it is assumed that the only possible source of emergency short-term borrowing is the reserve portion of the firm's bank credit line. However, other strategies may also be used to raise emergency short-term debt-generated funds; we will discuss hedging strategies using other sources of short-term debt in Chapter 12.

borrow a maximum of $1 million, but sets up the credit line for a maximum of $1.2 million. The additional $200,000 can be used to fund the firm if cash flows turn out to be less than expected.

This approach to the hedging problem is fairly convenient and low-cost. It requires that the firm negotiate with its banker(s) well in advance of any borrowing needs, providing the financial statements and projections necessary to apply for the loan. Any additional inconvenience and expense necessary to apply for the extra amount desired for hedging purposes is a cost of this hedging strategy. Also, the firm must advise the bank(s) when it wants to use ("draw down") the credit line, and it must arrange for the funds to be transferred to its disbursement account(s). Finally, banks generally require a "commitment fee" that varies with the maximum amount of the credit line. This fee is often in the 0.25 to 0.5 percent range (tax deductible): the additional commitment fee for the hedging portion of the credit line is another cost of this hedge. Note that since bank credit line commitments often cover substantial periods of time (a year is not uncommon), and the amount of needed hedge varies with the firm's projected cash flows and their uncertainty over such periods, there will be times when the credit line arrangement will provide much more hedge than is needed.

For large firms arranging to borrow large amounts, the fixed costs of application for the credit line are small relative to the variable costs of the commitment fees. Because these commitment fees are inexpensive relative to the costs of most other hedging strategies, the establishment of additional available borrowing capacity is often the cheapest hedge for large firms. This is true even though the use of reserve bank borrowing requires that firms must pay fees on the *maximum* needed hedge, which results in excess hedging capacity during some times of the year.

Investing Temporary Surpluses in Near-Cash Assets If the yield curve is upsloping, the firm has an incentive to invest surplus funds for the longest possible time, matching the maturity of the investment made with the surplus funds to the length of time until the funds will be needed. However, if there are unexpectedly low cash flows before the maturity of the investment, the firm may be forced to sell before the maturity date. This exposes the firm to interest rate risk. One method of addressing this risk is to invest the surplus funds in near-cash investments. When the firm pursues this strategy, it incurs two costs which would not have occurred had the maturity of the instrument been matched to the time of future cash needs. First, the firm will obtain less interest income. Second, the firm will incur more investment transaction costs. To see this, assume that the firm has cash available that will not be needed for the next 90 days. It can invest the cash by purchasing an instrument maturing in 90 days and yielding a yearly interest rate of 6.5 percent. Alternatively, it can purchase a series of 10-day instruments that currently yield 6 percent per year. If the firm chooses to hedge the interest rate risk by using the second strategy, it will lose 0.5 percent interest. However, the firm will also have to purchase nine different instruments to reinvest the cash (one every 10 days) rather than one instrument. Also, there are transaction costs incurred when the near-cash assets are liquidated to cover shortages. These transaction costs and interest differentials are the costs of this hedging strategy.

Note that, while this strategy removes the interest rate risk from the 90-day investment, another type of risk is generated. Since the reinvestment of the 10-day instruments will be made at market rates at the time of the reinvestment, a decline in these rates during the 90-day period will cause still-lower yields for this strategy.

HEDGING VIA INTEREST RATE FUTURES AND OPTIONS ON FUTURES

Up to this point in the text, we have alluded to the use of interest rate and other futures without any extensive discussion of these vehicles. In this section, we present discussion of interest rate futures, options on these futures, and how these futures and options can be used in hedging two types of uncertainties that arise from the cash forecast.[32] First, like the holding of cash balances and near-cash assets, these futures and options can hedge the *interest rate risk inherent in the temporary investment of short-term funds where unexpected future needs for these funds can cause premature liquidation of the temporary investment*. Second, interest rate futures and options can also be used to hedge interest rate risks that do not arise as the result of uncertainties in the firm's cash flow, but instead occur solely because of *changing interest rates between the time of the forecast and the planned investment or financing*. The intent in this section is to review the basics of futures and options and to provide an introduction to the hedging of risks in the cash forecast with futures and options on financial instruments.

Basics of Interest Rate Futures Contracts The discussion of futures can be obscured by the jargon of the futures market, leaving the reader bewildered and uninformed. If a few basic principles are kept in mind, much of this confusion can be avoided. First, we must always remember that the proper

[32]For more on interest rate futures contracts and options on these futures contracts, see two articles by Anatoli Kuprianov, both of which apeared in *Economic Review* (published by the Federal Reserve Bank of Richmond): "Short Term Interest Rate Futures" (September/October 1986), pp. 12–26, and "Options on Short-Term Interest Rate Futures" (November/December 1986), pp. 3–11. For additional discussion of hedging strategies using futures contracts, see Michael T. Belongia and G. J. Santoni, "Hedging Interest Rate Risk with Financial Futures: Some Basic Principles," *Review*, published by the Federal Reserve Bank of St. Louis (October 1984), pp. 15–25.

name for any future is a *futures contract*, with the emphasis on *contract*. A futures contract is just a contract between one party and another for the future delivery of a commodity. In this contract, the price and delivery date are specified. By specifying the price, both the buyer and seller are hedged against price fluctuations between the date on which the contract is sold and the delivery date. Futures contracts are commonly made on numerous types of goods. In this text, we will discuss the use of three types of futures contracts in the context of working capital management: interest rate futures (which hedge interest rate risk), foreign exchange futures (which hedge exchange risk among currencies), and commodity futures (which hedge the price risk of commodities purchased for inventory). Interest rate futures are discussed in this chapter.

Since the futures contract specifies delivery at a *fixed* price but the *market* price of the commodity fluctuates with supply and demand, *the value of the futures contract will fluctuate with the market price of the commodity*. If the price of the commodity rises, so will the value of the futures contract specifying the purchase of the commodity at a lower price. However, one major difference between run-of-the-mill legal contracts for future delivery of goods and the futures contracts discussed here is that *these futures contracts are traded on exchanges*. This enables the parties to satisfy the contract and to realize gains or losses before the maturity of the contract by selling the contract to a third party.

In these exchanges, the *clearinghouse* (which manages the exchange) guarantees the performance of both parties to the contract and offsets opposing transactions. An example of this offset procedure is useful. Suppose that a firm *purchases* a contract for the future delivery of a commodity. Later, it decides to take its gain or loss on this contract. It may do so by *selling* a contract for the delivery of the same commodity on the same delivery date at the same price. In the language of the futures market, the firm is both *long in the contract* (because it contracted to take delivery of the commodity) and *short in the contract* (because it contracted to deliver the commodity). In futures markets, the clearinghouse will net out these offsetting transactions, and the firms need not be involved thereafter.

When a firm decides to take its gain or loss on a futures contract, a large transfer of cash between the firm and its futures broker is not required. Most futures contracts are purchased *on the margin*; the firm gives the futures broker a relatively small deposit toward the total price of the contract. In the futures market, the amount of the deposit (the *margin*) is adjusted every day, and the firm gains or loses the difference in value. If the value of its contract goes up, the margin account with the futures broker is credited; if it goes down, the margin account is reduced. This process is called *marking to market*. When the futures transaction is closed, the firm reclaims the balance in its margin account.

A very common mistake regarding futures contracts is to think of the margin requirement as an out-of-pocket transaction cost. Like a deposit on any purchase contract, *the margin is eventually applied to the purchase price* should the buyer take delivery. If the buyer cancels the contract by taking an opposing position, the margin is returned to the trader (less any losses and plus any gains). Thus, the margin requirement is a partial payment for the final goods, not a transaction cost.

While futures contracts on other financial instruments are traded, the major hedging instrument is the contract for the *future delivery of Treasury bills*. The major trading volume occurs in the contracts traded on the International Money Market (IMM). These contracts are for the delivery of 91-day Treasury bills with a maturity value of $1 million maturing in March, June, September, and December of the following two years. Therefore, eight contracts are being traded at any time, and the furthest delivery date for the Treasury bills is 24 months in the future. Transactions cost for the purchase of these futures contracts (represented by the difference between the prices at which the same contracts are bought and sold at the same time on the IMM) is quite small.

Basics of Options on Interest Rate Futures Contracts An *option* is a contract to purchase or sell something at a fixed price *which may be exercised or not at the buyer's discretion*. This is distinct from a futures contract, which *must* be exercised, unless the futures contract is canceled via an opposing transaction. In the case of a futures contract, once the contract is canceled, the cost or benefit to the trader is the difference in price between the original cost of the contract and its cancellation cost, which is the difference in the trading price of the contract between when the trader went long and when he or she canceled via the short (or vice versa). In the case of the option, *the cost of the option does not count toward the purchase price of the items in the contract*, and the option does not have to be canceled; it merely expires.

Thus, for an option, the firm faces an initial out-of-pocket cost. But relative to the futures contract, which locks in the future price of the commodity, the option offers greater flexibility. Since the option need not be exercised, the firm's costs are limited to the initial price of the option. If it is not profitable to exercise the option, the firm need not do so. However, if movement in the price of the commodity on which the option is written turns out to be such that exercising the option is profitable, the firm may make gains by exercising the option or by taking an opposing position to the option and offsetting the positions. An option to *sell* an item for a fixed price over a fixed period is called a *put option*. An option to *buy* an item for a fixed price over a fixed period is called a *call option*.

Options on the purchase or sale of interest-bearing instruments are not widely used. Instead, the popular option is the *option on a contract for the future purchase of a Treasury bill*, that is, an option on a Treasury bill futures contract. Options on futures contracts for Treasury bills are traded on the

IMM for the three-month bills. The options expire about three weeks before the maturity of the futures contract on the Treasury bill. Thus, the holder of the option must decide at the time of the option's maturity whether or not to take delivery on a three-week futures contract to purchase 90-day Treasury bills or to let the option expire (the option can of course be exercised, sold, or canceled via an offsetting transaction at any time before this).

The market prices of futures contracts on financial instruments and options on these contracts depends on the market price of the underlying financial instrument. For futures contracts, while the cash price of the instrument and the price of the instrument implied in the price future on this instrument are always closely related, they may diverge when the futures contract is far from maturity. However, as the futures contract moves closer to maturity, the prices of the cash purchase of the good and the price of the good implied by the price of the futures contract for the good *converge*, until *just before maturity the cash price of the good and the price implied by the futures contract on this good are the same*. This occurs because purchasing a futures contract with a short time to maturity is virtually the same as purchasing the instrument itself.

For options on these futures contracts, the market price of the option depends on the relationship between the market price of the instrument and the *exercise price* of the option. The exercise price is the price at which an option is executed. For a put option, it is the price at which the instrument is *sold* to satisfy the option; for a call option it is the price at which the instrument is *bought*. If the exercise price of a put option on a financial future is greater than the current market price of that future, then the value of the option must be at least the difference between the prices. This is necessary because, if it were less, any investor could buy the future, exercise the option to sell the future, and make a gain of the difference. If the current market price of the future is more than the exercise price of the put option, the only value of the put option is that, over the remaining period, the market price might fall below the exercise price, giving the ability to make money. The reverse case between exercise price, market price, and option value occurs for call options.[33]

Using Futures and Options on Futures to Hedge the Risk in the Cash Forecast As previously discussed, interest rate futures contracts, and options on these contracts, can be used in two ways to hedge risk in a cash forecast: (1) they can be used to hedge the interest rate risk on *future borrowings and*

---

[33]Additional discussion of the relationship between the price of the futures contract on a Treasury bill and the market price of the bill can be found in Kuprianov, "Short-Term Interest Rate Futures," pp. 24–25. Additional discussion of the pricing of options on futures can be found in Kuprianov, "Options on Short-Term Interest Rate Futures," pp. 4–7.

investments, or (2) they can be used to hedge the interest rate risk inherent in investing in *longer-term instruments where an unexpected cash shortage may lead to selling* these instruments before maturity. Each of these uses will be discussed in turn.

Let us first consider the hedging of interest rates on future expected borrowing and investing. Futures contracts on Treasury bills or options on these contracts can be used in conjunction with the cash forecast to lock in future rates on this expected borrowing and investment, and thus to hedge interest rate risk from the fluctuation in these rates between the time the cash forecast is generated and the time the borrowing or investing is to be executed. Using futures in this way is a classic futures application. Futures contracts were originally developed to hedge the risk of price fluctuations in agricultural commodities; by selling contracts for future delivery at a specified price, both buyer and seller were protected against price fluctuations in the intermediate period.

To hedge the risk of changes *in interest yields on investments*, the firm may *purchase a financial future* in the investment instrument. For example, assume that it is January and the firm has just completed its cash forecast which shows a surplus of $1.96 million beginning in June and lasting through September. To invest these funds from June to September (90 days), it intends to purchase Treasury bills. The current interest rate on a 90-day T-bill is 2 percent. If interest rates do not change and no hedging is undertaken, the firm may purchase $2 million (maturity value) in Treasury bills in June for $1,960,784.31 (since $1,960,784.31 times 1.020 is $2 million). The resulting cash flows are portrayed in Panel A of Table 3-11.

The firm will receive $39,215.69 in interest income using this strategy (ignoring any commissions). This unhedged strategy requires no initial investment or cash flows between January and June. The problem with the unhedged strategy is risk. If interest rates fall to 1.50 percent (per 90 days) between January and June, the firm will have to pay $1,970,443.35 for the Treasury bills, and will receive only $29,556.65 in interest.

However, if the firm purchases a futures contract in January for the acquisition in June of 90-day Treasury bills (September maturity), it is guaranteed that the rate of investment will be that of the futures contract. The disadvantage of this strategy is the requirement of initial margin and the possibility of other cash flows from January through June. If the initial requirement is 1.0 percent, the firm will have to deposit $19,607.84 with its futures broker. Also, if interest rates rise so that the value of the future falls, the firm may be subject to margin calls. Of course, any margin the firm deposits with its broker will be used to offset the cost of the contract when it is executed in June. The expected cash flows from this hedging strategy, ignoring any cash flows from margin calls, are portrayed in Panel B of Table 3-11.

The difference between Panel A and Panel B is that part of the cash flow to purchase the T-bills (the initial margin deposit) occurs at time zero

Table 3-11. *Net Cash Flows from Various Hedging Strategies for Example Investment Situation.*

	Day 0 *(January)* NCF Transactions		*Day 180* *(June)* NCF Transactions		*Day 270* *(September)* NCF Transactions
Panel A: No Hedge					
0	None	− $1,960,784.31	Purchase of T-Bills	$2,000,000	Maturity of T-Bills
Panel B: Futures Hedge, Contract Executed to Obtain T-Bill					
− $19,607.84	Futures Contracts Purchased	− $1,941,176.47	Futures Contracts Executed	$2,000,000	Maturity of T-Bills
Panel C: Futures Hedge, Contract Sold, Interest Rates Decline					
− $19,607.84	Futures Contracts Purchased	− $1,970,443.35	Purchase of T-Bills	$2,000,000	Maturity of T-Bills
		9,659.04	Gain on Futures		
		19,607.84	Return of Margin		
		− $1,941,176.47	Net Cash Flow		
Panel D: Futures Hedge, Contract Sold, Interest Rates Rise					
− $19,607.84	Futures Contracts Purchased	− $1,955,034.21	Purchase of T-Bills	$2,000,000	Maturity of T-Bills
		− 5,750.10	Loss on Futures		
		19,607.84	Return of Margin		
		− $1,941,176.47	Net Cash Flow		

in Panel B, whereas the entire cost of the T-bills is paid at 180 days in Panel A. Since money has a time value, the firm would prefer the cash flows in Panel A to those in Panel B *if these two sets of flows were equal in risk, but they are not.* The cash outflow at 180 days in Panel A is *risky* because of potential changes in interest rates, while the cash flows in Panel B are *riskless.* Therefore, many firms would prefer the cash flows in Panel B, and will choose the hedging strategy.

For illustrative purposes, Panels C and D portray the cash flows that would occur if the firm chose to liquidate the futures contract and purchase T-bills directly rather than via the futures contract. Panel C presents the cash flows associated with a decline in the 90-day interest rate to 1.50 percent, and Panel D presents the flows associated with a rise in this interest rate to 2.30 percent. The important thing to note in these two panels is that, once the firm has entered into the futures contract, *the cash flows (ignoring margin transactions) are the same regardless of any changes in interest rates.* By purchasing the futures contract, *the firm is truly locked into the rate on that contract.* If interest rates go up before the June surplus is available for investment (Panel D, which would be advantageous if the firm were unhedged), the firm must still either honor the futures contract (and take a lower rate on its investment than the market rate), or sell the contract (and take a loss on this sale). The firm is protected against declines in rates, but cannot profit from rises.

Because the use of a futures contract to hedge the interest rate risk of a future investment precludes the firm from investing should rates fall, some firms use options on futures contracts (rather than the futures contracts themselves) to hedge future investments even though there is an out-of-pocket cost to use the option. If options are used, the exercise of the option is at the discretion of the firm, and it may purchase securities directly in the market rather than through the option. In this way, it may benefit from rises in rates, though it is protected from their decline. To do this in the prior example, the firm would *purchase a call option on the June futures contract.* This option would mature in early May. At that time, the firm could either (1) exercise the option, or (2) let the option expire, go unhedged for the remaining three weeks, and purchase the bills in June. The first strategy would lock in the rate via the futures contract, and would be advantageous if rates had dropped, while the second strategy would be advantageous if rates had risen.

The process of hedging the interest cost on future needed financing is parallel to hedging the interest yield on future investing. However, with regard to financing, the firm wants to hedge a rate of *borrowing* (equivalent to selling debt securities) as opposed to *lending* (equivalent to buying debt securities). To hedge future borrowings, the firm may *sell a futures contract* on an investment instrument for future delivery (go short in the contract). To see how this hedges borrowings, consider the firm that, as of January, expects to borrow $3 million from September until December. If it sells a futures contract for September delivery of Treasury bills, it is hedged against changes in overall interest rate levels. If interest rates increase between January and September, the costs of its borrowing will increase, but the price of the futures contract will decline. When the firm must buy the investments for delivery to fulfill (cover) the short in the futures contract, the price of these instruments will have fallen, and the firm will make a gain on the futures transaction between the original selling price of the instrument (in the short sale) and the eventual covering price. If interest rates decline, the opposite effect occurs; the firm's borrowings are cheaper, but it takes a loss on the futures transaction (since it will now cost more to buy the securities to cover the short sale than the original short sale netted to the firm).[34]

Like the purchase of a futures contract in anticipation of investment, the short sale of a futures contract in anticipation of borrowing locks in the rate of borrowing. Similar to the investment case, the use of options on futures (rather than futures themselves) enables the firm to profit from fortuitous interest rate movements, but at the cost of the option. To use an option to hedge future borrowing rates, the firm should *purchase a put option on the futures contract.* In the prior financing example, the firm would purchase a put option on a futures contract for Treasury bills to be issued in September. This would mature in early August. If interest rates had increased, the firm's cost of borrowing will have increased, but so will the value of the put. The firm can sell the put (or exercise it and then sell the futures contract), and use these gains to offset the increased cost of borrowing. If interest rates have not increased, the firm would let the put expire, go unhedged over the remaining three weeks, and borrow at the lower rates.

Now let us consider the second application of these contracts in hedging the risks from the cash forecast: *the risk of funds shortage.* We previously discussed how hedges such as keeping a stock of cash and near-cash assets, investing temporarily surplus cash in near-cash assets rather than longer maturities, or arranging for excess borrowing capacity can address this risk. Recall that when the firm has invested temporary cash in investments with maturities matching the expected future times when the cash will be needed (to take advantage of upsloping yield curve effects), the firm is subject to interest rate risk should actual cash flows be such that the firm must liquidate these investments before maturity. Futures contracts themselves will not work in this situation because the firm does not know whether there will be a shortage which will necessitate the selling of the investments. The firm needs an instrument it can exercise *if the shortage occurs,* and it is forced to sell its investments. One possible strategy is to *purchase a put option* on a futures contract for investment securities.

To see how this strategy would work in practice, assume that it is January and the firm has $1 million in surplus which it will need in March. If the yield curve is upsloping, it is more advantageous to invest this by purchasing a Treasury bill with a March maturity than to buy bills of shorter maturity and reinvest the proceeds as these bills mature. But if the cash is needed before

---

[34]As before, the firm does not actually have to purchase the securities to fulfill the contract for delivery (the short sale). The same losses and gains occur if the firm merely purchases a futures contract to cover the short and has the clearinghouse offset the firm's short and long positions in the contract. The difference between the prices of the short and long contracts is the firm's gain or loss, which offsets the changes in the cost of borrowing.

this, the firm may have to liquidate the investment (depending on the amount of the deficit and the amount of the firm's other hedges). Since interest rates may rise, this possibility exposes the firm to interest rate risk. However, *if the firm also purchases a put option* on a futures contract for the future delivery of Treasury bills, this interest rate risk will have been partially hedged. If the firm is forced to liquidate the investment before maturity *and interest rates have fallen*, it will allow the put option to expire, sell the investment, and realize a gain. (Since interest rates have fallen, the value of the bill will have risen by more than its normal appreciation.) If the firm is forced to liquidate the investment in February *and interest rates have risen*, it will sell its securities *and sell the put*, which will have risen in value. The increase in the value of the put because of increased interest rates will offset the lessened rise in the value of the bill.

Problems in Using Interest Rate Options and Futures for Hedging   There are two factors inhibiting the firm in efforts to construct hedges that completely eliminate the risk of interest rate fluctuations via futures contracts or options on these futures contracts. These problems are *thin markets* and *basis risk*.

In order to close out any position in futures or options on futures, the firm must either (1) fulfill the contract by taking delivery of the instrument, (2) take a position opposite to the original contract by selling a contract (for a long) or buying a contract (for a short), take the loss or gain, and have the clearinghouse offset the transactions. The latter strategy is by far the most popular; however, it requires that the firm make at least one additional transaction in the futures marketplace. In making these market transactions, it is very useful for the firm to be able to find a ready buyer or seller without the action of buying or selling affecting the market price of the contract. In *thin markets*, there are so few contracts traded that this may not be possible; the very act of closing out the position may reduce the firm's returns via the act's effect on the market price of the contracts. While volume on near-term IMM futures contracts is quite high, volume in contracts with maturities beyond nine months is significantly lower, and may not be sufficient for large firms that wish to close out positions far in advance of maturity.[35] The same thin market condition exists in many options on financial futures contracts.

---

[35]To avoid this problem of thin markets and still hedge interest rate risk for longer time horizons, the firm may purchase a future on a relatively near-term instrument, close out the futures position just before maturity, and purchase another future. This procedure hedges most of the interest rate risk and is called "rolling the hedge forward." The same procedure can be used to hedge interest rate risk beyond the longest available future. See George M. McCabe and Charles T. Franckle, "The Effectiveness of Rolling the Hedge Forward in the Treasury Bill Futures Market," *Financial Management* (Summer 1983), pp. 21–29, and Dwight Grant, "Rolling the Hedge Forward: An Extension," *Financial Management* (Winter 1984), pp. 26–28.

The other problem, *basis risk*, also is related to trading volume. While Treasury bills are issued weekly, the futures contracts are traded on only eight different Treasury bill issues. This standardization of trading in a relatively few instruments generates the economies of scale and exchange that make modern futures trading possible. However, this standardization means that firms can rarely find a futures contract or option that *exactly* matches their hedging needs in terms of maturity date, amount, and instrument. For example, suppose it is January and that the firm expects to borrow $1.3 million in May from its bank for 60 days. To try to hedge this, it may purchase a futures contract on $1 million in Treasury bills to be issued in June with a maturity of 90 days (if this were the closest match available). This contract is different in instrument (Treasury bills versus bank lending), amount ($1 million versus $1.3 million), and maturity (the Treasury bills will mature in September, but the loan will mature in July). As long as the *difference in rates* between the future loan and 90-day Treasury bills (the *basis*) stays the same, the changes in the value of the futures contract will offset changes in the cost of borrowing for $1 million of the firm's future loan. But if the basis changes, or if the firm is not able to exactly match the principal value of the instrument with the principal value of the hedge (as in this case), *the changes in the value of the instrument will not be exactly offset with changes in the value of the future or option.*

While basis risk is a significant consideration in using futures and options to hedge risk, its importance should not be overemphasized. When the firm uses these hedges, the prime variable it is attempting to hedge is the overall level of interest rates. Compared to changes in these general levels, changes in the basis are often rather small. Despite problems of thin markets and basis risk, the use of futures, and options on these futures, provides results that are significantly safer than unhedged strategies.

HEDGING STRATEGIES IN PERSPECTIVE

One final note on the hedging of the risk implied in the cash forecast is useful. In the prior pages, we have discussed several different types of hedges: keeping a stock of cash, keeping a stock of near-cash assets, arranging for extra borrowing capacity, investing temporary surpluses of cash in near-cash rather than longer-term instruments, and using interest rate futures and options on these futures. It is important to remember that these differ significantly in their cost, flexibility, and the types of risk that they can hedge. Keeping a stock of cash or near-cash assets will hedge the risk of cash stockout (unexpectedly low cash balance). Cash is expensive but very flexible. Near-cash assets are less expensive but entail transaction costs. Excess borrowing will also hedge cash stockout risk but requires prearrangement and commitment fees. Investing surpluses in near-term instruments rather than in longer-

Table 3-12. *Features of Some Hedging Strategies for Risks in the Cash Forecast.*

Hedge	*Risks of Cash Shortage When Applicable*	*Costs*
1. Keep stock of extra cash.	Hedges any shortage.	1. Opportunity loss on investment in amount of the firm's cost of capital.
2. Keep stock of near-cash assets.	Hedges any shortage.	1. Opportunity loss on investment in amount of the difference between the after-tax return on the near-cash investments and the firm's cost of capital. 2. Transaction costs of purchase, reinvestment, and sales of assets.
3. Arrange for extra borrowing capacity.	Hedges any shortage.	1. Out-of-pocket expenses of applying for and drawing down extra borrowing. 2. Commitment fees on extra borrowing capacity for maximum needed hedge.
4. Invest temporary surpluses in near-cash assets rather than longer-term assets.	During surpluses only.	1. If yield curve is upsloping, difference in yield between near-cash and longer-term investments. 2. Transaction costs of purchase, reinvestment, and sale of assets.
5. Invest temporary surpluses in longer-term investments and hedge interest rate risk with options on financial futures.	During surpluses only.	1. Cost of the options contracts. 2. Possible losses due to changes in the basis.

Interest Rate Risk on Future Investments and Borrowings

Hedge	*When Applicable*	*Costs*
1. Buy futures contract on T-bills.	Future investment.	1. Small transactions costs of purchase. 2. Opportunity cost of lost income if rates rise before time of expected investment.
2. Buy call option on a futures contract for T-bills.	Future investment.	1. Cost of the options contract. 2. Possible losses during three-week unhedged period if rates decline during this period.
3. Sell futures contract on T-bills.	Future borrowing.	1. Small transactions costs of purchase. 2. Opportunity cost of lost income if rates decline before time of expected investment. 3. Possible losses due to change in basis between T-bill and borrowing rates.
4. Buy put option on a futures contract for T-bills.	Future borrowing.	1. Cost of the options contract. 2. Possible losses during three-week unhedged period if rates rise during this period. 3. Possible losses due to change in basis between T-bills and borrowing rates.

term investments will provide a hedge only in times of surplus. Its costs are the difference in yield between near-term and longer-term investments and the cost of the additional transactions required. The use of put options on financial futures will hedge the interest rate risk inherent in using longer-term temporary investments when cash flows are uncertain. Interest rate futures and options can also hedge the interest rate risk involved in planned future investments and borrowings. Options have significant transaction costs, but allow the firm to profit from fortuitous changes in interest rates. Futures contracts do not allow such profit, but lock in future interest rates and have low transactions costs. Table 3-12 summarizes the features and risks of the various hedging strategies used as a result of uncertainty in the cash forecast. This mix of applicability and cost means that firms have a rather difficult strategic decision in hedging the cash shortage uncertainties inherent in the cash forecast. To correspond with this mix of advantage and disadvantage, it makes sense to use a mix of hedging strategies, and *many firms use more than one of these strategies* to address the uncertainties they face.[36]

SUMMARY

In this chapter, the methods and uses of cash forecasting have been discussed. Firms make and use cash forecasts in order to be able to plan for expected surpluses and deficits. This planning process produces lower borrowing costs during periods of cash need and higher interest income during periods of temporary cash surplus than would otherwise be the case. The early portions of this chapter discussed methods of generating cash forecasts. The receipts and disbursements approach to cash forecasting was reviewed in detail. This method requires the estimation of individual cash inflows and outflows for each of the periods within the forecast. Many of the inflows and outflows are prescribed by the firm's other financial plans and forecasts, such as its capital budget and its sales forecast. Forecasting methods used for cash flows are usually the spot or percent of sales methods; the use of these methods is a consequence of the near-term nature of the forecasting period. Accounts receivable collections, an important inflow for many firms, can be forecast by the payment patterns approach. In this approach, expected collections on the sales of a particular period are spread over other periods based on historic payment proportions. An example spreadsheet cash forecast was executed, illustrating these forecasting techniques.

To use the cash forecast for more comprehensive planning, it is necessary to estimate the uncertainty in it and to develop strategies to deal with this uncertainty. Even though the cash forecast is a very near-term estimate, there are significant uncertainties involved. These uncertainties can be costly if ignored. Major uncertainties come from sales forecasts, estimates of receivables collection proportions, forecasts of production costs, and schedules of capital expenditures. One approach to assessing uncertainty is sensitivity anal-

---

[36]Because the cheapest strategies for hedging the risk of cash shortages often involve arranging for the availability of extra borrowing capacity, we defer the remaining discussion of hedging such shortages to Chapter 12, which deals with short-term financing. In that chapter, a methodology for developing the optimal hedging strategy for a limited variety of hedging vehicles will be presented.

ysis. This involves trying alternate estimates, forecasts, and assumptions to assess their effect on the timing and amount of cash surpluses and required borrowings.

The sensitivity analysis approach provides useful insights, but major concerns of the firm regarding its future cash position require the more complex technique of simulation analysis. Simulation analysis yields probability distributions of required borrowings and surpluses. These probabilities can then be used to develop hedging strategies to address the possible variations of the firm's borrowings and surpluses from their expected values. The choice of hedging strategies employed by the firm depends on the costs of the hedges and the costs of shortage. Possible hedges include keeping a stock of extra cash or near-cash assets, arranging for the availability of extra borrowing capacity, keeping temporary surpluses in near-cash investments rather than longer maturities, and using long-term investments but hedging the interest rate risk in these temporary investments with options on interest rate futures. Futures and options can also be used to hedge the interest rate risk in planned borrowings and investments, though the construction of perfect hedges is difficult.

Problems

3-1. It is January and the XYZ Company wishes to prepare a monthly cash forecast over the next four months. Sales for December were $1,100,000. Expected sales for the next four months are:

Month	January	February	March	April
Expected Sales	$600,000	$800,000	$1,100,000	$800,000

Thirty percent of the firm's sales are for cash; the remainder are collected in the month following the sale (there are no bad debts). Disbursements consist of payments for raw materials, direct labor, other operating expenses, purchases of fixed assets, and taxes. Costs of sales are 75 percent of sales. Of these costs of sales, 38 percent are raw material costs and 62 percent are direct labor costs. Direct labor costs are paid in the month incurred, while raw materials are purchased on net 30-day terms. Other operating expenses total $150,000 per month. Expenditures for fixed assets of $75,000 are to be made in February and April, and tax payments of $110,000 are to be made in January and March. As of January 1, there are no surpluses or deficits and the firm's cash balance is $83,000. The firm keeps a cash balance equal to 10 percent of the month's cost of sales. Generate a monthly cash forecast for the upcoming four months.

3-2. A firm makes monthly cash forecasts and distributes these forecasts to a daily basis. For the upcoming month, anticipated cash inflows are $1,000,000. Each of the first two weeks has five working days. Twenty percent of the month's total cash receipts are expected to be received during the first week and 28 percent are expected to be received during the second week. Within each week, receipts are expected to be received as follows:

Day	Monday	Tuesday	Wednesday	Thursday	Friday
Proportion	0.20	0.23	0.07	0.20	0.30

The firm writes checks on Tuesday for the entire week's expenses, except for taxes. Ten percent of these checks are cashed on Tuesday, 5 percent on Wednesday, 60 percent on Thursday, and the remainder on Friday. Checks totaling $250,000 are to be written on Tuesday of the first week, and checks totaling $200,000 are to be written on Tuesday of the second week. A tax payment in the amount of $100,000 will be made on Wednesday of the second week via wire transfer. Beginning cash is $50,000; this is also the desired cash at all times during the first two weeks of the month. Generate the distributed daily cash forecast for the first two weeks of the upcoming month.

3-3. A firm has generated a cash forecast that shows the following pattern of surpluses over the next four months:

Month	March	April	May	June
Surplus	$2,500,000	$1,700,000	$2,000,000	$0

The yield curve is upsloping and has the following rates and maturities:

Time to Maturity	Uncompounded Yearly Rate
1 month	9.00%
2 months	9.60%
3 months	10.00%

Generate a bar chart of the surpluses over time. Using this bar chart, formulate an investment strategy for the investment of surplus funds. In formulating this investment strategy, assume that the firm has hedged the cash stockout risk; the surplus amounts can thus be treated as certain. Ignoring transaction costs, calculate the interest income from your investment strategy.

3-4. A firm has performed a simulation of its cash budget, with the following results:

Month	Expected Surplus or (Deficit)	Standard Deviation of Expected Surplus or (Deficit)
1	($80,000)	$100,000
2	($20,000)	$150,000
3	$70,000	$200,000
4	$20,000	$250,000

The firm keeps two hedges against cash flow uncertainty: excess borrowing capacity with its bank and a $50,000 cash reserve. It must commit to its maximum level of borrowing over the next four months, at a commitment fee of 0.2 percent of the maximum amount of borrowing arranged. The opportunity cost of holding the cash hedge is 10 percent per year (3.33 percent for the upcoming four months). The firm wishes to limit its probability of running out of cash (of exceeding the total available hedge) to a maximum of 5 percent in any month. Calculate the amount of borrowing capacity that the firm should arrange for with its bank and the total cost of its hedges of cash flow uncertainty, assuming that the probability distributions of surpluses and deficits are normal and serially uncorrelated. (Hint: The maximum amount of borrowing required will be the maximum needed for hedging and for expected borrowings less that needed for expected borrowings only.)

Selected Readings

Belongia, Michael T., and G. J. Santoni, "Hedging Interest Rate Risk with Financial Futures: Some Basic Principles," *Review*, published by the Federal Reserve Bank of St. Louis (October 1984), pp. 15–25.

Kuprianov, Anatoli, "Short Term Interest Rate Futures," *Economic Review*, published by the Federal Reserve Bank of Richmond (September/October 1986), pp. 12–26.

Kuprianov, Anatoli, "Options on Short-Term Interest Rate Futures," *Economic Review*, published by the Federal Reserve Bank of Richmond (November/December 1986), pp. 3–11.

Lerner, E. M., "Simulating a Cash Budget," *California Management Review* (Winter 1968), pp. 79–86.

Pan, J., D. R. Nichols, and O. M. Joy, "Sales Forecasting Practices of Large U.S. Industrial Firms," *Financial Management* (Fall 1977), pp. 72–77.

Shim, J. K., "Estimating Cash Collection Rates from Credit Sales: A Lagged Regression Approach," *Financial Management* (Winter 1981), pp. 28–30.

Smith, K. V., *Guide to Working Capital Management* (New York: McGraw-Hill, 1979), Chapters 2 and 3.

Stone, B. K., "The Payment-Patterns Approach to the Forecasting and Control of Accounts Receivable," *Financial Management* (Autumn 1976), pp. 65–82.

Calais Belting Company Cash Forecasting

Calais Belting Company was a subsidiary of a French firm with a similar name. The American subsidiary was headquartered in a relatively remote section of the Virginia countryside. When asked why that particular section of the country was selected, Jacques Beaudine, the president of the subsidiary, cited the physical similarity to the terrain near the firm's main plant and headquarters facility in France. "One of the considerations in plant location is that the region should make you comfortable," he said, "and when executives from our parent firm come to visit us here, it seems like home to them."

The firm's primary business line was plastic industrial belting for applications in motion transfer (between pulleys) and material transfer (via conveyor belts). Some belts were fabric-backed while others were made only of resilient plastic materials. The raw material used in making the firm's products was mostly rolled plastic sheet which was manufactured at the firm's headquarters facility and shipped to the United States by the parent firm. Some sales were directly to end users, while other sales were made via jobbers. All sales to customers from the U.S. subsidiary were made on stated terms of net 30 days from date of invoice.

The U.S. firm's production facility was a modest one-story plant. The plant was previously used as a regional warehouse by an auto parts firm. While Calais Belting considered the building to be a good investment because of its excellent condition and location, floor space was only partially utilized; the firm had substantial room to expand their production facilities. This was an advantage since the firm felt that there were excellent market opportunities for high quality belt products in the American market. The firm intended to make substantial capital investment purchases during the 1984 calendar year, including a new roof for part of the plant, shelves, grinders, racks, and similar equipment. Some of this would be purchased from the French parent firm while some would be bought locally.

The firm was financed by a package of equity (invested by the parent firm), long-term notes to the firm's bank (principal and interest payments on these notes were made on a monthly basis), and temporary short-term bank borrowings to cover deficits, in addition to the usual accruals and amounts due trade suppliers.

One problem faced by Mr. Beaudine was that of cash forecasting and control. Arrangements for shipments from the parent firm had

Exhibit 1

Calais Belting Company
Forecast of Monthly Sales
(thousands of dollars)

Month 1984	Pessimistic Estimate	Realistic Estimate	Optimistic Estimate
January		468.00 (actual)	
February		455.00 (actual)	
March	426.08	448.50	470.93
April	389.03	409.50	429.98
May	389.03	409.50	429.98
June	401.38	422.50	443.63
July	397.80	442.00	486.20
August	409.50	455.00	500.50
September	418.50	465.00	511.50
October	427.50	475.00	522.50
November	412.25	485.00	557.75
December	425.00	500.00	575.00
1985			
January	437.58	514.80	592.02
February	420.75	495.00	569.25

Note: For any month, the probability of the expected sales estimate is 0.6, and the probabilities of the optimistic and pessimistic estimates are 0.2 each. Each month's outcome is independent of the result in any other month.

Exhibit 2

Calais Belting Company
Projected Future Purchases of Franc
Currency
(thousands of dollars)

Month 1984	Purchase
March	299.00
April	234.00
May	208.00
June	299.00
July	234.00
August	208.00
September	328.90
October	257.40
November	228.80
December	328.90
1985	
January	257.40
February	228.80

to be made many months in advance, and these purchases were a large portion of the firm's cash outflows. The firm had only limited opportunities to adjust purchases (and thus cash outflows) downward to reflect lower sales (and thus cash inflows). Further, it was the firm's policy not to lay off workers in the event of a temporary sag in demand. Within a short planning horizon, the firm's payroll expenses were also fixed. Without the ability to quickly cut payrolls and material purchases in response to any circumstances involving unexpectedly lower sales, the firm could face significant cash shortages. In light of these facts, Mr. Beaudine was very careful about his cash forecasting procedures. At the beginning of each month, he generated a monthly cash forecast for the following twelve months, showing months where surpluses and deficits could be expected. These deficits were financed by short-term bank borrowings.

Exhibit 3

Calais Belting Company
Estimates of Several Types of Cash Expenses (thousands of dollars)

	1984										1985	
	March	April	May	June	July	Aug.	Sept.	Oct.	Nov.	Dec.	Jan.	Feb.
Salaries and Taxes	61.10	65.00	67.60	67.60	67.60	67.60	70.00	70.00	70.00	70.00	70.00	70.00
Travel and Entertainment	17.55	22.75	26.65	26.65	26.65	26.65	30.00	30.00	30.00	30.00	30.00	30.00
Interest Payments	4.03	26.39	4.03	4.06	26.39	4.03	4.03	26.39	4.03	4.03	26.39	4.03
Principal Pays.—Notes	6.63	6.63	6.63	6.63	6.63	6.63	6.63	6.63	6.63	6.63	6.63	6.63
Insurance Payments	5.20	5.20	11.96	5.20	5.20	11.96	5.20	5.20	11.96	5.20	5.20	11.96
Overheads	18.85	18.85	18.85	18.85	18.85	18.85	18.85	18.85	18.85	18.85	18.85	18.85
Equipment Purchases	10.56	22.50	18.99	10.10	2.30	7.80	20.50	7.30	5.40	5.70	19.80	24.50

In early March of 1984, Mr. Beaudine was making a cash forecast for the upcoming year. He first made optimistic, realistic, and pessimistic estimates of monthly sales (see Exhibit 1). Naturally, he felt that his estimates of near-term sales figures were more certain than those further in the future. He also knew the schedule of purchases of materials from the parent firm in France. As a matter of policy, when the materials were shipped from France, the U.S. subsidiary entered into a futures contract for the delivery of francs at the time the bills were due. A schedule of projected currency purchases is presented in Exhibit 2. Mr. Beaudine also made schedules of expected payments for several other types of expenses which were estimated over the planning period via the spot method. These are presented in Exhibit 3.

Mr. Beaudine knew that two types of expenses were likely to vary with sales volume. These were sales commissions and shop materials. Sales commissions were paid to the firm's sales force during the month of the sale and were 2.3 percent of sales volume. Shop materials were materials, other than those shipped from the parent firm, that were used in the production process. These could be varied in the short term to reflect sales volume and were projected as 6.5 percent of sales. These materials were purchased on net 30-day terms from local suppliers.

Exhibit 4

Calais Belting Company
Results of Regression Analysis of Collection Patterns

$$C_t = 0.075 \, S_t + 0.800 \, S_{t-1} + 0.120 \, S_{t-2}$$
$$(0.023) \quad\;\; (0.120) \quad\quad\; (0.055)$$

This is an ordinary least squares suppressed-constant regression. The equation is not serially correlated according to the appropriate statistical test. Dummy variables were tried to assess seasonality but these were not significant. The numbers in parentheses under the estimated coefficients are their respective standard errors.

Mr. Beaudine had previously done a regression analysis to estimate the firm's collection rates. The results are presented in Exhibit 4. He decided to follow the European practice of keeping a fairly substantial cash balance in his firm's account; he intended to keep a cash balance of 12 percent of the month's sales. This cash balance, along with reserve borrowing capacity at the firm's bank, formed the firm's hedge against funds shortages. The beginning cash balance for the forecasting period (that is, the firm's actual cash balance at the end of February 1984) was $58,240. As of this time, the firm had no outstanding temporary borrowings or temporary investments.

Models for the Management of Cash And Temporary Investments

This is the final chapter concerning the management of cash and marketable securities. In Chapter 2, we discussed the gathering and disbursing of cash by the firm. In Chapter 3, we discussed cash forecasting, the temporary investment of cash, and the hedging methods that the firm can use to address the risk inherent in its forecasts of cash flows. This chapter, Chapter 4, has two purposes. First, we discuss models to decide whether it is worthwhile to make short-term investments of cash and to make strategic decisions regarding such investments. Second, we review survey evidence regarding the actual practices used by financial managers in the management of cash and temporary investments.

IS IT WORTHWHILE TO MAKE A SHORT-TERM INVESTMENT?

In the prior two chapters, we discussed strategies for (1) the investment of temporary surpluses of funds until they are needed, and (2) the use of short-term investments as interest-bearing repositories for funds kept as reserves against cash flow shortages. In this discussion, we deemphasized the role of the transactions costs of investing and disinvesting in these investment strategies. In general, it was assumed that the amounts involved were sufficiently large and the time of investment sufficiently long that *transactions costs were very small in comparison to investment income*. For example, in Chapter 3 we discussed cash forecasting, and concentrated on the monthly cash forecast. For most firms, surplus cash that is available for more than a month can be profitably invested. For investments of this duration, the period of investment is sufficiently long that the interest income from the investment will far outweigh the costs of making and withdrawing that investment.

However, the predominance of investment income over transaction costs of investment does not hold *if the amounts of funds are small or the periods of investment are very short*. For example, assume that the total costs of investing and disinvesting are $50, and that the monthly interest rate is 0.6 percent (0.02 percent per day). If a firm had $100,000 to invest for a month, it would be profitable to make the investment; the interest income of $600 would far outweigh the transaction costs of investment and disinvestment. But if the firm had the funds for only two days, it would be better not to invest; the interest income of $40 would be less than the $100 total cost of making and withdrawing the investment. Since many firms have small surpluses available for short periods of time, a set of models is needed to address temporary investment decisions for circumstances where transactions costs play an important part.

In this chapter, we discuss four models that provide strategies in these circumstances. These models are named after their authors; the models are the Baumol model, the Beranek model, the Miller-Orr model, and the Stone model. Each of these models provides optimum strategies *for a given time pattern of cash flows*. Each model assumes a particular pattern of future cash flows and develops an optimum strategy for investment and disinvestment for that assumed pattern based on the trade-off between investment income and transaction costs.

While these models provide interesting and useful approaches, their limitations must be stressed. Like all optimization models, their domain is constrained by the assumptions made in their derivation. While all models are robust to deviations from these assumptions to a greater or lesser extent, the use of an optimization model outside its intended domain is dangerous, and may lead to uneconomical and perhaps disastrous results. Thus, it makes good sense to pay close attention to the assumptions and derivation of a model in deciding whether to use that model in addressing a particular management decision.

THE BAUMOL MODEL

In this model, the firm is assumed to receive cash periodically but to pay out cash continuously at a steady rate.[1] That is, the firm's inflows are lumpy but its outflows are not. This time pattern of cash balance is portrayed in Panel A of Figure 4-1. When the cash inflow is received, the firm puts enough cash in its disbursement account to cover outflows until the next inflow is received. There are several types of businesses that experience a time pattern of cash flows similar to this. For example, for firms that manage rental

[1]See William Baumol, "The Transactions Demand for Cash: An Inventory Theoretic Approach," *Quarterly Journal of Economics* (November 1952), pp. 545–56.

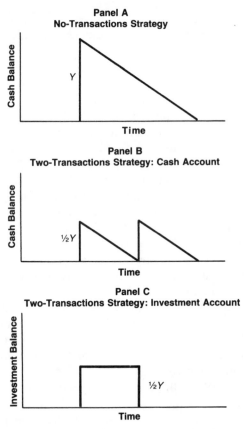

Figure 4-1. *Time Pattern of Cash Balance for the Baumol Model.*

property, rents are often received over a short period early in the month but other expenses (such as maintenance) continue evenly throughout the month.

The Baumol model also makes several assumptions about the firm's situation. It assumes that investments yield a fixed rate of return per period, regardless of the length of the investment (that is, it assumes that yield curve effects are small over the time period of investment). This is an appropriate assumption if the firm is limited to investments in money market accounts, negotiated order or withdrawal accounts, or similar small-dollar investments. The model assumes, as do all the other models discussed in this chapter, that the transaction cost of investing and disinvesting is a fixed cost that is independent of the amount of the investment.[2] These transaction costs consist of all the out-of-pocket costs of making or selling the investment: commissions, postage, telephone charges, the opportunity cost of diverted managerial effort, and so forth.

[2]Situations where the transaction cost of investing is variable in the amount of the investment are addressed in mathematical programming models of investment, such as Gary Eppen and Eugene Fama, "Cash Balance and Simple Dynamic Portfolio Problems with Proportional Costs," *International Economic Review* (June 1969), and Hans Dallenbach, "A Stochastic Cash Balance Model with Two Sources of Short-Term Funds," *International Economic Review* (June 1969).

Given that the firm has periodic inflows and steady outflows, what is the appropriate strategy for investing the funds until they are needed? This is the question addressed by the Baumol model. To understand the trade-offs in this situation, let us evaluate some possible strategies. One possible strategy is:

1. When the cash inflow is received, invest one-half of the total inflow; put the remaining one-half in the disbursement account.
2. During the first half of the period, pay disbursements from the disbursement account. This account will be drained one-half of the way through the period. At that time, sell the investments and place the resulting funds in the disbursement account.
3. Use these funds to pay disbursements during the remainder of the period.

This is called the *two-transactions strategy* because it involves one investment of funds and one disinvestment of funds. The effects of this strategy on the cash and investment accounts is portrayed in Panels B and C of Figure 4-1. To see the net gain from this strategy, let Y be the amount of the cash inflow and i be the interest rate per period (that is, the interest rate from one periodic cash inflow to the next). Since in this strategy one-half the inflow is invested for one-half the period, the interest income is:

$$\text{Investment Income} = (1/2)(1/2)iY = (1/4)iY \qquad (4\text{-}1)$$

But there are two transactions in this strategy: one investment and one disinvestment. If the cost per transaction is a, the transactions cost of this strategy is $2a$, and the profit is:

$$\text{Profit} = (1/4)iY - 2a \qquad (4\text{-}2)$$

While the simple two-transactions strategy captures one-half of the cash inflow into the investment account for one-half the period, other strategies will capture more of this flow for longer periods and thus earn more interest. Consider the *three-transactions strategy*:

1. When the cash flow is received, initially invest two-thirds of it. Place the remaining one-third in the disbursements account.
2. One-third of the way through the period, the disbursements account will be exhausted. At this time, disinvest one-half of the funds in the investment account [the amount is $(1/2)(2/3)Y = (1/3)Y$] and put this in the disbursement account. Leave the remaining $(1/3)Y$ in the investment account.
3. Two-thirds of the way through the period, the disbursements account will again be exhausted. Disinvest the remaining $(1/3)Y$ in the investment account and move the proceeds to the disbursement ac-

count. This will fund disbursements through the remainder of the period.

This strategy involves one investment transaction and two disinvestment transactions. The balances in the investment and disbursement accounts are portrayed in Figure 4-2. This strategy captures a greater portion of the initial cash inflow in the investment account. Two-thirds of the initial cash inflow resides in the investment account for one-third of the period (until the first withdrawal) and one-third of the cash inflow resides in the investment account for the second one-third of the period (until the second withdrawal). The interest income is then:

$$\text{Interest Income} = (2/3)\,(1/3)iY + (1/3)\,(1/3)iY = (1/3)iY \qquad (4\text{-}3)$$

And since there are now three transactions, the profit is:

$$\text{Profit} = (1/3)iY - 3a \qquad (4\text{-}4)$$

Whether the three-transactions strategy is more profitable than the two-transactions strategy depends on the amount of additional interest earned versus the additional transaction cost paid. The Baumol model addresses the question of the optimal strategy by deriving a general expression for the *optimal number of transactions* for a firm with periodic inflow and steady outflows. In general, the interest income from investment strategies in this situation is:

$$\text{Interest Income} = [(n-1)/2n]iY \qquad (4\text{-}5)$$

Figure 4-2. *Time Pattern of Cash Balance for the Baumol Model Three-Transactions Strategy.*

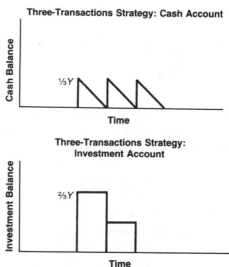

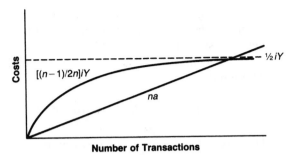

Figure 4-3. *Costs and Revenues versus Number of Transactions for the Baumol Model.*

where n is the number of transactions. The student may verify that this expression gives the proper income for the two- and three-transactions strategies. Since the transactions cost is na, the profit for n transactions is:

$$\text{Profit} = [(n-1)/2n]iY - na \qquad (4\text{-}6)$$

As the number of transactions increases, the interest income increases but so does the total transactions cost. This relationship is plotted in Figure 4-3. Since the total interest income is limited to capturing the entire initial cash inflow in the investment account, which would result in an interest income of $(1/2)iY$, the interest income is asymptotic to this level.[3] For some level of n, the profit (equal to the vertical distance between the cost and interest income functions) is at a maximum. To find this, we take the first derivative of the profit function [equation (4-6)], set this equal to zero, and solve for the optimal n. The result is:

$$n^* = (iY/2a)^{1/2} \qquad (4\text{-}7)$$

where n^* is the optimal number of transactions. In the Baumol model, the firm will always make one deposit and $n^* - 1$ withdrawals from the investment account. The amount of the initial deposit will be $[(n^* - 1)/n^*]Y$; the amount of the withdrawals will be $(1/n^*)Y$. The profit from this strategy can be computed via equation (4-6).

An example in the use of the Baumol model is in order. A firm runs an apartment complex. Cash comes in at the beginning of the month (from rental payments) and is disbursed uniformly throughout the following month. For the upcoming month, the firm expects to have cash expenses of $250,000.

---

[3]This occurs because:

$$\lim_{n \to \text{Inf.}} [(n-1)/2n]iY = 1/2iY$$

By investing in a money market account, it can earn 0.5 percent per month. Transactions costs are estimated at $50 per transaction. What is the firm's best investment strategy and how much will this earn?

To formulate this strategy, the optimal number of transactions is first computed:

$$n^* = (iY/2a)^{1/2} = [(0.005) \, (250,000)/2(50)]^{1/2} = 5.0 \qquad (4\text{-}8)$$

The five-transactions strategy is optimal; there should be one deposit and four withdrawals from the investment account. The amount of the initial deposit will be $(4/5) \, (\$250,000) = \$200,000$; each of the four withdrawals will be $50,000, as will the initial deposit in the disbursement account. This initial deposit will fund the firm for one-fifth of the month $(50,000/250,000)$, or about six days; then the first withdrawal will be made from the investment account. Withdrawals will occur every six days (on the sixth, twelfth, eighteenth, and twenty-fourth days of the month). The profit from this strategy will be:

$$\text{Profit} = [(n-1)/2n]iY - na$$

$$= (5-1)/2(5) \, (0.005) \, (250,000) - 5(50)$$

$$= 500 - 250 = \$250 \qquad (4\text{-}9)$$

Like all the models in this chapter, the applicability of the Baumol model is limited to situations where the cash flow pattern fits that assumed in the model's derivation. Other patterns are addressed by other models, such as the Beranek model, which is discussed in the next section.

THE BERANEK MODEL

Beranek hypothesized firms where the cash *inflows* were steady, but the *outflows* were periodic.[4] This is the mirror image of the time pattern of cash flows within the Baumol model, where inflows were periodic and outflows were steady. The time pattern of cash balances in the Beranek model is pictured in Panel A of Figure 4-4. Balances build over time, then are disbursed all at once. This time pattern represents the situation faced by many firms. For example, a firm that ships and bills uniformly throughout the month on net 30-day terms but which writes checks only a few times per month would experience this pattern. Cash would be collected continuously at a uniform rate, but would be disbursed over a short time as a group of the firm's checks reached its bank and were paid.

[4]See William Beranek, *Analysis for Financial Decisions* (Homewood, Ill.: Richard D. Irwin, 1963), Chapter 11.

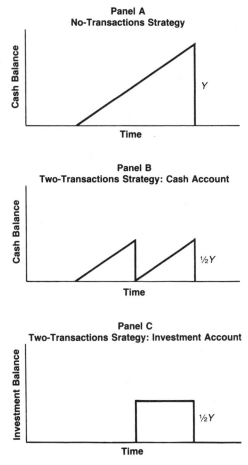

Figure 4-4. *Time Pattern of Cash Balance for the Beranek Model.*

In this pattern of cash flows, the challenge is to profitably invest the funds between the time of their receipt and the time when a group of checks are presented to the bank for payment. The trade-off between interest income and transactions expense and the strategies employed are parallel to those of the Baumol model. For example, the firm could wait until one-half of the incoming cash has been accumulated, then invest this cash until the end of the period when it is needed. In this two-transaction strategy (see panel B of Figure 4-4), the interest income would be $(1/4)iY$, as in the Baumol model, and the transaction expense would be $2a$. The formula for the optimum number of transactions is the same as that for the Baumol model, and is given in equation (4-7). In the Beranek model, however, *the cash is accumulated gradually* (rather than disbursed gradually), so the transactions pattern would involve *a series of investments followed by one disinvestment* at the end of the period.

Let us try an example. A firm receives $100,000 per day, which it will eventually need to make disbursements, and follows a policy of writing checks every two weeks. Over a two-week period, it accumulates $1,400,000. It can invest at an interest rate of 6.825 percent per year (0.2625 percent for two weeks). The transaction cost of investment or disinvestment is $37.50. What investment strategy should the firm follow and how much will this strategy earn?

From equation (4-7), the optimal number of transactions is:

$$n^* = (iY/2a)^{1/2}$$

$$= [(0.002625)\ (1,400,000)/2(37.50)]^{1/2} = 7.0 \qquad (4\text{-}10)$$

In the Beranek model, these seven transactions consist of six deposits and one withdrawal. The amount of the final withdrawal is:

$$[(n^* - 1)/n]Y = 6/7\ (1,400,000) = \$1,200,000 \qquad (4\text{-}11)$$

The amount of the periodic investments will be $(1/n)Y$, or $200,000. The initial investment will require two days to accumulate, and will be made at the end of the second day. The other investments, in the same amount, will be made at the end of the fourth, sixth, eighth, tenth, and twelfth days. The accumulated balance of $1,200,000 will be withdrawn on the fourteenth day, and with the cash accumulated during days 13 and 14, will constitute the $1.4 million needed to cover the checks presented to the bank at that time. From equation (4-6), the profit from this strategy will be:

$$\text{Profit} = [(n-1)/2n]iY - na$$

$$= [(7-1)/2(7)]0.002625(1,400,000) - 7(37.50)$$

$$= 1575 - 262.5 = \$1,312.50 \qquad (4\text{-}12)$$

While they address parallel time patterns of cash flow, neither the Baumol nor the Beranek models deal with risk; they both assume that the amounts of cash inflows and outflows are known with certainty. In using these models, the firm must use a hedging strategy similar to those outlined in the prior chapter to deal with cash flow uncertainty. For example, a firm facing the cash flow pattern in the Beranek model might keep a reserve of cash. If cash inflows then turned out to be less than expected for a particular part of the period, the firm could temporarily draw from the cash reserve to make deposits of economical size.

The remaining two models presented in this chapter (the Miller-Orr model and the Stone model) do not require these additional hedges. Instead, they incorporate uncertainty explicitly within the strategies which they derive.

THE MILLER-ORR MODEL

As in the prior two models, Miller and Orr assume that the yield curve for investments made via their model is flat and that there is a fixed cost of investing and disinvesting that does not vary with the amount of investment or disinvestment.[5] They also assume that investments and disinvestments can take place instantaneously and that there is a lower limit below which the firm's cash balance is not to fall. This lower limit is set by management and is not determined within their model; it may be a zero cash balance (so that the firm does not overdraft) or the firm's minimum compensating balance.

The major difference between the Miller-Orr model and the prior two models concerns the assumed time pattern of cash flows. Baumol and Beranek assume a rise-and-fall pattern of net inflows and outflows. Miller and Orr assume that net cash flows are normally distributed with a mean of zero, that the standard deviation of this distribution does not vary across time, and that there is no correlation of the cash flows across time. Under these assumptions, cash flows must follow a random walk around a zero average net flow. Based on these assumptions, and using the advanced mathematical technique of stochastic calculus, they formulate a profit-maximizing strategy based on *control limits*.

This control-limits approach involves exactly the same decision rules as does the control-limits approach in production management theory. In production management theory, a production process is initially adjusted for optimum performance. However, it is recognized that variations in materials, machine wear, and so forth will cause random fluctuations in the output of the process. Since it is costly to adjust the process, control limits are set up based on the expected variation in the process. Only when these limits are breached is the process adjusted. The Miller-Orr cash management model is basically an application of control-limits theory to the cash/investment decision. Control limits are set up using a formula derived by Miller and Orr. When the firm's total cash goes outside the *upper control limit*, *investments are made* to bring the cash balance back down to the *return point*; when the firm's cash balance goes below the *lower control limit*, *disinvestments are made* to bring the balance back up to the return point. The formula developed by Miller and Orr is:

$$R = (3aV/4i)^{1/3} \qquad (4\text{-}13)$$

---

[5]See M. H. Miller and D. Orr, "A Model of the Demand for Money by Firms," *Quarterly Journal of Economics* (August 1966), pp. 413–35. For an interesting discussion of the relationship between the Baumol and Miller-Orr models, see B. D. Bagamery, "On the Correspondence Between the Baumol-Tobin and Miller-Orr Optimal Cash Balance Models," *Financial Review* (May 1987), pp. 313–19.

where V is the variance of daily cash flows, i is the daily interest rate on investments, and a is the transactions cost of investing or disinvesting. If L is the lower control limit (set by management), the optimal return point is $R + L$ and the optimal upper control limit is $3R + L$.

To see how this model would work in practice, let us address an example problem. A firm has confirmed that its cash flows satisfy the requirements of the Miller-Orr model (by procedures we will discuss later). It can earn 0.02 percent per day in investments. Based on historic data, the firm has estimated the standard deviation of its daily cash flows at $50,000 and its transaction costs of investment or disinvestment at $45.00. It wishes to maintain a minimum cash balance of $100,000 at all times. Based on this data, the R statistic would be calculated as:

$$R = (3aV/4i)^{1/3} = [3(45)(50,000^2)/4(0.0002)]^{1/3}$$
$$= \$75,000 \tag{4-14}$$

Using this statistic, the firm would set the lower control limit at $100,000, the return point at $175,000, and the upper control limit at $325,000 (3(75,000) + 100,000). Let us track the effects of this strategy for some example cash flows. Assume that the firm's starting balance was $150,000 and the following cash flows occur:

Day	Net Cash Flow
1	– $25,000
2	– $75,000
3	$100,000
4	– $25,000
5	$125,000

The control limits, the return point, and the effects of these cash flows are portrayed in Figure 4-5. At the end of day 1, the cash balance would be $125,000; since this is between the control limits, no action would be taken. At the end of day 2, however, the cash balance would be reduced to $50,000 if the firm did nothing. Since this is below the lower control limit, the firm would disinvest sufficient securities to get back the return point. In this case, a disinvestment of $100,000, equal to the return point of $150,000 less the ending cash balance of $50,000, would be made and the firm would start day 3 at the return point. At the end of days 3 and 4, the cash balance would be $250,000 and $225,000 respectively, but no action would be taken since these balances are within the control limits. However, during day 5, $125,000 is collected, and the balance would be $350,000 if no action is taken. However, in the Miller-Orr model, this is a sufficient balance to justify investment, and $200,000 would be invested, bringing the cash balance back to the return point to start day 6.

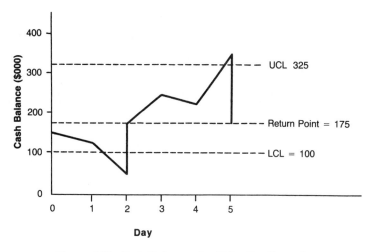

Figure 4-5. *Cash Balances for Miller-Orr Example.*

Concerns About the Assumptions of the Miller-Orr Model While the Miller-Orr model has intuitive appeal as a control-limits approach, the time pattern of cash flows hypothesized within the model has been subject to substantial criticism. The random walk nature of this time pattern assumes that management has no knowledge at all about the direction of future cash flows; in reality, management may forecast these flows, but with a substantial error component within the forecast.[6] Also, while existence of the time patterns of cash flows in the Baumol and Beranek models may be suspected by the business patterns and policies of the firm, the assumption of normality in the Miller-Orr model relies on the central limits theorem, and the convergence to normality of a sample under this theorem depends on the shape of the underlying population distribution.

Because of doubts about the normality of firms' cash flows, and about the Miller-Orr assumptions of no correlations in cash flows over time and no changes in standard deviation over time, several researchers in finance have conducted empirical studies of the probability distributions of firms' net cash flows. These studies have produced mixed results. In their original study, Miller and Orr found that the distributions of cash flows for the Union Tank Car Corporation were more "fat tailed" (had more outlying observations) than would be expected under normality.[7] Homonoff and Mullins also found the cash flows to be nonnormal for their sample firm.[8] Emery tested cash

[6]See Bernell Stone, "The Use of Forecasts and Smoothing in Control-Limit Models for Cash Management," *Financial Management* (Spring 1972), pp. 72–84, and Hans Daellenbach, "Are Cash Management Optimization Models Worthwhile?" *Journal of Financial and Quantitative Analysis* (September 1974), pp. 607–26.

[7]See Miller and Orr, "A Model of the Demand for Money."

[8]See R. Homonoff and D. W. Mullins, Jr., *Cash Management* (Lexington, Mass.: Lexington Books, 1975).

Table 4-1. *Example Net Cash Flows and Summary Statistics.*

Day	NCF
1	−100
2	100
3	−200
4	0
5	−100
6	300
7	0
8	200
9	−200
10	−100
Sample Mean	−10.00
Sample Standard Deviation	157.80
Standard Deviation for Mean = 0	158.11

flow data from three firms in different industries.[9] He found that daily net cash flows from two of these firms were normally distributed, but the distributions changed over time. He also found evidence regarding the existence of correlations in cash flows over time. Further, his simulation of the Miller-Orr model found that the existence of such a correlation affected the behavior of this model.

In summary, these empirical results suggest that a firm should not automatically adopt the Miller-Orr if no discernible time pattern of cash flows is obvious. Instead, the firm needs to perform statistical tests to assess the agreement between the probability distributions of the firm's cash flows and the distributions assumed in the model. Tests for nonnormality and for the correlation of the cash flow over time (autocorrelation) are generally sufficient to confirm or deny this agreement. To illustrate this procedure, let us test the data in Table 4-1 for these two properties.[10]

[9]See Gary Emery, "Some Empirical Evidence on the Properties of Daily Cash Flow," *Financial Management* (Spring 1981), pp. 21–28.

[10]In the following discussion, we treat the test for equality of distribution over time as tested simultaneously with that of normality, since shifting distribution parameters over time would bias the statistical tests against normality. (See Emery, "Some Empirical Evidence," for discussion.) We test only for first-order autocorrelation (correlation between one day's cash flow and the next) because this is the correlation that Emery found to be important. Finally, we use an impractically small sample in the interests of simplicity; the chi-square test we use to test for normality requires that the expected number of outcomes in each range be greater than five, though it is robust to deviations from this condition.

Summary statistics regarding this distribution of cash flows are presented at the bottom of the table. The Miller-Orr model requires that the cash flows be normally distributed with a mean of zero,[11] so for testing purposes an additional standard deviation of 158.11 has been calculated using a zero mean, and the other test statistics will be calculated using a mean of zero.

To test for normality, the frequency distribution of the sample is compared with the frequency distribution that would be expected of a normally distributed sample with the same mean and standard deviation. We will use a chi-square test for this purpose.[12] A test of this sort is illustrated in Table 4-2. To use this test, the data are first divided up into ranges. This division is rather arbitrary; we have used four ranges with endpoints of -150, 50, and 250 (four ranges is the minimum number for using this test). The upper limits of these ranges are in column A. To compare the expected frequency if the distribution is normal with a mean of zero to the observed frequencies, we need to calculate the probability that an outcome will fall in each range. The first range extends from minus infinity to -150. If the mean is zero and the standard deviation is 158.11, -150 is 0.95 standard deviations to the left of the mean $[(-150-0)/158.11 = -0.95]$; cell B5 contains "(A5-0)/158.11." This formula is then copied into cells B6 and B7 to obtain the Z scores for the upper cutoffs for each range (the

!	A !!	B !!	C !!	D !!	E !!	F !!	G !
	Upper	Z for	Prob.	Prob.	Expected	Actual	Cont.
1	Cutoff	Upper	for Upper	for	Number	Number	to Chi-
2	of Range	Cutoff	Cutoff	Range	for Range	in Range	Square
3							
4							
5	-150	$-.95$	.1711	.1711	1.71	2	.0260
6	50	.32	.6255	.4544	4.54	5	.0004
7	250	1.58	.9430	.3175	3.18	2	.1435
8	+ Inf.	+ Inf.	1.0000	.0570	.57	1	.0086
9							
10	Totals			1.0000	10.00	10.00	.1786

Table 4-2. *Test for Nonnormality for Example Net Cash Flows.*

[11]Alternately, if the firm has a positive or negative level of expected cash flows (for example, if it has expected cash inflows of a certain amount per day), it might deduct or add this expected amount from the actual net cash flow during each day and use the Miller-Orr model to manage the remainder, which would then have a zero mean. The net cash flows in Table 4-1 have been adjusted in this way.

[12]A more powerful test, particularly for small samples, is the Kolmogorov-Smirnov goodness-of-fit test [see J. V. Bradley, *Distribution-Free Statistical Tests* (Englewood Cliffs, N.J.: Prentice-Hall, 1968)]. We use the chi-square test here because it is more familiar to students and because it is simpler.

upper cutoff for the topmost range is infinity). A cumulative probability up to these Z scores (from a cumulative normal distribution table) is then entered as data in column C. The probability between these cutoffs is the probability for the range, which is calculated in column D. For example, cell D6 contains "C6-C5." The total in cell D10 verifies that the probabilities of the ranges sum to 1.0. The probabilities in column D times the sample size of 10 give the expected frequencies in column E.

These frequencies in column E are those that would be expected if the distribution is normal with a mean of zero and a standard deviation of 158.11. The actual frequency counts in the sample appear in column F. The larger the differences between the expected frequencies and the actual frequencies, the less likely that the distribution is normal. The chi-square statistic measures the differences between the expected and actual frequencies. The overall chi-square statistic is the sum of the contributions to that statistic based on the differences between the expected and actual frequencies for each range. The contribution to the chi-square statistic for each range is calculated as:

$$\frac{(|\text{actual frequency} - \text{expected frequency}| - 0.5)^2}{\text{expected frequency}} \qquad \text{(4-15)}$$

The particular spreadsheet used here has an absolute value function denoted by @ABS. Therefore, cell G5 contains "((@ABS(F5-E5) − 0.5)^2)/E5" and parallel entries are in cells G5 through G8. The contributions to the chi-square statistic are summed in cell G10; this total chi-squared statistic measures the difference between the actual and the expected frequencies, and the distribution of this statistic is known. The number of degrees of freedom is the number of ranges minus three, so in this case the number of degrees of freedom is 1. From a table of critical chi-square values, at the 90 percent confidence level with one degree of freedom, a chi-square statistic of greater than 2.71 is required to accept the hypothesis that the two frequency distributions are not the same. Since the calculated chi-square statistic is 0.1786, *the hypothesis of nonnormality is not supported* at the 90 percent confidence level.

The second test is for autocorrelation. Autocorrelation has to do with the existence of positive or negative trends. Does knowing one value tell us anything about the next value? If it does, there is autocorrelation. If a higher-than-average value on an outcome is associated with a higher-than-average value in the next outcome, there is a positive correlation coefficient among the cash flows and positive autocorrelation. If a higher-than-average value on an outcome is associated with a lower-than-average value in the next outcome, there is a negative correlation coefficient among the cash flows and negative autocorrelation. Any significant autocorrelation, positive or negative, is a violation of the assumptions of the Miller-Orr model.

In a testing for autocorrelation, one possible approach is based on the statistical significance of the correlation coefficient between one day's cash flow and the next day's cash flow. To perform such a test, the correlation coefficient is first calculated, then tested to see if it is significantly different from zero. A significantly nonzero correlation coefficient, either positive or negative, is evidence of autocorrelation. The formula for the Pearson product-moment correlation coefficient between these two cash flows is:

$$r = \frac{\sum_{\text{all } t} (NCF_t - E(NCF_t))(NCF_{t-1} - E(NCF_{t-1}))}{(SS_{NCFt} SS_{NCFt-1})^{1/2}} \quad (4\text{-}16)$$

where r is the correlation coefficient, NCF_t is the net cash flow on day t, $E(NCF_t)$ is the expected net cash flow on day t, NCF_{t-1} is the net cash flow on day $t-1$, and $E(NCF_{t-1})$ is the expected net cash flow on day $t-1$. Also, SS_{NCFt} and SS_{NCFt-1} are the *sums of squared deviations* for NCF_t and NCF_{t-1} respectively. The sum of squared deviations for NCF_t is:

$$SS_{NCFt} = \sum_{\text{all } t} (NCF_t - E(NCF_t))^2 \quad (4\text{-}17)$$

and SS_{NCFt-1} is a corresponding formula. In this test, we want to constrain the expected net cash flows ($E(NCF_t)$ and $E(NCF_{t-1})$) to zero (if they are not actually zero) since a zero mean is required by the Miller-Orr model. In this special case, equation (4-16) reduces to:

$$r = \frac{\sum_{\text{all } t} (NCF_t)(NCF_{t-1})}{(SS_{NCFt} SS_{NCFt-1})^{1/2}} \quad (4\text{-}18)$$

and equation (4-17) reduces to:

$$SS_{NCFt} = \sum_{\text{all } t} (NCF_t)^2 \quad (4\text{-}19)$$

A spreadsheet to perform this test for the data from Table 4-1 is presented in Table 4-3. The original data are in columns A and B. Column C contains the prior day's net cash flow (for example, cell C6 contains "B5"). Because no prior data is available for day 1, that data point is lost, and analysis proceeds using data from days 2 through 10. We use these data to calculate the numerator and denominator of equation (4-18). The sums of squared deviations from zero required for the denominator are calculated in columns D and E.

Table 4-3. Calculation for First-Order Correlation Coefficient for Example Net Cash Flows.

! A !!	B !!	C !!	D !!	E !!	F !
1		Prior	Day's	Prior Day's	Product of
2	Day's	Day's	Squared	Squared	Deviations
3 Day	NCF	NCF	Deviation	Deviation	from Zero
4			from Zero	from Zero	
5 1	−100				
6 2	100	−100	10000	10000	−10000
7 3	−200	100	40000	10000	−20000
8 4	0	−200	0	40000	0
9 5	−100	0	10000	0	0
10 6	300	−100	90000	10000	−30000
11 7	0	300	0	90000	0
12 8	200	0	40000	0	0
13 9	−200	200	40000	40000	−40000
14 10	−100	−200	10000	40000	20000
15					
16 Sums of Squared Deviations			240000	240000	
17 Sum of Product of Deviations					−80000
18 Correlation Coefficient					−0.333

In column D, each of the day's cash flows from column B is squared, and the sum of these is presented in cell D16; column E performs a parallel calculation for the prior day's cash flows. For this particular example, the sums of square deviations from zero for the day's cash flows and the prior day's cash flows are both 240,000.

The numerator of equation (4-18) is calculated in column F. The numerator is the sum of the products of the day's cash flow and the prior day's cash flow, so each row in column F contains the day's cash flow (from column B) times the prior day's cash flow (from column C). Thus, cell F6 contains "B6*C6". Cell F17 gives the sum of cells F6 through F14, which is the numerator of equation (4-18). Cell F18 contains the formula for the correlation coefficient, which in this spreadsheet is "F17/((D16*E16)^1/2)."

The calculated value for the correlation coefficient is −0.333. To test whether this is significantly different from zero, we use a Student's t-test. The formula for converting a correlation coefficient into a t-score is:

$$t = r[(N-2)/(1-r^2)]^{1/2} \qquad (4\text{-}20)$$

where t is the t statistic and N is the number of data points used (nine in this example). This statistic has $N-2$ degrees of freedom. The t statistic for the example is then:

$$t = r[N-2)/(1-r^2)]^{1/2}$$
$$= -0.333[(9-2)/(1-(-0.333)^2]^{1/2} = -0.935 \qquad (4\text{-}21)$$

The assumptions of the Miller-Orr model are violated if the correlation coefficient is significantly different from zero in a positive or negative direction, so a two-tailed test is required. With seven degrees of freedom, 90 percent of the Student's t distribution is contained between t statistics of -1.895 and $+1.895$. Since the calculated statistic is within this range, *the hypothesis of significant autocorrelation is not accepted* at the 90 percent confidence level. Since the data are neither significantly nonnormal nor significantly autocorrelated, the firm might consider applying the Miller-Orr model as part of its management strategy for cash and temporary investments.

The Miller-Orr model is intended to apply when the firm has no valid future information about day-to-day cash flows; that is, when these cash flows follow a random walk. However, firms may know parts of their cash flows with considerable certainty (such as disbursements), though other parts may be quite uncertain. In the case where the firm has some (though not error-free) knowledge of future cash flows, the Miller-Orr model may produce nonoptimal strategies. For example, if the upper control limit in the Miller-Orr model is pierced, the model suggests that the firm invest. But if the firm knows that a major cash outflow is imminent, this investment may not be the best strategy. It may be better for the firm to ignore the signaled purchase, keep the funds in cash to cover the outflow, and save the transactions costs on the investment and disinvestment. The Stone look-ahead model described in the next section allows the firm to modify investment and disinvestment decisions based on expected future cash flows.

THE STONE MODEL

Like the Miller-Orr model, the Stone model takes a control-limits approach; when cash balances fall outside the control limits, the firm is signaled to do something.[13] But in the Stone model, the signal does not automatically result in an investment or disinvestment: the recommended action depends on management's estimates of future cash flows. That is, the model signals an *evaluation* by management rather than an *action*. To do this, the Stone model uses *two sets* of control limits (see Figure 4-6); the *inner control limits* (UCL_1 and LCL_1) and the *outer control limits* (UCL_2 and LCL_2).

Under the Stone model, strategy proceeds as follows. The firm performs no evaluation until its cash balance falls outside the *outer* control limits. When this occurs, the firm *looks ahead* by adding the expected cash flows for the

[13]This model is presented in Stone, "The Use of Forecasts."

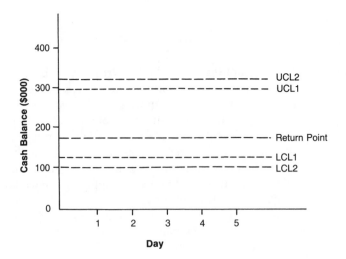

Figure 4-6. Control Limits for the Stone Model.

next few days to the current balance. If the sum of the current balance and these expected future cash flows (which is the expected cash balance a few days hence) falls outside the *inner* control limits, a transaction is made; otherwise, the transaction is foregone. The transactions are the same as those in the Miller-Orr model. Investments are made sufficient to bring the cash balance back to the return point if the upper control limit is exceeded; corresponding disinvestments are made if the lower control limit is exceeded. Optimal procedures for setting the return point, the two sets of control limits, and the number of days a firm looks ahead are not specified; the outer control limits could be set by the Miller-Orr model or could be based on the cash manager's feeling for the best limits.

To see how the Stone model would function in practice, let us consider the first example used in the discussion of the Miller-Orr model. In this discussion, the beginning balance was $150,000, the upper control limit was $325,000, the return point was $175,000, the lower control limit was $100,000. The cash flows for the first five days were:

Day	Net Cash Flow
1	− $25,000
2	− $75,000
3	$100,000
4	− $25,000
5	$125,000

Let us also assume that the inner control limits are set $20,000 inside the outer control limits (at $305,000 and $120,000), and that the firm looks ahead at the next two days' cash flows. At the end of day 1, the cash balance is

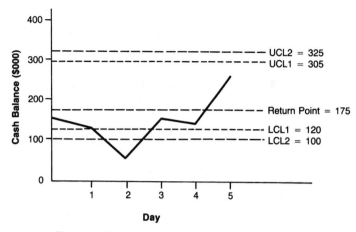

Figure 4-7. *Cash Balances for the Stone Example.*

$125,000, but since the outer control limits have not been breached, no evaluation is made. At the end of day 2, however, the cash balance has been reduced to $50,000. At this point, the firm totals the next two days' cash flows. Let us assume that this forecast is correct; the total obtained is $75,000 (100,000 − 25,000) as the expected future cash flow. Adding this to the current balance of $50,000 gives an expected balance of $125,000. *Since this expected cash balance is within the inner control limits, no transaction is made.* The pattern of cash balances that would result is illustrated in Figure 4-7; there are no investments or disinvestments over the five-day period of the example (recall the Miller-Orr model required one investment and one disinvestment).

When the firm has some knowledge of future daily cash flows, the Stone model offers an advantage over the Miller-Orr model in reducing the number of investment and disinvestment transactions, though investment income may also be reduced. Also, the Stone model is very flexible in that it does not assume a flat yield curve, and in that the parameters of the model may be changed over time to accommodate the firm's needs. For example, the control limits may be tightened during periods when cash control is critical, or the look-ahead period may be lengthened when the firm has better information about future cash flows. Set against these advantages is a substantial disadvantage: *the model does not specify the optimal levels of the parameters* (the control limits, the return point, and the look-ahead period). Stone states that these parameters should be set by the manager by trying various strategies on past data and observing the results; this is a sensitivity analysis approach. There is no guarantee that this process will lead to optimal (or even near-optimal) strategies. Indeed, though it is flexible and has substantial intuitive appeal, the Stone method might be more properly regarded as an *approach* to the daily management of cash and temporary investments rather than an *optimization model* for this management.

Table 4-4. *Time Pattern of Cash Flow Assumed in Four Models of Short-Term Investment.*

Model	Assumptions Regarding Cash Flow Pattern
Baumol	1. All cash flows are certain. 2. Cash inflows are periodic and instantaneous. 3. Cash outflows occur at a constant rate.
Beranek	1. All cash flows are certain. 2. Cash outflows are periodic and instantaneous. 3. Cash inflows occur at a constant rate.
Miller-Orr	1. Firm has minimum required cash balance. 2. Cash flows are normally distributed. 3. The expected cash flow is zero. 4. There is no autocorrelation in cash flows. 5. The standard deviation of cash flows does not change over time.
Stone	1. Firm has minimum required cash balance. 2. Firm has some knowledge of future cash flows, although this knowledge contains an error component.

OPTIMIZATION MODELS FOR SHORT-TERM INVESTMENTS IN PERSPECTIVE

In the past sections, we have discussed four models that generate strategies for the short-term investment of funds.[14] All of these models are oriented toward small- and medium-sized firms where the amounts of cash available for investment are sufficiently small that transaction costs are an important consideration in formulating strategy. All of these models take a similar approach: they first hypothesize a time-pattern of cash flows, then develop a strategy appropriate for that time pattern. The Miller-Orr and Stone models explicitly address the risk in the net cash flows, while the Baumol and Beranek models assume certainty. In the latter cases, risk must be addressed outside the methods by using the hedging strategies for cash flow uncertainty outlined in Chapter 3.

In deciding whether to use these models, the firm must examine the yield on its investments versus the transactions costs of making such invest-

---

[14]Numerous models besides those discussed or referenced in this chapter have also been developed to address other cash flow patterns. Many of these models are discussed in G. Gregory, "Cash Flow Models: A Review," *Omega*, Vol. 4, No. 6 (1976), pp. 643–56.

ments. If transaction costs are large relative to investment income and the firm has foregone investments because of such transaction costs, these models should be considered. To choose among these models, the first step is to match the time pattern of the firm's cash flows to the time patterns assumed in the models; Table 4-4 relates the four models to their assumed time patterns. This match should be based on the specifics of the firm's business policies that affect cash flows (how often payments are made to suppliers, the firm's terms of sale, and so forth) and on empirical investigations of the time patterns of cash flow. The latter investigation might include time plots of net cash flow and statistical comparisons of net cash flows with known probability distributions.

THE MANAGEMENT OF CASH AND TEMPORARY INVESTMENTS IN PRACTICE

The first purpose of this chapter was to review several optimization models for the short-term investment decision. The second purpose is to present survey evidence of the practices actually used by the cash managers of firms. Unlike some other areas of working capital management, there is a good deal of available survey evidence describing current practice in the management of cash and marketable securities. Such evidence is helpful because it gives the student useful knowledge in two areas. First, it tells the student which material presented in the past three chapters is likely to be used in the firms that may employ them. Second, it tells which areas of current practice are candidates for improvement by the adoption of new and better analysis methods. For ease of discussion, the survey information will be presented according to the major topics covered in the past three chapters. We will refer to the survey articles in this area by the initials of their authors. For students concerned about the samples used and the dates of the surveys, or who wish to read the original articles, details of the surveys are presented in Table 4-5.

Management of Cash Inflows In general, firms perceive that the acceleration of the receipt of cash is more important than the control of disbursements (GMW, p. 34). To achieve this acceleration, the use of lockboxes is widespread (GMW, pp. 35–36; SS, pp. 54, 65). Virtually all large firms use lockbox systems as do a large percentage of smaller firms (GMW, p. 36). This somewhat lower use by smaller firms is a reflection of the costs versus the gains from lockbox systems; for such systems to be economical, the gain for the acceleration of receipts must be sufficient to offset the costs of the system, and large firms have higher average receipts. To bring collected funds together for use, over one-half of all large firms use concentration banking (GMW, p. 36), with wire transfers and depository transfer checks being the

Table 4-5. *Facts Regarding the Survey Articles on the Management of Cash and Short-Term Investments Used.*

Abbre-viation	Authors	Article Title	Reference	Date of Survey	Sample(s) Used	Response Rate
BG	S. Block and T. Gallagher	"The Use of Interest Rate Futures and Options by Corporate Financial Managers"	*Financial Management* (Autumn 1986), pp. 73–78.	1985	Fortune 500	38.6%
GG	L. Gitman and M. Goodwin	"An Assessment of Marketable Securities Management Practices"	*Journal of Financial Research* Vol. II, No. 2 (Fall 1979), pp. 161–69.	1977	300 firms ranging from number 201 to number 631 of Fortune 1,000	50.0%
GMW	L. Gitman, E. Moses, and I. White	"An Assessment of Corporate Cash Management Practices"	*Financial Management* (Spring 1979), pp. 32–41.	1977*	Largest 150 and smallest 150 of Fortune 1,000	32.6%
KKMW	R. Kamath, S. Khaksari, H. Meier, and J. Winklepleck	"Management of Excess Cash: Practices and Developments"	*Financial Management* (Autumn 1985), pp. 70–77.	1984**	Fortune's Second 500	41.5%
RGG	A. Rappaport, P. Goulet, and L. Goulet	"Marketable Securities Portfolio Management: A Survey of Theory and Practice"	Eastern Finance Association, 1985; available from the authors at the University of Northern Iowa.	1984	All publicly traded firms with marketable securities of over $5 million in 1982 (373 firms)	26.5%
SS	K. Smith and S. Sell	"Working Capital Management in Practice"	*Readings in the Management of Working Capital*, 2d. Ed. (N.Y.: West Pub., 1980), pp. 51–84.	1978	668 of Fortune's 1,000, with selection based on size and profitability	31.4%

*Estimated; date not given.

primary means of moving funds from one bank to another (GMW, p. 35; SS, p. 65).

Temporary Investments   Almost all large firms (96 percent) invest surplus cash in money market instruments (KKMW, p. 71). To select the instruments for investment, the criteria used (in descending order of importance) are default risk, liquidity, yield, time to maturity, and price risk (KKMW, p. 74; GG, p. 165; SS, p. 66). Firms typically use three of four types of investment instruments over the course of a year (KKMW, pp. 71–2), but at any particular time they have over one-half of their total portfolio in a single type of security (RGG, p. 6). These investments are almost always held to maturity (KKMW, p. 76; GG, p. 164). If differences in the time to maturity of the different instruments are ignored, the most popular investments (in descending frequency of use) are: commercial paper, certificates of deposit, repurchase agreements, treasury securities, and banker's acceptances (KKMW, p. 73, provides a summary of KKMW, GG, SS, and GMW). However, the most popular type of investment varies with the length of time that the funds are available for investment. Repurchase agreements and commercial paper are the most popular investments for maturities under 30 days, while certificates of deposit and commercial paper are most popular investments for maturities over 30 days (KKMW, p. 73). Eurodollar deposits have become more popular over time (KKMW, p. 72). This trend is based on the higher interest rates available on such deposits (RGG, p. 7), a phenomenon which will be discussed in Chapter 13 of this text.

Management of Cash Outflows   The primary tools for the management of cash outflows are zero-balance accounts and centrally controlled disbursing. Central control of disbursements is the major tool for about 70 percent of large firms (SS, p. 65; GMW, p. 37). Zero-balance accounts are used by the vast majority of larger firms, although they are used less frequently by smaller firms (GMW, p. 35). There appears to be substantial disagreement among firms as to whether the further delay of payments to suppliers (via maximization of mail float, for example) is useful. Some firms report the use of this technique (GMW, p. 37), while others think it is a bad idea (SS, pp. 54, 65).

Cash Forecasting   Almost all large firms prepare cash forecasts (GMW, p. 35; GRR, p. 11). Smaller firms are less likely to prepare such forecasts (GMW, p. 35). These cash forecasts are the primary method used to determine the amount and duration of temporary investments in marketable securities (KKMW, p. 76).

In hedging the risk that cash flows may be less than forecast, many firms use more than one technique. A substantial number of firms keep a stock of short-term investments for precautionary reasons (GMW, p. 37; RGG, pp. 3, 12). Many firms also borrow to address unanticipated cash needs, either directly from banks or through the commercial paper market (GRR, pp. 12, 26).

Futures and Options for Hedging The number of firms using futures and options on financial instruments to hedge the risk of future borrowings and lendings or to protect against interest rate risk in temporary investments is not yet very large. About 20 percent of large firms use these contracts, and they use them almost exclusively for hedging rather than speculation (BG, pp. 75–6). Bigger firms are much more likely to use the contracts than are smaller firms (BG, p. 75). Treasury bill futures and Eurodollar futures are the most frequently used contracts, with the most important uses being the hedging of expected future borrowings and lendings (BG, p. 76). The reason for the relatively low use of these hedging vehicles appears to be top managements' resistance to these contracts, caused by a lack of knowledge about their characteristics, advantages, and costs (BG, pp. 77–8).

Models for Temporary Investments While, in general, quantitative and statistical models are in wide use in working capital management (GMW, p. 36), the models discussed in this chapter (which balance the transactions costs of investment against interest revenues) have not found wide acceptance. They are in use by less than 10 percent of large firms (SS, p. 68; GRR, p. 26). Further, smaller firms do not use them at all (SS, p. 68). This is perhaps due to an interaction between the need for models of these sorts and the financial sophistication of firms. These models are primarily oriented toward small- and medium-sized firms, where the amounts of investment are such that transaction costs are an important offset to interest income. Yet smaller firms tend to be less financially sophisticated, as much research on the adoption of other advanced financial techniques has shown.[15]

SUMMARY

This chapter addresses two topics. The majority of the chapter is concerned with cost-balancing models for decisions regarding the temporary investment of cash into interest-bearing investments. These models balance the interest revenues from these investments against the fixed cost of making investments and disinvestments. Each of the four models assumes a different time pattern of cash flow, then derives a strategy based on this time pattern. In choosing among these models, the firm must first compare its time pattern of cash flows against those assumed by the various models. The Baumol and

[15]See, for example, J. W. Petty and O. D. Bowlin, "The Financial Manager and Quantitative Decision Models," *Financial Management* (Winter 1976), pp. 32–41.

Beranek models assume certainty, and thus require a hedging strategy outside the context of the model, while the Miller-Orr and Stone models explicitly account for the uncertainty of cash flows within their formulation.

The second part of the chapter reviewed several surveys in the current practice of the management of cash and marketable securities. In general, the management techniques discussed in the text concerning the management of cash inflows, temporary investment of surplus funds, cash budgeting, and hedging cash uncertainties are in use by a substantial portion of larger firms. For the management of cash outflows, some of the techniques we described are frequently used, but some firms also use techniques (such as increasing mail float on outgoing checks) that other firms believe are inappropriate, and which we have not addressed in depth. We have also devoted considerable space in this text to two techniques not in wide use: hedging with interest rate futures and cost-balancing models. The most probable reason for the relatively infrequent use of these techniques is management's lack of familiarity with them. These are areas where employees might make significant contributions to the current practices of their firms, if the circumstances are appropriate for the use of these methodologies.

Problems

4-1. A firm has periodic cash inflows and steady cash outflows and wants to use the Baumol model to formulate a strategy for the temporary investment of some of its cash. The firm receives an inflow of cash every 15 days (use a 360-day year). The yield on invested cash is 12 percent per year. It costs $500 to invest or disinvest, and the portion of the next cash inflow that will be retained to pay bills over the following 15 days is $3.2 million. Calculate:

   a. The optimal number of transactions.

   b. The amount of the initial investment.

   c. The amount of the periodic withdrawals.

   d. The net profit from this strategy.

4-2. A firm has steady inflows and periodic outflows and wants to use the Beranek model to manage its cash. Cash outflows occur once per month; the amount of the next outflow is $2.16 million. It costs $200 to make an investment or a disinvestment. The yearly interest rate is 8 percent. Calculate:

   a. The optimal number of transactions.

   b. The amount of the periodic investments.

   c. The amount of the final withdrawal.

   d. The net profit from this strategy.

4-3. A firm is trying to decide whether its cash flows fit the assumptions of the Miller-Orr model. A sample of 15 cash flows has been obtained:

Day	Net Cash Flow	Day	Net Cash Flow
1	$ 0	9	$500
2	$100	10	− $600
3	− $200	11	$200
4	− $300	12	− $200
5	$100	13	$100
6	$ 0	14	− $100
7	$200	15	− $200
8	$400		

a. Calculate the standard deviation of these cash flows assuming a zero mean.

b. Using a chi-square test, assess whether the data are normally distributed under that assumption of a zero mean. Utilize five ranges: less than −250, −250 to −75, −75 to +75, +75 to +250, and greater than +250.

c. Using a Student's t-test, assess whether the data are serially correlated.

4-4. A firm has confirmed that its daily cash flows are in accord with the assumptions of the Miller-Orr model. Based on historic data, it has been determined that the standard deviation of daily cash flows is $400,000 with a mean of zero. Interest rates on short-term investments are 6 percent per year (use a 360-day year). Each investment or disinvestment costs the firm $100 in paperwork costs, etc. The firm's bank requires a minimum cash balance of $500,000; this is the firm's lower control limit.

a. Calculate the return point and the upper control limit.

b. Assume that the firm's initial cash balance is $1,000,000 and that it experiences the following cash flows over the first seven days:

Day	Net Cash Flow
1	− $300,000
2	− $400,000
3	$500,000
4	− $200,000
5	$900,000
6	$200,000
7	$700,000

Using the control limits and return points calculated in part a, indicate the transactions that would occur for this series of cash flows. Give the amounts of any puchases or sales of short-term investments.

4-5. A firm wishes to use the Stone look-ahead model with a one-day look-ahead. It has determined that the outside upper control limit is $1,600,000, the inside upper control limit is $1,300,000, the return point is $1,000,000, the inside lower control limit is $750,000, and the outside lower control limit is $500,000. Assuming that the starting cash balance is $1,000,000 and using the seven days of cash flows from Problem 4, find the transactions that would occur during the first six days.

Selected Readings

Baumol, William, "The Transactions Demand for Cash: An Inventory Theoretic Approach," *Quarterly Journal of Economics* (November 1952), pp. 545–56.

Block, S., and T. Gallagher, "The Use of Interest Rate Futures and Options by Corporate Financial Managers," *Financial Management* (Autumn 1986), pp. 73–78.

Beranek, William, *Analysis for Financial Decisions* (Homewood, Ill.: Richard D. Irwin, 1963), Chapter 11.

Daellenbach, Hans, "Are Cash Management Optimization Models Worthwhile?" *Journal of Financial and Quantitative Analysis* (September 1974), pp. 607–26.

Emery, Gary, "Some Empirical Evidence on the Properties of Daily Cash Flow," *Financial Management* (Spring 1981), pp. 21–28.

Eppen, Gary, and Eugene Fama, "Cash Balance and Simple Dynamic Portfolio Problems with Proportional Costs," *International Economic Review* (June 1969).

Gregory, G., "Cash Flow Models: A Review," *Omega*, Vol. 4, No. 6 (1976), pp. 643–56.

Kamath, R., S. Khaksari, H. Meier, and J. Winklepleck, "Management of Excess Cash: Practices and Developments," *Financial Management* (Autumn 1985), pp. 70–77.

Miller, M. H., and D. Orr, "A Model of the Demand for Money by Firms," *Quarterly Journal of Economics* (August 1966), pp. 413–35.

Rappaport, A., P. Goulet, and L. Goulet, "Marketable Securities Portfolio Management: A Survey of Theory and Practice," available from the authors at the University of Northern Iowa.

Stone, Bernell, "The Use of Forecasts and Smoothing in Control-Limit Models for Cash Management," *Financial Management* (Spring 1972), pp. 72–84.

The Polyurethane Company[1] — Cash and Marketable Securities: The Miller-Orr Model

The Polyurethane Company was the largest division of a middle-sized chemical company and was a primary manufacturer of the chemicals used in the production of polyurethane foam. Polyurethane foam is made by mixing chemicals together under controlled conditions. The chemical reaction is exothermic (that is, it gives off heat). The exact chemicals used determine the consistency of the foam produced: hard or soft, with large or small bubbles. Hard, large-bubbled urethane foams were often used as insulating materials; softer, small-bubbled foams were used in shoe soles. However, the most common use of urethane foam was in cushions and mattresses. To produce mattresses, 80/20 toluene diisocyanate, the largest-selling urethane chemical (80/20 indicates the mix of monomers), was mixed with another chemical and extruded into long, rectangular "buns." These buns were then cut into mattress sizes by means of a hot wire system. The foam produced for this application was large-bubbled and soft. In the early 1980s the Polyurethane Company sold about

[1]This case has been adapted from Frederick C. Scherr, *Cases in Finance* (New York: Macmillan, 1984), pp. 51–55.

$200 million in 80/20 toluene diisocyanate and similar chemicals annually.

In middle-sized firms such as the Polyurethane Company, managers often "wear many hats": they do several jobs which in a larger firm would be handled by specialists. Thomas Charles, who held an undergraduate degree and an M.B.A. from a large land-grant university, was the company's assistant credit manager, accounts receivable manager, cash reporter, and cash forecaster. Also (but less frequently), he assisted the accounting department in computing break-even points, performed accounting functions, and helped the firm's planning department with statistical analysis. When the firm's finance department moved to a new office building, Mr. Charles was heard to remark (somewhat jovially), "I hope my new office isn't near the boiler; they'll have me shoveling coal, too!"

Mr. Charles's duties as cash forecaster of the company had become increasingly important (a sample of one of his cash forecasts is presented as Exhibit 1). The firm had recently undertaken a program of active management of its cash and near-cash assets. Because the Polyurethane Company was the firm's largest division, Mr. Charles's forecasts were

Exhibit 1

The Polyurethane Company
Forecast of Daily Cash Flows For the
Business Week of 1/11/82 to 1/15/82
(rounded thousands of dollars)

	Monday 1/11/82	Tuesday 1/12/82	Wednesday 1/13/82	Thursday 1/14/82	Friday 1/15/82
Starting cash balance	200	827	387	(53)	174
Receipts	1667	600	600	1267	1100
Total funds	1867	1427	987	1214	1274
Disbursements	1040	1040	1040	1040	1040
Cash balance, end of day	827	387	(53)	174	234
Desired cash balance	140	140	140	140	140
Surplus or (deficit)	687	247	(193)	34	94

critical to the process of planning short-term investments and financings. However, Mr. Charles was not happy with the accuracy of his forecasts of daily cash flow. If the forecasts proved to be substantially in error, the cash manager had to alter investment or borrowing plans. This was inconvenient, and the resulting transactions costs were expensive.

Mr. Charles found the inaccuracy of the daily forecasts to be quite perplexing. While the company's sales were somewhat seasonal, by using appropriate estimates of the firm's collection rates, he could make fairly accurate estimates of monthly cash flows. The difficulty was in forecasting daily flows within the monthly periods. Mr. Charles had been distributing the monthly forecasts to daily forecasts based on his feel for the patterns of cash flow within the month. His initial efforts to improve his daily forecasts centered on the statistical estimation of week-of-the-month and day-of-the-week effects. It was his plan to use these estimates in his cash flow distribution system.

He first examined the firm's cash flow patterns near the tenth and twenty-fifth of the month. He knew that, in the past, some customers had tended to concentrate their payments around these dates. However, he found no statistically significant differences between the cash flow patterns around these dates and other times during the month. He then tested cash flow patterns for days early in the week versus those later in the week. He had suspected that there would be heavier cleared cash flows at some point during the week since the firm's bank credited checks received in the mail on Saturday and Monday to the company's account on Monday (on book but not cleared basis). Again, he found no statistically significant differences in cleared balances. Finally, he ran regressions looking for daily and weekly forecasting tools, but the explanatory power of these regressions was minimal.

In desperation, he talked the problem over with his friend and golfing partner, David Feldstein. "Tom," Mr. Feldstein had said, "has it occurred to you that there may be no time

Exhibit 2

The Polyurethane Company

Changes in Cleared Bank Balances (Cleared Daily Net Cash

Flows) Month of January 1982 (Business Days Only; Rounded

Thousands of Dollars)

Date	Day No.	Change in Cleared Balances
4	1	−445
5	2	−137
6	3	376
7	4	−34
8	5	445
11	6	−479
12	7	274
13	8	−96
14	9	294
15	10	501
18	11	239
19	12	34
20	13	171
21	14	308
22	15	−342
25	16	−205
26	17	−103
27	18	−117
28	19	616
29	20	−137

of cash and investments on the basis of your daily forecasts is counterproductive. Maybe what we need is a new approach to the daily cash management problem."

Mr. Charles considered this for a time and decided to try a new approach. Instead of looking for a pattern, he assumed that the net cash flows fluctuated randomly around their mean. He knew that if, in such a cash, the cash flows of the firm met certain statistical requirements, the Miller-Orr model of cash and marketable securities management and not the firm's current procedure, was the appropriate strategy. He decided to test the daily cash flow data within the months to assess whether the pattern of cash receipts met these requirements. To perform the necessary tests, he collected daily net cash flow data for several months; an example of the data for the 20 working days in January 1982 is presented in Exhibit 2. For this month, total cash inflows were expected to exceed total cash outflows by $800,000, so Mr. Charles decided to deduct $40,000 per day from these figures under the assumption that this amount would be removed daily from the firm's temporary pool of funds and invested in a more permanent fashion. Once the results of these tests were in hand, he intended to present them to the treasurer of the firm with a recommendation regarding the most advantageous strategy for the management of daily cash flows.

pattern in these net cash flows at all? If there is not really a time pattern, all this churning

chapter 5

Terms of Sale Decisions

This is the first of three chapters concerning the *management of accounts receivable*. Accounts receivable management *starts* where the management of inventory *ends* (with the shipment of goods or the performance of services by the seller) and *ends* where the management of cash *begins* (when the remittance in payment for the goods or services is on its way to the seller from the buyer). Accounts receivable management is also known as *credit management*. Credit management is primarily concerned with two questions:

☐ What terms of sale should the firm use?
☐ To whom should the firm grant credit?[1]

This chapter, Chapter 5, has two purposes. First, it provides an introduction to the management of accounts receivable. Second, it discusses decision methodologies with respect to the first of the above questions: what terms of sale should the firm use? Chapter 6 addresses the second of these questions: to which applicants should credit be granted? Included in Chapter 6 is a substantial discussion of the effects of the costs of information on such credit-granting decisions. Chapter 7, the final chapter concerned with the management of accounts receivable, discusses the monitoring of accounts receivable. Monitoring receivables is a mechanism for assessing the accuracy and stability of the estimates used in making the terms of sale and credit-

---

[1] Another question sometimes discussed in this area is *collection policy*—how much should the firm spend on collecting from buyers and what mechanisms should be used? While the collection policy problem is not trivial, the amounts of money involved in such policy decisions are usually much smaller than those involved in the other credit policy decisions. Also, the principles used in the analysis of collection policy decisions are the same as those used in the analysis of terms of sale policy decisions. In the interests of space, we do not discuss collection policy in this text.

granting decisions. Chapter 7 also contains a review of survey evidence regarding the methods currently in use by credit managers.

WHY GRANT CREDIT?

If you ask a practicing businessperson *why* his firm grants credit to customers for the purchases of goods and services, the businessperson is likely to be rather perplexed. The use of credit in the purchase of goods or services is so common that it is taken for granted. The granting of credit from one business to another for the purchase of goods or services—*trade credit*—has been part of the American business scene for hundreds of years. Trade credit provided the major means of obtaining debt financing by businesses before the existence of banks.[2] Over 200 years ago, Benjamin Franklin was a founding member of a trade credit organization. Trade credit continues to be a very important source of funds for firms; it provides more financing to businesses than does commercial borrowing or corporate bond financing.[3] Further, the accounts receivable assets that result from granting trade credit are a major investment for the firm. As of 1981, accounts receivable assets averaged 26.5 percent of the total assets of industrial firms.[4]

But business procedures such as the granting of trade credit do not persist and do not provide major financing and investment merely because of historical tradition. They persist because they perform useful economic functions. Trade credit may perform at least three useful functions: it may provide the opportunity for *financial arbitrage*, it may help overcome an *information problem in the sale of goods*, and it may *make the payment for goods less difficult.*[5]

Let us first discuss the possibility of *financial arbitrage*. If firms operated in perfectly competitive capital markets, there would be no financial impetus for trade credit. The extension of time to pay in granting credit is equivalent to the granting of a loan from the seller to the buyer. The seller bears the cost of this loan. If the seller chose not to grant trade credit to buyers, in perfect capital markets, the buyer could obtain the same financing by taking out a loan in these markets and paying cash for the product or service. But

[2]See R. Barzman, *Credit in America* (New York: National Association of Credit Management, 1975).

[3]See M. H. Seiden, *The Quality of Trade Credit* (New York: National Bureau of Economic Research, 1964).

[4]See G. Emery, "A Pure Financial Explanation for Trade Credit," *Journal of Financial And Quantitative Analysis,* Vol. 19, No. 3 (September 1984), pp. 271–85.

[5]If customers are differentially allowed to pay beyond the stated terms of sale, credit policy can also be used to circumvent the equal-price restrictions of the Robinson-Patman Act. We do not discuss this potentially illegal strategy here; see G. J. Alexander and J. M. Gahlon, "Can Credit Terms Cause Stretching?" available from the authors at the University of Minnesota.

this loan would be costly to the buyer, and the buyer would then require a lower price from the seller. In perfect capital and product markets, the lower price that the buyer requires if the seller does not grant trade credit exactly offsets the costs to the seller if trade credit is granted. There is no advantage to the seller of granting or not granting credit, and therefore no financial reason for the existence of trade credit.[6]

However, capital markets may not be perfectly competitive. For one reason or another, buying firms may not be able to borrow at economical interest rates, and thus may not be able to economically replicate the delay in payment that is inherent in trade credit. When such imperfections occur, trade credit can serve as a conduit for funds from the capital markets to buying firms. Sellers can borrow in the capital markets, then lend to buyers via trade credit. This process of borrowing cheaply by sellers in order to relend to buyers substitutes for buyers' access to capital markets and is thus a type of financial arbitrage.

What imperfections exist that might make this financial arbitrage profitable? Several observed imperfections of capital markets might account for it, particularly if the buying firms are smaller than the selling firms. Various restrictions on the amount of borrowing occur for smaller firms. Since they are less well-known than bigger firms, they are less able to borrow in the capital markets. If they do borrow in these markets, their interest costs will be higher than for larger firms because of this information effect and because the fixed costs of issuing securities bear more heavily on their smaller issues. If they instead borrow from banks, usury laws and restrictions on banks' lending to particular customers limit the availability of funds. Finally, as a result of the selling (and possibly the product development) process, the seller may have acquired quite a bit of information about the buyer. For the buyer to borrow, this information would have to be transmitted to the bank (a costly process), while the seller already possesses it. All these factors work to give advantage to an arbitrage transaction where the seller borrows in the capital markets, then relends to buyers.[7]

Another possible function of trade credit has to do with the *buyer's imperfect knowledge regarding the quality of the products purchased*.[8] When payment is delayed until some time after the goods have been received, the

[6]See W. Lewellen, J. McConnell, and J. Scott, "Capital Market Influences on Trade Credit Policies," *Journal of Financial Research,* Vol. III, No. 2 (Fall 1980), pp. 105–13.

[7]For discussion of these effects, see Dana Johnson, "Market Justifications for Trade Credit in Imperfect Capital Markets," available from the author at Virginia Polytechnic Institute and State University. Also see Emery, "A Pure Financial Explanation," and R. Schwartz, "An Economic Model of Trade Credit," *Journal of Financial and Quantitative Analysis* (January 1974), pp. 643–57.

[8]For a review of the literature, see W. Beranek, "Towards a Positive Theory of Working Capital," available from the author at the University of Georgia, pp. 17–19.

buyer has the opportunity to count and inspect the goods. If the goods are not up to the required standards, the buyer may short-remit or not pay at all until the defect is fixed. If the buyer has paid cash for the goods, much of the leverage that the buyer has in obtaining satisfaction on such matters is lost.

Still a third potential function of trade credit concerns the payment process itself. *It is simply less costly, and to some extent, less risky for buyer and seller alike if payment on delivery can be avoided.* The payment of cash on delivery requires that the buyer and seller entrust large sums to employees dealing with the deliveries, opening the firms to the possibility of theft. Alternatively, the seller could obtain a certified check to be presented on delivery, but this is an inconvenient and expensive process, and the check may be lost by delivery personnel. From both the buyer's and seller's viewpoints, there are substantial advantages to the payment for goods or services via the normal check remittance process, even if the time from the receipt of the goods to payment is only a few days.

In addition to these three potential functions of trade credit, more complex explanations for its existence have also been put forward. One of these concerns the use of trade credit as a potentially effective means of dealing with temporary fluctuations in demand for the firm's products or services. In this explanation, terms of sale exist so that firms lengthen them to stimulate demand when it is less than expected and shorten them to curtail demand when it is more than expected.[9] Another explanation centers around the use of the cash discount amount, cash discount date, and net date to obtain information regarding the probability of the buyer's default. Buyers who do not take advantage of generous cash discounts may be more prone to default. Since the financing they obtain by delaying payment is very expensive, they must be foreclosed from cheaper sources because of their poor financial condition.[10]

By this discussion, we see that there are several possible functions of trade credit in the selling of goods from one firm to another. It is not presently known which of these explanations is correct; they may all be true to some extent. But whatever its reasons for existence, trade credit is pervasive. It has been employed for centuries and will likely persist for some time to come.

This section has deliberately discussed credit in the context of *one firm granting credit to another* rather than *a firm granting credit to an individual*. This orientation toward interfirm credit rather than consumer credit will continue throughout this text. This orientation is an outgrowth of this text's direction toward the management of working capital *within business firms* and recent trends in the granting of credit. While the granting of credit from

---

[9]See G. Emery, "An Optimal Financial Response to Variable Demand," *Journal of Financial and Quantitative Analysis,* Vol. 22, No. 2 (June 1987), pp. 209–25.

[10]See J. K. Smith, "Trade Credit and Information Asymmetry," *Journal of Finance* (September 1987), pp. 863–72.

one firm to another shows no sign of abating, the granting of credit *by firms directly to individuals* is rapidly fading from the economic scene. It is fading because there are substantial economies of scale in credit investigation and administration when granting credit to individuals. This has led to a substantial growth of *financial institutions* such as credit-card companies whose business it is to grant credit to *individuals* for the purchase of goods *from business firms*. By aggregating the sales of many businesses, these institutions achieve the economies of scale in investigation and administration necessary to reduce the costs of consumer credit-granting.[11] These institutions *enable individuals to buy on credit without the seller having to extend credit*. While the study of such institutions is an important part of finance, it is not a topic for this text. Since this text is concerned with the management of business firms rather than financial institutions, we deal with firms granting credit to other firms, rather than with the granting of credit to individuals.

COSTS, REVENUES, AND CREDIT DECISIONS

It should be obvious to most students that *the granting of trade credit is an aspect of price*. The time that the buyer gets before payment is due is one of the dimensions of the product (like quality, service, and so forth) which determine the attractiveness of the product. Like other aspects of price, the firm's terms of sale and credit-granting decisions affect its sales volume. All other things being equal, longer terms of sale and more liberal credit-granting policies increase sales, while shorter terms and more stringent credit-granting policies decrease sales. These policies also affect the level and timing of certain costs. Evaluation of policy changes must *compare these sales and cost effects*. In this section, we list and discuss the various types of costs and revenues that may be affected by the firm's accounts receivable management decisions.

While the discussion of these decisions' effects is usually phrased in terms of costs and revenues, we should recognize that what is really being discussed is the *timing and amount of the firm's cash flows*. Cash flows are critical to firms, and the different types of costs and revenues are just labels for the various cash flows that result from credit management policies. The analysis of terms of sale policy to be presented later in this chapter centers on the timing and amount of these cash flows.

Collections on Sales Whenever the firm institutes a new credit policy, it is anticipated that changes in the firm's sales volume and in the timing of

---

[11]However, there are a few major firms that still run their own consumer credit operations. Some retailers continue to issue their own credit cards, as do many large oil companies. In such circumstances, sellers must be aware of the morass of constantly changing state and federal legislation dealing with the granting of credit to individuals and the collection of debts from them.

receipts from sales will result. For example, suppose that the firm lengthens its terms of sale. Since this is in effect a lowering of price, sales volume would be expected to increase.[12] However, since the terms of sale are longer, customers would be expected to pay later, and the cash inflows from these sales would occur further into the future.

Investment in Inventory Many credit policy decisions result in an increase or decrease in sales volume. This change in sales volume in turn requires an increase or decrease in inventory.[13] For example, suppose that the firm makes a change in credit policy that reduces sales by $200,000, and that the firm follows a policy of keeping inventory so as to produce an inventory turnover ratio of 5.0 based on sales volume (that is, sales divided by inventory is 5.0). Because of this change in policy, the firm can then liquidate $40,000 in inventory ($200,000/5.0) and retain the same turnover ratio on the remaining inventory balance. This liquidated inventory can be used to make sales that would normally require the firm to spend $40,000 in additional costs of materials. The $40,000 represents a net cash inflow (a saved cash outflow) for the firm.

Cost of Sales When sales change, the firm will have to produce different amounts of goods. This in turn will affect several types of cash outflows, such as direct labor, direct materials, and so forth. The change in the amounts of these cash outflows is relevant to credit policy decisions.

Discount and Bad Debt Expenses These expenses are really deductions from the expected level of cash inflows from future sales. For example, suppose that the firm changes credit policy in such a way that sales increase from $1 million to $1.3 million in a particular period. Assume that the levels of discount and bad debt expense increase from 2 percent and 0.5 percent of sales to 3 percent and 1 percent of sales respectively. Under the old policy, the collections on sales from that period would have been $975,000 ($1 million − (0.02 + 0.005) ($1 million)), but under the new policy collections will be $1,248,000 ($1.3 million − (0.03 + 0.01) ($1.3 million)). The differences in bad debt expense and in discount expense are thus reflected in the changes in future cash flows.

---

[12]The amount of this increase depends in part on market structure facing the firm and the reactions of competitors to the change in terms. See F. Scherr, "Credit, Oligopoly, and the Prisoners' Dilemma," *Credit and Financial Management,* Vol. 80, No. 1 (January 1978), pp. 14–15, 41, and J. M. Collins, "The Multiperiod Approach to Credit Policy Decision," available from the author at the University of Tulsa, pp. 13–14.

[13]We will discuss inventory policy in later chapters. For now, we assume that the firm's policy relating inventory and sales has already been determined.

Collection Costs The administration of accounts receivable is costly. To collect the monies owed, the credit departments of firms generally employ telephone calls, letters, visits to customers, and other mechanisms. These entail postage, telephone charges, travel expenses, lost management time and effort, and other out-of-pocket and opportunity costs. While these costs usually rise with sales volume, their amounts vary among types of customers; risky customers with financial problems require disproportionate collection costs. However, the out-of-pocket costs of collection are almost always very small relative to the other cash flows that occur in credit policy decision making (such as sales, cost of sales, changes in inventory levels, and so forth). Thus, their effects are frequently ignored in the interests of simplicity when analyzing terms of sale and credit-granting policies.

Timing of Capital Expenditures When a credit policy change affecting sales volume is made, this change may also affect the timing and amount of future capital expenditures. For example, suppose that a firm expects sales of 100,000 units for the upcoming year and that sales are expected to grow at 10 percent per year. Assume also that the life of the product being sold is six years and that the production capacity of the firm's plant is 130,000 units. The firm is trying to decide whether to implement a credit policy change that would increase next year's sales to 115,000 units but result in the same rate of future sales growth and the same product life. The projected future sales volumes for the present and proposed policies are presented in Table 5-1. If no change in credit policy was made, the firm would reach capacity near the end of the fourth year. At that time, if they wanted to continue to service demand through the life of the product, the firm would have to expand the plant to accommodate an eventual demand of 161,051 units (the sales volume for year six under the present policy). But if the change in credit policy was made, the plant would reach capacity between the second and third years, and the final required capacity would be 185,209 units; a larger capacity expansion would be required. Changes such as these in the timing and amount of the capital expenditures for plant expansion may be caused by alterations in the terms of sale, and any such changes need to be considered in conjunction with terms of sale policy.

Income Tax Effects Changes in credit policy may also affect the firm's tax bill. The most obvious effect involves the change in the firm's depreciation

Table 5-1. *Future Sales in Units for Change in Credit Policy.*

Year	1	2	3	4	5	6
Sales–Old Policy	100,000	110,000	121,000	133,100	146,410	161,051
Sales–New Policy	115,000	126,500	139,150	153,065	168,372	185,209

schedule that results from alterations in the timing and amount of the firm's capital expenditures. However, changes in sales and in cost of sales will also have an impact on the firm's required income tax payments by changing other portions of its pretax income.

Salvage and Recovery Values Since changes in credit policy affect the firm's investments in accounts receivable, inventory, and capital assets, they will naturally affect the recoveries on these assets at the end of the life of the product.

All these changes in costs and revenues affect the cash flows of the firm, and therefore the firm's value to shareholders. To properly evaluate credit policy, a methodology is needed to reflect the differences in timing and amount of these cash flows. In the next section, we present the standard methodology for evaluating terms of sale decisions. Variations on this methodology are presented in many textbooks. Unfortunately, this simple methodology does not sufficiently capture many of the changes in cash flows that result from many terms of sale decisions. The presentation of this textbook methodology is followed by a technique, based on spreadsheet analysis, that adequately addresses the cash flows from these terms of sale decisions.[14]

TERMS OF SALE DECISIONS: STANDARD APPROACH

Before getting into the details of technique, a general discussion of terms of sale decisions is appropriate. First, under U.S. antitrust statutes, *terms of sale must, in almost all cases, be the same for all the firm's customers*, although the selling firm may require some specific buyers to pay cash because of the high costs of granting credit to these buyers.[15] Second, terms of sale decisions involve the setting of the three parameters: the cash discount (the amount of discount allowed for payment within a specified period of time), the period of time this discount is to be allowed, and the net date (the due date of the invoice if the cash discount is not taken). For example, the setting of terms of 2 percent 10 days, net 30 days, requires three decisions (the three numbers in these terms). Finally, for any firm selling any product in any competitive situation, there is almost certainly a set of *optimum terms of sale*, that is, a set of terms of sale for a product or service that results in the highest possible

---

[14]The author is grateful to Tirlochan S. Walia, who is coauthor of the remainder of this chapter.

[15]There are two exceptions to this rule. The selling firm may charge different terms of sale to different customers if the costs of selling to these customers are different (the "cost justification defense") or if other sellers are selling to the customers on terms that are of more advantage to buyers (the "meeting competition" defense).

net present value to the selling firm from that product or service. However, the firm often has little insight into what that set of optimum parameters may be. Consequently, it is usually recommended that the firm analyze the effects of *changes* in its terms; if the proposed change increases the value of the firm, then the change is a move toward the optimum and should be implemented.

To illustrate the traditional methodology for evaluation of the effects of terms of sale changes, let us address a simple example problem. A firm is considering changing its terms of sale from net 30 days to net 60 days (the firm does not offer a cash discount). The change in terms will not affect collection expense or bad debt expense. All the firm's customers pay promptly. The firm's current sales are $50 million per year, and the marketing department estimates that such a change would cause sales to immediately increase to $53 million. The out-of-pocket costs of materials are 80 percent of sales and the required rate of return on accounts receivable is 12 percent. Should the firm make the change in its terms?

To address this question, the traditional terms of sale analysis method compares the one-period, before-tax effects on "profit" of the present and proposed terms of sale. Changes in sales, costs of sales, discount expense, bad debt expense, collection expense, and the opportunity cost of changes in the investment in accounts receivable are netted to determine the advantage of the change in terms. In the example problem, there are no changes in discount expense, bad debt expense, or collection expense. The traditional analysis is presented in Table 5-2. Projected accounts receivable are calculated as the expected time for payment divided by 360 times sales, and opportunity cost for this asset is calculated as the receivables balance times a required return.[16] Since there is an increase in "profit" for this example problem, the change in terms of sale is recommended.

While this analysis methodology is very simple, it turns out to have substantial problems in representing the situations faced by firms and in evaluating the net cash flow effects from terms of sale decisions. Several of these problems stem from a particular assumption made in this methodology regarding the time pattern of future cash flows. To see this assumption, let us look a little more closely at the algebra of this analysis. Let ΔS be the change in sales resulting from the change in policy and V/P to be the cost ratio. For purposes of simplicity, let this cost ratio capture all the costs of the decision (production costs, bad debt expense, and so forth) except for the opportunity cost of investment in receivables. The change in margin can be expressed as $\Delta S(1 - V/P)$; in our example, this is $3,000,000 (1 - 0.8)$, or

---

[16]Other methods can also be used to compute this opportunity cost. We do not discuss these methods here because we will later present a better approach to the problem that does not require the use of this opportunity cost methodology to compute the cost of investment in accounts receivable.

Table 5-2. Traditional One-Period Analysis of a Terms of Sale Change (thousands).

Analysis of Terms of Sale Change

Item	Old	New	Change
Sales	$50,000	$53,000	$3,000
COGS	40,000	42,400	2,400
Margin	$10,000	$10,600	$600
Expected Time for Payment	30	60	
Accounts Receivable	$4,167	$8,833	$4,667
Required Return	0.12	0.12	0.12
Accounts Receivable Carrying Cost	$500	$1,060	$560
Profit	$9,500	$9,540	$40

$600,000. Letting ΔR be the change in accounts receivable, the increased carrying cost is $k\Delta R$, where k is the required return. Algebraically, this decision rule becomes:

$$\text{if } \Delta S(1 - V/P) - k\Delta R > 0, \text{ accept} \qquad (5\text{-}1)$$

Or, rearranging the terms:

$$\text{if } (\Delta S(1 - V/P))/k - \Delta R > 0, \text{ accept} \qquad (5\text{-}2)$$

Finance theory states that cash flows are the things of importance to firms, and that the net present value of future cash flows is the proper evaluation statistic for decisions. Under what conditions does the rule expressed in equation (5-2) agree with the net present-value rule as applied to the terms of sale decision? Except by luck, *the one-period rule will only give the net present value of the decision when the future cash flows from the decision are a perpetual* in the amount of $\Delta S(1 - V/P)$. If the future cash flows are a perpetual in this amount, then their net present value is $(\Delta S(1 - V/P))/k$, since $1/k$ is the discount rate for a perpetual starting at period 1. Netting this present value of the perpetual future cash flows against the initial cash outflow of ΔR yields the traditional decision rule.

Unfortunately, the sales of most firms are not perpetual nor do the managers of firms expect them to be. The sales of actual firms, both in terms of dollar sales and unit sales, *change over time*. Sometimes these changes are due to the market penetration of new products or the maturity of old ones;

sometimes they are due to external factors such as economic conditions or competition. With these changes in sales come changes in bad debt expense, costs of production, and so forth. Since the traditional decision methodology assumes a perpetual, *the effect of changes in sales and costs over time cannot be captured in the net present value implied within this rule.* For firms whose sales are expected to change over time, the rule therefore misrepresents the effects of the present and proposed terms of sale policies.

In addition to this, there are *other problems* within the traditional decision methodology. There is no provision made within this methodology for assessing the effects of changes in capital expenditures, salvage values, or taxes that occur because of changes in terms of sale. Also, if the rule is portrayed in the form of equation (5-1), there is a substantial question as to the proper specification of both the investment in accounts receivable and the opportunity cost of this investment.[17]

To be fair, the traditional one-period approach to the terms of sale decision can be viewed as an attempt to introduce beginning students to trade-offs required in analyzing terms of sales decisions. The effects of changes in all the different types of costs and revenues relevant to terms of sale decisions are not easy to address. By ignoring some of these costs and revenues and assuming a perpetual, it is possible to reduce the problem in size. But the cost of this simplicity is accuracy and realism. In the next section, we introduce a spreadsheet approach to the problem which, by sequentially considering the various types of cash flows inherent in the terms of sale decision, can give a reasonably accurate representation of the net present values in such decisions.

TERMS OF SALE DECISIONS: MULTIPERIOD APPROACH

The discounted net cash flow approach presented here is based on the net present-value procedures for evaluating terms of sale decisions outlined by Collins and by Sartoris and Hill.[18] To illustrate this spreadsheet application, we model the various types of cash flows for an example terms of sale decision problem. This problem is described in the following paragraph.

[17]The debate about the proper specification of investment in accounts receivable and the opportunity cost of these investments spawned a series of articles on the topic during the late 1970s and early 1980s. These articles are too numerous to reference here. See, for example, E. Dyl, "Another Look at the Evaluation of Investment in Accounts Receivable," and T. S. Walia, "Explicit and Implicit Cost of Changes in the Level of Accounts Receivable and the Credit Policy Decision of the Firm," both in *Financial Management* (Winter 1977), pp. 67–70 and 75–78 respectively.

[18]Collins, "The Multiperiod Approach" and W. Sartoris and N. Hill, "A Generalized Cash Flow Approach to Short-Term Financial Decisions," *Journal of Finance*, Vol. 38, No. 2 (May 1983), pp. 349–60.

An Example Terms of Sale Decision Problem Sweets, Incorporated, is the manufacturer of Joybeans, an "executive" jellybean. This year's sales of Joybeans were $1,904,762. The firm expects to sell $2,000,000 worth of Joybeans during the upcoming year with sales expected to grow at 5 percent per year. It is considering lengthening its terms of sale. This change in policy would result in a decreased accounts receivable turnover from eight times per year (45 days) to six times per year (60 days). Under the proposed terms, next year's sales are expected to increase to $2,200,000, although the growth rate of sales would be the same as that under the present policy for all years after this. Variable costs of production are 65 percent of gross sales, and the appropriate risk-adjusted discount rate for cash flows is 15 percent. The life of the product is five years. The production equipment currently in place will produce enough Joybeans for a maximum of $2,300,000 in sales. Under the present policy, the firm will have to purchase additional production capacity at the end of the fourth year at a cost of $150,000; this capacity will be scrapped at the end of the life of the product at a salvage value of $80,000. If the firm implements the proposed policy, the capital expenditure for additional capacity will be made at the end of the second year in the amount of $175,000 and will have a salvage value of $75,000 at the end of the product's life. The firm's policies are such that inventory turnover is 20 times per year, with this ratio based on gross sales. Under the present policy, bad debts total 2 percent of sales; under the proposed policy, this would increase to 2.5 percent of sales. Collection costs for the firm will not change if the new policy is adopted, and the firm does not offer a cash discount. The firm is in the 34 percent tax bracket. For simplicity, assume that the firm depreciates assets from their initial value to their expected salvage value by the straight-line method. At the end of the product's life, inventory will be liquidated and accounts receivable will be collected. It is anticipated that these will be recovered at book value. Should the firm make the proposed change in its terms of sale?

A Spreadsheet Solution This is a relatively complicated problem, but by modeling the various costs and revenues one at a time, the problem can be solved in a tractable and reasonably accurate fashion. We want to know the net present value of the cash flows from the product under two conditions— with the proposed change in terms of sale and without it. To do this, we start by modeling the cash flows that would occur if the policy is not changed. The required analysis for the present policy is presented in Table 5-3. It will pay the student to study this table in detail, as it will be reviewed on a line-by-line basis.

Much of the basic data is contained in cells B8 through B13. This data has been separated, rather than embedded in the contents of later cells, for two reasons: first, so that the analysis of the proposed policy can be carried out using this same spreadsheet by changing this basic data; and second, to facilitate sensitivity analysis for the assessment of risk in terms of sale decisions (a procedure we will discuss later). Using this basic data, gross sales and net sales figures are computed in rows 15 and 16. Since there is no discount expense, net sales are gross sales minus expected bad debts. The cell entries here are straightforward; for example, cell C15 contains "B9", cell D15 contains "C15*(1+(B10/100))", and cell D16 contains "D15*(1−(B12/100))". These gross and net sales entries will be used later in the spreadsheet in calculating cash inflows and outflows.

Because sales in this problem are growing, so also will the accounts receivable balances; the amount of uncollected sales will increase over time. At present, ⅛ of last year's net sales are outstanding (assuming that the firm keeps a reserve for bad debt). The amount of $233,333 appears in cell B19, which contains "B16/8" since the turnover for last year was eight times per year. Over the next year, the firm will make $1,960,000 in net sales; $245,000 will remain outstanding at the end of the year (cell C19 contains "C16/B11" since next year's turnover rate is in cell B11). Thus, of the $1,960,000 in net sales, an additional $11,667 will be uncollected at year-end; *this is the amount of the increase in the firm's accounts receivable* ($245,000 − $233,333). The *net cash flow from the collection of sales* will then be only $1,948,333 because of the increase in receivables over the year. This amount is calculated in cell C20, which contains "C16−(C19−B19)"; the remaining cells in this row contain parallel entries. This row contains the timing and amount of the firm's cash inflow from sales, allowing for the growth of the firm and for increasing investment in accounts receivable.[19]

The sale of Joybeans requires that Sweets, Inc., keep inventory on hand. Like the accounts receivable balance, the required inventory balance will increase over time with increases in sales, as will the cost of materials and labor (variable cost of production). Cash outflows associated with the production of goods thus have two parts: (1) cash outflows to increase inventory levels, and (2) cash outflows to produce goods that are actually sold (the costs of sales actually made). These two parts are calculated in rows 22 through 26 of the spreadsheet. The required inventory balances are calculated in row 23 as 1/20 of the gross sales figures in line 15 (cell B23 contains "B15/20"). The required increase in these balances, equal to last year's balance minus this year's balance, appears in line 24 (cell C24 contains "C23−B23"). Costs of sales, at 65 percent of gross sales, are in line 25. Line 26 adds the cash outflows for additions to inventory to the cash outflows for goods actually sold to calculate the total cash outflows for goods produced in line 26.

---

[19]This is an approximate presentation of this timing and amount because the cash flows are grouped at the end of each year. This is the same grouping generally used in the evaluation of other multiperiod decisions, such as those related to the management of capital assets. A more accurate presentation could be achieved by using more columns (for example, one column for each month rather than for each year).

Table 5-3. Sweets, Inc. Example Problem—Analysis of Present Policy.

	A	‼	B ‼	C ‼	D ‼	E ‼	F ‼	G ‼
3	!							5
4	Year		0	1	2	3	4	5
5								
6	Present Policy:							
7								
8	Last Year's Gross Sales		1904762					
9	First Year's Gross Sales		2000000					
10	Growth Rate		5 percent					
11	Accounts Receivable Turnover		8 Times/Yr.					
12	Bad Debt Expense		2 percent of sales					
13	Discount Rate		15 percent					
14								
15	Gross Sales		1904762	2000000	2100000	2205000	2315250	2431013
16	Sales Net of Bad Debts		1866667	1960000	2058000	2160900	2268945	2382392
17								
18	Collections:							
19	Accounts Receivable Balance		233333	245000	257250	270113	283618	297799
20	Cash Receipts from Sales			1948333	2045750	2148038	2255439	2368211
21								
22	Inventory Investment:							
23	Inventory Balance		95238	100000	105000	110250	115763	121551
24	Increase in Inventory			4762	5000	5250	5513	5788
25	Cost of Goods Produced for Sale			1300000	1365000	1433250	1504913	1580158
26	Total Cost of Goods Produced			1304762	1370000	1438500	1510425	1585946
27								

28 Capital Expenditures		150000			
29 Salvage Value—New Equipment	80000				
30					
31 Income Tax Calculations:					
32 Sales Net of Bad Debts	2382392	2268945	2160900	2058000	1960000
33 Cost of Goods Produced for Sale	1580158	1504913	1433250	1365000	1300000
34 Depreciation	70000				
35					
36 EBT	732234	764033	727650	693000	660000
37 Taxes at 34 percent	248960	259771	247401	235620	224400
38					
39					
40 Net Cash Flow Table:					
41 Cash Receipts from Sales	2368211	2255439	2148038	2045750	1948333
42 Total Cost of Goods Produced	−1585946	−1510425	−1438500	−1370000	−1304762
43 Capital Expenditures		−150000			
44 Salvage Value—New Equipment	80000				
45 Recovery on Receivables	297799				
46 Recovery on Inventory	121551				
47 Taxes Paid	−248960	−259771	−247401	−235620	−224400
48					
49 Net Cash Flow from Joybeans	1032655	335243	462137	440130	419171
50					
51 Present Value Interest Factors	.4971768	.5717532	.6575162	.7561437	.8695652
52 Contribution to NPV	513412	191676	303862	332802	364497
53 Total Net Present Value	1706249				

Table 5-4. Sweets, Inc. Example Problem—Analysis of Proposed Policy.

	A	!!	B !! 0	C !! 1	D !! 2	E !! 3	F !! 4	G ! 5
3	!	!!	!!	!!	!!	!!	!!	!
4	Year		0	1	2	3	4	5
5								
6	Proposed Policy:							
7								
8	Last Year's Gross Sales		1904762					
9	First Year's Gross Sales		2200000					
10	Growth Rate		5 percent					
11	Accounts Receivable Turnover		6 Times/Yr.					
12	Bad Debt Expense		2.5 percent of sales					
13	Discount Rate		15 percent					
14								
15	Gross Sales		1904762	2200000	2310000	2425500	2546775	2674114
16	Sales Net of Bad Debts		1866667	2145000	2252250	2364863	2483106	2607261
17								
18	Collections:							
19	Accounts Receivable Balance		233333	357500	375375	394144	413851	434543
20	Cash Receipts from Sales			2020833	2234375	2346094	2463398	2586568
21								
22	Inventory Investment:							
23	Inventory Balance		95238	110000	115500	121275	127339	133706
24	Increase in Inventory			14762	5500	5775	6064	6367
25	Cost of Goods Produced for Sale			1430000	1501500	1576575	1655404	1738174
26	Total Cost of Goods Produced			1444762	1507000	1582350	1661468	1744541
27								

#		Year 1	Year 2	Year 3	Year 4	Year 5
28	Capital Expenditures		175000			
29	Salvage Value—New Equipment					75000
30						
31	Income Tax Calculations:					
32	Sales Net of Bad Debts	2145000	2252250	2364863	2483106	2607261
33	Cost of Goods Produced for Sale	1430000	1501500	1576575	1655404	1738174
34	Depreciation			33333	33333	33333
35						
36	EBT	715000	750750	754954	794369	835754
37	Taxes at 34 percent	243100	255255	256684	270085	284156
38						
39						
40	Net Cash Flow Table:					
41	Cash Receipts from Sales	2020833	2234375	2346094	2463398	2586568
42	Total Cost of Goods Produced	−1444762	−1507000	−1582350	−1661468	−1744541
43	Capital Expenditures		−175000			
44	Salvage Value—New Equipment					75000
45	Recovery on Receivables					434543
46	Recovery on Inventory					133706
47	Taxes Paid	−243100	−255255	−256684	−270085	−284156
48						
49	Net Cash Flow from Joybeans	332971	297120	507059	531846	1201120
50						
51	Present Value Interest Factors	.8695652	.7561437	.6575162	.5717532	.4971768
52	Contribution to NPV	289540	224665	333400	304084	597169
53	Total Net Present Value					1748859

Table 5-5. Sweets, Inc. Example Problem—Analysis of Proposed Policy, No Increase in Sales.

	A	!!	B !!	C !!	D !!	E !!	F !!	G !
3								
4	Year		0	1	2	3	4	5
5								
6	Proposed Policy:							
7								
8	Last Year's Gross Sales		1904762					
9	First Year's Gross Sales		2000000					
10	Growth Rate		5 percent					
11	Accounts Receivable Turnover		6 Times/Yr.					
12	Bad Debt Expense		2.5 percent of sales					
13	Discount Rate		15 percent					
14								
15	Gross Sales		1904762	2000000	2100000	2205000	2315250	2431013
16	Sales Net of Bad Debts		1866667	1950000	2047500	2149875	2257369	2370237
17								
18	Collections:							
19	Accounts Receivable Balance		233333	325000	341250	358313	376228	395040
20	Cash Receipts from Sales			1858333	2031250	2132813	2239453	2351426
21								
22	Inventory Investment:							
23	Inventory Balance		95238	100000	105000	110250	115763	121551
24	Increase in Inventory			4762	5000	5250	5513	5788
25	Cost of Goods Produced for Sale			1300000	1365000	1433250	1504913	1580158
26	Total Cost of Goods Produced			1304762	1370000	1438500	1510425	1585946
27								

#						
28	Capital Expenditures		150000			
29	Salvage Value—New Equipment	80000				
30						
31	Income Tax Calculations:					
32	Sales Net of Bad Debts	2370237	2257369	2149875	2047500	1950000
33	Cost of Goods Produced for Sale	1580158	1504913	1433250	1365000	1300000
34	Depreciation	70000				
35						
36	EBT	720079	752456	716625	682500	650000
37	Taxes at 34 percent	244827	255835	243653	232050	221000
38						
39						
40	Net Cash Flow Table:					
41	Cash Receipts from Sales	2351426	2239453	2132813	2031250	1858333
42	Total Cost of Goods Produced	−1585946	−1510425	−1438500	−1370000	−1304762
43	Capital Expenditures		−150000			
44	Salvage Value—New Equipment	80000				
45	Recovery on Receivables	395040				
46	Recovery on Inventory	121551				
47	Taxes Paid	−244827	−255835	−243653	−232050	−221000
48						
49	Net Cash Flow from Joybeans	1117243	323193	450660	429200	332571
50						
51	Present Value Interest Factors	.4971768	.5717532	.6575162	.7561437	.8695652
52	Contribution to NPV	555467	184787	296316	324537	289193
53	Total Net Present Value	1650299				

The capital expenditures required of Sweets, Inc., under this credit policy are input as data in line 28 as is the salvage value of these new purchases in line 29. With these and the prior data, the firm's tax bills can now be computed. This is done in lines 31 through 37. In this calculation, *accrual accounting must be used*, since this is the method required under the federal tax statutes. Thus, in line 32 of these pro forma income statements, sales appears rather than collections. Under these statutes, only the costs of goods actually sold (and not those produced to increase inventory) are deductible, so these are the costs reproduced in row 33. Therefore, cell C32 contains "C16" and cell C33 contains "C25". The depreciation deductions appear in row 34. Since we are assuming for simplicity that the firm depreciates assets from their acquisition cost to their expected salvage value by the straight-line method, and since the asset will be held for only one year, cell G34 contains "(F28 − G29)/1". Row 36 contains the contribution to the firm's taxable earnings; cell C36 contains "C32 − (C33 + C34)". The tax bill associated with the Joybeans product is 34 percent of these earnings, and appears in row 37.

At this point, data for all the various types of cash flows associated with the present terms of sale for Joybeans have been calculated; it is just a matter of summing these cash flows and discounting them. For clarity, a separate summary section of this spreadsheet in rows 40 through 49 presents the cash flow data; the discounting is carried out in rows 51 through 53. The contents of the cells in rows 41 through 49, where the different types of net cash flows are detailed, are simply cell addresses referring to other parts of the spreadsheet. For example, cell C41 contains "C20", cell C42 contains " − C26", and cell G45 contains "G19". Rows 41 through 47 are summed in row 49 (cell C49 contains "@SUM(C41 . . . C49)"). Present value interest factors are computed in row 51 by using the discount rate in cell B13 and the year number data in row 4. For example, cell D51 contains "1/(((1 + (B15/100))^D4)". These are multiplied by the net cash flow estimates in line 49 to obtain the contributions to net present value in line 52. The formula in cell G53 is "@SUM(C52 . . . G52)", and gives the total net present value of the cash flow stream from Joybeans under the present terms of sale. This NPV is $1,706,249.

To decide whether the new terms of sale should be adopted, this net present value of the present policy must be compared to the net present value of the cash flows under the proposed policy. To obtain this analysis, the turnover, sales, and bad-debt data in cells B9, B10, and B11 and the data and formulas elsewhere in the spreadsheet on capital expenditures and their depreciation are changed to reflect the results of the new policy. The results are presented in Table 5-4. The net present value is $1,748,859 for the cash flows under the proposed policy, so by this analysis *the change should be made*; it increases the value of the cash flows to Sweets, Inc., by $42,610.

ASSESSING RISK IN TERMS OF SALE DECISIONS

This approach to the analysis of terms of sale decisions is comprehensive and reasonably accurate. It avoids many of the problems inherent in the traditional approach to these decisions and is very flexible. Numerous time patterns of sales, costs, and so forth can be modeled quite easily. This methodology takes the basic capital budgeting view of discounting expected cash flows to obtain their value. Since the changes in net cash flows inherent in terms of sale decisions are generally of similar risk to other cash flows of the firm (since they result from greater or lesser sales and costs for an existing product or service), it makes sense to use a risk-adjusted rate in discounting, with this rate based on the firm's cost of capital. Adjustments to this cost of capital (via benchmarks or via the CAPM) can be made to reflect differences in risk among the firm's products. In this way, the value of the flows to the firm is adjusted for risk as part of the discounting process.

While this risk-adjusted discounting procedure is a reasonable approach to the problem of addressing risk in terms of sale decisions, many firms will want to do additional analysis of risk with respect to these decisions, particularly if the net present values of the cash flow streams are large and the differences in net present value between alternate credit policies are small. The evaluation of various terms of sale policies involves the estimation of future cash flows, and there are numerous sources of potential error that may make actual results different from estimates. Sartoris and Hill cite four sources of possible error in estimates of future outcomes in terms of sale decisions: estimates of the fraction of sales paid with a discount, estimates of the accounts receivable turnover, estimates of sales volume, and estimates of bad debt expense.[20] To this list could be added sources of error in numerous other estimates, including estimates of future production expenses, capital expenses, salvage values, product life, and even future tax rates. Sartoris and Hill suggest several methods for addressing this estimation risk, including the use of risk-adjusted discount rates (as we used previously), simulation, and sensitivity analysis.

Simulation, as was used in Chapter 3 to assess the risk of cash stockout in the cash forecast, is a potentially fruitful avenue for assessing risk in many situations. However, the additional estimation cost inherent in simulation is of most advantage when there are a number of important parameters of the decision which exhibit large variations and which are likely to substantially change the outcome of the analysis. In many terms of sale problems, there is one parameter that plays an extremely important part in the analysis and about which there is considerable uncertainty. That parameter is *the change in future sales resulting from a change in credit policy*. It is our experience

---

[20]See Sartoris and Hill, "A Generalized Cash Flow Approach," p. 357.

that other parameters of the analysis (future accounts receivable turnover, bad debt expense, and so forth) may be estimated relatively accurately based on the firm's past experience, data from other product lines where the firm offers different terms of sale, publicly available data on turnover ratios, and so forth. However, *the estimation of the change in future sales requires substantial insight into demand curve effects and the reactions of competitors*; accurate estimation in these areas is a good deal harder to achieve.[21] Consequently, we believe that the most useful tool for risk assessment in terms of sale decisions is *sensitivity analysis of the anticipated sales change resulting from a terms of sale decision.*

To understand the criticality of the sales effect, let us return to the example problem used previously. While a change in terms of sale policy could well affect other aspects of the time pattern of future sales, in this problem the firm's first-year sales were expected to undergo a substantial increase, with sales thereafter growing at the same rate regardless of whether the proposed policy is adopted or the present policy is continued. Assume that Sweets, Inc., changes its terms of sale, and that the firm's accounts receivable turnover slows and bad debt increases as a result, but that the first year's sales do not increase. Perhaps the firm is in an oligopolistic industry and other manufacturers of executive jellybeans elect to match the change in terms initiated by Sweets. In such a case, the firm will experience decreased cash inflows due to (1) decreased accounts receivable turnover, and (2) increased bad debt losses, but will experience no offsetting increases in cash inflows due to additional sales volumes (although the firm's time pattern of capital expenditures will be the same as under the present terms of sale policy).[22] The analysis of this possible result is presented in Table 5-5. The net present value of the cash flows from Joybeans is $1,650,299, which is $55,950 less than the net present value for the current terms of sale, so the change reduces the value of the firm. Using this example, we see that the relationship between the firm's terms of sale and the resulting sales volume is a critical element affecting the desirability of any proposed changes in these terms.

Since the changes in sales that result from a change in terms are so critical and so uncertain, sensitivity analysis of the effects of these changes versus the advantage of the proposed new policy is a reasonable approach to addressing the major risk factor in this analysis. A sensitivity analysis of the first-year sales level for the proposed terms of the Sweets, Inc., example problem is presented in Table 5-6 and graphed in Figure 5-1. In this example

[21]The substantial difficulty experienced by firms in estimating future sales levels, even without the added complication of changes in terms of sale, is discussed in J. Pan, D. R. Nichols, and O. M. Joy, "Sales Forecasting Practices of Large U.S. Industrial Firms," *Financial Management* (Fall 1977), pp. 72–77.

[22]This discussion ignores any increases in industry sales from industry demand curve effects in the interests of simplicity.

Table 5-6. Sensitivity Analysis of Increase in NPV for Various First Year's Sales.

First Year's Gross Sales	% Above Present	Year of Cap. Exp.	Amount of Cap. Exp.	Amt. of Salvage	NPV	Increase in NPV
$2,000,000	0.00	4	$150,000	$80,000	$1,650,299	− $55,950
$2,050,000	2.50	4	$156,250	$78,750	$1,682,340	− $23,909
$2,100,000	5.00	3	$162,500	$77,500	$1,701,523	− $4,726
$2,150,000	7.50	3	$168,750	$76,250	$1,733,123	$26,874
$2,200,000	10.00	2	$175,000	$75,000	$1,748,859	$42,610
$2,250,000	12.50	2	$181,250	$73,750	$1,779,947	$73,698
$2,300,000	15.00	1	$187,500	$72,500	$1,791,535	$85,286
$2,350,000	17.50	1	$193,750	$71,250	$1,822,030	$115,781

problem, the initial sales figure for the new policy affects the future schedule of capital expenditures because it affects the levels of future sales; estimates of the required capital expenditures for various sales levels must be generated. Such estimates are also provided in Table 5-6. As can be seen from this table and figure, unless the change in terms increases sales to approximately $2,110,000 (about a 5.5 percent increase), the difference in the old and new net present

Figure 5-1. Increase in NPV Versus First-Year Sales.

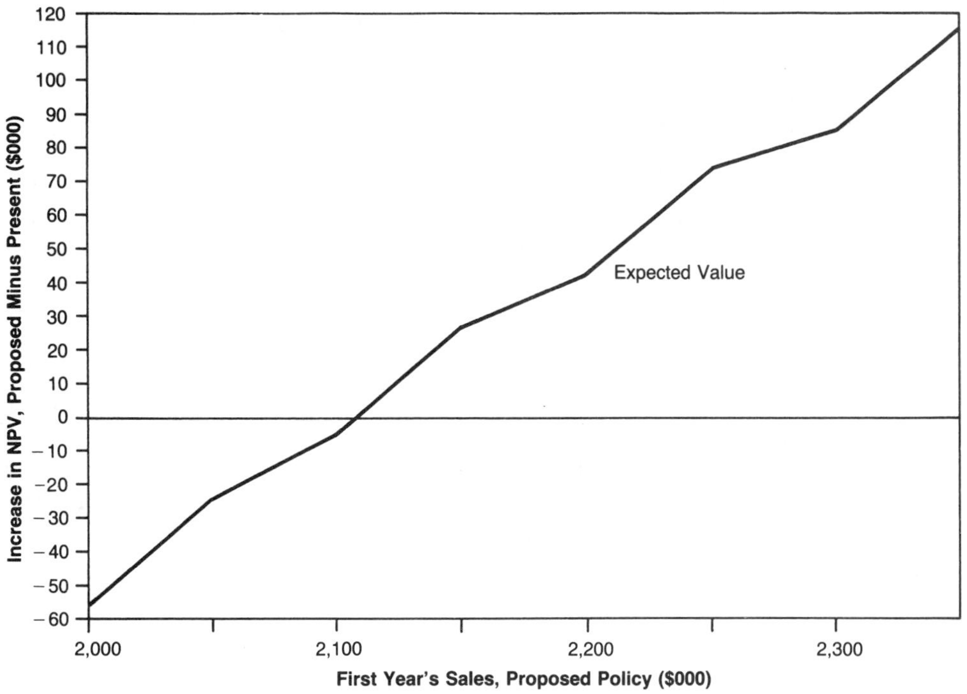

values is negative, and the change will not be of advantage to the firm. The expected increase is 10 percent, but Sweets, Inc., needs to take a *very close look at this estimate* and the way in which it was made. What assumptions and procedures were used to make it? How certain is it? What is the chance that the actual increase will be less than 5.5 percent? If the management of Sweets is confident that this estimate was made in a reasonable fashion and that the probability is small that the increase in sales will be less than 5.5 percent, the change in the terms of sale should be made. If not, the results of the analysis need to be considered carefully.

STRATEGIC ASPECTS OF TERMS OF SALE POLICY[23]

In the prior discussion and example of the analysis of terms of sale decisions, it was assumed that the decision to change the firm's terms of sale did not affect the life of the product. However, it is the policy of many firms to exit the market for a particular product as the product moves toward the maturity stage of its product life cycle. In such a case, the firm may use credit policy and other price-related tools to change the *time pattern* of future cash flows as well as the *level* of future cash flows. This strategy may, in turn, affect the optimal life of the product. Assume, for example, that the firm has used credit and other pricing policies to accelerate the acceptance of a new product but at the cost of higher-margin sales over a longer period. Such a maneuver may also have shifted the time pattern of the firm's capital expenditures and costs. This may result in a higher net present value for a product but a shorter optimal product life.

An example of this is presented in Figure 5-2. Here, it is assumed that the firm has used price-related policies to shift the pattern of costs and revenues. In this figure, the present policy is policy A and the proposed policy is policy B. Under the old policy, the optimal product life was $LIFE_A$ (since for this product life the net present value is at a maximum), and the net present value of the product under this policy was NPV_A. If the firm adopts proposed policy B, the optimal life is $LIFE_B$, and the optimal net present value is NPV_B. Since NPV_B in this case is greater than NPV_A, the optimal choice is to adopt Policy B and to exit the product at $LIFE_B$.

To illustrate the principles involved, let us introduce an example problem. Sweets, Inc., has a product line of hard candy which has recently been introduced and is sold under the name "Moonrocks." It is considering changing the terms of sale for this product line. Present terms of sale have resulted in an accounts receivable turnover of 12 times per year and bad debt expense of 2 percent of sales. The new terms of sale will result in an accounts receivable

[23]This section relies heavily on T. S. Walia, "Credit Policy of the Firm as a Tool for Implementing Strategic Decisions," presented at the Eastern Finance Association, April 1984, and available from the author at Indiana University of Pennsylvania.

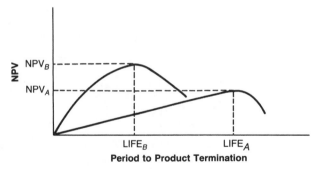

Figure 5-2. *Net Present Value Versus Project Life for Two Terms of Sale Policies.*

turnover of 4 times per year and bad debt expense of 5 percent of sales. The appropriate risk-adjusted discount rate for this product is estimated at 10 percent per year (the cash flows from Moonrocks are considered to be less risky than those of Joybeans), and inventory turnover will be 15 times per year. Last year's gross sales were $10 million. No capital expenditures will be required under either policy, although the rate of production and length of production will affect the after-tax salvage value of existing fixed assets.

The expected effect of this policy change on sales for Moonrocks is portrayed in Table 5-7. After seven years, sales are expected to be zero for either policy, and the product will be abandoned then in any case. The policy change is expected to increase sales from $123 million to $139 million over the life of the product. However, the new terms will increase sales only in the first two years of the product (due to market penetration effects). After that, the present policy will produce higher sales volumes in the remaining years. In such a case, the changes in the time pattern and level of sales may change the optimum product life.

Analysis of the present and proposed policies is presented in Tables 5-8 and 5-9. Rows 1 through 34 are virtually the same as the spreadsheets

Table 5-7. *Sales for Moonrocks Example Problem.*

Year	Sales— Present Policy	Sales— Proposed Policy	Difference in Sales
1	$ 20,000	$ 35,000	− $15,000
2	$ 30,000	$ 60,000	− $30,000
3	$ 30,000	$ 25,000	$ 5,000
4	$ 15,000	$ 10,000	$ 5,000
5	$ 12,000	$ 5,000	$ 7,000
6	$ 10,000	$ 3,000	$ 7,000
7	$ 6,000	$ 1,000	$ 5,000
Total	$123,000	$139,000	

Table 5-8. Moonrocks Example Problem—Analysis of Present Policy (rounded thousands of dollars)

	A	!!	B	!!	C	!!	D	!!	E	!!	F	!!	G	!!	H	!!	I	!!
4																		
5	Year		0		1		2		3		4		5		6		7	
6																		
7	Present Policy:																	
8																		
9	Last Year's Gross Sales		10000															
10	First Year's Gross Sales		20000															
11	Accounts Receivable Turnover		12	Times/Yr.														
12	Bad Debt Expense		2	percent of sales														
13	Discount Rate		10	percent														
14	Inventory Turnover (GS/Inv.)		15															
15																		
16	Gross Sales		10000		20000		30000		30000		15000		12000		10000		6000	
17	Sales Net of Bad Debts		9800		19600		29400		29400		14700		11760		9800		5880	
18																		
19	Collections:																	
20	Accounts Receivable Balance		817		1633		2450		2450		1225		980		817		490	
21	Cash Receipts from Sales				18783		28583		29400		15925		12005		9963		6207	
22																		
23	Inventory Investment:																	
24	Inventory Balance		667		1333		2000		2000		1000		800		667		400	
25	Increase in Inventory				667		667		0		-1000		-200		-133		-267	
26	Cost of Goods Produced for Sale				13000		19500		19500		9750		7800		6500		3900	
27	Total Cost of Goods Produced				13667		20167		19500		8750		7600		6367		3633	

28							
29 Income Tax Calculations:							
30 Sales Net of Bad Debts	19600	29400	29400	14700	11760	9800	5880
31 Cost of Goods Produced for Sale	13000	19500	19500	9750	7800	6500	3900
32							
33 EBT	6600	9900	9900	4950	3960	3300	1980
34 Taxes at 34 percent	2244	3366	3366	1683	1346	1122	673
35							
36 Net Cash Flow Table:							
37 Cash Receipts from Sales	18783	28583	29400	15925	12005	9963	6207
38 Total Cost of Goods Produced	−13667	−20167	−19500	−8750	−7600	−6367	−3633
39 Taxes Paid	−2244	−3366	−3366	−1683	−1346	−1122	−673
40							
41 Net Cash Flow Selling Moonrocks	2873	5051	6534	5492	3059	2475	1900
42							
43 Recovery on AR and Inv.	2967	4450	4450	2225	1780	1483	890
44 Recoveries on Equipment	6000	4800	3840	3072	2458	1966	1573
45							
46 Present Value Interest Factors	.9090909	.8264463	.7513148	.6830135	.6209213	.5644739	.5131581
47 Contribution to NPV from Oper. NCF	2612	4174	4909	3751	1899	1397	975
48							
49 NPV of Recoveries	8152	7645	6228	3618	2631	1947	1264
50							
51 Net Present Value of Termination	10763	14430	17923	19064	19976	20689	20981

Table 5-9. Moonrocks Example Problem—Analysis of Proposed Policy (rounded thousands of dollars)

!	A	!!	B	!!	C	!!	D	!!	E	!!	F	!!	G	!!	H	!!	I	!
5	Year		0		1		2		3		4		5		6		7	
6																		
7	Proposed Policy:																	
8																		
9	Last Year's Gross Sales		10000															
10	First Year's Gross Sales		35000															
11	Accounts Receivable Turnover		4		Times/Yr.													
12	Bad Debt Expense		5		percent of sales													
13	Discount Rate		10		percent													
14	Inventory Turnover (GS/Inv.)		15															
15																		
16	Gross Sales		10000		35000		60000		25000		10000		5000		3000		1000	
17	Sales Net of Bad Debts		9800		33250		57000		23750		9500		4750		2850		950	
18																		
19	Collections:																	
20	Accounts Receivable Balance		817		8313		14250		5938		2375		1188		713		238	
21	Cash Receipts from Sales				25754		51063		32063		13063		5938		3325		1425	
22																		
23	Inventory Investment:																	
24	Inventory Balance		667		2333		4000		1667		667		333		200		67	
25	Increase in Inventory				1667		1667		-2333		-1000		-333		-133		-133	
26	Cost of Goods Produced for Sale				22750		39000		16250		6500		3250		1950		650	
27	Total Cost of Goods Produced				24417		40667		13917		5500		2917		1817		517	

28							
29 Income Tax Calculations:							
30 Sales Net of Bad Debts	33250	57000	23750	9500	4750	2850	950
31 Cost of Goods Produced for Sale	22750	39000	16250	6500	3250	1950	650
32							
33 EBT	10500	18000	7500	3000	1500	900	300
34 Taxes at 34 percent	3570	6120	2550	1020	510	306	102
35							
36 Net Cash Flow Table:							
37 Cash Receipts from Sales	25754	51063	32063	13063	5938	3325	1425
38 Total Cost of Goods Produced	−24417	−40667	−13917	−5500	−2917	−1817	−517
39 Taxes Paid	−3570	−6120	−2550	−1020	−510	−306	−102
40							
41 Net Cash Flow Selling Moonrocks	−2233	4276	15596	6543	2511	1202	806
42							
43 Recovery on AR and Inv.	10646	18250	7604	3042	1521	913	304
44 Recoveries on Equipment	6000	4200	2940	2058	1441	1008	706
45							
46 Present Value Interest Factors	.9090909	.8264463	.7513148	.6830135	.6209213	.5644739	.5131581
47 Contribution to NPV from Oper. NCF	−2030	3534	11717	4469	1559	679	414
48							
49 NPV of Recoveries	15133	18554	7922	3483	1839	1084	518
50							
51 Net Present Value of Termination	13103	20058	21144	21173	21088	21012	20860

presented in the prior analysis of terms of sale policy, except that (1) the capital expenditure effects have been deleted (since there are no differential effects between the policies on capital expenditures), and (2) the future sales figures are now input as data, since they are being forecast by the spot method. For purposes of this analysis, the cash flows associated with the Moonrocks product are split into two types: the cash flows from sales and the recoveries in the termination of the product line. The cash flows from sales are calculated in rows 37 through 41. In this particular example problem, there are three types of cash flows resulting from sales: the cash receipts from sales (row 37), the cost of goods produced (row 38), and the taxes paid (row 39). As in prior spreadsheet analyses, these figures are taken from calculations performed in prior rows (cell C37 contains "C21", and so forth). The sum of these three, which is the cash flow from sales of Moonrocks, appears in row 41 (cell C41 contains "@SUM(C37 . . . C39), for example).

Rows 43 and 44 contain the recovery amounts to the firm *if the product is terminated at the end of the year*. The recovery amount for accounts receivable and inventory (row 43) is the sum of the balances of these two accounts at the end of the year from rows 20 and 24 (a 100 percent recovery is assumed in this problem). The recoveries on equipment in line 44 are spot estimates and are input as data. The sum of these two is the cash recovery that the firm would receive if it terminates the product at the end of that year. For example, if the product was terminated at the end of year 2 (column D), the firm would receive a total of $4.45 million on the recovery of receivables and inventory ($2.45 million from receivables and $2 million from inventory) and $4.8 million on the salvage of equipment. The contributions to the net present value from the operating net cash flow (from selling the product) and from liquidation are presented in rows 47 and 49 respectively. These are the future cash flows times the present value interest factors in row 46.

The net present value of the flows from the Moonrocks product line for termination in various years is presented in row 51. To understand how these figures were derived, recognize that if the firm terminates the product line at any time, it receives the cash flows from sales *up through that time* plus the cash flow from recovery that is applicable *at that time*. For example, if the firm terminates the product at the end of the third year, it will receive the cash flows from sales for years 1 through 3 and the recovery for year 3. Therefore, the net present value of termination of the product at the end of the third year is $17.923 million, which is composed of the net present value of the operating cash inflows from years 1, 2, and 3 in the amounts of $2.162 million, $4.174 million, and $4.909 million plus the net present value of the recoveries at the end of year 3 in the amount of $6.228 million. That is, cell E51 contains "@SUM(C47 . . . E47)+E49". The other cells in row 51 contain similar entries, with the summation function always beginning at cell C47

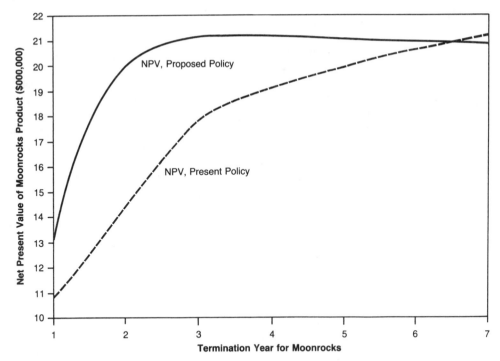

Figure 5-3. *NPV Versus Termination Year—Two Policies.*

and continuing to the column involved. From row 51, the optimal strategy for the present terms of sale is to continue to sell the product for the entire seven-year life, with a net present value of $20.981 million.

The parallel analysis for the proposed terms of sale in Table 5-9 shows a different picture. Here, the optimum product life is only four years, with a net present value of $21.173 million. Since this net present value is higher than the net present value for the optimum product life under the present policy, *the proposed terms of sale should be adopted, and the product should be terminated after four years.* A graph of the net present values for the two policies is presented in Figure 5-3. This graph highlights the necessity that the analyst consider the effects of optimal product life in assessing any multi-period decision (including terms of sale policy decisions). In this particular problem, if Sweets, Inc., assumes that the change in policy has not affected the optimal life and incorrectly evaluates both the present and proposed policies using a seven-year life, it will continue with the present terms of sale since the net present value of the present policy is higher than that of the proposed policy for a seven-year product life. Stockholders would then not gain the additional value that would accrue to the firm from adopting the proposed terms of sale and terminating the product in the fourth year.

SUMMARY

This chapter introduced the management of accounts receivable. Trade credit, which is the granting of credit from one firm to another for the purchase of goods or services, has historically been an important source of financing for firms. Trade credit continues to exist because it performs several useful functions: it allows firms that are best able to borrow to access capital markets and then relend funds to other firms; it allows firms to check the quality of goods and services before paying for them; and it avoids the conveyance problems associated with the payment of cash on delivery.

This chapter also discussed one of the two major decision areas in the management of accounts receivable: terms of sale policy. The analysis of terms of sale decisions requires that the selling firm estimate the effects of these decisions on the timing and amount of its cash flows. There are several types of cash flows that may be affected by terms of sale decisions. Unfortunately, the standard approach to terms of sale policy deals with only a few of these types, and assumes an unrealistic time pattern for those that it does consider. An alternate spreadsheet analysis system is presented in which the analyst estimates all the major types of cash flows effects from the terms of sale decision, then sums and discounts these to obtain the net present values of alternative terms of sale policies. This approach to terms of sale analysis is very flexible and is reasonably accurate in capturing the timing and value of cash flows. Further, this approach facilitates the assessment (via sensitivity analysis) of the major risk factor in terms of sale decisions: the expected change in future sales from a change in terms of sale policy.

Finally, we present analysis of the strategic aspects of terms of sale policy. In this analysis, the firm may use terms of sale policy to change the time pattern (as well as the level) of future cash flows. By the technique presented, firms may analyze the alternative terms of sale policies which may involve the termination of products before the maturity stage of the product life cycle.

In addition to the analysis of terms of sale policy, the other major decision to be made in the management of accounts receivable is the *credit-granting decision*: to whom should the firm grant credit? We take up the analysis of the credit-granting decision in the next chapter.

Problems

5-1. A firm is considering changing its terms of sale for a particular product. The product has a three-year life. Last year's sales were $1 million. The current terms are net 30 days; 99 percent of customers pay promptly and the remainder default. Under the current terms, expected sales for the upcoming year are $1.1 million. If these terms are continued, the firm will make a fixed asset purchase in the amount of $30,000 in the second year. The salvage value for this asset is $10,000. The proposed terms are net 60 days. If these terms are instituted, next year's sales are expected to be $1.15 million, and it is expected that 97 percent of all customers will pay promptly and the remaining 3 percent will default. Under the proposed terms, a fixed asset purchase in the amount of $40,000 will be required in the first year; the salvage value of this asset will be $15,000. Whether or not the terms change is instituted, sales are expected to grow at 10 percent per year after the first year. Costs of goods are 80 percent of sales. Inventory levels are kept at 10 percent of sales. The firm's cost of capital is 12 percent, and federal and state income taxes total 40 percent of earnings before taxes. The firm depreciates assets using the straight-line method from the initial purchase price to the expected salvage value.

a. Compute the net present value of the product under the present terms of sale.

b. Compute the net present value of the product under the proposed terms of sale.

c. Indicate whether the proposed terms change should be instituted. Give a rationale for your answer.

5-2. The increment to sales volume resulting from a change in terms of sale is always uncertain. Investigate the sensitivity of your answer to Problem 1 by recalculating the net present value of the proposed policy for initial sales volumes of $1.1 million, $1.2 million, $1.25 million, $1.3 million, $1.35 million, and $1.4 million. Assume that these sales amounts do not require any other capital expenditures beyond the $40,000 amount to be spent in the first year, and do not affect the salvage value of this expenditure. How does this analysis influence your conclusions with respect to the adoption of the proposed terms of sale change?

Selected Readings

Barzman, R., *Credit in America* (New York: National Association of Credit Management, 1975).

Collins, J. M., "The Multiperiod Approach to Credit Policy Decisions," available from the author at the University of Tulsa.

Emery, G., "A Pure Financial Explanation for Trade Credit," *Journal of Financial And Quantitative Analysis,* Vol. 19, No. 3 (September 1984), pp. 271–85.

Emery, G., "An Optimal Financial Response to Variable Demand," *Journal of Financial and Quantitative Analysis,* Vol. 22, No. 2 (June 1987), pp. 209–25.

Johnson, Dana, "Market Justifications for Trade Credit in Imperfect Capital Markets," available from the author at Virginia Polytechnic Institute and State University.

Lewellen, W., J. McConnell, and J. Scott, "Capital Market Influences on Trade Credit Policies," *Journal of Financial Research,* Vol. III, No. 2 (Fall 1980), pp. 105–13.

Sartoris, W., and N. Hill, "A Generalized Cash Flow Approach to Short-Term Financial Decisions," *Journal of Finance,* Vol. 38, No. 2 (May 1983), pp. 349–60.

Smith, J. K., "Trade Credit and Information Asymmetry," *Journal of Finance* (September 1987), pp. 863–72.

Walia, T. S., "Credit Policy of the Firm as a Tool for Implementing Strategic Decisions," presented at the Eastern Finance Association, April 1984, and available from the author at Indiana University of Pennsylvania.

Alloyed Companies, Inc.[1]
Terms of Sale Analysis

Alloyed Companies, Inc., was one of the more successful miniconglomerates, perhaps because of two policies: (1) no firm was acquired that Alloyed did not think it could manage properly, and (2) after acquisition, certain functions of the acquired firms were centralized to take advantage of economies of scale. One of these centralized functions was receivables management. Mr. Juliett, assistant treasurer of Alloyed, acted as credit and receivables manager for all of Alloyed's five divisions.

Sales had been expanding over the past few years, as had Alloyed's customer base, in each of the five divisions. The average receivables balance for each of the credit department's three accounts managers had reached $9 million, which Mr. Juliett thought was uncomfortably high. Though there had been no complaints from the accounts managers (who reported to Mr. Juliett directly) he felt that they could do a better job with a decreased work load and had decided to add another accounts manager to the force. Mr. Juliett also felt that the time was right to re-

view the firm's credit and receivables management policies in general.

Despite the fact that Alloyed's five divisions were similar in terms of the processes used and the physical products sold, they each sold to different markets. There were no common customers. As each firm had been acquired, its receivables had been centralized and sorted into Alloyed's receivables system. This system was a fairly complex one, using much computer assistance and capable of producing the numerous reports requested by management. All sales were within the continental United States.

Credit and receivables management was one of the areas where Alloyed felt that future financial executives should have experience, and so the company rotated promising people into the accounts manager positions on a regular basis. Average tenure within these positions was about two and one-half years, after which time the employee would go on to another position within the firm. The accounts of all five divisions were sorted alphabetically and assigned to the accounts managers in this fashion. Each manager had about the same total dollar exposure and total number of accounts. The management strategy for handling accounts had been to treat each account

[1]This case has been adapted from Iqbal Mathur and Frederick C. Scherr, *Cases in Financial Management* (New York: Macmillan, 1979), pp. 50–55.

Exhibit 1

Alloyed Companies
Divisional Statements of Income for Fiscal 1977
(rounded thousands of dollars)

	Imported Products Division	Paint Supplies Division	Plastic Resin Division	Consumer Products Division	Chemical Division
Gross Sales	$41,800	$24,200	$61,600	$26,400	$66,000
Bad Debt Allowance	100	121	462	610	660
Other Allowances	109	121	154	182	0
Net Sales	$41,591	$23,958	$60,984	$25,608	$65,340
Cost of Goods Sold:					
Direct Labor	$ 0	$ 1,978	$ 3,297	$ 1,512	$ 5,213
Direct Materials	36,421	14,916	32,450	15,026	29,657
Direct Overhead	1,011	1,412	1,932	1,020	1,764
Depreciation[1]	0	1,100	4,400	880	4,620
Gross Margin on Sales	$ 4,159	$ 4,552	$18,905	$ 7,170	$24,086
Selling and Administrative Expenses:					
Sales Salaries[2]	$ 1,501	$ 1,121	$ 8,703	$ 3,121	$13,101
Marketing Department[3]	539	1,962	5,232	1,127	3,020
Headquarters Staff[4]	190	110	280	120	300
Computer Department[4]	152	88	224	96	240
Nonplant Depreciation[5]	836	484	1,232	528	1,320
Other Indirect Overhead[4]	105	61	154	66	165
Operating Margin	$ 836	$ 726	$ 3,080	$ 2,112	$ 5,940
Interest Expense[6]	167	97	246	106	264
Other Income[7]	50	0	0	0	111
Profit Before Tax	$ 719	$ 629	$ 2,834	$ 2,006	$ 5,787
Gross Margin on Sales (%)	10	19	31	27	36
Operating Margin (%)	2.0	3.0	5.0	8.0	9.0
Profit Before Tax (% Sales)	1.7	2.6	4.6	7.6	8.8

Notes to Divisional Statements of Income

[1]This depreciation refers to that on the actual facilities producing the materials for sale. It is computed on an accelerated basis, and transferred to the divisional income statements from the corporate tax reports.

[2]Sales salaries are only for the salesmen who are actually selling the division's products. A salesman's time is highly utilized and each salesman has about as much volume as he can handle.

[3]Marketing department expenses include all salaries for this department for the related division. In general, this department's time is not fully utilized.

[4]For all costs with this footnote number, costs were allocated based on sales volume. Charges of this type continue, regardless of changes in the sales volume of the individual divisions.

similarly, and to try to keep the time spent on each account proportional to the dollar exposure. Accounts managers were instructed to be courteous to all, but not to make concessions from the stated terms of sales, which had been set at net 30 days for all divisions. These standardized terms were a policy decision and were an outgrowth of the centralization of the firm's receivables management. To assure that none of the accounts managers grew bored with his or her group of customers, assignments within the department were rotated on a regular basis. Mr. Juliett wondered if these policies were optimal, particularly in view of the differences between the divisions in customer characteristics, competitive situation, and profitability (see Exhibit 1 for divisional statements of income for 1977, the year just completed).

The Imported Products Division brought products into the United States from other countries. Sales were by contract to large, very creditworthy firms. Though the division sold a substantial portion of Alloyed's sales volume in terms of dollars, it handled relatively few orders, and consequently had relatively few employees in the sales and marketing areas. Because bargaining power was on the buyer's side, profit margins tended to be slim. Despite the low risk of default, the collection effort of the credit and receivables management department tended to be fairly high for this division. This was because of paperwork problems. The large firms sold by this division did not respond to computer-generated form letters, which were effective collection tools in dealing with some of the smaller firms sold by other divisions. Also, the sales management

of this division tended to make special deals with customers that, because they were not reflected in paperwork, caused some nonpayment of invoices. When this occurred, the division was slow to correct the matter. Consequently, the accounts managers spent a significant amount of time following up unpaid items on a personalized basis and attempting to get the sales management of the division to correct errors so that payments could be collected. The average time to receive payment for an invoice issued by this division was 42 days. Customers of this division almost never requested extended time for payments.

The Paint Supplies Division dealt with paint manufacturers of various sizes. Risk of default for these customers was in the medium range, but payments were often received far beyond terms. Accounts could be collected in a routine fashion with computer assistance. There had been numerous requests in the past for lengthened terms of sale to meet competitive situations, but in keeping with the firm's policy of standard terms, these had been denied. The average time taken to pay an invoice was 60 days.

The Plastic Resin Division represented the highest degree of default risk of any of the divisions. The customers were small job shops with highly variable cash flows, little management expertise, and almost no profitability. Though market power should have been on the seller's side, with few sellers of resin and many buyers, a "huckster" attitude prevailed among the industry sellers, and there were constant requests for extended terms to meet competition. Because of poor financial circumstances, customers of this division were

---

[5]Nonplant depreciation includes tax-statement depreciation on administrative buildings, recreational facilities, and so on. It is allocated to the divisions based on sales volume.

[6]This interest-expense entry is an allocation based on the sales volume of interest expense on corporate debt to support assets. Accounts receivable are a minor part of these assets.

[7]Other income is basically royalties on the patents which divisions have licensed out to other firms.

continuously harangued by creditors, and did not generally respond to computer-assisted collection methods; personal collection effort was necessary. Average time to pay an invoice by the customers of this division was 55 days.

The Consumer Products Division sold items to wholesalers and jobbers. Though customers tended to be highly leveraged, and therefore very risky from a default standpoint, their asset turnover was very high and their cash flows substantial; they tended to pay promptly. Routine follow-up was sufficient to collect any past-due items. Though analysis of the financial condition of these customers was necessary on a regular basis, less than an average amount of time of the accounts receivable managers was taken up with accounts from this division. Because demand for the Consumer Products Division's products at the retail level was high, bargaining power was on Alloyed's side, and there were few requests for concessions in terms of sale. The average time taken to pay an invoice was 35 days.

The Chemical Division had the largest share of company sales. The average time to pay an invoice by the customer of this division was 36 days, and customers were average in terms of default risk. The Chemical Division sold to a moderately large group of medium-sized, well-established firms, and it held a major share of the market. However, because the number of buyers of the division's individual product lines was not large, bargaining power was about equally distributed between buyer and seller. There had been frequent requests for extended terms of sale, all of which had been refused. This had resulted in some lost sales. Most of this division's customer base had dealt with Alloyed for several years, and had developed working relationships with the accounts managers. When there was some payment problem (which occurred in a small minority of cases, as indicated by this division's 36-day payment average) some personal contact by accounts managers was required.

Mr. Juliett had already decided that an additional accounts manager would be added to the staff. He was also considering changing the assignment system of these managers from alphabetical to divisional. In a divisional system, the firm's accounts receivable would be sorted by division, and each manager would handle accounts from only one or at most two divisions. His tentative plan was to have one manager handle each of the Imported Products, Plastic Resins, and Chemical Divisions and have the other manager handle the Paint Supplies and Consumer Products Divisions. He felt that this would enable the department to enforce different terms of sale policies for different divisions without confusion. The question then was which divisions should receive terms of sale other than the firm's regular net 30 terms.

To address this question, Mr. Juliett first eliminated from consideration the Imported Products Division and the Consumer Products Division. He knew that firms incur costs when terms of sale are lengthened; to make changes in terms of sale advantageous, these costs must be offset with sales increases. For both these divisions, Mr. Juliett felt that any increases in sales were likely to be very small, and this made terms changes unattractive.

Mr. Juliett approached the divisional sales managers for the remaining three divisions and asked them to prepare proposals for terms of sale adjustments. These proposals were to include the estimated effects of changes in terms on sales, receivables turnover, and bad debt expense (it was assumed that collection expense would not change). These proposals are summarized in Exhibit 2. He then used the standard single-period analysis technique to evaluate the proposed changes in terms. This analysis was presented at the next meeting of the firm's Policy Committee (a committee of

Exhibit 2

Alloyed Companies
Proposed Changes in Terms of Sale

	Paint Supplies	*Plastic Resin*	*Chemical*
Present Terms	*Net 30 Days*	*Net 30 Days*	*Net 30 Days*
Proposed Terms	*3% 10, N 90*	*Net 45 Days*	*Net 60 Days*
Percent of Customers Taking Discount: Present Terms	0		
Expected Percent of Customers Taking Discount: Proposed Terms	70		
Expected 1978 Gross Sales (Thousands, Present Policy)	$25,410	$64,648	$70,620
Expected 1978 Gross Sales (Thousands, Proposed Policy)	$26,681	$71,148	$75,917
Current Accounts Receivable Turnover (Based on Net Sales)	60 Days	55 Days	36 Days
Expected Accounts Receivable Turnover (Based on Net Sales)	40 Days	70 Days	66 Days
Current Bad Debt Expense (Percent of Gross Sales)	0.5%	0.75%	1%
Expected Bad Debt Expense (Percent of Gross Sales)	0.4%	1.2%	1.5%
Inventory Turnover (Based on Gross Sales)	8.0	9.0	9.0

executives that considered strategic proposals which might affect several departments). His recommendation was that changes in the terms of sale proposed by the Plastic Resin and Chemical Divisions should be accepted, but that the Paint Supplies Division should continue with the current terms. Following the lively discussion (to put it mildly) of this rec-

ommendation, Fred Turner (Manager of Long-Term Planning for the firm) cautioned against a hasty decision on credit policy. He raised the following specific objections to the analysis presented:

1. The analysis showed only the first-year impact of the proposed changes in credit

---

Exhibit 3

Alloyed Companies, Inc.
Fred Turner's Memo to Frank Juliett

Subject: Credit Policy for Plastic Resin Division
To: Frank Juliett
From: Fred Turner

John and I have put together the information requested in our last Policy Committee meeting. The necessary data are summarized in Table 1 of this memo. You will notice that John projects the market for the products produced by the Division to last for ten years.

Table 1

	Present	Proposed
Estimated Gross Sales for 1978	$64,680	$71,148
Growth Rate of Sales	6%	8%
Capital Expansion Cost	$50,000	$60,000
Required Year for Capital Expansion	Seventh	Fourth
Salvage Net of Restoration, Tenth Year	$8,000	$15,000

Notes: The product life is ten years. Recovery on accounts receivable on product termination is expected to be 100 percent of the book value of receivables at that time; recovery on inventory is expected to be 70 percent of book value of these assets at that time. Depreciation will be via the straight-line method from the initial book value to the estimated salvage value. The firm is in the 46 percent tax bracket. The firm's weighted-average, after-tax marginal cost of capital is 12 percent, and the cash flows from the products sold by the Plastic Resin Division are about as risky as the firm's average project.

---

policy, and as such it was difficult to gauge its effect on the value of the firm.

2. The analysis was based on the present idle capacity for manufacturing these products. However, he felt that the new terms of sale would have an impact on the timing and amount of capital investments required for future plant expansion. This would be especially true for the Plastic Resin Division, since the proposed terms were expected to increase first-year sales by about 10 percent.

Fred suggested that the proposed credit policy be evaluated in a net present-value framework. The ensuing discussion indicated that the other members were sympathetic to Fred's concerns. Linda Harper, from the treasurer's staff, indicated special interest in such an analysis since it would indicate future cash flows from the product line, and thus would aid in her financial forecasting tasks. Mr. Juliett agreed to make the analysis, provided he was supplied with future sales figures and plant expansion data. John Lambert, who was responsible for marketing research, and Fred agreed to supply the necessary figures within a week's time (Fred's response is contained in Exhibit 3). Furthermore, because of the time and effort involved, the committee agreed to limit the initial analysis to the Plastic Resin Division.

chapter 6

Credit-Granting Decisions

This chapter concerns the *credit-granting decision*: which of the selling firm's credit applicants will be allowed to purchase goods and services on credit, and which will be required to pay cash. This is a critical decision for the seller. Since credit granting has economic value to buyers, the decision concerning which potential buyers can purchase on credit determines, to a large extent, the base of customers to which sales can be made. The size of the firm's customer base is in turn an important determinant of the firm's sales, cash flows, and value to shareholders.

The outcomes of the firm's credit-granting decisions are sometimes called its *credit standards policy*. The methods used to make these decisions are quite different from those used to make terms of sale decisions. This difference stems from a divergence in the law that governs terms of sale and credit-granting decisions. Under U.S. antitrust statutes, *the selling firm must grant the same terms of sale to all buying firms, if they grant credit to these firms.* This means that some buyers will receive longer terms than are necessary to make the sale. For example, if the seller's terms of sale are net 30 days, it will be able to sell to all buyers who require 30 days *or less* to pay for goods. Buyers that require only 20 days, for example, get an additional 10 days in which to pay that the seller would not have to grant if it could negotiate with each buyer individually.

But in credit-granting decisions, the firm is not constrained to offer the same conditions of sale to all possible buyers so some buyers gain a windfall. *It may instead analyze each potential buyer and grant credit or not based on the attributes of that particular buyer.* Thus, while the seller makes *one* terms of sale decision for *all* the customers purchasing a particular good or service, the firm may elect to make credit-granting decisions *individually* for *each* of the customers purchasing that good or service.[1] While the level of analysis

---

[1] Whether it is optimal for the seller to consider each applicant individually or to group applicants according to common characteristics is a question we will consider later in this chapter.

for the firm's terms of sale policy is *in aggregate across customers*, the level of analysis for credit-granting policy can be *at the level of the individual customer*. Because of the expense involved in changing the firm's terms of sale to *all* customers, terms-of-sale decisions are made *infrequently* (once a year or less).[2] Credit-granting decisions, on the other hand, *occur constantly* as new customers come to the firm, and old customers are reviewed.

It is easy to see that credit-granting decisions are a major task in financial management of the firm. The policies necessary for the proper management of credit granting are extremely important and need to be carefully formulated, as the questions involved in credit granting are complex and their impact is substantial. Among the policy questions that must be addressed are:

☐ How much information should the firm collect on each credit applicant?

☐ What method of analysis should the seller use to determine which applicants should be granted credit?

☐ How many periods should be considered in evaluating the expected cash flows from selling to an applicant?

☐ How should the credit-related parameters of credit applicants be estimated?

We examine these questions in this chapter. The first of these, which concerns the amount of information that should be gathered on each applicant, is called the *credit investigation problem*. Following discussion of this, we present the traditional and net present value methods for determining which applicants should receive credit. The remaining questions, which concern the number of periods to model and the estimation of credit-related parameters regarding applicants, are discussed with reference to this net present value approach.

INFORMATION COSTS AND THE CREDIT-GRANTING DECISION

In a wealth-maximizing approach to the credit-granting decision, the selling firm evaluates the cash flows that would result from granting credit to a credit applicant versus those that would result if credit were not granted to that applicant. As in terms-of-sale analysis, these cash flows result from *the cost and revenue effects of the decision*. These are the changes in sales and collections, the costs of production, bad debt expense, and so forth that are

[2]The costs of changing the firm's terms of sale include the costs of printing new invoices, manuals, and price specifications, as well as the costs of notifying all the firm's customers and salespeople of the new terms.

contingent on the granting or not granting of credit. The analyst must estimate each of these effects in making the decision. Estimates of some of these costs and revenues are easy to obtain, while others are difficult and costly to estimate. Estimates of potential sales to a particular customer are usually obtained from the firm's sales or marketing departments or directly from the customer. Factors such as costs of production and service are obtained from the selling firm's accounting records. However, the remaining costs (such as bad debt expense) must be estimated via the available *sources of credit information* about potential customers. These sources vary in their cost and the type of information they provide. The following paragraphs list and discuss several sources of credit information, proceeding from the least costly to the most costly.

The Seller's Prior Experience with the Customer One of the cheapest and most reliable sources of information about expected future payment patterns is that customer's history of dealings with the seller. If the customer has paid promptly for the last 20 orders, it is very likely that the customer will pay promptly for the twenty-first. To obtain information on the customer's history of payments to the seller, the credit analyst queries the seller's data base of prior customer payments.

Credit Agency Ratings and Reports Several firms are in the business of collecting and selling credit-related information to sellers. Some of these investigation firms report on wide varieties of buyers (such as Dun and Bradstreet) while others report only on buyers in a single industry. Most of these agencies provide several types of service. They issue ratings based on buyers' financial strength and payments to sellers. They provide reports which may include the buyer's financial statements and the results of an investigation into legal records regarding the buyer's business dealings. They collect and distribute *trade clearances*, which are lists of amounts owing, amounts past due, and histories of payments by buyers to their trade creditors.

Personal Contact with the Applicant's Bank and Other Creditors A more expensive (but very reliable) source of information is the applicant's current creditors and its bank. To obtain such information, the analyst may personally contact these sources to discuss their experiences with the applicant. In this way, the analyst can verify the information in credit agency reports and gain other insights that are not available from these reports. Unfortunately, such an investigation is usually quite time consuming.

Analysis of the Applicant's Financial Statements Any credit applicant's ability to pay is in great part dependent on its financial condition. Analysis of this financial condition can thus considerably aid in credit evaluation. Financial statements must first be obtained. This may entail significant effort if the applicant firm is not publicly traded. These statements must then be examined and analyzed. This analysis often begins by making adjustments to these statements to utilize accounting conventions other than those chosen by the applicant's accountants. Such adjustments are made if the analyst believes that the conventions used did not do the best job of portraying the economic health of the firm. Once these adjustments are made, ratio analysis and/or statistical analysis is then applied to these statements to assess the financial health of the applicant.

Customer Visit One very expensive option in the collection of information is for the credit analyst to visit the applicant. An on-site viewing of the applicant's facilities and discussions with the applicant's management can provide insights and information that cannot be obtained in other ways. For example, the credit analyst can obtain impressions on the competence of the applicant's management and on the physical condition of the applicant's plant, service facilities, and equipment.

One important question in the formulation of policies for credit granting asks: Which source of information should be used and how much information should be collected on credit applicants? This is an important consideration in credit management. The proper strategy for the collection of information in any decision situation revolves around the relative *cost of the information* versus the resulting *cost of errors in decisions*. In many other financial decisions, such as the purchase of a new manufacturing facility, the expected effects on the firm's cash flows are fairly large, often on the order of hundreds of thousands of dollars. In such situations, the firm may spend considerable time and money estimating the resulting cash flows, evaluating their likely effects on the firm, and investigating the risks associated with the decision. The money and time spent on the decision is very small relative to the effects of the decision on the firm. However, in many credit-granting decisions, the revenues and costs associated with selling to some individual buyers may be quite small. In such cases, *it may not make sense to spend much management time or cost on the investigation of these buyers*. The cost of information and analysis may outweigh the costs of any errors that might be made.

To see the effects of the cost of information in credit-granting decisions, assume that the seller is making a credit decision with respect to a particular credit applicant firm. The seller has already spent some money on investigation and, given the information already in hand, the expected cost of an error (either granting credit to a firm which will eventually default or not granting credit to a firm which will not default) is $15. The next step in the investigation process, however, costs $20. In this case, it is clear that *the cost of information is greater than the cost of error without the information*. Therefore, the firm should not spend the additional $20; it should forego the collection of this information since the cost of the error is less than the information cost.

To see how the principles of information cost versus error cost apply to the collection of credit information, let us present an extensive and reasonably realistic example problem. It will pay the student to read the statement of this problem several times for comprehension before proceeding.

AN EXAMPLE PROBLEM IN THE COSTS OF CREDIT INVESTIGATION

A firm receives orders in the amounts of $50, $1,000, and $10,000. Out-of-pocket costs of the product are 80 percent of sales, and are paid when the order is shipped. Collection costs are trivial. The seller's risk-adjusted discount rate for credit decisions is 12 percent. For purposes of this example, we will assume that there is no recovery if the applicant defaults, and we will ignore taxes. When an order is received, the firm may investigate via one or more sources of credit information. These sources, in sequence of cost, are:

Source of Information	Cost per Query
Record of past payments	$ 2
Credit agency rating and report	$ 15
Comprehensive analysis (includes personal contact with banks and other creditors, analysis of financial statements, and so forth)	$300

If the firm performs no investigation (and incurs no investigation costs), it must make a credit decision with no information regarding the applicant. For the average applicant, there is a 3 percent chance that the applicant will default (that is, the *expected default rate* is 3 percent); if the applicant pays, the average time taken to pay will be 45 days. (These estimates could be taken from publicly available statistics of default rates and payments.) At this point, the analyst may choose to grant credit, reject the applicant, or investigate further. If the firm chooses to investigate the applicant, it will first query its data base of past payments by customers (since this is the cheapest source of information available). These are four possible outcomes from this query. First, the customer may have paid promptly (net 30 days are the terms of sale). Second, the customer may have paid 30 days beyond terms. Third, the firm may have no prior experience selling to the customer. Finally, the firm may have previously sold to the customer and the customer may have defaulted. The probabilities of these four outcomes in querying the data base of past customer payments are 0.50, 0.29, 0.20, and 0.01. If the applicant has previously purchased from the seller, it is assumed that the applicant will pay as it has in the past.

If the query to the data base shows no past experience, the analyst again faces the choice of granting credit, rejecting the applicant, or investigating further. If the analyst chooses to grant credit, the expected default rate and days to pay are 3 percent and 45 days as before, since the query to the data base provided no new information. If the analyst chooses to investigate, a credit agency report and rating is ordered at a cost of $15. This report may show ratings designated 1, 2, or 3. A rating of 1 indicates that the applicant pays promptly and has no chance of default. A rating of 2 indicates that the applicant has a 15 percent probability of default but is expected to pay in 60 days if payment is received. A rating of 3 indicates that the applicant has a 25 percent probability of default, but is expected to pay in 90 days if payment is received. Overall, 84 percent of firms are rated 1 by the credit agency, 10 percent are rated 2, and 6 percent are rated 3. The ratings of the credit agency for applicants rated 2 or 3 are, however, open to some degree of error and represent only average default rates and payment periods.

At this point, the analyst may grant credit, reject the applicant, or perform an extensive credit analysis. Because applicants rated 1 are granted credit (since they have no chance of default) this procedure is used only for applicants with ratings of 2 or 3. The outcome of this analysis will show the applicant's financial position to be strong or weak relative to the average firm with that credit rating. The probability of each outcome is 50 percent. If the applicant is rated 2 and the analysis shows a relatively strong financial position, the expected default rate is 1 percent and the expected time to pay is 30 days. If the applicant is rated 2 and is financially weak, the default rate is 29 percent and the expected time to pay is 90 days. If the applicant is rated 3 and shows a strong financial position, the expected default rate is 15 percent and the expected days to pay is 60. If the applicant is rated 3 and shows a weak financial position, these statistics are 35 percent and 120 days respectively. All the information on probabilities, expected default rates, and days to pay if default does not occur are summarized in Table 6-1.

This credit investigation problem involves *discrete probabilities and events.* When a problem in finance involves discrete, sequential events and decisions, one method of analysis is the *decision-tree approach.*[3] The decision tree for the example credit investigation problem for an order size of $10,000 is presented in Figure 6-1. This tree is quite complex, but we will review it on an item-by-item basis. In this tree, later time is to the right and earlier time to the left. In a decision tree, a *square* represents a *decision node* and a *circle* represents a *chance-event node.* All the nodes in this decision tree have been numbered, and we will be referring to them by these numbers. Most of the

---

[3]This approach to the credit investigation problem is found in D. Mehta, "The Formulation of Credit Policy Models," *Management Science*, Vol. 15, No. 1 (October 1968), pp. B30–B50. Problems of this sort can also be solved via integer programming; see J. D. Stowe, "An Integer Programming Solution for the Optimal Investigation/Credit Granting Sequence," *Financial Management* (Summer 1985), pp. 66–76.

Table 6-1. Summary of Outcomes in Example Problem in Credit Investigation—4 Stages.

Stage 1: No Investigation

Expected default rate: 3%
Expected time to pay: 45 days
Probability: 1.00

Stage 2: Check of History of Applicant's Payment to Firm

Outcome:	Prompt in Past	Slow in Past	No Data	Default in Past
Expected default rate:	0%	0%	3%	100%
Expected time to pay:	30 days	60 days	45 days	—
Probability:	.50	.29	.20	.01

Stage 3: Credit Agency Report and Rating

Credit Rating:	1	2	3
Expected default rate:	0%	15%	25%
Expected time to pay:	30 days	60 days	90 days
Probability:	.84	.10	.06

Stage 4: Comprehensive Credit Investigation

Credit Rating:	2	2	3	3
Financial Position:	Strong	Weak	Strong	Weak
Expected default rate:	1%	29%	15%	35%
Expected time to pay:	30 days	90 days	60 days	120 days
Probability:	.50	.50	.50	.50

branches of this decision tree are labeled with the capital letters "A," "R," "I," "P," "D," "S," or "W." An "A" indicates that the applicant is *accepted* (granted credit), an "R" indicates that the applicant is *rejected* for credit, an "I" indicates that further *investigation* is undertaken, a "D" indicates that the applicant has *defaulted*, a "P" indicates that the applicant has *paid*, an "S" indicates that the credit applicant's financial position is relatively *strong*, and a "W" indicates that this position is relatively *weak*. The decimal numbers near branches after a chance-event node represent the probabilities of events occurring at that node. At decision nodes, the firm chooses one of the possible paths leading from that node. Dollar amounts beneath "I" symbols indicate that investigation costs have been incurred; dollar amounts at the ends of branches indicate the net present value for that outcome. The cash flows and

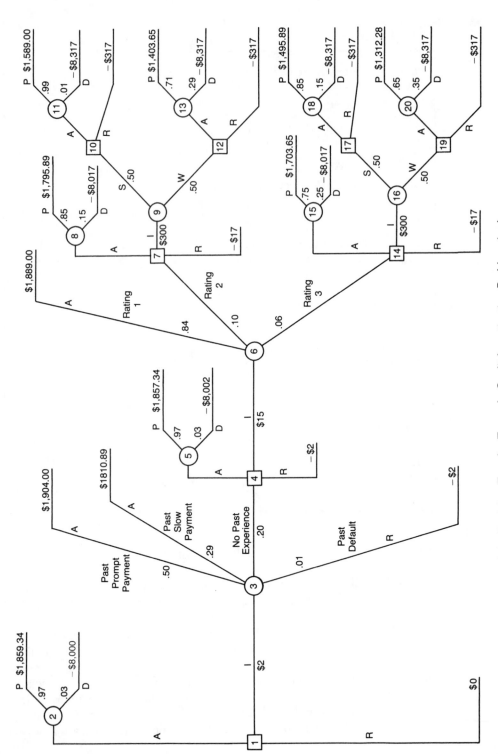

Figure 6-1. Decision Tree for Example Credit Investigation Problem (order = $10,000).

net present values for each possible outcome are presented in Table 6-2.[4] For example, for outcome 5P (the "applicant pays" outcome from node 5), the net present value of the cash flows is calculated as $-\$8,000 - \$2 + (10,000)(1.12^{-45/360})$, which equals the $\$1,857.34$ shown.

We now review how this tree represents the events of the example problem. We start with the firm's *initial decision* at node 1: it may grant credit without investigation, investigate, or reject the applicant. If the analyst grants credit at this stage, the expected default rate is 0.03 and the expected time to pay is 45 days for all applicants. If credit is granted here, the process moves to node 2, the chance event which represents the uncertain process of payment or default for the applicant given the information available. Before granting credit, the selling firm must pay $\$8,000$ for the goods to service the order. This payment occurs regardless of whether the applicant pays for the order or not. If the applicant pays, the firm receives $\$10,000$ in 45 days, and the net present value is $\$1,859.34$. If the applicant does not pay, the net present value is $-\$8,000$. The expected value of granting credit, given that no investigation has been undertaken, is $\$1,563.56$, equal to $(0.97)(1,859.34) + (0.03)(-\$8,000)$. At node 1, if the firm rejects the credit applicant without having spent any funds on investigation, a net present value of zero results. The third alternative is to investigate further, the net present value of which is unknown at this stage of the analysis.

The collection of more data, even though this data collection is costly, *may result in strategies with higher expected net present values* than the $\$1,563.56$ obtained from granting credit with no investigation. The possibility of further investigation therefore must be evaluated. If the firm spends $\$2$ to check its prior experience with the applicant (moding to node 3), it can gain some important information regarding a majority of the applicants. Specifically, *it will be able to better evaluate the net present values from selling to 80 percent of applicants*: those that paid promptly, those that paid slowly (but eventually paid), and those that defaulted. Since the net present values are positive for the "prompt payment" and "slow payment" groups, they would be granted credit at this point, while credit to the "default" group should not be granted.

If the firm has no past experience with the applicant (which occurs 20 percent of the time in this problem), it must decide whether to grant credit, reject the applicant, or investigate further via the credit agency rating and report. If it grants credit, the expected net present value is $\$1,561.56$ at node 5 $(0.03)(-8,002) + (0.97)(1,857.34)$. If the applicant is rejected, the net present value is $-\$2$, representing the costs of credit investigation spent to this point. If the seller seeks more information, $\$15$ is spent for the credit report, the firm moves to node 6. The result will be a rating of 1, 2, or 3 for

[4]The information in Table 6-2 and in Tables 6-3, 6-4, and 6-5 (to be presented later) can be generated via a spreadsheet. However, because the main analytic thrust here is the decision tree, and because the spreadsheets involved are very simple, we suppress discussion of spreadsheet aspects in this analysis.

Table 6-2. Net Present Values for Decision-Tree Credit Investigation Problem (order = $10,000).

Outcome	Costs of Product ($)	Stage 2 Invest. Costs ($)	Stage 3 Invest. Costs ($)	Stage 4 Invest. Costs ($)	Inflow from Payment ($)	Days to Pay	Net Present Value ($)
1 R							0.00
2 P	8,000				10,000	45	1,859.34
2 D	8,000						-8,000.00
3 Prompt	8,000	2			10,000	30	1,904.00
3 Slow	8,000	2			10,000	60	1,810.89
3 Default		2					-2.00
4 R		2					-2.00
5 P	8,000	2			10,000	45	1,857.34
5 D	8,000	2					-8,002.00
6 Rtg. 1	8,000	2	15		10,000	30	1,889.00
7 R		2	15				-17.00
8 P	8,000	2	15		10,000	60	1,795.89
8 D	8,000	2	15				-8,017.00
10 R		2	15	300			-317.00
11 P	8,000	2	15	300	10,000	30	1,589.00
11 D	8,000	2	15	300			-8,317.00
12 R		2	15	300			-317.00
13 P	8,000	2	15	300	10,000	90	1,403.65
13 D	8,000	2	15	300			-8,317.00
14 R		2	15	300			-17.00
15 P	8,000	2	15	300	10,000	90	1,703.65
15 D	8,000	2	15	300			-8,017.00
17 R		2	15	300			-317.00
18 P	8,000	2	15	300	10,000	60	1,495.89
18 D	8,000	2	15	300			-8,317.00
19 R		2	15	300			-317.00
20 P	8,000	2	15	300	10,000	120	1,312.28
20 D	8,000	2	15	300			-8,317.00

the applicant. If the applicant is rated 1, the net present value of granting credit is $1,889.00 for certain, since applicants with this rating have a zero probability of default, and credit should be granted.

If the applicant is rated 2 or 3, the analyst again may elect to grant credit, reject the applicant, or investigate further. These decisions occur at nodes 7 and 14 respectively. At node 7, if the applicant is granted credit without further investigation, the default rate is 0.15 and the expected days to pay is 60 (node 8). The decision to grant credit will result in an expected net present value of $323.96 $((0.85)(1,795.89) + (0.15)(-8,017))$. If the firm elects not to grant credit at node 7, the net present value is $-$17$, since investigation costs in this amount have been spent. If the firm elects to in- vestigate further, it must spend $300 (node 9) to find out whether the firm is relatively strong (node 10) or relatively weak (node 12). At nodes 10 and 12, the firm must decide whether to grant credit (nodes 11 and 13) or to reject the applicant (these are the only two alternatives, since no further investi- gation is possible). The firm is faced with parallel decisions and chance events if the credit rating of the applicant is 3; this process starts at node 14.

With this model of the credit investigation process in hand, we can use *inductive reasoning* to develop a set of strategies regarding credit investigation and credit granting. In this inductive process, we start at the furthest point in time and work backward, calculating expected values and making choices along the way, *given the circumstances implied by our location on the decision tree.* Each point on the decision tree implies a set of circumstances. For example, at node 10 the circumstances are: "A decision on credit granting has not yet been made. The seller has no past experience with the applicant, the applicant's credit rating is 2, and the applicant has a strong financial position relative to those with this rating. The seller may reject the applicant (with a net present value of $-$317$) or may accept the applicant. If the applicant is accepted, a net present value of $1,589.00 will result with a probability of 0.99 and a net present value of $-$8,317$ will result with a probability of 0.01."

The use of inductive reasoning to assess strategies is called *rolling back the decision tree.* Two rules are used in this process:

1. At any chance-event node, calculate the value of the node by taking the expected value of all the future decisions and events leading forward in time from this node.

2. At any decision node, assume that the firm will choose the branch that results in the highest expected value. This highest expected value is then the value of that node.

The roll-back inductive reasoning procedure as applied to the decision tree in Figure 6-1 is presented in Figure 6-2. The supporting calculations of the expected net present values for chance event nodes are presented in Table

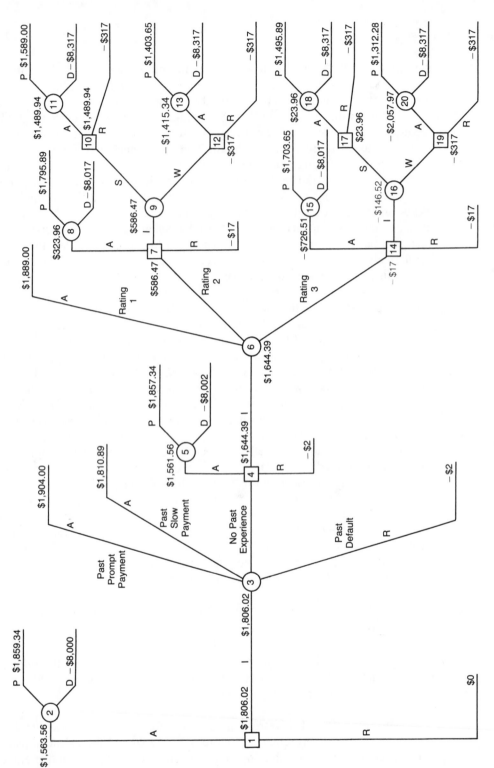

Figure 6-2. Roll-Back of Decision Tree for Example Problem (order = $10,000).

Table 6-3. Computation of Expected Net Present Values for Roll-Back of Decision Tree (order = $10,000).

Node	NPV 1	Prob. 1	NPV 2	Prob. 2	NPV 3	Prob. 3	NPV 4	Prob. 4	E(NPV)
11	1,589.00	.99	−8,317	.01					1,489.94
13	1,403.65	.71	−8,317	.29					−1,415.34
18	1,495.89	.85	−8,317	.15					23.96
20	1,312.28	.65	−8,317	.35					−2,057.97
9	1,489.94	.50	−317	.50					586.47
16	23.96	.50	−317	.50					−146.52
8	1,795.89	.85	−8,017	.15					323.96
15	1,703.65	.75	−8,017	.25					−726.51
6	1,889.00	.84	586.47	.10	−17	.06			1,644.39
5	1,857.34	.97	−8,002	.03					1,561.56
3	1,904.00	.50	1,810.89	.29	1,644.39	.20	−2	.01	1,806.02
2	1,859.34	.97	−8,000	.03					1,563.56

6-3. In the interests of simplicity, the costs of investigation and the probabilities of the uncertain events are not shown on Figure 6-2. The dollar figures proximate to the nodes are the optimum expected net present values at these nodes after the application of the two rules given above. To see the strategies implied by the roll-back procedure, let us review its application to see how the various node values were developed.

We start at the furthest point in time, which is the right of the decision tree. Moving left, the first nodes encountered are nodes 11, 13, 18, and 20. These are the chance events associated with granting credit to strong and weak applicants with ratings 2 and 3. Using the first of the prior rules, the statistics summarizing the worth of these nodes are their expected net present values. At nodes 10, 12, 17, and 19, the firm must choose between these expected values of granting credit and the net present value of rejecting the applicant (which is −$317 in each case). If the applicant has a rating of 2 and is financially strong, or has a rating of 3 and is financially strong, the expected net present value of granting credit is greater than the expected value of refusing credit, and the applicant should be granted credit. The net present values of $1,489.94 at node 10 and $23.96 at node 17 are then the expected net present values of accepting the credit applicant. If, however, the credit applicant is relatively weak, the alternative of rejecting the applicant produces the highest expected net present value, and is the proper choice at nodes 12 and 19 by the second rule. The values at these nodes are the −$317.

If the applicant is rated 2 and the selling firm investigates further, there is a 50 percent chance that the applicant will be weak and a 50 percent chance that the applicant will be strong. At node 9, *given the optimal future decision to reject the applicant if a weak position is found*, there is a 50 percent chance of an expected net present value of $1,489.94 and a 50 percent chance of an expected net present value of −$317.00. The expected net present value at this node is $586.47; by similar logic, it is −$146.52 at node 16.

At node 7, the selling firm has a choice of three expected net present values: $323.96 (from granting credit without further investigation), $586.47 (from investigating further), and −$17 (from rejecting the applicant). The highest net present value results from investigating further. The spending of $300 in additional investigation expenses enables the firm to economically assess the financial strength of applicants with a rating of 2, after which it will reject the applicants with relatively weak financial positions and grant credit to stronger applicants.

The decision faced by the firm at node 14, where the applicant firm has a rating of 3, is quite different. Here, the highest net present value (of −$17) is achieved by *rejecting all applicants with this rating*. The number of applicants with relatively strong financial positions and the expected value of granting credit to these applicants is sufficiently small that *it makes more sense to reject all applicants with this rating and save the $300 in investigation expenses*. Note that by this strategy the selling firm will reject the 50 percent of the applicants *that in fact have positive expected net present values* of $23.96. However, since it costs the firm $300 to find out which half of the applicants possess this quality, *it is better to reject them all.*

The remainder of the roll-back procedure is straightforward. The expected value at node 6 is $1,644.39. At node 4, the firm faces the choice of investigating further (with an expected net present value of $1,644.39), granting credit to all firms with whom the firm has had no prior credit experience (node 5, with an expected net present value of $1,561.56), or rejecting such applicants (with an expected net present value of −$2). Investigating by checking the firm's credit rating and credit report is the optimum choice. At node 3, the four possible outcomes give the firm an expected net present value of $1,806.02, which is the optimum choice at node 1.

It is useful at this point to summarize the credit investigation rules that we have developed for the example problem and an order size of $10,000. These rules are:

1. When an order of size $10,000 is received, always check the past experience in selling the firm. If the firm has paid promptly or slowly, grant credit without further investigation. If the firm has defaulted, reject credit without further investigation.

2. If the seller has no past experience with the firm, always obtain a credit rating and report. If the applicant's rating is 1, grant credit without further investigation. If it is 3, reject credit without further investigation.

3. If the applicant's rating is 2, investigate further via a comprehensive credit analysis. If the applicant's financial position is strong relative to other firms with ratings of 2, grant credit. If this position is weak, refuse credit.

These rules balance the costs of information and the expected returns from credit granting for orders of $10,000. Using this strategy, the expected net present value of evaluating applicants for a purchase of $10,000 is $1,806.02. However, *for smaller orders, different rules may be optimal* because the costs of investigation bear more heavily on the value of credit granting. Table 6-4 presents the net present values for the various outcomes of the example decision tree problem for an order size of $1,000, Figure 6-3 presents the roll-back of the decision tree for orders of this size, and Table 6-5 presents the expected net present value calculations for this tree. For an order size of $1,000, the optimal credit investigation strategy is:

1. When an order of size $1,000 is received, always check the past experience in selling to the firm. If the firm has paid promptly or slowly, or if the applicant has no previous experience with the selling firm, grant credit without further investigation. If the firm has de-faulted, reject credit without further investigation.
2. For orders of size $1,000, never obtain a credit agency report and rating for any applicant.

The expected value of this strategy is $177.64 for order sizes of $1,000. Because of the costs of investigation, for orders of this size the selling firm will grant credit to firms with credit ratings of 3 and also to firms with ratings of 2 whose financial positions are relatively weak. *These two groups would be rejected if this information were known*. However, given the proportion of such firms in the population of firms with whom the seller has no previous credit experience, and given the expected costs of investigation, *it is more economical to grant credit to these firms than to find out who they are*. The student may verify that for orders of $50 the optimum policy is to grant credit to all applicants without checking on the seller's prior experience with them. The expected value of this strategy is $7.82 per order.[5]

Some Lessons from the Decision-Tree Credit-Investigation System The decision-tree approach balances the costs of investigation of credit applicants with the costs of error in granting credit to them. Costly errors may occur in

[5]Both Mehta, "The Formulation of Credit Policy Models," and Stowe, "An Integer Programming Solution," provide general procedures for the formulation of credit investigation policies for orders of any size, not just for the discrete sizes used in this example.

Table 6-4. Net Present Values for Decision-Tree Credit Investigation Problem (order = $1,000).

Outcome	Costs of Product ($)	Stage 2 Invest. Costs ($)	Stage 3 Invest. Costs ($)	Stage 4 Invest. Costs ($)	Inflow from Payment ($)	Days to Pay	Net Present Value ($)
1 R							0.00
2 P	800				1000	45	185.93
2 D	800						−800.00
3 Prompt	800	2			1000	30	188.60
3 Slow	800	2			1000	60	179.29
3 Default		2					−2.00
4 R		2					−2.00
5 P	800	2			1000	45	183.93
5 D	800	2					−802.00
6 Rtg. 1	800	2	15		1000	30	173.60
7 R		2	15				−17.00
8 P	800	2	15		1000	60	164.29
8 D	800	2	15				−817.00
10 R		2	15	300			−317.00
11 P	800	2	15	300	1000	30	−126.40
11 D	800	2	15	300			−1,117.00
12 R		2	15	300			−317.00
13 P	800	2	15	300	1000	90	−144.93
13 D	800	2	15	300			−1,117.00
14 R		2	15	300			−17.00
15 P	800	2	15	300	1000	90	155.07
15 D	800	2	15	300			−817.00
17 R		2	15	300			−317.00
18 P	800	2	15	300	1000	60	−135.71
18 D	800	2	15	300			−1,117.00
19 R		2	15	300			−317.00
20 P	800	2	15	300	1000	120	−154.07
20 D	800	2	15	300			−1,117.00

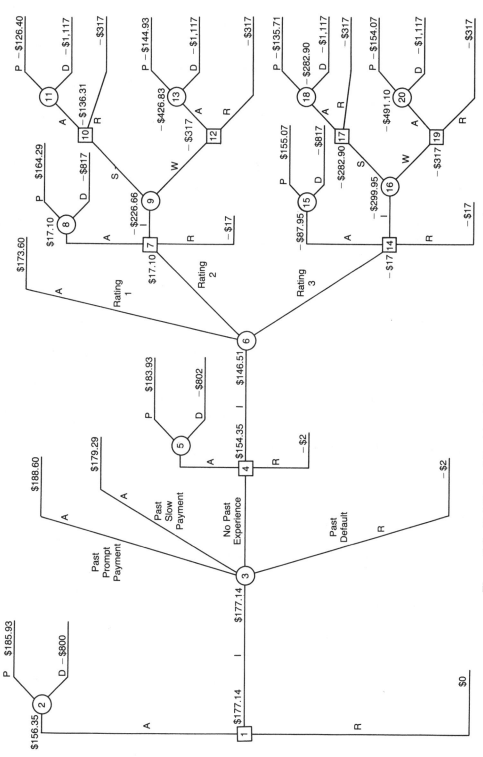

Figure 6-3. Roll-Back of Decision Tree for Example Problem (order = $1,000).

Table 6-5. *Computation of Expected Net Present Values for Roll-Back of Decision Tree (order = $1,000).*

Node	NPV 1	Prob. 1	NPV 2	Prob. 2	NPV 3	Prob. 3	NPV 4	Prob. 4	E(NPV)
11	− 126.40	.99	− 1117	.01					− 136.31
13	− 144.93	.71	− 1117	.29					− 426.83
18	− 135.71	.85	− 1117	.15					− 282.90
20	− 154.07	.65	− 1117	.35					− 491.10
9	− 136.31	.50	− 317	.50					− 226.66
16	− 282.90	.50	− 317	.50					− 299.95
8	164.29	.85	− 817	.15					17.10
15	155.07	.75	− 817	.25					− 87.95
6	173.60	.84	17.10	.10	− 17	.06			146.51
5	183.93	.97	− 802	.03					154.35
3	188.60	.50	179.29	.29	154.35	.20	− 2	.01	177.14
2	185.93	.97	− 800	.03					156.35

(1) granting credit to negative-NPV applicants, and (2) not granting credit to positive-NPV applicants. Besides providing a general method for formulating strategy for credit investigation procedures, there are some lessons to be learned from the logic of this procedure that are not generally obvious.

First, as long as credit investigation is costly, there will be some firms granted credit who will default. This is in large part due to the cost of obtaining the information necessary to separate these firms from other firms whose probability of default is lower. The goal of having a minimum bad debt expense (which is occasionally voiced by some managers) thus entails excessive credit expenses, and is not an optimal policy.[6]

Second, as long as credit investigation is costly, the amount of time and money spent on the investigation of individual applicants will vary with the size of the order. For smaller orders, less time and money will be spent, and rather crude but cheap methods (such as credit ratings) will be the economical approach to investigation. Because these methods entail significant errors in the classification of firms (since firms within ratings classes are not homogeneous), applicants will be refused credit who would receive credit if more was spent on investigation. The opportunity cost of these lost profits is a result of the costliness of credit investigation.

Finally, if this approach to optimal credit investigation is adopted by the seller, it prescribes simple and low-cost strategies for the handling of routine orders. We have taken care to make the example problem repre-

---

[6]Also, such a goal would require that the firm refuse credit to many firms with a very low probability of default (and thus a positive expected net present value) because of the small chance that they might default.

sentative of typical industrial situations, and it illustrates strategies of these sorts. Orders of $50 are serviced without any investigation, and orders of $1,000 require only a query to the selling firm's data base of past experience with customers. For orders of $10,000, routine transactions with existing customers (80 percent of the total number of such orders) are also handled after the data base query. Of the remaining 20 percent, all those orders from very healthy firms (rated 1) and very unhealthy firms (rated 3) are approved or rejected via a check of the applicant's credit rating (from a credit agency report). The only firms that require extensive and comprehensive investigation are those where the *order amounts are large and the applicant's financial health is neither excellent nor awful*. Because credit-granting decisions for *all other orders* are handled in a quick and low-cost fashion, the credit analyst is free to devote time and effort to this important class of credit applicants. For these applicants, the amount of the order is sufficiently large and the applicant's financial situation sufficiently uncertain to justify spending a substantial amount of time, money, and effort in the analysis of the applicant. In credit parlance, such applicants are called *marginal accounts*.

The analysis of marginal accounts requires a *different approach* than that used for other customers. Rules for the acceptance or rejection of these *other* customers come from the decision tree of credit investigation. The probabilities and days-to-pay statistics that appear on the decision tree are *aggregate probabilities* for *classes* of applicants. These statistics can be developed from survey evidence. For example, by examining a history of applicants and defaults, the firm might find that 100 of the 2,000 applicants with a particular credit rating have defaulted. For any new applicant with that rating, it may then estimate the probability of default at 5 percent (100/2,000).

However, for marginal accounts, the size of the order is large enough that the selling firm should not use inexpensive but inherently inaccurate estimation methodologies to evaluate the value of granting credit. Instead, the seller should *examine the credit-related attributes of the individual applicant* rather than rely on proxies for these attributes (such as credit rating). The intent is to directly estimate the value of granting credit *to that particular applicant*, with all the eccentricities of that applicant incorporated in the investigation. Discussion of procedures for the evaluation of such marginal accounts constitutes the balance of this chapter.

CREDIT GRANTING TO MARGINAL ACCOUNTS: TRADITIONAL APPROACH

In the traditional approach to the credit-granting decision on marginal accounts, the credit analyst tries to assess the *creditworthiness* of the applicant. Creditworthiness is a concept related to the positive and negative aspects of granting credit to the applicant. These aspects include the business history of the applicant, the manner in which the applicant makes payments to other trade suppliers, the profitability of the products that the applicant wants to purchase, the applicant's financial position, and so forth. Much of this information is gathered via the sources of credit information previously discussed. In the traditional approach to the credit-granting decision, it is the credit analyst's job to *synthesize all information that has been collected and reach a judgment* regarding the applicant's creditworthiness.

To perform this synthesis, it is useful to have some mechanism for organizing the information that has been collected. One traditional way of organizing this information is by characterizing the applicant along five dimensions. These dimensions are called the *Five Cs of Credit*—capital, character, collateral, capacity, and conditions. These are discussed in the following paragraphs.

Capital The evaluation of the applicant's capital refers to an analysis of the applicant firm's *financial position*. What are the applicant firm's financial strengths? What are its weaknesses? Overall, is it stronger or weaker than other firms that the seller believes are creditworthy?

To assess the capital dimension, the credit analyst considers the data obtained from the applicant's financial statements. The usual procedure is to perform an extensive ratio analysis, comparing the applicant's financial ratios to ratios for the applicant's industry and performing trend analysis of the applicant's ratios over time. This ratio analysis can be quite sophisticated, using graphical presentations of ratio trends and statistical comparison of the applicant's ratios with industry standards.[7] Spreadsheet analysis can aid in this ratio analysis process. Indeed, the ratio analysis of firms is a typical introductory exercise in spreadsheet application and is found in most textbooks on the financial applications of spreadsheets.[8]

The assessment of the financial position of an applicant from a morass of ratio data is not an easy task. To aid in this process, some credit analysts choose to emphasize a few of the financial aspects of the applicant and deemphasize others. Frequently, analysts will focus on the applicant firm's *aggregate liquidity position* and its *total debt position*. The first is measured by ratios such as the current ratio and the quick ratio, while the latter is measured by the total debt to total equity and total debt to total assets ratios. Analysts emphasize these ratios because the seller wishes to know the likelihood of payment from the applicant, how long it will take to receive the payment, and what is likely to happen if the applicant defaults. Ratios that measure

---

[7]For statistical procedures in the comparison of ratios with industry standards, see F. Scherr, "Ratio Analysis for Credit Decisions on Marginal Accounts: A Statistical Approach," *Akron Business and Economic Review*, Vol. 11, No. 3 (Fall 1980), pp. 12–16.

[8]See, for example, N. Cohen and L. Graff, *Financial Analysis with Lotus® 1-2-3®* (Bowie, Md.: Brady Communications, 1984), Chapter 5.

aggregate liquidity assess the relative amounts of current assets and current debt, and thus the funds received and disbursed as part of the applicant's working capital cycle. As discussed in Chapter 1, problems within the working capital cycle are a major cause of default. Measures of aggregate liquidity are thus related to the applicant's ability to pay.

Total debt position tells the relationship between the applicant's assets, equity, and debt. Debt position is also related to the possibility of default, since more debt means a greater probability of default. However, in conjunction with the analysis of collateral (to be discussed later), ratios measuring debt position tell something about the likely recovery of trade creditors if the applicant defaults and is forced to liquidate. The more debt and the fewer assets, the lower will be the recoveries of individual creditors in such liquidations.

Character In order to make payments to trade suppliers, the applicant must have both the *funds to pay the debts* and the *willingness to pay the debts*. The capital dimension involves the former, while the character dimension involves the latter. In assessing character, the credit analyst considers all the information that relates to willingness to pay by the applicant's management. What is the applicant's history of payments to the trade? Has the firm defaulted to other trade suppliers? Does the applicant's management make a good-faith effort to honor debts as they come due? Information in these areas bears on the analyst's assessment of the applicant's character.

Collateral If the applicant experiences financial difficulty, it may be forced to liquidate. In such a situation, the recoveries to trade creditors will depend on (1) the recoveries on assets sold, (2) the amount of debt owed by the firm, and (3) the extent to which these debts are secured. If the firm liquidates, the recoveries on assets that are security for debt will go to the holders of that secured debt. That is, the secured creditors get paid first from the revenues of selling the assets that have been granted to them as security. Since, in general, it is very difficult for trade creditors to obtain secured positions, this means that the recoveries to trade creditors are significantly lower when the applicant has financed by using secured borrowings.[9] Information on secured borrowings is gleaned from the applicant's financial statements, from the applicant's bank, from credit reports on the applicant, or directly from conversations with the applicant. More existing secured financing means lower creditworthiness from the trade creditor's standpoint.

Capacity This dimension has two aspects: *management's capacity to run the business* and the applicant firm's *plant capacity*. Management's capacity

---

[9]For more discussion on the recoveries to creditors in bankruptcy, see the "Bankruptcy and Reorganization" chapter in any good corporate finance text.

to run the business relates to the competency (ability) of the management personnel in the applicant's operations. Any information relevant to this capacity is assessed, including personal impressions, the history of success or failure by the managers running the applicant business, the number of years that the applicant has been in business, and so forth. The better is management's capacity to run the firm, the lower is the chance of default.

Physical capacity refers to the value and technology of the applicant's production or service facilities. Accounting conventions can paint an unrealistic picture of the value of such assets, particularly if the technology of the applicant's industry is subject to rapid change. The more up-to-date and well-maintained are the applicant's facilities, the more likely that the applicant will be able to stay in business and to take advantage of business upturns.

Conditions These are the economic conditions in the applicant's industry and in the economy in general. If there is a good deal of foreign and domestic competition in the applicant's industry, the possibility of failure and default to trade creditors is larger, since profit margins are likely to be lower. If the economy in general is undergoing a contraction, failures are more likely to occur than during an expansionary period.

Once the credit analyst has gathered information on these dimensions of the marginal credit applicant and information on the profitability of the product to be purchased, the traditional approach requires that all this information be *analyzed* and *synthesized*. By this process, the analyst is to make an *informed judgment* on the overall creditworthiness of the applicant. Unfortunately, there are some problems endemic to this traditional analysis methodology which call its usefulness into substantial question. These problems are discussed in the next section.

PROBLEMS WITH THE TRADITIONAL APPROACH

The traditional judgmental approach to credit-granting decisions on marginal accounts is very flexible. In the process of synthesis, the analyst can take into account any and all of the special features that may affect the desirability of the applicant as a customer. Set against this flexibility are several substantial disadvantages inherent in this decision methodology.

No Analytic Framework Most financial decision methods start with a basic analysis technique, such as net present value. It is then up to the financial analyst to make the necessary estimations to execute the technique. However, there is no such analytic framework in the traditional credit analysis methodology. The analyst is asked to make a *judgment*, with few guidelines on what the appropriate criteria for that judgment should be. Given the large amount of information encompassed in the five Cs and the lack of specific evaluation criteria, this judgment is not easy to make. Consequently, the traditional analysis method is very difficult to execute effectively.

No Link to Shareholder Wealth Maximization In most financial decision methods, the analyst starts with a technique that is theoretically and empirically linked to shareholder wealth maximization. For example, it is known that shareholders value cash flows, so techniques such as net present value concentrate on the evaluation of these flows. The traditional credit-granting decision technique does not contain such an explicit link to the creation of shareholder wealth, so there is no necessity that decisions based on this technique will be consistent with that goal.

No Consistency of Analysis Because the synthesis process is almost totally judgmental, the results it produces can be inconsistent. The same analyst considering the same applicant on different days can reach different decisions, as can two different analysts considering the same applicant. This inconsistency gives the impression to those outside of the credit department that decisions are being made in an arbitrary fashion. This seeming arbitrariness can cause friction between the credit and other departments of the firm.

Difficult for the Inexperienced Analyst to Execute Over time, a credit analyst, through trial and error, will become experienced at assessing the strengths and weaknesses of applicants, but any judgments will be biased by the analyst's experience. For example, if the analyst grants credit to several applicants who are below-average with respect to a particular ratio and these applicants then default, the analyst will tend to be biased against applicants with such ratios in the future even if the default of these applicants was an aberration, and the particular ratio involved was not truly related to the default. The longer an analyst continues with the traditional method, the larger will be the sample of applicants analyzed, and the less will be the likelihood of such bias.

However, the generation of experience through years of wrong decisions is costly to the selling firm. Inexperienced analysts will have great difficulty with the synthesis process and will make numerous costly errors. Credit will be granted to applicants that are not of advantage to the firm, and it will not be granted to many firms that would be advantageous customers.

In an attempt to overcome some of these substantial problems with the traditional analysis method, firms and authors have developed *judgmental scoring systems* for the evaluation of marginal credit applicants. There are two basic versions of these systems. In *checklist systems*, a series of questions is asked about the applicant, such as: "Is the applicant's current ratio above 2.0?" and "Is the applicant's total debt to total assets ratio below 0.5?" If the applicant gets positive responses on a predetermined portion of the questions, the applicant is granted credit. In checklist systems, all the questions receive the same weight in decision making. In *weighted scoring systems*, however, the weights can vary from question to question, reflecting the importance of a particular dimension in the evaluation of the applicant.[10] Such weighted evaluation methods often use *point scores* to assess the overall creditworthiness of the applicant. For example, an applicant may receive no points if the current ratio is below 1.5, 2 points if it is between 1.5 and 2.0, 3 points if it is between 2.0 and 2.5, and 4 points if it is above 2.5. The sum of the points scored on various measures of creditworthiness is then compared to some preset number of points when making the credit-granting decision.

Judgmental scoring systems are developed by consultation among experienced credit analysts. These are *expert systems* in that they simulate the decisions an expert (the experienced credit manager) would make when considering the applicant.[11] They have advantages over the traditional judgmental approach in that they provide an analytic framework for analysis, they produce consistent results, and they can be used by a novice credit analyst to make decisions.

Despite their advantages over the traditional judgmental approach, judgmental scoring systems still have one substantial problem. Like the traditional approach, judgmental scoring systems *are not developed from the benchmark of shareholder wealth maximization*. Since they are not developed from this benchmark, *there is little certainty that the decision systems they use will produce a wealth-maximizing result*. A more useful system, from the standpoint of shareholders, would *start with the idea of maximizing shareholder wealth*, and develop decision rules based on this precept. Such a system for the evaluation of marginal credit applicants is developed in the remainder of this chapter.

A ONE-PERIOD NET PRESENT-VALUE MODEL WITH NONZERO RECOVERIES

Since net present value is based on shareholder wealth maximization, the net present-value evaluation method is a logical approach to the credit-granting decision problem. This was the approach taken in the prior discussion

---

[10]When we talk about judgmental scoring systems here, we are referring to systems based on the opinions of credit analysts (their judgments) rather than to systems based on the statistical analysis of defaulted and nondefaulted firms. See, for example, the systems described in "Credit Limits Established by Formula and Computer," Occasional Paper, Credit Research Foundation, and J. E. Kristy, *Analyzing Financial Statements: Quick and Clean* (Buena Park, Cal.: Books on Business).

[11]For an interesting attempt to replicate the decisions of experienced credit managers via statistical analysis, see V. Srinivasan and Y. Kim, "Credit Granting: A Comparative Analysis of Classification Procedures," *Journal of Finance* (July 1987), pp. 665–83.

of the credit investigation decision. In the balance of this chapter, we apply analysis based on net present value to the credit-granting decision.[12]

In the prior analysis of the credit investigation decision, it was assumed that if the applicant was granted credit, either payment was made in the expected number of days (outcomes designated P in prior decision trees) or the applicant defaulted and the seller recovered nothing. It was assumed that only the cash flows from the current order (the $50, $1,000 and $10,000 order amounts) were relevant to the analysis of the credit applicant. Also, the effects of taxes on decisions were ignored. Since we are now centering on the analysis of credit granting to large customers, we can afford to build models of the cash flows from credit granting that are a bit more sophisticated than those based on these assumptions but require more information and cost to execute. In particular, it is useful to consider situations in which: (1) the recoveries if the applicant defaults are nonzero; (2) there may be other future cash flows that are dependent on the firm's credit-granting decision; and (3) taxes play an important part in the analysis. A model for the first of these is developed in this section. The other two situations are considered in future sections.

To develop a model of the cash flows from credit granting that incorporates recoveries in default, it is first necessary to understand the potential events within the default process. When an applicant defaults on a debt to a trade creditor, it is sometimes because the applicant has adopted the policy of default to that particular creditor. That is, the applicant may be able to pay but may be unwilling to do so. The applicant will then usually pay after the creditor sues. However, in many cases, the applicant may be willing to pay but simply does not have the funds to pay. Several courses of action are available to the applicant firm in this situation. The firm may try to reach an accommodation with creditors, may seek the protection of the courts by filing for bankruptcy, or may liquidate immediately. In the case where the applicant files for bankruptcy and the applicant's attempts at reorganization are unsuccessful, an eventual liquidation also results.[13]

The important point to recognize is that *when the buyer defaults, future cash flows to the seller are delayed, and their amount may be reduced* relative to payment in nondefault. Both of these effects occur in the liquidation of the buyer. Also, liquidation is one of the most common outcomes of the default process. Therefore, we will phrase the discussion of recoveries from defaults in terms of liquidation.

In a liquidation, the amount of the recovery depends on the market value of the applicant's assets, the security arrangements that are in force

---

[12]For an alternate approach using the option pricing model, see J. A. Miles and R. Varma, "Using Financial Market Data to Make Trade Credit Decisions," presented at the Eastern Finance Association's 1984 annual meeting, and available from the authors at Pennsylvania State University.

[13]For a detailed discussion of the court procedures and negotiations which the defaulted firm faces, see F. Scherr, "The Bankruptcy Cost Puzzle," *Quarterly Journal of Economics and Business*, Summer 1988.

regarding these assets, the size of priority claims (which are paid before any funds are disbursed to creditors), and the total amount of debt owed by the applicant. While recoveries in some defaults will be zero, recovery in others may be substantial. This model developed in this section, which incorporates such recoveries, serves as a basis for our discussion of multiperiod credit-granting models. We will also use this model later in the chapter as a basis for modeling the effect of taxes on credit-granting decisions.

Let us develop a mathematical expression for the net present value of granting credit with recoveries. The decision tree for granting credit is in Panel A of Figure 6-4. Investigation and collection costs can safely be ignored here: we are dealing with marginal applicants of sufficient size that these costs are small relative to the other revenues and costs that relate to the sale. With no investigation costs, the net present value of rejection is zero. Let S be the amount of the sale and c be the expected time from the sale to the payment if the applicant pays. Let V be the costs of making the sale, payable immediately. Let X be the probability of default (thus, $1 - X$ is the probability of payment). The net present value of the sale, should outcome $2P$ occur, is then:

$$\text{NPV}_{2P} = -V + S(1 + k)^{-c} \tag{6-1}$$

where k is the required rate of return on the expected value of the future cash inflow. Let the recovery rate in default be R (as a proportion of the sale) and let the time until this recovery is received be d. The net present value of the sale, should outcome $2D$ occur, is then:

$$\text{NPV}_{2D} = -V + RS(1 + k)^{-d} \tag{6-2}$$

Rolling back the decision tree, the value of node 2 is then:

$$E(\text{NPV})_2 = (1 - X)(-V + S(1 + k)^{-c} + X(-V + RS(1 + k)^{-d})$$
$$= -V + (1 - X)S(1 + k)^{-c} + XRS(1 + k)^{-d} \tag{6-3}$$

This is the decision statistic for the two-state, one-period, no-tax decision-tree model of the credit-granting decision. The alternative of rejecting the applicant has a net present value of zero, so if equation (6-3) is positive, the applicant should be granted credit. This is a two-state model because it has been assumed that only two outcomes can result: payment in the expected time and default.[14] To see how this model would be used to make credit-granting decisions, assume that an applicant has placed an order with the seller for $75,000 worth of goods or services. These goods or services will

---

[14]If the additional complication is warranted, no-tax, single-period models can be made more comprehensive than this. W. Beranek and W. Taylor ("Credit-Scoring Models and the Cut-Off Point—A Simplification," *Decision Sciences* (July 1976), pp. 394–404) present a model with a third branch: collection beyond the expected time to payment in nondefault.

Panel A
Decision Tree for One-Period Credit-Granting with Recoveries

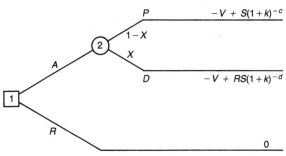

Panel B
Roll-Back of Decision Tree for Example Problem

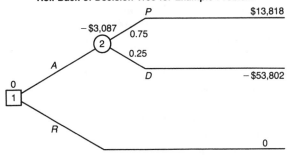

Figure 6-4. *Decision Tree for One-Period Credit Granting with Recoveries.*

cost $60,000 to provide. If the applicant pays, it is expected that payment will be received in 60 days. If the applicant defaults, a 10 percent recovery is expected, and it is expected that the courts will take two years to liquidate the firm and disburse the proceeds. The estimated probability of default is 25 percent and the required return is 10 percent per year.[15] Should credit be granted?

To answer this question, we insert the estimates of the variables into equation (6-3).

$$E(\text{NPV})_2 = -V + (1 - X)S(1 + k)^{-c} + XRS(1 + k)^{-d} \qquad (6\text{-}3)$$

$$= -60{,}000 + (1 - .25)75{,}000(1.10)^{-60/360}$$

$$+ (.25)(.10)75{,}000(1.10)^{-2}$$

$$= -60{,}000 + 55{,}363.53 + 1{,}549.59$$

$$= -\$3{,}086.88 \qquad (6\text{-}4)$$

[15]Methods for the estimation of these parameters will be discussed later in the chapter.

Since the net present value is negative, the appropriate choice at node 1 is to reject the applicant. The analysis in decision tree format is presented in Panel B of Figure 6-4. The student may verify that if the recovery rate in liquidation is above 30 percent, the proper decision is to grant credit to the applicant (the net present value for $R = 0.30$ is $12.29).

MULTIPERIOD MODELS FOR CREDIT-GRANTING DECISIONS

The one-period approach to the credit-granting problem should leave the sophisticated student a bit uneasy. It implies that, in making credit-granting decisions, the selling firm needs to look only at the order in hand and not at any future orders that may be forthcoming from the applicant once a selling relationship is established. In this section, decision methodologies for credit granting which consider cash flows beyond one period are discussed. These models are extensions of the one-period model previously presented. The *main objective* of this section is to *assess the conditions under which multiperiod analysis is necessary*.

To understand the implications of the multiperiod approach, let us expand our one-period example problem to two periods. We will assume that the applicant orders every 90 days. If the applicant does not default on the initial sale, the seller has the opportunity to make another sale in the second 90-day period. All other facts are the same as for the prior single-period problem. The decision tree, with the rollback figures, is presented in Figure 6-5; the supporting calculations are presented in Table 6-6. Despite the possibility of a future sale in the second period, the rollback of the decision tree shows that *at node 1 the firm faces exactly the same decision that it faced when only one sale was considered*: the firm has the choice of an expected net

Figure 6-5. *Two-Period Decision Tree Example Problem.*

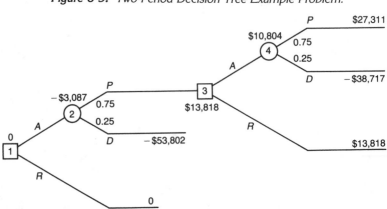

Table 6-6. Supporting Figures for Roll-Back of Two-Period Decision Tree.

Day	0	60	90	150	720	810	
Outcome			Cash Flow at Day				NPV
4P	– $60,000	$75,000	– $60,000	$75,000			$27,311
4D	– $60,000	$75,000	– $60,000			$7,500	– $38,717
3R	– $60,000	$75,000					$13,818
2D	– $60,000				$7,500		– $53,802
1R							0

Node	Outcome 1	Prob. 1	Outcome 2	Prob. 2	E(NPV)
4	$27,311	0.75	– $38,717	0.25	$10,804
2	$13,818	0.75	– $53,802	0.25	– $3,087

present value of – $3,087 from granting credit or a net present value of $0 by refusing it. What is going on here?

The answer is fairly simple. For the same problem parameters (default rate, cost of the sale, and so forth), *if it is not of advantage to grant credit to the applicant firm for the initial sale, it will not be of advantage to grant credit for any future sales either.* This is true because, for any number of periods, it will not be advantageous to grant credit in the *last* sales period of the analysis. If credit is refused for this last sale, there will be no contribution of that *last* sale to the net present value of the *next-to-last* period's decision, and thus the period before that, and so forth. Since there are no contributions to the net present value from selling in any future periods, *in the initial period the firm is faced with the same decision as if only one period were analyzed.* That is, adding the opportunity to make negative-NPV credit sales in the future does not affect the decision as to whether to make a credit sale initially.[16]

To make multiperiod analysis necessary, there has to be some expectation that *profitable future sales opportunities will be missed* if the applicant is not granted credit for the unprofitable current sale. For future profitable sales to occur when current sales are unprofitable, *some parameter of the credit-granting decision must change over time.* For example, let us alter the previous problem by assuming that, if the applicant pays for the first order, there is only a 5 percent (rather than a 20 percent) chance that the applicant will default on the second order. The required rolled-back decision tree and

---

[16]This conclusion is not affected by the size of the future sale. As long as the ratio of V/S and the other parameters of the credit-granting decision (X, c, and so forth) remain the same, the size of the order will not affect the decision as to whether credit granting for that order has a positive expected net present value.

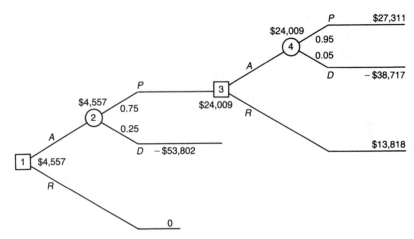

Figure 6-6. Two-Period Decision Tree Example Problem with Changing Default Probabilities.

supporting calculations are presented in Figure 6-6 and Table 6-7. The optimal decision at node 1 is now to *grant credit* for the initial sale, with an expected net present value of $4,557.

The multiperiod analysis in Figure 6-6 assumes that the firm must make the first sale in order to make the second one. That is, it assumes that the applicant is *brand loyal* and tends to purchase from the same supplier for repeat sales. If the applicant is brand loyal, *refusing credit at node 1 prohibits the seller from granting credit at a future time when the parameters of the credit-granting decision have changed.* An alternate analysis where the applicant is *not* brand loyal is presented in Figure 6-7, with supporting calculations in

Table 6-7. Supporting Figures for Roll-Back of Two-Period Decision Tree with Changing Default Probabilities.

Day	0	60	90	150	720	810	
Outcome			Cash Flow at Day				NPV
4P	– $60,000	$75,000	– $60,000	$75,000			$27,311
4D	– $60,000	$75,000	– $60,000			$7,500	– $38,717
3R	– $60,000	$75,000					$13,818
2D	– $60,000				$7,500		– $53,802
1R							0

Node	Outcome	Prob.	Outcome	Prob.	E(NPV)
	1	1	2	2	
4	$27,311	0.95	– $38,717	0.05	$24,009
2	$24,009	0.75	– $53,802	0.25	$4,557

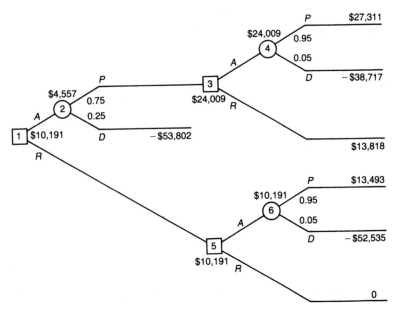

Figure 6-7. *Two-Period Decision-Tree Example Problem with Changing Default Probabilities and No Brand Loyalty.*

Table 6-8. Since the customer is not brand loyal, the refusal of credit at node 1 does not preclude the seller from receiving orders and granting credit in the future (at node 5). Further, the analysis shows that *this is the optimal strategy*. If the applicant is not brand loyal, the seller should refuse credit for the order in the current period. If the applicant has not defaulted to other trade suppliers by the end of the *first* period, the seller should grant credit for orders in the *second* period.

Let us summarize this discussion of the need for multiperiod analysis in credit-granting decisions on marginal accounts. It is assumed that the credit analyst has performed a single-period analysis of a credit applicant. If the expected net present value is positive, credit is granted; when future orders are received from this customer, these can be analyzed as needed. If the one-period expected net present value is negative, however, the analyst may be concerned that refusing credit to the applicant may result in the loss of future positive-NPV orders. In the latter situation, the analyst should perform multi-period analysis *only if both of the following are true*:

1. The parameters of the credit-granting situation (such as the expected recovery rate or the expected default rate) are expected to change over time.
2. The applicant is brand loyal.

Table 6-8. Supporting Figures for Roll-Back of Two-Period Decision Tree with Changing Default Probabilities and No Brand Loyalty.

	Day	0	60	90	150	720	810	
Outcome				Cash Flow at Day				NPV
4P		−$60,000	$75,000	−$60,000	$75,000			$27,311
4D		−$60,000	$75,000	−$60,000			$7,500	−$38,717
3R		−$60,000	$75,000					$13,818
2D		−$60,000				$7,500		−$53,802
6P				−$60,000	$75,000			$13,493
6D				−$60,000			$7,500	−$52,535
5R								0

Node	Outcome 1	Prob. 1	Outcome 2	Prob. 2	E(NPV)
4	$27,311	0.95	−$38,717	0.05	$24,009
2	$24,009	0.75	−$53,802	0.25	$ 4,557
6	$13,493	0.95	−$52,535	0.05	$10,191

As previously illustrated, if the first is not true, future opportunities for unprofitable sales will not change the initial decision. If the second is not true, the seller can wait and see if the applicant defaults, granting credit in the future if default does not occur. Only in the case where both are true is a multiperiod approach to credit-granting decisions required.

The application of a complete multiperiod analysis to credit-granting decisions requires some rather complex calculations and programming methodologies; the methodology is presented in an article by Bierman and Hausman, and is not reviewed here.[17] However, the two conditions listed above that require multiperiod analysis are relatively restrictive. For the parameters of the credit-granting decision to change over time, the applicant must be in a period of changing financial structure or policy. Also, the applicant must be brand loyal. The likelihood of these two conditions occurring simultaneously is rather small. Therefore, for most circumstances a single-period anal-

[17]See H. Bierman, Jr., and W. H. Hausman, "The Credit-Granting Decision," *Management Science* (April 1970), pp. B591–B532. Note however that the techniques in this article are primarily directed toward situations where the credit-granting firm has incomplete information on applicants (and thus the experience of payment or nonpayment affects the estimation of the applicant's parameters for future sales) rather than to marginal accounts with changing financial positions (and therefore changes in the expected parameters of credit granting over time). Extensions of Bierman and Hausman's analysis may be found in Y. M. I. Dirickx and L. Wakeman, "An Extension of the Bierman-Hausman Model for Credit-Granting," *Management Science*, Vol. 22, No. 11 (July 1976), pp. 1229–1237.

ysis is adequate, although the analyst should be aware of the limitations of such an approach.

A ONE-PERIOD MODEL WITH NONZERO RECOVERIES AND TAXES

For the balance of this chapter, we assume that multiperiod analysis is not necessary and continue discussion using models that consider only the next sale to the customer. In a prior section, we developed a one-period model that allowed for recoveries in the event of default. In this section, we extend this one-period model with recoveries to the evaluation of credit-granting decisions where the seller is taxable.[18] This one-period model with taxes and recoveries is the one we recommend as a practical and realistic approach to credit-granting decisions on marginal accounts. Later sections will discuss the estimation of the parameters and the assessment of the risk inherent within this model.

In the prior analysis, three types of cash flows were considered: the initial cost of producing the goods or services for sale (which occurs whether or not the applicant pays), the future cash flow from this payment (occurring with probability $X - 1$) and the future cash flow from recovery in liquidation (occurring with probability X). If the selling firm is taxable, there is a fourth type of cash flow from the sale: the firm's tax payments and refunds. *The timing and amount of these tax flows will affect the value of granting credit to a particular applicant.* Further, the timing and amount of these cash flows depends on the treatment of bad debts that the selling firm elects for tax purposes. Two treatments are common: recognizing bad debts as they occur, and accruing bad debt reserves based on average loss rates. We will develop net present value rules based on expected net present value for each of these two popular tax treatments.

Bad Debts Recognized as They Occur In this tax treatment, the firm does not keep a reserve for bad debt. Instead, it recognizes and deducts bad debt expenses when buyers default. This alternative is simple from an accounting standpoint, but it requires that the firm defer the tax reduction that comes with bad debt expense until defaults actually occur. Let V_T be the firm's cost of goods sold for tax purposes. Due to tax accounting rules, this may not be equal to V, the cash cost of such goods. Since no reserve for bad debt is accrued, the firm will face an initial tax bill on the entire profit from the sale. The amount of this tax bill will be $(S - V_T)T$, where T is the seller's corporate tax rate. Let us assume that this tax bill is payable at the time of

---

[18]Much of the discussion in this section parallels F. Scherr, "The Industrial Credit-Granting Decision: Two-State Models Including Tax Effects," *Akron Business and Economic Review*, Vol. 16, No. 4 (Winter 1985), pp. 7–11.

the sale.[19] The initial cash flow will then be $-V - (S - V_T)T$ instead of $-V$. If the applicant pays, there is no tax loss, and the net cash flow in the event of payment is the same as in prior models. However, if the applicant defaults, the uncollected balance is a tax deduction that results in a tax refund or a tax reduction. Assume that the firm takes this deduction at the time the recovery occurs. The net present value of the tax reduction is then $T(1 - R)S$, and the net cash flow at the time of recovery will be $RS + T(1 - R)S$. Applying the probability of X to the cash flows from default and the probability $1 - X$ to the cash flows in nondefault and discounting these expected cash flows gives the expected net present value of the credit-granting decision where the firm does not accrue a bad debt reserve:

$$E(\text{NPV}) = -V - (S - V_T)T + (1 - X)S(1 + k)^{-c}$$

$$+ X[RS + T(1 - R)S](1 + k)^{-d} \tag{6-5}$$

Let us address an example problem. A seller facing a tax rate of 33 percent has received an order for $100,000. The cost of materials for servicing this order will be $85,000; the cost of these goods for tax purposes is the same as the cash cost. The estimated probability of default for the applicant is 10 percent and the estimated recovery rate, should the applicant default, is 20 percent. If the applicant does not default, payment is expected in 75 days; if the applicant does default, it is expected that disbursements from the court will be received in three years. The required rate of return is 13 percent per year. The initial tax bill will be $(100,000 - 85,000)(0.33) = \$4,950$. If the applicant defaults, $20,000 will be recovered (that is, $RS = (0.20)(100,000) = \$20,000$), and the remaining $80,000 will be written off, resulting in a tax reduction of $26,400 ($T(1 - R)S = (0.33)(1 - 0.2)\$100,000$). The expected net present value is then:

$$E(\text{NPV}) = -V - (S - V_T)T + (1 - X)S(1 + k)^{-c}$$
$$+ X[RS + T(1 - R)S](1 + k)^{-d} \tag{6-5}$$

$$= -85,000 - 4,950 + (1 - 0.\blacklozenge)100,000(1.13)^{-75/360}$$
$$+ (0.10)(20,000 + 26,400)(1.13)^{-3}$$

$$= -85,000 - 4,950 + 87,737 + 3,216 = \$1,003 \tag{6-6}$$

Under this tax election decision, the expected net present value granting credit for the sale is positive; the sale is of advantage to the firm, and credit should be granted.

[19]We assume that any tax flows occur concurrently with other events for simplicity of presentation. If, however, the tax flows occur at other times, they can be separately discounted to obtain their values without affecting the basic structure of the model. The same procedure would apply if the cash flow for the cost of the order (V) does not occur at time zero.

Reserve for Bad Debt is Accrued Another tax option is to accrue a reserve for bad debts. Firms accrue this reserve based on average loss rates and average recovery rates for particular types of customers, such as all the customers purchasing from the unit of the firm that is considering the applicant. This reserve is accrued as a deduction from the profit on each sale by that unit. The reserve builds up over time, and when customers default, the amounts of the losses are offset against the reserve. This offset has no tax effect. In this system of tax accounting for bad debts, there are no tax effects after the initial reduction of taxable profit to increase the reserve.

Let P_a be the average default rate for the customers of a particular unit of the selling firm, and let R_a be the average recovery rate on these defaults. The tax-deductible addition to the reserve for bad debt from a sale will then be $P_a (1 - R_a)S$, and the initial tax bill on the profit from this sale will be $(S - V_T - P_a(1 - R_a)S)T$. In this tax option, there will be no tax effects beyond this initial tax bill, so the remaining terms in the net present-value equation are the same as in those of the no-tax model portrayed in equation (6-3). The expected net present value will be:

$$E(\text{NPV}) = -V - (S - V_T - P_a(1 - R_a)S)T$$

$$+ (1 - X)S(1 + k)^{-c} + XRS(1 + k)^{-d} \qquad (6\text{-}7)$$

To illustrate this tax option, we use the same facts as in the last prior example problem, but also assume that the average default rate of customers of this unit of the selling firm is 1 percent and that the average recovery rate on defaults is 15 percent. The addition to the bad debt reserve is $850 $(P_a(1 - R_a)S = (0.01)(1 - 0.15)100,000)$, so the initial tax bill is $4,670 $(S - V_T - P_a(1 - R_a)S)T = (100,000 - 85,000 - 850)(0.33))$. The expected net present value is then:

$$E(\text{NPV}) = -V - (S - V_T - P_a(1 - R_a)S)T$$
$$+ (1 - X)S(1 + k)^{-c} + XRS(1 + k)^{-d} \qquad (6\text{-}7)$$

$$= -85,000 - 4,670 + 87,737 + (0.10)(0.20)(100,000)(1.13)^{-3}$$

$$= -\$546 \qquad (6\text{-}8)$$

Under *this* tax election option, granting credit is not advantageous to the firm.[20]

[20]The difference in expected net present value between the two tax elections for this particular problem is due mainly to the difference in default rates. In the second tax treatment, the firm may accrue a reserve at only average default rates, and the probability of default for this applicant is higher than average, so some tax benefit of this applicant is lost. In this problem, this lost benefit more than compensates for the fact that in the second election option, the benefit is received sooner (immediately, rather than when the loss is realized).

The important point made by this analysis is that *the existence of taxes and the different tax treatments of bad debts elected by the firm may affect the credit-granting decision for some applicants*. If taxes did not exist, equation (6-3) applies, and the expected net present value is:

$$E(NPV) = -V + (1 - X)S(1 + k)^{-c} + XRS(1 + k)^{-d} \qquad (6\text{-}3)$$

$$= -85,000 + (1 - 0.10)100,000(1.13)^{-75/360}$$

$$+ (0.10)(0.20)100,000(1.13)^{-3}$$

$$= -85,000 + 87,737 + 1,386 = \$4,123 \qquad (6\text{-}9)$$

This result suggests that the applicant should be granted credit. Yet, we know that for firms accruing a bad debt reserve at average loss rates, granting credit is not of advantage. Thus, *it is important to incorporate tax flows into the analysis of marginal credit applicants*. Since the models portrayed in equations (6-5) and (6-7) account for taxes (and for possible recoveries in default), they are our preferred models for credit analysis.

ESTIMATING PARAMETERS FOR MARGINAL CREDIT APPLICANTS

To use the after-tax models for credit-granting decisions that are presented in equations (6-5) and (6-7), the analyst must make estimates of the values for each of the variables which appear in these equations. A recap of these variables is presented in Table 6-9. One variable, the time to recovery if the applicant defaults and is liquidated (d), is a function of efficiency of the court system in the area where the applicant resides, and must be estimated by the seller based on the seller's knowledge of the typical delays that occur in the required legal proceedings. The remaining variables can be divided into two classes: variables that originate with the *seller* and variables that originate with the *applicant*. Estimation of many of the variables that originate with the seller requires only a reference to the seller's accounting system aided by basic financial analysis. Most selling firms have no trouble constructing data on the out-of-pocket costs of servicing the order (V), the tax cost of this service (V_T), the selling firm's tax rate (T), the average default rate (P_a), and the average recovery rate on defaults (R_a). The size of the order (S) is usually available, since it is often an order which precipitates the analysis. If the impetus for evaluation is an anticipated order, information on the likely size of orders from the applicant can often be provided by the seller's sales force.

The one parameter of the decision that originates with the selling firm and that is a bit more difficult to estimate is the appropriate discount rate for the expected future cash flows (k). This is a risk-adjusted rate that reflects both the time value of money and the risk of the cash flows. However, these

Table 6-9. *Variables That Must Be Estimated for Equations (6-5) and (6-7).*

For Equation (6-5):

V = Out-of-pocket cost of materials to service order from applicant, in dollars.

S = Size of order from applicant, in dollars.

V_T = Tax cost of materials to service order from applicant, in dollars.

T = Seller's tax rate on profits.

X = Probability of applicant's default.

k = Required rate of return on cash flows (a risk-adjusted discount rate).

c = Expected time for payment to be received from the applicant if the applicant does not default.

R = Recovery rate if applicant defaults (a proportion).

d = Time to recovery inflow if applicant defaults.

Additional Variables for Equation (6-7):

P_a = Average default rate for customers of this unit of the selling firm.

R_a = Average recovery rate for customers of this unit of the selling firm.

cash flows are from the additional sales of an ongoing product, and it is thus appropriate to use the risk-adjusted discount rate that is relevant to that product line. For most firms, this is the firm's cost of capital adjusted for differences in risk among the lines of business in which they deal.

This leaves three variables that must be estimated in order to compute equations (6-5) and (6-7). Each of these variables originates not with the selling firm but with the credit applicant. The estimation of each requires some sophistication and insight. These three variables are the expected time that payment is to be received if the applicant does not default (c), the recovery rate in default (R), and the probability of the default (X).

Estimating the Time to Pay in Nondefault As previously discussed, the pattern of payments to trade creditors by a debtor firm depends on both the debtor's *financial position* (ability to pay) and *management policies* (inclination to pay). Measures of ability to pay, such as the applicant's current and quick ratios, thus have some bearing on the estimation of the time to pay in nondefault. However, these are not perfect measures. Debtors with seemingly few available funds sometimes show a startling ability to pay trade debts as they come due, and debtors with strong financial positions sometimes leave creditors unpaid for extended periods.

A pragmatic approach to the required estimation is to obtain the applicant's historical pattern of payments to the trade and assume that this pattern will continue into the future. This information can be gleaned from other suppliers of the applicant. For example, if conversations with other suppliers or the examination of the applicant's current trade clearance shows a general pattern of paying promptly, it may be expected that the applicant will be most likely to pay an additional seller on this basis.

Another pragmatic approach is to compute the applicant's *accounts payable turnover ratio* based on the latest data that is available. The accounts payable turnover ratio is:

Annual Cost of Materials and Services Purchased/Payables to Trade   (6-10)

This ratio measures the average turnover of trade debts, and therefore the average time that the creditor has taken to pay these debts. For example, assume that an applicant is being considered and that the analyst has a copy of the applicant's financial statement for the fiscal year just passed. By examining the income statement, the analyst finds that purchases from the trade of goods and services (which are part of cost of goods sold) were $12 million and that year-end accounts payable were $3 million.[21] The accounts payable turnover ratio is $12/3 = 4.0$ times per year. On average, the applicant paid creditors in $360/4.0 = 90$ days. While some types of creditors may have been paid more rapidly and some more slowly than this average indicates, this ratio is a good indicator of the applicant's policies and its ability to pay trade creditors.

Estimating the Recovery in Default   The model we are using assumes that the applicant will be liquidated if default occurs. The challenge is to estimate the recoveries from this liquidation. While ratios such as debt to assets are useful in this context, they are relatively crude proxies for expected recovery. One method for estimating this recovery is the *simulated asset sale approach*. In this approach, the analyst uses the applicant's latest financial statement, estimated recovery rates based on the type and quality of assets, and knowledge about any security interests that the applicant has granted. With this information, the analyst simulates the recoveries and transactions that would occur in liquidation. The calculated recovery rate is used as an estimate of R.

Estimating the Probability of Default   Of all the estimates required in the analysis of credit applicants, this one is the most difficult to address. What is the chance that an applicant will not pay? Much of the traditional approach to the credit-granting decision centers on this question. One possible method

---

[21]The use of an average accounts payable figure rather than year-end accounts payable in this calculation would be more descriptive, but requires that both beginning and ending figures are available.

of estimating this probability is to start with the industry failure rate, which represents the average chance that the applicant will default, and adjust this rate up or down to reflect the applicant's strength relative to the average firm in the industry. This approach is very flexible in that any information on the applicant, quantitative or nonquantitative, can be incorporated in the estimation process. For example, the analyst's opinion of the ability of the applicant's management team can be used in the analysis. However, an accurate estimate using such a methodology clearly requires very extensive insight by the analyst.

Another approach is to develop a *failure forecasting function* and use this function to estimate the probability of default by the applicant. There has been very substantial academic research on the estimation of these functions, and this research has shown that such functions can produce excellent results in the classification of firms as future failures or nonfailures, if the required data are available.[22] To estimate such a function, five steps are required.

First, the firm must gather a sample of failed and nonfailed firms. The population from which this sample is drawn will determine the applicability of the estimated failure-forecasting function. If the firm gathers a sample of defaulted and nondefaulted firms from the general population of all the firms in an industry, then the estimated failure forecasting function is applicable to any applicant from that industry. If the sample is limited to those firms that have passed the selling firm's initial credit screening criteria, then the function should be applied only to such applicants.

One problem that can arise at this point is that of sample size. To estimate a reliable failure-forecasting function, the sample should contain at least 20 default firms and 20 nondefaulted firms and preferably more. Since for statistical purposes the size of the smaller group acts as a constraint on the effectiveness of the technique, the usual procedure is to use an industry's entire population of defaulted firms and a randomly selected, equal-sized sample of nondefaulted firms. Even then, the size of the defaulted group of firms in a particular industry may be insufficient, and the selling firm may be forced to combine defaulted firms from several industries to obtain a sufficient sample size. This mixing of industries in estimating the function is an empirical trade-off; there are substantial disadvantages to this procedure if there are divergent causes of default among the industries that are mixed.[23]

Second, the analyst must select variables that are believed to be related

[22]The literature on failure forecasting is extensive. Most of the seminal studies were published between 1969 and 1980; for a review of this literature, see E. I. Altman, R. B. Avery, R. A. Eisenbeis, and J. F. Sinkey, Jr., *Application of Classification Techniques in Business, Banking and Finance* (Greenwich, Conn.: JAI Press, 1981), pp. 255–306.

[23]See F. Scherr, "Estimating and Using Failure-Forecasting Functions: Some Problems and Some Proposed Solutions," *Baylor Business Studies* (January 1982), pp. 23–27.

to default and obtain measures of these for each defaulted and nondefaulted firm in the sample. Financial ratios are typically selected; these ratios have to be good predictors of default in numerous studies (although other variables capturing firm age, firm size, and the state of the economy can also be incorporated). Ratios measuring liquidity and debt are often included, since these reflect potential causes of default.[24]

Third, the analyst must select a statistical technique to relate these variables to the default/nondefault of the firms in the sample. There are several alternative statistical techniques available, including linear probability models, probit models, logit models, discriminant analysis models, and recursive partitioning models. These models have different statistical requirements and require different interpretations.[25]

Fourth, the function must be estimated and adjusted. Estimation is done via a computerized statistical package. Once the initial output is received, the analyst may add or drop variables in an attempt to achieve a superior formulation, then reestimate the function. The goal in the estimation of this function is accurate prediction, and this goal should be kept in mind in the development process.

Finally, the developed failure-forecasting function must be tested on data outside that on which it was developed. This process is called *validation* and is critical in the assessment of the accuracy of the function. The ability of the function to assess the default potential of a *new* applicant is, of course, the proper index of its usefulness.

Once the failure-forecasting function has been estimated and validated, it can then be used to calculate the estimated probability of default for new applicants. This calculation requires two steps. First, data on the applicant is inserted into the function, and a probability of default is calculated. However, *the probability of default calculated in this way assumes that the proportion of defaults among applicants is the same as that in the sample* that was used to estimate the function. That is, this unadjusted probability assumes that the chance of default is 50 percent for any applicant if this is the proportion of defaults in the sample. On average, a much smaller proportion of applicants than this will actually default. To adjust for this difference in probability between that of the sample and that of the population of applicants, Bayes' rule can be used. Bayes' rule states:

$$\text{Posterior odds} = (\text{prior odds})\ (\text{information odds}) \qquad (6\text{-}11)$$

For example, suppose a failure-forecasting function is estimated using an equal

---

[24]See Scherr, "Failure-Forecasting Functions," pp. 20–23 and 27–29.

[25]Discussion of the linear probability, probit, logit, and discriminant analysis models can be found in Altman et al., *Classification Techniques*, pp. 1–58. Discussion of the recursive partitioning technique can be found in H. Frydman, E. Altman, and D. Kao, "Introducing Recursive Partitioning for Financial Classification: The Case of Financial Distress," *Journal of Finance* (March 1985), pp. 269–91.

proportion of defaulted and nondefaulted firms. This function is then used to calculate the probability of default for a credit applicant. Assume that the calculated probability of default for the applicant is 60 percent. Thus, the *information odds* given by the failure-forecasting function are 60/40 (60 defaults and 40 nondefaults in 100 applicants with these characteristics). However, suppose that in the overall population of credit applicants, only 2 firms in 100 default. The *prior odds* are then 2/98. The applicant's true default odds are:

$$(2/98) \ (60/40) = 0.0306 \tag{6-12}$$

The proper estimate of X for equation (6-5) or (6-6) is then 3.06 percent.

Failure-Forecasting Functions in Perspective The estimation of the probability of failure via statistical techniques is a relatively new technology and deserves additional discussion. The use of these techniques to estimate the probability of default avoids any personal biases of credit analysts, provides a probability estimate of default, and has been shown, in several studies, to be quite accurate. An additional advantage is that most statistical techniques used to estimate failure-forecasting functions also provide estimates of the error inherent in the forecast. However, failure-forecasting functions require considerable data collection and statistical sophistication to develop. In particular, the selection and adjustment of the appropriate statistical model requires expertise that most businesspersons do not possess. To successfully develop a reliable failure-forecasting function, this expertise must be available within the selling firm, or it must be purchased from a consultant. Further, the resulting failure-forecasting function can be used most advantageously to estimate the default probability only when data on the applicant is available for each of the variables in the failure-forecasting function. Difficulties such as these do not invalidate the failure-forecasting function as a way to estimate default probability, but they do make this technique more difficult to execute.

UNCERTAINTY IN CREDIT-GRANTING DECISIONS

The risk of the applicant's default in the credit-granting decision is captured by the expected value process and the use of a risk-adjusted discount rate. What has not yet been addressed is the *uncertainty in the estimation of parameters* for the evaluation of the applicant. What if the estimates of the parameters used in making the credit-granting decision are subject to error? How does this affect the decision process?

To address this question, we must look at the estimates made in order to calculate equations (6-5) and (6-7) and assess the effect of possible variations in these estimates on the decision to grant or not to grant credit. In examining the variables in Table 6-9, there is likely to be considerable uncertainty about the values of some of these, while the values of others are relatively certain. For example, the selling firm is likely to know its near-term tax rate (T) with considerable certainty. However, the estimations of three important variables are likely to be very uncertain: the expected time to payment in nondefault (c), the recovery rate in default (R), and the probability of default (X).

The estimated time to pay in nondefault is subject to error in part because of the different policies that debtors use in paying various suppliers. For example, some debtors follow the policy of paying continuing suppliers more promptly than they pay suppliers from which they buy only occasionally. In such a case, the *average* payment time to suppliers may misrepresent the expected payment time to a particular supplier. Also, the use of past data (past payment patterns in this case) to estimate future behavior always carries with it the risk that the applicant will change policies.

The estimated recovery rate in default is uncertain for two reasons. First, this recovery rate is usually estimated based on the applicant's financial structure *at the time of the sale*. Between that time and the time of liquidation, however, this structure may have changed considerably. Second, in the simulated asset sale approach, estimated recovery rates are applied to the applicant's assets. However, the actual recovery rates in the liquidation of these assets may be much higher or lower, depending on the condition of the assets at the time of liquidation.

Finally, the estimated default probability is uncertain, even if the most careful estimation techniques are used. No statistical or other estimation technique can capture all the peculiarities that are inherent in the survival or failure of firms. For example, an intelligent and skillful manager can keep a financially strapped business going for a surprising amount of time, while inept management can run a strong firm out of business in months. Because of such peculiarities, any failure-forecasting methodology will always have error in the estimate of default probability.

Because there is a distinct cutoff between acceptance and rejection (based on the expected net present value of granting credit for the sale to the applicant), a *simulation* of the effect of these uncertainties on this net present value can go a long way to investigating risk in the credit-granting decision. In such a simulation methodology, an estimated probability distribution of the applicant's payment pattern to trade suppliers and of the recovery rate, along with the standard error of the estimate of the failure-forecasting function, can be used to develop the probability distribution of the expected net present value from granting credit to the applicant. This probability distribution is then examined relative to the cutoff of zero expected net present value. Two examples are presented in Figure 6-8. In both of these, the expected net present value is positive, so the applicant will be granted credit in the absence of uncertainty considerations. However, in Panel A, there is very little chance that the errors in the estimation of the parameters

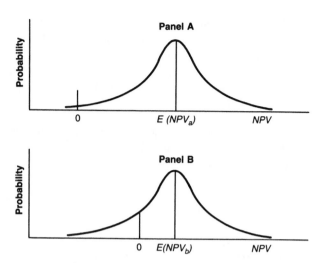

Figure 6-8. *Two Probability Distributions of Net Present Value from Granting Credit.*

are such that the true expected net present value is negative; the seller can have considerable confidence that granting credit to this applicant is an appropriate decision. In Panel B, however, there is a very substantial chance that the true expected net present value is negative, and the seller should carefully examine the estimates made in assessing this applicant before proceeding with the granting of credit.

CREDIT LIMITS: AN UNANSWERED QUESTION

Up to this point, we have treated the credit-granting decision as dichotomous: the selling firm either granted credit to the applicant for the amount of the order or it did not. However, there is a third option: the seller may grant a *limited amount* of credit, called a *credit line* or a *credit limit*. In such a credit-granting system, the seller will specify a maximum amount of outstanding debt from each customer. If an additional order is placed so that the credit limit is exceeded, the order may be refused or the customer may be required to pay for prior orders so that this maximum is not violated. We will see in the next chapter that many selling firms limit credit granting in this way.

Except in special cases, the credit limit approach does not seem to agree with the maximization of shareholder wealth as expressed by equations (6-5) and (6-7). For the credit limit approach to be in line with the maximization of shareholder wealth, the net present value in these equations *must go through a maximum in sales* (S) then fall with additional sales. In such a situation, it would be optimal for the seller to limit sales to that particular customer to the amount that results in this maximum NPV.[26] The prevalent use of credit limits by industrial sellers has left researchers in accounts receivable management searching for some cost or revenue that may be a function of sales volume and may produce the NPV optimum, explaining the behavior of firms. Several such costs and revenues have been suggested. We discuss them and other possible reasons for limiting credit in the following paragraphs.

Overbuying One possibility is that industrial purchasers will "overbuy" if granted credit beyond their needs.[27] In such a case, the purchaser will take on trade debt beyond that needed for purchases; the purchaser will also become less liquid, as its inventory turnover will fall. This overbuying will then increase the probability of the purchaser's default (X) for some levels of additional sales and, at some point, produce a maximum in NPV.

Increases in Production Costs Another possibility is that the cost of goods produced to service the order (V) may rise disproportionately with sales. In this case, net present value may rise initially with sales volume, then decline with increases in sales to the customer as unit production costs rise.

Funds Constraints Another circumstance that can lead to credit limits as an optimal policy occurs when the seller faces funds constraints in the firm's investment in accounts receivable. In such circumstances, the selling firm must optimize net present value given this constraint, and limiting sales volumes to customers is one possible response. Note that this situation implies the rejection of sales that have positive net present values.[28]

Changes in the Firm's Systematic Risk Granting credit can raise the systematic risk of the firm and therefore alter its required returns via the CAPM.[29] Recall from Chapter 1 that in the CAPM the required return on an asset is:

$$R_i = R_f + b_i(R_m - R_f) \tag{1-5}$$

[26]For discussion of this issue, see F. Scherr, "Marginal Cost and Revenue Industrial Credit-Granting Models: Decision Implications and an Example Application," *Akron Business and Economic Review*, Vol. 13, No. 4 (Winter 1982), pp. 38–42.

[27]See Jess H. Chua, "A Trade Credit Granting Model with Order-Size Dependent Credit Risks," available from the author at the University of Calgary and S. Besley and J. S. Osteryoung, "Accounts Receivable Management: The Development of a General Credit-Granting Algorithm for Determining Credit Limits Under Funds Constraints," presented at the Financial Management's 1984 annual meeting and available from Besley at the University of South Florida. This overbuying phenomenon is almost certainly the reason that credit limits are commonly used in the management of consumer credit.

[28]See Besley and Osteryoung, "Accounts Receivable Management."

[29]See T. E. Copeland and N. T. Khoury, "Analysis of Credit Extensions in a World of Uncertainty," in K. V. Smith, ed. *Readings in the Management of Working Capital*, Second Edition (St. Paul: West Publishing, 1980), pp. 323–30.

In this equation, the beta for the asset (b_i) is the comovement between the asset's returns and the returns on the market portfolio. Beta is directly proportional to the covariance between the asset's returns and the returns on the market portfolio. This covariance is:

$$\text{Cov}(R_i, R_m) = SD_{Ri}SD_{Rm}\text{Cor}_{RiRm} \qquad (6\text{-}13)$$

where SD_{Ri} is the standard deviation of the returns on the asset, SD_{Rm} is the standard deviation of the returns on the market portfolio, and Cor_{RiRm} is the correlation coefficient between these returns. If granting credit to an applicant adds to the dispersion of returns on the firm's assets (SD_{Ri}), it will increase the firm's beta, and thus its overall level of risk in a CAPM context. If the cash flows from the applicant are correlated with returns in the economy (Cor_{RiRm}), this can also increase risk. In either case, the required returns on the firm's assets will increase. The resulting decrease in the value of the firm's assets because of this increase in required return may offset the increased expected cash flows from credit granting, resulting in an optimum in NPV.

Changes in the Variance of the Receivables Portfolio As additional credit is granted to a buyer, the variance of the cash flows from the seller's portfolio of accounts receivable is altered. Depending on the correlation between the cash flows from additional receivables and the amount of such receivables, the variance of the cash flows from the receivables portfolio may increase. If the seller is averse to this variance, the seller will price it by increasing the required return on new receivables (k) with the amount of credit granted. This can cause a maximum in the NPV of additional credit sales.[30]

Agency Problems Another possibility is that managers are not acting in the shareholders' interests; that is, they are not maximizing net present value. In such a case, they may not use decision processes that parallel equations (6-5) and (6-7); the decision processes they do use may require credit limits. Situations where managers do not act in the shareholders' best interests (which are called *agency problems*) may be caused by an unintentionally faulty implementation of the rules of shareholder wealth maximization in the development of policies for the selling firm.[31] In the context of setting policies for the evaluation of credit management personnel, firms may have chosen statistics such as accounts receivable turnover or bad debt expense as their measures of credit-manager effectiveness, with the implication that higher turnover and lower bad debts indicate better management. In such a case, credit managers may tend to be more conservative in their credit-granting

[30]See F. Scherr, "A Portfolio Approach to Credit-Granting Decisions" available from the author at West Virginia University.

[31]See A. Barnea, R. Haugen, and L. Senbet, *Agency Problems in Financial Contracting* (Englewood Cliffs, N.J.: Prentice Hall, 1985) for a discussion of agency problems in finance.

decisions than the net present value rules would dictate, since they are penalized for defaults and slowness but are not credited when positive-NPV sales are made.[32] They may use credit limits to reduce bad debt expense, even though the orders refused have positive expected net present values.

Credit Limits and Credit Investigation Another possibility is that credit limits are used within firms as *monitoring tools*, but these limits are not as enforced as limits on the amounts that customers can purchase. Credit managers are often charged with making the proper credit investigation decisions, in addition to credit-granting decisions. If they assign credit limits to customers based on the amount of credit information that has been collected on that customer, the violation of the credit limit can be used as a trigger for additional credit investigation. When the credit limit set for this purpose is violated, this violation provides a signal to the credit analyst to collect additional credit information and to reexamine the applicant based on this information. Based on this additional information, the credit analyst may approve the order by raising the applicant's credit line or may withdraw credit altogether.

Financial research has not yet provided an answer to why firms use credit limits. The link between shareholder wealth and the determination of credit limits is not understood. There may be several reasons for this use, or the reasons may vary from firm to firm. Given the current state of research, the most that can be said is that this use is widespread but the general explanation for it is unknown.

SUMMARY

This chapter dealt with the credit-granting decision: to whom should the firm grant trade credit? There are numerous sources of information that give the selling firm insight into the costs and revenues from credit granting. However, the collection of information from these sources is costly. These costs of information play an important part in developing strategies for credit granting. For small order sizes, it is not economical for the selling firm to spend large amounts on the investigation of the credit applicant. The decision-tree approach to the credit investigation gives optimal rules for investigation based on order size. This approach was illustrated for three order sizes in an extensive example problem.

For large orders from customers of uncertain financial strength, it is optimal for the selling firm to collect a great deal of information on the credit applicant. With this information in hand, some method must be used to

---

[32]We will see in the next chapter that the proper way to use measures of accounts receivable turnover and bad debt is with reference to budgets, with these budgets being set up based on the terms of sale and credit-granting decisions of the selling firm.

integrate the facts regarding these marginal applicants and decide whether or not to grant credit. In the traditional approach to this credit-granting decision on marginal accounts, the credit analyst uses the Five Cs of Credit as a framework to assess the creditworthiness of the applicant, and makes a judgment on credit granting. Unfortunately, there are several problems with this method, the most serious of which is that there is no direct link to shareholder wealth maximization.

To directly link the credit-granting decision on marginal accounts to the desires of shareholders, a net present-value model for credit-granting decisions was developed. This model allows for taxes and recoveries in the default of the credit applicant. The model should be used in its one-period form unless the applicant is brand loyal and the estimated parameters of the credit applicant are expected to change over time. (If the applicant is brand loyal and estimated parameters are expected to change, a multiperiod approach is required.) Methods of estimating the parameters necessary to execute this model were discussed. The risk associated with this model originates with the uncertainty in the estimation of these parameters, and can be assessed via simulation analysis.

The terms of sale and credit-granting policies that the firm adopts will imply some level of expected revenues and costs. Unfortunately, comparing the actual levels of some of these revenues and costs with the expected levels is a relatively tricky business. Yet such a comparison is necessary to enable the firm to monitor the effectiveness of its policy decisions. In the next chapter, we discuss the monitoring of these revenues and costs for accounts receivable. We also review the literature on the practices currently used in credit management.

Problems

6-1. A firm is trying to formulate a credit investigation policy for order amounts of $500. When an order is received, the firm can accept the order, reject the order, or investigate further. If the order is accepted without further investigation, the probability of default is 5 percent and it is expected that payment will be received in 45 days (terms of sale are 30 days). If the firm elects to investigate, the costs of this investigation are $5, and three results are possible: the applicant may have paid promptly in the past, the applicant may have defaulted in the past, or the firm may have no experience with the applicant. The probabilities of these outcomes are 0.75, 0.05, and 0.20. If the seller has experience with the applicant, it is assumed that future credit granting will have the same result as past credit granting. At this stage, the seller may grant credit to the applicant without further investigation, reject the applicant, or investigate further. If the seller has no experience with the applicant and credit is granted without further investigation, the probability of default is 5 percent and the expected time to pay is 45 days. If additional credit investigation is undertaken, investigation costs will be $25 and two outcomes are possible: the applicant may have a strong or a weak financial position. Financially strong firms pay promptly; there is a 70 percent chance the applicant will be financially strong. If the applicant is found to be financially weak, the probability of its default is 15 percent. If the financially weak firm does not default, it is expected that payment will be received in 80 days. Construct the necessary decision tree and develop the appropriate credit investigation strategy. The firm's cost of capital is 10 percent and costs of materials are 85 percent of sales (payable immediately). Ignore taxes and recoveries in default in your calculations.

6-2. A credit applicant has placed three orders with a seller, and the seller must make a credit-granting decision regarding the applicant. The first order is to be delivered immediately, the second in 120 days, and the third in 240 days. Each order is for $10,000. Costs of goods sold are 85 percent of sales, payable at the time the order is delivered. If the applicant defaults, no recoveries are expected. The applicant is undergoing a period of expansion and is brand loyal. The seller has estimated that the probability of default for the initial order is 20 percent, and that payment for this order is expected in 75 days if the applicant does not default. If the applicant does not default in paying for the initial order, it is expected that the probability of default for the second order will be 10 percent and the expected time to pay for that order will be 60 days. If the applicant does not default on the second order, the probability of default on the third order is 5 percent, and the expected time to pay for that order is 45 days. Indicate whether credit should be granted for the initial order. The seller's cost of capital is 13 percent; ignore taxes in your calculations and assume that all credit investigation costs have been spent.

6.3. A selling firm is taxable and wants to evaluate a credit applicant via the one-period, after-tax, net present-value approach. The appropriate discount rate for expected future flows is 10 percent per year. If the applicant does not pay in the normal course of business, it is expected that the applicant will be liquidated. The liquidation process will take two years, and trade creditors are expected to experience a 50 percent recovery rate, though the average recovery by the seller in such cases is 20 percent. If the applicant does not default, it is expected that payment will be received in 90 days. Based on a failure-forecasting function estimated with equal sample sizes of defaulted and nondefaulted firms, a probability of default of 80 percent for the applicant has been computed. However, only 1 percent of applicants actually default. The seller is in the 35 percent tax bracket, and the order amount is $30,000. The tax cost of the inventory to service the order will be $27,000, although the actual out-of-pocket cost to replenish inventory when the order is shipped will be only $26,000. Use a 360-day year.

a. Calculate the expected net present value of the sale if the firm accrues a reserve for bad debt based on average loss rates.

b. Calculate the expected net present value of the sale if the firm does not accrue a reserve, but instead writes off bad debts as they occur.

Selected Readings

Altman, E. I., R. B. Avery, R. A. Eisenbeis, and J. F. Sinkey, Jr., *Application of Classification Techniques in Business, Banking and Finance* (Greenwich, Conn.: JAI Press, 1981), pp. 255–306.

Beranek, W., and W. Taylor, "Credit-Scoring Models and the Cut-off Point—A Simplification," *Decision Sciences* (July 1976), pp. 394–404.

Bierman, H., Jr., and W. H. Hausman, "The Credit-Granting Decision," *Management Science* (April 1970), pp. B591–B532.

Mehta, D., "The Formulation of Credit Policy Models," *Management Science*, Vol. 15, No. 1 (October 1968), pp. B30–B50.

Scherr, F., "Estimating and Using Failure-Forecasting Functions: Some Problems and Some Proposed Solutions," *Baylor Business Studies* (January 1982), pp. 23–27.

Scherr, F., "Marginal Cost and Revenue Industrial Credit-Granting Models: Decision Implications and an Example Application," *Akron Business and Economic Review*, Vol. 13, No. 4 (Winter 1982), pp. 38–42.

Scherr, F., "The Industrial Credit-Granting Decision: Two-State Models Including Tax Effects," *Akron Business and Economic Review*, Vol. 16, No. 4 (Winter 1985), pp. 7–11.

Stowe, J. D., "An Integer Programming Solution for the Optimal Investigation/Credit Granting Sequence," *Financial Management* (Summer 1985), pp. 66–76.

Vopal Plastics[1]
Credit-Granting Decisions

On January 7, 1976, Dick Smith (the assistant credit manager of Gymbal Plastic Resins) had just finished a meeting with his boss, Bob Little. Mr. Little had received a call the previous day from Gymbal's salesman for Michigan regarding Vopal Plastics, a firm located in Muskegon. Vopal had been a customer in 1971 and 1972, but had not purchased anything from Gymbal for the past three years.

"I haven't looked at the Vopal file, Dick," Mr. Little had said. "You weren't here then, but when we were selling to them in 1972, they were slow payers. The salesman tells me that they lost money in 1974 and 1975; things are probably pretty grim there now from a financial standpoint. However, the salesman says that they are buying a lot of materials from our competitors. We could make some money if we could sell some plastic there, payments aren't too far beyond our terms of sale, and the risk of default isn't too great. The salesman says we might sell them as much as $50,000 per month, though the order we have in hand is for less than that. Check it out and get back to me."

[1]This case has been adopted form Iqbal Mathur and Frederick C. Scherr, *Cases in Financial Management* (New York: Macmillan, 1979), pp. 7–11.

Gymbal had maintained a running credit file on Vopal Plastics. This file contained credit agency reports and trade clearances (lists of amounts owing, amounts past due, terms of sale, and payment patterns to suppliers). Stock in Vopal was traded over-the-counter; audited financial statements from annual reports had been reproduced in credit agency presentations. The auditor was a major accounting firm, and the auditor's opinion contained no disclaimer.

From reading the credit agency reports, Dick ascertained that Vopal's recent history had contained some peaks and valleys. The firm had been founded in the late 1940s and was one of the oldest plastic-molding firms in the Muskegon area. Sales volumes had grown steadily in the 1969–1974 period, but had suffered a severe decline in 1975. In a mid-1975 message to stockholders, Vopal's president had attributed this decline to customers' caution in responding to the economic upturn underway at the time.

Profits, too, had recently declined. The years 1971 to 1973 had been profitable, but 1974 and 1975 had been loss years. The losses in these years had been attributed by Vopal's management to several factors. Profits in 1974 were good through three quarters, but significant losses were incurred in the fourth quarter due to diminished demand, rising raw material costs, customer resistance to price increases, rises in indirect costs, and a write-down of some assets. The latter factor alone had increased the net loss by $130,000. In 1975, the firm had attempted to return to profitability by reducing its selling and administrative expenses. An unprofitable operation was also closed. This closing resulted in a nonrecurring item that reduced income by $126,000. However, operations still resulted in a small net loss due to decreased sales volumes. Vopal's financial statements from 1971 through 1975 are presented in Exhibit 1.

According to their banker's comments, Vopal's relationships with their banks had always been satisfactory. In 1969, Vopal had consolidated a number of term loans from their bank into a medium-term secured loan. In 1973, this loan had been renegotiated. The firm's current banking arrangements were comprised of a long-term secured loan and a revolving credit arrangement in which three local banks participated. The covenants of this loan agreement were given in Vopal's annual report, and included restrictions on net worth, working capital, cash dividends, and capital spending. These loans were secured by all the firm's assets.

Dick Smith noted that the raw materials purchased by Vopal were not sold on cash discount terms. Vopal had always had a reputation in the trade as a slow-paying account, but Vopal's management had always made some excuse for this condition. Dick Smith used his credit file's trade clearances to make a table of Vopal's payment pattern to the trade over time and the reasons given for slowness (see Exhibit 2).

The usual credit-granting decision method used by Gymbal was the traditional approach. After analyzing Vopal Plastics via this judgmental analysis procedure and coming to a conclusion regarding the granting of credit to

the firm, Dick Smith was quite unsatisfied. It seemed to him that his analysis had been unnecessarily lengthy and time consuming. He also felt that his conclusion regarding the granting of credit to Vopal, while based on his best judgment regarding the positive and negative aspects of the applicant, was to some extent arbitrary and thus could easily be incorrect relative to the goals of his firm. These difficulties, which he felt made the judgmental analysis of credit applicants more of an art than a science, had troubled him for some time. Therefore, he decided to attempt a net present value analysis of the initial monthly order from Vopal, which was for 200,000 pounds of high-density polyethylene plastic pellets, to be sold to Vopal for $0.13 per pound.[2]

To obtain an estimate of Gymbal's cost for this material, Mr. Smith consulted with his firm's cost accounting department. After a period of discussion and analysis, Mr. Smith determined that the out-of-pocket costs of replacing the inventory sold to Vopal Plastics would be about $0.10 per pound for materials (chiefly ethylene gas and catalysts) and direct labor. However, because of the method used by Gymbal in valuing inventory for tax purposes, the tax bill for the sale would be based on a unit cost of $0.105 per pound. The sale to Vopal, were it made, would not affect Gymbal's present or future levels of capital expenditure; Gymbal's polyethylene production facility had substantial excess production capacity. Gymbal's terms of sale for polyethylene were net 30 days.

---

[2]While Gymbal's salesman for Michigan had estimated the potential sales volume to Vopal as ". . . as much as $50,000 per month," this estimate assumed that Gymbal would be the sole supplier of polyethylene to Vopal. Vopal's actual order represented only part of this total material use. Vopal usually bought product simultaneously from several suppliers of each type of plastic, placing a particular order with whichever supplier offered the best unit price and delivery terms at that time.

Exhibit 1

Vopal Plastics
Financial Statements for the Fiscal Years Ending 12/31/71 to 12/31/75
(rounded thousands of dollars)

Year End	12/31/71	12/31/72	12/31/73	12/31/74	12/31/75
			Statements of Income		
Sales	$4,639	$5,850	$7,184	$8,282	$6,207
Cost of Goods Sold	3,841	4,899	6,084	7,148	5,115
Gross Margin on Sales	798	951	1,100	1,134	1,092
Selling and Admin. Expenses	739	724	970	1,373	1,105
Operating Income.	59	227	130	−239	−13
Extraordinary Profit and Loss	−5	−28	84	0	−126
Earnings Before Tax	54	199	214	−239	−139
Income Taxes	−12	98	86	−98	0
Earnings After Taxes	$ 66	$ 101	$ 128	$−141	$−139
			Balance Sheets		
Cash	$ 48	$ 90	$ 90	$ 184	$ 319
Accounts Receivable	630	766	939	1,090	1,015
Inventories	888	725	958	1,261	785
Prepaid Expenses	40	52	61	60	47
Other Current Assets	19	19	21	114	17
Total Current Assets	$1,625	$1,652	$2,069	$2,709	$2,183
Fixed Assets less Depreciation	$1,288	$1,311	$1,298	$1,796	$1,791
Other Assets	259	121	78	43	22
Total Assets	$3,172	$3,084	$3,445	$4,548	$3,996
Accounts Payable	$ 722	$ 390	$ 510	$ 706	$ 685
Due on Credit Line			100	325	312
Current Long-Term Debt	218	210	404	373	352
Accruals	80	110	124	229	248
Other Current Liabilities	73	156	99	52	22
Total Current Liabilities	$1,093	$ 866	$1,237	$1,685	$1,619
Long-Term Debt	$ 596	$ 634	$ 499	$1,295	$ 951
Common Stock	96	96	93	93	90
Paid-In Capital	440	440	440	440	440
Retained Earnings	947	1,048	1,176	1,035	896
Total Equity	$1,483	$1,584	$1,709	$1,568	$1,426
Total Liabilities and Equity	$3,172	$3,084	$3,445	$4,548	$3,996

Exhibit 2

Vopal Plastics
Summary of Trade Payments and Management Comments, 1971 to 1975.

Year	Trade Payment Habit	Reasons Given for Slowness
1971	Generally pays 30 days beyond terms. Some supplies paid promptly.	"Surplus" cash was invested in Treasury bills.
1972	Generally pays 60 days beyond terms.	Lack of working capital.
1973	Generally pays promptly; some minor slowness of up to 20 days beyond terms.	Funds being used for expansion.
1974	Generally pays promptly; some minor slowness up to 20 days beyond terms.	Increases in cost of raw materials.
1975	Some prompt payment; some slowness up to 10 days beyond terms.	Slow-moving inventory.

In estimating a probability of default, Mr. Smith considered several approaches. One method was to start with the average default rate for firms in Vopal's industry and then judgmentally adjust this average rate based on the particular characteristics of Vopal Plastics. For example, if he decided that Vopal was less prone to default than the average firm in industry, the default rate would be adjusted downward.[3] Another method was to statistically analyze the characteristics of defaulted versus nondefaulted firms. To execute this last procedure, Mr. Smith first collected data on a sample of 10 recently defaulted firms and 10 randomly selected nondefaulted firms in Vopal's industry.[4] He decided to limit his analysis to the firms' liquidity and debt positions, which he considered to be the most important affectors of default from a financial standpoint. He then selected the current ratio and the ratio of total debt to total assets as measures of these financial aspects of firms. Exhibit 3 presents the data collected by Mr. Smith.

---

[3]On average, 30 of every 1,000 firms in Vopal's industry defaulted on trade debts. The average recovery by Gymbal on defaults was 10 percent and the average time from credit granting to default was three years. These later averages were very similar to those experienced by other firms in Gymbal's industry.

[4]This is too few data points for a complete statistical investigation, but Mr. Smith was experimenting with the technique.

Exhibit 3

Vopal Plastics
Ratio Data on a Sample of Firms.

Case No.	CA/CL	TD/TA
Defaulted Group:		
1	1.15	0.72
2	0.48	0.60
3	0.38	0.73
4	0.89	0.98
5	0.55	1.06
6	0.78	0.88
7	0.65	0.71
8	0.49	1.16
9	0.88	1.20
10	0.55	1.32
Mean	0.68	0.94
Nondefaulted Group:		
11	2.12	0.50
12	1.09	0.62
13	1.32	0.27
14	1.81	0.49
15	0.73	0.61
16	2.05	0.40
17	0.56	0.85
18	1.03	0.73
19	1.78	0.29
20	1.16	0.80
Mean	1.37	0.56

Exhibit 3 presents the data collected by Mr. Smith.

To estimate recovery rates to unsecured trade creditors if Vopal should default, Mr. Smith decided to assume that default would result in the liquidation of the firm. It was his experience that this outcome was the result of default on debts in the majority of cases in Vopal's industry. To estimate the recovery to creditors, Mr. Smith decided to use a "simulated asset sale" procedure. In this procedure, the most recent book values of the assets of the applicant were multiplied by estimated recovery rates to obtain estimated dollar re-coveries. The estimated liquidation recovery rates used by Mr. Smith, which were based on his evaluation of the quality of Vopal's assets, are presented in Exhibit 4. The liquidation of Vopal Plastics, should it occur, would be a relatively simple procedure. As soon as the firm defaulted, the banks participating in Vopal's bank borrowings would "offset" Vopal's cash balances against the debt owed them by the firm. This offset procedure would reduce their claims by the amount of the cash offset. Then, from the recovery on the sale of the remaining assets, "priority claims" would be paid first. Included here would be court and attorney fees, accrued wages, and accrued taxes.[5] Vopal owed no accrued taxes. Accrued wages were estimated by Mr. Smith at 75 percent of "Accruals"; he also estimated court and attorney fees at 15 percent of the total estimated recovery on assets. After priority claims were paid, recoveries on assets that had been pledged as security for Vopal's bank debts would then be assigned to secured creditors. If these recoveries were insufficient to satisfy these creditors, then the excess claims of these creditors would be classified with the claims of unsecured creditors. If there were more recoveries from these pledged assets than needed to satisfy the claims of secured creditors, then this excess would be available to satisfy the claims of the unsecured creditors. Unsecured creditors would then be paid on a pro rata basis (that is, if there was not enough money available to pay unsecured creditors in full, the same percentage of each claim would be paid). If there were any funds left over after priority claims and unsecured creditors were paid, these funds would go to equity holders.

---

[5]The priority portion of accrued wages is limited to a certain figure per employee, but this limitation would not be surpassed for any of the employees of Vopal, given the firm's current salary schedule and pay policies.

Exhibit 4

Vopal Plastics
Estimated Recoveries, Percent of Book Value

Account	Estimated Recovery
Accounts Receivable	85%
Inventories	65%
Prepaid Expenses	40%
Other Current Assets	0%
Fixed Assets less Depreciation	40%
Other Assets	0%

In discounting cash flows, Mr. Smith decided to use Gymbal's after-tax, weighted-average cost of capital. As of 1976, Gymbal's capital structure was composed of 46 percent debt and 54 percent equity. New bonds with covenants similar to those of the firm had recently been sold near par with promised coupon rates of 8.1 percent. Gymbal's marginal tax rate was 48 percent. Gymbal's stock was selling at $53 per share, and during 1975 had paid a dividend of $2.40 per share. Gymbal's dividends had historically grown at 6.1 percent per year.

chapter 7

Monitoring Accounts Receivable

In this, the final chapter in the management of accounts receivable, we discuss the *monitoring* of this asset. Accounts receivable is a major investment, and the continuous assessment of the state of this asset is a necessary function in the financial management of the firm. Monitoring is intended to fulfill this assessment function. We also review survey evidence on current practice in the management of accounts receivable.

WHY MONITOR ACCOUNTS RECEIVABLE?

In the prior two chapters, we discussed the formulation of the firm's terms-of-sale and credit-granting policies. These policies are made and implemented based on expectations regarding the behavior of the accounts receivable asset. In particular, the firm has expectations regarding the *turnover* of this asset and the amount of *bad debt* resulting from it. If these expectations are not fulfilled, this is a signal to management that the assumptions used in making the firm's terms-of-sale and credit-granting policies may be faulty, or that these policies are not being implemented properly. Deviations from the expected levels of turnover and of bad debt can signal several different problems. Three of these problems are discussed in the following paragraphs.

Changing Customer Payment Characteristics In contrast to longer-term assets and liabilities, working capital accounts turn over rapidly. If the average customer pays in 45 days, then in the course of a year, the accounts receivable asset will turn over eight times. The accounts receivable manager is dealing with *a constantly changing portfolio of receivables* as customers pay invoices, and new sales are made. Because of the rapid maturation of the assets in this portfolio, changes in the firm's customers or in economic and competitive conditions can impact receivables with remarkable suddenness. For example, economic slowdowns first manifest themselves in slowing sales *and in slowing collections on these sales*. Since turning receivables into cash is a critical part of the selling firm's working capital cycle, changes in the pattern of cash flows from the receivables assets have important implications for management.

Inaccurate Policy Forecasts In the interests of shareholders, managers formulate terms-of-sale and credit-granting policies based on net present value rules. To calculate these net present values, management must estimate the effects of these policies on bad debt, turnover, and other relevant variables. For example, in deciding whether to change its terms of sale, the firm will make estimates of the new turnover of receivables, bad debt levels, and sales effects. There is substantial uncertainty in this estimation process. If there are deviations from these expectations, the policies need to be reconsidered and reanalyzed so that shareholder wealth is maximized. Therefore, firms need to compare the outcomes of policy with what was estimated in their formulation.

Improper Policy Implementation When the managers of a firm set policies, these policies must be implemented. The details of the policies, the rationales for them, and the means to carry them out must be given to the employees who will execute them. If the implementation is faulty, shareholder wealth will not be enhanced. Difficulties in the implementation of policies may stem from problems in communicating the policies to employees, from inappropriate evaluations of employees relative to these policies, or from any number of other sources.

Deviations from the expected levels of turnover and bad debt expense can signal such implementation problems. For example, suppose that a firm sells on net 30-day terms. The firm's top marketing and credit managers have analyzed the firm's credit-granting and terms-of-sale policies and determined that the most advantageous level of accounts receivable turnover is 40 days and that bad debt expense should be 1 percent of sales. Suppose further that the individuals who manage credit relations with the firm's customers do not understand this, but believe that the lower these statistics, the better for the firm. Alternatively, the evaluation systems for these employees could be such that they are penalized for bad debts and payments beyond terms, despite top management's beliefs about the most advantageous levels of these variables. In such circumstances, the employees may make decisions in such a way as to produce turnover of 35 days and bad debt expense of 0.5 percent of sales. To achieve these results, the employees may be turning away profitable but risky customers. By monitoring these statistics, the firm's management can detect and correct deviations from the intended policy that result from improper policy implementation.

Monitoring *provides signals* of deviations from expectations. When a signal is detected, *it is up to managers to investigate and to assess the reason for deviation*. The managers must then take the necessary corrective action, and the type of necessary action will vary with the cause of the deviation. If the problem is changing customer payment patterns or inaccurate prior estimations, the credit-granting and terms-of-sale decisions of the firm need to be reanalyzed based on this new data. However, if the problem is in implementation, the firm's managers need to assess why the firm's policies are not being executed. In any case, *both positive and negative deviations* in accounts receivable statistics need to be investigated, since deviations in either direction signal differences from the results that management believe to be the most advantageous for the firm.

The monitoring process is a comparison of expectations and outcomes. Within the firm, these expectations are captured in the form of *budgets*. These budgets are part of the accounting control system of the firm, a system intended to detect deviations from policy. Some of the deviations from budgeted figures will represent one or more of the problems outlined previously, while others will represent random events. For example, a delay in the receipt of some customer checks (and thus a slowing of accounts receivable turnover) might be due to a strike of postal employees (a random event), and not due to any factors controllable by the selling firm. Since the investigation of deviations from expectations is a costly and time-consuming process, managers do not want to expend effort on this process when the deviations from expectations occur because of such random processes. The task of monitoring receivables, then, is to signal *nonrandom deviations from the budgeted receivables statistics*.

The statistics that have a primary bearing on credit decisions are levels of sales, collection expense, receivables turnover, and bad debt expense. The monitoring of sales levels and collection expense can be addressed in a straightforward fashion via the firm's systems of accounting controls.[1] However, *the monitoring of accounts receivable turnover and bad debt expense is a relatively tricky process when firms experience fluctuations in sales over time*. Unfortunately, fluctuations in the sales of firms due to economic, seasonal, and product life-cycle effects are more the rule than the exception. In the following sections, biases in the simpler monitoring tools when sales fluctuate are discussed, and better tools for this monitoring process are developed.

BIAS IN SIMPLE MEASURES OF RECEIVABLES TURNOVER

The sales volumes of firms fluctuate, and therefore so do dollar investments in receivables. In monitoring the collection (turnover) of accounts receivable, management wants to use a methodology that measures the re-

---

[1]For an approach to the assessment of sales effects in accounts receivable management decisions, see G. W. Gallinger and A. J. Ifflander, "Monitoring Accounts Receivable Using Variance Analysis," *Financial Management* (Winter 1986), pp. 69–76 and particularly pp. 74–76. As discussed in prior chapters, collection costs are usually very small relative to other credit-related costs; we do not discuss the monitoring of collection costs in this text.

lationship between the firm's receivables and its sales, *regardless of fluctuations in sales level*. Ideally, the methodology meets at least three criteria: (1) it *should not* signal a deviation from expectations in the payment behavior of the firm's customers when *none* has occurred; (2) it *should* signal a deviation when one *has* occurred; and (3) it should be simple to implement and to understand.[2] Two common methods of receivables' monitoring are used for this purpose: the *days' sales outstanding* statistics (also known as average collection period) and the *aging fraction* statistics.[3] Unfortunately, both of these approaches to the accounts receivable monitoring problem are seriously flawed with regard to the first two of these three criteria. When sales vary over time, both days' sales outstanding and aging fractions will give inappropriate signals. To see this and to understand how these statistics are computed, let us calculate them for an example situation.

Assume that a firm makes 5 percent of sales for cash. Sixty-five percent of a month's sales are paid in the next month, 25 percent in the second month following, and the remaining 5 percent in the third month following the sale. This pattern of customer payment does not vary over the year, but monthly sales volume is seasonal. The firm experiences constant sales volumes of $5 million per month from November through March; sales then increase through April to a seasonal peak of $9 million per month in May, then decrease to a low of $1 million per month in September, finally climbing back to $5 million a month in November. The important thing to remember is that, by assumption, the payment habits of customers are the same throughout the year: customers pay in an average 39.0 days.[4] Sales average $5 million per month, and there is no overall trend in sales except for seasonality.

This situation is presented in Table 7-1. The accounts receivable balances are computed using the collection rates in the upper left-hand corner of this table. For example, let us examine the $10.9 million receivables balance for May. May's sales are $9 million. Of these, 5 percent are for cash, so 95 percent ($8.55 million) are outstanding as of the end of May. Also outstanding at the end of May are receivables from sales in April and March. April's sales were $7 million. Of these, 5 percent were for cash, and 65 percent were collected during May. As of the end of May, the remaining 30 percent ($2.1 million) are outstanding. March's sales were $5 million; by the end of May, all but 5 percent have been collected (these will be collected in June); this 5 percent is $0.25 million. The firm's end-of-May receivables are thus $8.55 million plus $2.1 million plus $0.25 million, or $10.9 million.

---

[2]For an excellent discussion of these points, see W. G. Lewellen and R. W. Johnson, "Better Way to Monitor Accounts Receivable," *Harvard Business Review* (May–June 1972), pp. 101–109.

[3]See B. K. Stone, "The Payment-Patterns Approach to Forecasting and Control of Accounts Receivable," *Financial Management* (Autumn 1976), pp. 65–82.

[4]This is the weighted average based on the assumed payment pattern, and equal to 5 percent times zero days to pay, plus 65 percent times 30 days to pay, plus 25 percent times 60 days to pay, plus 5 percent times 90 days to pay.

Table 7-1. Days' Sales Outstanding and Aging Fractions Statistics for Example (dollar figures in rounded thousands).

Cash Sales	5%	
Coll., First Prior Mo.	65%	
Coll., Second Prior Mo.	25%	
Coll., Third Prior Mo.	5%	

Month	Jan.	Feb.	March	April	May	June	July	August	Sept.	Oct.	Nov.	Dec.	Jan.
Sales	$5,000	$5,000	$5,000	$7,000	$ 9,000	$7,000	$5,000	$3,000	$1,000	$3,000	$5,000	$5,000	$5,000
Out., Current Month	4,750	4,750	4,750	6,650	8,550	6,650	4,750	2,850	950	2,850	4,750	4,750	4,750
Out., First Prior Mo.		1,500	1,500	1,500	2,100	2,700	2,100	1,500	900	300	900	1,500	1,500
Out., Second Prior Mo.			250	250	250	350	450	350	250	150	50	150	250
Receivables Outstanding			$6,500	$8,400	$10,900	$9,700	$7,300	$4,700	$2,100	$3,300	$5,700	$6,400	$6,500
DSO (2-Month Average)			39.00	42.00	40.88	36.38	36.50	35.25	31.50	49.50	42.75	38.40	39.00
Aging Fractions:													
0 to 30 days old			0.73	0.79	0.78	0.69	0.65	0.61	0.45	0.86	0.83	0.74	0.73
31 to 60 days old			0.23	0.18	0.19	0.28	0.29	0.32	0.43	0.09	0.16	0.23	0.23
61 to 90 days old			0.04	0.03	0.02	0.04	0.06	0.07	0.12	0.05	0.01	0.02	0.04
Total			1.00	1.00	1.00	1.00	1.00	1.00	1.00	1.00	1.00	1.00	1.00

The days' sales outstanding (DSO) statistic is interpreted as the average number of days of sales that are still owed at the end of the month being evaluated. It is computed as:

$$\text{DSO} = (\text{month-end receivables/average sales}) (30 \text{ days/month}) \quad (7\text{-}1)$$

The average sales figure may use any of several averaging periods; in Table 7-1, it is computed as the average of the last two months' sales. Thus, for May, average sales are $8 million (May's sales are $9 million and April's sales are $7 million) and the DSO is:

$$\text{DSO} = (10.9 \text{ million/8 million}) (30 \text{ days/month}) = 40.88 \text{ days} \quad (7\text{-}2)$$

The aging fractions are computed by dividing the outstanding receivables of a particular age by the total receivables balance at the end of that month. For example, at the end of May, $8.55 million in receivables are one month old or less. Since there are $10.9 million in total receivables, the aging fraction for receivables less than one month old (between zero and 30 days) is 8.55/10.9 = 0.78. The remaining figures for May are similarly computed.

An examination of the monthly DSO and aging fractions figures in Table 7-1 shows substantial variation, to say the least. DSO reaches a minimum of 31.5 days in September and a maximum of 49.5 days in October. The aging fraction for zero to 30 days, for example, ranges from 0.45 to 0.86. *This should seem distressing since by construction, customer payments followed exactly the same pattern in every single month.* What has happened relates to *the comparison of receivables and sales from different months.* It is a "comparing-apples-and-oranges" problem. When we equally weight receivables resulting from varying sales, we get distorted results. Both of these measures of receivables do this, and therefore both give inappropriate signals. The manager of a credit department using DSO to monitor receivables behavior and who observes the set of measures in Table 7-1 may believe that payment patterns had varied widely over the year, when in fact they were uniform. Further, this example is for a firm with only one variation in sales pattern, that of seasonality. In other situations, there may be an overall trend in sales and changes in the proportion of sales made under various terms of sale. These fluctuations, because of measurement errors, can mask true differences between actual and expected payment behavior. Because of the way they compare sales and receivables, *DSO and aging fractions give the proper signals of receivables movement only in the special case where sales exhibit no fluctuations over time.*

Adherents of these methods may counter that some simple modification may negate this measurement problem. In particular, it can be contended that the judicious selection of a longer or shorter averaging period for sales in computing DSO may result in a more accurate representation of true payment behavior. Unfortunately, this is not correct. As Lewellen and Johnson put it:

> [N]o single averaging period will consistently yield a correct appraisal where there are fluctuations in sales. In fact, within any given sales interval, even the *direction* of the signal depends on the averaging period chosen.[5]

To see this, examine Table 7-2, in which the DSO figures for the example are presented for sales averaging periods of one month, two months, and three months. The errors in these assessments, relative to the known payment pattern, are also given. These errors vary widely among the averaging periods, with none of the periods consistently producing an accurate measure. In fact, the two-month averaging period turns out to be the most accurate for this example problem in the sense that the greatest absolute error for this method is "only" 10.5 days, as opposed to 24.0 days for the one-month averaging period and 18.0 days for the three-month averaging period.[6]

Better Tools for Monitoring Accounts Receivable While knowledgeable managers might try to judgmentally adjust DSO or aging fraction figures to reflect these inaccuracies, it would be very hard for them to know how much adjustment is necessary. A more appropriate approach is to use a tool that is not subject to distortions caused by sales fluctuations. In this section, three such tools are examined: the ratios of receivables outstanding to original sales,[7] customer's payment proportions,[8] and the sales-weighted DSO.[9,10]

---

[5]Lewellen and Johnson, "Better Way to Monitor."

[6]The conclusion that the two-month period is the least inaccurate is a product of the particular data used in this example and does not hold for all receivables monitoring situations.

[7]The measure is recommended in Lewellen and Johnson, "Better Way to Monitor." Also see W. G. Lewellen and R. O. Edminster, "A General Model of Accounts Receivable Analysis and Control," *Journal of Financial and Quantitative Analysis* (March 1973), pp. 195–206.

[8]See Stone, "The Payment-Patterns Approach."

[9]See M. D. Carpenter and J. E. Miller, "A Reliable Framework for Monitoring Accounts Receivable," *Financial Management* (Winter 1979), pp. 37–40.

[10]One method not discussed in this chapter is the Markov chain approach to monitoring payment behavior. The Markov chain approach is primarily oriented toward monitoring payments on consumer installment credit where payment patterns may not exhibit seasonal or cyclical fluctuation, rather than patterns of trade credit which may fluctuate with sales. For an example in the application of this approach, see J. G. Kallberg and K. Parkinson, *Current Asset Management* (New York: Wiley, 1984), pp. 182–84.

Table 7-2. Days' Sales Outstanding for Various Sales Averaging Periods (dollar figures in rounded thousands).

Cash Sales — 5%
Coll., First Prior Mo. — 65%
Coll., Second Prior Mo. — 25%
Coll., Third Prior Mo. — 5%

DSO Averaging Per. — 60 days

Month	Jan.	Feb.	March	April	May	June	July	August	Sept.	Oct.	Nov.	Dec.	Jan.
Sales	$5,000	$5,000	$5,000	$7,000	$ 9,000	$7,000	$5,000	$3,000	$1,000	$3,000	$5,000	$5,000	$5,000
Out., Current Month	4,750	4,750	4,750	6,650	8,550	6,650	4,750	2,850	950	2,850	4,750	4,750	4,750
Out., First Prior Mo.		1,500	1,500	1,500	2,100	2,700	2,100	1,500	900	300	900	1,500	1,500
Out., Second Prior Mo.			250	250	250	350	450	350	250	150	50	150	250
Receivables Outstanding			$6,500	$8,400	$10,900	$9,700	$7,300	$4,700	$2,100	$3,300	$5,700	$6,400	$6,500
DSO (1-Month Average)			39.00	36.00	36.33	41.57	43.80	47.00	63.00	33.00	34.20	38.40	39.00
Actual Collections Rate			39.00	39.00	39.00	39.00	39.00	39.00	39.00	39.00	39.00	39.00	39.00
Over or (Under)			0.00	−3.00	−2.67	2.57	4.80	8.00	24.00	−6.00	−4.80	−.60	0.00
DSO (2-Month Average)			39.00	42.00	40.88	36.38	36.50	35.25	31.50	49.50	42.75	38.40	39.00
Actual Collections Rate			39.00	39.00	39.00	39.00	39.00	39.00	39.00	39.00	39.00	39.00	39.00
Over or (Under)			0.00	3.00	1.88	−2.63	−2.50	−3.75	−7.50	10.50	3.75	−.60	0.00
DSO (3-Month Average)			39.00	44.47	46.71	37.96	31.29	28.20	21.00	42.43	57.00	44.31	39.00
Actual Collections Rate			39.00	39.00	39.00	39.00	39.00	39.00	39.00	39.00	39.00	39.00	39.00
Over or (Under)			0.00	5.47	7.71	−1.04	−7.71	−10.80	−18.00	3.43	18.00	5.31	0.00

Table 7-3. Example of Ratios of Receivables Outstanding, Payment Proportions, and Sales-Weighted DSO.

	A	B	C	D	E	F	G	H	I	J	K	L	M	N
1	Cash Sales	5%							5%					
2	Coll., First Prior Mo.	65%							55%					
3	Coll., Second Prior Mo.	25%							20%					
4	Coll., Third Prior Mo.	5%							20%					
5														
6	Month	Jan.	Feb.	March	April	May	June	July	August	Sept.	Oct.	Nov.	Dec.	Jan.
7	Sales	5000	5000	5000	7000	9000	7000	5000	3000	1000	3000	5000	5000	5000
8														
9	Out., Current Month	4750	4750	4750	6650	8550	6650	4750	2850	950	2850	4750	4750	4750
10	Out., First Prior Mo.		1500	1500	1500	2100	2700	2100	2000	1200	400	1200	2000	2000
11	Out., Second Prior Mo.			250	250	250	350	450	1400	1000	600	200	600	1000
12														
13	Receivables Outstanding			6500	8400	10900	9700	7300	6250	3150	3850	6150	7350	7750
14														
15	Ratios of Receivables Outstanding:													
16														
17	Current Month			.95	.95	.95	.95	.95	.95	.95	.95	.95	.95	.95
18	First Prior Month			.30	.30	.30	.30	.30	.40	.40	.40	.40	.40	.40
19	Second Prior Month			.05	.05	.05	.05	.05	.20	.20	.20	.20	.20	.20
20														
21	Payment Proportions:													
22														
23	Current Month			.05	.05	.05	.05	.05	.05	.05	.05	.05	.05	.05
24	First Prior Month			.65	.65	.65	.65	.65	.55	.55	.55	.55	.55	.55
25	Second Prior Month			.25	.25	.25	.25	.25	.10	.20	.20	.20	.20	.20
26														
27	Sales-Weighted DSO:													
28														
29	Contribution, Current Month's Sales			28.50	28.50	28.50	28.50	28.50	28.50	28.50	28.50	28.50	28.50	28.50
30	Contribution, Fst Prior Month's Sales			9.00	9.00	9.00	9.00	9.00	12.00	12.00	12.00	12.00	12.00	12.00
31	Contribution, Snd Prior Month's Sales			1.50	1.50	1.50	1.50	1.50	6.00	6.00	6.00	6.00	6.00	6.00
32														
33				39.00	39.00	39.00	39.00	39.00	46.50	46.50	46.50	46.50	46.50	46.50

An example spreadsheet for the computation of these three measures is presented in Table 7-3. In this spreadsheet, the sales figures for all months and the receivables balances for March through July are the same as in Tables 7-1 and 7-2. We have assumed that a change in payment patterns occurs in August and that this change is in effect through the remainder of the table. The outstanding receivables in this table have been calculated by applying the collection rates in cells B1 to B4 and I1 to I4 to the sales in row 7. For example, cell D10 contains "$(1-((B1-B3)/100))*C7$"; since 5 percent of sales are for cash (B1) and 65 percent of sales are collected during the first month (B2), the receivables balance after one month will be $(1 - (0.05 + 0.65))$, or 30 percent. Applying this to sales for February (cell C7) gives the $1.5 million balance outstanding from February at the end of March. This spreadsheet is intended to show that these three tools *do not* provide improper signals when *no* deviation from expected payment patterns has occurred and *do* provide signals when a change *has* in fact occurred.

The *ratios of receivables outstanding to original sales* remove the confusion caused by fluctuating sales levels by comparing only "oranges and oranges." That is, receivables outstanding at any particular time are compared *only to sales in the period during which the receivables were generated.* This gives a true picture of receivables payment behavior. The ratios of receivables outstanding in Table 7-1 appear in rows 17 through 19 and are computed by dividing the receivables outstanding from a particular month by the sales from that month. For example, in May, the ratios of receivables outstanding are 0.95, 0.30, and 0.05. These are computed in cells F17 through F19. For example, F18 contains "$F10/E7$" since cell F10 contains the balance of receivables which are one month old and cell E7 contains last month's sales (that is, sales for April). The ratio of 0.30 is receivables of $2.1 million (the receivables still outstanding from April as of the end of May) divided by $7 million (sales for April).

The *payment proportions* figures displayed in rows 23 through 25 of the table are computed as the proportion of a month's sales that are collected in the month being analyzed. Looking again at the figures for May, the payment proportions are 0.05, 0.65, and 0.25. These are calculated by comparing changes in receivables balances with sales for the month during which the receivables originated. For example, during May, the receivables balance from sales in April was reduced from $6.65 million (the balance as of the end of April from April's sales, in cell E9) to $2.1 million (in cell F10); therefore during May, $4.55 million of receivables from April's sales must have been collected. This figure divided by April's sales of $7 million gives the 65 percent payment proportion. Thus, cell F24 contains "$(E9-F10)/E7$" since sales for April are found in cell E7.

Sales-weighted DSO allows for fluctuations in sales by weighting the receivables balances by the sales incurred in the month during which the receivables were generated. The sales-weighted DSO (SWDSO) can be calculated as:

$$SWDSO = \sum_{t=0}^{n} \left(\frac{AR_t}{S_t} \right) (30 \text{ days/month}) \qquad (7\text{-}3)$$

where t is the month of sale, n is the number of months for which receivables are outstanding, AR_t is the outstanding accounts receivable balance from month t, and S_t is the sales in month t. However, the sales-weighted DSO is actually a good deal simpler than this. Recognizing that AR_t/S_t is the ratio of receivables outstanding from month t (call this RRO_t) then equation (7-3) becomes:

$$SWDSO = \sum_{t=0}^{n} (RRO_t) (30 \text{ days/month}) \qquad (7\text{-}4)$$

and factoring out the 30 days/month:

$$SWDSO = (30 \text{ days/month}) \sum_{t=0}^{n} (RRO_t) \qquad (7\text{-}5)$$

The sales-weighted DSO is therefore the sum of the ratios of receivables outstanding times 30 days/month.

To calculate the SWDSOs in Table 7-3, equation (7-4) was used. The contributions to the SWDSO for each month were computed by multiplying each of the ratios of receivables outstanding in rows 17 through 19 by 30 days per month. These figures appear in rows 29 through 31 of the spreadsheet. For example, the contribution of April's receivables outstanding based on April's sales to the SWDSO for May can be found in cell F30, which contains "F18*30". The SWDSO for May is the sum of the contributions to this statistic for the three months from which receivables are outstanding, and appears in cell F33. This cell contains "@SUM(F29 . . . F31)".

All these three methods do a much better job than aging fractions or traditional DSO in monitoring payment behavior since they do not give false signals when no deviations from the expected payment pattern have occurred and do give proper signals when such deviations have actually occurred. While aging fractions and DSO fluctuate considerably during the period from January through July (see Table 7-1), when there are really no deviations from historic payment patterns, all three new measures do not vary over this period. However, when payment patterns actually *do* change in August, all three new methods accurately show this change.

Using These Tools to Monitor Payment Patterns The proper use of these measures as management-by-exception tools requires the construction of confidence intervals around their expected values. In this way, the chance that

Table 7-4. *Example Historic Data on Ratios of Receivables Outstanding.*		
	Mean	*Standard Deviation*
Current Month	0.950	0.015
First Prior Month	0.300	0.020
Second Prior Month	0.050	0.003

costly management investigation will be triggered by random events is reduced. To construct these confidence intervals, the analyst may obtain a sample of data on these measures from the period of time during which fluctuations in the measures are thought to have been random. The frequency distribution of these measures can then be compared to various probability distributions based on goodness-of-fit tests, or it can be assumed that the data fits some known probability distribution.[11] Given the probability distribution, the appropriate confidence intervals are then constructed based on statistics calculated from the sample.

For example, suppose that a firm had decided that there were no variations, except for random ones, in its collection patterns over the last two years. These patterns were, on average, in keeping with those expected from the firm's accounts receivable management strategies. The firm's managers monitor their receivables via ratios of receivables outstanding. Using the last two years of monthly data, the standard deviations for these ratios have been computed; these are presented in Table 7-4. The firm believes that the data are distributed as Student's t.[12] The managers of the firm want to investigate if there is a 90 percent chance that deviations from the expected payment patterns have occurred. Deviations either above or below the expected levels are to be investigated.

To signal the managers of such deviations, a two-tailed test is needed with 5 percent of the distribution in each tail. Since there are 24 observations, the sample statistics in Table 7-4 have 23 degrees of freedom. From a table of the Student's t distribution, for a one-tailed test, the appropriate t-statistic is 1.714. That is, with 23 degrees of freedom, 90 percent of the Student's t distribution occurs between t-statistics of -1.714 and $+1.714$. For the ratio of receivables outstanding from the first prior month, the confidence interval is then 0.300 plus and minus 1.714 times the standard deviation of 0.020, or between 0.265 and 0.334. If, in the future, the ratio of receivables outstanding

[11]If lagged regression has been used to estimate payment proportions, then the estimated standard errors of the payment proportions can be used in construction of confidence intervals.

[12]We use the Student's t-test here for simplicity. However, students with some sophistication in statistics should note that the distributions of ratios of receivables outstanding are bounded (they cannot take on values above one or below zero).

Table 7-5. Example Confidence Intervals for Ratios of Receivables Outstanding.

	Mean	Standard Deviation	LCL	UCL
Current Month	0.950	0.015	0.924	0.976
First Prior Month	0.300	0.020	0.266	0.334
Second Prior Month	0.050	0.003	0.045	0.055

The lower confidence limit (LCL) and the upper confidence limit (UCL) are based on a 90 percent confidence interval, 23 degrees of freedom, and a Student's t-distribution; see text.

from the first prior month falls outside this range, management would investigate payment behavior for payments from this month. Otherwise, no investigation of these payments would be undertaken. Similarly computed control limits for the other two ratios of receivables outstanding in Table 7-4 are presented in Table 7-5.

In examining these tables, readers will notice that the example standard deviations are much smaller than the expected values of these ratios of receivables outstanding. The coefficients of variation are less than 10 percent. The small standard deviations relative to the means in this example are not atypical. Indeed, random shifts in payment patterns are usually relatively minor for firms of substantial size. Large- and medium-sized firms receive hundreds of checks per month; this large sample size tends to negate deviations in payment patterns caused by the random receipt or nonreceipt of checks from individual customers or groups of customers.[13] This is why the choice of an accounts receivable monitoring tool that accurately measures payment patterns is so useful. Since random movements are minor, small deviations in payment patterns can be quickly detected and acted upon. Monitoring instruments that allow the measurement of nonrandom changes in payment patterns to be overwhelmed by measurement errors caused by fluctuations in sales are therefore a good deal less effective than are more accurate measures.

Deciding Which Method to Use in Monitoring Collections In prior sections, we had discussed five monitoring methods: traditional DSO, aging fractions, ratios of receivables outstanding, payment proportions, and the sales-weighted DSO (SWDSO). The practicing manager must choose one or more methods of monitoring the firm's receivables portfolio. While the first two methods can be inaccurate in their measurement of payment behavior,

---

[13]However, for smaller firms who receive fewer checks per month, the standard deviations of collection patterns may be larger relative to their expected values.

other arguments are sometimes made in their favor. Typical arguments for these methods include: (1) they are simple to compute, and (2) industry figures are reported—particularly with regard to DSO—giving management some standard of comparison in assessing trends in the payment behavior of customers. However, none of these arguments holds much weight. Regarding the first, the additional effort necessary to compute performance statistics for more accurate methods is very small. The second argument would be important only if the firm was limited to the computation of one measure of payment behavior. However, there is no reason that the firm cannot use an accurate measure of payment behavior to assess its *own* patterns of receipts and *another* measure to compare this behavior to published figures.

The choice of receivables monitoring methods for internal control purposes is then among the more accurate methods: ratios of receivables outstanding, payment proportions, SWDSO, and other similar measures.[14] Each of these measures has advantages and disadvantages. Measures such as ratios of receivables outstanding and payment proportions indicate payment performance via a series of numbers, while SWDSO is a single-number measure. Therefore, SWDSO is simpler to interpret. However, this single figure (while an accurate aggregate measure) may hide deviations from expectations among the collection rates from the various sales periods. One possible system is to utilize SWDSO as a screen for the examination of payment behaviors. In this system, confidence limits would be computed for SWDSO based on the firm's expected payment patterns and an estimate of the random variation around these expectations. If the firm's actual SWDSO fell outside these confidence limits, investigation would be triggered. The first step in this investigation might be the examination of some measure of collection rates or receivables balances from individual periods. Such an investigation process is described in the next section.

INVESTIGATING PAYMENT PATTERNS USING "VARIANCE ANALYSIS"

Let us assume that some event (such as the SWDSO falling outside its confidence limits) has triggered an analysis of the payment behaviors of the firm's customers. Investigation of the deviations from expectations is then

---

[14]The accuracy of these methods should not be overstated. They will not detect changes in payment behavior that occur *within* the month. For example, if customers who had paid near the middle of the month choose instead to pay near the end of the month, this would go undetected by all the measures discussed herein. More microscopic measures of receivables performance are necessary to detect changes of this sort; see G. N. Engler and D. V. Considine, "Excess Collection Days: A New Concept in Monitoring Accounts Receivable," paper presented at the Eastern Finance Association's 1985 Annual Meeting, available from Considine at California State University, Los Angeles.

required. One possible tool in this investigation to determine the sources of the problem and the amounts involved is "variance analysis."[15] This tool will determine how much of the total fluctuation of the balance in the accounts receivable account has been caused by sales discrepancies and how much has been caused by collection discrepancies.[16]

Variance analysis is a very simple tool. The differences between the *actual* and *budgeted* accounts receivable balances are affected by two variables: the level of sales and the ratios of receivables outstanding. In variance analysis, the effects of sales and collections on balances are separated by generating a third set of balances: the accounts receivable balances given the *actual* sales figures but *as if the expected ratios of receivables outstanding had occurred*. In this system, the *total dollar variance* is the difference between the actual and budgeted receivables balances. The portion of this variance caused *by collections* is the difference between the actual receivables and the third set of balances (actual sales times expected ratios of receivables outstanding). The remaining variance, which is equal to this third set of balances minus the budgeted accounts receivable balance, is due to sales effects.[17]

To see how this system works and the insights it can lend, let us address an example problem. A firm has made a three-month budget assuming sales of $100,000 for the first month, $200,000 for the second month, and $300,000 for the final month. Ratios of receivables outstanding are projected as 0.90 for sales from the month just completed, 0.40 for sales two months ago, and 0.10 for sales three months ago. Therefore, the expected SWDSO statistic is 42.00 ((0.90 + 0.40 + 0.10) times 30 via equation (7-5)). The expected

---

[15]The basic published references on this technique are Gallinger and Ifflander, "Monitoring Accounts Receivable," and J. A. Gentry and J. M. De La Garza, "A Generalized Model for Monitoring Accounts Receivable," *Financial Management* (Winter 1985), pp. 28–38. Here, "variance analysis" takes the accounting meaning of variation from budget, rather than the statistical meaning of variation around the mean.

[16]Some firms monitor receivables balances rather than payment behavior. When these balances are larger or smaller than budgeted balances, these firms want to know how much of this discrepancy is caused by sales effects and how much by collection effects. Also, while this discussion concentrates on the firm's expectations regarding collection rates, the variance analysis technique can also be used to assess the changes in sales from a change in credit policy. See Gallinger and Ifflander, "Monitoring Accounts Receivable," pp. 74–76.

[17]There is actually another type of variance, called the "joint effect" variance, which occurs because of the interaction between the sales and collection effects. Following Gallinger and Ifflander, "Monitoring Accounts Receivable," we have included joint effect variance with the variance caused by differences in collection rates. For more discussion of joint effect variance and its implications in monitoring accounts receivable, see V. Srinivasan and Y. Kim, "Credit Management: A Variance Framework for Monitoring Accounts Receivable," paper presented at the Financial Management Association's 1987 Annual Meeting and available from Srinivasan at Northeastern University.

accounts receivable balance at the end of the third month is $360,000 ((0.90) (300,000) + (0.40) (200,000) + (0.10) (100,000)). At the end of the third month, the actual SWDSO statistic is 46.80, which is outside the confidence limits set by management, and the accounts receivable balance is $513,000. Since the SWDSO statistic is outside the confidence levels, investigation of differences from expectations is undertaken. Actual sales for the first month were $120,000, for the second month were $250,000, and for the third month were $400,000. At the end of the third month, there is $380,000 outstanding from the third month's sales, $115,000 outstanding from the second month's sales, and $18,000 outstanding from the first month's sales.

We want to assess the differences between expected and actual collections and the effect of these differences on the firm's accounts receivable balances. Note first that since the SWDSO statistic is corrected for sales trends, the difference from the expected value of this statistic *cannot be merely a sales effect; it must arise from collections*. Variance analysis helps highlight the source of this deviation in collections and assess its effect on accounts receivable investment.

The required analysis is presented in Table 7-6. Columns B and C contain the budgeted sales for the three-month period (starting with the last month) and the budgeted accounts receivable balances. Column D contains the budgeted ratios of receivables outstanding. Columns E, F, and G contain the actual sales, actual ending accounts receivable, and actual ratios of receivables outstanding, with these ratios computed as the receivables from a month divided by the actual sales for that month. The total variance is the difference between the actual ending receivables balance of $513,000 and the projected balance of $360,000, and appears in cell H12 (which contains "F9-C9").

However, not all of this variance of $153,000 is due to differences from expectations in the collection rates from customers. Column H contains accounts receivable balances projected by using *actual* sales figures but *projected* ratios of receivables outstanding. For example, the budgeted ratio of receivables outstanding from the first prior month is 0.90. If 90 percent of the prior month's actual sales were outstanding as of the end of the third month, the accounts receivable balance for that month would be $360,000 (0.90 times $400,000). Thus, cell H5 contains "D5*E5", and cells H6 and H7 contain parallel entries. The projected accounts receivable balance, *using budgeted collection rates*, is $472,000, which appears in cell H9. Of the $153,000 variance, $41,000 ($513,000 minus $472,000) is caused by the unexpectedly slow collection rates from customers. The remaining $112,000 ($472,000 minus $360,000) was caused by unexpectedly large sales. These two parts of the total variance appear in cells H13 and H14, which contain "F9-H9" and "H9-C9" respectively.

An examination of the ratios of receivables outstanding in columns D and G shows that each is larger than original expectations. Therefore, col-

Table 7-6. Computation of Sales and Collection Variances for Example Problem.

! A !!	B !!	C !!	D !!	E !!	F !!	G !!	H !!	I !
1 Month	Proj. Sales	Proj. A.R. Balance	Proj. RRO	Actual Sales	Actual A.R. Balance	Actual RRO	Actual Sales, Proj. RRO	Collection Variance by Month
2								
3								
4								
5 3	300	270	.90	400	380	.95	360	20
6 2	200	80	.40	250	115	.46	100	15
7 1	100	10	.10	120	18	.15	12	6
8								
9 Totals	600	360	1.40	770	513	1.56	472	41
10		SWDSO	42.00			46.80		
11								
12					Total Variance		153	
13					Collection Var.		41	
14					Sales Variance		112	

lections have been unexpectedly slow from sales made in *all months* of the forecast. However, since sales have been rising over time, the major collection effect that has caused an increase in receivables balances *has come from the final month's sales*. This is seen in column I, where the variance in the receivables balances is computed for receivables from each month. Cells I5 through I7 contain formulas for the difference in the corresponding cells in columns F and G (for example, I5 contains "F5-G5"). Slower receipts from sales in the third month account for $20,000 of the $41,000 variance which is due to collections.

Now that the patterns and amounts of the differences between the expected collection rates and accounts receivable balances are known, the management of the firms must assess why this difference has occurred. Are customers paying more slowly than expected because of economic or competitive effects? Is there something wrong with the forecasting procedures used to estimate collection rates? Are the firm's policies being improperly implemented? While the across-the-board decrease in collection rates from those that were expected suggests an economic or competitive effect, the other explanations remain possible, and management must assess the cause of these deviations in reexamining its strategies.

MONITORING BAD DEBT LOSSES

The usual measure of bad debt losses is the ratio of bad debts to sales. The basic approach to comparing actual bad debt losses to those that are expected is the same as that for the monitoring of payment patterns. Confidence limits are determined based on the expected value of this ratio (given the firm's credit policies) and the historic random variation in this ratio. If the firm's actual ratio of bad debt expense to sales falls outside these confidence limits, investigation is undertaken. As with collection experience, either a positive or negative deviation from expectations is cause for concern.[18]

However, there are some difficulties inherent in this comparison process that must be recognized and addressed. These difficulties are illustrated in the spreadsheet presented in Table 7-7. The first difficulty concerns the matching of debt expense *with its proper period of origin*. Before recognizing that a sale has resulted in a bad debt, the seller must make every effort to collect from the buyer. This usually takes some period of time. Thus, bad debts are *recognized* in a period *far after the sale occurs*. In this spreadsheet, we have assumed that bad debts are recognized after sales are 120 days old. Thus, the bad debts of $180 recognized in *May* (cell F5) occurred because of sales in

---

[18]As with payment patterns, unexpectedly low bad-debt loss is just as much a concern as is unexpectedly high bad-debt loss. For example, unexpectedly low bad-debt loss might signal overestimation of the default risks of applicants in the firm's credit granting process, causing credit-granting decisions to be overly restrictive.

Table 7-7. Example Problem in Monitoring Bad Debt Expense.

!	A	!!	B	!!	C	!!	D	!!	E	!!	F
1	Month		Jan.		Feb.		March		April		May
2											
3	Sales for Month		10000		15000		20000		25000		30000
4											
5	Bad Debts Recognized		50		105		0		5		180
6											
7	Percent of Sales		.50		.70		0.00		.02		.60
8											
9	Bad Debts Originated		180		0		0		150		100
10											
11	Percent of Sales		1.80		0.00		0.00		.60		.33
12											
13											
14											
15											
16	Qly. Percent of Sales						.40				
17											
18											
19											

January. The comparison in row 7 of bad debts recognized as a percent of the *current* month's sales is misleading. Sales from January resulted in bad debts of $180 (recognized in May), which is 1.80 percent of January's sales, rather than the 0.5 percent that appears in cell B7. The correct calculation of bad debt expense ratios is presented in row 11, where the dollar bad debt expenses are compared with sales in the month in which the sales occurred. For example, cell B11 (the ratio of bad debts from January to sales for January) contains "(B9/B3)*100" since the bad debt expense originating in January appears in cell B9 and sales for January appear in cell B3.

The second difficulty in monitoring bad debt expense has to do with the "lumpy" pattern by which bad debt expenses occur to the firm and the effect of this lumpiness on estimates of dispersion of bad debt expense. In general, the credit policies of most firms and the failure rates of trade customers are such that *a few defaults account for most of the firm's bad debt expense.* Most firms experience *very few* defaults by trade debtors, but when a debtor does default, a significant amount of money is often lost. This lumpiness in defaults means that *the dispersion of bad debt losses over time is substantial,* particularly for short time periods. An industrial seller can go for months without a major default, then several defaults may occur over a short period. This dispersion of loss is portrayed in row 11 of Table 7-7; losses range from 1.80 percent of sales (for January) to 0.0 percent of sales (for February, March, and November). The mean loss as a percent of the originating month's sales is 0.47 percent (cell M13), with a standard deviation of 0.95 percent.

| ! G !! | H !! | I !! | J !! | K !! | L !! | M ! |
June	July	Aug.	Sept.	Oct.	Nov.	Dec.
35000	35000	30000	25000	20000	15000	10000
0	0	150	100	20	75	100
0.00	0.00	.50	.40	.10	.50	1.00
20	75	100	250	20	0	120
.06	.21	.33	1.00	.10	0.00	1.20
					Mean	.47
					S.D.	.95
.30			.47			.31
					Mean	.37
					S.D.	.08

Because of this large standard deviation relative to the mean, the confidence limits for bad debt loss as a percent of monthly sales are too wide to be of practical use; the month-to-month random variation overwhelms any nonrandom effects. To monitor bad debt expense, most firms must use a longer averaging period than a month so that there is a sufficient number of bad-debt events to obtain a reasonably sized sample of bad-debt experience. Quarterly figures are presented in row 16, with the mean and standard deviation of these figures in cells F18 and F19.[19] These quarterly figures are computed as the sum of the bad debts originating in the quarter divided by the sum of the sales over the quarter. Thus, cell D16, which shows the bad debt experience for the first quarter, contains "(@SUM(B11...D11)/@SUM(B3 ... D3))*100". Note that, in this quarterly averaging procedure, the standard deviation of bad debt expense is much smaller relative to its mean than for the monthly averaging procedure. Because of this, reasonable confidence intervals for quarterly bad debt expense can be generated.

However, because of the delay in the recognition of bad debt expense and the necessity of averaging bad debt expense over several periods, there will always be a substantial time lag in the detection of differences between expected and actual bad debt losses. This makes the current level of bad debt

[19]The difference in the mean losses between cells M13 and M18 occurs because these are averages of averages for fluctuating sales and are not weighted by sales volume.

expense a good deal harder to assess than current payment patterns from customers. To monitor the current payment patterns from customers, the firm merely computes the appropriate statistics at the end of a period and compares these to their confidence limits. This calculation and comparison can be made almost immediately as periods end, and quick action can be taken to investigate and correct any collection problems. For bad debt expense, however, a significant waiting period is necessary before such a comparison and investigation can proceed. The firm must wait until the bad debts associated with a sale have been recognized, a process of several months' duration. Further, because of the necessary averaging of bad debt losses over several months, differences from historic patterns can have occurred for several prior periods without detection. These lags between occurrence and detection make the management of current bad debt expense a difficult business.

THE MANAGEMENT OF ACCOUNTS RECEIVABLE IN PRACTICE

Since this is the last chapter on the management of accounts receivable, it is appropriate to contrast the techniques described in this text with current practice in the management of this asset. This discussion of current practice is organized according to the major topics discussed in the last three chapters. As in our discussion of practice in the management of cash and marketable securities, in the interests of brevity the surveys will be referred to by abbreviation; details of the surveys are given in Table 7-8.

Interestingly, this assessment of current practice will find a substantial divergence between the techniques displayed in the academic literature and those commonly used in credit management. Some of the techniques discussed in these chapters are extensively used, while others have not yet been widely adopted.

The Prevalence of Trade Credit in the Sale of Goods The vast majority of manufacturing output is sold via trade credit; 87 percent of manufacturing firms report that between 91 and 100 percent of their sales are made on a credit basis (BO, p. 73). The availability of trade credit does not depend on economic conditions or interest rates. This is so because, in general, firms do not adjust their credit policies to reflect changes in these conditions (HWS; Walker, p. 20).

Terms-of-Sale Decisions Since credit terms are an aspect of price but have implications for the financial management of selling firms, it is logical that terms-of-sale decisions should be made jointly by the finance and marketing departments. Survey evidence confirms this logic (HWS). In evaluating the terms-of-sale policy, firms consider the effect of terms changes on sales, investments, bad debt losses, and returns (SS, pp. 56 and 70). In general, these considerations are in keeping with the terms-of-sale evaluation methodologies portrayed in this text.

However, once set, firms rarely consider changes in their terms of sale (HWS). Most firms simply utilize the traditional terms of sale in their markets (HWS; Scherr, p. 14). When competitors change terms, other sellers typically will "follow the leader" (HWS). This is in sharp contrast to the aggressive marketing policies followed by many firms, where other price-related variables are manipulated to influence sales volume. The management of terms-of-sale policies to obtain desired patterns of sale is certainly an area where current practice can be reconsidered.

Credit Investigation Policies There is considerable evidence that firms follow cost-of-information principles in setting their credit investigation policies. Small firms, who on average receive orders for small dollar amounts, tend to use low-cost sources of credit information, such as past experiences with the applicant and credit ratings from credit agencies (Walker, pp. 17–19, 24). Larger firms tailor the amount of information collected to the amount of the order, with more information being collected in making credit-granting decisions on larger orders (Scherr, p. 15).

Credit-Granting Decisions on Marginal Accounts Most firms find the credit-granting decision to be more difficult to make than decisions regarding terms of sale or credit investigation policy (Scherr, p. 15). There appears to be substantial disagreement within surveys regarding these credit-granting decisions. Several surveys have shown that firms use the traditional "Cs of Credit" to make judgmental decisions on credit applicants, though a substantial fraction use some type of credit-scoring approach (Scherr, p. 16; SS, pp. 55 and 69). However, there is also survey evidence that firms can and do make reasonably accurate estimates of default probability, delinquency, and discount rates (BO, p. 79; Scherr, p. 16). If the seller can make an accurate estimate of these statistics, why should firms bother with a judgmental approach to credit-granting decisions? Why not just compute the net present value of expected cash flows, since such a technique is straightforward and is consistent with shareholder wealth maximization? It would seem that knowledge about current practice in credit-granting decisions is incomplete.

Monitoring Accounts Receivable Unfortunately, most of the published survey information on practice in the monitoring of accounts receivable is fairly old. Published survey results from the mid-1970s showed aging fractions to be the most popular method of monitoring customer payment patterns at the time (SS, pp. 55–56 and 69; Stone, pp. 70–71). The use of this and other traditional measures of payment behavior (such as DSO) may continue to

Table 7-8. *Facts Regarding the Survey Articles on the Management of Accounts Receivable Referenced.*

Abbreviation	Authors	Article Title
BO	S. Besley and J. Osteryoung	"Survey of Current Practices in Establishing Trade-Credit Limits"
HWS	N. Hill, R. Wood, and D. Sorenson	"Factors Influencing Corporate Credit Policy: A Survey"
Scherr	F. Scherr	"Managing Accounts Receivable"
Stone	B. Stone	"The Payments-Pattern Approach to the Forecasting and Control of Accounts Receivable"
SS	K. Smith and S. Sell	"Working Capital Management in Practice"
Walker	D. Walker	"Factors Influencing Trade Credit for Small Businesses"

*Estimated from discussion in article.

the present.[20] It is not known how or if managers correct for the bias caused in these measures by variations in sales. If firms use aging fractions or DSO, switching to a more accurate method of monitoring can significantly enhance their ability to detect nonrandom changes in payment behavior.

SUMMARY

The major discussion in this chapter concerned the monitoring of accounts receivable. Monitoring means comparing the actual payment patterns and bad debt losses from this asset to those that are expected because of the firm's terms-of-sale and credit-granting policies. Monitoring is important because the rapid turnover of accounts receivable means that the characteristics

[20]In a reference to an unpublished survey, Srinivasan and Kim ("Credit Management") indicate that aging fractions and DSO continue to be popular as payment monitoring methods.

Reference	Date of Survey	Sample(s) Used	Response Rate
Financial Review (February 1985), pp. 70–81	1982	510 members of the Credit Research Foundation, mostly engaged in manufacturing.	45.9%
Journal of Cash Management, Vol. 1, No. 2 (Fall 1981)	1979	500 members of the National Association of Credit Management	55.4%
Nevada Review of Economics and Business, Vol. 8, No. 2 (Summer 1984), pp. 14–16	1981	Fortune's 500 Industrials	49.0%
Financial Management (Autumn 1976), pp. 65–82	1975*	Executives of 148 firms participating in executive development seminars	100.0%*
Readings in the Management of Working Capital, 2nd. Ed. (N.Y.: West Pub., 1980), pp. 51–84	1978	668 of Fortune's 1000, with selection based on size and profitability	31.4%
Eastern Finance Association, 1985; available from the author at Georgetown University	1983*	27 small businesses near Washington, D.C.	100.0%*

of this asset can change quickly, and because cash inflows from the collections of accounts receivable are important in the seller's working capital cycle. Deviations from expectations can signal changing customer payment characteristics, inaccurate forecasts, or improper implementation of terms-of-sale or credit-granting policies.

The simplest methods of monitoring the payment patterns are aging fractions and traditional days' sales outstanding statistics. Unfortunately, both of these measures are biased when sales fluctuate over time: they may show a deviation from expectations when no change has occurred and may not signal a deviation when one has occurred. Tools that do not contain this inherent bias include payment proportions, ratios of receivables outstanding, and sales-weighted days' sales outstanding. These tools compare outstanding receivables and collections with sales from the period in which these receivables and collections originated. In deciding among these unbiased tools, the choice is between simplicity and descriptive power. Sales-weighted days' sales outstanding is the simplest measure of payment patterns, but will not signal offsetting deviations in payment patterns among collections from different periods. Payment proportions and ratios of receivables outstanding will signal such deviations, but are more complex to use. One possible compromise is to monitor payment patterns via sales-weighted days' sales outstanding, and then use payment proportions, ratios of receivables outstanding, or the accounting technique of "variance analysis" to pinpoint the sources of deviations once the need for investigation has been signaled.

As in the monitoring of payment patterns, the monitoring of bad debt losses requires the analyst to carefully match the event with original sales. For bad debt losses, this process is complicated by two factors. First, there is a substantial time lag between sales and the eventual recognition of bad debts from sales. Second, due to the "lumpiness" of bad debt losses, effective detection of trends requires that these losses be averaged over a period of time. Consequently, it is often many months before a deviation from expected bad debt levels can be detected.

A review of surveys in the practice of accounts receivable management showed areas where this practice is in accord with the latest developments in the theory of working capital management and areas where there are substantial differences between theory and practice. Firms use the expected criteria in evaluating terms-of-sale policy, but do not change these terms very frequently. Unlike other price-related variables, firms do not use terms-of-sale policy to aggressively pursue the goals of the firm. Firms follow cost-of-information principles in setting their credit-investigation policies; more information is gathered for applicants when expected sales are greater. Contradictions appear in the surveys of procedures that firms use to make credit-granting decisions. Surveys report that firms use judgmental procedures in these decisions. However, these surveys also report that firms make accurate estimates of default probabilities and of opportunity costs; estimation of these parameters is not required in judgmental methods, but is critical to a net present value analysis of credit applicants. No recent published information is available with regard to the measures that firms use in monitoring accounts receivable. If firms use aging fractions or DSO, switching to more accurate techniques will improve their ability to monitor this asset.

This concludes our discussion of the management of accounts receivable. The next chapter starts a new topic: the management of inventory.

Problems

7-1. A firm's sales have been as follows:

Month	June	July	August	September	October
Sales	$5,000	$10,000	$25,000	$35,000	$20,000

And its receivables balances at the end of September and October were:

	September	October
From Current Month	$32,000	$17,000
From First Prior Month	$15,000	$21,000
From Second Prior Month	$3,500	$12,000
From Third Prior Month	$500	$1,500
From All Other Months	$0	$0

a. Compute the firm's traditional DSO at the end of September and October using a 90-day sales averaging period.

b. Compute the firm's ratios of receivables outstanding at the end of September and October.

c. Compute the firm's sales-weighted DSO at the end of September and October.

d. Compute the firm's payment proportions for October.

7-2. A firm has observed sales-weighted DSOs of 50.1 days, 62.2 days, 53.1 days, 49.8 days, and 57.6 days over the prior five months. For the current month, the sales-weighted DSO is 59.2 days. Using a Student's t test, assess whether the current month's sales-weighted DSO is significantly different from those of the prior five months at the 10 percent confidence level using a two-tailed test.

7-3. Referring to the data presented in Problem 1, assume that the firm had the following expected sales:

Month	June	July	August	September	October
Sales	$7,500	$20,000	$30,000	$30,000	$25,000

Assume also that the firm expected the following ratios of receivables outstanding:

Month	Current	First Prior	Second Prior	Third Prior
RRO	0.90	0.50	0.25	0.05

Using these data, compute the expected SWDSO and the collection, sales, and total dollar variances of accounts receivable for the month of October.

Selected Readings

Besley, S., and J. Osteryoung, "Survey of Credit Practices in Establishing Trade-Credit Limits," *Financial Review* (February 1985), pp. 70–81.

Carpenter, M. D., and J. E. Miller, "A Reliable Framework for Monitoring Accounts Receivable," *Financial Management* (Winter 1979), pp. 37–40.

Gallinger, G. W., and A. J. Ifflander, "Monitoring Accounts Receivable Using Variance Analysis," *Financial Management* (Winter 1986), pp. 69–76.

Gentry, J. A., and J. M. De La Garza, "A Generalized Model for Monitoring Accounts Receivable," *Financial Management* (Winter 1985), pp. 28–38.

Hill, N., R. Wood, and D. Sorensen, "Factors Influencing Corporate Credit Policy: A Survey," *Journal of Cash Management*, Vol. 1, No. 2 (Fall 1980).

Lewellen, W. G., and R. W. Johnson, "Better Way to Monitor Accounts Receivable," *Harvard Business Review* (May–June 1972), pp. 101–109.

Scherr, F., "Managing Accounts Receivable," *Nevada Review of Economics and Business*, Vol. 8, No. 2 (Summer 1984), pp. 14–16.

Srinivasan, V., and Y. Kim, "Credit Management: A Variance Framework for Monitoring Accounts Receivable," available from Srinivasan at Northeastern University.

Stone, B. K., "The Payment-Patterns Approach to Forecasting and Control of Accounts Receivable," *Financial Management* (Autumn 1976), pp. 65–82.

Foxtrot Incorporated[1]
Monitoring Accounts Receivable

Foxtrot Incorporated, a medium-sized manufacturer of chemicals and machinery, had personnel policies that fostered long-term employment. Promotions were made when vacancies arose; there was little hiring from outside the firm. Employees who seemed promising were nurtured slowly and given an opportunity to learn the various areas of their specialty in anticipation of the eventual promotion or retirement of their boss.

However, the accidental death of Foxtrot's treasurer, Louis Newington, had disturbed the firm's plans. Lucy Krenn, the assistant treasurer, had been elevated suddenly to the treasurer's job. Ms. Krenn had started with the firm about five years ago and had previous experience with a larger firm in the areas of capital planning and acquisitions. Since being promoted to assistant treasurer three years ago, her principal assignments had been related to the firm's cash management system. Her experience with credit and receivables management was very limited. Early in her tenure as treasurer, she was reviewing the firm's

[1]This case has been adapted from Iqbal Mathur and Frederick C. Scherr, *Cases in Financial Management* (New York: Macmillan, 1979), pp. 45–49.

recent financial statements and noted that receivables balances had been rising rapidly. Bad-debt levels, however, seemed normal. Ms. Krenn had scheduled an appointment with Jay Natalli (the firm's General Credit Manager) to discuss the receivables balances. In Foxtrot's organizational structure, the "Accounts Receivable Management Department" was part of the firm's accounting section and reported to the controller. This department was charged with applying incoming cash receipts to accounts receivable records and keeping these records current. The firm's "Credit Department," by contrast, was part of the firm's finance function and was charged with administering policy with regard to collections, credit granting, and terms of sale. The general credit manager reported directly to the firm's treasurer. Therefore, Mr. Natalli was the appropriate person with whom to discuss terms of sale and credit-granting policies and the effects of the policies on accounts receivable levels.

"I recognize that the monitoring system used in the past was not very sophisticated, Lucy, but it suited Mr. Newington," said a seemingly harried Mr. Natalli. "We gave him data on days' sales outstanding and aging fractions. His critical indicator was the figure representing the overall DSO for all our receivables. We used a ninety-day sales averaging period for DSO calculations. Any tools of these sorts are, of course, just aids to the manager in understanding and evaluating customers' payment patterns relative to the estimates we anticipate because of our credit policies. As you know, our sales are not very seasonal, and until recently haven't been growing substantially. This recent surge of sales has really put my department in a bind. We've been hit by a rash of new credit applicants and requests for increased credit from old customers. My staff is working very hard analyzing customers' financial statements and making credit-granting decisions. This, and the increased collection work from the higher sales volume, doesn't make for short days. By Mr. Newington's standards, we were doing fine."

Ms. Krenn then examined Mr. Newington's file of reports from Mr. Natalli. These reports had been prepared on a quarterly basis; the most recent report was for the last quarter of the year just passed. (This report is presented as Exhibit 1.) She was surprised to see that the overall DSO statistic had risen substantially during 1984, but on closer examination decided that this was probably due to a greater concentration of receivables in export accounts, which were sold on substantially longer terms than domestic accounts. DSO figures for disaggregated domestic and export accounts seemed essentially level for the year. She wondered, however, if patterns of customer payments were, in fact, in accord with the firm's expectations based on prior years' experience. She also had on hand a breakdown, generated from the firm's aging schedules of accounts receivable, of dollar re-

---

Exhibit 1

Foxtrot Incorporated
DSO and Aging Fractions for 1984

Quarter Ending	*March 31*	*June 30*	*Sept. 30*	*Dec. 31*
Domestic DSO	44.98	46.46	45.23	44.92
Due from Current Month	0.697	0.657	0.680	0.657
Due from First Prior Month	0.241	0.252	0.262	0.280
Due from Second Prior Month	0.040	0.054	0.045	0.051
Due from Third Prior Month	0.020	0.032	0.012	0.011
Due from Fourth Prior Month	0.002	0.005	0.001	0.002
Export DSO	153.20	160.10	155.11	153.27
Export Receivables Balances:				
Due from Current Month	0.212	0.191	0.209	0.206
Due from First Prior Month	0.194	0.185	0.174	0.200
Due from Second Prior Month	0.180	0.185	0.196	0.181
Due from Third Prior Month	0.203	0.177	0.172	0.187
Due from Fourth Prior Month	0.132	0.140	0.136	0.125
Due from Fifth Prior Month	0.069	0.089	0.086	0.084
Due from Sixth Prior Month	0.010	0.033	0.027	0.018
Overall DSO	61.71	64.50	63.25	63.62

Exhibit 2

Foxtrot Incorporated
Quarterly Receivables Aging for 1984

Quarter Ending	March 31	June 30	Sept. 30	Dec. 31
Domestic Receivables Balances:				
Due from Current Month	$17,500	$18,400	$19,800	$19,500
Due from First Prior Month	6,050	7,060	7,620	8,320
Due from Second Prior Month	1,000	1,500	1,300	1,500
Due from Third Prior Month	500	900	360	320
Due from Fourth Prior Month	50	140	20	60
Total Domestic Receivables	$25,100	$28,000	$29,100	$29,700
Export Receivables Balances:				
Due from Current Month	$ 3,305	$ 3,480	$ 4,087	$ 4,343
Due from First Prior Month	3,029	3,377	3,406	4,219
Due from Second Prior Month	2,817	3,360	3,837	3,816
Due from Third Prior Month	3,176	3,222	3,358	3,948
Due from Fourth Prior Month	2,062	2,548	2,668	2,646
Due from Fifth Prior Month	1,082	1,622	1,689	1,776
Due from Sixth Prior Month	155	596	521	383
Total Export Receivables	$15,626	$18,205	$19,566	$21,131

Exhibit 3

Foxtrot Incorporated
Domestic and Export Monthly Sales
(thousands of dollars)

Year	Month	Domestic Sales	Export Sales
1983	September		$2,575
1983	October	$18,000	$2,775
1983	November	$15,400	$2,864
1983	December	$15,780	$3,312
1984	January	$16,000	$2,846
1984	February	$16,720	$3,029
1984	March	$17,500	$3,305
1984	April	$17,850	$3,377
1984	May	$17,990	$3,377
1984	June	$18,400	$3,480
1984	July	$19,000	$3,860
1984	August	$19,100	$3,406
1984	September	$19,800	$4,087
1984	October	$19,700	$3,846
1984	November	$20,300	$4,219
1984	December	$19,500	$4,343

ceivables outstanding in various age categories as of the end of each quarter of 1984 (see Exhibit 2) and a schedule of monthly sales for 1984 and late 1983 (see Exhibit 3). As a first step toward additional evaluation of the firm's collection patterns during 1984, she calculated Foxtrot's sales-weighted days' sales outstanding statistics as of the end of each month for the prior three years (1981 through 1983). This 36-month period was a time when the firm's sales volumes and customer payment patterns were considered to be more or less as anticipated. She found the average sales-weighted days' sales outstanding figure to be 43.3 days with a standard deviation of 1.0 days for domestic sales, and the average sales-weighted days' sales outstanding figure to be 152.6 days with a standard deviation of 7.8 days for export sales.

chapter 8

Inventory Management: Certainty Approaches

This is the first of two chapters on the management of *inventory*. The management of this asset is unlike the management of any of the other assets and liabilities discussed in this text, in that the assets are *physical* rather than purely *financial* in nature. A dollar of accounts receivable, for example, represents a debt owed by one firm to another. Such a debt may be evidenced by an invoice, but it is primarily a financial transaction. However, inventory represents items with a physical existence: a bushel of corn, an automobile headlamp, or another good. In the management of inventory, our models relate to physical rather than financial circumstances.

The management of inventory is one of the oldest concerns of management science. As such, there is a broad and deep volume of literature on the management of this asset in various situations, the interaction of this asset with other assets, and similar issues. A complete and comprehensive discussion of the issues in inventory management is beyond the scope of this text. We limit our coverage to only the most basic inventory problem: the determination of ordering strategies for individual items of inventory. These ordering strategies are formulated by the application of mathematical models. A limited set of these models is developed in the following chapters.[1] Readers who are interested in other inventory issues, such as material requirements planning and the use of inventory to improve the quality of goods produced, are referred to the many available texts in the area.[2]

[1]For a more extensive description of the various models available, see S. Love, *Inventory Control* (New York: McGraw-Hill, 1979).

[2]Love, *Inventory Control*, provides a good discussion of many of these issues. See J. Orlicky, *Material Requirements Planning* (New York: McGraw-Hill, 1975), for a discussion of material requirements planning. A good text relating inventory decisions to other strategies in operations management is J. Evans and others, *Applied Production and Operations Management*, Second Edition (St. Paul: West Publishing, 1984).

In the inventory situations addressed in this text, the challenge is to formulate strategies for the ordering and holding of inventory that will be the most advantageous to the firm. However, because of uncertainties regarding the various parameters that are estimated in making these decisions, there is risk associated with these strategies. Two approaches are used in addressing this risk. One method, called the "certainty approach," is discussed in this chapter. In this approach, a strategy is first formulated to deal with the *expected values* of these inventory parameters, under the unrealistic assumption that these parameters are certain. Then, a *hedging strategy* is formulated to address the uncertainties in these parameters. This is called the *certainty approach* not because the parameters are certain, but *because they are treated as certain in the first phase of policy making*. An alternate methodology, in which the risk of these parameters is considered simultaneously with their expected values, is called the "uncertainty approach" to inventory management. The uncertainty approach to inventory management is discussed in Chapter 9.

WHY CARRY INVENTORY?

Like all other assets, inventory represents a costly investment to the firm. In order for this investment to be worthwhile, there must be some advantage in making it. In this section, we discuss some reasons why the firm may want to carry inventory. These reasons vary with the *type of inventory* carried. For purposes of discussion, we will use the accountant's convention of dividing inventory into three types: raw materials inventory, work-in-process inventory, and finished goods inventory.

Raw Materials Inventory There are several reasons why firms might want to carry inventories of raw materials. First, having an available stock of raw materials inventory *makes production scheduling easier*. Since the raw materials for the production process are on hand, scheduling of the firm's production equipment can proceed without concern over when these goods will arrive. Without a stock of raw materials on hand, this scheduling would be tentative, and subject to the arrival of such materials.

A second reason to keep raw materials inventory is to *avoid price changes* for these goods. If the firm keeps a stock of raw materials, the firm can purchase these materials when it believes prices are low and can decline to purchase when it believes prices are high. This reduces the firm's costs and also the variability of these costs. By keeping a stock of raw materials for this purpose, the firm is pursuing a hedging strategy against price fluctuations of these materials.

Third, the firm may keep extra raw materials inventory to *hedge against supply shortages*. When prices of raw materials are controlled (such as by laws regarding the maximum price that can be charged), there will be times when goods are unavailable at the controlled price. During these times, the firm may draw down its existing inventory to continue production.

Finally, the firm may order and keep additional inventories of raw materials to *take advantage of quantity discounts*. Quantity discounts are reductions in the price per unit purchased that occur when the firm orders larger amounts. For example, the firm may pay $10 per unit if orders are less than a truckload, and $9.75 if a truckload or more is ordered. By ordering more, the purchasing firm may reduce the price paid per unit, but it must hold more inventory on average.[3]

Work-In-Process Inventory In manufacturing firms, a certain amount of work-in-process inventory occurs as products move from one production process to another. A major reason that firms keep work-in-process inventory beyond this minimum level is to *buffer production*. Buffering is part of the planning process and allows flexibility and economies that would not otherwise occur. Buffering is diagrammed in Figure 8-1. In Panel A, a production line with three processes produces goods. Without buffer stocks, production is not very flexible. For example, the production line can produce continuously only at the pace of the slowest process. If, at maximum, Process A can produce 10 units per hour, Process B can produce 7 units per hour, and Process C can produce 9 units per hour, the production line must be set up at a rate of 7 units per hour. Otherwise, because A's rate of production is greater than B's, inventory will accumulate between A and B. Also, if one process breaks down, the entire line must be shut down, resulting in the unplanned idling of the machinery and workers involved with all the processes.

If buffer stocks of inventory are employed between the production processes, these problems are avoided. (The production process with buffer stocks is portrayed in Panel B of Figure 8-1.) Process A can be run at its maximum output, accumulating inventory for Process B. Once sufficient in-

Figure 8-1. *Work-In-Process Inventory as a Production Buffer (arrows indicate flow of materials).*

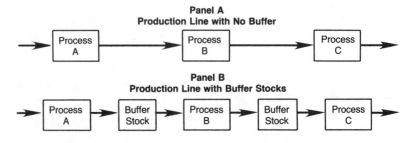

[3]Later in this chapter, we will formulate a model to assess whether ordering higher volumes to take advantage of quantity discounts is of advantage to the firm.

ventory is accumulated to employ Process B for a time, the firm can plan to take Process A out of the production line temporarily and redeploy its workers and machinery to other useful endeavors. Also, if one of the processes breaks down, the other processes can continue to run. For example, if Process B is shut down for maintenance, Process A can continue to produce goods. These goods are accumulated as inventory in the first buffer stock. Further, Process C can continue to operate using materials from the second buffer stock. Once Process B is reactivated, the excess inventory in the first buffer stock can be depleted and the reduced inventory in the second buffer stock can be re-plenished.

Finished Goods Inventory One reason to keep finished goods inventory is to *provide immediate service*. When customers want to purchase goods and services, ready availability of these is a substantial advantage in making a sale. Sellers who do not have goods available will find buyers ordering else-where.

Intertwined with this notion of providing immediate service is the pre-sumption that demand for goods or services is uncertain. If demand and the future arrivals of goods could be known for certain, there would be no need to keep inventories of finished goods (beyond those inventories resulting from the minimization of production and ordering costs). Plans could be made for the goods to be produced or to arrive from suppliers just as the buyer wished to purchase them. We will see later in the chapter that dealing with uncertainty of demand is a major consideration in the formulation of inventory strategies.

A second reason for keeping finished goods inventory is to *stabilize production*. When firms produce several types of products using the same equipment, there are costs and delays in changing from the production of one product to another. The longer are the firm's production runs, the lower are these transition ("setup") costs. However, longer production runs result in higher finished goods and work-in-process inventories.

ALTERNATIVES TO HOLDING INVENTORY

In the prior section, rationales for holding various types of inventory were listed. The holding of inventory for these various reasons are *solutions* to different *problems* that the firm faces: fluctuations in the prices of raw materials, the formulation of economical production strategy, the need for goods availability, and so forth. *However, the holding of inventory is not the only possible approach to these problems.* Like investment in any other asset, *investment in inventory should be carefully considered in light of the alternative approaches to the problem at hand.* A little thought will show that each of these problems can be addressed via alternative strategies to holding inventory, and that in some cases, these alternative strategies may result in lower costs. Let us discuss a few examples.

One reason for holding raw materials inventory is to avoid fluctuations in prices of these materials. However, holding inventory is not the only way to avoid these fluctuations. The firm could enter into long-term private contracts with the producers of these raw materials. These contracts would specify the prices to be paid. Alternatively, if the raw material involved is one on which a futures contract is traded, the firm can purchase such a contract for future delivery. This futures strategy is pursued by many firms—producers of chocolate do not keep inventories of cocoa; they purchase futures contracts on this commodity to ensure delivery and price.

One reason for using buffer stocks of work-in-process inventory is to hedge against the breakdown of one of the processes within the production line. The same effect can be achieved by replacing processes prone to breakdown with others that are more reliable. In this circumstance, the capital expenditure made in improving the processes substitutes for the buffer stock.

Similar strategies can be formulated to reduce finished goods inventories. For example, one common reason to keep finished goods is to provide immediate availability of goods to customers. By satisfying customer needs promptly, the seller hopes to increase sales. However, there are other techniques that will obtain the same effect. For example, the firm could offer longer terms of sale or lower prices as an alternative to immediate availability. Many customers will be willing to wait for goods if they can obtain them on more advantageous terms or at a lower price.

Just-In-Time Systems   One of the newest and most interesting alternatives to holding inventory is to use *just-in-time* (JIT) systems. JIT systems were developed by Japanese firms. In these systems, holding inventory is considered to be an uneconomical solution to the various problems facing the firm. Inventories are minimized. Instead, JIT substitutes demand-based systems based on flexible production, small lot sizes, and high-quality output.[4] To reduce inventory, goods are produced and delivered only as they are needed. JIT systems can be used within the firm to reduce work-in-process inventories and, in conjunction with suppliers, to reduce raw materials inventories. Let us discuss each of these applications in turn.

Within the firm, the JIT system is, to some extent, an alternative to traditional production planning systems. Production planning is done only in the aggregate, and is based on total output. After this aggregate plan is made,

---

[4]The just-in-time inventory system is discussed in most texts on production and operations management; see, for example, Evans and others, *Applied Production*, pp. 530–543. For a report of its application in the United States, see E. Hoeffer, "GM Tries Just-In-Time American Style," *Purchasing*, August 19, 1982.

a signaling system is used among the production processes, starting with the last process. The last process signals the next-to-last that goods are needed, the next-to-last signals the process before that, and so forth. This signaling is done by means of *Kanbans* (Japanese for cards). Kanbans travel through the processes, indicating the need for goods. In response to these Kanbans, the employees set up production processes and produce the needed goods. Because goods are produced only as needed, work-in-process buffer stocks are minimized.

The JIT system requires quite different procedures than does the typical American production system. The biggest differences concern the lot sizes and quality of production runs. In order to achieve a reduction in inventory, set-up costs for processes must be small so that small lot sizes can be economically produced in response to demand. Small lot sizes also require that workers be flexible; they must be able to change their work stations from one production process to another in response to demand (as signaled by the Kanbans). Workers cannot be specialists performing only one task. Also, because goods move directly from one production process to another, there are few en route quality control inspections. Workers must perform their own quality control as they execute the production processes. Finally, since there are no buffer stocks, output must be of very high quality (or later processes will not be able to function, since they have no inventory from which to draw if the delivered goods are defective).

In JIT, suppliers are treated as another step in the production process. They are required to produce small lots of high-quality goods for frequent delivery. This minimizes the producer's raw materials inventory. To obtain the necessary quality, buyers frequently must work with their suppliers to assure that the output from supplier's manufacturing processes fits as perfectly as possible with the producer's manufacturing processes.

Japanese firms have proved that JIT is a viable alternative to the costly holding of inventory. However, JIT systems have their own costs. JIT essentially substitutes worker education costs and capital costs for inventory costs. For JIT to work properly, workers must be highly skilled and flexible, and the machinery they use must be capable of high-quality output while being cheap and quick to set up.

The point of this section is that *there are alternative potential strategies in response to each of the problems that holding inventory addresses.* JIT is one of these strategies. Because of the existence of these alternatives, the firm should think *very broadly* about the problem to be addressed and about other possible solutions before adopting an inventory approach. The costs and benefits of these other solutions should be compared to the costs and benefits of holding inventory, given an optimal inventory management strategy. The costs to the firm in inventory-based solutions to such problems are discussed in the next section of this chapter.

COSTS IN INVENTORY SYSTEMS

Any changes in the firm's cash flows that are caused by inventory management strategies are relevant in the evaluation of these strategies. Inventory strategies can have several different effects on cash flows. As in accounts receivable management, the different types of cash flow effects that occur in inventory management decisions are usually discussed in terms of the different costs faced by the firm in making these decisions. These different types of costs are discussed in the following paragraphs.

Costs Directly Proportional to Amount of Inventory Held Certain costs are directly proportional to the level of inventory carried by the firm. These are usually called "carrying costs of inventory" or "holding costs of inventory." Included here are any costs that fluctuate directly with the level of inventory, such as the opportunity cost of inventory investment, insurance on the inventory, storage costs of inventory, taxes on inventory investments, and so forth. The formula for this type of cost is:

$$\text{Cost} = (a) \text{ (amount of inventory)} \qquad (8\text{-}1)$$

where a is a coefficient representing the sum of all costs that are directly proportional to the level of inventory.

Costs Not Directly Proportional to the Amount of Inventory Held In addition to those costs that are directly proportional to the amount of inventory held, there is also a group of costs that vary with inventory size but not in direct proportionality. Instead, they assume some other mathematical relationship with the amount of inventory held. Consider costs such as spoilage and obsolescence. These costs vary with the length of time that an item is in inventory. The more inventory ordered at one time, the higher the firm's average inventory, and the longer, on average, that items are in inventory. For several reasons, the cost of spoilage and obsolescence is nonlinear in this average time in inventory. For example, some types of spoilage are caused by bacterial action, and bacteria multiply at a geometric rather than arithmetic rate. For technological obsolescence, the inventory often retains a substantial part of its value until a new technological advance is made. Initial time periods involve little loss of value, then value declines in an accelerating fashion. While some processes of this sort can be approximated by linear relationships, there are many cases in which such an approximation distorts results. The general formula for these costs is:

$$\text{Cost} = f(\text{inventory level}) \qquad (8\text{-}2)$$

where f(inventory level) means that the cost is a function of inventory level, with the particular mathematical relationship depending upon the type of cost being considered.

Costs Directly Proportional to the Number of Orders Whether the firm produces its own materials for inventory or orders goods from another firm, there are costs to the ordering, delivery, and payment processes. These costs depend directly on the number of times that orders are placed and received. Costs of this sort include set-up costs on machines to produce inventory, costs of generating a purchase order for the inventory, costs of writing a check and mailing it in payment for the order, fixed costs of unloading the order, and so forth. The formula for this type of cost is:

$$\text{Cost} = (c)(\text{number of orders}) \tag{8-3}$$

where the c is a coefficient representing the sum of all the costs of this type.

The Price per Unit of Inventory Obtained Due to quantity discounts and economies of scale in production, the price per unit of goods purchased or produced for inventory may vary with the amount ordered. When this occurs, the change in the total cost of the inventory that results can be a major determinant of the most advantageous order quantity. The formula for the total cost of the inventory is:

$$\text{Cost} = P_q S \tag{8-4}$$

where P_q is the unit price for the quantity ordered by the firm and S is the yearly usage of the good.

Stockout Cost Another cost that is dependent on the firm's inventory strategy is stockout cost. Stockout cost occurs when immediate service is required but inventory is unavailable. If the inventory is raw materials or work-in-process, the cost of stocking out will include the cost of changing the firm's production plans, costs of idling or rescheduling equipment, and so forth. If the inventory is a finished good, stockout costs may include the lost cash flow from the sale if the customer does not make the purchase because immediate service cannot be provided. Also, when stockouts of finished goods occur, customers are less likely to purchase from the firm in the future, so the opportunity costs of lost *future* cash flows (in addition to lost flows from missing the current sale) can also occur.

All these types of inventory costs will vary with the type of inventory under consideration. Some types of bulky or high-value inventory may have high storage costs, while other inventory may be stored for years at relatively little expense. The size of these costs, plus the other characteristics of the inventory situation, help determine the best approach to inventory strategy. These other characteristics of inventory situations are discussed in the next section.

OTHER CHARACTERISTICS OF INVENTORY SITUATIONS

Besides the various types of costs involved, there are other characteristics of the situation that vary among types of inventory, and must be captured if the decision model is to be an accurate representation of the physical circumstances. Several of these characteristics are listed here.

Lead Times Obtaining inventory usually requires a time lag from the initiation of the process until the inventory starts to arrive. This lead time may be a few minutes or it may be many months, and depends in part on whether the firm is producing goods for its inventory or is ordering these goods from another firm. To produce goods for its own use, the firm must schedule, set up, and adjust manufacturing equipment. When purchasing from a vendor, the firm must order the goods and await delivery. Deliveries from a vendor may be almost immediate, or may be months away from imported or specially built items.

Sources and Levels of Risk Uncertainties play a significant role in inventory situations. Uncertainties usually involve lead times and demand levels, but situations where other variables are uncertain also occur. Where there are substantial uncertainties and where the costs of stockout are important, strategies for addressing risk must be formulated.

Static versus Dynamic Problems Inventory problems are usually divided into two types based on the characteristics of the goods involved. In *static inventory problems*, the goods have a one-period life; there can be no carryover of goods from one period to the next. Inventory situations where decisions involve the number of newspapers to print, the number of Christmas trees to purchase, or the number of calendars to produce are static inventory problems. In *dynamic inventory problems*, the goods have value beyond the initial period; they do not lose their value completely over time. Inventory situations such as that faced by a service station in determining how much gasoline to purchase are dynamic inventory problems.

Replenishment Rate Once goods start to be received from a vendor or from the firm's own production processes, there are differences among goods in the *rate* at which they are received. Small orders from vendors are likely to be received all at once. For example, assume that a firm has placed an order for 10 cases of paper towels. For such a small order, the rate of replenishment is essentially infinite; the firm's inventory will go up by 10 cases in a very short time as the goods are quickly unloaded. For larger orders from vendors, or for inventory produced within the firm, the replenishment rate may be slower. For example, suppose that the firm orders 10 *truckloads* of paper towels. Given the size of such an order, it is likely to take some time to unload. During this time, inventory will increase as cases of paper towels are removed from the trucks and added to the firm's inventory. Because inventory increases slowly, this is called a "finite replenishment rate" situation.

DECIDING ON AN APPROACH IN INVENTORY STRATEGY

To formulate an inventory strategy, the firm first considers the costs and characteristics of the particular inventory item involved. What costs are important? What are the characteristics of the inventory situation? Once this is assessed, the analyst then chooses a basic approach: either the *certainty approach*, in which the expected values of uncertain variables and their risk are addressed separately, or the *uncertainty approach*, in which these facets are addressed simultaneously. The certainty approach is tractable, well-tested, and easy to implement. However, because of the way it handles risk, the certainty approach is not applicable to *static* inventory problems. In the certainty approach, risk is usually addressed via the use of a *safety stock*. A safety stock is an additional amount of inventory kept permanently on hand to absorb fluctuations in inventory usage. However, a safety stock strategy is inappropriate in *static* inventory situations because such a safety stock would have no value after the initial period. The uncertainty approach, on the other hand, is applicable in these static inventory problems, because this approach does not rely on the safety stock methodology to handle risk. The uncertainty approach can also address dynamic inventory problems, but simulation is required and the resulting methodology does not lead to a definitive strategy. Thus, in our two chapters on inventory management we will concentrate on illustrating the *certainty* approach for *dynamic* inventory problems and the *uncertainty* approach for *static* inventory problems.

Once the costs and characteristics of the problem are identified and a modeling approach is chosen, a model must be developed for the formulation of policy. This model must capture the costs and characteristics of the inventory situation. This modeling process is critical; it cannot be stressed sufficiently that the *domain of a mathematical model is limited to situations covered by the model's assumptions*. The application of a model to other situations can lead to nonoptimal and sometimes *disastrously incorrect* strategies. For example, assume that an analyst applies an inventory model that does not allow for spoilage to a grocery chain's ordering policy for lettuce and formulates the strategy of ordering lettuce in large amounts every 14 days. A little thought will show that *this is obviously nonsense*. This strategy implies that lettuce will be on the shelves for an average of seven days, and in seven days most lettuce will be spoiled. However, *this is not a failure of the inventory model*: *it is a failure to apply the correct model*. With this firmly in mind, let us proceed to discuss inventory models of dynamic inventory situations using the certainty approach.

THE BASIC EOQ MODEL

The economic order quantity (EOQ) model is presented in most introductory textbooks in finance and in management science. In this section, we present the basic version of this model under the assumption that all variables are certain. In later sections, we present other versions of this model for other inventory situations and present methods for developing safety stock strategies to address risk. The basic EOQ model is simple, but it is applicable only to those inventory situations described by its assumptions, which are:

1. There are only two types of costs: costs that are directly proportional to the amount of inventory held and costs that are directly proportional to the number of orders received. Call the former *carrying or holding cost* and the latter *ordering cost*. There are no costs that are indirectly proportional to the amount of inventory held, and the price per unit of inventory obtained does not vary with the amount of inventory received (there are no quantity discounts). Stockout costs are modeled separately and are not considered in the EOQ model.

2. There may be lead times of any length.

3. There is no risk (risk is modeled separately in determining safety stock strategy).

4. The replenishment rate is infinite.

The time-pattern of inventory for these assumptions is portrayed in Panel A of Figure 8-2. When an order arrives, the level of inventory held by the firm increases instantaneously from zero to Q_A, the order quantity. It is a right triangle because of the instantaneous increase in inventory. (Remember, the replenishment rate is infinite, so replenishment occurs in zero time.) Over time, inventory is used up, and the level of inventory declines; let the usage rate be S, which will be the slope of hypotenuse of the triangle. During the inventory cycle, Q_A units are used up, and a new order is received just as inventory falls to zero.

The Optimal Order Quantity The question in this inventory situation is *how much to order*; that is, what should be the order quantity, Q? A relatively

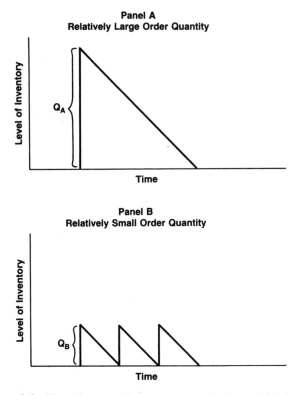

Figure 8-2. *Time Pattern of Inventory Level for Basic EOQ Model.*

large Q (as in Panel A) results in a high average inventory but infrequent orders. A smaller order quantity (Q_B in Panel B) results in lower average inventory but more frequent orders.[5] The first strategy will result in higher holding cost but lower ordering cost; the latter strategy will have the reverse effect. To decide on the optimal Q, we need a mathematical model of the trade-offs between the two costs. This requires the development of expressions for the holding cost and carrying cost of inventory; these are operationalizations of equations (8-1) and (8-3) for this inventory situation. Equations (8-1) and (8-3) are:

$$\text{Cost} = (a) \text{ (amount of inventory)} \qquad (8\text{-}1)$$

$$\text{Cost} = (c) \text{ (number of orders)} \qquad (8\text{-}3)$$

Taking equation (8-1) first, inspecting the time-pattern of inventory in

[5]Note that the usage rate, as represented by the slope of the hypotenuse, is the same for the smaller triangles in Panel B as for the larger triangle in Panel A.

Figure 8-2 shows that the inventory level goes from Q to zero in a linear fashion. The average amount of inventory, in units, is then:

$$\text{Average inventory} = (Q + 0)/2 = Q/2 \qquad (8\text{-}5)$$

The logical way to value this inventory investment is in dollars. If the dollar investment per unit is P, and the yearly cost of holding a dollar of inventory (equal to the sum of all the costs that are directly proportional to inventory level) is C, then equation (8-1) becomes:[6]

$$\text{Cost} = (a) \text{ (amount of inventory)} \qquad (8\text{-}1)$$

$$= CP(Q/2) \qquad (8\text{-}6)$$

since $a = CP$. This is our expression for the holding cost of the inventory for this inventory situation.[7]

Turning now to equation (8-3), for any level of order quantity, over an entire year the amount ordered must be sufficient to cover the yearly usage (S). The number of orders required to do this is:

$$\text{Number of orders} = S/Q \qquad (8\text{-}7)$$

For example, if the firm uses 10,000 units of a product per year and obtains 1,000 units each time it orders, 10 orders must be placed per year. Letting F be the cost of ordering, equation (8-3) becomes:

$$\text{Cost} = (c) \text{ (number of orders)} \qquad (8\text{-}3)$$

$$= F(S/Q) \qquad (8\text{-}8)$$

[6]In this equation, P represents the price (out of pocket investment) per unit; this was represented by P_q in equation (8-4). However, since P is invariant to Q (there are no quantity discounts), the use of the P_q notation from equation (8-4) is unnecessary for this inventory situation. The simpler P notation is therefore used.

[7]In this method of calculating the holding cost, a required rate of return is applied to the inventory investment to account for the time value of money. This required return is part of C. This approach to the time value of money was also used in Chapter 2, where lockbox location problems were discussed. As discussed in that chapter, this approach is not quite equivalent to discounting cash flows, which is the proper technique for making decisions that result in shareholder wealth maximization. However, the opportunity cost approach is much simpler and has been shown empirically to produce almost exactly the same strategies for inventory situations; see W. R. McDaniel, "The Economic Ordering Quantity and Wealth Maximization," *Financial Review*, Vol. 21, No. 2 (November 1986), pp. 527–36. For more on the relationship between inventory models and net present value, see Y. H. Kim, G. C. Philippatos, and K. H. Chung, "Evaluating Investment in Inventory: A Net Present Value Framework," *Engineering Economist*, Vol. 31, No. 2 (Winter 1986), pp. 119–25.

since $c = F$. This is our expression for the cost of ordering in this inventory situation. Looking at equations (8-6) and (8-8), we see that the holding cost rises linearly with the order quantity, while the ordering cost declines inversely with the order quantity. The total cost in this situation is the sum of these two cost types:

$$\text{Total cost} = CP(Q/2) + F(S/Q) \qquad (8\text{-}9)$$

To see how the two cost types interact, let us examine an example inventory problem. We will use several variations of this problem at different times in this chapter.

A firm purchases 10,000 units of a particular product per year. The product costs $8 per unit. The sum of insurance, storage, and the opportunity cost of invested funds is 20 percent per year of the average dollar investment in inventory. Each time the firm places an order, it costs $50 in out-of-pocket expenses to generate the purchase order, receive the goods, and so forth. How much should the firm order each time an order is placed?

One possible approach to the problem is to compute the costs for several possible order quantities [from equations (8-6), (8-8), and (8-9)] and graph the costs versus order quantity. Cost data for order quantities between 100 and 1,200 units are presented in Table 8-1. To see how these data were computed, let us examine the cost figures of an order quantity of 500. For this order quantity, the average inventory will be 250 units (equal to $Q/2$). At $8 per unit, this results in an average investment of $2,000, which generates a yearly holding cost of $400 since the sum of all the costs that are directly related to inventory level is 20 percent. Since yearly demand is 10,000 units, an order quantity of 500 necessitates that 20 orders be placed per year. At a cost of $50 per order, this is an ordering cost of $1,000. The total cost of the inventory strategy for an order quantity of 500 is then $1,400 per year.

The cost data from Table 8-1 are graphed in Figure 8-3. Inspection of this graph shows that the minimum total cost occurs for an order quantity of about 800 units. We also note from this graph that the total cost function attains a minimum.[8] This suggests a more direct way to obtain the optimal ordering strategy: we could take the derivative of the total cost function, set this derivative equal to zero, and solve for the optimum Q:

$$\text{Total cost} = TC = CP\,(Q/2) + F(S/Q) \qquad (8\text{-}9)$$

$$dTC/dQ = CP/2 - F(S/Q^2) \qquad (8\text{-}10)$$

---

[8]For some products this function is not quite continuous, since the order quantity can take only integer values. A fractional unit of such products would be quite useless to the firm. An integer restriction does not, however, affect the major conclusions of the analysis in this chapter.

Table 8-1. Holding, Ordering, and Total Costs for Basic EOQ Example Problem.

Initial Data:

Yearly Usage (S)		10,000 units
Yearly Cost per Dollar of Inventory (C)		$.20/yr.
Investment per Unit of Inventory (P)		$8
Fixed Cost of Placing an Order (F)		$50/order

Order Quantity	Avg. Inv. in Units	Holding Cost	Orders per Year	Ordering Cost	Total Cost
Q	$Q/2$	$CP(Q/2)$	S/Q	$F(S/Q)$	$CP(Q/2)$ $+F(S/Q)$
100	50	$ 80	100	$5,000	$5,080
200	100	$160	50	$2,500	$2,660
300	150	$240	33	$1,667	$1,907
400	200	$320	25	$1,250	$1,570
500	250	$400	20	$1,000	$1,400
600	300	$480	17	$ 833	$1,313
700	350	$560	14	$ 714	$1,274
800	400	$640	13	$ 625	$1,265
900	450	$720	11	$ 556	$1,276
1,000	500	$800	10	$ 500	$1,300
1,100	550	$880	9	$ 455	$1,335
1,200	600	$960	8	$ 417	$1,377

$$0 = CP/2 - F(S/Q^2) \tag{8-11}$$

$$Q^* = (2FS/CP)^{0.5} \tag{8-12}$$

where Q^* is the optimum (lowest total cost) ordering strategy. Substituting the figures from the example problem into this formula, the optimum order quantity is calculated:

$$Q^* = (2FS/CP)^{0.5} \tag{8-12}$$

$$= [2(50) \ (10,000)/(0.20(8))]^{0.5}$$

$$= 790.57 \tag{8-13}$$

The optimal order quantity is therefore 791 units per order. This will result in 12.64 orders per year (equal to 10,000/791). For a 360-day year, orders will be placed about every 28 days (equal to 360/12.64). The total cost of holding and ordering the inventory will be:

$$\text{Total cost} = CP(Q/2) + F(S/Q) \tag{8-9}$$

$$= 0.20(8) \ (791/2) + 50(10,000/791) = \$1,264 \tag{8-14}$$

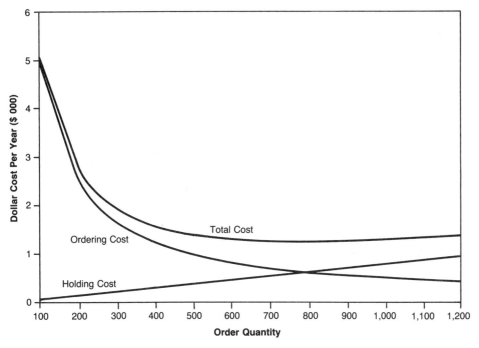

Figure 8-3. *Example Problem Data From Table 8-1.*

The Order Point The order quantity strategy outlined above is very simple to implement: order 791 units every 28 days. However, rather than using a *timed* ordering approach, it is often advantageous to place orders based on *inventory levels*. In this way, if the usage rate is greater than expected, an order will be placed earlier and the goods received sooner. The triggering of orders based on inventory levels is called the *order point system*, and it works well with modern methods of inventory record keeping. If the firm's data base of inventory levels is adjusted each time a unit of inventory is used (as occurs, for example, when a sale is recorded on an electronic cash register), then the firm's computer can compare inventory levels to order points and generate a list of items to be ordered.

The order point is calculated as the expected usage during the lead time. For the prior example problem, assume that the lead time is seven days. The usage over this time will be $(7/360) (10,000) = 194$ units. When the level of inventory reaches 194 units, the firm should place an order for 791 units. Just as this order arrives (seven days later), the firm will have run out of inventory. The optimal strategy and the order point for this example problem are portrayed in Figure 8-4.

This basic EOQ model with order points is easy to understand and to put into practice, but its range is limited to those situations described by its assumptions. Other situations require different models to portray their different circumstances.

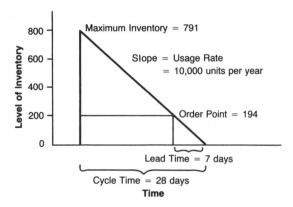

Figure 8-4. *Optimal Strategy for Example EOQ Problem.*

VARIATIONS ON THE BASIC EOQ MODEL

In this section, we present three variations of the basic EOQ model: the production order quantity model, the EOQ model with quantity discounts, and the EOQ model with decay. These variations are intended to illustrate how models are developed to capture the relevant aspects of the various situations faced by firms in managing inventory.

The Production Order Quantity Model There are many inventory situations where the increase in the inventory level during the replenishment portion of the inventory cycle is not instantaneous. While such situations may occur because of other circumstances (such as limitations in the ordering firm's ability to unload materials quickly), one common circumstance happens when the firm *produces its own goods for inventory*. For example, as a manufacturing firm turns work-in-process inventory into finished goods, the finished goods inventory increases *gradually rather than all at once*. This *finite replenishment rate* situation results in a different time-pattern of inventory than does the basic EOQ model. This time-pattern is portrayed in Panel A of Figure 8-5. Here, the triangle representing inventory level is not a right triangle; there is a gradual buildup of inventory over time. However, the problem of how much to order remains the same. Either infrequent large orders (Panel A) or frequent small orders (Panel B) will get the job done, although different ordering strategies have divergent effects on ordering and holding costs.

The primary difference between the basic EOQ model and the model for the finite-replenishment case (which is called the *production order quantity* (POQ) model) concerns the maximum inventory that occurs during the inventory cycle, and therefore the level of holding costs of inventory. Since the replenishment portion of the inventory cycle takes place over time, and there is a continual usage of inventory, *the maximum inventory that occurs in the POQ model is less than the order quantity*. For example, assume a firm makes

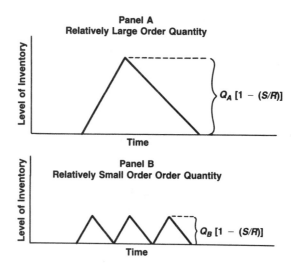

Figure 8-5. *Time Pattern of Inventory Level for Finite Replenishment Rate.*

500 units of a product for inventory and takes a week to produce these units. Also assume that usage is 20 units per day. Over the seven-day week during which the firm is producing these goods, 140 units of product will be used, so the *net increase* in inventory will be 360 units: the 500 units that were *added* to inventory, less the 140 units that were *withdrawn* from inventory during this week. If inventory started the week at zero, the final inventory after replenishment will be 360 units, not 500.

Since the physical situation is different from that of the basic EOQ model, a different mathematical model is needed. Let R be the *replenishment rate*, the rate at which items are put into inventory. During the replenishment portion of the inventory cycle, Q items will be received. The length of the replenishment portion of the inventory cycle must then be equal to Q/R (for example, if the firm wants to receive 1,000 items, and the items arrive at the rate of 250 per day, the replenishment will take 4 days). During the replenishment portion of the cycle, inventory will be used up at rate S; since this part of the cycle is Q/R in length, the usage over this portion of the cycle will be $S(Q/R)$. For example, if usage is 50 units per day, the order quantity is 1,000, and replenishment is 250 units per day, 200 units will be used during the replenishment part of the inventory cycle. The *maximum inventory* will then be the *increase* in inventory due to replenishment minus the *usage* during replenishment, or:

$$\text{Maximum inventory} = Q - S(Q/R) = Q[1 - (S/R)] \qquad (8\text{-}15)$$

Since the inventory level varies from zero to this maximum in a linear fashion, the average inventory will be one-half of the maximum, or:

$$\text{Average inventory} = Q[1 - (S/R)]/2 \qquad (8\text{-}16)$$

Applying the pricing and holding cost parameters to this average inventory gives the holding cost expression for the finite replenishment case:

$$\text{Holding cost} = CPQ[1 - (S/R)]/2 \qquad (8\text{-}17)$$

The number of orders is S/Q as before, so the ordering cost is $F(S/Q)$. The total cost equation for the finite replenishment case is then:

$$\text{Total cost} = CPQ[1 - (S/R)]/2 + F(S/Q) \qquad (8\text{-}18)$$

To see how the finite replenishment rate affects strategy, let us modify our prior example problem by assuming that the firm produces the product (rather than purchases it) and that the production process results in replenishment at a rate of 40,000 units per year during the portion of the inventory cycle when replenishment occurs. As before, yearly usage is 10,000 units, the yearly cost per dollar of inventory is $0.20, investment per unit is $8, and it costs $50 to place each order. The cost terms are calculated in Table 8-2 and plotted in Figure 8-6. As can be seen from these presentations, the optimum for the finite replenishment case is about 900 units per order.

To obtain an exact optimum, we can follow the same procedure as for the infinite replenishment rate situation by taking the derivative of the total

---

Table 8-2. Costs for Finite Replenishment Rate Example Problem.

Initial Data:

Yearly Usage (S)	10,000 units/yr.
Yearly Cost per Dollar of Inventory (C)	$.20/yr.
Investment per Unit of Inventory (P)	$8
Fixed Cost of Placing an Order (F)	$50/order
Replacement Rate (R)	40,000 units/yr.

Order Quantity Q	Avg. Inv. in Units $Q[1 - (S/R)]/2$	Holding Cost $CPQ[1 - (S/R)]/2$	Orders per Year S/Q	Ordering Cost $F(S/Q)$	Total Cost $CPQ[1 - (S/R)]/2 + F(S/Q)$
100	38	$ 60	100	$5,000	$5,060
200	75	$120	50	$2,500	$2,620
300	113	$180	33	$1,667	$1,847
400	150	$240	25	$1,250	$1,490
500	188	$300	20	$1,000	$1,300
600	225	$360	17	$ 833	$1,193
700	263	$420	14	$ 714	$1,134
800	300	$480	13	$ 625	$1,105
900	338	$540	11	$ 556	$1,096
1,000	375	$600	10	$ 500	$1,100
1,100	413	$660	9	$ 455	$1,115
1,200	450	$720	8	$ 417	$1,137

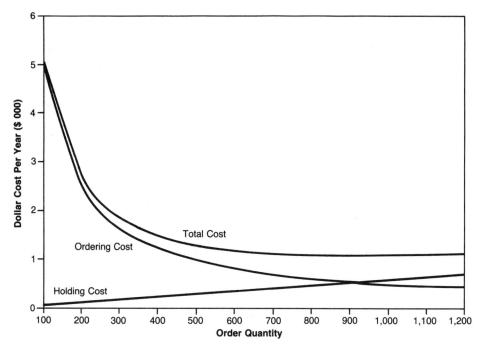

Figure 8-6. *Finite* R *Problem Data from Table 8-2.*

cost function with respect to Q, setting this derivative equal to zero, and solving for the optimal Q:

$$\text{Total cost} = TC = CPQ[1 - (S/R)]/2 + F(S/Q) \qquad (8\text{-}18)$$

$$dTC/dQ = CP[1 - (S/R)]/2 - F(S/Q^2) \qquad (8\text{-}19)$$

$$0 = CP[1 - (S/R)]/2 - F(S/Q^2) \qquad (8\text{-}20)$$

$$Q^* = (2FS/CP[1 - (S/R)])^{0.5} \qquad (8\text{-}21)$$

where Q^* is again the optimum order quantity.[9] Substituting the figures for the problem into equation (8-21):

$$Q^* = (2FS/CP[1 - (S/R)])^{0.5} \qquad (8\text{-}21)$$

$$= [2(50)\,(10{,}000)/(0.20)(8)(1 - (10{,}000/40{,}000))]^{0.5}$$

$$= 912.87 \qquad (8\text{-}22)$$

[9]Note that formula (8-21) reduces to formula (8-12) as the replenishment rate tends toward infinity:

$$\lim_{R \to \text{Inf.}} (2FS/CP[1 - (S/R)])^{0.5} = (2FS/CP)^{0.5}$$

since, as $R \to$ Infinity, $1 - (S/R) \to 1$.

so the optimal order quantity is 913 units per order. This will result in 10.95 order per year: for a 360-day year, orders will be placed about every 33 days. The order point, for a seven-day lead time from the time when the firm decides to produce the material until production is started, is 194 units. The total cost of holding and ordering the inventory will be:

$$\text{Total cost} = CPQ[1 - (S/R)]/2 + F(S/Q) \qquad (8\text{-}18)$$

$$= 0.20(8)913(1 - (10{,}000/40{,}000))/2 + 50(10{,}000/913)$$

$$= \$1{,}095 \qquad (8\text{-}23)$$

Quantity Discounts The prior model deals with cases where the replenishment rate is finite. Let us return to the basic infinite replenishment rate situation but now model the circumstance where the cost of acquiring inventory varies with the amount acquired. The most common circumstance that would cause this is the existence of quantity discounts. In this case, there is an additional cost that varies with the firm's ordering strategy and that must be included in the model: the cost of materials. Equation (8-4) gives this cost as:

$$\text{Cost} = P_q S \qquad (8\text{-}4)$$

Here, the P variable (which represents the investment in each unit of inventory) has a q subscript since it varies with order quantity. In situations where there are no quantity discounts, the cost of materials does not vary with order quantity, and this term need not appear in the total cost equation. But with quantity discounts, the firm's ordering strategy affects the total cost of materials, and this effect must be incorporated in the decision model. Adding the cost of materials term to equation (8-9), the total cost function for the infinite replenishment case becomes:

$$\text{Total Cost} = CP_q(Q/2) + F(S/Q) + P_q S \qquad (8\text{-}24)$$

To find the optimum order quantity, it would be useful if we could take the derivative of equation (8-24) with respect to Q, set this equal to zero, and solve for Q^* as before. Unfortunately, the quantity discount policies of most selling firms (the manner in which P_q varies with Q) are not such that P_q is a continuous function of Q. One alternative approach to the problem is to evaluate the total cost function of various levels of Q via a spreadsheet. Let us develop an inventory policy for an example problem in this way.

Most of the parameters of the problem are as before. The replenishment rate is infinite, the fixed cost of ordering (F) is $50, the carrying cost parameter (C) is 20 percent per year, and yearly usage (S) is 10,000 units. However, the product is to be purchased from a vendor who has established a pricing schedule that includes quantity discounts. If the buyer places an order for less than 500 units of the product, the price is $8.25 per unit. For order quantities between 500 and 1,499, the price is $8 per unit. If the firm's order is for more than 1,500 units, the price is $7.75 per unit. We know that if the price is $8 per unit, the optimal order quantity is 791 units. However, this analysis did not allow for the quantity discounts. The minimum order quantity to obtain the $7.75 price is about twice the EOQ with no quantity discounts. What is the optimal ordering strategy?

A spreadsheet evaluating equation (8-24) for various levels of Q is presented as Table 8-3. The data on yearly usage, the holding cost parameter, and the fixed cost of ordering is entered in cells B6 through B8. Cells A15 through B17 contain a table detailing the relationship between the order quantity and the price per unit. Column A contains the *minimum* order quantity necessary to receive this price. For example, the buyer must order at least 500 units (cell A16) in order to receive the price of $8 per unit (cell B16).

The parts of equation (8-24) are calculated in rows 25 through 44. Order quantities from 100 through 2,000 are listed in column A. Column B contains the unit prices for these order quantities. To obtain these prices, the "LOOKUP" function contained in most spreadsheets is utilized. The LOOKUP function reports the value of a cell based on a table contained elsewhere in the spreadsheet. In this spreadsheet, the values in cells B25 through B44 depend on the order quantities and the quantity/price relationship in cells A15 through B17.[10]

With the price data now available, the holding, ordering, and material costs can be calculated for each order quantity. Holding cost appears in column C; cell C25, for example, contains "B7*B25*(A25/2)". Ordering cost is calculated in column D; cell D25 contains "B8*(B6/A25)". The total cost of materials for the orders appears in column E, with cell E25 containing "A25*B6". These three costs are summed to obtain the total cost figures in column F.

These total cost figures are plotted in Figure 8-7. The total cost function is discontinuous because of the quantity discount pricing schedule. While, for the $8 price, total cost obtains a minimum for an order quantity of 791, placing an order sufficient to obtain the $7.75 price will reduce total cost still further. However, beyond the minimum necessary to get the price break, total cost again rises (because of the higher holding costs for these larger order quantities). Thus, if the seller offers the assumed quantity discount schedule, the

---

[10]LOOKUP functions vary substantially from program to program; some allow both vertical and horizontal references within tables while others do not. This particular spreadsheet was generated using a program which allows only horizontal lookups. Cell B25, for example, contains "@LOOKUP(A25,A15 . . . A18)".

1 **Table 8-3.** *Spreadsheet for Evaluation of EOQ Problem with Quantity Discounts.*

	Q	P_q	$CP_q(Q/2)$	$F(S/Q)$	P_qS	$CP_q(Q/2) +$ $F(S/Q) + P_qS$

2

3 ! A !! B !! C !! D !! E !! F !

4 Initial Data:

5

6 | | S | 10000 |

7 | | C | .20 |

8 | | F | 50 |

9

10 Lookup Table

11 for Price:

12

13 | | Q | P_q |

14

15 | | 0 | 8.25 |

16 | | 500 | 8.00 |

17 | | 1500 | 7.75 |

18

19 O. Q.   Price   Hold. Cost   Ord. Cost   Mtl. Cost   Total Cost

O. Q.	Price	Hold. Cost	Ord. Cost	Mtl. Cost	Total Cost
Q	P_q	$CP_q(Q/2)$	$F(S/Q)$	P_qS	$CP_q(Q/2) +$ $F(S/Q) + P_qS$
100	8.25	83	5000	82500	87583
200	8.25	165	2500	82500	85165
300	8.25	248	1667	82500	84414
400	8.25	330	1250	82500	84080
500	8.00	400	1000	80000	81400
600	8.00	480	833	80000	81313
700	8.00	560	714	80000	81274
800	8.00	640	625	80000	81265
900	8.00	720	556	80000	81276
1000	8.00	800	500	80000	81300
1100	8.00	880	455	80000	81335
1200	8.00	960	417	80000	81377
1300	8.00	1040	385	80000	81425
1400	8.00	1120	357	80000	81477
1500	7.75	1163	333	77500	78996
1600	7.75	1240	313	77500	79053
1700	7.75	1318	294	77500	79112
1800	7.75	1395	278	77500	79173
1900	7.75	1473	263	77500	79236
2000	7.75	1550	250	77500	79300

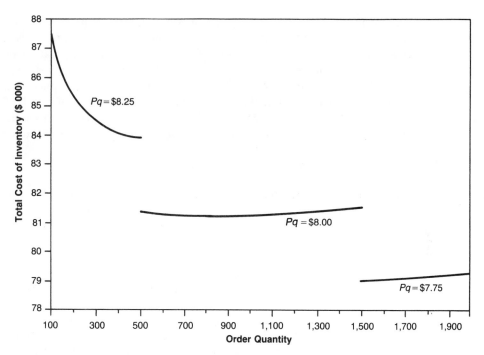

Figure 8-7. *Total Cost Versus Q with Quantity Discount.*

optimum ordering strategy is to order 1,500 units, incurring higher holding costs but lower material and ordering costs.[11]

Nonlinear Decay Inventory situations will occur where one or more costs are a continuous, but nonlinear, function of order quantity. Since costs of this type are not directly proportional to Q, they cannot be accurately represented as part of the holding cost of inventory. As in the modeling of quantity discounts, the appropriate method is to add a term to the total cost equation representing this cost. Equation (8-2) gives the general form of this additional term:

$$\text{Cost} = f(\text{inventory level}) \qquad (8\text{-}2)$$

Here, the functional notation indicates that there is a mathematical relationship between the cost and the level of inventory. The specific mathematical

[11]In this particular example, the minimum-cost order quantity occurs at an endpoint of a price range. Note that, if an optimum does not occur at a price range endpoint, but instead occurs for some value of Q between the price range endpoints, equation (8-12) could be used to compute the exact optimum order quantity for that price.

relationship will depend on the type of cost involved. For processes such as decay and obsolescence, the cost may be nonlinearly related to the *average time that a unit is in inventory*. In the EOQ model, the length of an inventory cycle is Q/S. For example, if the firm orders 250 items and yearly demand is 1,000, the inventory cycle will last one-fourth of a year. Since usage is linear, any particular unit will be in inventory an average of one-half this time, or $(1/2)(Q/S) = Q/2S$. The relationship between this average time in inventory and loss of value of inventory due to decay might be exponential:

$$\text{Cost} = Ge^{HQ/2S} \qquad (8\text{-}25)$$

where G and H are parameters that depend on the characteristics of the decay or obsolescence process. Alternately, higher powers of the average time in inventory might be involved:

$$\text{Cost} = G_1(Q/2S)^2 + G_2(Q/2S)^3 \ldots \qquad (8\text{-}26)$$

where the G_i $(i = 1, 2, \ldots)$ are the coefficients of the various terms of the polynomial. The ease of finding an optimum for a total cost function including such terms depends on the functional form of the relationship. The derivative of some functional forms is not easily taken. Further, for some functional forms the derivative of the total cost function is not easily solved for the optimum order quantity. When it is reasonable to take the necessary derivative and solve for the optimal order quantity, this approach will directly yield an optimization formula. However, for other functions, as long as the function relating decay costs to order quantity is well-behaved (always increases with increasing order quantity), there will be one global optimum. This optimum can be found using a spreadsheet approach.

Let us try an example problem. The replenishment rate is infinite and the fixed cost of placing an order, the holding cost of inventory, the price per unit, and the usage rate are $50, 20 percent, $8, and 10,000 respectively as before. However, inventory loses value over time because of decay. This decay is proportional to the square of the average time that a unit is in inventory. The formula for total inventory cost is then:

$$\text{Total Cost} = CP(Q/2) + F(S/Q) + G_1(Q/2S)^2 \qquad (8\text{-}27)$$

The firm has researched this particular decay process and found that the appropriate coefficient of the decay term (the value of G_1) is 400,000 when the average time in inventory is expressed in years.[12] Let us find the optimum order quantity via the spreadsheet method.[13]

---

[12] The units of this coefficient are dollars per year squared. Such a coefficient would be estimated based on historical or theoretical data regarding the decay process.

[13] The derivative of equation (8-27) is easily taken but the derivative is not readily solved for Q^*, since it is a polynomial.

1 **Table 8-4.** *Spreadsheet for Evaluation of EOQ Problem with Decay.*

3 ! A !!	B !!	C !!	D !!	E !!	F !
4 Initial Data:					
5					
6 S	10000				
7 C	.20				
8 F	50				
9 P	8.00				
10 G_1	400000				
11					
12 O. Q.	Hold. Cost	Ord. Cost	Avg. Time in	Decay Cost	Total Cost
13			Inv. (yrs)		
14					CP(Q/2)
15 Q	CP(Q/2)	F(S/Q)	Q/2S	$G_1(Q/2S)^2$	+F(S/Q)
16					$+G_1(Q/2S)^2$
17 By 100s					
18					
19 100	80	5000	.005	10	5090
20 200	160	2500	.01	40	2700
21 300	240	1667	.015	90	1997
22 400	320	1250	.02	160	1730
23 500	400	1000	.025	250	1650
24 600	480	833	.03	360	1673
25 700	560	714	.035	490	1764
26 800	640	625	.04	640	1905
27 900	720	556	.045	810	2086
28 1000	800	500	.05	1000	2300
29 1100	880	455	.055	1210	2545
30 1200	960	417	.06	1440	2817
31					
32					
33 By 10s around 500					
34					
35 450	360	1111	.0225	203	1674
36 460	368	1087	.023	212	1667
37 470	376	1064	.0235	221	1661
38 480	384	1042	.024	230	1656
39 490	392	1020	.0245	240	1653
40 500	400	1000	.025	250	1650
41 510	408	980	.0255	260	1648
42 520	416	962	.026	270	1648
43 530	424	943	.0265	281	1648
44 540	432	926	.027	292	1650
45 550	440	909	.0275	302	1652

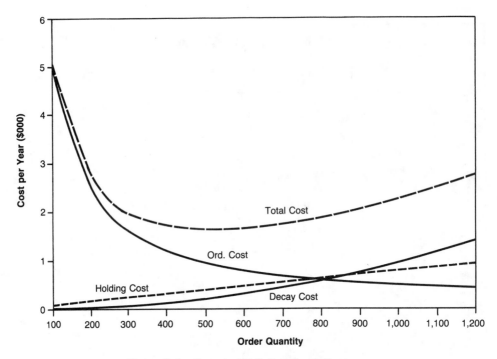

Figure 8-8. *Costs in EOQ Model with Decay.*

The necessary analysis is presented in Table 8-4 and graphed in Figure 8-8. The formulas for the holding cost and ordering cost in columns B and C are similar to those in Table 8-3 except that price does not vary among order quantities. The average time that a unit is in inventory is calculated in column D. Cell D19, for example, contains "A19/(2*B6)" since the order quantity for this row is in cell A19 and the usage rate is in cell B6. The decay cost is calculated in column E based on the G_1 coefficient in cell B10 and this average time; cell E19 contains "B10*(D19^2)". The total cost in column F is the sum of the holding, ordering, and decay costs.

In rows 19 through 30, the order quantity is iterated by 100 units to search for the approximate optimum. Among these order quantities, the lowest-cost outcome is found to be 500 units, with a yearly total cost of $1,650. In rows 35 through 45, the order quantity is increased by 10 per row starting at 450 units in order to find a more precise optimum. The order quantity of 520 units per order produces the lowest yearly cost (of $1,648 per year). Ordering 520 units is the firm's optimum strategy.

In this section, we have developed three additional models that extend the basic EOQ model to other inventory situations. However, given the diversity of inventory situations faced by firms, no complete listing of such models is possible. Instead, the intent has been to introduce the student, by example, to the principles of *how these models are developed*. In this way, students may understand the models presented in other texts addressing the particular situations they face in their business experiences.

Thus far, the models presented have not addressed the risk aspects of inventory modeling. Instead, it was assumed that all variables were certain. Since many situations do not fit this assumption, some mechanism for addressing uncertainty is needed. The formulation of safety stock strategies to address this uncertainty and the possible stockout costs caused by it is discussed in the next section.

SAFETY STOCK STRATEGIES FOR ADDRESSING UNCERTAINTY

There are two major uncertain variables in inventory situations: the *demand for the goods* and the *lead time from the order to the arrival of the goods*. If neither of these variables is uncertain, the firm can plan perfectly: inventory will arrive just as it is needed, and the firm will never face an unplanned stockout of goods. However, when either or both of these variables is uncertain, there will be times when the firm will not have sufficient goods available, and will then incur stockout costs. To avoid these stockout costs in dynamic inventory situations, the firm may keep a permanent safety stock of inventory, trading off the holding costs of this safety stock against the stockout costs that would result from not maintaining it. The important question, of course, is *how much safety stock to hold*, given the firm's order quantity strategy. In the next few pages, models for the optimal level of safety stock are developed based on the trade-off between stockout costs and the holding costs of the safety stock. Models will be developed for three circumstances regarding uncertainty: (1) only demand is uncertain, (2) only lead time is uncertain, (3) both lead time and demand are uncertain. In these models, the following assumptions will be made:

1. The firm uses the EOQ/order-point system to generate order quantity strategies.
2. If the firm stocks out of the good, it incurs a one-time cash cost which is independent of the amount of the shortage.[14]
3. Holding costs of the safety stock are a linear function of the amount of safety stock held.
4. The probability distributions of the uncertain variables are normal.[15]

---

[14]This is the simplest possible assumption regarding stockout cost. A more realistic assumption is that the firm incurs a stockout cost that is proportional to the amount of the shortage. Unfortunately, the latter assumption considerably complicates model building; interested readers are referred to more comprehensive texts in inventory management.

[15]Some safety stock strategies for Poisson and discrete distributions can be found in J. Kallberg and K. Parkinson, *Current Asset Management* (New York: Wiley, 1984), pp. 217–26.

Uncertain Demand Levels Since, for most firms, sales are uncertain, so is their usage of finished goods, work-in-process, and raw materials. To assess the probability of stockout for a given level of safety stock, we need an estimate of the uncertainty in demand. If the firm is using the EOQ/order-point system, the relevant uncertainty of demand is the uncertainty from the time the order is placed until the order is received, that is, *uncertainty of demand during the lead time*. To see this, consider a firm that has highly uncertain demand but can obtain goods immediately as needed. Such a firm need never stock out; if demand is greater than expected, the firm can immediately obtain goods to satisfy this demand. However, when there is a *significant lead time* between order and acquisition of the goods, there may be stockouts. When demand during this lead time is larger than expected, a stockout will occur. For example, assume that the firm has calculated an optimum order quantity of 100 units and an order point of 15 units, based on a lead time of 10 days. During a particular inventory cycle, an order will be placed when inventory reaches 15 units. If, over the next 10 days (until the order is received) demand is greater than 15 units, then the firm will stock out. Thus, *it is the uncertainty of demand between order and delivery that is relevant in formulating safety stock policy*.

Let us present an example problem, and then look at its implications for the optimum safety stock. Recall that, in our basic EOQ example, the optimal ordering strategy was to order 791 units when the level of inventory reached an order point of 194 units, given a lead time of 7 days and a yearly demand of 10,000 units. There were 12.64 inventory cycles per year. The price was $8 per unit and the carrying cost of inventory was 20 percent per year. Assume that the yearly demand is uncertain, with a coefficient of variation of 0.10. Assume also that the lead time is certain and that the cost of a stockout is $100. How much safety stock should the firm keep?

Let A be the level of the safety stock in units. The yearly holding cost of this safety stock will then be CPA. Let the probability of stockout during an inventory cycle based on this level of safety stock be X_a. The expected cost per cycle of stocking out will then be X_aK, where K is the cost of the stockout. Since there are S/Q^* cycles per year, the expected stockout cost will be $X_aK(S/Q^*)$, and the cost associated with the safety stock will be:

$$\text{Total Safety Stock Cost} = CPA + X_aK(S/Q^*) \qquad (8\text{-}28)$$

Equation (8-28) is evaluated for the example problem in Table 8-5; these data are plotted in Figure 8-9. Note here that since the coefficient of variation is 0.10, the standard deviation of demand during the lead time is (0.10)(194) = 19.4. In this table, the calculations are straightforward with the exception of the calculation of the probability of stockout. Let us review this calculation for a safety stock of 10 units. The expected usage during the lead time is 194 units. If the firm carries 10 units of safety stock, actual demand must be greater than 204 units (194 plus 10) in order for a stockout to occur. The Z-

Table 8-5. Evaluation of Safety Stock Strategies for Example with Demand Uncertainty Only.

Initial Data:

Carrying Cost per Year (C)	$.2
Stockout Cost (K)	$100
Price per Unit (P)	$8
Standard Deviation of Demand	19.4
Yearly Usage (S)	10,000 units/yr.
Economic Order Quantity (Q*)	791 units

Level of Safety Stock A	Holding Cost CPA	Z-Score for Stockout	Probability of Stockout X_a	Expected Yearly Stockout Cost $X_a K(S/Q^*)$	Total Cost $CPA + X_a K(S/Q^*)$
0	$ 0	0.00	0.5	$632	$632
10	$ 16	0.52	0.3015	$381	$397
20	$ 32	1.03	0.1515	$192	$224
30	$ 48	1.55	0.06057	$ 77	$125
40	$ 64	2.06	0.01970	$ 25	$ 89
50	$ 80	2.58	0.00494	$ 6	$ 86
60	$ 96	3.09	0.001001	$ 1	$ 97
70	$112	3.61	0.0006119	$ 1	$113
80	$128	4.12	0.00008222	$ 0	$128
90	$144	4.64	0.00000843	$ 0	$144

score for this outcome is $(204-194)/19.4 = 0.52$. From a table of the cumulative normal distribution, the probability that an outcome over 0.52 standard deviation above the mean will occur is 0.3015. Thus, the probability of stockout during each cycle for a safety stock of 10 units is 0.3015.

From this table and figure, the minimum-cost strategy is to keep about 50 units of safety stock, which results in a yearly total cost of $86. The optimum can be found more directly by taking the derivative of equation (8-28), setting this equal to zero, and solving for the optimum A. The derivative of equation (8-28) is:

$$dTC/dA = CP + (dX_a/dA)K(S/Q^*) \qquad (8-29)$$

A closed-form solution to this equation requires an expression for dX_a/dA. For the normal distribution, this expression is:[16]

$$dX_a/dA = -\frac{1}{SD_d\sqrt{2\pi}} e^{-(1/2SD_d^2)A^2} \qquad (8-30)$$

where SD_d is the standard deviation of demand during the lead time. Sub-

[16]See W. Peters and G. Summers, *Statistical Analysis for Business Decisions* (Englewood Cliffs, N.J.: Prentice Hall, 1968), p. 83, or any good statistics text.

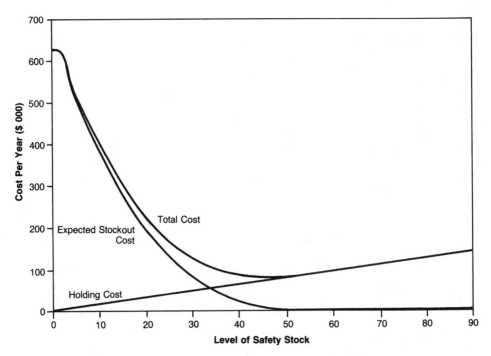

Figure 8-9. Data for Safety Stock Example Problem.

stituting this into equation (8-29), setting this equal to zero, and simplifying, we obtain:

$$A^* = [-2SD_d^2 ln(CPQ^* SD_d \sqrt{2\pi}/SK)]^{0.5} \qquad (8\text{-}31)$$

Inserting the data from the example problem into this equation, the optimum safety stock can be calculated:

$$A^* = [-2(19.4)^2 ln\{0.2(8)791(19.4)[2(3.14159)]^{.5}/10,000(100)\}]^{.5} \qquad (8\text{-}32)$$
$$= [-752.72 ln\{61,544.32/1,000,000\}]^{.5} = 45.81$$

So the optimal strategy is to carry a safety stock of 46 units. Since the expected usage during the lead time is 194 units, the firm should place an order for 791 units when the inventory level reaches 240 units. This order point reflects an expected usage of 194 units and a safety stock of 46 units. This level of safety stock results in a Z-score of $46/19.41 = 2.37$ and a stockout probability of 0.008894 for each inventory cycle. Substituting these figures into equation (8-28) gives the yearly cost of the optimal safety stock strategy:

$$Total\ Safety\ Stock\ Cost = CPA + X_a K(S/Q^*) \qquad (8\text{-}28)$$

$$= 0.20(8)46 + 0.008894(100)(10,000/791)$$

$$= \$74 + \$11 = \$85 \qquad (8\text{-}33)$$

Uncertain Lead Times Firms may also face situations where demand is certain but the *lead time between order and the arrival of the inventory is uncertain*. Uncertainty lead times often occur when the firm orders materials from a supplier. In such a case, if the firm kept no safety stock, 50 percent of the time the order would be received after the firm had stocked out, and stockout costs would have been incurred.

The appropriate model for determining the optimum safety stock with uncertain lead time is essentially the same as that where only demand is uncertain. To see this, recall that in this model the measure of uncertainty was the *standard deviation of demand from the order point to the receipt of the goods*. Variation in lead time produces uncertainty in demand *over this period* in the same way that a simple variation in demand would produce this uncertainty. For example, suppose that a firm's demand for a particular good was 5 units per day for certain, but the lead time from order to delivery was 10 days with a standard deviation of 2 days. This is the same as saying that, *between the placing of an order and its receipt*, the expected demand is 50 units with a standard deviation of 10 units (2 days times 5 units per day). If SD_1 is the standard distribution of demand during the time from order to receipt due to uncertainty regarding the lead time, formula (8-31) still gives the optimum order quantity, but SD_1 is substituted for SD_d.

Uncertain Demand and Uncertain Lead Times There are many circumstances where both demand and lead time are uncertain. In such cases, *both uncertainties* must be taken into account in formulating safety stock strategy. Here, the probability distributions of demand and lead time uncertainty must be combined to obtain an estimate of the total uncertainty during the time between the placing of the order and its receipt. The formula for the standard deviation of two combined probability distributions is:

$$SD_c = (SD_a^2 + SD_b^2 + 2SD_aSD_b\text{COR}_{ab})^{0.5} \qquad (8\text{-}34)$$

where SD_c is the standard deviation of the combined distributions, SD_a is the standard deviation of the first distribution, SD_b is the standard deviation of the second distribution, and COR_{ab} is the correlation coefficient between the two distributions. If both of the probability distributions are normal, the resulting probability distribution will be normal. Further, if the correlation coefficient between the distributions of demand and lead time is zero, then the standard deviation of the combined distributions is simply:

$$SD_c = (SD_a^2 + SD_b^2)^{0.5} \qquad (8\text{-}35)$$

To illustrate the appropriate safety stock levels with uncertainty in both demand and lead time, return to our example problem where demand was uncertain over the seven-day lead time, with a standard deviation of 19.4 units. Let us also assume that lead time is uncertain, with a standard deviation of 1.2 days, and that the two uncertainties are uncorrelated. Since demand is $10,000/360 = 27.78$ units per day, the standard deviation of the lead time translates into a standard deviation in usage of 33.33 units (1.2 times 27.78). The standard deviation of the combined probability distributions of lead time and demand uncertainty is:

$$SD_c = (SD_d^2 + SD_1^2)^{0.5} \tag{8-34}$$

$$= (19.4^2 + 33.33^2)^{0.5} = 38.56 \tag{8-36}$$

This figure can then be used in equation (8-31) to obtain the optimal safety stock:

$$A^* = [-2SD_c^2\ln(CPQ^*SD_c\sqrt{2\pi}/SK)]^{0.5} \tag{8-31}$$

$$= [-2(38.56)^2\ln\{0.2(8)791(38.56)\,[2(3.14159)]^{.5}/10,000(100)\}]^{.5}$$

$$= [-2,973.75\ln(122,327.26/1,000,000)]^{0.5} = 79.04 \tag{8-37}$$

so the optimum strategy is to carry 79 units of safety stock. This strategy will minimize the total costs to the firm, where these costs are composed of the expected stockout costs (due to uncertainty regarding demand and lead time) and the carrying costs of the safety stock.

SUMMARY

Firms make costly investments in inventory to address problems they face. These problems include variability in the price of goods over time, the need for flexibility in production processes, and the need for ready availability of goods to sell. Holding raw materials, work-in-process, and finished goods inventories will address these problems, but so will other strategies. For example, the problem hedging variability in the price of future purchases of raw materials can be addressed via futures contracts (for materials on which these contracts are available). Similarly, the just-in-time system can provide materials to the firm's production processes without the necessity of extensive investments in inventories.

In this chapter and the following one, we discuss optimal strategies for holding and ordering inventory for firms that choose to use the inventory approach to address some of their problems. We discuss strategies only for single-item inventory problems; those interested in more advanced inventory management topics are referred to the extensive literature in the area. The development of mathematical models for these single-item inventory situations requires that these models describe the physical circumstances regarding the purchasing and holding of these items. The great diversity of these physical situations leads to the great diversity of inventory models that appear in the literature.

In this chapter, the basic EOQ model was first developed. This model describes situations where the replenishment rate is infinite, and there are only two types of relevant costs in the inventory decision: ordering costs and holding costs. Other inventory models were then developed to address situations where the replenishment rate was finite, where there were quantity discounts on materials purchased, and where there were decay costs. These models were developed to illustrate the process of model building in inventory situations. Like all inventory models, these optimization routines are limited to situations described by the assumptions under which they are derived.

In the "certainty" approach to inventory management, an ordering and holding strategy is developed assuming that the levels estimated for each of the parameters in the inventory situation are certain. A separate safety stock strategy is then developed to address the uncertainty inherent in these estimates. This strategy trades off the holding costs of the permanent safety stock with the expected stockout costs inherent in that level of safety stock. Under restrictive assumptions, models were developed to generate optimal safety stock levels where demand and/or lead time were uncertain.

While this two-phase approach to the generation of inventory strategies is tractable, it is primarily oriented toward dynamic inventory situations, where a permanent safety stock can be used as a hedge against uncertainty since this stock does not become worthless after the initial period. "Uncertainty" approaches can also address such dynamic inventory situations, but are of most use in static inventory problems. Uncertainty approaches to inventory problems are the primary topic of the next chapter.

Problems

8-1. A firm is trying to decide on an ordering strategy for a particular item. The item can be delivered in unlimited quantities; unloading times are inconsequential. The firm uses 3,000 units of the item per year. Each item has a purchase price of $3. The firm has calculated that storage and insurance costs of inventory are 12 percent per year. The firm's cost of capital is 10 percent per year. Out-of-pocket paperwork costs associated with generating a purchase order total $10 per order. Costs of writing a check for an order are $5. Unloading costs are $12, regardless of the amount of the order. In general, the items ordered are expected to arrive 7 days after the order is placed. Using a 360-day year, calculate the optimum order quantity, the order point, and the total cost of the ordering strategy assuming that the firm does not keep a safety stock.

8-2. A firm is trying to decide how much of a particular liquid should be ordered. The liquid is kept in a storage tank; there are separate inflow and outflow pipes for the tank. The firm uses 500 gallons of liquid per day. When an order is placed with the supplier of the liquid, the truck arrives 7 days later to pump liquid into the tank. Because of the small size of the input pipe, only 2,500 gallons per day can be pumped into the tank. The fixed costs of placing an order are $500 per order. Carrying costs are 20 percent per year, and each gallon of liquid costs $10. The firm keeps a safety stock of 1,000 gallons of liquid on hand at all times. Use a 360-day year.

a. Calculate the economic order quantity and the order point.

b. Assume that the maximum capacity of the tank is 10,000 gallons. For your ordering strategy, will the tank overflow? Explain why or why not.

8-3. You are manager of the Manero Paint Store, a large paint outlet. One big-demand item is Color Number 107 (Passion Fire) latex paint in one-gallon containers. Manero Paint sells 10,000 containers of this paint per year. Demand is normally distributed with a standard deviation of 2,000 units. Passion Fire costs $7.50 per container. The lead time from order to delivery is 10 days with a standard deviation of 3 days. Holding costs are 16 percent per year and the fixed costs of placing an order are $80. If Manero Paint stocks out of Passion Fire, it incurs $500 in stockout costs. The replenishment rate is infinite. Use a 360-day year.

a. Calculate the optimum order quantity.

b. Calculate the optimum safety stock.

c. Calculate the cost of this inventory strategy per year.

8-4. A firm uses 7,500 units per year of a particular item. Holding costs are 15 percent per year and the fixed costs of ordering are $15 per order. The replenishment rate is infinite. If the firm orders in quantities of 1,000 units or less, the item costs $6 per unit. If the firm orders in quantities of greater than 1,000 units, the item costs $5.95 per unit. Find the optimum ordering strategy by evaluating the total costs (including material costs) of ordering strategies between 250 and 1200 units per order.

Selected Readings

Austin, L., "Project EOQ: A Success Story in Implementing Academic Research," *Interfaces*, Vol. 7, No. 4 (August 1977).

Kallberg, J., and K. Parkinson, *Current Asset Management* (New York: John Wiley, 1984), Chapter 6.

Kim, Y. H., G. C. Philippatos, and K. H. Chung, "Evaluating Investment in Inventory: A Net Present Value Framework," *Engineering Economist*, Vol. 31, No. 2 (Winter 1986), pp. 119–35.

Love, S., *Inventory Control* (New York: McGraw-Hill, 1979), Chapters 1, 2, and 4.

McDaniel, W. R., "The Economic Ordering Quantity and Wealth Maximization," *Financial Review*, Vol. 21, No. 2 (November 1986), pp. 527–36.

Snyder, A., "Principles of Inventory Management," *Financial Executive*, Vol. 32, No. 4 (April 1964), pp. 13–21.

Koss TBA[1]
Inventory Management

In April of 1985, Dan Olson (the manager of retail sales for Koss TBA, Inc.) had asked the operations research staff of the firm to develop an inventory management system for the company's chain of TBA stores. TBA, in the automotive business, stands for "tires, batteries, and accessories." TBA stores cater to the do-it-yourself trade in auto maintenance. In the early 1970s, a trend had developed in automobile maintenance. Due to the high cost of labor, automobile owners had started to do their own routine maintenance chores rather than pay a service station to do the work. Included among the routine chores were changing oil and oil filters, replacing windshield wipers, and changing spark plugs. (Another manifestation of this do-it-yourself attitude was the self-service gas station). A growing portion of the market for oil, oil filters, and so forth was therefore the car owner rather than the service station operator. To service this demand, enterprising firms had opened chains of retail stores selling auto parts to the gen-

eral public. Koss TBA was a chain of such stores. Koss purchased TBA items from suppliers, warehoused them in central locations, and distributed them from the warehouse network to their retail stores.

Mr. Olson did not consider the existing inventory system at the retail stores to be very effective. In this system, managers were given the authority to place orders from the warehouses at their discretion. This worked fairly well when the store manager had considerable experience, since their "feel" for demand levels was sufficient for effective inventory control. However, less experienced managers frequently had considerable trouble and often kept either too much inventory or too little. Too much inventory resulted in excessive carrying costs, but too little resulted in overly frequent orders and stockouts.

Once an ordering system was developed, implementation at the store level would be fairly simple. When customers paid for their purchases, checkout personnel at the firm's electronic cash registers input the item numbers. The current price for each item was then automatically drawn from the store's computer system; checkout personnel did not input prices. The computer system also kept

[1]This case has been adapted from Iqbal Mathur and Frederick C. Scherr, *Cases in Financial Management* (New York: Macmillan, 1979), pp. 56–61.

running records of the amount of inventory for all parts, updating this based on sales (via the register checkouts) and parts received. The accuracy of these computer records was maintained via periodic physical checks of inventory level (these checks are, of course, known as "taking inventory"). It would be a fairly easy programming task to have the computer system print daily lists of items on which inventory levels had fallen below critical cutoffs. These lists of merchandise would then be ordered from the warehouses and sent to the stores via one of the firm's trucks. The problem for the operations research staff was to set the cutoffs.

Any inventory system involves trade-offs among different types of costs. For TBA items, at the retail level, these costs were of three types: ordering costs, carrying costs, and stockout costs. Ordering costs have to do with the costs of placing and receiving the ordered quantity of the item. In Koss's system, these costs consisted of the incremental costs of adding a quantity of another item to the daily delivery which was made to each store. Compared to ordering from an outside source, these costs were relatively small. Since there was a daily delivery to each store regardless of what items were ordered, there were no additional shipping costs. Since there was no check to be written to an outside vendor, there were no check generation costs. The only additional costs, the operations research staff reasoned, would relate to any additional computer and paperwork expenses necessary to process the order, plus the additional labor necessary to unload the items from the delivery truck. They estimated the computer and paperwork expenses at $5 per order. While the personnel necessary to unload such items were already employed at the store, the unloading of trucks diverted their time from more profitable endeavors, such as servicing customers. Thus, the cost of the unloading crew

was not a sunk cost. The bulkier the item, the longer it took to unload each order of the item, and the higher were unloading costs.

To test the feasibility of the new inventory system, the operations research staff decided to estimate ordering and other costs and to formulate an inventory strategy for six sample items for a sample store: a particular brand of GR-78/14 tires, F22 batteries, 323 filters, 16-inch windshield wiper blades, 5-inch lamps, and 6C tuneup kits. These items varied in size, yearly demand, uncertainty of demand, bulk, unloading cost, and out-of-pocket investment. Estimates of some of these parameters for the six sample items were developed by the operations research department based on sampling and on some calculations. A summary is presented in Exhibit 1.

The costs of carrying inventory for the retail stores consisted of taxes, insurance, and cost of tied-up capital. Taxes occurred because some states in which the stores were located levied inventory taxes on the value of the inventory stored. For the sample store, taxes were 4 percent per year of inventory investment. Insurance was 3 percent per year of investment. The firm's cost of capital was 10 percent.

Stockout costs occurred when the store did not have inventory on hand to service a customer. In such a case, the profit on the sale was lost. However, the firm's true loss was more than this. The TBA business was very competitive; several other firms in areas where Koss stores operated could provide essentially equivalent auto parts. A prime selling feature of TBA stores was the ability to service demand with a minimum of inconvenience. When a customer tried to purchase an item and did not find it in stock, the customer was far less likely to return for future purchases, and most TBA customers needed auto parts and accessories several times per year. The operations research staff decided to model

Exhibit 1

Koss TBA
Statistics on Six Items Sold

Part	Expected Yearly Demand (Units)	Investment Per Item	Standard Deviation of Yearly Demand	Unloading Cost Per Order
GR-78/14 Tires	757	$30	298	$30
F22 Batteries	252	$30	78	$30
323 Filters	720	$ 5	150	$10
16-Inch Wiper Blades	360	$ 2	100	$10
5-Inch Lamps	108	$ 2	20	$10
6C Tuneup Kits	720	$15	168	$10

the stockout process by assigning a $50 stockout cost if the store was unable to service demand.

The operations research staff decided to use a two-step strategy for addressing the costs of inventory. To address the ordering and carrying costs associated with the normal inflow and outflow of material from the stores, they would assume that the demand for the item was certain, and they would develop an ordering strategy using standard economic order quantity methods. The uncertainty of this demand would be addressed via the use of a safety stock, the level of which would depend on the holding costs of this stock and the penalties for stockout. The store's computer would be programmed to place an order for the order quantity in such a way as to have the order arrive just as the store's inventory for the item was expected to reach the safety stock level. This order would then be scheduled for a truck making deliveries to the store. Given the firm's delivery system, lead times from order to delivery were five days for all items. Orders could be received later or earlier in the day, de-

Exhibit 2

Koss TBA
Monthly Sales Data for GR-78/14 Tires

Month Number	Sales in Units	Month Number	Sales in Units
1	84	21	55
2	36	22	101
3	62	23	90
4	30	24	20
5	5	25	72
6	70	26	55
7	54	27	65
8	24	28	87
9	65	29	91
10	77	30	36
11	39	31	74
12	81	32	20
13	66	33	90
14	83	34	86
15	44	35	87
16	86	36	57
17	42	37	61
18	40	38	99
19	70	39	40
20	91	40	88

pending on the amounts delivered to the other stores on the truck's delivery route. For this reason, the lead time was not certain, but had a standard deviation of 0.20 days.

The determination of the safety stock for each item posed one additional problem. To formulate a strategy based on the trade-off between the holding costs of a level of safety stock and the expected stockout costs that would result from that level, it was necessary to assess the probability distribution of demand. The operations research staff suspected, for several reasons, that demand and

lead time were normally distributed, but sound and careful business practice required that this suspicion be checked. In collecting the data on demand presented in Exhibit 1, the staff had gathered monthly sales data for the last 40 months for each of the six products. These data for the GR-78/14 tires are presented in Exhibit 2.[2]

[2]The operations research staff also checked this data for seasonality. Note that, while this is monthly data, if these data are normally distributed, the probability distribution of sales is also normal for any longer or shorter period.

chapter 9

Inventory Management: Uncertainty Approaches

In Chapter 8, we discussed the "certainty" approach to inventory management. In that approach, a strategy for inventory management was developed in two parts. First, a minimum-cost ordering strategy was formulated using the expected parameters of the particular inventory situation. This involved the computation of an economic order quantity based on expected demand, carrying costs, ordering costs, and so forth. Second, a separate hedging strategy was developed to handle deviations from these expectations. This involved the computation of an optimum safety stock, the level of which minimized the sum of the holding costs and the stockout costs associated with this safety stock.

The "uncertainty" methods discussed in this chapter are an alternate approach to inventory management problems. We label as "uncertainty methods" those methods that incorporate the riskiness of the situation, in addition to the firm's expectations, as a primary part of the analysis procedures. In this chapter, we consider uncertainty methods for both static and dynamic inventory problems. However, "static" problems (in which no carryover of inventory is allowed from one inventory cycle to the next) receive the major portion of our attention. We address static problems using three methods: (1) the Black-Scholes option pricing model; (2) risk-return analysis using the expected net present value of the cash flows and the coefficient of variation of this net present value; and (3) net present value using risk-adjusted discount rates. For simplicity, in our analysis of static problems, risk is assumed to occur only because of uncertainty regarding demand levels.

The second type of inventory problem allows carryover of inventory from one cycle to the next. This is called the "dynamic" inventory problem. We address this problem via simulation analysis, with the relative merits of various strategies assessed via their expected net present values and the risk of these net present values. Since simulation can incorporate the variability in any number of parameters without undue difficulty, our analysis of dynamic inventory problems allows for uncertainty in both lead times and demand levels. The chapter concludes with sections on the monitoring of inventory and on the management of inventory in practice.

THE STATIC INVENTORY PROBLEM

The static inventory problem is the simplest of all inventory problems. One and only one order is placed; there is no variation in ordering costs from one strategy to another. The question is how much of the good in question to order. Cash flows may include those related to initial purchase, overstocking, stockout costs, liquidation of excess inventory, and so forth. This type of problem occurs when the product is perishable in a physical or stylistic sense. Fashion or fad items, seasonal items, and other items with one and only one selling period (such as calendars) are typical items of this sort.

To enable the student to get a feel for such inventory problems and the methods by which they may be addressed, it is useful to introduce an example problem.[1] A nontaxable firm is deciding how many Christmas trees to purchase. The order must be placed in early October and prepaid. These trees are to be resold to the public during late December (90 days after ordering). Each tree costs $12. If there is demand for a particular tree, it will be sold for $20. Overstocked trees will sell for $2. The firm has estimated a discrete distribution of potential demand levels; it is expected that there will be a 20 percent chance that demand will be 100, 125, 150, 175, or 200 trees.[2] There are no repeat customers and thus no stockout costs of unfilled demand. How many trees should the firm order?

The simplest way, though not the best way, to address this problem is to calculate the expected profits from ordering strategies of 100 trees, 125 trees, and so forth. The profit from each strategy-outcome pair is presented in Table 9-1. For example, the entry of $950 for an ordering strategy of 175 trees and an outcome of 150 trees (cell D8) is computed as $-175(12)$ plus

---

[1]This problem is abstracted from J. D. Stowe and A. K. Gehr, Jr., "An Arbitrage Solution to the Christmas Tree Problem," a paper presented at the Financial Management Association Meeting in October, 1984, and available from authors at the University of Missouri at Columbia.

[2]In this problem and throughout this chapter, we have used discrete distributions of uncertain variables because we have found that managers are more comfortable estimating ranges and probabilities of these variables than estimating means and standard deviations. However, when historical data is used to estimate probability distributions, continuous distributions may be more appropriate. For a treatment of the static inventory problem where demand is distributed as a truncated normal distribution, see Y. H. Kim and K. H. Chung, "Inventory Management: A Financial Theory of the Firm Under Uncertainty," available from Kim at the University of Cincinnati.

Table 9-1. *Expected Profits for Example Problem.*

!	A	!!	B	!!	C	!!	D	!!	E	!!	F	!!	G !
1	Demand		100		125		150		175		200		
2	Prob.		.2		.2		.2		.2		.2		
3													
4	O. Q.				PROFIT								E(Prof)
5	100		800		800		800		800		800		800
6	125		550		1000		1000		1000		1000		910
7	150		300		750		1200		1200		1200		930
8	175		50		500		950		1400		1400		860
9	200		−200		250		700		1150		1600		700

20(150) plus 2(25) equals $950. All the entries above the diagonal running from the upper left to the lower right of the profits matrix are situations where quantity demanded exceeds that supplied (that is, the firm stocks out). Entries on this diagonal represent situations where just enough is ordered to satisfy demand. For entries below the diagonal, the firm has ordered more than is sold. Cell entries in the profits matrix take the form of "if statements." In this example problem, if quantity demanded is less than quantity supplied for a particular cell, the spreadsheet returns $8 (the margin per unit sold) times quantity demanded minus $10 per unit on overages (the loss per extra unit). If quantity demanded is greater than quantity supplied, the spreadsheet returns $8 times quantity supplied. Cell D8 thus contains "@ IF (D1 $\Leftarrow$ A8, D1*8, (D1*8) − ((A8−D1)*10))". The expected profits are calculated by multiplying the probabilities times the outcomes for each strategy; for example, the expected profit of $930 for the strategy of ordering 150 trees is 0.2(300) + 0.2(750) + (0.2 + 0.2 + 0.2) (1,200). To perform this operation on the spreadsheet, the contents of the probabilities row is multiplied by the contents of the outcomes row and these contributions summed. Thus, cell G7 contains "(B2*B7) + (C2*C7) + (D2*D7) + (E2*E7) + (F2*F7)". Since the strategy of ordering 150 trees produces the highest expected profit, this strategy would be preferred under this simple methodology.

This methodology is unsatisfactory from a financial analysis standpoint for two reasons. First, it does not take into account the time value of money; all the cash flows are lumped together without discounting. Since many static inventory problems involve cash flows that are spread over substantial periods, ignoring time value is a serious problem with this methodology. Second, this method does not address risk. For example, it is clear in our sample problem that the 150-trees order strategy is considerably more risky than the 125-trees order strategy in the sense that the variation in outcomes is more substantial. A method is needed to account for time value and risk. Three such methods are described in the following sections.

USING THE OPTION PRICING MODEL

There are interesting parallels between the put options that are available on some common stocks and the purchase of inventory in static inventory situations. A put is a contract to sell the stock at a predetermined price, which can be exercised or not at the holder's option.[3] The value of this contract depends on the future market price of the stock, which is uncertain. European put options (which can be exercised only on their maturity date) derive their value from the chance that the market price of the stock will be higher than the exercise price of the option on the maturity date. Similarly, in static inventory problems the value of a unit of inventory depends on the uncertain level of demand at the time of sale. The acquisition of a unit of inventory can be thought of as *an option to sell that unit, the value of which will depend on the eventual demand level.*

Because of these parallel circumstances, an option pricing approach has appeal as an analysis method in static inventory situations. One possible approach involves the application of the Black-Scholes option pricing model (OPM).[4] The OPM is a method of determining the current value of an option where the future payoffs from the option depend on the level of an exogenous variable at the option's maturity. In the OPM, the current value of the option depends on (1) the relationship between the current level of the exogenous variable and the exercise level of the option, (2) the variability of the exogenous variable, (3) the time remaining until the option's maturity, and (4) the risk-free rate of interest.

The relationships between these variables and the value of the put option are almost all obvious. The value of the put option increases directly with the probability that the level of the exogenous variable will be above the exercise price of the option at the option's maturity (and thus the probability that the holder of the option will be able to exercise it at a gain). This probability (and thus the value of the put option) is larger when:

1. The current price of the exogenous variable is higher relative to the exercise price. The higher the current price of the exogenous variable

---

[3]The basics of options contracts were described in Chapter 3.

[4]A complete presentation of the OPM is beyond the scope of this text. See F. Black and M. Scholes, "The Pricing of Options and Corporate Liabilities," *Journal of Political Economy* (May–June 1973), pp. 637–54. In this article, the option pricing model is derived using the advanced mathematical technique of stochastic calculus. For a derivation of the OPM without the use of this technique, see J. R. Garven, "A Pedagogic Note on the Derivation of the Black-Scholes Option Pricing Formula," *Financial Review*, Vol. 2, No. 2 (May 1986), pp. 337–44. A good overview of the OPM is presented in T. Copeland and J. F. Weston, *Financial Theory and Corporate Policy*, Second Edition (Reading, Mass.: Addison-Wesley, 1983), pp. 230–84.

is, the more likely that this price will be above the exercise price at maturity.

2. The variability of the price of the exogenous variable is greater. The greater this variability is, the greater is the spread of the probability distribution of the price of the exogenous variable at maturity. The greater the spread of this probability distribution, the greater is the probability that the price of the exogenous variable at maturity will be higher than the exercise price.

3. The time to maturity is longer. The longer is the time to maturity, the greater the chance that the value of the exogenous variable will rise above the exercise price.

By more obtuse reasoning, the value of the option in the OPM will increase with the risk-free rate of interest.

The primary figure to be calculated in the option pricing model is the "d_2 statistic" and its cumulative normal value. The cumulative normal value of the d_2 statistic can be thought of as the probability that the level of the exogenous variable will be less than the exercise level of the option. The formula for the d_2 statistic is:

$$d_2 = -\{[ln(P_0/Y) + (r + (1/2)SD^2)t]/SD(t^{.5}) - SD(t^{.5})\} \qquad (9\text{-}1)$$

where P_0 = the current level of the exogenous variable
Y = the exercise level for the option on the exogenous variable
r = the yearly risk-free rate of interest
SD = the instantaneous standard deviation of the exogenous variable
t = the number of years to maturity of the option

Once the d_2 statistic is calculated, its cumulative normal value is obtained, and this cumulative normal value is discounted to the present to obtain the value today of an option that pays \$1 at the maturity date if and only if the level of the exogenous variable is less than the exercise level for the option. The formula (using continuous discounting) is:

$$P(Y) = e^{-rt}[N(d_2(Y))] \qquad (9\text{-}2)$$

where $P(Y)$ is the value of the option with an exercise price of Y and $N(d_2(Y))$ is the cumulative normal value of the d_2 statistic for this Y.

In applying the option-pricing model to static inventory problems, it is useful to value an option that pays off if the value of the exogenous variable falls in a particular *range* (rather than merely falling below a particular level). In such a case, the $P(Y)$ statistics are first computed for the upper and lower cutoffs of the range and their normal values obtained. The following formula is then applied to obtain the value of an option which can be exercised only if the level of the exogenous variable falls within the range:

$$P(Y_1, Y_2) = e^{-rt}[N(d_2(Y_2)) - N(d_2(Y_1))] \tag{9-3}$$

where $P(Y_1, Y_2)$ is the value of the option, $N(d_2(Y_2))$ is the normal value of the d_2 statistic for the *upper limit* of the range, and $N(d_2(Y_1))$ is the normal value of the d_2 statistic for the *lower limit* of the range.

In option pricing, the exogenous variable can be almost any uncertain variable, but it is usually the market price of a traded asset; this asset is then referred to as the "comparison asset." The comparison asset is often an issue of common stock. The firm's own common stock or the stock of any other firm not expected to pay a dividend over the period can be used.

The OPM and the formulas associated with it may seem daunting, but their application to the static inventory problem is quite straightforward. Estimates or actual data on four parameters are needed:

1. The risk-free rate of interest.
2. The current price of the comparison asset.
3. The instantaneous variance of the price of the comparison asset.[5]
4. The future price ranges of the comparison asset for the various levels of demand.

Let us illustrate the use of the OPM per our example Christmas tree problem. Assume that the firm's common stock is to be used as the comparison asset and that the current price of this stock is $42. The risk-free rate is 8 percent per year, and the instantaneous standard deviation (square root of the variance) of the price of the firm's stock is 20 percent. The firm expects that 100 trees will be demanded only if economic conditions near Christmas are very poor. In that case, the firm's stock price might be expected to decline from its present level to less than $36. Similarly, it has estimated that if its stock price falls in the range of $36 to $40, demand will be 125 trees; if the price falls in the range of $40 to $46, demand will be 150 trees; if the price falls in the range of $46 to $52, demand will be 175 trees; and if price is greater than $52, demand will be 200 trees. With this information in hand, we can now execute the option pricing model's formulas and derive an optimum strategy.

In the example problem, P_0 is $42, the first comparison stock range is

[5]See H. Latane and R. J. Rendleman, Jr., "Standard Deviations of Stock Price Ratios Implied in Option Prices," *Journal of Finance* (May 1976), pp. 369–82, and M. Parkinson, "Option Pricing: The American Put," *The Journal of Business* (January 1977), pp. 21–36, for methods of obtaining estimates of the instantaneous variance of the price of common stock.

that below $36, and the inventory cycle is 1/4 year. The d_2 statistic for the price of the comparison stock being less than $36 is:

$$d_2 = -\{[ln(42/36) + (0.08 + (1/2)0.2^2)0.25]/0.2(0.25^{.5}) - 0.2(0.25^{.5})\}$$

$$= -1.69 \tag{9-4}$$

The normal value of this statistic, from a cumulative normal distribution table, is 0.04551. This is the probability that the stock price for the comparison stock will be less than $36. The second calculation needed in the option pricing model is to discount this probability back to the present. For the "below $36" range, the lower limit of the range (Y_1) is minus infinity (with a probability of zero), and the upper limit is $36 (with a probability of 0.04551). The $P(Y_1,Y_2)$ statistic for this range is:

$$P(Y_1,Y_2) = e^{-0.08(0.25)}(0.04551 - 0) = 0.04461 \tag{9-5}$$

This calculated result can be regarded as the value of an option which pays $1 if the price of the comparison stock falls below $36 and nothing otherwise. Calculation of this value for the other ranges of the comparison stock's future price is parallel. The d_2 statistics are first computed for the two values of Y, and the difference between the normal values of these statistics ($N(d_2(Y_2))$ minus $N(d_2(Y_1))$) is then discounted via equation (9-3).[6] Let us examine the next stock price range, which extends from $36 to $40. We already know the value of d_2 and the normal value for a Y of $36 (the d_2 value is -1.69, and the cumulative normal value for this d_2 statistic is 0.04551). The d_2 statistic for a Y of $40 is -0.64, and its normal value is 0.2611. The difference in cumulative normal values is 0.2611 minus 0.04551 or 0.21559. Using equation (9-3), the value of an option that pays $1 if the price of the comparison stock is between $36 and $40 is $0.21132.

Since these calculations are quite burdensome, it makes sense to set up the entire procedure on a spreadsheet, particularly if more than a very few ranges of the comparison stock are to be used. The results of the analysis for the sample problem are presented in Table 9-2. The possible demand levels and comparison stock upper limits are presented in lines 1 and 2. Additional needed data are in cells C3 through C6. These cells are referenced in the computation of the d_2 statistics and the option values in lines 8 through 13; the formulas for the d_2 statistics, option values, and so forth, are contained in the appropriate cells in these rows.

Once the option values (line 13) are calculated, these are applied to the future cash flows to assess the present values of these flows. For example, the value of an option that pays $1 if the comparison stock price is between

---

[6] See D. T. Breeden and R. H. Litzenberger, "Prices of State-Contingent Claims Implicit in Option Prices," *Journal of Business* (October 1978), pp. 621–51.

Table 9-2. *Net Present Values for Example Problem From Option Pricing Model.*

! A !!	B	!!	C !!	D !!	E !!	F !!	G !!	H !
1 Demand			100	125	150	175	200	
2 Comp. Stock Upper			36	40	46	52		
3 Comparison Stk. Var.			.04					
4 Yearly Risk-Free Rt.			.08					
5 Period Length			.25					
6 Init. Comp. Stk.			42					
7								
8 d2(Y1)			− Inf.	−1.69	−.64	.76	1.99	
9 N(d2(Y1))			0.00	.04551	.2611	.7764	.9767	
10 d2(Y2)			−1.69	−.64	.76	1.99	+ Inf.	
11 N(d2(Y2))			.04551	.2611	.7764	.9767	1.00	
12 N(d2(Y1))−N(d2(Y2))			.04551	.21559	.5153	.2003	.0233	
13 P(Y1,Y2)			.04461	.21132	.50510	.19633	.02284	
14								
15	O. Q. Int. Flow			Future Cash Flows				NPV
16	100	−1200	2000	2000	2000	2000	2000	760.40
17	125	−1500	2050	2500	2500	2500	2500	930.42
18	150	−1800	2100	2550	3000	3000	3000	1005.4
19	175	−2100	2150	2600	3050	3500	3500	852.99
20	200	−2400	2200	2650	3100	3550	4000	612.28

$36 and $40 is $0.21132. If we order 100 trees and this state occurs, the future net cash flow will be $2,000. The present value of this potential future cash flow is thus 0.21132 times $2,000 or $422.64. This is the contribution to the net present value of this ordering strategy from this potential future cash flow. Summing these contributions for all the potential cash flows and including the initial expense gives the total net present value of the strategy as computed via the option pricing approach. We see from the net present value column (column H) that the maximum net present value occurs for the 150-trees ordering strategy; based on the option pricing model, this strategy should be selected.

While the option pricing model provides an interesting and well-based approach to the one-period inventory problem, its application is not without difficulty. First, it requires a particular input that is fairly difficult to estimate: the set of price ranges of the comparison stock that are associated with each level of demand. Second, while this approach accounts for the time value of money, the option pricing model is risk-neutral; it does not price risk. In the option pricing model, risk in the option is not relevant because this risk can be hedged completely via an appropriate investment position in the comparison asset. While it is possible for the firm to make the necessary transactions so as to hedge an investment in an inventory position with an investment in the comparison asset, such strategies may be costly. Other uncertainty models of static inventory decisions provide more direct methods of dealing with risk.

USING THE EXPECTED NPV AND ITS COEFFICIENT OF VARIATION

Another approach to time value and risk in the static inventory problem is to employ a two-phase strategy in which time value is addressed first and then risk is assessed. The time value of money is properly addressed if the net present value technique is used to calculate the worth of cash flows. Since risk is to be addressed separately, discounting need only reflect time value, and the risk-free rate is the appropriate discount rate. In this technique, the expected net present value of each strategy is calculated first. Once these expected net present values are computed, one possible measure of their relative risk is the coefficient of variation of each net present value. A risk-return decision can then be made among strategies, based on their expected net present values and their dispersions of net present value. Let us execute this technique for the example problem.

In this problem, there is a three-month time lag between the initial cash outflow and the final cash inflow. Assuming an 8 percent yearly risk-free rate gives a discount factor of $1/1.02 = 0.9804$ for this interval. Multiplying this factor times the future cash flows for each strategy-outcome pair and incorporating the initial expense gives the result presented in Table 9-3. For example, cell D8 has a value of $890.20, which is a net present value. For this cell, the initial cash outflow is $175(12) = \$2,100$. The future cash inflow is $20(150) + 2(175 - 150) = \$3,050$. The value of this future flow discounted at 2 percent is $2,990.20, so the net present value is $890.20. The cell contains "@IF (D1 $\Leftarrow$ A8, $-(D1*12) + (D1*20)/1.02$, $-(D1*12) + ((D1*20) - ((A8-D1)*2)))/1.02$". Columns H and I contain the standard deviation and coefficient of variation of these net present values for each order quantity strategy. Examining these, it is clear that strategies involving order quantities above 150 trees are ruled out on dominance grounds; they have *lower* expected net present values and *higher* risk (in a coefficient of variation sense) than do other alternatives. It is *not* clear, however, whether the strategy of ordering

Table 9-3. *Expected Net Present Value and Coefficient of Variation of Net Present Value for Example Problem.*

! A !!	B !!	C !!	D !!	E !!	F !!	G !!	H !!	I !
1 Demand	100	125	150	175	200			
2 Prob.	.2	.2	.2	.2	.2			
3								
4 O. Q.			NPV			E(NPV)	SD(NPV)	COV(NPV)
5 100	760.78	760.78	760.78	760.78	760.78	760.78	0	0
6 125	509.80	950.98	950.98	950.98	950.98	862.75	176.4706	.20454545
7 150	258.82	700	1141.2	1141.2	1141.2	876.47	352.9412	.40268456
8 175	7.8431	449.02	890.20	1331.4	1331.4	801.96	514.4958	.64154728
9 200	−243.1	198.04	639.22	1080.4	1521.6	639.22	623.9177	.97606764

150 trees is superior to that of ordering 125 trees when risk is considered. The expected net present value of the 150-tree order strategy is $13.72 higher ($876.47 − $862.75), *but this strategy is also much riskier*; the coefficient of variation for this order strategy is about 0.40 versus 0.20 for the 125-tree order quantity strategy.

It should be obvious that while this approach is easy to understand and allows us to rule out some strategies and to assess the risk of others, the procedure could still be improved upon in at least one respect: it does not lead to a definitive recommendation in terms of strategy. Once risk and expected net present value are assessed and dominated strategies eliminated, the risk-return trade-off decision must still be made among the remaining alternatives. In the example problem, the manager still has to decide among the 100-, 125-, and 150-tree ordering strategies, although his or her decision is now a more informed one.

NPV WITH RISK-ADJUSTED DISCOUNT RATES

One method that leads to a definitive recommendation on strategy is to use risk-adjusted discount rates to incorporate the differential risk among the expected future cash flows from the various strategies. In this technique, the risk of future cash flows is assessed first and then addressed in the discounting process simultaneously with the time value of money. The discount rate does double duty: it reflects the time value of money and also the risk of the cash flows.

In using risk-adjusted discount rates (RAD), an important decision involves the choice of an RAD that properly reflects the amount of risk in the uncertain cash flows. If the firm uses the market risk concept and can estimate the beta of the cash flows from the decision, this estimate could form the basis for using the CAPM to obtain a risk-adjusted rate.[7] However, let us assume for example purposes that the firm uses the benchmark method, comparing the risk of the cash flows from the various inventory strategies with the risk of other cash flows and selecting a RAD accordingly. To make such an assignment of rates, the firm might assess the risk of the uncertain future cash flows by calculating their standard deviation and then use this measure of variability to assign a RAD.[8] Let us illustrate this procedure for the example problem.

The standard deviations of the future cash flows for the various ordering

---

[7]Kim and Chung, "Inventory Management," use this technique.

[8]Note the difference from the technique presented in the prior section. In that procedure, the NPV was computed first (to account for time value) and the coefficient of variation of this NPV formed the basis for second-phase risk assessment. However, if RADs are used, the risk adjustment is concurrent with discounting, and risk must be assessed before discounting is done.

Table 9-4. *Risk-Adjusted Net Present Values for Example Problem.*

!	A !!	B	!! C !!	D !!	E !!	F !!	G !!	H !!	I	!! J !!	K !
1		Demand	100	125	150	175	200				
2		Prob.	.2	.2	.2	.2	.2				
3											
4	O. Q.	Int. Flow		Future Cash Flows				E(FCF)	SD(FCF)	RAD	NPV(RAD)
5	100	−1200	2000	2000	2000	2000	2000	2000	0	.02	760.78
6	125	−1500	2050	2500	2500	2500	2500	2410	175.442	.03	839.81
7	150	−1800	2100	2550	3000	3000	3000	2730	339.146	.04	825.00
8	175	−2100	2150	2600	3050	3500	3500	2960	465.918	.05	719.05
9	200	−2400	2200	2650	3100	3550	4000	3100	492.950	.055	538.39

strategies are presented in column I of Table 9-4. Risk-adjusted discount rates are then assigned. (Note that the rates shown in the table are for the 90-day discounting period of the example problem, not yearly rates.) These appear in column J. The order quantity of 100 trees has a certain return, so its future cash flow is discounted at the risk-free rate. Various premiums have been added to this rate to reflect the relative riskiness of the other strategies. Risk-adjusted net present values are then computed using these rates (for example, cell K6 contains "B6 + (H6/(1+J6))"). From this analysis, it would seem that the 125-tree ordering strategy (not the 150-tree strategy) is superior, since it has the highest risk-adjusted net present value (column K).

This risk-adjusted discount approach is similar to standard capital budgeting procedures. It allows for the time value of money and prices risk. The problem, as in many situations where risk-adjusted discount rates are used, is the selection of the appropriate rates in line with the risk of each alternative strategy. The betas of demand for individual products may be difficult to estimate. If the benchmark method is used, the assignment of RADs may require substantial judgment, even though the analyst has reference discount rates from which to make adjustments.

THE DYNAMIC INVENTORY PROBLEM

In dynamic inventory problems, just as in static inventory problems, different ordering strategies produce divergent patterns of future cash flows. The major difference between the static and dynamic problems is that for dynamic problems, the cash flows occur over longer periods of time (since inventory can be carried from one period to another) and are, therefore, more complex. One uncertainty technique that can be applied to dynamic inventory problems is to discount future cash flows to obtain their NPVs, then assess risk via the coefficients of variation of these net present values.[9]

[9]Recall that we applied exactly this technique to the static inventory problem in the second prior section.

However, because the static inventory problem involves uncertainty in several future periods, simulation analysis is required to assess the risk of the various ordering strategies.[10]

While simulation is a more complex analysis technique, there are some advantages to its application. Recall that simulation analysis enables the management of the firm to assess the level of risk of a particular strategy by generating a mathematical model of the system under consideration and the random processes that affect it. These random factors are then allowed to vary, and the effects on important outcome variables are observed. In the inventory situation, a major random factor is sales volume, and the previous discussion of static problems centered on addressing the effects of sales fluctuations. However, within a simulation, the effects of other uncertain variables (such as delivery time, interest rate, and so forth) can be easily introduced.

Rather than continue the discussion in the abstract, let us introduce a sample dynamic inventory problem and address it via simulation analysis.[11] An appliance retailer is trying to formulate a strategy for managing the inventory of a particular major appliance (a dishwasher, clothes dryer, or similar item). His strategy variables are the number of appliances ordered (the order quantity) and the level of inventory at which an order is placed (the order point). Each appliance has an out-of-pocket cost of $300 and sells for $400. It costs $10 to place an order (no matter how many units are ordered). Orders can be placed only once a month. If a customer goes to the store to make a purchase and the appliance is out of stock, the retailer bears a $20 stockout cost per unit stocked out, representing the present value at the time of the stockout of lost future sales to the customer. All sales are for cash. Terms of sale from the appliance supplier to the retailer are net 30 days from the date of delivery, and the retailer pays these bills on the net date. Sales are not seasonal, and the retailer wants to formulate a policy to be in effect for the next 12 months.[12] The yearly risk-free rate of interest (used as the discount rate in simulation analysis) is 8 percent. Five appliances are currently in stock.

In this problem, assume that both the monthly demand and the delivery time from the month the order is placed are uncertain. The firm has collected demand and delivery time data from the last 50 months; these are presented in Table 9-5. Assuming that the future is like the past, the observed frequencies can be interpreted as probabilities, and random numbers can be assigned to the frequencies to stimulate the probability distributions of demand and delivery time.

---

[10]Simulation analysis was discussed in general in Chapter 1. This analysis technique was used in Chapter 3 to assess the risk of future cash balances in cash forecasting.

[11]This example problem is adapted from Ali Mansour, "Monte Carlo Simulation," available from the author at West Virginia University.

[12]For simplicity we assign a zero value to any remaining inventory at the end of this time.

Table 9-5. Historical Data on Demand and Delivery Times for Example Dynamic Inventory Problem.

Demand/Month	Frequency	Relative Frequency	Cumulative Frequency
0	2	0.04	0.04
1	4	0.08	0.12
2	14	0.28	0.40
3	20	0.40	0.80
4	8	0.16	0.96
5	1	0.02	0.98
6	1	0.02	1.00
	50	1.00	

Delivery Time (Months)	Frequency	Relative Frequency	Cumulative Frequency
1	6	0.60	0.60
2	3	0.30	0.90
3	1	0.10	1.00
	10	1.00	

To obtain expected net present values and coefficients of variation for these net present values, the usual procedure would be to utilize a simulation package. However, simulation analysis of small problems can also be conducted on a spreadsheet. A spreadsheet simulation of this inventory situation, with a set of random uniform numbers to illustrate the procedure, is presented in Table 9-6. The initial data and test values for the strategy variables are presented in columns A and B. The rest of the spreadsheet draws on these for the values in the remaining columns. The demand data in cells A7 through B15 and the delivery time data (time from order to delivery) in cells A18 through B22 are used in conjunction with the spreadsheet's lookup feature to turn random uniform numbers into demand and lead time statistics with the appropriate historically based probability distributions. In this speadsheet, we use two-digit random uniform numbers between 0.00 to 0.99. Cutoff points in the lookup tables must be specified such that the proper probabilities occur for each possible outcome. To do this, the cutoff points have been generated by deducting 0.005 from the cumulative frequencies given in Table 9-5. Thus, for example, if the random number for demand is 0.00, 0.01, 0.02, or 0.03, the lookup feature will return a demand of 0, since all these numbers are less than the cutoff for the first range of 0.0395. These four possible outcomes, which produce this demand level, are 4 percent of the 100 possible random numbers between 0.00 and 0.99, so the proper historic probabilities are represented.

To see how this simulation works, let us examine the results in columns E through P in detail. The random uniform numbers to generate demand and delivery time are in cells E3 through P4. These could be input manually from a uniform random number table or generated internally if the spreadsheet has this facility. Reading down column E, the beginning inventory is 5. The demand uniform random number for the first month is 0.19 (cell E3), so demand for this month is 2 appliances (because 0.19 is greater than 0.115 but less than 0.395 on the demand lookup table). We assume that there are no previous orders yet to be delivered, so the cells representing deliveries for this month (E8 through E10) are zero. The ending inventory is thus three units. Since this is equal to or less than the reorder point (cell B27), an order for the order quantity (cell B26) is placed. That is, cell E13 contains an "if statement"—that if ending inventory (cell E11) is equal to or less than the reorder point, an order for the order quantity is placed. The delivery time random number is 0.20 (cell E4), so the delivery time assigned to this order is one month (via the lookup table for delivery time). This order then appears as an addition to inventory in the next month (cell F8). For the second month, the beginning inventory is three units, the demand is three units, and a delivery of five units is received. The ending inventory is thus five units, and no order is placed. The simulation continues on this basis for the remaining months. Note that in month three, a stockout occurs; demand is six units, but available inventory is only five units.

Sales in units are recorded in cells E16 through P16. These sales figures are the lesser of (1) demand, or (2) available inventory (beginning inventory plus deliveries) for each month. Using these sales and inventory transactions, cash flows are calculated in cells E18 through P23. Since all sales are for cash, cash receipts from this particular appliance are sales from the month (row 16) times the selling price per unit (cell B3). Terms are net 30 days, and so are calculated as the prior month's deliveries (rows 8 through 10) times the cost per item (cell B2). A stockout cost (cell B4) is included for each unit by which demand exceeds available inventory (row 20 thus contains a series of if statements referring to rows 6 through 10), and row 21 contains an ordering cost (cell B4) in each month during which an order is placed (the if statements in row 21 refer to the contents of the "orders placed" row, which is row 13). Looking at the cash flow for month three, for example, cash receipts are $2,000, representing the sale of five units at $400 per unit. Payments for purchases are $1,500, representing $300 per unit paid for the five units received in month two (which were ordered in month one). While sales in month three were five units, demand was six units, so a stockout charge of $20 is incurred ($20 per unit times the one unit stockout). The net cash flow for the month is therefore $470, equal to the $2,000 inflow minus the $1,530 in outflows. The net present value of $4,265.60 for this simulation run is presented in cell P25, using 1/12 of the yearly risk-free rate (cell B29) as a monthly discount factor.

Table 9-6. Spreadsheet Simulation of Example Dynamic Inventory Problem.

!	A	!!	B	!!	C	!!	D	!!	E	!
1	Data:						Month:		1	
2	Cost per Item				300					
3	Selling Price per Item				400		Demand Random Number		.19	
4	Ordering Cost				10		Delivery Time Random Number		.2	
5	Stockout Cost				20					
6							Beginning Inventory		5	
7	Demand Data:						Demand		2	
8			R. N.		Demand		Rec. From Fst. Prior Mo.		0	
9			0		0		Rec. From Snd. Prior Mo.		0	
10			.0395		1		Rec. From Trd. Prior Mo.		0	
11			.115		2		Ending Inventory		3	
12			.395		3					
13			.795		4		Orders Placed		5	
14			.955		5		Delivery Time		1	
15			.975		6					
16							Sales (units)		2	
17										
18	Delivery Time Data:						Cash Receipts		800	
19			R. N.		Lead Time		Payments for Pur.		0	
20			0		1		Stockout Costs		0	
21			.595		2		Ordering Cost		10	
22			.895		3				——	
23							Cash Flows		790	
24										
25	Strategy Variables:									
26	Order Quantity				5					
27	Reorder Point				3					
28										
29	Yearly Risk-Free Rate:				8					

The value of simulation analysis lies not in the results of any particular simulation run but in the results of numerous simulation runs, which together give estimates of both the expected values of outcome variables and their riskiness. In the context of this example dynamic inventory problem, the strategy variables are order quantity and order point, and the outcome variable is net present value. The retailer wants to know what combinations of order point and order quantity strategy will yield his preferred combination of risk and return. To assess the risk and expected return from various order point and order quantity strategies, the analyst generates a number of simulation runs for each order-point/order-quantity strategy. The resulting net present values are recorded and the mean and standard deviation of the net present value calculated for each strategy combination. The mean net present value and the estimated coefficients of variation of these net present values

! F	!! G	!! H	!! I	!! J	!! K	!! L	!! M	!! N	!! O	!! P !
2	3	4	5	6	7	8	9	10	11	12
.45	.99	.8	.15	.34	.1	.74	.02	.13	.73	.43
.95	.13	.14	.45	.61	.54	.67	.87	.39	.23	.36
3	5	0	1	4	2	1	8	8	6	3
3	6	4	2	2	1	3	0	2	3	3
5	0	5	5	0	0	5	0	0	0	5
0	0	0	0	0	0	5	0	0	0	0
0	0	0	0	0	0	0	0	0	0	0
5	0	1	4	2	1	8	8	6	3	5
0	5	5	0	5	5	0	0	0	5	0
3	1	1	1	2	1	2	2	1	1	1
3	5	4	2	2	1	3	0	2	3	3
1200	2000	1600	800	800	400	1200	0	800	1200	1200
0	1500	0	1500	1500	0	0	3000	0	0	0
0	20	0	0	0	0	0	0	0	0	0
0	10	10	0	10	10	0	0	0	10	0
1200	470	1590	−700	−710	390	1200	−3000	800	1190	1200

Net Present Value 4265.60

for combinations of order points from 1 to 7 and order quantities from 1 to 7 using the simulation model previously presented are given in Table 9-7. These sample statistics are estimates of the true population parameters; the more simulation runs are made for each possible strategy, the closer will these estimates converge on the actual parameters.

Assessing the risk-return trade-offs encompassed in a table of this sort seems foreboding at first, but fortunately a substantial number of the possible strategies can be eliminated on dominance grounds. However, in looking for dominated strategies, we must keep in mind that we are examining estimates of population parameters and not true population parameters. Thus, small differences among results can be sampling variation and not actual differences in expected risk and return.

A detailed examination of Table 9-7 gives some very interesting infor-

Table 9-7. *Results of Simulation Analysis of Example Dynamic Inventory Problem.*

Order Quantity

		1	2	3	4	5	6	7
	1	1371	1368	1671	3017	3570	3107	3171
		(0.06)	(0.05)	(0.24)	(0.23)	(0.22)	(0.30)	(0.18)
	2	1333	1348	1737	3128	3948	3676	3039
		(0.05)	(0.06)	(0.30)	(0.17)	(0.20)	(0.26)	(0.25)
	3	1363	1341	1853	3214	3826	3604	2978
		(0.05)	(0.04)	(0.30)	(0.22)	(0.24)	(0.32)	(0.36)
Order	4	1342	1363	1730	3158	3697	4028	3208
Point		(0.05)	(0.05)	(0.21)	(0.28)	(0.23)	(0.22)	(0.36)
	5	1342	1365	1800	3397	3351	3735	2731
		(0.05)	(0.04)	(0.26)	(0.23)	(0.37)	(0.27)	(0.61)
	6	1367	1345	1781	2979	3373	3724	2685
		(0.04)	(0.05)	(0.25)	(0.27)	(0.31)	(0.23)	(0.43)
	7	1348	1300	1684	2867	3085	3272	2017
		(0.04)	(0.05)	(0.18)	(0.25)	(0.40)	(0.30)	(0.85)

Estimated means, standard deviations, and coefficients of variation are based on 25 simulation runs per order-point/order-quantity combination (a total of 960 runs). Numbers without parentheses are mean net present values for each set of 25 runs; numbers in parentheses below these are the associated estimated coefficients of variation.

mation. It can be calculated from Table 9-5 that the expected demand is 2.70 units per month. The problem specifies that only one order can be placed per month, and that the beginning stock is five units. As a result, for strategies involving order quantities of less than 3 the firm sells out in almost every month and incurs frequent stockout costs. This produces relatively low but safe profits, as can be observed in the entries in the columns representing order quantities of 1 and 2. The order point has little effect on these results; the retailer orders in virtually every period in most of the simulation runs for these order quantities.

Reading across the rows of the table, it would seem that the strategies using order quantities of 6 and 7 for order points of 1, 2, and 3 are less advantageous than lower order quantity strategies for these same order points. For example, looking at the row for a two-unit order point, the maximum mean profit occurs for an order quantity of 5 (at $3,948); higher order quantities for this order point produce lower and riskier profits. Similar logic allows us to discard order quantities of 7 for order points of 5, 6, and 7.

The patterns of expected return and risk are less clear when looking down the columns. It appears that order points of 5, 6, and 7 for a seven-unit order quantity produce lower and riskier profits than do lower order points for this same order quantity. Similarly, order points of 7 seem to produce inferior expected results to lower order point strategies for order quantities of 4, 5, and 6.

Finally, a sizable increase in expected profitability comes from increasing an order quantity of 3 to an order quantity of 4 for all order points. This occurs with no estimated increase in risk. The average coefficient of variation across all order points for the three-unit order quantity is 0.25, while the average for the four-unit order quantity is 0.24; yet the respective average net present values are $1,751 and $3,109. It would thus seem that the three-appliance order strategy is less advantageous than the four-appliance order strategy.

Figure 9-1 presents the results of this examination of dominance among the simulated strategies. Managers representing very risk-averse shareholders would choose order quantity strategies of one or two units; for these strategies, order point is irrelevant. Less risk-averse shareholders would choose to undertake more risk in exchange for more expected present value. Such strategies are represented in the rightmost unshaded portion of the chart. Within this portion of the chart, the estimated coefficients of variation indicate that risk is fairly uniform among strategies. It would seem that the strategies involving either: (1) an order quantity of 5 and an order point of 2; (2) an order quantity of 5 and an order point of 3; and (3) an order quantity of 6

Figure 9-1. *Dominated Strategies in Example Dynamic Inventory Problem.*

Order Quantity

Order Point		1	2	3	4	5	6	7
	1	1,371 (0.06)	1,368 (0.05)	1,671 (0.24)	3,017 (0.23)	3,570 (0.22)	3,107 (0.30)	3,171 (0.18)
	2	1,333 (0.05)	1,348 (0.06)	1,737 (0.30)	3,128 (0.17)	3,948 (0.20)	3,676 (0.26)	3,039 (0.25)
	3	1,363 (0.05)	1,341 (0.04)	1,853 (0.30)	3,214 (0.22)	3,826 (0.24)	3,604 (0.32)	2,978 (0.36)
	4	1,342 (0.05)	1,363 (0.05)	1,730 (0.21)	3,158 (0.28)	3,697 (0.23)	4,028 (0.22)	3,208 (0.36)
	5	1,342 (0.05)	1,365 (0.04)	1,800 (0.26)	3,397 (0.23)	3,351 (.037)	3,735 (0.27)	2,731 (0.61)
	6	1,367 (0.04)	1,345 (0.05)	1,781 (0.25)	2,979 (0.27)	3,373 (0.31)	3,724 (0.23)	2,685 (0.43)
	7	1,348 (0.04)	1,300 (0.05)	1,684 (0.18)	2,867 (0.25)	3,085 (0.40)	3,272 (0.30)	2,017 (0.85)

Data are from Table 9–7. The dominated strategies are indicated by shading. The remaining strategies are not dominated by others and will be preferred by some decisionmakers.

and an order point of 4 would be prime candidates for implementation, since these produce the highest (and nearly equivalent) mean net present values.

Even a small simulation analysis of this sort is complicated and expensive relative to the certainty approaches to the dynamic inventory problem. Also, as seen by our example, simulation analysis does not produce a definitive recommendation regarding strategy; the choice among nondominated risk-return combinations must be made by the firm's management. However, simulation analysis is very flexible in the probability distributions that it can address. In addressing risk in the certainty method, we generated optimal safety stock strategies by taking the derivative of the total cost expression for the safety stock. Included in this expression was the probability density function for uncertainty in usage. Obviously, there will be probability density functions that are discontinuous (as in our example) and others where obtaining or solving a mathematical expression for the derivative is very difficult. However, the simulation method can address these situations. This is a prime advantage of the simulation approach to dynamic inventory problems.

MONITORING INVENTORY BALANCES

As with accounts receivable balances, inventory balances turn over rapidly. Also, inventory is a major investment for many firms, particularly firms engaged in manufacturing, retailing, or wholesaling. For these reasons, the continuous monitoring of inventory investments is a necessary function in the management of working capital.

The monitoring of inventory entails several problems not encountered in the monitoring of accounts receivable. First, there is a *cost-of-information problem* in keeping track of the physical inventories of some goods. Second, because of the number of variables involved, *it is very difficult to develop an accurate measure of inventory turnover*. We will discuss these two problems in the following paragraphs. To add interest to the discussion, we will contrast the monitoring of inventory with that of accounts receivable, which was discussed in detail in Chapter 7.

The cost-of-information problem in the monitoring of inventory levels has to do with the nature of inventory and the many types of inventory that are held by firms. Records of accounts receivable are kept in electronic form; the cost of maintaining such records is not large. But the electronic records of inventory are only *representations of the actual physical items* that are the firm's inventory. Physically counting large numbers of items to update electronic records is extremely expensive because it is a labor-intensive process. Also, because of the great number of items kept by some firms and the costliness of the monitoring process, there is always a question about how much time and money should be spent on the monitoring of the levels of some inventory items. If the carrying costs and stockout costs associated with holding some types of inventory are small, it makes sense to avoid spending substantial amounts to access the level of these types of inventory; the costs of monitoring outweigh the benefits.

To address these information cost problems, many firms use the *A-B-C System* of inventory management. In this system, types of inventory are given ratings of A, B, or C based on their cost and criticality to the firm. Items rated A are large-dollar investments or are critical to the operations of the firm. Items rated C are small-dollar items or items where immediate availability is not required. For example, in a hospital, oxygen supplies would be type A inventory, while pencils would be type C inventory. Items of middle rank in terms of investment and need are classified as type B inventory items. Depending on the type of firm, inventory rated A and B will encompass a relatively small proportion of the *number of items* in the firm's inventories, but will include the majority of the *dollar inventory investment* and of the items that are absolutely necessary in order for the firm to function. When using this system, the firm will keep very close track on the ordering and inventory levels of type A items, spend somewhat less effort in the management of type B items, and be fairly cavalier about inventories of type C items. In this way, information and management costs are minimized.[13]

The second problem in the monitoring of inventory is developing a procedure to accurately measure the behavior of inventory. Recall that this problem also occurred in the measurement of customer payment patterns of accounts receivable balances. In monitoring accounts receivable, changes in sales caused distortions in turnover-based measures of receivables' quality, such as days' sales outstanding. Measures such as sales-weighted days' sales outstanding were developed to correct for this problem. These measures eliminated the distortions caused by fluctuating sales levels. Unfortunately, the problem of distortion in turnover-based monitoring statistics is even more severe in the management of inventory. For inventory, distortions occur not only because of variations in *sales*, but also variations in *unit investment* in inventory, *usage rates* (unit turnover), and the *mix of different types* of inventory carried by the firm.

To see this, let us address an example problem. Using the A-B-C System of inventory management, a firm has decided to divide its inventory into three types: inventories of Product 1 and Product 2 (which are type-A inventory items) and all other inventories (which are type-C items). Based on expected costs of obtaining inventories, sales rates, inventory management procedures, and so forth, the firm has estimated that year-end inventory will be $40.25 million, and that aggregate dollar inventory turnover (cost of sales divided by inventory) will be 6.32. Sales turn out to be somewhat higher than expected,

---

[13]The A-B-C System is widely discussed in the literature on inventory management. For more on this system, see S. Love, *Inventory Control* (New York: McGraw-Hill, 1979), pp. 244–47.

Table 9-8. Example Inventory Monitoring Problem.

Projected Inventory Balances

	Sales (Units)	Unit Turnover	Investment per Unit	Cost of Goods Sold	Inventory (Units)	Inventory (Dollars)
Product 1	40,000	8.00	2.50	100,000	5,000	12,500
Product 2	18,000	6.00	7.25	130,500	3,000	21,750
All Other Prdts.	48,000	4.00	.50	24,000	12,000	6,000
Totals				254,500	20,000	40,250
CGS/Inventory						6.32

Actual Inventory Balances

	Sales (Units)	Unit Turnover	Investment per Unit	Cost of Goods Sold	Inventory (Units)	Inventory (Dollars)
Product 1	35,000	5.83	2.75	96,250	6,000	16,500
Product 2	25,000	7.14	6.75	168,750	3,500	23,625
All Other Prdts.	50,000	4.55	.60	30,000	11,000	6,600
Totals				295,000	20,500	46,725
CGS/Inventory						6.31

and inventory turnover is actually 6.31 (data are presented in Table 9-8). Is any review of inventory policies and levels needed, or should the firm be satisfied with this result?

While the actual dollar inventory turnover is very near the expected levels, even a cursory glance at the data shows that something may be happening that the firm did not expect. Some unit inventory turnovers (calculated based on units sold and held) and investments in the three types of inventory items were much more or less than expected; *it is only a coincidence that these differences balance out* in the aggregate dollar turnover ratio calculated for this firm.

To find out what has actually occurred, one useful technique is *variance analysis.* We also used this accounting-based procedure in connection with the monitoring of accounts receivable in Chapter 7. However, this procedure is even more useful in connection with the monitoring of inventory. Because of the difficulty in obtaining and interpreting a measure of inventory behavior that corrects for the biases introduced by changes in sales, price, and so forth, variance analysis is our primary means of monitoring inventory patterns. The variance analysis technique addresses changes in the *mix* of inventory by disaggregating the various types of inventory kept by the firm. Then, for each type of inventory, dollar variances due to the differences between actual and expected levels of *sales, unit turnover,* and *price* (where price is the investment in each unit of inventory) are computed to isolate the effects of each of these important variables on inventory investment.

The variance analysis technique for inventory monitoring is best illustrated by example. Table 9-9 presents a spreadsheet variance analysis of the data in Table 9-8. Let us examine this spreadsheet in detail.[14]

The computation of the three variances occurs in rows 4 through 40. In these rows, column B contains sales in units, column C contains unit turnover (based again on units sold and held), D contains investment (price) per unit of inventory, E contains inventory in units, F contains inventory in dollars (computed as inventory in units times investment), and G contains the variances for each type of inventory. Rows 4 through 13 contain the projected (budgeted) figures for each of these items; rows 33 through 40 contain the actual outcomes. The total variance is $6.475 million, computed as the actual inventory balance of $46.725 million minus the projected balance of $40.25 million. The intervening rows are used to calculate the portions of this variance resulting from sales, turnover, and price for each type of inventory held.

In rows 15 through 22, the actual sales volumes in units are used and the inventory investment computed assuming that the investment per unit and the turnover were as projected. Because of these variations in sales, inventory balances are lower than expected for Product 1 and higher than expected for the remaining products. When sales are greater or less than expected, changes in inventory investments are required, and this type of variance in inventory balances due to sales is to be anticipated.

The variances due to unit turnover are computed in rows 24 through 31 by using the actual ending inventories in units. These appear in column E. For example, actual sales on Product 1 were 35 million units and actual ending inventory in units was 6 million, so unit inventory turnover was 5.83 (cell C27) for this inventory item. We see in column G that there are large variances caused by the differences between projected and actual turnovers. All these differences should cause substantial concern regarding the inventory management procedures of the firm. If the firm keeps too much inventory (has too low a turnover), there is excessive investment. This has occurred for Product 1. However, if the firm keeps too little inventory, it risks stockouts. This has occurred for Product 2 and for the type-C inventory items.

The variance in inventory investment due to price is calculated in rows 33 through 40. There are substantial variances for each of the three inventory types. Product 1 costs more than expected to purchase or make, as did the type-C items. Product 2 costs less than expected to obtain.

A summary of the variances for the three products is presented in rows 42 through 50. Since the effect of sales is factored out, we can discuss the effects of turnover and price in isolation. The pattern of these two variances differs among the three types of inventory. Product 1 has a large turnover variance; turnover has slowed from expected levels. The firm may be carrying

---

[14]Additional discussion of variance analysis for the monitoring of inventory balances is provided in G. Gallinger and P. Healey, *Liquidity Analysis and Management* (Reading, Mass.: Addison-Wesley, 1987), pp. 417–42.

Table 9-9. *Variance Analysis of Example Monitoring Problem via Spreadsheet*

	A	B	C	D	E	F	G
4	Projected Sales, Projected						
5	Turnover, and Projected Price						
6							
7		Sales	Turnover	Inv./	Inventory	Inventory	
8		(Units)		Unit	(Units)	(Dollars)	
9	Product 1	40000	8.00	2.50	5000	12500	
10	Product 2	18000	6.00	7.25	3000	21750	
11	All Other Prdts.	48000	4.00	.50	12000	6000	
12							
13	Totals				20000	40250	
14							
15	Actual Sales, Projected						
16	Turnover, and Projected Price						
17							Sales
							Variance
18	Product 1	35000	8.00	2.50	4375	10938	−1563
19	Product 2	25000	6.00	7.25	4167	30208	8458
20	All Other Prdts.	50000	4.00	.50	12500	6250	250
21							
22	Totals				21042	47396	7146
23							

Actual Sales, Actual Turnover, and Projected Price

	Proj. Balance				Actual Balance	Turnover Variance
27 Product 1	35000	5.83	2.50	6000	15000	4063
28 Product 2	25000	7.14	7.25	3500	25375	−4833
29 All Other Prdts.	50000	4.55	.50	11000	5500	−750
30						
31 Totals				20500	45875	−1521

Actual Sales, Actual Turnover, and Actual Price

						Price Variance
36 Product 1	35000	5.83	2.75	6000	16500	1500
37 Product 2	25000	7.14	6.75	3500	23625	−1750
38 All Other Prdts.	50000	4.55	.60	11000	6600	1100
39						
40 Totals				20500	46725	850

Summary of Variances

	Proj. Balance	Sales Var.	Turn. Var.	Price Var.	Actual Balance
46 Product 1	12500	−1563	4063	1500	16500
47 Product 2	21750	8458	−4833	−1750	23625
48 All Other Prdts.	6000	250	−750	1100	6600
49					
50 Totals	40250	7146	−1521	850	46725

too much of this type of inventory. The firm has also paid more than expected for inventory of this product.

For Product 2, turnover was much faster than expected, resulting in inventory being $4.833 million lower than expected, given actual sales levels. Investigation is needed to assess whether this has resulted in excessive stockouts for this type-A inventory item. The firm also paid less than expected for this inventory over the period of the analysis.

The turnover variance for the type-C inventory items is negative, indicating that these items turned over less rapidly than expected. This is of a good deal less concern than the turnovers of the type-A items, since (by their classification as C items) these inventories are not critical to the firm's operations. However, the price variance for these items is substantial ($1.1 million) and requires investigation.

By this example, we see the usefulness of variance analysis in the monitoring of inventory patterns. By applying variance analysis to each type of inventory, we are able to separate the effects of mix, sales, turnover, and price. With these effects isolated, investigation of any disadvantageous deviations from expectations can be undertaken.

INVENTORY MANAGEMENT IN PRACTICE

This is the final chapter concerning the management of inventory. In this chapter and the prior one, techniques have been presented for managing inventory and for monitoring inventory levels. Students are naturally interested in the extent to which these techniques are used in the practice of inventory management.

Unlike the decision methodologies presented in many other parts of this text, the basic technologies of inventory management are not new; many of them date from the 1940s or before. Consequently, there has been relatively little recent interest in assessing whether firms have adopted such basic methodologies as the EOQ approach, safety stock strategies, the A-B-C System, and so forth. However, a review of trade publications, where businessmen often discuss their views on management, indicates that the understanding of these basic methodologies is widespread.

Some supporting evidence on the use of these basic approaches to inventory management is presented in Smith and Sell's questionnaire survey of large firms, which was conducted in 1978.[15] As part of this survey, they asked firms to specify the technique used for establishing inventory restocking points (reorder points). Sixty-eight percent of respondents indicated that they used

[15]K. V. Smith and S. B. Sell, "Working Capital Management in Practice," in K. V. Smith, Editor, *Reading on the Management of Working Capital*, Second Edition (St. Paul: West Publishing, 1980), pp. 51–86.

either cost-balancing models (such as the models presented in Chapter 9) or computerized inventory control. This result depended to some extent on the size of the firm; 82.4 percent of larger firms indicated the use of these two types of reorder point determination, while 53.1 percent of smaller firms made similar indications. If firms' computerized inventory order point systems are based on EOQ-type models, it would seem that certainty methodologies are a widely used approach to the order strategy problem, particularly for larger firms.

Smith and Sell also found that changes in profits and return on investment were important criteria in evaluating changes in inventory policy. To the extent that criteria of these sorts are proxies for shareholder wealth maximization, they are generally in keeping with the approaches used in this text. This survey evidence, together with the discussion of these techniques in trade publications, suggests that the basic models of inventory management are widely used. However, much less is known about the use of more complex or more recently developed approaches (such as uncertainty models) to the management of inventory.

SUMMARY

In this chapter, we discussed several methods that simultaneously address the expected parameters of an inventory situation and their uncertainty. Both static and dynamic inventory problems were discussed. Three uncertainty methods for addressing static inventory problems were outlined: (1) valuation of the uncertain future flow via the option-pricing model; (2) the calculation of expected net present value, with risk assessed via the coefficient of variation of this net present value; and (3) net present value using risk-adjusted discount rates to adjust the value of the uncertain expected future flows for their riskiness. All three of these methodologies addressed both the time value and the riskiness of future cash flows in static inventory problems.

Dynamic inventory problems were addressed via simulation analysis of the expected net present value and the variability of net present value for various inventory strategies. Unlike certainty methods, simulation analysis can address any probability distribution of the uncertain variables in inventory problems. However, simulation analysis of inventory problems is costly to execute and eliminates only dominated risk-return strategy combinations; management must make the choice among the nondominated strategies.

The monitoring of inventory levels was discussed. This monitoring is a difficult process because of the effects of variations in sales, the price of the inventory, the mix of inventory among inventory types, and unit inventory turnover on monitoring statistics. These variations make the aggregate dollar turnover ratio (which compares sales to inventory investment) a misleading indicator of inventory behavior. To control for price, sales, unit turnover, and mix in assessing behavior, the accounting technique of variance analysis was used.

The available survey evidence, along with observations of businesspersons' contributions to the trade press, indicates that the basic inventory management concepts of economic order quantity, safety stock for hedging uncertainty, and so forth, are widely used and understood, particularly among larger firms. Less is known about the application of more advanced techniques to inventory management situations.

This chapter concludes our discussion of the management of working capital assets. Chapters thus far have concerned the management of the major short-term assets held by firms: cash, marketable securities, accounts receivable, and inventory. Numerous tools and concepts for determining the most advantageous composition of these various assets have been discussed. The next three chapters concern the management of short-term liabilities.

Problems

9-1. A student at Enormous State University (ESU) has decided to scalp tickets to ESU's football games. The prime question is, of course, how many tickets to purchase for a particular game. The student anticipates that the number of tickets that he or she can sell on the day of the game will be dependent on the level of the Dow-Jones Industrial Average (DJIA) at the time of the game:

Level of the DJIA	Less Than 1,500	1,500–1,900	Greater Than 1,900
Number of tickets sold	20	40	60

The DJIA is currently 1850. The first game is 6 months away. The risk-free rate of interest is 6.5 percent per year. Tickets cost $15, payable immediately, and sell for $25 if they are sold. There are no taxes or stockout costs. Assume that the instantaneous variance of the DJIA is 0.70. Calculate the number of tickets that the student should purchase (choices: 20, 40, or 60) using the option-pricing model.

9-2. A firm is trying to develop an inventory policy for an item with a one-period life using uncertainty methods. Items can be acquired now for sale three months hence. Each item costs $6, payable immediately, and will sell for $10 if it is sold at all. If there are not sufficient items to service demand, the firm will incur an after-tax stockout cost of $1 per unit stocked out. Excess items have no salvage value. Tax bills will be paid at the time of sale; the firm is in the 40 percent tax rate, and will have sufficient other earnings to utilize tax shields in the event of losses. The estimated probability distribution of demand is:

Probability	0.1	0.4	0.4	0.1
Demand (units)	100	200	300	400

The feasible ordering strategies are 100, 200, 300, or 400 units.

a. Generate a matrix of initial cash flows and future after-tax cash flows.

b. Calculate the expected net present value and the coefficient of variation of net present value for each ordering strategy. The risk-free rate of interest is 7.5 percent per year. Indicate which strategy should be chosen by this methodology.

c. Calculate the net present value of each ordering strategy using risk-adjusted discount rates. Use the following risk-adjusted rates (in percent per year):

Order Quantity	100	200	300	400
RAD	8	9	10	11

Indicate which strategy should be chosen by this methodology.

9-3. A firm carries two types of inventory, Type 1 and Type 2. Expected sales, turnover, and price were:

Inventory	Sales (in Units)	Unit Turnover	Price per Unit
Type 1	1,000	20.00	$150
Type 2	3,000	15.00	$75

Actual sales, turnover, and price were:

Inventory	Sales (in Units)	Unit Turnover	Price per Unit
Type 1	750	10.00	$170
Type 2	4,000	18.00	$65

Perform a variance analysis for the two types of inventory; calculate sales, turnover, and price variances for each inventory type.

Selected Readings

Copeland, T. E., and J. F. Weston, *Financial Theory and Corporate Policy*, Second Edition (Reading, Mass.: Addison-Wesley, 1983), pp. 230–84.

Gallinger, G., and P. Healey, *Liquidity Analysis and Management* (Reading, Mass.: Addison-Wesley, 1987), Chapter 15.

Kim, Y. H., and K. H. Chung, "Inventory Management: A Financial Theory of the Firm Under Uncertainty," available from Kim at the University of Cincinnati.

Love, S., *Inventory Control* (New York: McGraw-Hill, 1979), Chapter 9.

Mansour, Ali, "Monte Carlo Simulation," unpublished manuscript, available from the author at West Virginia University.

Stowe, J. D., and A. K. Gehr, Jr., "An Arbitrage Solution to the Christmas Tree Problem." Paper presented at the Financial Management Association Annual Meeting, October, 1984. Available from the authors at the University of Missouri at Columbia.

Simpson Stores Inventory Management: One-Period Products

In the clothing business, there are two general types of goods: fashion-related and nonfashion-related. Fashion-related items are those with a high "fad" component. Demand for items of this sort is heavily related to the strength and length of fashion trends, and thus is highly uncertain. Further, since these trends tend to disappear as quickly as they appear, the recovery value of unsold fashion items is usually minimal. Numerous retailers, left with stocks of unsalable merchandise, will sadly attest to this fact.

Nonfashion-related items become outmoded more slowly. Demand trends in such items are less perceptible from season to season. Basic athletic apparel and some types of blue jeans are examples of such items.

For Ms. Dora Lee, a merchandise buyer for Simpson Stores, this difference required a variation in purchase and inventory management techniques. For all types of goods, demand was seasonal, and overstocked items could not be returned to vendors. For nonfashion-related items, while some merchandise could be sold in end-of-season sales with minor price reductions, it was generally feasible to carry over some merchandise from one year to another. Many fashion-related

items, however, had a selling life of one season or less. Drastic markdowns were used to dispose of such merchandise as the end of the season approached. Any unsold merchandise of this sort was written off at cost at the end of the season and given to charity. Thus, nonfashion-related items represented a dynamic (multiperiod) inventory problem, while fashion-related items represented a static (one-period) inventory problem.

One item with a heavy fad component was a particular blouse (style number 111703) purchased from No Bikini Atoll Sportswear. The blouse was of a color and style that led Ms. Lee to believe that, while it might be quite popular this year, the market for the item next year was likely to be very limited. Further, the blouse could be ordered only once for the upcoming selling season (a common situation for fashion items). The order had to be placed six months before the selling season. Merchandise would be received about four months after the order was placed, and the invoice for the merchandise would be due one month after the merchandise was received. Based on her assessment of the demand for such items among the stores in the Simpson chain, Ms. Lee expected that 200 blouses could be sold

---

Exhibit 1

Simpson Stores
Estimated Main-Season Sales of Style
Number 111703 for Each Size Range

Economic Conditions	*Sales Range (units sold)*	*Price Range for Firm's Stock*
Very Poor	25–75	Below $75
Recession	76–125	$75–$90
Weak	126–175	$90–$105
Average	176–225	$105–$120
Good	226–275	$120–$135
Excellent	276–325	$135–$150
Boom	326–375	Above $150

---

in the upcoming year in each of the common sizes. There was, however, substantial uncertainty about this demand level. Ms. Lee estimated the continuous distribution presented in Exhibit 1 to represent demand and economic conditions. She decided to use the midpoints of the demand ranges to analyze the outcomes. Consultation with the firm's financial staff also gave her estimates of the levels of the firm's common stock for each of these economic conditions. The current price of the firm's common stock was $110 per share.

The blouses could be purchased from the vendor for $20 each. During the relatively short prime selling season, they would be priced at $30 each. At the end of this season, they would be marked down to $15 each; it was expected that 85 percent of the remaining stock would be sold at this price. The remaining 15 percent would be given to charity. The firm was taxable and was in the 46 percent marginal tax bracket. Ms. Lee felt, given the character of Simpson Stores and its customers, that stockout costs would be incurred if a customer wished to purchase the blouse and found the store to be out of stock. She decided to assign a $2 after-tax stockout cost for each unit stocked out. This cost would be incurred at the time of the stockout and would represent the present value of lost future after-tax cash inflows due to decreased customer patronage.

chapter 10

The Firm's Level of Aggregate Liquidity

Throughout this text, we are concerned with the effects of uncertainty on the management of the firm's current assets and liabilities. At each stage, we provide methods for addressing the risks that occur for a particular current liability or asset. What is not discussed in other chapters is the *gross* hedge that occurs via the relationship between *total* short-term assets and *total* short-term liabilities. The overall relationship between current assets (which produce cash inflows) and current liabilities (which require cash outflows) will determine the size of this gross hedge. If current assets can provide much more cash than is needed for current liabilities, then the chance of a cash stockout is lessened. We call this overall relationship between a firm's potentially available cash and its potential cash needs the firm's *aggregate liquidity position*. The proper measurement and management of aggregate liquidity position is the concern of this chapter.

The chapter begins with a section discussing why the measurement and management of aggregate liquidity is important to the firm. Following this, issues in the measurement of aggregate liquidity are discussed. A reliable measure of aggregate liquidity can serve several purposes, but we will see that the traditional measures of liquidity are not very accurate indicators of a firm's true aggregate liquidity position. After these traditional measures are reviewed, some that are more accurate and comprehensive are suggested. The risk-return trade-off that faces the firm in determining its aggregate liquidity position is then discussed, and some measures of the inherent risks and returns are illustrated. A section on the management of aggregate liquidity in practice concludes the chapter.

WHY MEASURE AND MANAGE AGGREGATE LIQUIDITY?

Firms measure and manage their aggregate liquidity positions because of the risk and return implications of this gross hedge for the firm. We will see later in the chapter that the amount of current debt relative to current assets affects the level of expected cash flows to shareholders and the risk of these cash flows. Since any such variations in the risk and return affect shareholder wealth, assessing and addressing these variations is a necessary function of financial management.

The management of aggregate liquidity starts with the measurement of the size of this hedge for various potential financial strategies. Since this management is facilitated by more precise measurement, the development and application of *accurate* measures of aggregate liquidity is of substantial advantage to the firm. However, the availability of accurate measures of aggregate liquidity has a side benefit. In addition to the measurement of the firm's own liquidity for the purpose of managing this position, measures of liquidity can also be applied to outside firms as an aid in making credit-granting decisions. Aggregate liquidity is an important determinant of the probability of default, and the accurate assessment of this aggregate liquidity position can therefore lend important insights in estimating the default probabilities of credit applicants.

TRADITIONAL MEASURES OF THE AGGREGATE LIQUIDITY OF THE FIRM

In prior chapters, we have discussed aggregate liquidity rather simplistically in terms of the relative amounts of current debt and current assets, but the concept is really more complex than this. Liquidity can be thought of as the *firm's ability to quickly generate cash versus the firm's need for cash on short notice.* Beginning textbooks usually cite several financial ratios as measures of liquidity. Unfortunately, each of the ratios that are traditionally cited has problems as an omnibus measure of the firm's liquidity position. Commonly cited ratios include:

Current Ratio. This is the ratio of current assets to current liabilities. The higher this ratio, the more liquid the firm is said to be. This ratio is widely used by practitioners and has substantial intuitive appeal. It uses the standard accounting convention in designating which assets and debts are "liquid" and which are not. The convention, of course, states that any asset or debt expected to mature in less than a year is "liquid" (that is, "current"). The problem with the current ratio is that it mixes assets and liabilities that are, in reality, quite different in terms of their nearness to cash (that is, in their time to maturity). A debt due in six months is treated the same way as a debt due in six days, since they are both part of current liabilities. Inventory, which requires a sale to become receivables and the collection of the resulting receivables to become cash, is treated in the same way as marketable securities, which can be sold quickly and thus are clearly more liquid.

Therefore, while it is widely used, the current ratio can be improved upon as a measure of aggregate liquidity.

Quick Ratio This is also called the "acid test" ratio. Here, inventories (which require a sale to become collectible) are deducted from the current assets account and the result divided by current liabilities.[1] Interpretation is similar to the current ratio. The idea behind the quick ratio is to generate an index that better compares short-term cash-generating ability with short-term cash needs by excluding the most obviously illiquid current asset (the one furthest from cash in the working capital cycle) from the near-cash assets total. This is a reasonable step since the sales of any firm are always quite uncertain; however, this ratio still entails a substantial mixing of maturities, particularly among liabilities.

Accounts Receivable Turnover This ratio is usually calculated as sales divided by accounts receivable. The inverse of this ratio times the number of days in a year gives the *average collection period*: the weighted-average time that a receivable is outstanding.[2] The higher the turnover (and the lower the average collection period), the quicker is a receivable turned into cash, and the more liquid is the firm said to be.

Inventory Turnover Ratio This is usually computed as cost of sales divided by inventory. Like the accounts receivable turnover ratio, the higher the turnover, the more liquid the asset.[3] The basic difficulty with the accounts receivable turnover ratio and the inventory turnover ratio as liquidity measures is that they focus on only one asset's nearness to cash, and thus by themselves do not tell much about the firm's *overall* liquidity position. That is really what we want to measure.

The four ratios discussed above are easy to understand and are commonly used in assessing the liquidity of firms. But as the discussion indicates, all are flawed to some extent as omnibus liquidity measures. *They may give the wrong signals, contradictory signals, or no signals at all of actual changes in liquidity position.* To see this, let us examine the liquidity position of Hacker Corporation, a designer and manufacturer of computer games. Hacker's year-

---

[1]Note that this procedure still leaves other, less liquid assets (such as prepaid expenses) included in the numerator of the ratio. This is usually justified because the amounts of these other assets are generally small; cash, marketable securities, accounts receivable, and inventories comprise the vast majority of current assets for most firms. A more careful but less common definition of the quick ratio is: (cash + marketable securities + accounts receivable)/current liabilities.

[2]When used for the monitoring of customer payments, this ratio is known as the firm's *days' sales outstanding*; it was discussed in Chapter 7.

[3]We discussed the use of this aggregate dollar inventory turnover ratio for the monitoring inventory in Chapter 9.

end financial data are presented in Table 10-1. The "Old" columns indicate Hacker's current financial position.

In assessing Hacker's financial position, the four traditional measures of liquidity can be computed:

Current Ratio: $140,000/$170,000 = 0.82$ \hfill (10-1)

Quick Ratio: $(\$140,000 - \$75,000)/\$170,000 = 0.38$ \hfill (10-2)

Accts. Rec. Turnover: $\$1,000,000/\$50,000 = 20$ times per year \hfill (10-3)

Inv. Turnover: $(\$200,000 + \$700,000)/\$75,000 = 12$ times per year \hfill (10-4)

To see the problems with these traditional measures, let us hypothesize some changes in Hacker's financial position. Suppose that buyers start paying more slowly, so that accounts receivable build up by $10,000. Hacker Corporation finances this by reducing cash by the same amount. This change is portrayed in Panel A of Table 10-1. The firm's overall liquidity has been reduced since it has less cash and more accounts receivable (which are less liquid than cash). However, *the firm's quick, current, and inventory turnover ratios are unchanged*. These measures do not show this change in liquidity. The accounts receivable turnover ratio would, however, decrease to 16.67 ($1,000,000/$60,000).

Even more startling examples are possible. Suppose that, due to better inventory management techniques, the firm is able to reduce inventory investment from $75,000 to $50,000 with no increase in total inventory costs. Assume that the funds freed from this reduction in inventory are used to reduce accounts payable. These effects are portrayed in Panel B of Table 10-1. The firm's current ratio would decline from 0.82 to 0.79, its quick ratio would climb from 0.38 to 0.45, its inventory turnover would increase from 12.0 to 18.0, and its accounts receivable turnover would be unchanged. The decreased current ratio indicates a *decline* in liquidity, the increased quick and inventory turnover ratios indicate an *increase* in liquidity, and the accounts receivable turnover ratio indicates that liquidity is *unchanged*. We see by these examples that the traditional measures of liquidity may not signal when changes in liquidity have occurred, or they may give conflicting signals regarding the direction of this change.

Problems and contradictions such as these in the use and interpretation of the traditional ratio measures have led to the development of several improved measures of the overall liquidity of the firm. These measures are discussed in the next section.

IMPROVED INDICES FOR MEASURING AGGREGATE LIQUIDITY

Several improved measures of aggregate liquidity have appeared in the literature. Four of these are: (1) the *Cash Conversion Cycle* of Richards and

Table 10-1. *Hacker Corporation: Analysis of Changes in Liquidity.*

Last Year's Sales $1,000,000
Cost of Sales $ 900,000

Panel A: Change in Accounts Receivable Turnover

Situation Number	1 Old	2 New
Cash	$ 15,000	$ 5,000
Accounts Receivable	50,000	60,000
Inventory	75,000	75,000
Total Current Assets	140,000	140,000
Net Fixed Assets	150,000	150,000
Total Assets	$290,000	$290,000
Accounts Payable	$110,000	$110,000
Accrued Wages	60,000	60,000
Total Current Liabilities	170,000	170,000
Equity	120,000	120,000
Total Liabilities and Equity	$290,000	$290,000
Current Ratio	.82	.82
Quick Ratio	.38	.38
Accts. Rec. Turnover	20.00	16.67
Inventory Turnover	12.00	12.00

Panel B: Change in Inventory and Accounts Payable

	1 Old	3 New
Cash	$ 15,000	$ 15,000
Accounts Receivable	50,000	50,000
Inventory	75,000	50,000
Total Current Assets	140,000	115,000
Net Fixed Assets	150,000	150,000
Total Assets	$290,000	$265,000
Accounts Payable	$110,000	$ 85,000
Accrued Wages	60,000	60,000
Total Current Liabilities	170,000	145,000
Equity	120,000	120,000
Total Liabilities and Equity	$290,000	$265,000
Current Ratio	.82	.79
Quick Ratio	.38	.45
Accts. Rec. Turnover	20.00	20.00
Inventory Turnover	12.00	18.00

Laughlin,[4] (2) a version of the *Comprehensive Liquidity Index* developed by Melnyk and Birati,[5] (3) the *Net Liquid Balance* measure of Shulman and Cox,[6] and (4) the *Lambda* index developed by Emery.[7] While each of these improved indices measures one or more aspects of liquidity more accurately than do the traditional measures, each is, nonetheless, limited in some respect; none is a perfect liquidity measure. We discuss them in turn in the following paragraphs.

Cash Conversion Cycle This measure is based directly on the concept of the working capital cycle as discussed in Chapter 1 of this text. Recall in this cycle that the firm purchases labor and materials, which it uses to make inventory, which is sold to generate receivables, which are in turn collected to produce cash. Within this cycle, there are two assets, generated at different times, that must be financed (inventory and accounts receivable), and one set of liabilities that provides the financing (accounts payable and wages payable). The Cash Conversion Cycle is the *net time interval* between the expenditure of cash in paying the liabilities and the receipt of cash from the collection of receivables. The lower the Cash Conversion Cycle, the more liquid the firm is said to be. It is calculated as the firm's average collection period plus its "inventory conversion period" (Richards and Laughlin call the sum of these two the "operating cycle") minus the "payment deferral period." The "inventory conversion period" and the "payment deferral period" are turnover statistics similar to the average collection period. They represent, respectively, the weighted-average time that a dollar is tied up in inventory or financed by payables. Inventory conversion period is calculated as the inverse of the inventory turnover ratio times 360 days. The payment deferral period is calculated as the sum of all the sales-related accrual and payable accounts divided by cost of sales, with this calculated figure multiplied by 360 days.

The Cash Conversion Cycle may seem a bit difficult at first, but it is, in fact, quite easily calculated. Let us perform an example calculation using the original data from Hacker Corporation presented in Table 10-1. The firm's accounts receivable turnover is 20 times per year, so its average collection period is 360 divided by 20 or 18 days. The firm's inventory turnover is 12

[4]See V. D. Richards and E. J. Laughlin, "A Cash Conversion Cycle Approach to Liquidity Analysis," *Financial Management* (Spring 1980), pp. 32–38.

[5]See Z. L. Melnyk and A. Birati, "Comprehensive Liquidity Index as a Measure of Corporate Liquidity," *Scientific and Behavioral Foundations of Decision Sciences* (Atlanta, Ga.: Southeastern Region of the American Institute for Decision Sciences, 1974), pp. 162–65.

[6]J. Shulman and R. Cox, "An Integrative Approach to Working Capital Management," *Journal of Cash Management* (November/December 1985), pp. 64–67.

[7]G. Emery, "Measuring Short-Term Liquidity," *Journal of Cash Management* (July/August 1984), pp. 25–32.

times per year, so its inventory conversion period is 360 divided by 12 or 30 days. The sum of these two statistics is 48 days; this is the firm's operating cycle. Hacker's cost of sales is $900,000. Hacker's accounts payable and accrued wages totaled $170,000, so the firm's payment deferral period was $170,000 divided by $900,000 times 360 or 68 days. Hacker's Cash Conversion Cycle is 48 days minus 68 days or minus 20 days.

The Cash Conversion Cycle is an excellent quantification of the working capital cycle. It is often a more accurate measure of overall liquidity than is the current ratio. However, it does not capture the effects of current assets or liabilities other than accounts receivable, inventory, accounts payable, and sales-related accruals. For example, *cash*, the most liquid of assets, is not involved in the calculation. Yet few would argue that a firm with less cash is more liquid than a firm with more cash, all other things being equal.

Comprehensive Liquidity Index This is a liquidity-weighted version of the popular current ratio. Recall that one of the problems with using the current ratio is that it treats all the current assets and liabilities as being of equal liquidity, when in reality their liquidity is quite different. In the prior example of an increase in receivables and a corresponding decrease in cash, the current ratio would not be affected. The Comprehensive Liquidity Index overcomes this by weighting each current asset and liability based on its nearness to cash (its turnover). In computing the Comprehensive Liquidity Index, the dollar amount of each current asset or liability is multiplied by one minus the inverse of the asset or liability's turnover ratio. If there are more than two turnovers required to generate cash from the asset, the inverse of each of these ratios is deducted. The results are summed over all current assets and current liabilities. The summed totals are liquidity-adjusted measures of total current assets and total current liabilities. The current ratio is then computed based on these adjusted figures; in the notation of Melnyk and Birati, X is the adjusted total current assets figure, and Y is the adjusted total current liabilities figure. The Comprehensive Liquidity Index is just X divided by Y.

Again, let's compute this measure for the original data on Hacker in Table 10-1. The cash figure of $15,000 needs no adjustment. Receivables turnover is 20, so the adjusted receivables figure is:

$$\$50,000(1 - (1/20)) = \$47,500 \tag{10-5}$$

The generation of cash from inventory requires both the turnover of inventory to receivables and the turnover of receivables to cash. Inventory turnover is 12, so the adjusted value of inventory is:

$$\$75,000(1 - (1/20) - (1/12)) = \$65,000 \tag{10-6}$$

The adjusted current assets figure (X) is then $15,000 plus $47,500 plus $65,000 or $127,500 (in thousands). The slower the turnovers, the lower this adjusted figure will be relative to the book figure.

For the adjusted current debt figure, we must compute some new turnover ratios. Accounts payable of $110,000 are the result of materials purchases; assume that such purchases totaled $400,000 for the year. The accounts payable turnover ratio is then $400,000 divided by $110,000 or 3.64. The adjusted accounts payable figure is:

$$\$110,000(1 - (1/3.64)) = \$79,750 \tag{10-7}$$

Wages payable are $60,000; assume that the firm's total wage bill is $500,000, so the turnover of wages payable is 8.33. The adjusted wages payable amount is:

$$\$60,000(1 - (1/8.33)) = \$52,800 \tag{10-8}$$

The adjusted current debt figure (Y) is the sum of these adjusted liability figures, or $132,550. The Comprehensive Liquidity Index is then $127,500 divided by $132,550 or 0.96.

Net Liquid Balance Both this index and the Lambda measure (discussed next) center on the firm's balance of cash and marketable securities. The argument is that this balance represents the firm's true reserve against unanticipated cash needs, since other remedies for cash shortages can be very costly.[8] For example, if the firm runs out of cash, it might try to liquidate inventory via a distress sale, but this would generate costs that would not otherwise occur. The Net Liquid Balance does not view the firm's investments in accounts receivable and inventory as contributions to aggregate liquidity, but, rather, considers them as additional assets to be financed. The accounts payable and accruals that are part of current liabilities are treated not as maturing obligations but as part of the firm's permanent financing package (similar to long-term debt). Only notes payable (short-term, interest-bearing debts) are treated as maturing obligations. The Net Liquid Balance (NLB) is defined as:

$$\text{NLB} = (\text{Cash} + \text{Mar. Sec.} - \text{Notes Payable})/\text{Total Assets} \tag{10-9}$$

---

[8]Recall from the discussion in Chapter 3 that holding cash and marketable securities beyond those amounts necessary for transactions and for the temporary investment of surplus funds is one mechanism for hedging cash flow risk. Note, however, that Net Liquid Balance ignores other possible hedges of this risk, such as the availability of reserve borrowing capacity.

In the original situation, Hacker Corporation has cash of $15,000 and no marketable securities or notes payable balances. Total assets are $290,000, so the NLB is:

$$\text{NLB} = 15,000/290,000 = 0.052 \qquad (10\text{-}10)$$

Lambda This approach is different from the previous ones in four respects. First, in the Lambda measure, the firm's available credit line (if known) is counted as part of the firm's package of liquid reserves. Second, this index uses a measure of uncertainty to evaluate the firm's potential need for liquidity. Third, this is the only measure that incorporates the firm's expected cash *flows* in addition to its cash and near-cash *stocks* of assets. Finally, the other measures consider only cash flows relating to current assets and liabilities; that is, they consider only flows around the working capital cycle. While working capital flows are extremely important, they are not the only flows of funds within the firm; there are also cash inflows and outflows on the long-term accounts. Lambda considers all the flows through the firm, regardless of whether they originate from short-term or long-term transactions.

The use of a measure of uncertainty in this context makes particularly good sense. By measuring aggregate liquidity, we are attempting to develop an index that indicates the possibility the firm will run out of cash, and thus be forced to take costly actions to remedy this problem. A firm with more certain cash flows will be less likely to default. The Lambda index uses this cash flow uncertainty along with the level of the firm's initial reserve and the expected future cash flows to generate an index akin to a Z-score. The formula is:

$$\text{Lambda} = (\text{Initial Reserve} + E(NCF))/\text{Uncertainty} \qquad (10\text{-}11)$$

In this formula, the initial reserve is defined as cash plus marketable securities plus available credit lines. The expected cash flow ($E(NCF)$) and the uncertainty regarding this expected cash flow depend on the period being forecast. For example, if a firm is using this index to formulate its liquidity strategy over the next year, these expected flows and the uncertainty of these flows would be defined on a yearly basis. However, if the firm is using this index to assess a credit applicant for a trade credit sale on 30-day terms, these flows and their uncertainty are defined on a 30-day basis.

For Hacker Corporation, assume that our analysis is over the next year, and that Hacker's expected cash flow is $50,000 over this year (a net cash inflow). The appropriate measure of uncertainty is the standard deviation of this flow; assume that this is $100,000. Hacker has no reserve line of credit. The corporation's Lambda is then:

$$\text{Lambda} = (15,000 + 50,000)/100,000 = 0.65 \qquad (10\text{-}12)$$

The problem with the net liquid balance and Lambda measures as indices of liquidity is that they ignore all assets other than cash, marketable securities, and available borrowings in determining the firm's liquidity position. While these are certainly major contributors to liquidity, the natural process of the working capital will turn other current assets into cash as time progresses. Also, current liabilities will reduce cash as they mature and are retired. Leaving these other assets and liabilities out of a liquidity measure or dealing with them indirectly can introduce distortion in the measurement of aggregate liquidity. This is the opposite problem from that of the cash conversion cycle, which counts the *other* assets and liabilities but *does not* count cash or marketable securities.

To assess the advantages and disadvantages of these new indices, let us apply them to the two hypothetical changes in Hacker's financial position, as previously postulated. The calculations and results are presented in spreadsheet format in Table 10-2. The Cash Conversion Cycle statistics appear in cells B46 through D46, the Comprehensive Liquidity Index statistics in cells B53 through D53, the Net Liquid Balance in cells B55 through D55, and the Lambda index in cells B57 through D57.

Recall that in going from situation 1 (the firm's original financial position) to situations 2 and 3, the firm's liquidity seemed to have changed, but the common liquidity ratios did not indicate this change or provide contrary indications. In going from situation 1 to situation 2, Hacker's cash is reduced, and accounts receivable are increased. This clearly makes the firm less liquid. *All four of the new measures decline and thus properly detect this change.*

The change in liquidity in going from situation 1 to situation 3 is more complicated. Both current assets and current liabilities decline by the same amount, but the current asset (inventory) that is reduced in this process is further from cash than is the current liability (accounts payable). Inventory requires that a sale and a collection be converted to cash, while cash for accounts payable will be required as these payables mature. Further, initial current assets are less than current liabilities; an equal dollar reduction in both bears more heavily on asset reserves than it does on liability requirements. In comparing situations 1 and 3, then, aggregate liquidity probably decreases. The Net Liquid Balance (cells B55 and D55), however, incorrectly signals an increase in liquidity. The Cash Conversion Cycle (cells B46 and D46) and Lambda (cells B57 and D57) signal no change in liquidity. The Comprehensive Liquidity Index (cells B53 and D53) signals a decrease in liquidity.

The two examples in Table 10-2 of changes in liquidity illustrate the positive and negative features of the improved measures of liquidity relative to traditional measures. The first example illustrates that the new measures are more accurate than traditional ones, and will frequently detect changes in liquidity where traditional methods fail to detect such changes. However, the second example shows that since the four measures do not measure exactly

Table 10-2. Hacker Corporation: Analysis of Liquidity Changes with New Liquidity Indices.

	A	!!	B !!	C !!	D !
5	Last Year's Sales		1000000		
6					
7	Last Year's Materials		400000		
8	Last Year's Wages		500000		
9					
10	Last Year's Cost of Sales		900000		
11					
12	This Year's E (NCF)		50000		
13	This Year's SD (NCF)		100000		
14					
15	*Situation Number*		*1*	*2*	*3*
16					
17	Cash		15000	5000	15000
18	Accounts Receivable		50000	60000	50000
19	Inventory		75000	75000	50000
20					
21	Total Current Assets		140000	140000	115000
22	Net Fixed Assets		150000	150000	150000
23					
24	Total Assets		290000	290000	265000
25					
26	Accounts Payable		110000	110000	85000
27	Accrued Wages		60000	60000	60000
28					
29	Total Current Debt		170000	170000	145000
30	Equity		120000	120000	120000
31					
32	Total Lia. and Equity		290000	290000	265000
33					
34	Current Ratio		.82	.82	.79
35	Quick Ratio		.38	.38	.45
36	Accts. Rec. Turnover		20.00	16.67	20.00
37	Inventory Turnover		12.00	12.00	18.00
38					
39	Cash Conversion Cycle:				
40	Average Collection Period		18.00	21.60	18.00
41	Inventory Conv. Period		30.00	30.00	20.00
42					
43	Operating Cycle		48.00	51.60	38.00
44	Payment Deferral Period		68.00	68.00	58.00
45					
46	Cash Conversion Cycle		−20.00	−16.40	−20.00
47					
48	Comprehensive Liquidity Index:				
49	Accounts Pay. Turnover		3.64	3.64	4.71
50	Accrued Wages Turnover		8.33	8.33	8.33
51	Calculated X		127500	125650	107222
52	Calculated Y		132550	132550	119737
53	Calculated X/Y		.96	.95	.90
54					
55	Net Liquid Balance:		.052	.017	.057
56					
57	Lambda:		.65	.55	.65

the same aspects of liquidity, they will sometimes produce contradictions in the same way as do the traditional measures.[9]

Some Caveats Regarding Liquidity Measures While all four of these measures are improvements, no index of this sort will *completely* measure the concept we call "aggregate liquidity," particularly when the index is used to assess the liquidity of a firm other than one's own. Two problems in the measurement of liquidity that are not addressed by these new indices concern the effect of *off-balance-sheet relationships* and the *treatment of current long-term debt.*

The existence of off-balance-sheet affectors of liquidity creates special circumstances that may make these indices less than complete representations of a firm's position. These indices measure only "normal course of business" transactions. A firm with seemingly poor liquidity may have hidden reserves (such as some relatively liquid and valuable fixed assets) for use in times of emergency. If such a firm needs cash, it can be raised quickly, and possibly with little cost. Conversely, a firm in a seemingly good liquidity position can be forced into financial difficulties by an unforeseen occurrence, such as the bankruptcy of a major customer or a lawsuit. It is extremely difficult for an outsider to assess the quantity and quality of such special circumstances, and thus to measure the aggregate liquidity of such firms.

A second problem concerns the treatment of the current portion of the firm's long-term debt. Should this be included among current liabilities in assessing liquidity or not? Whether this current long-term debt will actually result in a cash outflow (and a reduction in liquidity) depends on the analyzed firm's long-term financing plans. If the firm considers its long-term debt to be *permanent* financing, it will refund this debt with new debt of the same type as it comes due. In this case, the current portion of its long-term debt will be paid via the sale of new debt, and not from maturing current assets; the existence of current long-term debt does not decrease the firm's liquidity. However, if the firm being analyzed is *paying off* long-term debt as it becomes due (perhaps because it has too much debt in its financial structure), then current long-term debt must be serviced from working capital flows and should be counted among current liabilities.[10] Unfortunately, a firm's plans for managing its long-term debt are not often available to outside analysts.

[9]See J. W. Henderson and T. S. Maness, "An Integration of the Net Liquid Balance and the Financial Flexibility Approach in Analyzing Liquidity," paper presented at the 1987 Southern Finance Association Meeting and available from Maness at Baylor University, for more discussion of the Net Liquid Balance and the signals it gives relative to other approaches in measuring liquidity. This reference also reviews several improved measures of liquidity in addition to those discussed in this text.

[10]For discussion of the effect of current long-term debt on the firm's liquidity measures, see E. F. Brigham and L. C. Gapenski, *Intermediate Financial Management* (New York: Dryden, 1985), p. 620.

Both of these two problems add uncertainty to the measurement of the liquidity of outside firms, regardless of the measure of liquidity employed. The analyst must be aware of these problems in using measures of aggregate liquidity in the analysis of credit applicants. However, in using any measure in the formulation of the firm's *own liquidity management strategy,* these problems are of less concern, since the analyst will have information on off-balance-sheet relationships and on the firm's plans regarding its long-term debt. The next sections of this chapter concern the formulation of such liquidity management strategies.

LIQUIDITY AND THE FIRM'S FINANCIAL MANAGEMENT PROCESS

Now that we have developed measures of the firm's aggregate liquidity position, we can talk about the management of that position within the firm's financial management process. The author of this text sees the firm's financial management process as composed in part of the following steps:[11]

1. The firm decides what assets, current and long-term, it wants to hold using methodologies related to shareholder wealth maximization. Such procedures for various current assets were discussed previously in this text; for fixed assets, the procedures are those of capital budgeting.[12]

2. The firm decides on a target structure of financing based on a desired ratio of total debt to total assets.[13] This ratio determines the amount of debt and equity the firm needs but not the maturity structure of

[11]In reality, no firm operates in the clean, step-by-step fashion described here; the steps are all going on at the same time. The steps represent instead, a *thinking process* about financial management that is consistent with much of financial theory. Other approaches to the problem are also possible. For a classic summary of possible approaches to the liquidity level decision and to several other topics in the management of working capital see K. V. Smith, "State of the Art of Working Capital Management," *Financial Management* (Autumn 1973), pp. 50–55.

[12]The idea that the firm can make these decisions concerning which assets to purchase without regard to how these assets will be financed is called a *separation principal* in finance because the investment and financing decisions are made separately. For discussion, see T. E. Copeland and J. F. Weston, *Financial Theory and Corporate Policy,* Second Edition (Reading, Mass.: Addison-Wesley, 1983), pp. 408–409.

[13]This may be based on the firm's belief about its optimal capital structure: the mix of debt and equity that minimizes the firm's cost of capital. Whether optimal capital structure exists is an issue of significant debate in financial theory. The literature on this debate is extensive; see A. Barnea, R. A. Haugen, and L. W. Senbet, "Market Imperfections, Agency Problems, and Capital Structure: A Review," *Financial Management* (Summer 1981), pp. 7–22 for a partial literature review.

this debt (that is, how total debt is to be split into short- and long-term portions).

3. The firm decides on a target level of aggregate liquidity. This decision may be based on a desired index of aggregate liquidity (such as the current ratio, Cash Conversion Cycle, Comprehensive Liquidity Index, and so forth). In doing this, the firm may evaluate several potential positions to determine the appropriate target. Once the aggregate level of liquidity is chosen, the firm determines a target structure for its current and long-term debt.[14]

4. The firm compares this plan with its present financial structure and makes necessary and cost-effective adjustments to move toward the targeted financial structure. In a particular planning period, the costs of transition (such as the costs of refunding debt) may prevent the firm from achieving these targets; however, the firm moves toward the targets when it is cost-effective to do so.

The part of step 3 in which the firm determines its target level of liquidity and the structure of current debt is the thrust of the remainder of this chapter and of the next two chapters of this text. Procedures and models for choosing among liquidity positions are discussed in this chapter. Procedures for achieving a minimum-cost structure for current debt are discussed in Chapters 11 and 12.

To show how these decisions fit into the financial management process outlined above, let us illustrate this process for an example problem. Assume that the management of GenuSplice, a biological research firm, wants to plan its future financial position. Data on the current financial position of the firm is presented in Table 10-3. In step 1, the firm has assessed its asset position based on shareholder wealth maximization and determined that its desired level of assets is $270 million; fixed assets must be increased by $20 million. An additional investment of $10 million is also required for accounts receivable, as the firm has decided that it would be in the shareholders' interest to lengthen terms of sale. Based on considerations of optimal capital structure

---

[14]Note that in the methodology presented, the target composition of current debt is determined after its target level is determined. Since the relative costs of long-term and short-term debt are an important determinant of this target level, one alternative approach to the problem would be to use a global optimization procedure that would codetermine the level of short-term debt and its composition. However, such a procedure would be very cumbersome. For purposes of discussion, we assume that the firm can approximate the cost of short-term debt when determining its target level of aggregate liquidity. This estimate can be refined later when the target composition of debt for this target level is determined. If this cost of short-term debt is significantly different from that used in the analysis of aggregate liquidity, the firm may perform this analysis again based on this new data regarding short-term debt cost.

Table 10-3. GenuSplice
Actual and Desired Financial Positions (thousands of dollars).

	Actual	*Desired*
Cash	$ 10,000	$ 10,000
Accounts Receivable	100,000	110,000
Inventory	20,000	20,000
Current Assets	130,000	140,000
Fixed Assets	110,000	130,000
Total Assets	$240,000	$270,000
Accounts Payable	$ 5,000	$ 10,000
Accrued Wages	30,000	30,000
Short-Term Bank Borrowings	50,000	30,000
Total Current Debt except Current LTD	85,000	70,000
Current Portion of LTD	10,000	
Long-Term Debt (LTD)	90,000	
Total Long-Term Debt	100,000	92,000
Total Debt	185,000	162,000
Owners' Equity	55,000	108,000
Total Liabilities and Equity	$240,000	$270,000

(step 2), the firm determined that the desired debt-to-assets ratio is 0.60 (a rather highly leveraged position, for one reason or another), so the preferred amount of total debt for this asset structure is 0.60 times $270 million, or $162 million, and equity is the remaining $108 million. Step 3 requires the firm to set a target aggregate liquidity level and to structure current debt. Assume for simplicity that the firm has used the current ratio as its measure of aggregate liquidity and has decided that their preferred aggregate liquidity position involves a current ratio of 2.00 (where current long-term debt is not included in current liabilities in computing this ratio because this debt will be refunded at maturity). Since the desired level of current assets is $140 million, this entails that all current liabilities except the current portion of long-term debt total $70 million. The firm would then make a minimum-cost financing plan for current liabilities to total this amount; assume that this plan requires $10 million in accounts payable, $30 million in accrued wages, and $30 million in short-term bank borrowings. The firm would then compare these desired positions in its assets and liabilities with its planned positions and make cost-effective changes to move toward its desired future financial structure (step 4). In this very simplified example, over the planning period the firm would consider purchasing $20 million in fixed assets, increasing accounts receivable by $10 million, retiring $8 million in long-term debt (since the desired total is $92 million and the present total is $100 million), issuing $53 million in equity, lengthening payments to trade creditors, and decreasing reliance on short-term bank borrowings.

EVALUATING STRATEGIES FOR AGGREGATE LIQUIDITY

Left unsaid thus far is how the firm decides on the best level of aggregate liquidity. For a given structure of current assets (step 1) and a given amount of total debt (step 2), the level of aggregate liquidity depends mainly on how the total amount of debt is divided into short- and long-term portions. This division of total debt into short- and long-term portions has substantial implications for the risk and return position of the firm. In particular, the use of relatively more short-term debt and less long-term debt is a *higher risk and higher expected return liquidity strategy*. This is due to the way the division of total debt affects the firm's *expected level of interest payments, variability of interest payments,* and *cash shortage risk.* Let us discuss each of these effects in turn.

Expected Level of Interest Payments The use of more permanent, short-term debt (with this debt refinanced as it matures) and less long-term debt will generally reduce the firm's cash outflows for interest expense. There are two reasons for this reduction. First, the interest rates on short-term debt are usually lower than the interest rates on long-term debt (that is, the yield curve is usually upsloping). Second, if the firm is in a business where seasonality affects its need for funds, and it uses a relatively large proportion of long-term debt financing, there may be times during which the firm has excess financing. During these times, the firm will invest these excess funds in short-term instruments, since they will be needed later in the year. However, since the yield curve is usually upsloping, the interest revenue from these investments will be less than the interest cost of the long-term debt financing. During these slack periods, if short-term financing had been used instead, the firm could pay off this financing and incur no interest expense. We see that since the yield curve is usually positively sloped, the strategy of relatively more short-term and less long-term debt financing produces a lower expected interest outflow, and therefore a higher residual cash flow for the shareholders.

Variability of Interest Expense However, the strategy of more short-term debt and less long-term debt involves higher risks. One source of risk in using short-term financing is the changeable nature of short-term interest rates. Minimum-cost, short-term financing strategies for firms often involve the use of interest-bearing obligations, such as bank credit line borrowings or commercial paper. While interest rate variations can be hedged to some extent with forwards and futures,[15] when the firm uses short-term, interest-bearing obligations, and refunds these with similar instruments at maturity (instead of financing with fixed-rate, long-term obligations) it subjects itself to the interest rate variability, because it must bear market interest rates at the time of refunding. This variability adds an additional component of uncertainty into the firm's cash flow stream. Further, if monetary conditions become such that the yield curve becomes downsloping, the strategy of using more short-term and less long-term financing will result in a *higher* interest outflow (since short-term rates would then be higher than long-term rates).

Cash Shortage Risk Another risk associated with the use of more short-term debt and less long-term debt is the cash shortage risk that accompanies the lower liquidity in this strategy. The higher the short-term borrowing, all other things being equal, the more principal to be refinanced, and consequently, the higher the firm's average inflows and outflows of cash. And the higher the required cash outflows, the greater the chance that a difficulty with inflows will cause a financial crisis and that a financially painful solution (dividend reduction, rushed liquidation of assets, unplanned borrowing, and so forth) will be needed. This cash shortage risk is measured by the indices of aggregate liquidity developed previously.

The trade-offs involved in setting the level of aggregate liquidity by partitioning total debt are pictured in Figure 10-1.[16] As the proportion of long-term, fixed-rate financing increases, the expected total interest cost increases, but the expected shortage cost and the risk cost of varying interest payments declines. As a result, there is an optimum proportion of long-term versus short-term debt at the minimum of the total cost function.[17] The task

---

[15]The main reason that the interest rate risk from the strategy of financing with short-term debt and refunding cannot be completely hedged revolves around the maturities of long-term debt, short-term debt, and futures contracts. To obtain the minimum interest expense, short-term financing should be of short maturity, say 90 or 180 days. The interest rate risk from future refundings of such debt can be hedged by the standard futures contracts for a maximum of only 24 months ahead (see Chapter 3). However, long-term instruments (such as corporate bonds) usually have maturities of 10 years or longer. This gap in hedging between the maximum available futures contract and the maturity of corporate bonds results in interest rate risk. Further, strategies where the futures position is closed out and a new futures position is undertaken ("rolling the hedge") do not eliminate all interest rate risk (see footnote 35, Chapter 3).

[16]For additional discussion, see R. Gilmer, "The Optimal Level of Liquid Assets: An Empirical Test," *Financial Management* (Winter 1985), pp. 39–43.

[17]The conclusion that there is an optimal level of aggregate liquidity (that is, for a given structure of current assets, an optimal debt maturity structure) is not without challenge. Under some assumptions about the nature of markets and costs, this structure is irrelevant. See, for example, C. M. Lewis, "A Multiperiod Theory of Corporate Financial Policy under Taxation," available from the author at Vanderbilt University.

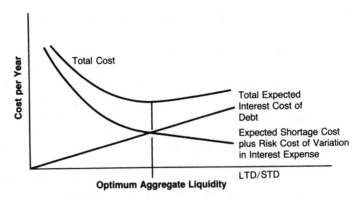

Figure 10-1. *Optimum Level of Aggregate Liquidity.*

in the management of aggregate liquidity is to find this optimum. Several partial models of the risk-return trade-offs inherent in liquidity decisions have been developed,[18] but a complete model of these trade-offs and their effect on firm value has not yet emerged. In the following section, the methods of financial analysis are used to quantify some of the risk and return aspects of this decision.

AN EXAMPLE SPREADSHEET ANALYSIS OF AGGREGATE LIQUIDITY

The Gridlock Corporation is trying to decide on an aggregate liquidity plan for the upcoming year. The firm wishes to maintain a total debt to total assets ratio of 0.50. Since total assets are expected to be $174.5 million, both total debt and total equity will then be $87.25 million. The firm is evaluating two liquidity strategies: these have been designated Plan 1 and Plan 2 (most firms would, of course, evaluate more than two alternative plans). Both plans would utilize minimum accounts payable and accrued wages of $11.4 and $13.2 million respectively.[19] Plan 1 calls for the use of $30 million in interest-bearing, short-term financing, while Plan 2 calls for the use of $50 million in such financing. The firm expects that, with proper structuring, this interest-

[18]Included among these models are those in J. C. Van Horne, "Corporate Liquidity and Bankruptcy Costs," Research Paper Number 205, Graduate School of Business, Stanford University; H. Bierman, K. Chopra, and L. J. Thomas, "Ruin Considerations: Optimal Working Capital and Capital Structure," *Journal of Financial and Quantitative Analysis* (March 1975), pp. 119–28; and K. Borch, "The Capital Structure of the Firm," *Swedish Journal of Economics* (1969), pp. 1–13.

[19]There is a minimum level of these liabilities below which it is uneconomical for the firm to reduce these items. Beyond this minimum, the firm may utilize these liabilities for financing, or may utilize other financing vehicles. These effects will be discussed in Chapters 11 and 12.

bearing, short-term financing will result in a yearly interest cost at approximately the prime rate. Neither plan will result in excess financing at any time during the current year. The question, of course, is which plan should be undertaken. To address this question, we need to develop measures of the cash stockout risk, expected interest cost, and potential variation in interest cost for the two strategies.[20]

To assess cash stockout risk, the firm could use any or all of the improved indices of aggregate liquidity that were presented previously. The Comprehensive Liquidity Indices for the two strategies are calculated in Table 10-4. The structures of current assets do not depend on the financing plan utilized. We have assumed that the firm's marketable securities mature every seven days, that the firm's "Other Current Assets" contribute nothing to liquidity, and that the interest-bearing, short-term liabilities turn over eight times per year (assuming that 45 days is the average maturity). We have also assumed the long-term debt is permanent; the current portion of this debt is then irrelevant in liquidity calculations. All the remaining calculations are straightforward: the Comprehensive Liquidity Index is 1.91 for Plan 1 and 1.41 for Plan 2.

To calculate the expected interest expense and fluctuations in this expense, we need to know the current rates of interest and the probability distribution of interest expense for interest-bearing, short-term debt (which is assumed to be floating-rate). Gridlock's long-term debt carries a 13.5 percent fixed coupon rate. The current prime rate is 10.5 percent. The firm believes there is a 50 percent chance that this rate will stay the same over the planning period, a 10 percent chance that this rate will fall to 9.5 percent, a 30 percent chance that it will rise to 11.5 percent, and a 10 percent chance that it will rise to 12.5 percent.

A spreadsheet analysis of the firm's after-tax interest expense is presented in Table 10-5. We have assumed a 34 percent tax rate in this example. The basic data for the problem appears in cells B5 through E7. Each column represents an interest rate outcome. Thus, column B, cells B10 through B37, models the interest expenses that will occur to Gridlock under Plans 1 and 2 if the prime rate averages 9.5 percent. The interest-bearing, short-term financing for Plan 1 is in cells B10 through E10; the data were put in column B and replicated into columns C, D, and E. The interest expense calculations in cells B11 through E11 are the interest rates from the "Basic Data" section times the short-term balance (for example, cell B11 contains "B6 * B10"). Multiplying this times 0.66 (equal to 1.0 minus the tax rate of 34 percent) gives the after-tax interest outflow figures in row 12. Similar calculations are performed in rows 14 through 16 for the long-term debt in Plan 1. These two

---

[20]We assume in this example that the fluctuations in short-term interest rates are undiversifiable or unhedged. In such a case, interest rate fluctuations represent relevant risk even in a CAPM sense.

Table 10-4. *Gridlock Corporation: Data on Two Liquidity Plans (rounded thousands for dollar figures).*

Sales	$698,000	

Cost of Materials	209,400	
Cost of Labor	349,000	
Total Cost of Sales	558,400	

Cash	5,400	
Marketable Securities	12,000	
Accounts Receivable	54,300	
Inventory	32,000	
Other Current Assets	5,400	
Total Current Assets	109,100	

Fixed Assets	65,400	
Total Assets	$174,500	

	Plan 1	Plan 2
Minimum Accounts Payable	$ 11,400	$ 11,400
Minimum Accrued Wages	13,200	13,200
Other Short-Term Financing	30,000	50,000
Total Current Liabilities	54,600	74,600
Long-Term Borrowings	32,650	12,650
Common Equity	87,250	87,250
Total Liabilities and Equity	$174,500	$174,500

Comprehensive Liquidity Index:

Marketable Securities Turnover	52.00	
Accounts Receivable Turnover	12.85	
Inventory Turnover	17.45	
Accounts Payable Turnover	18.37	
Accrued Wages Turnover	26.44	
Turnover for Other Short-Term Financing	8.00	

Contributions to CLI:

Cash	$ 5,400	
Marketable Securities	11,769	
Accounts Receivable	50,076	
Inventory	27,677	
Calculated X	$ 94,922	$ 94,922

Minimum Accounts Payable	$ 10,779	$ 10,779
Minimum Accrued Wages	12,701	12,701
Other Required Financing	26,250	43,750
Calculated Y	$ 49,730	$ 67,230

CLI (X/Y)	1.91	1.41

Table 10-5. *Gridlock Corporation: Spreadsheet Analysis of Alternative Liquidity Strategies.*

	A	!!	B	!!	C	!!	D	!!	E	!
1	Gridlock Corporation									
2	Analysis of Debt Structure Plans									
3										
4	Basic Data:									
5	Interest Rate on Long-Term Debt		.135		.135		.135		.135	
6	Prime Rate		.095		.105		.115		.125	
7	Prime Rate Probabilities		.1		.5		.3		.1	
8										
9	Plan 1:									
10	Short Term Financing		30000		30000		30000		30000	
11	Before-Tax Interest Expense		2850		3150		3450		3750	
12	After-Tax Interest Expense		1881		2079		2277		2475	
13										
14	Long-Term Borrowings		32650		32650		32650		32650	
15	Before-Tax Interest Expense		4408		4408		4408		4408	
16	After-Tax Interest Expense		2909		2909		2909		2909	
17										
18	Total After-Tax Interest Expense		4790		4988		5186		5384	
19										
20	Expected Interest Expense								5067	
21	Standard Deviation of Interest Expense								158	
22										
23										
24	Plan 2:									
25	Short Term Financing		50000		50000		50000		50000	
26	Before-Tax Interest Expense		4750		5250		5750		6250	
27	After-Tax Interest Expense		3135		3465		3795		4125	
28										
29	Long-Term Borrowings		12650		12650		12650		12650	
30	Before-Tax Interest Expense		1708		1708		1708		1708	
31	After-Tax Interest Expense		1127		1127		1127		1127	
32										
33	Total After-Tax Interest Expense		4262		4592		4922		5252	
34										
35	Expected Interest Expense								4724	
36	Standard Deviation of Interest Expense								264	
37										
38										
39							*Ratio*			
40	*Summary of Results*		*Plan 1*		*Plan 2*		*P1/P2*			
41										
42	Comprehensive Liquidity Index		1.91		1.41		1.35			
43	Expected Interest Expense		5067		4724		1.07			
44	Standard Deviation of Interest Expense		158		264		.60			

after-tax interest figures are totaled in row 18 to obtain total interest expense for each level of the prime interest rate for Plan 1. The expected after-tax interest expense appears in cell E20, and is calculated by multiplying the total interest expense figures in row 18 by the probabilities in row 7. For Plan 1, the expected interest expense is $5.067 million. The standard deviation of this interest expense is calculated in cell E21, given the probabilities in row 7. The analysis for Plan 1 was replicated into cells B25 through E37 and the short-term balance data changed to produce the parallel analysis for Plan 2.

A summary of the risk and return measures for the two plans appears in rows 39 through 44. For comparison purposes, we have divided the statistics from Plan 1 by those from Plan 2 in cells D42 through D44. The Comprehensive Liquidity Index for Plan 1 is 35 percent higher than that for Plan 2, indicating that Plan 1 produces a considerably lower stockout risk. Because of the use of less short-term debt, the variability of interest expense due to changes in the prime rate (in a standard deviation sense) for Plan 1 is only 60 percent of that of Plan 2. However, the after-tax interest expense for Plan 1 is 7 percent higher than for Plan 2; Plan 1 will cost an additional $343 thousand in after-tax expense.

In this decision methodology, it is now up to the firm to choose among the plans based on management's assessment of current shareholders' risk preferences. If the firm was one that in the past had pursued high-risk, growth-oriented financial and operating strategies, then it probably would have attracted investors with a preference for strategies such as this, and management should adopt a liquidity strategy in line with these preferences. That is, in this example, it should probably adopt Plan 2. If the firm had in the past been very conservatively managed, then its shareholders would probably prefer a less risky strategy, and Plan 1 should be adopted.[21] Of course, since most firms' operating and financial policies are neither extremely aggressive nor conservative, and since they are likely to consider several alternative strategies with diverse risk-return characteristics, their decisions will rarely be so obvious.

LIQUIDITY MANAGEMENT IN PRACTICE

It is useful to compare the approaches to the management of working capital outlined in this text with those used by practicing financial managers. When this comparison was made in past chapters, survey evidence was used

---

[21]In this discussion, we assume the existence of shareholder clienteles. These may be induced by the different tax consequences of high-risk, high-growth vs. conservative management policies. The existence of shareholder clienteles is currently under investigation by finance researchers, and the issue is still in doubt; see Copeland and Weston, *Financial Theory*, pp. 506–509.

to assess management practice. We will also cite evidence from surveys in assessing the practice of liquidity management. However, unlike the results of many other decisions in working capital management, the results of decisions regarding the management of aggregate liquidity are *observable*: from published financial statements, measures of aggregate liquidity can be calculated for samples of firms. Using this data, researchers in finance have been able to ascertain patterns in firms' aggregate liquidity decisions. This empirical research provides additional evidence on practice in the management of aggregate liquidity.

Let us first review the available survey evidence. Two surveys that addressed current practices regarding the management of aggregate liquidity were conducted in 1978. Both of these surveys utilized all or part of the Fortune listing of large firms. Smith and Sell found that about 30 percent of responding firms had a formal overall working capital policy, 60 percent had an informal policy, and 10 percent had no policy.[22] Larger firms were more prone to have a formal policy than were smaller firms. With regard to liquidity level, 22 percent of the firms indicated that they had a cautious (high liquidity) working capital policy, 28 percent indicated that they had an aggressive (low liquidity) policy, and the remainder indicated that they changed policy over time. Ratios used to assess liquidity position (in order of popularity) were the current ratio, the working capital turnover ratio (sales divided by net working capital), and working capital as a percentage of total assets. The use of the improved measures of liquidity management described in this chapter was not investigated in this survey.

Where Smith and Sell investigated the types of tools and policies used by firms, Johnson, Campbell, and Wittenbach were primarily concerned with the *importance* of several tools in the management of liquidity.[23] They found that the most popular objective of liquidity management was a very general one: to meet temporary financial problems as they arise. This overall objective was more popular than specific ones related to individual parts of liquidity management, such as the ability to meet creditor obligations. However, they found that measures of aggregate liquidity were important to firms relative to this objective mostly during periods when the firm was having liquidity difficulties. They did not investigate the techniques by which firms manage aggregate liquidity.

Let us now turn from survey evidence to empirical investigations of liquidity choice based on firms' financial statements. If the previously presented logic regarding an optimal level of aggregate liquidity is true and the

---

[22]K. V. Smith and S. B. Sell, "Working Capital Management in Practice," in K. V. Smith, Editor, *Readings on the Management of Working Capital* (St. Paul: West Publishing, 1980), pp. 51–84.

[23]J. Johnson, D. Campbell, and J. Wittenbach, "Problems in Corporate Liquidity," *Financial Executive* (March 1980), pp. 44–53.

liquidity policies of firms are based on this optimum, then there should be industry-to-industry variations in the aggregate liquidity structures of firms, because there is variation among firms in shortage costs should the firm run out of funds. For example, firms in some industries hold more illiquid fixed assets than others, and consequently, will take greater losses if the firm runs out of cash and is forced to sell these assets. These shortage costs, along with the risk cost of interest rate fluctuations, act to offset the lower expected interest expense on short-term debt and cause an optimum in aggregate liquidity. If there are variations in shortage costs, then the optimal level of liquidity should vary among industries. That is, the minimum point on the total cost curve of aggregate liquidity portrayed in Figure 10-1 should vary among firms in different business lines.

Two empirical studies have confirmed this variation. Gilmer found that the optimal level of liquid assets varied among industries and over time.[24] Gardner and Mills found the level of current liabilities to be associated with the level of assets and the firm's industry.[25] These findings suggest that there is an optimal liquidity position that firms seek, and that this position is dependent on the characteristics of a firm's business.

Another interesting result of these empirical investigations is that firms' aggregate liquidity positions have been declining over time. Gardner and Mills cite such evidence using the quick and current ratios as liquidity measures.[26] Belt finds the same trend when using the Cash Conversion Cycle as the measure of aggregate liquidity.[27] This suggests that either expected costs of cash shortages have declined over time or firms have become less averse to the risk of cash shortage.

These surveys and empirical investigations lead to important conclusions regarding the practice of liquidity management. Most firms have either a formal or informal aggregate liquidity policy. These policies may be aggressive, conservative, or may change over time, and are most important when firms are having problems within the working capital cycle. While not all firms have a formal policy and while many regard the measurement of liquidity as important only at certain times, empirical evidence suggests that *there is an optimal level of liquidity that depends on the characteristics of the firm*. The average value of this optimal level seems to be declining over time.

[24]Gilmer, "The Optimal Level of Liquid Assets."

[25]M. Gardner and D. Mills, "Determinants of Working Capital Policy in Non-Financial Industries, 1969–1979: Some Empirical Evidence," presented at the Financial Management Association Annual Meeting, 1982, and available from the authors at Illinois State University. Gardner and Mills also found that the size of the firm influenced the proportion of current assets held.

[26]Gardner and Mills, "Determinant of Working Capital Policy," p. 2.

[27]B. Belt, "The Trend in the Cash Conversion Cycle and Its Components," *Akron Business and Economic Review* (Fall 1985), pp. 48–54.

SUMMARY

This chapter addressed one of the firm's major decisions: the level of aggregate liquidity. Aggregate liquidity is the relationship between the firm's ability to generate cash and the firm's potential needs for cash on short notice. The level of the firm's aggregate liquidity constitutes a multiasset hedge against multiliability cash demands.

We first discussed issues in the measurement of the firm's aggregate liquidity position. Some traditional measures of the aggregate liquidity are the current ratio, quick ratio, accounts receivable turnover, and inventory turnover. Unfortunately, all of these are seriously flawed in some way as measures of aggregate liquidity. For example, the most popular of these measures (the current ratio) treats the liquidity of several types of current assets and liabilities as equivalent when in reality they are not. These ratios do not always properly signal changes in liquidity when such changes occur.

To accurately measure liquidity, improved indices are required. Four of these were illustrated: the Cash Conversion Cycle, the Comprehensive Liquidity Index, the Net Liquid Balance, and the Lambda index. While the signals regarding liquidity that these measures provide may sometimes conflict, all of these are improvements over the traditional measures in the assessment of liquidity position.

In prior chapters of this text, the structuring of current assets was discussed. For a given structure of current assets and a given amount of total debt, the firm's aggregate liquidity position is determined by how the total amount of debt is divided into floating-rate, short-term borrowings and fixed-rate, long-term borrowings. Even if financial futures are used to hedge against interest rate swings, the use of relatively more floating-rate, short-term debt increases the variability of interest expense. The use of more short-term debt also results in a higher risk of cash shortage. However, expected cost of short-term debt is usually lower, since the yield curve is usually upsloping. In setting the level of aggregate liquidity, the firm is therefore faced with a risk/return trade-off: more short-term debt means more risk but lower expected interest expense. Procedures were outlined to estimate the risk and return effects of various liquidity strategies.

Once the firm has decided on its level of aggregate liquidity, it must generate an advantageous structure for current debt that yields this level of liquidity. The next two chapters deal with the generation of a plan for current liabilities that results in the targeted level of liquidity while minimizing the cost of this financing.

Problems

10-1. A firm is trying to formulate its aggregate liquidity policy. One alternative involves financing with $600,000 in short-term notes payable, and will result in the following projected financial position at the end of the upcoming year:

Projected Income Statement
Year Ending 12/31/8X

Sales	$3,000
Cost of Sales:	
Materials	$1,000
Labor	$1,500
Depreciation	$100
Interest Expense	$90
Earnings Before Taxes	$310
Taxes	$109
Earnings After Taxes	$201

Projected Balance Sheet
Year Ending 12/31/8X

Cash	$100	Accounts Payable (materials)	$200
Marketable Securities	$300	Accrued Labor	$400
Accounts Receivable	$500	Notes Payable	$600
Inventory	$700	Total Current Debt	$1,200
Total Current Assets	$1,600		
		Long-Term Debt	$200
Fixed Assets	$500	Equity	$700
Total Assets	$2,100	Total Lia. and Equity	$2,100

The average maturity of marketable securities is 90 days. The maturity of all notes payable is 120 days. Ignore the effects of any maturing of long-term debt. With this structure, the firm will have $100 in available borrowing remaining on its credit line. Use a 360-day year.

a. Compute the firm's projected Cash Conversion Cycle.

b. Compute the firm's projected Comprehensive Liquidity Index.

c. Compute the projected Net Liquid Balance.

d. Compute the firm's projected Lambda. In this calculation, assume the firm's cash flows are defined as its projected cash flow from operations (earnings after taxes plus depreciation) and that the standard deviation of these flows for the upcoming year is $250.

10-2. A firm is trying to decide on the structure of its debt financing. Based on capital structure considerations, the firm has decided to utilize a total of $10 million in total debt. It expects to have $1 million in unavoidable short-term funding and $5 million in existing long-term debt which it does not wish to refund. The total amount of debt to be structured is thus $4 million. Two alternatives are being considered. In alternative A, the firm would issue $1.5 million in long-term, fixed-rate debt and 2.5 million in short-term, floating-rate debt. In alternative B, the firm would issue $3 million in long-term, fixed-rate debt and $1 million in short-term, floating-rate debt. In either case, the interest rate on long-term debt will be 10 percent. The estimated probability distribution of interest rates on short-term debt for the upcoming year is:

Probability	.2	.5	.3
Interest Rate	7%	8%	9%

The firm is in the 35 percent tax bracket. For the upcoming year, compute the standard deviation of after-tax interest expense on the $4 million in new interest-bearing debt for each of the alternative structures.

Selected Readings

Bierman, H., K. Chopra, and L. J. Thomas, "Ruin Considerations: Optimal Working Capital and Capital Structure," *Journal of Financial and Quantitative Analysis* (March 1975), pp. 119–28.

Cohn, R. A., and J. J. Pringle, "Steps Toward an Integration of Corporate Financial Theory," in K. V. Smith, ed., *Readings on the Management of Working Capital*, Second Edition (St. Paul: West Publishing: 1980), pp. 35–42.

Emery, G., "Measuring Short-Term Liquidity," *Journal of Cash Management* (July/August 1984), pp. 25–32.

Gilmer, R., "The Optimal Level of Liquid Assets: An Empirical Test," *Financial Management* (Winter 1985), pp. 39–43.

Melnyk, Z. L., and A. Birati, "Comprehensive Liquidity Index as a Measure of Corporate Liquidity," *Scientific and Behavioral Foundations of Decision Sciences* (Atlanta, Ga.: Southeastern Region of the American Institute for Decision Sciences, 1974), pp. 162–65.

Richards, V. D., and E. J. Laughlin, "A Cash Conversion Cycle Approach to Liquidity Analysis," *Financial Management* (Spring 1980), pp. 32–38.

Shulman, J., and R. Cox, "An Integrative Approach to Working Capital Management," *Journal of Cash Management* (November/December 1985), pp. 64–67.

Van Horne, J. C., "A Risk-Return Analysis of a Firm's Working Capital Position," *The Engineering Economist* (Winter 1969), pp. 71–89.

Van Horne, J. C., "Corporate Liquidity and Bankruptcy Costs," Research Paper Number 205, Graduate School of Business, Stanford University.

The Jones Company
Deciding on the Level of Liquidity

The Jones Company was the product of a financial transaction called a "leveraged buyout." In such a transaction, the managers of a unit of a large company purchase the unit from the parent, usually financing the purchase with a relatively small equity contribution. The bulk of the financing is provided by loans secured by the purchased unit's assets and by loans from the selling firm. This method of divestiture is sometimes used by large firms to rid themselves of unwanted divisions.

Four years ago, the Jones Company had been the Jones Division of FCS Incorporated, a large conglomerate. The division manufactured and sold office furniture, a business that the top management of FCS had come to regard as low-growth, marginally profitable, cyclical, and generally not compatible with FCS's long-term corporate strategy. The three upper-level managers of the division were not of the same opinion. Consequently, when the division became available for purchase, they put in a bid, which was accepted. The purchase of the unit by the managers was advantageous in that it preserved their jobs, which would have been at risk under other ownership. The purchase was financed via a $1.5 million equity contribution,

a $50 million unsecured note from FCS, and short- and long-term secured loans from a financial intermediary.

Things went well for the first few years. Though sales did not grow much, the new owners were able to use their knowledge of the industry to lessen the effects of the business cycle on the firm's earnings. Equity grew, and the long-term portion of the loan from the financial intermediary was reduced on schedule. (The firm's financial statements as of December 31, 1983, are presented in Exhibit 1.) The beginning of the firm's fifth year brought a crisis, however. The note from FCS allowed the Jones Company to make interest payments only for the first four years to allow the firm to "get on its feet." Very substantial principal payments ($10 million per year) were scheduled to be due starting in 1984, however, and it was clear that these payments could not be made from the firm's cash flow, even if needed fixed asset purchases were delayed (see Exhibit 2). It seemed that a restructuring of the FCS note would be necessary. At the same time, the owners decided to give serious thought to the firm's capital structure and its mix of short- and long-term borrowings.

Exhibit 1

Financial Statements
The Jones Company
Fiscal Year 1983
Rounded Thousands of Dollars

Balance Sheet
December 31, 1983

Cash	$ 4,200
Marketable Securities	410
Accounts Receivable	24,996
Inventories	34,421
Other Current Assets	1,127
Total Current Assets	$ 65,154
Gross Fixed Assets	$ 55,832
Less: Accum. Depreciation	22,333
Net Fixed Assets	33,499
Other Assets	3,790
Total Assets	$102,443
Accounts Payable	14,547
Notes Payable (FCS)	10,000
Accruals, etc.	10,859
Short-Term Borrowings	1,365
Current Portion–LTD	1,000
Total Current Liabilities	$ 37,771
Long-Term Debt	$ 15,000
Long-Term Note to FCS	$ 40,000
Common Stock	$ 1,500
Retained Earnings	8,172
Total Common Equity	9,672
Total Lia. and Equity	$102,443

Statement of Income and Retained Earnings
Fiscal Year Ending December 31, 1983

Sales	$174,972
Cost of Goods Sold	121,605
Selling and Administrative Expenses	42,173
Interest Expense — FCS Note	5,000
Other Interest Expense	2,084
Earnings Before Taxes	$ 4,110
Taxes	1,891
Earnings After Taxes	$ 2,219
Common Dividends	0
Changes in Retained Earnings	$ 2,219

Exhibit 2

The Jones Company
Proforma Statement of 1984 Net Operating Cash Flow
if FCS Note is Not Refinanced

Sales[1]	$180,221
Cost of Goods Sold[1]	125,254
Selling and Admin. Exp.[2]	43,270
Interest Expense — FCS Note[3]	4,500
Other Interest Expense[4]	2,090
Earnings before Tax	$ 5,107
Taxes[5]	2,120
Earnings after Taxes	$ 2,987
Depreciation Addback	5,583
Cash Dividends	0
Operating Net Cash Flow	$ 8,570
Principal Payment — FCS Note	10,000
Principal Payment — Other LTD	1,000
Operating Net Cash Flow after Principal Payments	− $2,430

[1]All entries with this mark are forecast strictly on a 3 percent growth over 1983.

[2]This entry consists of fixed operating expenses plus depreciation. Depreciation is expected to be the same as 1983.

[3]It is assumed that the $10 million payment is made about one-half of the way through the year, and thus average balance on the note is $45 million.

[4]Due to financial intermediary. Includes interest on new required short-term financing.

[5]Based on the firm's expected tax rate.

The owners believed that there was an optimal overall mix between debt and equity that minimized a firm's cost of capital. They also recognized that the capital structure of the Jones Company as of early 1984 was probably far from this optimum. Specifically, with 90 percent debt and 10 percent equity, they knew that interest rates on debt and the risk of returns to equity were far higher than need be. However, they did not want to make additional equity contributions or dilute their ownership interest by selling equity to outside investors. Therefore, they decided not to issue any new equity financing, but instead decided to slowly reduce the firm's level of debt by paying off long-term debt as it became due, at least for the next few years.

The refinancing problem then resolved into how the required total debt financing should be divided into short- and long-term portions. The owners contacted the financial intermediary and were advised that the intermediary would be willing to lend the $50 million needed to refinance the FCS note. The firm's other borrowings from the intermediary would be renegotiated at the same time. Because of the Jones Company's very highly leveraged position, rates on all short-term borrowings would be 13 percent per year. Further, it was standard that such borrowings would have to be reduced to a zero balance for at least 60 consecutive days per year to evidence that such borrowings were truly short term and intended to cover seasonal needs only. The owners calculated that this would limit short-term borrowings to (at most) an average short-term balance of $12 million. All long-term borrowings would then carry an interest rate of 16 percent per year, with principal payments made in equal installments over the next 20 years (a repayment schedule similar to that for a sinking fund debenture).

The Management of Short-Term Liabilities: Introduction

In Chapter 10, we developed methods of measuring the aggregate liquidity of the firm. These measured the relative nearness to cash of the firm's short-term assets versus the possible needs for cash from the firm's short-term liabilities. Given the availability of these measures, the firm's planned structure of assets, and the firm's target capital structure, the firm's management can determine its target level of aggregate liquidity.

In this chapter, we begin discussion of the structuring of the firm's current liabilities. This structure should achieve two goals. First, it should provide the necessary amounts of short-term financing. Second, it should be in keeping with the target level of aggregate liquidity. The challenge in the management of current liabilities is to *achieve these goals at a minimum cost*.

Before proceeding with the discussion of current liability structuring, one clarification of the material in the prior chapter is necessary. In that chapter, the firm's projected financial statements were used in two ways: to provide a basis for the measurement of aggregate liquidity and to estimate the amount of required financing. It should be recognized that, in the second application, the amount of financing estimated is only an approximation, since the firm's financial statements are computed on an *accrual basis* while the actual amount of financing needed must be calculated on a *cash basis*. This approximation was made in the interests of simplicity. More accurate estimates of the firm's cash financing needs can be obtained via cash forecasting, a topic that was discussed in Chapter 3.

This chapter covers two major topics. First, some commonly used sources of short-term financing for firms are listed and discussed. The availability and cost of these sources, we will see, varies considerably from firm to firm and from source to source. Second, a technique (the *sequential method*) for generating a minimum-cost structure of current liabilities in some situations is presented.

WHY USE SHORT-TERM FINANCING?

Before moving on to these major topics, it is useful to ask why firms use short-term financing at all. In considering this issue, it is useful to think of current debt as composed of two parts: *temporary* short-term financing and *permanent* short-term financing. Temporary short-term financing is used to provide funds for transient cash flow shortages, such as those caused by seasonality in sales. When it is cheaper to borrow funds to cover such deficits than to keep a reserve of funds against them, temporary borrowings are attractive to the firm.

Permanent short-term borrowings are another matter. They are used by firms on a continuing basis and are refinanced with new short-term debt as they mature. There are at least three reasons for the use of permanent short-term borrowings. First, as discussed in Chapter 5, there are minimum amounts of accounts payable and of accruals. It is uneconomical for the firm to reduce short-term debt below those levels. Second, as long as the yield curve is upsloping, the expected interest expense of short-term debt is less than that on long-term debt, though the use of short-term debt is riskier (this effect was discussed in Chapter 10). Finally, financing with permanent short-term debt allows the firm substantial *flexibility* in its package of permanent financing. Unlike long-term debt, the amount of short-term debt can be easily expanded or contracted to meet business conditions and opportunities. This flexibility is a big advantage to the firm in dealing with uncertain conditions in product and capital markets. For all these reasons, it makes sense for firms to use some permanent short-term debt financing. The next section provides discussion of the important sources of short-term financing for firms.

SOURCES OF SHORT-TERM FINANCING

In attempting to obtain an advantageous structure of short-term liabilities, the firm must consider its alternative sources of short-term debt. The characteristics of these sources vary considerably. They are of different maturity and cost. Also, some types of short-term financing are available only to certain firms. In this section, we discuss the availability, cost, maturity, and other characteristics of nine common types of short-term financing:

1. Commercial paper
2. Bankers' acceptances
3. Accounts payable
4. Accruals
5. Unsecured credit line borrowings
6. Unsecured notes and term loan borrowings

7. Secured borrowings with marketable securities as collateral

8. Secured borrowings with accounts receivable as collateral

9. Secured borrowings with inventory as collateral

The first six of these are unsecured borrowings, while the last three involve secured transactions. Together, these sources of short-term funding comprise the vast majority of the current debt of most business firms.

Commercial Paper We briefly discussed this financial instrument and the following one (bankers' acceptances) in Chapter 2 as possible investment instruments for the firm's excess cash. Commercial paper is discounted large-denomination unsecured debt sold by corporations for financing purposes. Commercial paper has been one of the fastest growing sources of short-term financing for major firms. Most of the participants in the commercial paper market are bank holding companies, finance companies, or industrial firms. While longer maturities are possible, the most common maturity for commercial paper is 30 days.[1] Firms issuing commercial paper must have lines of credit available from their banks to substitute for their commercial paper borrowings if needed.

To use commercial paper to obtain short-term financing, the firm first applies for a commercial paper rating from one or more of the major rating services (Fitch, Moody's, or Standard and Poors). Firms that are not able to obtain satisfactory ratings may obtain a bank-guaranteed letter of credit which obligates the bank to make good on the commercial paper if the issuing firm does not. The dual responsibility of the firm and the bank is then sufficient to allow access to the market. Once the firm has obtained either the necessary rating or bank support, it must decide whether to sell its paper directly to investors or to use a commercial paper dealer. Large firms generally place their commercial paper directly with investors, while smaller firms use dealers.

The interest rate on commercial paper financing is generally below the banks' prime rate of interest. Even allowing for the cost of the required backup lines of credit and payments to rating agencies, the net cost of borrowing via commercial paper is usually cheaper than bank borrowing; this accounts for its substantial use.[2] However, there are some disadvantages in the use of

---

[1] For instruments with maturities longer than 270 days, the Securities and Exchange Commission requires a securities registration. To avoid the expensive and time-consuming registration process, commercial paper is not issued in maturities longer than this.

[2] The difference between bank lending rates and commercial paper rates stems from banks' reserve requirements and operating costs. If banks borrow to relend to firms, they must keep part of their funds in reserves. This, along with the costs of operating the bank, keeps the banks' lending rates above their cost of borrowing. Borrowers can avoid these higher bank lending rates by going directly to the money markets and borrowing via commercial paper.

commercial paper for financing. For all intents and purposes, only the largest firms and their financing subsidiaries can use it. Refunding is impractical, so once the paper is outstanding it generally remains so until maturity; this limits the flexibility of the issuing firm with respect to this financing. Still, for firms that are large enough to participate in this market, commercial paper is often a very advantageous form of short-term financing.

Bankers' Acceptances Like commercial paper, bankers' acceptances are negotiable discounted short-term instruments.[3] However, for bankers' acceptances the default risk *never* rests solely with the issuing entity; a bankers' acceptance is *always* backed by both a bank and a firm. This dual responsibility makes bankers' acceptances very safe, and consequently their interest cost is quite low.

Most bankers' acceptances are generated in connection with international trade. They exist because of two problems faced by exporting firms. First, terms of sale in international commerce are much longer than terms of sale for domestic transactions. Second, many firms that sell to buyers in other countries do not have the necessary expertise in the nondomestic accounting conventions, business practices, and so forth necessary to make reliable credit-granting decisions on export customers. Further, even if the exporting firm has the necessary expertise, credit information on international customers may be hard to obtain.[4] Consequently, selling firms need a method of obtaining guaranteed payment for goods and of receiving this payment in a reasonable amount of time.

The bankers' acceptance is a response to this need. The typical series of events that generates a bankers' acceptance starts once the exporter and importer agree to a shipment. The importer then arranges with its bank for a *letter of credit* to be issued. This letter of credit commits the importer's bank to make payment for the goods once proper documentation is presented. The exporter then ships the goods and forwards the shipping documents and a *time draft* through the exporter's bank to the importer's bank. (A time draft is similar to a note; it is a promise to pay a certain sum at a certain time.) The importer's bank then *accepts the draft* and sends the shipping documents to the importer who uses them to claim the goods when they arrive. The accepted draft is called a bankers' acceptance and obligates the importer and the importer's bank to make a set payment at a set time. At this point, the exporter usually sells the draft to the importer's bank on a discounted basis and takes the cash. The bank may resell the draft or hold it to maturity.

---

[3]Good discussions of both bankers' acceptances and commercial paper can be found in K. Brown and B. Summers, eds., *Instruments of the Money Market*, Fifth Edition (Richmond: Federal Reserve Bank of Richmond, 1981).

[4]We will discuss these problems in making international credit-granting decisions in Chapter 13.

The most popular maturity for bankers' acceptances is 90 days, although maturities of as short as 30 days or as long as 180 days are common. Bankers' acceptances are usually issued by moneycenter banks and are traded through dealers. Because both the importer and the importer's bank stand behind the instrument, interest rates on bankers' acceptances lie between the rate on treasury bills of similar maturity and the prime rate. However, borrowers must also pay a fee to their bank of about 1 percent per year for services in connection with generating these acceptances. Still, even with this fee, the net cost of borrowing via bankers' acceptances is often less than the prime rate.

Accounts Payable The trade credit granted from one firm to another for the purchase of goods provides more financing to businesses than all the other sources of short-term financing put together, including bank borrowing. The ready availability of trade credit relative to bank credit stems partly from the different margins experienced by selling firms and by banks in granting credit. The margin for banks is the difference between the interest cost of funds raised and the interest income from loans; this difference often averages about 3 percent. For firms, however, the margin is the difference between the selling price and the cash cost of the goods sold, which may be twenty percent or more. Consequently, firms often find it quite profitable to grant credit to buyers whose probability of default is sufficiently large that banks would deny credit. Further (as discussed in Chapter 5), even if buyers preferred to purchase goods for cash, imperfect knowledge by buyers of the quality of sellers' goods and the inconvenience of handling cash make the use of a minimum amount of trade credit almost mandatory. The ready availability of trade credit, along with the minimum mandatory use of this debt, accounts for its prevalence in providing short-term financing.

Strategies for the use of trade credit as a financing vehicle revolve around *the payment dates of invoices*. The later the firm pays, the more financing will be generated. For example, suppose the firm purchases $100,000 per year in goods from a particular supplier, with these purchases evenly distributed throughout the year. If this supplier is paid 10 days from the date of the invoice, the average amount of financing will be $2,777.78 (equal to $100,000 times 10/360). If the supplier is paid 30 days from the date of the invoice, the average financing will be $8,333.33 (equal to $100,000 times 30/360). This difference in the level of accounts payable is due solely to the different payment policies. Three typical policies for the payment of invoices (from the soonest possible payment to the latest) are:

1. Pay on the discount date of the invoice if the supplier offers a cash discount as part of its terms of sale.

2. Pay on the due date of the invoice.
3. Pay after the due date of the invoice.[5]

Let us discuss each of these policies in turn. Under the first policy, payment is made on *the latest date that will allow the buyer to take the cash discount* offered in the sellers' terms of sale. This usually entails mailing the check on the discount date; many U.S. firms have traditionally used the postmark date of checks as the date for assessing whether terms of sale have been honored.[6] Under this policy, the firm obtains financing from the time the goods are received until cash is deducted from the firm's bank account. It should be stressed that this financing *should not be regarded as free.* A possible alternative would be to arrange with the supplier to pay cash on delivery or in advance for goods, and receive an additional discount for this payment. However, the most common cash discount date is 10 days from the date of receiving the goods. For most firms, the additional discount that would be received from the seller for paying 10 days earlier *is much smaller than the costs associated with not being able to check the quality of the goods and the costs associated with the transmittal of cash.* However, the firm should investigate the possibility of cash payment with suppliers; there may be some cases where the total elimination of this trade credit may be of advantage.

One way of generating additional short-term financing from trade creditors is to delay payment to trade creditors *beyond the discount date.* To do this, the firm could follow a policy of paying on the due date of invoices rather than their discount date; this is the second strategy listed above. This strategy is called *skipping the discount.* In doing this, the buyer still honors the seller's terms of sale, but incurs the penalty of having to pay more for the goods. For example, if the terms of sale are 2 percent 10 days, net 30

---

[5]Other policies are, of course, possible, but they make little sense except in very unusual circumstances. For example, the firm could elect to pay as soon as the goods are inspected (but before the discount date of the invoice). However, if the firm uses trade credit as a mechanism for monitoring goods and to avoid problems in transmitting cash, it makes sense to extend this utilization and generate financing if there is no penalty for doing so. The first penalty in utilizing trade credit almost always comes when the firm takes sufficiently long to pay an invoice so as to be unable to take the cash discount. Because there is no penalty for delaying payment up to the discount date of the invoice, most firms do not pay before this date, if they utilize trade credit at all. Similarly, if the firm takes sufficiently long to pay that it misses the discount date, the next date at which a penalty occurs is the due date. Therefore, if a firm misses the discount date, it makes no sense to pay before the due date.

[6]For survey results contrasting the views of credit managers and payables managers on the accepted payment date in honoring terms of sale, see N. Hill, W. Sartoris, and D. Ferguson, "Corporate Credit and Payables Policy: A Survey of Size and Industry Effects," paper presented at the Financial Management Association's 1983 Annual Meeting, and available from Hill at Brigham Young University.

days, and the invoice size is $1,000, the buyer will have to pay $20 more for the goods ($1,000 rather than $980) in order to delay payment for an additional 20 days.

Additional penalties are incurred if the buyer chooses to pay *beyond the due date*. This strategy is called *stretching accounts payable* (strategy number three above). Such a strategy may result in a lower credit agency rating for the buyer and, consequently, higher interest costs of borrowing from financial intermediaries. However, the primary effect of stretching accounts payable is a *loss of bargaining power with the seller*. In dealings between buyers and sellers, various aspects of the conditions of sale are continually being negotiated, including goods availability, shipping schedules, and so forth. Customers who pay in compliance with the seller's terms of sale are in a better position to negotiate these aspects than are customers who do not. The penalty costs of payment beyond the terms of sale therefore depend on the effects of these slow payments on bargaining, and may be substantial or trivial depending on the market conditions for the product in question. The firm must weigh these penalty costs against the financing provided in deciding whether to pay suppliers beyond their stated terms.

Accruals Accounts payable are generated when firms purchase goods and services on credit. However, firms also incur other types of debts for which immediate payment is not required. For example, the firm may obtain the labor of executive and hourly employees, incur liabilities for future tax payments, and accumulate interest expense on borrowed funds without paying cash for these items. Any such accrual involves a delay in payment, and thus it is a potential source of financing.

As with accounts payable, it would be uneconomical for the firm to avoid minimum levels of many accrued liabilities. For example, the firm could cut the size of accrued wages by paying each employee at the end of each day. By such a strategy, the firm might reduce its labor expense relative to that which would be required for longer pay cycles; employees who are paid more frequently may accept a lower wage, since they can spend or save their wages sooner. However, the paperwork expense of frequent payments to labor would probably outweigh any such savings. Similar minimum levels occur for many types of accrued liabilities.

Beyond these minimum levels of accruals, the firm needs to consider the penalty costs of extending payment in determining whether additional short-term debt should be raised in this fashion. The penalty cost will depend on the type of accrual under consideration. For example, the discounts given for the early payment of taxes are often very small; in such cases the firm may elect to pay later and obtain financing.

It should be noted that these minimum levels of accounts payable and accrued liabilities reduce the amount of other short-term financing that must be obtained to achieve a specific level of total short-term debt. For example, if the firm desires that total short-term debt be $250,000 and has already determined that trade credit and accruals cannot economically be reduced below $50,000, the remaining $200,000 is the amount the firm must plan to raise. It is this $200,000 that is the subject of the remaining portion of the firm's planning process in the minimization of short-term debt cost.

Unsecured Credit-Line Borrowings This is the simplest way to obtain financing from a financial intermediary. To use it, the firm presents its financial statements to its bank and requests a credit line. The lending officer then either approves or disapproves the request. No security agreements or complicated bookkeeping are required; the bank is a general creditor of the firm. The firm then draws on the credit line and repays as needed. Because of this simplicity, this type of borrowing arrangement is often the preferred lending method for many banks and the preferred borrowing method for many firms.

Unsecured credit-line borrowing is available to any firm with a sufficiently good financial position to justify the loan. There are two costs associated with unsecured credit-line borrowings: the *commitment fee* on the maximum credit line that has been arranged and the *interest cost* of borrowing.[7] The interest cost of borrowed funds is often based on the prime rate; large and financially strong firms pay the prime rate (or sometimes a little less). Less creditworthy firms pay based on a percentage of the prime (for example, 120 percent of prime) or on prime plus percentage points (for example, prime plus 3 percent).

While this source of short-term financing is simple to obtain and very flexible, it does have drawbacks. First, because of the narrow margin between their borrowing and lending rates, banks' credit criteria for unsecured lending is quite stringent; a strong financial position is required of unsecured borrowers. These financial requirements often prevent small and new firms from obtaining unsecured credit-line borrowing. Second, bankers usually regard credit-line borrowings as primarily intended to fund seasonal short-term financing needs rather than to provide permanent short-term debt. They prefer that permanent debt be arranged via long-term borrowing (at higher interest rates). Therefore, a common requirement is for the firm to be out of debt for a specific period of the year (often 60 or 90 days) to evidence that credit-line financings are temporary. If the firm uses an unsecured credit line containing this provision as part of its permanent short-term financing package, it needs to arrange for other financing during the out-of-debt period.

---

[7]As in prior chapters, we assume here that the bank does not use compensating balances to extract compensation for services, but instead uses fee-based procedures.

Unsecured Notes and Term Loan Borrowings These are other mechanisms used in borrowing on an unsecured basis from financial intermediaries.
As in borrowing by the use of an unsecured credit line, the bank lends to the
firm based on its overall financial position. However, in using unsecured notes
and term loan borrowings, the financing and repayment schedules (and sometimes the interest rates) are set beforehand. For notes, one future repayment
is scheduled to retire each note, whereas a term loan is retired via a schedule
of several future payments. These prescheduled payments offer less flexibility
than a credit-line arrangement that can be repaid at the borrower's option.
However, the use of these notes and term loans avoids the commitment fees
that the firm might have to pay in using credit-line borrowings. Note borrowings from intermediaries often carry a 90-day maturity; interest on notes
may be on a discounted basis or may be payable when the notes are due. As
with unsecured credit-line borrowings, the availability of short-term note and
term loan borrowings is limited to firms that can meet the intermediary's
credit criteria.

Secured Borrowings with Marketable Securities as Collateral The remaining three sources of short-term financing require that the firm pledge an
asset as security for borrowing. Such a pledging of any asset improves the
position of the lender. Since the lender has first claim on that asset, the lender
is in a superior position to unsecured creditors in the event of the borrower's
default. Because of this superior position, the terms of lending can be improved. More credit can be granted and/or credit can be granted at lower
rates than if borrowings were unsecured. This increased availability or decreased interest rate is often of great advantage to the borrowing firm.[8]

The advantage to the lender in secured borrowing comes if the borrowing
firm is liquidated. The proceeds from the liquidation of the assets that are
security for the loan go to the secured lender. Thus, the more liquid and
valuable is the security, the greater will be the dollar recovery in default.
This means more advantage to the lender in holding a secured position;
consequently the lender is able to offer better terms to the borrowing firm.
Since current assets are the most liquid assets of borrowing firms, secured
borrowings (particularly secured short-term borrowings) are frequently based
on the use of current assets as security. Therefore, in our discussion of secured
borrowing, we center on borrowing arrangements that are based on the pledg-

---

[8]Historically, secured short-term borrowing was used by firms whose financial
condition was so poor as to preclude unsecured financing. Banks were reluctant to
charge appropriate interest rates to such high-risk customers, instead choosing to refuse
credit entirely. However, during the 1970s, the advantages of secured short-term
borrowing were discovered by many firms that could have borrowed on an unsecured
basis. Today, secured short-term borrowing may be considered by any firm in pursuit
of lower interest costs.

ing of the firm's major current assets as security for these borrowings: marketable securities, accounts receivable, or inventory.[9]

To finance with marketable securities as collateral, the firm could institute a reverse repurchase agreement (a reverse repo), pledging its marketable securities as collateral against a loan of short-term funds. However, the major volume of short-term secured borrowings use accounts receivable or inventories as security, since most firms have far larger holdings of these assets than they do of marketable securities.

Secured Borrowings with Accounts Receivable as Collateral In borrowing on a secured basis, lending does not depend only on this general financial position, but also on the value of the specific assets that are pledged as security. In the case of accounts receivable, the value of the asset (that is, its potential for recovery in liquidation) depends on the *number and type of customers to which the firm grants credit*. The more creditworthy the buyers of the borrower's products, the more that can be lent against receivables from those buyers.

The two methods of financing using accounts receivable as security are *pledging* and *factoring*.[10] Let us discuss pledging first. To institute this borrowing system, the firm contacts a financial intermediary who makes such loans. This is often a commercial lending company, but banks may also lend in this fashion. Participating banks may also choose to utilize, as their agents, other firms that are specialists in the monitoring of secured transactions. The lender or its agent then inspects the firm's accounts receivable portfolio and proposes a lending agreement based on this portfolio. This lending proposal will specify three important parameters that vary among such proposals: (1) the *receivables to be used as security*, (2) the *percent advance*, and (3) the *notification system*. The first of these is the designation of which receivables are to be pledged as collateral—all of the borrower's receivables portfolio or only part of this portfolio. The percent advance gives the amount of credit line to be granted relative to the receivables pledged. The more liquid the firm's receivables, the greater the advance. The notification system specifies whether the seller's customers will be notified to send remittances directly to the lender or will continue to send these payments to the borrowing firm.

The firm that finances by pledging accounts receivable can borrow up

---

[9]Cash, the remaining major current asset, cannot be used as security in borrowing arrangements from the firm's bank because it offers no advantage to the bank. In default, the bank will use its right of offset to seize the cash if any borrowings are outstanding, secured or unsecured. Since the bank will seize the cash in any case, offering this asset as security to a lending bank will not improve its position.

[10]For a good discussion of the basics of financing using accounts receivable and inventory as security, see G. Gallinger and P. Healey, *Liquidity Analysis and Management* (Reading, Mass.: Addison-Wesley, 1987), pp. 467–83.

to the advance at any time. For example, if the firm has $1 million in receivables outstanding and all the firm's receivables are to be used as security, with an advance rate of 80 percent, it may borrow up to $800,000, and will pay interest only on the borrowed amount. Interest rates in the pledging of accounts receivable are negotiated and are always lower than rates on the firm's unsecured borrowings.

Borrowing by pledging accounts receivable is a very useful strategy for many firms. If the firm's sales increase, so does needed financing, but so does the receivables collateral to obtain this financing. However, the paperwork necessary in the pledging of accounts receivable is substantial. The lender must be continually apprised of the state of the firm's accounts receivable portfolio. As receivables are paid, the firm's credit line decreases; new invoices and shipping papers must be presented to the lender as sales occur in order to restore the amount of available credit.

The *factoring* of receivables is substantially different from pledging receivables. In fact, factoring is not really secured borrowing at all. In factoring, the firm *sells its receivable asset to the financial intermediary* (the factor). Essentially, the factor takes over the firm's credit-granting function (for the receivables to be factored) and buys the resulting assets.

The procedures for factoring are outlined in the factoring agreement between the firm and the factor, but the events in the factoring of a receivable usually occur in the following sequence. When an order is received from a potential buyer, the seller requests permission from the factor to ship the order. If the factor approves the order, the order is shipped and the firm presents the paperwork (the invoice and the shipping documents) to the factor. The firm may then wait until the invoice matures and obtain the face value of the invoice less the factor's fee. The factor's fee compensates the factor for credit investigation expense, bad debt expense, and other expenses related to credit granting, and averages about 1 percent of the face value of the invoice.[11] Waiting to obtain the funds until the maturity of the invoice is called *maturity factoring*. The seller also has the option of taking cash for the receivable at the time the paperwork is presented to the factor. The amount of cash received for each invoice will be the face value of the invoice less the factor's fee and an interest charge. Taking a cash settlement when the receivable is presented to the factor is called *discount factoring*. In either case, the factor may retain a percentage of the face value as a holdback against material quality problems (which remain the seller's responsibility); this holdback is remitted to the selling firm when the invoice is actually paid by the buyer.

---

[11]See E. Farragher, "Factoring Accounts Receivable," *Journal of Cash Management* (March/April 1986), page 39. We assume in this discussion that the firm is factoring *without recourse*; when this is true, the factor bears the bad debt expense. If factoring is done *with recourse*, the firm bears the bad debt expense, but the factor's fees are lower.

Factoring is widely used by some firms in some lines of business, but is not an attractive financing vehicle for all firms because of noninterest costs, the constraints that factoring imposes on the seller, and the amount of paperwork entailed. If a firm factors all its receivables, it may eliminate the expense associated with its credit-granting function. However, such credit-granting expenses rarely total as much as the factor's fee. Also, when the firm factors its receivables, it subjects itself to the *factor's* credit-granting criteria. These may be considerably different from the credit-granting criteria which *the firm* finds to be optimal. In particular, the factor may institute credit criteria which are much more stringent than those preferred by the firm since its factoring fee is much smaller than the firm's margin on goods sold. Finally, there is usually a substantial paperwork cost entailed in passing invoices, shipping records, credit requests, and other documents back and forth between the firm and the factor. These disadvantages must be set against the reduction in interest expense and increase in availability that comes with factoring.

Secured Borrowings with Inventory as Collateral As with any secured financing system, the advantage for the lender of having the security determines how much will be lent and the interest rate that will be charged. Since the advantage to the lender revolves around the liquidation value of the asset, *the type of inventory that the firm holds will be a major determinant of the availability and cost of financing* when using inventory as collateral. The more salable the inventory, the more it is worth as security. Work-in-progess inventory rarely has any resale value, and therefore is useless as collateral. However, firms with substantial raw materials and finished goods inventories may find this form of financing of use. The more fungible these inventories, the more advantageous the financing that will result.

Besides its liquidity, another characteristic of the firm's inventory that will have a major impact on its value as collateral is *the ease with which the inventory can be monitored and controlled by the lender*. To make inventory worthwhile as security, the lender must be able to claim and liquidate the inventory if the borrower defaults. From the lender's view, the safest situation is when the lender can hold title to the goods or have them stored by a trusted third party. For example, in some states autos are titled and cannot be sold without these titles. If these titles are held by the lender, the inventory is fairly safe from misappropriation. Another strategy to secure the collateral is to use a *bonded warehouse* or *field warehouse* to store the goods until they are needed by the borrower. These are warehouses controlled by bonded personnel. Inventory stored there can be released to the borrower only by the lender. Such control insures inventory security.

However, arrangements can be made so that inventory that is not titled and does not lend itself to warehousing can, nevertheless, be used as collateral. For example, assume that the borrower is a retailer of appliances; an inventory of appliances would make excellent collateral, since appliances have substantial liquidation value. However, if it is necessary to display these goods in order to make sales, it would not be feasible to keep substantial amounts of this inventory in a warehouse. Further, appliances are generally not titled. In such a case, if inventory is to be used as security, the lender must trust the borrower and use a *general inventory lien* or a *trust receipt* system to obtain a secured position. These are legal instruments in which the lender maintains a security interest in the inventory, but the inventory is in the possession of the borrower. In a general lien (also known as a blanket lien), the lender gets a security interest in all the borrower's inventory, but keeps no record of particular inventory items. For example, in the case of the appliance retailer, the lender would have a security interest in the appliances but would not know at any particular time the exact composition of the security, since appliances are continually sold and restocked. By contrast, in the trust receipts system, specific untitled items serve as collateral. The items that are security for the loan are identified (perhaps by their serial numbers), and the lender keeps records giving the exact composition of the inventory at any time. When an item is sold, the borrower must offer additional collateral or must repay that portion of the loan. The trust receipt system is often used by automobile dealers in states where cars are untitled. However, under either system, the security is out of the lender's control and the firm will be able to borrow less and/or borrow at higher interest rates than in situations where the lender has more surety that the collateral will be available in the event of default.

Like financing using receivables as collateral, the use of inventory as security results in lower interest rates but has some offsetting costs. There are additional paperwork costs entailed in all types of inventory borrowings. If warehousing is used, there may be fees to warehousing and collateral-monitoring firms. These fees may have fixed and/or variable components and may be based on the size of the loan or the amount of inventory. The advantage to the borrowing firm of using inventory financing will depend on the magnitude of these additional costs compared to the reduced interest expense and increased availability that this borrowing system provides.

It is useful to summarize the mechanisms for obtaining short-term financing. Some important characteristics of the nine commonly used sources of short-term debt are presented in Table 11-1. One vital point to draw from the discussion and from this table is that *the types and costs of the various possible sources of short-term financing available to the firm will depend critically on other characteristics of that firm.* The firm's choice of capital structure and aggregate liquidity, the types of products and services (domestic and imported) that it purchases, its labor and tax payment situation, and the types of current assets that it holds will all bear on the types and costs of the short-term financing that will be available to it.

Table 11-1. *Characteristics of Sources of Short-Term Financing.*

Source of Financing	Who May Use	Interest and Other Costs	Maturity
Commercial Paper	Large firms and smaller firms with bank guarantee.	Interest cost plus cost of reserve bank credit; sum of two is usually below prime.	Up to 270 days; most common is 30 days.
Bankers' Acceptances	Firms importing goods.	Interest cost plus fees to bank; sum is often less than prime.	Usually 30 to 180 days; 90 days most common.
Accounts Payable	Any purchaser of goods or services.	1. For delay from discount date to due date: loss of discount.	1. Depends on terms; 30 days most common.
		2. For stretching beyond due date: higher borrowing costs, loss of bargaining power with supplier.	2. Until supplier sues.
Accruals	Firms who may defer labor, taxes, etc.	Depends on penalty cost of delay.	Depends on specific accrual.
Unsecured Credit Line	Firms with strong financial position from lender's view.	Interest cost, which depends on financial position of firm; Strong firms pay at prime. There may also be commitment fees.	Can be drawn down or paid off at any time.
Unsecured Short-Term Notes and Term Loans.	Firms with strong financial position from lender's view.	Interest cost, which depends on financial position of firm. Interest on notes may be discounted or paid at maturity.	90 days common for notes; varies for term loans.
Secured Borrowings Using Marketable Securities.	Firms holding marketable securities.	Interest at repo rate.	Reverse repos are typically very short maturities.
Secured Borrowings Using Accounts Receivable.	Firms with liquid and substantial accounts receivable.	1. Pledging: Interest expense lower than for unsecured borrowings; also large paperwork costs.	1. Loans due when invoices are paid.
		2. Factoring: Interest expense plus factor's fee averaging 1 percent of invoice (for discount factoring).	2. Firm sells assets; payment can be received immediately.
Secured Borrowings Using Inventory.	Firms with liquid and substantial inventory.	Interest similar to pledging accounts receivable; also monitoring, warehousing, and certification fees, depending on specifics of borrowing.	Loans are made when inventory is acquired and are due when inventory is used.

CALCULATING THE COST OF A SOURCE OF SHORT-TERM FINANCING

The first step in structuring the firm's liabilities is to generate a list of the types of short-term debt that are available to the firm. If this listing shows that the minimum levels of the firm's accounts payable and accruals are such that no additional financing is needed and aggregate liquidity targets are satisfied, then the process need go no further; these two sources of financing will comprise the firm's short-term debt package. However, the minimum levels of these liabilities do not provide sufficient short-term financing for most firms. In such cases, it is often useful to calculate measures of the maximum amount of financing and the cost of the alternative sources of short-term debt. We call measures of these characteristics the *net availability* and the *compounded effective annual interest rate*.

Calculating Net Availability To obtain the net availability from each source, the maximum amount of *net cash provided* by that source is calculated. This calculation is not as simple as it seems. The first thing to remember is that *cash financing* is what the firm requires. Thus, it is the *amount of cash that the firm receives* or the *amount of the delayed cash outflow* that comprises the relevant net availability.

Two problems often occur in determining this net availability from a potential source of financing. The first of these is *up-front expenses* that may make the amount of cash financing different from the face value of the debt. To see this, assume that one option in a firm's short-term financing package is a 180-day discounted note with a $1,000 principal amount. The interest for the 180-day period will be 5 percent. Such a note *will not provide $1,000 in financing*. Since the interest is discounted, the $1,000 note will net the firm only $950.00 in cash (equal to $1,000 minus interest of 0.05(1000)). Similar up-front expenses occur for several other types of current debts, including skipping the discount on accounts payable. Assume that the firm has the option of skipping the discount on invoices with a face value of $50,000 that have terms of 2 percent 10 days, net 90 days. If the firm pays in 10 days, the cash outflow will be $49,000; if it skips the discount, *only this amount of cash outflow is delayed*. The maximum financing from this source is $49,000, not $50,000. Any time that interest or other expenses are paid when financing is undertaken, and not at maturity, the net availability will be less than the face value of the liability.

A second problem in calculating the net availability from a liability occurs when *the financing from the liability changes over time*. There are several types of short-term financing with this characteristic, including short maturity term loans and accruals. For example, if the firm takes out a 180-day term loan with monthly amortization payments, the financing will not be the principal amount of the term loan. Since the principal decreases over time (in a nonlinear fashion), the average financing will be some lesser amount.

Table 11-2. *Average Financing From Example Term Loan.*

Month	Beginning Principal	Interest Payment	Principal Payment	Ending Principal
1	$10,000.00	$100.00	$1,625.48	$8,374.52
2	$ 8,374.52	$ 83.75	$1,641.74	$6,732.78
3	$ 6,732.78	$ 67.33	$1,658.16	$5,074.62
4	$ 5,074.62	$ 50.75	$1,674.74	$3,399.88
5	$ 3,399.88	$ 34.00	$1,691.48	$1,708.40
6	$ 1,708.40	$ 17.08	$1,708.40	0.00
Average	$ 5,881.70			

For example, assume that the principal amount on such a loan was $10,000, the interest is 1 percent per month, and equal monthly amortization payments are required. An analysis of the net availability from such a loan is given in Table 11-2. The monthly payment is $1,725.48.[12] Assuming that the payments on the loans are made at the end of the month, the beginning principal amounts constitute the financing for the month. For example, the financing provided by the loan for the second month is $8,374. 52. The average financing over the term of the loan is $5,881.70.

Let us illustrate changing availability over time with another example. Assume that a firm has a quarterly property tax liability with a face value of $100,000. It may choose to pay this liability on a monthly basis or to make the total payment at the end of the quarter. An analysis of the financing provided appears in Table 11-3. If the firm elects to pay at the end of each month, no month-end accrual occurs. However, if the firm chooses to pay at the end of the quarter, the accrued balance builds up over time, then is reduced to zero just before the end of the quarter. The delayed payments of $33,333

Table 11-3. *Financing from Example Tax Deferral.*

Month	Outflow for Monthly Payment	Month-End Accrual	Outflow for Quarterly Payment	Month-End Accrual	Month-End Financing Provided
1	$33,333	0	0	$33,333	$33,333
2	$33,333	0	0	$66,667	$66,667
3	$33,333	0	$100,000	0	0

[12]The present-value interest factor for a six-period annuity at 1 percent per period is 5.7955. The per-period amortization payment is then $10,000/5.7955 = $1,725.48.

for the first and second months provide month-end financing for the next month. That is, the strategy of delaying payments from a monthly to a quarterly basis provides $33,333 in financing during the second month and $66,667 in financing during the third month.

These two types of difficulties must be kept in mind in calculating the maximum amount of financing (the net availability) that is provided by each potential source of current debt. However, as long as the analyst focuses on the *net cash yielded* at various times from a source of financing, errors will be avoided.

Calculating the Compounded Effective Annual Interest Rate Once the firm knows how much financing a source will yield, a second natural question is the cost of this financing. We call this the compounded effective annual interest rate or *compounded EAI* of the funding source. The compounded EAI is calculated the same way for any source of funding: it is the yearly *compounded internal rate of return for the cash flows from the funding source*. To compute this cost statistic, the analyst obtains the cash flows for the funding source and their timing, calculates the internal rate of return (IRR), and compounds this IRR to a yearly basis. This gives a comparative cost statistic for the various available sources of funding which is based on net cash flows and is properly adjusted for the different maturities of the various funding sources. For purposes of this discussion, we will center on before-tax cash flows in calculating this cost measure.[13] To illustrate this procedure, let us do a few examples.

First, let us calculate the compounded EAI for the discounted note example previously presented. In return for the payment of $1,000.00 in 180 days, the firm can receive $950.00 in cash immediately. The IRR formula for this transaction is:

$$0 = 950.00 - 1,000.00/(1 + r) \tag{11-1}$$

where r is the IRR for the 180-day period. Solving this yields an r of 0.0526.[14]

---

[13]When all the expenses associated with the various sources of short-term debt have the same tax status and all tax bills are paid at the time of the expenses, ignoring taxes does not influence the relative costs of various sources. For discussion of the effects of taxes on the cost of financing with accounts payable where this does not hold, see I. Brick and W. Fung, "The Effect of Taxes on the Trade Credit Decision," *Financial Management* (Summer 1984), pp. 24–30. When expenses and tax bills are not concurrent, the IRR method presented in this chapter can be used to calculate after-tax EAIs by applying this method to after-tax (rather than before-tax) cash flows.

[14]The IRR method is employed in this chapter because it will give the effective rate for any set of cash flows, either the simple ones in this example or the more complex ones to be presented later. However, there is a shortcut method that will give the uncompounded rate *only for situations where there are exactly two cash flows*. In this shortcut method, the uncompounded EAI is calculated by dividing the difference in the cash flows by the net availability. Using this shortcut, the uncompounded EAI for this example would be calculated as (1,000.00 − 950.00)/950.00 = 0.0526.

The formula for compounding a rate is:

$$r_{comp} = (1 + r)^t - 1 \tag{11-2}$$

where r_{comp} is the compounded rate and t is the number of compounding periods. For a 360-day year, the 180-day note would be reborrowed twice, so the compounded rate is:

$$r_{comp} = (1 + 0.0526)^2 - 1$$

$$= 0.1080 = 10.80 \text{ percent} \tag{11-3}$$

This 10.80 percent is a yearly rate that can be used in comparing this source of short-term funds with other potential sources.

Another example presented previously concerned skipping the discount in payment to a trade supplier. The terms of sale were 2 percent 10 days, net 90 days, and the face value of invoices was $50,000. The IRR of this financing is computed as:

$$0 = 49,000 - 50,000/(1 + r) \tag{11-4}$$

The positive value of the $49,000 amount occurs because this cash outflow is avoided by skipping the discount, and therefore is a *net cash inflow*. Solving for r yields a rate of 2.04 percent for the 80-day difference in timing between the cash flows. On a yearly compounded basis, the rate is:

$$r_{comp} = (1 + 0.0204)^{360/80} - 1$$

$$= 0.0951 = 9.51 \text{ percent} \tag{11-5}$$

Let us now apply these principles to calculate the compounded EAI for a more complicated problem.[15] A firm is selling $1 million per month on terms of 2 percent 10 days, net 60 days. Historically, the firm has collected 20 percent of its receivables on the discount date; an additional 74 percent of sales are collected on the sixtieth day. Five percent of sales will be disputed on product quality grounds and will not be collected until 120 days from the date of sale. The remaining 1 percent are bad debts and are never collected. Credit department costs are 1.2 percent of sales and are paid 30 days after sales occur. A factor has made an offer of discount factoring. In this offer, the firm will receive the face value of invoices, less a 2.5 percent factor's fee, 1.75 percent interest, discount expense, and a 5 percent product quality hold-back; the cash will go to the seller immediately after sales are made. In this factoring arrangement, the factor absorbs any bad debts. The product quality

---

[15]This problem is adapted from E. Farragher, "Factoring Accounts Receivable," p. 41.

holdback will be settled on the 120th day, and the borrower will receive the remaining five percent at that time. What is the effective cost of this factoring?

The necessary analysis is presented in a spreadsheet format in Table 11-4. The basic data in cells B1 through B12 is used to compute the cash flows that appear in rows 17 through 21. The cash flows without factoring appear in column B of these rows while those with discount factoring appear in column C. The total net cash flow without factoring is $20,500 greater than that with factoring, but the cash flows from factoring occur earlier in time. The cash flow at day 120 happens to be the same in either case and thus has no bearing on the analysis. Since the last difference in the cash flows occurs at day 60, the present-value interest factors in column E have been computed for a 60-day period using the 60-day rate in cell E12. The rate of 2.7462 percent for this 60-day period produces a net present-value of zero in the differential cash flows (which appear in column D). This rate was found by iterating the contents of cell E12 until a zero NPV in cell F23 resulted. The yearly compounded rate is 17.65 percent, which is computed in cell E25 using equation (11-2).

Table 11-4. Cost Analysis of Example Discount Factoring.

!	A	!!	B	!!	C	!!	D	!!	E	!!	F	!
1	Sales		1000000									
2	Discount		.02									
3	% Taking Disc.		20%									
4	Disc. Exp.		4000									
5												
6	Factor Fee		.025 of sales									
7	Factor Exp.		25000 for sales of 1,000,000									
8	Interest Rate		.0175 of sales									
9	Interest Exp.		17500 for sales of 1,000,000									
10												
11	Bad Debt Rate		.01 of sales									
12	Credit Department Costs		.012 of sales		60-day Disc. Rate		.027462					
13												
14		Day	Cash Flow,		Cash Flow,		Diff. in				Cont.	
15			No Factoring		Disc. Factoring		Cash Flows		PVIF		to NPV	
16												
17		0	0		903500		−903500		1.00		−903500	
18		10	196000		0		196000		.995495		195117	
19		30	−12000		0		−12000		.986545		−11839	
20		60	740000		0		740000		.973272		720221	
21		120	50000		50000		0		.947258		0	
22												
23	Total NCF		974000		953500				NPV		0	
24												
25					Compounded Disc. Rate		.176507					

The computation of the net availabilities and compounded EAIs for each of the firm's potential sources of short-term financing may (under certain circumstances) be used to formulate a financing plan for the firm.[16] Such a procedure for formulating a structure of short-term liabilities is described in the following section.

THE SEQUENTIAL METHOD FOR FORMULATING A STRUCTURE OF CURRENT DEBT

In the prior section, we presented methods of assessing two important characteristics of each possible source of current debt for the firm. These were the net availability (which measures the maximum cash financing from the source) and the compounded EAI (which measures the costliness of a source). Under some limited conditions, these two parameters alone may be used to obtain an optimum structure for the firm's current liability package. To be used in this fashion, the net availability and compounded EAI for a source must *completely* capture the relative desirability of that source. For this complete capturing to occur, there must be no interactions among the EAIs and availabilities of the various sources. All sources must be divisible (utilizable in part) without affecting their EAIs. All sources must provide funding for one planning period only, or must be refundable at no cost. Finally, the firm must not be concerned with the differential effects of the various sources on aggregate liquidity.[17]

If these conditions are satisfied, the procedure for generating a minimum-cost plan for the structure of current liabilities is straightforward, and consists of the following steps:

1. List all the potential sources of short-term financing for the firm, starting from the lowest EAI and proceeding to the highest.
2. Starting with the source having the lowest EAI, proceed to utilize

---

[16]The internal rate of return has been used in this chapter without discussion of the problems in the use of this statistic to compare different sets of cash flows. Included among the problems are those related to rediscount rate and the possibility of multiple-root solutions in the calculation of the IRR. For discussion of these features of the internal rate of return, see T. Copeland and J. F. Weston, *Financial Theory and Corporate Policy*, Second Edition (Reading, Mass.: Addison-Wesley, 1983), pp. 29–36.

[17]If the firm is concerned with differences in liquidity, the net availability and the compounded EAI will not completely capture the desirability of any source of funding to the firm, since the various sources of funding will differ in their effects on aggregate liquidity. For the sequential method to be applicable, the firm must measure aggregate liquidity in some way that is not sensitive to differences in liquidity among different sources of current debt. For example, this would occur if the firm sets aggregate liquidity targets via the current or quick ratio.

sequentially more expensive sources until the firm's financing needs are fulfilled.

We call this method the *sequential method* because sources are chosen sequentially based on their costliness, from the cheapest to the most expensive. An illustrative example of this procedure is useful. Assume that a firm needs short-term financing totaling $1.5 million. Five sources of financing are available. Source A has an EAI of 9.32 percent and a net availability of $750,000. Source B has an EAI of 8.47 percent and a net availability of $340,000. Source C has an EAI of 21.81 percent and a net availability of $650,000. Source D has an EAI of 10.72 percent and a net availability of $134,000. Source E has an EAI of 8.05 percent and a net availability of $450,000. There is no interaction among the EAIs or availabilities for these sources (any source may be adopted without affecting the cost or availability of any other source). All the sources are completely divisible; the first dollar of financing from a source has the same EAI as all other dollars of financing from that source. All the sources are refundable at no cost, and the firm is unconcerned about differences in liquidity among the sources. What is the minimum-cost financing package?

The necessary analysis, performed according to the sequential method, is presented in Table 11-5. Data on the potential short-term financing sources are entered in columns A through C, starting with the lowest-cost source and proceeding to the highest-cost source.[18] Columns D through F determine the financing plan. The total financing requirement is entered as data in cell D4. Cells E4 through E8 contain "if statements." If the net availability (in column C) is less than the required financing (in column D), the net availability is displayed; otherwise, the required financing is displayed (for example, cell E4 contains "@IF(C4<D4,C4,D4)"). Column F contains the remaining financing after the use of the source on that line; cell F4 contains "D4-F4". For source E, the starting requirement is $1,500,000. The availability is $450,000 from this source, which is less than the required financing, so cell E4 returns the availability. After utilizing this source, $1.05 million in required financing remains, which appears in cell F4. This amount is also the starting required financing for the next source, so cell D5 contains "F4"; remaining cells in this column contain parallel entries.

The optimum financing plan appears in column E, and utilizes $450,000 in financing from source E, $340,000 in financing from source B, and $710,000 from source A. Financing from sources D and C is not utilized. The weighted-average EAI for the plan is calculated in columns G and H, and appears in cell H10. The EAI for this plan is 8.75 percent, and represents the yearly cost of the minimum-cost financing package from these sources of short-term financing.

[18]Alternatively, if the spreadsheet has a sorting function, the sources could be entered in any order and then sorted based on their compounded EAIs.

Table 11-5. *Execution of Sequential Method for Example Problem.*

	A Source	B Compounded EAI	C Net Availability	D Starting Requirement	E Usage from Source	F Remaining Requirement	G Percent of Total	H Contribution to Weighted EAI
1								
2								
3								
4	E	8.05	450000	1500000	450000	1050000	.30	2.42
5	B	8.47	340000	1050000	340000	710000	.23	1.92
6	A	9.32	750000	710000	710000	0	.47	4.41
7	D	-10.72	134000	0	0	0	0.00	0.00
8	C	21.81	650000	0	0	0	0.00	0.00
9								
10			2324000		1500000		1.00	EAI for Plan 8.75

SUMMARY

This chapter introduces the management of individual short-term liabilities. The goal in this management is to develop a strategy which, at a minimum cost, provides the desired funds and satisfies the firm's target level of aggregate liquidity. Nine commonly used sources of short-term funding were discussed: commercial paper, bankers' acceptances, accounts payable, accruals, unsecured credit lines, unsecured term loans and notes, and secured borrowings with marketable securities, receivables, or inventory as security. The availability and costliness of these sources varies substantially among firms, and depends on the firm's financial strength, operating methods, and other characteristics.

In addressing the structuring of current debt, the firm should first investigate all the possible sources of short-term debt that are available to it. There will be minimum levels of accounts payable and accruals which it is generally uneconomical to eliminate from the firm's structure of current debt. For amounts beyond this, if there are no interactions among the various possible sources of short-term funding, if all sources are divisible without affecting their costliness, if all sources are refundable, and if the firm's policy regarding aggregate liquidity is such that it is not concerned about differences in liquidity among the sources, analysis can proceed using the sequential method. In this method, the firm calculates the maximum funding from each source (its net availability) and the costliness of each source (its compounded effective annual interest rate). The firm then funds using the least-costly sources first and proceeding to more costly sources. This yields the optimum financing plan.

Unfortunately, the conditions under which the sequential approach will yield the optimal plan are quite restrictive. In the next chapter, we present a more complicated mathematical methodology (the integer programming approach) that produces the minimum-cost financial structure in these and a wide variety of other situations.

Problems

11-1. A firm is considering foregoing the discount on payments to a particular supplier. The firm purchases $200,000 per year from this supplier; purchases are distributed evenly throughout the year. The supplier offers terms of 1.5 percent 15 days, net 60 days, and the firm currently pays in 15 days and takes the discount. Calculate the compounded yearly effective annual interest rate and the maximum available borrowing from foregoing the discount to this supplier. Use a 360-day year.

11-2. A firm is considering several sources of funding as part of its current liability structure. One possible source of funds is changing its payment policy regarding insurance premiums. Currently, the firm makes two premium payments per quarter (one on the 45th day and one on the 90th day). These payments are in the amount of $49,500 each, and reflect a discount from the insurance company for such a payment policy. The alternative strategy would be to pay $100,000 at the end of 90 days. Use a 360-day year.

a. Calculate the compounded yearly effective annual interest rate of the alternative strategy.

b. Calculate the average additional availability of funds over the quarter from the alternative strategy.

11-3. A firm needs $800,000 in financing during January and $1.5 million during February. The following sources of funding are available:

Source	Yearly Compounded EAI	Maximum Availability, January	Maximum Availability, February
Bank Borrowing	12.0%	$500,000	$500,000
Skip Discount, Supplier A	9.0%	$250,000	$350,000
Skip Discount, Supplier B	30.0%	$600,000	$800,000
Delay Payments on Accruals	25.0%	$150,000	$250,000

There are no interactions among the sources. Sources may be utilized in part without affecting their EAIs, and all sources have equal effect on the firm's aggregate liquidity. All sources have a one-month maturity. Formulate a financing plan for each month and compute the weighted-average EAI of the financing for each month.

Selected Readings

Brick, I., and W. Fung, "The Effect of Taxes on the Trade Credit Decision," *Financial Management* (Summer 1984), pp. 24–30.

Brown, K., and B. Summers, eds., *Instruments of the Money Market*, Fifth Edition (Richmond: Federal Reserve Bank of Richmond, 1981), Chapters 9 and 10.

Farragher, E., "Factoring Accounts Receivable," *Journal of Cash Management* (March/ April 1986).

Gallinger, G., and P. Healey, *Liquidity Analysis and Management* (Reading, Mass.: Addison-Wesley, 1987), Chapters 16 and 17.

Charles' Clamps Corporation—Structuring Short-Term Liabilities: Sequential Method

Charles' Clamps Corporation was a family-owned firm headquartered in western Pennsylvania. The firm produced clamps of various types, including those for automotive and home repair applications. Clamps were manufactured mainly from sheet metal; thus the basic production processes were stamping and related metal-forming work, though some painting and some fabrication of other materials was required. The founder's name was Charles Jackson (hence the corporate name). The firm had grown over time and was now run by Mr. Jackson's sons, James and John. Financial statements for the firm as of the fiscal year ending on December 31, 1984 are presented in Exhibit 1.

Upon reviewing the firm's performance for 1984, the Jacksons were concerned with the amount of interest and other debt-related expense that the firm had incurred. The firm had paid $204,000 in debt-related expense in 1984, to service their long-term and short-term debt. The total principal on short-term debt and long-term debt (except for minimum levels of accounts payable and accruals) had averaged about $1.6 million, giving an effective financing rate of about 12.75 percent. This overall rate was slightly above the prime rate for 1984, which had averaged 12.04 percent.

However, the firm's long-term debt consisted principally of mortgages on the firm's various properties and term loans secured by equipment. Some of these mortgages had been taken out years ago and carried below-market rates as low as 7.5 percent; the average rate on the firm's long-term debt was 9.3 percent. Since principal on long-term debt had averaged about 68 percent of total interest-bearing debt, the Jacksons had calculated that the average effective rate on the firm's short-term borrowings was about 20 percent, or about 8 percent above the average prime rate. This seemed quite high to them since they considered their firm's financial position to be strong. Therefore, the family decided to reexamine their firm's short-term financing strategy in detail.

Initial efforts centered on the estimation of next year's short-term financing needs. While the firm's sales were fairly stable from year to year, these sales exhibited some seasonality within each year. The Jacksons projected the firm's sales and asset patterns for 1985 based on this seasonality. In the first, third, and fourth quarters, additional short-term financing would be required. These projections are presented in Exhibit 2.

In making these projections, they had assumed for preliminary analysis purposes that

Exhibit 1

Charles' Clamps Corporation
Financial Statements
(rounded thousands of dollars)

Statement of Income and Retained Earnings
Fiscal Year Ending 12/31/84

Sales	$10,246
Cost of Materials	7,768
Interest and Other Financing Expenses	204
Gross Margin on Sales	2,274
Selling, Labor and Administrative Expenses	1,618
Earnings Before Taxes	656
Taxes (Federal and State Income)	342
Earnings After Taxes	314
Common Dividends	150
Changes in Retained Earnings	$ 164

Balance Sheet
12/31/84

Cash	$ 458
Marketable Securities	0
Accounts Receivable	1,404
Inventories	1,564
Other Current Assets	102
Total Current Assets	3,528
Gross Fixed Assets	3,346
Less: Accumulated Depreciation	1,886
Net Fixed Assets	1,460
Other Assets	336
Total Assets	$ 5,324
Accounts Payable (Materials)	$ 810
Notes Payable	540
Accruals	434
Current Portion—Long-Term Debt	176
Total Current Liabilities	1,960
Long-Term Debt	802
Common Stock and Paid-In Capital	100
Retained Earnings	2,462
Total Common Equity	2,562
Total Liabilities and Equity	$ 5,324

Exhibit 2

Charles' Clamps Corporation
Projected Quarterly Financial Statements
(rounded thousands of dollars)

Statement of Income and Retained Earnings

Quarter Ending	3/31/85	6/30/85	9/31/85	12/31/85
Sales	$3,120	$2,152	$2,582	$2.905
Cost of Materials	2,365	1,632	1,958	2.202
Interest and Other Financing Expenses	62	42	51	58
Gross Margin on Sales	693	478	573	645
Selling, Labor and Administrative Expenses	493	340	408	459
Earnings Before Taxes	200	138	165	186
Taxes (Federal and State Income)	104	72	86	97
Earnings After Taxes	96	66	79	89
Common Dividends	40	40	40	40
Changes in Retained Earnings	$ 56	$ 26	$ 39	$ 49

Balance Sheet

Quarter Ending	3/31/85	6/30/85	9/31/85	12/31/85
Cash	$ 558	$ 384	$ 461	$ 519
Marketable Securities	0	40	0	0
Accounts Receivable	1,710	1,180	1,415	1,592
Inventories	1,905	1,314	1,577	1,774
Other Current Assets	124	86	103	116
Total Current Assets	4,297	3,004	3,556	4,001

Gross Fixed Assets	3,346	3,346	3,646	3,646
Less: Accumulated Depreciation	1,970	2,053	2,144	2,236
Net Fixed Assets	1,376	1,293	1,502	1,410
Other Assets	409	282	339	381
Total Assets	$6,082	$4,579	$5,397	$5,792
Accounts Payable (Materials)	$ 987	$ 681	$ 816	$ 919
Approximate Required Short-Term Financing	1,015	0	442	686
Accruals	528	364	438	492
Current Portion—Long-Term Debt	176	176	198	198
Total Current Liabilities	2,706	1,221	1,894	2,295
Long-Term Debt	758	714	820	765
Common Stock and Paid-In Capital	100	100	100	100
Retained Earnings	2,518	2,544	2,583	2,632
Total Common Equity	2,618	2,644	2,683	2,732
Total Liabilities and Equity	$6,082	$4,579	$5,397	$5,792
Current Ratio (Ignores Current LTD)	1.70	2.87	2.10	1.91
Average Current Ratio				2.14

interest and other financing expenses would be the same percent of sales that it had been in 1985 and that the management policies they had followed in prior years would be continued. With regard to current liabilities, these policies were:

1. *Accounts Payable*—Invoices with terms of sale that allowed a cash discount were paid on the discount date and the discount taken. Invoices with terms of sale without discounts were paid on the net date. The Jacksons had felt that violating the terms of sale would harm relationships with suppliers. The firm's prompt payment policy made it a valued customer, and together with other factors allowed Charles' Clamps to secure the most advantageous delivery schedules and prices.

2. *Notes Payable*—The firm had in the past financed short-term swings in required funds by borrowing from their bank via discounted, unsecured short-term notes. In combination with the firm's other short-term and long-term debt, this approach resulted in an aggregate liquidity position (as measured by the current ratio) which the Jacksons considered satisfactory, though this position varied with financing needs. The bank had set the rates on these notes as prime plus 6.5 percent. The notes matured in 90 days.

3. *Accruals*—Included in this financing source were accrued wages, taxes, and numerous other miscellaneous items. The amounts of financing were widely distributed within accrual subclassifications, but one of the largest subclasses was accrued wages.

4. *Current Portion of Long-Term Debt*—This account was determined by the covenants of the firm's long-term debt agreements. For 1985, the firm had planned to purchase some equipment during the third quarter, and also planned to take out an amortized term loan to partially finance these purchases.

Therefore, projections showed an increase in gross fixed assets, long-term debt, and current long-term debt during this quarter. The firm intended to refund all long-term debt as it came due.

The Jacksons also felt that, except for wages payable, the amounts of the other accrual subclasses were either too small to provide any substantial amount of additional financing or could provide such financing only at inordinate cost. They decided, as part of their efforts to control interest expense on short-term borrowings, to investigate the increased use of accounts payable and accrued wages as sources of short-term financing as well as the continued use of note financing from their bank. To assess the viability and cost of delaying of payment to accounts payable as a potential financing source, the Jacksons first developed a list of the terms of sale given them by suppliers and the proportions of accounts payable outstanding with each of these terms of sale. This list is presented as Exhibit 3. They decided to consider the strategy of delaying the payment of discount invoices from the discount date to the due date. They did not anticipate that this strategy would harm their relationships with suppliers, since they would still be honoring the suppliers' stated terms of sale.

Wage expense for production employees was 50 percent of Selling, Labor, and Administration Expense. The current twice-a-month pay schedule had been negotiated along with other pay and benefit features in the firm's labor contract. One short-term financing option would be to negotiate for a monthly payment cycle when the contract was reviewed. However, the members of the union considered even the current schedule to be a hardship and had pushed for a weekly pay cycle. Given the workers' preferences, they felt that going to the monthly cycle would

Exhibit 3

Charles' Clamps Corporation
Proportions of Accounts Payable for Various Terms of Sale

Terms	Percent of Payables Balance
Net Terms (Averaging Net 60 Days)	56
2% 10, Net 30	22
1% 10, Net 30	8
3% 10, Net 60	6
2% 10, Net 90	2
Miscellaneous Other Terms	6

require that they pay the workers 2 percent more than if the current pay schedule was continued.

In assessing their short-term banking relationships, the Jacksons had a long and rather arduous conversation with Carl Grant, their bank's commercial lending officer. Mr. Grant was surprised to find the Jacksons taking a serious look at their short-term financing situation, as the majority of their concern had previously centered on the cost of the firm's long-term debt. He agreed that the firm's overall financial position was quite strong and that the interest rate on the firm's note financing was quite high. However, he explained that since the firm had secured the long-term portion of its borrowing with fixed assets (a common requirement among smaller firms), in his view these substantial fixed assets could not be considered in an analysis of their short-term borrowings. Nonetheless, he agreed to grant future note borrowings at 5 percent above prime with the interest discounted. Borrowings would be limited to a maximum principal balance of $1.25 million.

The Integer-Programming Approach to Structuring Current Debt

In the prior chapter, we described the commonly used sources of the firm's short-term debt and presented the sequential method for obtaining a minimum-cost structure of this debt. The main objective in this chapter is the presentation of another method for structuring current debt—the *integer-programming method*—which will produce an optimum structure under a wider variety of conditions than will the sequential method, but is more complicated mathematically. We will also illustrate the use of the integer-programming method to develop an optimum hedge for the uncertainties inherent in a firm's cash flows, where this hedge uses reserve borrowing capacity of current debt. A review of some survey evidence on practice in the management of current debt is also included in this chapter.

PROBLEMS WITH THE SEQUENTIAL APPROACH

While the sequential method of structuring current liabilities is simple to understand and to use, it is applicable only under some very limited conditions. Included among these conditions are: (1) the costs and available funding from each source of short-term debt must be independent of all other sources, (2) the cost of a source must not vary with the amount of funds obtained from that source, (3) all sources must be of one-period maturity or most be costlessly refundable, and (4) the firm must not be concerned with differences among sources in liquidity. Unfortunately, one or more of these four conditions are violated in the situations faced by many firms. In this section, we discuss some sources of these violations and the effect of these violations on the problem of determining an optimal structure for current debt.

Interdependencies Among Funding Sources If the cost or availability of financing from one source varies with the use of another source, the cost and availability figures employed in the sequential method do not fully capture the relative desirability of funding from the various sources. In assessing their list of possible sources of short-term financing, many firms will find instances of such interdependencies.

A major source of interdependencies occurs between secured and unsecured borrowings. Recall that lenders will lend more funds or will lend funds at lower rates when borrowing is secured because, in liquidation, they have a priority claim on the revenues from the sale of a valuable asset. However, there is another side to the secured financing story. The pledging of assets as collateral to *secured* lenders increases the recovery to them but lowers the expected recovery to *unsecured* lenders. Every dollar that goes to a secured lender in liquidation is one less dollar that can be recovered by unsecured lenders. With respect to the credit-granting decision of an *unsecured* lender, pledging an asset to a *secured* lender is the same as removing that asset from the creditor's balance sheet. The more liquid and valuable is the asset (and therefore the better collateral it provides to secured lenders), the worse is the effect on unsecured lenders. Consequently, the use of assets as security to *reduce* the cost or *increase* the available borrowing from one lender may *increase* the cost or *reduce* the availability from other lenders.

Such interactions are a violation of the assumptions of the sequential method. When they occur, the *calculated* costs and availabilities misrepresent the *true* costs and availabilities because the interactions among the various sources are not taken into account. Under these circumstances, the sequential method may not produce the minimum-cost financing strategy.

Variation in Cost with Amount Borrowed When the cost per dollar borrowed from a source varies with the amount of funding from that source, any one-number measure of this per-dollar cost (including the compounded EAI) misrepresents the relative desirability of that source. Several potential sources of short-term financing have this characteristic.[1] Such variations in EAI will happen, for example, if there is some fixed cost associated with borrowing from a particular source, where this fixed cost is independent of the amount borrowed. Such a fixed cost will bear more heavily on per-dollar financing if borrowings are small than it will if borrowings are large.

To illustrate the fluctuation of EAI with amount borrowed, an example is in order. Assume that the firm has arranged with its bank to borrow on an unsecured line of credit. The maximum principal is $5 million, the expected interest rate is 10 percent per year (paid monthly), and all interest is paid at maturity. However, to maintain the availability of this credit line, the firm must pay a monthly fee of 0.25 percent of the average unborrowed balance. This commitment fee effectively imposes a fixed charge on the credit line; the minimum cost that the firm can pay is $12,500 per year (equal to 0.0025

[1]For an illustration of variation in per-dollar financing cost, see C. T. Conover, "The Case of the Costly Credit Agreement," *Financial Executive*, Vol. 39, No. 9 (September 1971), pp. 40–48.

times $5 million), regardless of how little it borrows. The result is that the compounded EAI of the credit line varies with the amount borrowed; this variation is portrayed in Table 12-1. If the firm's borrowings average only $500,000, the compounded EAI will be 12.96 percent; if the firm borrows to the maximum, the EAI will be 10.47 percent. As this example illustrates, when the EAI varies with the amount borrowed, a single measure will not properly represent the cost of that potential source of funding.

Multiperiod Maturities Many of the sources of funding facing firms have maturities that do not match the firm's planning horizon. For example, if the firm is planning its current liability structure for the next month and it issues nonrefundable 90-day notes, these notes will provide funding in that month, *and also in the two following months*. Multiperiod sources of funding may be highly desirable during one part of the time during which they are outstanding, but a good deal less valuable in other parts because of the availability of cheaper sources at other times. The optimum structure in one period will then depend on the structure chosen in another period. Because it assumes that each source of funds has a maturity of one planning period (or is refundable at no cost), the sequential method cannot address these interperiod effects.

Differences in Liquidity In the sequential method, sources of short-term funding are assessed based on cost and availability, without regard to their liquidity. Yet the firm may be concerned about differences in liquidity among current liabilities and their consequent effect on the aggregate liquidity of the firm. Under the sequential method, there is no guarantee that the minimum-cost structure of current liabilities will yield the desired level of aggregate liquidity.

Table 12-1. *Variation in Effective Cost with Amount Borrowed.*

Average Principal Amount	Monthly Commitment Fee	Monthly Interest Expense	Monthly EAI (percent)	Yearly EAI (percent)
$ 0	$1,042	$ 0	Infinity	Infinity
$ 500,000	$ 937	$ 4,167	1.02	12.96
$1,000,000	$ 833	$ 8,333	.92	11.57
$1,500,000	$ 729	$12,500	.88	11.11
$2,000,000	$ 625	$16,667	.86	10.88
$2,500,000	$ 521	$20,833	.85	10.75
$3,000,000	$ 417	$25,000	.85	10.65
$3,500,000	$ 312	$29,167	.84	10.59
$4,000,000	$ 208	$33,333	.84	10.54
$4,500,000	$ 104	$37,500	.84	10.50
$5,000,000	$ 0	$41,667	.83	10.47

When any of these assumptions about the nature of the firm's potential current liabilities are violated, the sequential method is unreliable; it may or may not yield an optimum structure, depending on the characteristics of the potential sources of funding. Under some circumstances, the violations of the assumptions underlying the sequential method are not serious, and a little insight and analysis will allow the sequential method to be used anyway. For example, suppose that the only violation of these assumptions is that two of the possible sources of short-term borrowing are mutually exclusive (and thus their availabilities are independent). If the more expensive of these sources is eliminated, the sequential method can be properly applied to the remaining sources to yield an optimum package.

However, there are many other situations that involve simply too many violations of the assumptions of the sequential method for insight and analysis to yield an optimum result. When this occurs, the firm needs to utilize a technique that can capture the complex interdependencies, costs, and constraints involved in the current liability structure problem. The integer-programming approach can accomplish this task. It is described in the following sections.

INTEGER PROGRAMMING AND THE STRUCTURING OF CURRENT LIABILITIES

The problem of deciding on a package of current liabilities can be viewed as one of minimization of costs, with this minimization constrained by the various characteristics of the situation. The costs to be minimized are the cash outflows for interest, fees, and so forth, associated with the firm's short-term financing plan. The constraints concern the maximum amount that can be borrowed, the need for funds, the firm's level of aggregate liquidity, and other circumstances. When viewed in this way, it is clear that the generic approach to the problem must be that of *mathematical programming*, which is used in Chapter 2 of this text to address the lockbox location problem. Since several of the variables in the typical current liability structuring problem can assume only integer values, *integer programming* is the type of mathematical programming usually required.[2] In this section, we will describe the solution procedure for the current liability structure problem under the assumption that the future cash flows (and consequently the future financing needs) of

[2]Major references in the use of mathematical-programming techniques to structure current liabilities include A. Robickek, D. Tiechrow, and J. Jones, "Optimal Short-Term Financing Decision," *Management Science*, Vol. 12, No. 1 (September 1965), pp. 1–36; G. Pogue and R. Bussard, "A Linear Programming Model for Short-Term Financial Planning Under Uncertainty," *Sloan Management Review*, Vol. 13 (1972), pp. 69–98; and J. Kallberg, R. White, and W. Ziemba, "Short-Term Financial Planning Under Uncertainty," *Management Science*, Vol. 28, No. 6 (June 1982), pp. 670–82.

the firm are certain. That is, in this section we ignore the uncertainty inherent in these flows. In the following section, the effects of uncertainty in these flows are discussed.

Basics of the Constrained Structuring Problem Let us assume that the treasurer of a firm has projected the firm's future financing needs over the next several planning periods and has made a list of the possible sources of short-term financing over these periods. If none of the sources of short-term financing has a multiperiod maturity, the treasurer need plan only for the next period, and should be concerned with the minimization of costs only for that period.[3] However, if there are candidate sources of financing with multiperiod maturities, a multiperiod plan is required, and the value of financing charges over the entire period must be considered. The various aspects of the situation will generally impose the following types of constraints on the financing plan to be devised:

1. *Available Funds Constraints*—For each period covered by the plan, the cash generated by the sources of short-term borrowing must be sufficient to address the firm's short-term financing requirements.

2. *Limits of Borrowing Constraints*—In general, the maximum amounts of borrowing from each possible source of short-term funding will be constrained; principal amounts cannot be less than zero or exceed this maximum.

3. *Aggregate Liquidity Constraints*—During each period, the firm's short-term financing plan must satisfy the firm's aggregate liquidity targets.

4. *Constraints to Model Stepwise Costs*—If there are sources of borrowing that entail fixed costs, there can be no borrowing from these sources without these stepwise costs being incurred.

5. *Interaction Constraints*—These model the relationships among sources and over time. For example, the use of one source may preclude the use of another.

6. *Ending Condition Constraints*—While the horizon of the treasurer's plan is limited, the firm will continue beyond this period. Because of this, the firm may want to impose constraints on its condition at the end of the planning period.

7. *Miscellaneous Other Constraints*—These limit values of some variables to integers, and so forth.

To approach this problem, the treasurer may use integer programming. In formulating the problem in an integer-programming format, the task is to

---

[3]For simplicity, in this chapter we ignore the effect of the cost of financing on future financing requirements.

develop mathematical expressions for the objective function (which contains the costs of financing) and the various types of constraints faced by the firm. The precise mathematical formulations will vary from situation to situation, based on the types of current liability financing available to the firm. At this point, it is useful to demonstrate the required procedures by means of an example problem.

An Example Problem   A firm is trying to structure its current liabilities package to achieve minimum cost. It has determined that over the next three months it will need short-term cash financing in the total amounts of $10 million, $4 million, and $8 million respectively. Four sources of financing are available:

1. *Notes with a Maturity of 90 Days*—The interest cost of these notes will be 11 percent per year, paid on a discounted basis. Only one borrowing can be made. Notes may be paid only at maturity. The maximum principal is $6 million. There can be no borrowings on this basis if secured borrowings are used.

2. *Secured Borrowings*—If this borrowing source is used, no borrowings can be made on unsecured notes. The borrowing will be secured by the firm's accounts receivable. Interest will be paid at maturity at a rate of 9.5 percent per year. Borrowings are on a monthly basis. Availability is based on the size of the firm's receivables portfolio; maximum borrowings for the three months are $4 million, $2 million, and $3 million respectively.

3. *Commercial Paper*—Maturity here will be 30 days. Rates are expected to be 10 percent per year in all three months. Interest is on a discount basis. The firm's maximum borrowings are $8 million. To be able to borrow using commercial paper, the firm will first have to pay a $10,000 fee to its bank to obtain a bank guarantee of this paper.

4. *Skipping the Discount on Payables*—The cost will be 1.25 percent per month on a discount basis. The availability depends on the amounts owed to suppliers; for the three months in question, the available financing will be $2.5 million, $3.5 million, and $4.5 million respectively.

The firm controls for aggregate liquidity based on the Comprehensive Liquidity Index. The target level of this index is 1.80; any value above this is acceptable. Current assets have an X value of $21.6 million in the first month, $15 million in the second month, and $20 million in the third month; and the minimum levels of accounts payable and accruals contribute $3 million to the value of Y. The firm is not concerned with its ending condition.

The objective function for this problem reflects the goal of minimizing the sum of the costs of financing over the three-month period.[4] Let P_{ij} be the principal amount raised from source i in period j. Let an i value of A indicate the note borrowing source, B the secured borrowings with accounts receivable as security, C the commercial paper, and D skipping the discount on payables. Let A be the first month, B the second, and C the third. Thus, P_{BC} is the principal amount borrowed on a secured basis in the third month. Let the X_{ij} variables be zero-one integer variables denoting whether source i is used in period j; if there is no j designation on an X_{ij} variable, the variable is X_i and indicates whether source i is used in *any* of the planning periods. The objective function is then:

$$\text{Min} \sum_{\text{all } i} \sum_{\text{all } j} r_{ij} P_{ij} + \text{Other Costs of Financing} \qquad (12\text{-}1)$$

Where r_{ij} is the cost which is proportional to the amount financed from source i in period j. For most sources of financing, r_{ij} will be the interest rate for source i in period j, although r_{ij} can include any other costs that vary directly with the principal borrowed. In our problem, the only costs proportional to the principal amounts are interest expenses. The monthly interest rates are 0.91667 percent for the note borrowing (11 percent per year divided by 12 months), 0.79167 percent for the secured borrowings, 0.83332 percent for the commercial paper, and 1.25 percent for the payables. There is also a $10,000 fixed charge if commercial paper is used; let X_C be a zero-one variable indicating this use. The objective function based on these coefficients along with the important constraint equations for this example problem appear in Table 12-2. Let us review this formulation in detail.

The types of constraint equations necessary for this example problem appear in Table 12-2 in the same order in which these types were previously discussed. The available funds constraints appear in rows 2 through 4. There is one constraint equation for each planning period. Financing expense is on a discounted basis for the notes, commercial paper, and payables sources (sources A, C, and D), so their contributions to the needed cash financing are less than their principal values. For example, the coefficient of the principal amount variable for note financing is 0.9725, reflecting the discounting of three months' interest (since the notes mature in 90 days). The limits of borrowing (maximum principal) constraints appear in rows 5 through 16; there is one equation for each source in each period.

The aggregate liquidity constraints based on the firm's Comprehensive Liquidity Index (one constraint per period) appear in rows 17 through 19. In these three equations, the coefficients of the principal amount variables rep-

---

[4]A slightly more accurate portrayal would minimize the present value of the future financing costs. To do this, the coefficients of future costs in the objective function would include present-value factors representing relative timing of these future flows. For simplicity, we do not include these in the example problem.

Table 12-2. *Partial LINDO Formulation for Example Problem.*

MIN   10 XC + .0091667 PAA + .0079167 PBA + .0083333 PCA + .0125 PDA
       + .0091667 PAB + .0079167 PBB + .0083333 PCB + .0091667 PAC
       + .0079167 PBC + .0083333 PCC + .0125 PDB + .0125 PDC

SUBJECT TO

    2)   .9725 PAA + PBA + .9917 PCA + .9875 PDA >= 10000
    3)   .9725 PAB + PBB + .9917 PCB + .9875 PDB >= 4000
    4)   .9725 PAC + PBC + .9917 PCC + .9875 PDC >= 8000
    5)   PAA <= 6000
    6)   PAB <= 6000
    7)   PAC <= 6000
    8)   PBA <= 4000
    9)   PBB <= 2000
   10)   PBC <= 3000
   11)   PCA <= 8000
   12)   PCB <= 8000
   13)   PCC <= 8000
   14)   PDA <= 2500
   15)   PDB <= 3500
   16)   PDC <= 4000
   17)   .75 PAA + .9167 PBA + .9167 PCA + .9167 PDA <= 9000
   18)   .75 PAB + .9167 PBB + .9167 PCB + .9167 PDB <= 5333
   19)   .75 PAC + .9167 PBC + .9167 PCC + .9167 PDC <= 8111
   20) − 8000 XC + PCA <= 0
   21) − 8000 XC + PCB <= 0
   22) − 8000 XC + PCC <= 0
   23)   PAA − PAB = 0
   24)   PAB − PAC = 0
   25) − 6000 XA + PAA <= 0
   26) − 4000 XBA + PBA <= 0
   27) − 2000 XBB + PBB <= 0
   28) − 3000 XBC + PBC <= 0
   29)   XA + XBA <= 1
   30)   XA + XBB <= 1
   31)   XA + XBC <= 1
   32)   PAA >= 0
   33)   PAB >= 0
   34)   PAC >= 0
   35)   PBA >= 0
   36)   PBB >= 0
   37)   PBC >= 0
   38)   PCA >= 0
   39)   PCB >= 0
   40)   PCC >= 0
   41)   PDA >= 0
   42)   PDB >= 0
   43)   PDC >= 0

resent their contributions to the Y figure used in the Comprehensive Liquidity Index. The maturity of the secured borrowings, commercial paper, and payables is one month, so they turn over 12 times per year; their coefficients are therefore 0.9167 (equal to 1 minus 1/12). Similarly, the coefficient of the principal amount borrowed on notes is 0.75 because this source of financing matures four times per year.

The stepwise cost associated with the use of the commercial paper is modeled in rows 20 through 22. The X_C variable is constrained to zero or 1.0, and unless it is 1.0, no borrowings can take place from commercial paper in any of the three planning periods.

There are two interactions in this example problem. First, the principal borrowed under the note borrowings in the initial period will continue over the three months of the plan, and cannot be reduced or increased over time. Rows 23 and 24 insure this by requiring that the three principal amounts under the note borrowings (source A) be equal. The second interaction occurs between the unsecured note borrowings and the secured borrowings against receivables (source B). Row 25 requires that X_A be 1.0 if there are any note borrowings. Rows 26 through 28 make the same requirement based on X_{Bj} variables for periods A, B, and C. These four 0,1 integer variables are then used in rows 29 through 31 to insure that only one of these two possible sources can be used over the planning horizon. In these equations, the sum of X_A and an X_{Bj} variable are constrained to be less than 1.0. Since these X variables are zero-one integers, if one of them is 1.0, the other cannot be 1.0 (though both can be zero). If X_A is 1.0, all the X_{Bj} variables must be zero; if one of the X_{Bj} variables is 1.0, X_A must be zero.

The remaining rows constrain the principal amounts of the various borrowings to be greater than zero. Not shown here (in the interests of brevity) are the miscellaneous constraints necessary to confine the X_{ij} variables to zero or 1.0.

The solution to this formulation is presented in Table 12-3; some analysis of this solution is presented in Table 12-4. The financing cost is $201,210. In each of the periods, the 90-day notes and the commercial paper provide the necessary cash. The resulting Comprehensive Liquidity Indices are 1.81, 2.35, and 1.98 respectively.

This solution yields some interesting insights regarding the structure of this particular problem. These can be assessed by inspecting Tables 12-3 and 12-4. One interesting aspect concerns the nonuse of secured financing, which is the source of funding carrying the lowest interest rate. This lack of use is due to the constraint on the firm's level of aggregate liquidity. In the first period, the firm *must* use note financing in order to achieve its minimum desired Comprehensive Liquidity Index. Because of the coefficients of the principal amount variables in rows 17 through 19 of the formulation and because of the interactions among the sources, only the use of notes as part

Table 12-3. LINDO Solution for Example Problem.

OBJECTIVE FUNCTION VALUE

1)   201.208000

VARIABLE	VALUE	REDUCED COST
XA	1.000000	.000000
XC	1.000000	10.000000
XBA	.000000	− 14.219780
XBB	.000000	− .972750
XBC	.000000	− 1.459035
PAA	2124.833000	.000000
PBA	.000000	.000000
PCA	8000.000000	.000000
PDA	.000000	.001172
PAB	2124.833000	.000000
PBB	.000000	.000000
PCB	1949.783000	.000000
PAC	2124.833000	.000000
PBC	.000000	.000000
PCC	5983.261000	.000000
PDB	.000000	.004202
PDC	.000000	.004202

of the financing package will achieve the necessary liquidity in this period (since the notes have a lower contribution to the Comprehensive Liquidity Index than do the other sources of financing). Since note financing must be used, secured borrowings may not be used.

Another interesting aspect of this solution concerns the use of the commercial paper. Since there is a fixed fee associated with this source of funding, its cost per dollar financed is very high if it is used in small amounts. However, the integer programming solution uses this source in sufficient amount that its overall cost is less than that of alternative accounts payable financing (which is the other remaining potential source of funding, since note borrowings have been used and secured borrowings are precluded).

The integer programming method is a straightforward approach to the current liability-structuring problem. As illustrated in the prior example, it yields optimal solutions when there are various constraints and interactions in raising the necessary funds. However, this methodology may also be used to simultaneously develop (1) a plan for short-term borrowing, and (2) a hedging strategy against the cash stockout risk that is caused by uncertainties in the firm's cash flows. Recall from prior chapters that one approach to hedging this risk is to keep a target level of aggregate liquidity (as discussed in Chapter 10). Another is to maintain a safety stock of liquid assets and/or

Table 12-4. *Analysis of IP Solution.*

	Principal Amounts Month				Financing Amounts Month		
Source	A	B	C	Source	A	B	C
A	$2,125	$2,125	$2,125	A	$ 2,067	$2,067	$2,067
B	0	0	0	B	0	0	0
C	$8,000	$1,950	$5,983	C	$ 7,934	$1,934	$5,934
D	0	0	0	D	0	0	0
					$10,000	$4,000	$8,000

	Financing Costs Month				Contributions to CLI Month		
Source	A	B	C	Source	A	B	C
A	$19.48	$19.48	$19.48	A	$ 1,594	$ 1,594	$ 1,594
B	0	0	0	B	0	0	0
C	$76.67	$16.25	$49.86	C	$ 7,333	$ 1,787	$ 5,485
D	0	0	0	D	0	0	0
	$96.15	$35.73	$69.34		$ 8,927	$ 3,381	$ 7,078
	Three-Month Total		201.21	Other Y	$ 3,000	$ 3,000	$ 3,000
				Total Y	$11,927	$ 6,381	$10,078
				X	$21,600	$15,000	$20,000
				CLI	1.81	2.35	1.98

short-term borrowing capacity (as discussed in Chapter 3).[5] The integer-programming approach to the current liability structure problem can also be used to plan this short-term borrowing capacity hedge. This use of integer programming in conjunction with hedging cash flow uncertainty is discussed in the next section.

INTEGER PROGRAMMING AND THE HEDGING OF CASH STOCKOUTS

For most firms, the expected cash flows used to determine the firm's financing requirements in various periods are not certain. Because of deviations from expectations in the levels of sales, collection patterns, and so forth,

[5]In Chapter 3, we generally limited our discussion of the use of reserve borrowing capacity in the hedging of cash shortages to the availability of additional borrowings on bank credit lines. We limited discussion to this particular source of funding in the interests of simplicity. However, the availability of reserve borrowing capacity from *any* source of short-term funding (accounts payable, commercial paper, accruals, etc.) can provide such a hedge, as is recognized in the following section.

the expected amounts of required financing and surplus funds are actually the means of the probability distributions. However, the firm's potential sources of short-term borrowing provide a method of hedging this cash flow risk. If the firm structures its sources of short-term borrowing so as to allow for *the availability of additional borrowing capacity* to address potential shortfalls, it can obtain a short-term financing strategy that includes a hedge against cash stockouts.

To see this, let us assume that the firm has, based on the costs of running out of cash, set an acceptable probability of such an event for each planning period. This probability, combined with data on the probability distributions of borrowing amounts in various future periods (obtained via a simulation analysis of the firm's cash budget), gives the total dollar amount of the necessary hedge. The firm's current asset structure can provide part of this hedge; the remainder can be provided by structuring current liabilities so as to have the necessary amount of reserve borrowing capacity available in each period. However, it is important to note that this reservation of borrowing capacity *may change the optimal strategy for financing expected deficits.* Further, because adding an additional set of constraints (those that require reserve borrowing capacity in each planning period) may change the mix of liabilities used in financing, *expected financing costs may be increased.* That is, depending on the costs of potential current liabilities and their availabilities, *this hedging strategy may not be costless.*

An Example Problem   Let us modify the prior example problem to reflect uncertainty and to use available borrowing capacity as a partial hedge against cash stockouts. In addition to the data provided previously, assume that the firm has conducted a simulation of its cash budget and determined that the standard deviations of the expected levels of borrowings over the next three months are $3 million, $4 million, and $5 million, respectively. The levels of borrowings are normally distributed and uncorrelated over time. The firm has decided that it is willing to undergo a probability of cash stockout of 5 percent in each month. If the firm has extra cash (because it has borrowed more on the 90-day note arrangement than it needs for financing, and the note balance cannot be reduced) this cash will be invested at 3 percent per year less than the interest rate on the notes. This investment will be in securities of very short maturity. The firm plans to keep $1 million in other cash or near-cash instruments as part of current assets during each of the three months. Besides this cash reserve, the firm would like to formulate an additional hedge based on short-term borrowing capacity to deal with cash shortage risks.

To address this problem, we need to formulate the firm's short-term financing strategy in such a way that it allows for the required hedging availability in each period. Recognize first that each possible source of short-term debt can entail the funding of expected principal borrowings in each period

Table 12-5. *Partial LINDO Formulation for Example Problem with Hedging.*

MIN   10 XC + .0091667 PAA + .0079167 PBA + .0083333 PCA + .0125 PDA
           + .0091667 PAB + .0079167 PBB + .0083333 PCB + .0091667 PAC
           + .0079167 PBC + .0083333 PCC + .0125 PDB + .0125 PDC + .0025 HAA
           + .0025 HAB + .0025 HAC

SUBJECT TO

2)	.9725 PAA + PBA + .9917 PCA + .9875 PDA >= 10000
3)	.9725 PAB + PBB + .9917 PCB + .9875 PDB >= 4000
4)	.9725 PAC + PBC + .9917 PCC + .9875 PDC >= 8000
5)	PAA + HAA <= 6000
6)	PAB + HAB <= 6000
7)	PAC + HAC <= 6000
8)	PBA + HBA <= 4000
9)	PBB + HBB <= 2000
10)	PBC + HBC <= 3000
11)	PCA + HCA <= 8000
12)	PCB + HCB <= 8000
13)	PCC + HCC <= 8000
14)	PDA + HDA <= 2500
15)	PDB + HDB <= 3500
16)	PDC + HDC <= 4000
17)	.75 PAA + .9167 PBA + .9167 PCA + .9167 PDA + .2097 HAA <= 9000
18)	.75 PAB + .9167 PBB + .9167 PCB + .9167 PDB + .2097 HAB <= 5333
19)	.75 PAC + .9167 PBC + .9167 PCC + .9167 PDC + .2097 HAC <= 8111
20)	− 8000 XC + PCA + HCA <= 0
21)	− 8000 XC + PCB + HCB <= 0
22)	− 8000 XC + PCC + HCC <= 0
23)	PAA − PAB = 0
24)	PAB − PAC = 0
25)	− 6000 XA + PAA + HAA <= 0
26)	− 4000 XBA + PBA + HBA <= 0
27)	− 2000 XBB + PBB + HBB <= 0
28)	− 3000 XBC + PBC + HBC <= 0
29)	XA + XBA <= 1
30)	XA + XBB <= 1
31)	XA + XBC <= 1
32)	PAA >= 0
33)	PAB >= 0
34)	PAC >= 0
35)	PBA >= 0
36)	PBB >= 0
37)	PBC >= 0
38)	PCA >= 0
39)	PCB >= 0
40)	PCC >= 0
41)	PDA >= 0
42)	PDB >= 0

43) PDC >= 0
44) .9725 HAA + HBA + .9917 HCA + .9875 HDA = 3935
45) .9725 HAB + HBB + .9917 HCB + .9875 HDB = 5580
46) .9725 HAC + HBC + .9917 HCC + .9875 HDC = 7225
47) HAA − HAB = 0
48) HAB − HAC = 0
49) HAA >= 0
50) HAB >= 0
51) HAC >= 0
52) HBA >= 0
53) HBB >= 0
54) HBC >= 0
55) HCA >= 0
56) HCB >= 0
57) HCC >= 0
58) HDA >= 0
59) HDB >= 0
60) HDC >= 0

(P_{ij}), a hedging availability in that period, or both of these. Designate the principal amount of the hedging availability from source i in period j as H_{ij}. An integer program incorporating the modifications necessary to include this hedging strategy for the example problem is presented as Table 12-5.[6] Let us review the modifications that have been made to the original, unhedged program on a line-by-line basis.

In our example, for the sources of short-term financing involving secured borrowings, commercial paper, and skipping the discount on payables (sources B, C, and D), there are no costs directly associated with keeping reserve borrowing capacity. Therefore, no cost terms for the hedging availabilities from these sources appear in the objective function. However, to have cash available from the 90-day notes (source A), the firm must borrow this cash and invest it in short-term securities, since the principal amount owing on the notes cannot be changed over the three-month period. Consequently, the loss of these investments (interest expense minus investment income) must appear in the objective function. This is represented by the H_{AA}, H_{AB}, and H_{AC} terms that have been added to this function. The cost of these hedges is 3 percent per year (0.25 percent per month).

The availability constraints for the expected amounts of necessary funding (rows 2 through 4) are not affected by the inclusion of hedging strategy within the problem. However, the limits of borrowing constraints (rows 5 through 16) must now reflect the potential reservation of a portion of available

[6]As before, in the interests of space we do not present the constraint equations that limit the X_{ij} variables to zero or 1.0.

borrowing for hedging purposes. This is done by adding the hedging principal variable to the lefthand side of each of these constraint equations. For example, in row 5, the total principal available for borrowing *and* hedging from source A in period A is $6 million; if borrowings from this source in this period are $4 million, the maximum hedge from this source is $2 million.

The modified aggregate liquidity constraints are presented in rows 17 through 19. The use of reserve availability from the secured borrowings, commercial paper, or delayed payment to suppliers does not entail a change in the firm's expected level of assets and liabilities, and therefore does not affect these constraints.[7] However, the use of notes as a hedging vehicle requires that more funds be borrowed on these notes and that these funds be temporarily invested; this changes the firm's aggregate liquidity position. Take period A as an example. For each dollar of principal borrowed on notes, the firm receives $0.9725 in cash which is then invested in short-term securities. This increases X in the Comprehensive Liquidity Index by $0.9725; the new X is $21.6 million plus $0.9725H_{AA}$. For each dollar of principal borrowed on notes, Y in the Comprehensive Liquidity Index will increase by $0.75 (since the maturity of the notes is 90 days). Let Y_p be the contribution to Y from the firm's other short-term borrowings. The new Y is then Y_p plus $3 million plus $0.75H_{AA}$, since the contribution to Y from the unavoidable payables and accruals is $3 million. Since the desired ratio of X to Y is 1.80, the appropriate constraint equation is:

$$21.6 + 0.9725 \text{ H}_{AA} \geq 1.80(Y_p + 3 + 0.75\text{H}_{AA}) \qquad (12\text{-}2)$$

Which simplifies to:

$$9 \geq Y_p + 0.2097\text{H}_{AA} \qquad (12\text{-}3)$$

Therefore, the necessary modification to reflect the hedge from the notes is to add $0.2097H_{AA}$ to the left-hand side of row 17. The same coefficient of H_{Aj} occurs for the other two aggregate liquidity constraint equations in rows 18 and 19.

Rows 20 through 22 utilize a stepwise variable (X_C) that must be 1.0 if the commercial paper (source C) is used as part of the firm's financing package. This variable appears in the objective function to trigger the required guarantee fee from the firm's bank. If the firm plans to use commercial paper as a financing vehicle *or as a hedge*, this fee must be paid; consequently, the hedging variables must appear in these constraint equations. Similar hedging principal variables for the notes payable (source A) and the secured financing (source B) must also appear in rows 25 and 26 through 28, where X_{ij} variables

---

[7]We assume that these constraints are not enforced if the firm, because of an unexpected cash shortage, is forced to deplete cash reserves or to borrow additional funds.

are used to signal the use of these sources; if these sources are used for borrowing or hedging, their X_{ij} usage variables must be 1.0.

The remainder of the original integer-programming formulation (through row 43) is as it appears in the unhedged program. Rows 44 through 60 are additional constraints resulting from the use of borrowing sources as hedging vehicles. Rows 44 through 46 give the total amounts of the necessary hedges. For example, row 44 specifies the hedge needed in period A. The dollar amount of the hedge (the righthand side of this equation) is determined as follows. Recall that the standard deviation of the necessary borrowing in period A is $3 million, the probability distribution of this borrowing is normal, and that the firm wants to be 95 percent sure of having sufficient funds. The Z-score for 95 percent is 1.645, so the firm must have a total hedging reserve of $4.935 million (equal to 1.645 times $3 million). The firm's current asset position provides $1 million of this reserve; the remaining $3.935 must come from current liabilities. The total reserve hedging capacity must then be $3.935 million. Similar calculations give the figures on the righthand sides of the equations in rows 45 and 46. The coefficients of the H_{ij} variables on the lefthand side of these equations are the ratios of the cash raised from these sources to the amounts of principal borrowed and are the same as those in rows 2 through 4. The remaining rows impose constraints that the hedging from the 90-day notes be the same in all periods (rows 47 and 48) and that the principal amounts of the hedges be greater than zero (rows 49 through 60).

A LINDO solution to this formulation is presented in Table 12-6. In this table, the amounts specified as hedges for the sources that are not costly unless used (sources B, C, and D) are arbitrary; costs for these hedges do not appear in the objective function.

Analysis of the LINDO solution is presented in Table 12-7. There are several differences between this hedged solution and the solution where there is no hedging. While the same sources of borrowing appear (notes, source A, and commercial paper, source C), the amount of borrowing on the note arrangement has increased from $2.125 million to $3.633 million over the unhedged solution. This greater use of note financing reduces the amount of necessary commercial paper financing; along with the financing available from delaying payments to suppliers, this creates the necessary $3.935 million in reserve borrowing capacity for hedging purposes in the first period.[8] When borrowing is structured in this way, the firm will have the minimum required reserved borrowing capacity in period A and surplus reserve borrowing capacity in periods B and C.

The requirements of this hedging strategy increase the expected borrowing cost from $201,210 to $205,710. This increase in expected cost of $4,500 is the cost of this hedging strategy. This additional cost should be

---

[8]The availability of a secured borrowing arrangement contributes nothing to hedging, since secured borrowings cannot be used in combination with the note borrowings.

Table 12-6. *A LINDO Solution for Example Problem with Hedging.*

OBJECTIVE FUNCTION VALUE

1)   205.707300

VARIABLE	VALUE	REDUCED COST
XA	1.000000	.000000
XC	1.000000	10.000000
XBA	.000000	− 14.219780
XBB	.000000	− .972750
XBC	.000000	− 1.459035
PAA	3632.545000	.000000
PBA	.000000	.000000
PCA	6521.478000	.000000
PDA	.000000	.004202
PAB	3632.545000	.000000
PBB	.000000	.000000
PCB	471.261000	.000000
PAC	3632.545000	.000000
PBC	.000000	.000000
PCC	4504.739000	.000000
PDB	.000000	.004202
PDC	.000000	.004202
HAA	.000000	.004516
HAB	.000000	.000000
HAC	.000000	.000000
HBA	.000000	.000486
HCA	1478.522000	.000000
HDA	2500.000000	.000000
HBB	.000000	.000486
HCB	5626.702000	.000000
HDB	.000000	.000000
HBC	.000000	.000486
HCC	3495.261000	.000000
HDC	3806.329000	.000000

compared to the cost of other possible strategies, and the cheapest method of hedging cash flow uncertainty over the planning horizon should be used.

INTEGER PROGRAMMING AND CURRENT LIABILITIES IN PERSPECTIVE

The integer-programming structuring approach to current debt has many positive features. Properly used, it provides the minimum-cost constrained solution to any structuring problem whose relationships among variables are linear. It addresses multiperiod planning situations and can incor-

Table 12-7. Analysis of Solution with Hedging.

Maximum Principal Borrowings

| | | Month | |
Source	A	B	C
A	$6,000	$6,000	$6,000
B	$4,000	$4,000	$4,000
C	$8,000	$8,000	$8,000
D	$2,500	$3,500	$4,000

Principal Amounts

| | | Month | |
Source	A	B	C
A	$3,633	$3,633	$3,633
B	0	0	0
C	$6,521	$ 471	$4,505
D	0	0	0

Princ. Avail. for Hedging

| | | Month | |
Source	A	B	C
A	0	0	0
B	0	0	0
C	$1,479	$ 7,529	$3,495
D	$2,500	$ 3,500	$4,000

Financing Amounts

Source	A	B	C
A	$ 3,533	$3,533	$3,533
B	0	0	0
C	$ 6,467	$ 467	$4,467
D	0	0	0
	$10,000	$4,000	$8,000

Fin. Amts. Avail. for Hedge

Source	A	B	C
A	0	0	0
B	0	0	0
C	$1,466	$ 7,466	$3,466
D	$2,469	$ 3,456	$3,950
	$3,935	$10,923	$7,416
Req. Hedge	$3,935	$ 5,580	$7,225

Financing Costs

Source	A	B	C
A	$33.30	$33.30	$33.30
B	0	0	0
C	$64.35	$ 3.93	$37.54
D	0	0	0
	$97.64	$37.23	$70.84
		Three-Month	$205.71

Contributions to CLI

Source	A	B	C
A	$ 2,724	$ 2,724	$ 2,724
B	0	0	0
C	$ 5,978	$ 432	$ 4,129
D	0	0	0
	$ 8,703	$ 3,156	$ 6,854
Other Y	$ 3,000	$ 3,000	$ 3,000
Total Y	$11,703	$ 6,156	$ 9,854
X	$21,600	$15,000	$20,000
CLI	1.85	2.44	2.03

porate hedging strategies. It is relatively cheap to compute; except for very complex problems, large amounts of computer time are rarely used.

However, this approach to the problem is not without its difficulties. These difficulties relate to the programming effort necessary to implement the integer-programming methodology in this context. This necessary programming effort is in contrast to the application of integer programming to the lockbox location problem, which was discussed in Chapter 2. When the firm wants to use integer programming to address the lockbox location problem, the firm does not have to develop mathematical expressions for the objective function and the constraint equations. Since all firms' lockbox location problems have approximately the same structure, integer-programming formats have been developed to address this structure and are commercially available (often through the firm's bank). In using these formats, the firm needs only provide specific data sets (check origins, possible lockbox locations, and so forth), and the prewritten program finds the optimum combination of lockbox location and customer assignment. In such a case, no need for actual programming arises, unless the firm's lockbox location problem contains very special features.

The use of a prewritten integer-programming format is in contrast to the methodologies that a firm must employ in using integer programming for determining a structure of current debt. For most firms, *this* application of integer programming usually contains a sufficient number of unique features so that the firm must write its own objective function and set of constraint equations to model availabilities, costs, and interactions among its possible sources of financing. *The programming process of obtaining proper expressions for these functions is not trivial, and any errors made in the process may lead to costly mistakes.* For most firms, while its proper use will lead to an optimal structure of current debt, using integer programming in this application requires substantially more effort than does the application of this technology to the lockbox location problem.

The Management of Current Liabilities in Practice There is not a great deal of information available on the methods by which firms structure their current liability package. However, some very interesting survey results have been reported regarding firms' policies in the use of some *individual* sources of short-term funding. In this section, we present information on the firms' practices in the use of *accounts payable* and of *factoring* in funding their short-term liability needs.

In 1981, Hill, Sartoris, and Ferguson conducted a survey of the accounts payable managers of 1,479 firms of various sizes in various industries; 180 responses were received.[9] A major thrust of this survey was obtaining infor-

---

[9]The full results of this survey are reported in N. Hill, W. Sartoris, and D. Ferguson, "Corporate Credit and Payables Policies: A Survey of Size and Industry Effects," presented at the Financial Management Association's 1983 Annual Meeting, and available from Hill at Brigham Young University.

mation on firms' decisions regarding two methods of obtaining financing from accounts payable: skipping the discount and stretching accounts payable. Let us first discuss their results regarding the use of skipping the discount as a financing strategy. The survey revealed that the vast majority of firms generally take the discount. In deciding whether to take the discount, the primary criterion of most firms is the amount of the discount. This makes good financial sense, since the amount of the discount (along with the delay period from the discount date to the due date) determines the cost of skipping as a source of financing. The plurality of payables managers continue to use the postmark on the envelope as the appropriate date in determining whether their remittances are eligible for the discount.[10] Some accounts payable managers believed that the portion of payables offering discounts had decreased over time, but the majority of these managers felt that this proportion had stayed about the same.

The other financing strategy in connection with accounts payable is the stretching of payables beyond the due date. Hill, Sartoris, and Ferguson's survey revealed three important factors that are considered by firms in deciding whether to use this strategy: the value of using the funds (that is, the cost of the funds relative to other funding sources), the effects on relationships with suppliers, and the impact on the firm's credit rating. The relative significance of these three factors varied among large and small firms. For small firms, the value of the funds was the most important factor, followed by the impact on the firm's credit rating, and finally by the effect on relationships with suppliers. For large firms, relationships with suppliers are most important, followed by the value of the funds, and the effect on credit rating. While each of these three factors is related to the cost of stretching, the differences between large and small firms are interesting. The primary importance of supplier relations to larger firms versus its lesser importance for smaller firms may be an indicator of differences in the character of bargaining with suppliers. Large firms may be able to bargain effectively (so supplier relations are important), but small firms may have to take or leave whatever conditions of sale the supplier is willing to offer (in which case supplier relations would be of lesser importance).

Farragher surveyed 33 firms with an interest in factoring to determine patterns in the use of this financing method; 21 responses were received.[11] The types of firms with heavy and growing involvement in factoring continue to be those that have traditionally used this type of financing. These firms are manufacturers of textiles and clothing. However, there is also growing

[10]Interestingly, a parallel survey of credit managers (who are responsible for collections on these checks) indicated that the date when the check is received at the lockbox, and not the postmark date, was their preferred date for assessing discount eligibility. See Hill, Sartoris, and Ferguson, "Corporate Credit and Payables Policies," p. 11.

[11]See E. Farragher, "Factoring Accounts Receivable," *Journal of Cash Management* (March/April 1986), pp. 38–42.

involvement among firms manufacturing furniture and firms wholesaling toys and sporting goods. Firms see the most important services provided by factoring as (1) the credit analysis of customers, (2) the control of bad debt losses, (3) cash advances for sales, and (4) control of collection effort and expense. While, in this ranking, services that factors provide relating to credit management are at the top of the list, Farragher found that 55 percent of factoring volume is on a discount basis, while only 36 percent is maturity factoring. Together, these results suggest that *both* the factor's expertise in credit management functions *and* the financing that this process provides are important to firms in deciding whether to use factoring.

SUMMARY

In this chapter, the integer-programming approach to the problem of developing a minimum-cost structure for current liabilities was presented. This mathematical-programming approach to the current liabilities structuring problem is an improvement over the sequential method since it can incorporate interdependencies among funding sources, variations in the costs of borrowing for particular sources, multiperiod maturities, and other commonly occurring effects.

The disadvantage of this more robust approach is the programming effort necessary for its implementation. The various operating and industry characteristics of different firms result in substantially divergent opportunities for current liability financing. These divergent sources of potential funding make the precise form of the integer-programming problem vary substantially from firm to firm. Therefore, unlike cases where the firm uses integer programming to locate its lockboxes (a problem that is similar from firm to firm, and for which commercial software is available), the use of this technique for structuring current liabilities requires that the firm must develop its own mathematical expressions for the objective function and the constraint equations. The objective function will contain the costs of the various sources of funds in the various planning periods. Constraint equations may include those requiring that the funding raised be sufficient to meet the firm's needs, those limiting the funds available from each source, and those concerning the target level of the firm's aggregate liquidity. Additional constraints may be necessary to model stepwise costs, interactions among sources of funding (including mutually exclusive sources), the desired ending financial condition of the firm, and the need for available borrowing capacity as a hedge against cash flow uncertainty. Example problems were presented illustrating the integer-programming approach with and without the use of extra borrowing capacity to hedge this uncertainty.

The chapter also reviewed some survey results regarding the use of accounts payable and of factoring as part of the firm's current liability package.

In the use of accounts payable, most firms decide whether to skip the discount based on the amount of the discount; the amounts of discounts are such that most firms pay in sufficient time to take advantage of this discount. The plurality of payables managers believe they can take the discount if their firm's check is postmarked by the discount date. In deciding whether to stretch payables beyond the due date, firms consider the cost of the funds, the effects of this stretching on relationships with the supplier, and the impact of stretching on the firm's credit rating. The relative importance of these three factors varies among large and small firms.

The use of factoring continues to be dominated by firms in textile and clothing manufacturing. Most firms who use factoring discount their invoices, and thus obtain immediate cash from the factor. However, the nonfinancing services that the factor provides in making credit-granting decisions, in controlling bad debt loss, and in making collections are also important to firms who factor their receivables.

Once the firm has determined a structure for its current liabilities (given its previously determined structure of current assets), it has completed the main tasks of working capital management. However, firms that participate in international trade, investment, and financing face special problems in making decisions on short-term debt and assets. These special problems will affect their strategies regarding these items. The management of working capital in an international environment is the topic of the next chapter.

Problems

12-1. A firm is considering the use of a field warehousing arrangement as part of its financing strategy. The arrangement would require a $10,000-per-year fee for the maintenance of the warehouse, regardless of the amount borrowed. This fee would be paid at the beginning of the year. A collateral certification and monitoring fee of 2 percent of the amount borrowed would be required, also paid at the beginning of the year. Interest would be at a rate of 11 percent per year, paid at maturity. Assuming that the duration of all loans is one year, calculate the effective annual interest rates of this arrangement for principal borrowings of $100,000, $200,000, $300,000, $400,000, and $500,000.

12-2. A firm is trying to structure its current liabilities for the next two quarters using the integer-programming method. There are only two possible sources of financing:

a. Discounted notes with a maturity of 180 days (source A). The stated interest rate on these notes is 10 percent per year. Maximum principal borrowings are $5 million. Excess borrowings are not invested. The notes are not refundable.

b. Credit-line borrowings with the firm's bank (source B). For these borrowings there is a fixed application fee of $1,000, payable immediately. The firm must pay this fee if it intends to borrow in either quarter. Interest will be paid at maturity at a rate of 11 percent per year. Maximum principal borrowings are $4 million.

The firm requires net financing of $3 million in the upcoming quarter (quarter A) and $6 million in the following quarter (quarter B). For purposes of this problem, assume that the firm does not use the availability of either of these sources of funds to hedge uncertainties in its cash forecast.

Let: XB = a zero-one integer variable indicating whether the firm will borrow on the bank credit line.

  PAA = the amount of principal borrowings from source A in quarter A.

  PAB = the amount of principal borrowings from source A in quarter B.

  PBA = the amount of principal borrowings from source B in quarter A.

  PBB = the amount of principal borrowings from source B in quarter B.

Write the objective function and the constraint equations for this situation. Assume that the sources are independent. Ignore any effects of the choice of financing on aggregate liquidity and any restrictions on ending conditions.

12-3. The firm described in Problem 2 has decided to incorporate the hedging of cash flow uncertainties via reserve borrowing capacity as part of its structuring strategy for current debt. The firm has performed a simulation analysis on its cash forecast and determined that the standard deviation of needed borrowings is $1.5 million in the first quarter and $3.5 million in the second quarter. The levels of borrowing are normally distributed and serially uncorrelated. The firm has decided that it is willing to undergo a probability of cash stockout of 10 percent in each quarter. Excess borrowing capacity will provide the only hedge against cash flow uncertainty. Using these facts and the data presented in Problem 2, write the objective function and necessary constraint equations for this situation.

Let: HAA = the principal amount of excess borrowing hedge from source A in quarter A.

HAB = the principal amount of excess borrowing hedge from source A in quarter B.

HBA = the principal amount of excess borrowing hedge from source B in quarter A.

HBB = the principal amount of excess borrowing hedge from source B in quarter B.

Selected Readings

Farragher, E., "Factoring Accounts Receivable," *Journal of Cash Management* (March/April 1986), pp. 38–42.

Hill, N., W. Sartoris, and D. Ferguson, "Corporate Credit and Payables Policies: A Survey of Size and Industry Effects," presented at the Financial Management Association's 1983 Annual Meeting, and available from Hill at Brigham Young University.

Kallberg, J., R. White, and W. Ziemba, "Short Term Financial Planning Under Uncertainty," *Management Science*, Vol. 28, No. 6 (June 1982), pp. 670–82.

Pogue, G., and R. Bussard, "A Linear Programming Model for Short-Term Financial Planning Under Uncertainty," *Sloan Management Review*, Vol. 13 (1972), pp. 69–98.

Robickek, A., D. Tiechrow, and J. Jones, "Optimal Short-Term Financing Decision," *Management Science*, Vol. 12, No. 1 (September 1965), pp. 1–36.

Transformers, Inc.[1] Structuring Short-Term Liabilities: Integer-Programming Method

Transformers, Incorporated, was a manufacturer of transformers, generators, and similar electrical devices. Founded in the early 1950s, the company had substantial success until the early 1970s, when a series of problems beset the firm. The recession of 1970–71 had severely reduced sales. From 1969 to 1970, the firm's sales declined by 33 percent (see Exhibit 1 for the company's financial statements for the fiscal years ending 12/31/69 through 12/31/72). Sales remained at these lower levels during fiscal 1971, then recovered in 1972. However, the losses during 1970 and 1971 had put a severe strain on the firm's financial position. In part to finance these losses, the firm had borrowed heavily from their bank during this period, both on a short-term and on a long-term basis. Short-term borrowings were made via an unsecured line of credit, while long-term borrowings were secured by the firm's fixed assets. However, in early 1973 additional short-term borrowing had come to a halt when the bank had indicated that it would not be receptive to requests by Transformers, Inc., for more short-term unsecured financing.

Besides these difficulties, Transformers, Inc. was also having problems with its trade suppliers. Because of suppliers' pricing and delivery policies, many of the raw materials used by the firm had to be ordered in increasingly larger quantities. Some domestic suppliers had offered substantial price reductions for ordering in larger quantities (quantity discounts), making ordering in small lots uneconomical, and some overseas suppliers had required that the firm take large quantities of materials because they did not maintain warehouse facilities in the United States. Because of its past losses and heavy investment in inventories, Transformers had stretched payments far beyond suppliers' terms of sale. In early 1973, there was a very real possibility that some of these suppliers would refuse to make further shipments, resulting in severe production problems for the firm. Some sort of financial restructuring was obviously needed.

In a discussion of the problems Transformers was having, a credit manager of one of these supplier firms suggested to Roger Trexler (Transformers' treasurer) that the firm consider a secured, short-term financing arrangement. Though Mr. Trexler was not familiar with this type of borrowing, he was determined to investigate any potential source

[1]This case has been adapted from Frederick C. Scherr, *Cases in Finance* (New York: Macmillan, 1984), pp. 132–37.

of new financing. Mr. Trexler contacted Transformers' bank lending officer and found him receptive to the possibility of secured short-term borrowing. The banker also proposed that such a financing system could be used to replace some of the firm's unsecured short-term borrowings with a lower interest arrangement. However, the banker said that under current lending policies a general security agreement (a blanket lien) would not be sufficient. An independent company would have to be retained to monitor the collateral and perform certification services for the bank. This sounded expensive to Mr. Trexler, but he made an appointment to discuss the matter with the agent of the company that usually performed collateral certification monitoring and certification services for Transformers' bank. At the meeting, the agent presented details of two borrowing plans to Mr. Trexler: certified accounts receivable and field warehousing of inventory.

Under the certified accounts receivable system, the collateral monitoring and certification services company would examine the Transformers' receivables to see if these were adequate collateral. Usually receivables more than 90 days old or those due from customers of uncertain credit quality were not considered to be adequate collateral for borrowings. If all or part of the receivables were approved as collateral, the bank would prepare a security agreement, have it signed by Transformers, and have it filed as prescribed by law. Payments by customers against the receivables used as security would be made to a special bank account. As existing receivables were paid and new ones generated, the collateral monitoring and certification services company would verify receivables balances and prepare reports of receivables eligible as collateral. The bank would loan Transformers up to 75 percent of the certified and monitored balance. In return for its services, the collateral monitoring and certification services firm

would be paid a yearly fee of 2.5 percent of the average amount of the loan. The receivables loan would carry an interest rate of 4 percent over prime (rather than the current rate of 7 percent over prime charged for the firm's unsecured borrowings). Because of the high quality of Transformers' receivables, Mr. Trexler believed that all the firm's receivables would be adequate collateral for borrowing under the certified receivables system.

Under the field warehousing arrangement, the collateral monitoring and certification services company would physically inspect and verify the quality of Transformers' inventory as collateral. Only inventory with significant resale value was considered to be adequate collateral for borrowing. For Transformers, only raw materials inventory would meet this qualification. A security agreement would be executed and filed on the inventory, and the collateral monitoring and certification services firm would lease (for a nominal fee) a portion of the storage area at Transformers' facilities. This area would be used to store the inventory that was collateral for borrowings. Access would be restricted (by means of a locked gate), and the collateral monitoring and certification services firm would arrange for the bonding of personnel who would control materials flow to and from the restricted area. The certification firm would also prepare periodic reports to the bank on the amount of collateral in the storage area. The bank would loan Transformers up to 60 percent of the collateral value. The yearly field warehousing fee to the collateral monitoring and certification services firm would be $15,000 per year plus 1.5 percent of the average amount of the loan. The entire $15,000 fee would have to be paid if the field warehousing arrangement was used at any time during the year. Bank interest charges would be the same as for the receivables borrowing system.

To assess the available financing from these two arrangements, Mr. Trexler esti-

Exhibit 1

Transformers, Inc.

Income Statements and Balance Sheets, Ordered by the Accountant's Method

Fiscal Year Ending	12/31/72	12/31/71	12/31/70	12/31/69
Sales	$3,170,860	$2,090,918	$2,176,716	$3,259,708
Cost of Goods Sold				
Direct Labor	448,664	377,065	474,524	538,760
Direct Materials	1,652,972	1,445,416	1,604,344	1,885,659
Other	259,752	272,324	180,772	269,380
Gross Margin on Sales	809,472	(3,887)	(82,924)	565,909
Selling and Administrative Expenses	542,359	436,342	520,404	464,363
Interest Expense	138,005	108,882	38,924	12,300
Income from Operations	129,108	(549,111)	(642,252)	89,246
Other Income	53,083	0	53,066	0
Earnings Before Taxes	182,191	(549,111)	(589,186)	89,246
Taxes	59,287	(141,035)	(306,196)	48,902
Earnings After Taxes	122,904	(408,076)	(282,990)	40,344
Dividends	0	0	0	0
Changes in Retained Earnings	$122,904	($408,076)	($282,990)	$40,344

Cash	$17,975	$5,297	$76,753	$103,545
Accounts Receivable	494,484	509,829	451,615	472,008
Inventory	1,613,364	882,457	916,312	741,951
Other Current Assets	184,869	183,308	391,148	344,995
Total Current Assets	2,310,692	1,580,891	1,835,828	1,662,499
Net Property, Plant, and Equipment	1,874,369	1,909,177	1,708,438	1,199,262
Misc. Other Assets	562,571	510,851	376,253	223,229
Total Assets	$4,747,632	$4,000,919	$3,920,519	$3,084,990
Accounts Payable	$734,941	$771,894	$669,945	$214,807
Due to Bank, Short-Term	812,274	375,882	130,289	12,139
Total Current Liabilities	1,547,215	1,147,776	800,234	226,946
Due to Bank, Long-Term	646,201	797,106	642,783	169,122
Deferred Income Taxes	0	0	135,190	76,370
Common Stock	46,547	39,041	36,605	36,350
Paid-In Capital	1,841,909	1,474,140	1,354,775	1,342,280
Retained Earnings	665,760	542,856	950,932	1,233,922
Total Owners' Equity	$2,554,216	$2,056,037	$2,342,312	$2,612,552
Total Liabilities and Equity	$4,747,632	$4,000,919	$3,920,519	$3,084,990

Exhibit 2

Transformers, Inc.
Average Quarterly Figures for Several Items

Quarter	First	Second	Third	Fourth
Accounts Receivable	$ 611,128	$ 545,650	$ 480,172	$ 545,650
Raw Materials Inventory	$1,635,518	$1,460,284	$1,285,050	$1,460,284
Needed Short-Term Financing	$1,833,364	$1,532,531	$1,236,199	$1,462,031

mated the average receivables, inventory, and financing needs for Transformers for each quarter of the upcoming year. These figures are presented in Exhibit 2. The needed financings in this exhibit are net of minimum levels of accounts payable and accruals and all anticipated long-term financing. Mr. Trexler had already computed the firm's projected current ratios (Transformers' preferred measure of aggregate liquidity) under the assumption that this needed financing was raised via short-term debt and found the levels of this ratio to be in line with the company's target levels of aggregate liquidity. The needed financing amounts incorporated a reduction in the firm's accounts payable to levels sufficient to insure the continued flow of goods from suppliers.

With all this information in hand, Mr. Trexler scheduled another meeting with the firm's banker. They agreed that the introduction of lending with receivables and inventory as security would provide increased availability and lower interest rates, but would dilute the bank's unsecured position. Because of this, the bank would continue with its current levels of unsecured lending only if the firm did not borrow with receivables and inventory as security. If Transformers decided to borrow on this basis, the maximum available amount of unsecured financing would be reduced at the rate of $0.30 for every dollar of principal borrowings that were outstanding on these short-term secured loans. However, whether or not the firm decided to employ secured lending, the maximum principal on the unsecured balance was limited to the $812,274 amount outstanding as of December 31, 1972.

On inquiring into other possible sources of funding, Mr. Trexler also found the banker receptive to the possibility of short-term note borrowings. The long-term loans made by the bank to Transformers were secured by the firm's property, plant, and equipment. As of late 1972, the book value of this equipment was about $1.8 million, while the total principal on the loans was only about $.65 million. There was thus some free collateral value available from these assets. The banker agreed to approve borrowings on 180-day notes, secured by these assets, for amounts up to $250,000. Interest would be at 13 percent and would be paid on a discounted basis. If the firm elected to use this funding source, the first group of notes would be issued immediately and would be due in mid-1973; new notes would be issued when the first group was retired. No prepayment of the notes was allowed. Borrowing via these notes would not affect the terms or availability of borrowing on the firm's unsecured credit line or of borrowing with receivables or inventory as collateral.

Working Capital Management in International Settings

Since the 1960s, a major trend has been the internationalization of business. This trend is driven directly by shareholder wealth maximization. It is in the interests of shareholders that managers seek out profitable markets, less expensive sources of materials and labor, and less restrictive regulatory environments, regardless of the location of these conditions. By finding and using these advantageous circumstances on a worldwide basis, managers can maximize the value of the firm.

There are many institutional and cultural differences among countries that influence the firm's business practices. Differences in economic conditions, language, legal systems, regulatory climates, and cultural heritage require careful consideration and attention. However, the basic principle of financial decision making holds: the firm should maximize the risk-adjusted net present value of cash flows. In this chapter, we provide an introduction to the management of short-term assets and liabilities in international settings based on this principle.

The application of this principle requires estimates of the expected cash flows and their risk. The differences among countries in taxes, legal systems, and so forth will affect the expected levels of cash flows from working capital investments and sources of financing. There are also substantial differences in the risk of the cash flows from international transactions as compared to the risk of cash flows from transactions within the firm's host country. The sources of these risk differences, and the methods available to deal with these differences, will be a major topic of discussion in this chapter.

WHY HAVE INTERNATIONAL WORKING CAPITAL?

The firm may use several different methods to take advantage of superior business conditions in another country: *trade* (importing and exporting of goods and services to and from the other country), *investment* (establishing an affiliate to produce goods or services within the other country), and *financing* (raising funds in the other country). These three strategies are alternative ways of utilizing the nonhost country's relative advantage, and to a great extent they are substitutes. For example, suppose that another country has a lower interest rate on loans than does the firm's host country (for whatever reason). Businesses within the other country will have lower costs of capital, and can provide goods at cheaper prices. To exploit this advantage, a firm needing such goods could either: (1) import them from businesses operating in that country, (2) set up an affiliate to manufacture in that country, financed with inexpensive local borrowings, or (3) borrow funds in that country to finance production in the firm's host country.

While all three strategies can achieve the same result, trade, investment, and financing have different effects on the firm's working capital position. *Importing* from another country may require that the firm deal in the currency in which the exporters' invoices are denominated. That is, importing may require the firm to practice the cash management of disbursements in multiple currencies. *Exporting* requires that the firm practice both cash and credit management on an international scale, since the firm will be selling to businesses in other countries and collecting from them. *Investment* in a producing, wholesaling, or retailing affiliate requires that the firm keep cash, receivables, and inventory assets that are denominated in and/or are located in the foreign country. *Financing* in nonhost capital markets requires the comparison of vehicles for the acquisition of short-term debt that combine different financing rates and different denominated currencies.

SOURCES OF RISK IN INTERNATIONAL FINANCIAL MANAGEMENT

While there are differential effects of trade, investment, and exporting strategies, it should be clear that *any* attempt to take advantage of an opportunity outside the firm's host country will generally require *some* international exposure in the firm's working capital accounts. With this exposure come the various risks inherent in different types of international transactions. The sources of this risk are discussed in this section. Following sections will discuss strategies available for hedging these risks. For discussion purposes, let us break the additional risks inherent in international cash flows into three types: *exchange risk*, *political risk*, and *economic risk*.

Exchange Risk Whether the firm is engaged in trade, investment, or financing, it is almost inevitable that the firm must exchange cash denominated in one currency for cash denominated in another. For example, the firm may want to transfer cash to an affiliate for the purchase of inventory in the affiliate's host country, and it may later want to repatriate cash from the sale of that inventory. These transactions may both require that currency of the firm's host country and of the affiliate's host country be exchanged. Assume that the firm is located in the United States and the affiliate is located in West Germany. The currency used in West Germany is the deutsche mark (DM). If the firm wishes to purchase 10,000,000 DM worth of inventory in Germany for this affiliate and the exchange rate is 2.5 DM per dollar, it will have to exchange $4 million to obtain the necessary German currency. Later, once the inventory is sold, the firm will have to exchange the DMs received into dollars.

The *risk involved in currency exchange* transactions comes not in exchanging currencies to address *current* needs for cash, but concerns the risk inherent in *future* conversions. Since 1971, the value of U.S. currency has floated against many other major currencies; we are in a period of *floating exchange rates*. These exchange rates change rapidly in response to countries' economic policies and developments.[1] This exchange rate system adds volatility to estimates of future cash flows from foreign transactions. Returning to our inventory purchase example, the number of dollars needed for the *current* purchase of the inventory is certain, since the current exchange rate and the needed number of DMs are known. However, the *future* dollar cash flow from the sale is uncertain. Let us assume that the sale of the inventory by the firm's German affiliate is expected to net 11,000,000 DM in six months. If this revenue is to be repatriated to the parent firm for use in the United States, it must be converted back into dollars. The estimate of the future cash flow is uncertain due to the general nature of most business transactions, domestic and international; there is uncertainty with respect to the eventual number of units sold, the price of these units, and so forth. However, there is additional uncertainty in the amount of the future cash flow from this inventory investment *because of possible fluctuations over the six-month period in the DM/dollar exchange rate*. For example, suppose that the value of the DM rises relative to the dollar, so that at the end of six months there are 2.85 DMs required to obtain each dollar. The firm will then receive only about $3.86 million in return for the 11,000,000 DM from the inventory's sale. Because of this change in exchange rates, while the firm would make a profit on the transaction *as denominated in DM*, it would take a loss when the profits were repatriated into dollars.

Political Risks This source of variation from expectations is also known as *country risk* or *sovereignty risk*. It stems from the fact that any government

[1]The foreign exchange marketplace is a system of brokers and banks located in money centers throughout the world. For an excellent discussion of foreign exchange markets and the determination of exchange rates, see J. O. Grabbe, *International Financial Markets* (New York: Elsevier, 1986), pp. 57–76 and 151–220. For some views of corporate executives on the effects of foreign exchange fluctuations on their businesses, see G. Melloan, "Corporations Grow Weary of Dollar's Capers," *Wall Street Journal* (March 3, 1987), page 35.

may choose to change the conditions under which foreign and domestic firms operate within the governed country. The firm's expected cash flows may be estimated based on an anticipated set of these conditions, but the actual conditions in force at a future time may be quite different. For purposes of discussion, let us divide political risks into three types: the risk of *civil unrest*, the risk that *the rules of operation governing the firm's business within the country may be changed*, and the risk that *the firm may be unable to repatriate the expected amounts of cash to the host country*.

Of these risks, that of civil unrest (war, revolution, riot, and similar activities) receives most attention in the press because of its spectacular nature. When these conditions occur, normal business processes may be disrupted, and assets may be destroyed or cash flows from these assets may cease temporarily or permanently. These are disastrous results, and risk of civil disruption in many countries is substantial.

Once the firm has expended the effort and funds to establish a trading relationship within a foreign country, or has made an investment in that country, it is vulnerable to changes in the rules of operation within that country. This is a second type of political risk that comes with international dealings. These changes are made by governments for political reasons, and their likelihood varies with the political character of the foreign country. Changes in the rules of operation can take several forms. The following are common.

1. Cancellation of importing, exporting, or other operating permits and licenses or increases in the required fees to renew such permits and licenses

2. Expropriation or confiscation of assets without adequate compensation

3. Imposition of increased taxes or other fees

4. Imposition of new restrictions on collections, investments, and so forth

For example, suppose that the firm has established an affiliate to hold and sell inventory in a foreign country. However, while the firm has inventory within that country, the country's political leadership imposes a new tax on inventory held there, including existing inventory. This tax would reduce net expected revenues from the affiliate. The possibility of the imposition of such a tax is a risk that the firm takes in holding inventory in that particular country.

In addition to the risk of civil unrest and the risk of possible changes in the rules of operation, countries may also directly inhibit firms' transfers of funds from the foreign country to the firm's host country. The firm may want to repatriate funds, but the foreign government may block or delay this transfer in various ways. One mechanism is to *regulate the dividends that an affiliate can make to its parent firm*. A typical restriction that can accomplish this regulates the affiliate's yearly dividends to a set percentage of its net worth.

Another mechanism that affects the cash flows from affiliates to parent firms is *exchange controls*. For their own political purposes, governments may regulate both the *exchange rate* at which outgoing cash is changed from their country's currency into other currencies and the *amount of exchange* that is allowed among currencies. With regard to exchange rates, the government may require an affiliate of a foreign-owned firm or a firm importing products into its country to exchange for local currency at a rate that gives a higher value to that currency than does the market rate. For example, suppose that the government of a country with currency denominated in pesos imposes a new mandated exchange rate of 50 pesos per dollar when the market rate is 25 pesos per dollar. Effectively, this action reduces the value of all cash leaving the country by 50 percent and is exactly equivalent to a tax on such cash flows.[2] The potential for such an action adds additional risk to investments in a country where such an action can be taken. Note that this risk of *politically imposed* changes in the rate of exchange is separate from the risk of *market-determined* changes in the rate of exchange.

A similar reduction in value occurs if a foreign government imposes new controls on the *maximum amount of exchange* among currencies. Such controls typically require that those wishing to exchange local currency for the currency of other countries do so only through a central exchange where the amount of exchange is regulated. The possibility that the firm will not be able to execute a planned exchange of an affiliate's currency into that of its host country adds risk to future cash flows. For example, suppose that a firm expects to receive monthly cash flows of $1 million from an affiliate in another country. The affiliate may have the local currency available to make these payments, but if the local government has imposed new currency controls such that the affiliate may obtain only $500,000 per month, regardless of the amount of local currency it wishes to exchange, only $500,000 may be paid to the parent firm.

Economic Risks In addition to exchange and political risks, international trade, investment, and financing also carry economic risks that vary from country to country. The volatility of a country's wage rates, material costs, interest rates, product demand, and other variables are related to the structure of its economy. The economies of some countries are based primarily on the production and export of one product (oil, for example). Fluctuations in the price of that particular commodity will affect such countries much more than those with more diversified economic bases.

While we have discussed them separately for convenience, it is important to realize that international exchange risk, political risk, and economic risk

---

[2] For a discussion of the effects of exchange rate regulation on the foreign country's economy, see Grabbe, *International Financial Markets*, pp. 70–74.

are not independent. Indeed, there is substantial overlap among them; political, economic, and exchange rate outcomes are quite intertwined. For example, suppose that for political reasons the government of a country imposes controls on the amount of local currency that may be exchanged for the currency of other nations. This *political* action may reduce the potential amount of cash repatriations, but the effect does not stop there. Industries within the country will have difficulty obtaining advantageous foreign goods since foreign suppliers will recognize the increased problems in being paid for such goods in their home currencies. This will reduce the efficiency of operation of these local industries. The reduced efficiency will have adverse effects on the level of local *economic* activity. Further, the reduced economic activity in the country may adversely affect the *exchange* value of its currency relative to that of other countries.

This chain of events need not start with a political action. Any change in any one of the political, economic, or exchange conditions will affect the other two. A change in economic conditions, for example, will certainly affect political circumstances within a country and the exchange rate of that country's currency with the currencies of other countries.

Assessing Risk in International Transactions To deal with the additional sources of risk that the firm faces in international dealings, the level of this risk must first be assessed. The available mechanisms for addressing and/or hedging this risk and the relative costs of these methods are then considered in developing a risk-management strategy. Information on exchange, political, and economic risks in international transactions is available from several sources.

Information on the relative volatility of currencies (and therefore their exchange risk) is presented in most textbooks on international finance and international economics. These analyses can be used to gain long-term historical perspectives. Historic conversion data is also available in *International Financing Statistics*. To assess more recent trends, the analyst may obtain data on the exchange rates of major currencies for immediate delivery (called *spot rates*) on a daily basis from the *Wall Street Journal*.

The political and economic risks in dealing with various countries are more difficult to assess. A number of organizations provide analyses of the political and economic climate in various countries on a commercial basis, and information of this type is sufficient if the firm's exposure is relatively small. However, if the firm is considering substantial investment or financing, an in-depth study of the potential host country's political and economic climate is required.[3]

---

[3]For an excellent discussion of the assessment of political and economic risks in international management, including a listing of the information sources on these risks, see two papers by E. G. Roberts: "The 'Debt Bomb' Shelter: How to Evaluate Foreign Credit Risk," *Cashflow* (October 1984), pp. 55–57 and "Evaluating Country Risk," Occasional Paper of the Credit Research Foundation, 1984.

HEDGING EXCHANGE RISK IN INTERNATIONAL TRANSACTIONS

Once it assesses the sources of risk in a proposed international transaction, the firm most incorporate this risk in its decision process. The firm may perform this incorporation by (1) *hedging the risk* (where hedges are available) and including the cost of the hedge in its evaluation of the transaction, or (2) *pricing the risk* by increasing the risk-adjusted discount rate for future cash flows from the transaction. In this section, we discuss several techniques that may be used to hedge the exchange risk in international transactions.[4]

Denominating Transactions in Dollars The simplest method of hedging exchange risk is to require that all transactions be conducted in dollars (or whatever is the currency of the firm's host country). By doing this, the firm avoids involvement in currency exchange. This technique is most applicable when the firm is importing or exporting.

While a relatively simple strategy, requiring that invoices be paid in dollars presents other problems. First, by making this requirement, the firm is merely shifting the exchange risk to its trading partner; the exchange risk is not really eliminated. For example, suppose that a U.S. firm is exporting to a West German firm on terms of sale requiring payment in 90 days. The dollar value of the shipment is $250,000 and it currently takes 2.5 DMs to obtain one dollar; the U.S. firm requires payment in dollars. Thus, at the current exchange rate the German firm will require 625,000 DM to obtain the necessary dollars. But over the 90-day terms of sale the DM may fall in value relative to the dollar. If, when payment is due, there are 2.6 DMs required to obtain each dollar, the German firm will have to exchange 650,000 DM to obtain the necessary U.S. currency. From the German firm's standpoint, this decrease in the value of the mark relative to the dollar has resulted in an increase in the cost of the shipment.

One difficulty in denominating invoices in dollars relates this shift in risk to the price at which the sale is made. *The trading partner will not accept the risk of adverse currency movements without compensation.* To make a sale with payment denominated in dollars, the U.S. firm must offer a lower price than if the trading partner can pay in foreign currency. This lower price

---

[4]We assume that the firm has no internal hedging mechanisms available to it, and thus must rely on the external mechanisms described in this section. However, some firms will have hedging mechanisms available to them within the structure of the firm's operations. For example, when the firm holds cash in several countries, it is diversified; fluctuations that affect one currency adversely may affect another positively. In such circumstances, external hedging is of less concern, and netting (a procedure discussed later in the chapter) can be a useful hedging strategy. Inventory strategies may also be used as hedging mechanisms. For example, an affiliate could purchase, pay for, and hold larger amounts of inventory from the parent firm. By purchasing the inventory at current exchange rates rather than purchasing it as needed, transfers at uncertain future rates are avoided.

compensates the trading partner for the currency risk and is the cost of this hedge.

Another problem with denominating export invoices in dollars is that this tactic subjects the exporter to the political risk of controls on the amount of exchange. When the foreign firm wants to pay the invoice, it must obtain dollars to do so. If there are government controls on the amount of exchange, it may not be able to accomplish this currency transaction, and thus may not be able to pay the invoice when due. A related approach that avoids this is to invoice in the local currency, but to *index the amount of the invoice* to the exchange rate between the dollar and the local currency. If the value of the local currency falls, the amount of the invoice rises. However, like denominating in dollars, this indexing system requires the trading partner to bear the exchange risk.

Invest Surplus Cash in the Eurodollar Market International investment of surplus funds need not be made in the local currency of the country in which the investment is made; it can also be conducted in dollars. In this way exchange risk is avoided. The major marketplace for international dollar-denominated investment is the *Eurodollar market*, which was discussed briefly in Chapter 2. A more complete discussion is appropriate at this point because of the importance of the Eurodollar market in offshore investment of surplus funds.[5]

Eurodollars are dollar-denominated deposits located outside the United States. The "Euro" in "Eurodollar" originally referred to Europe as the place of residency of these dollar deposits, but there are now centers of Eurodollar commerce throughout the world. The Eurodollar market is a "wholesale" money market for large deposits and loans. These deposits and loans are mostly bank-to-bank transactions, but large commercial firms may participate if they have sufficient amounts to invest or are of sufficient creditworthiness to borrow. Many U.S. firms invest in the Eurodollar market, and firms such as Gulf Oil, Martin-Marietta, and Warner Communications have been active in borrowing there. One-week and six-month maturity instruments are the most common *investment* vehicles; both fixed-rate and floating-rate investments are available. However, *borrowing* is mostly on terms of longer than one year, so the Eurodollar market is not a popular source of short-term financing.

While investment in dollar-denominated securities avoids exchange rate risk, this is not the basic reason for the substantial popularity of the Eurodollar market; firms can achieve the same result by investing domestically. The Eurodollar market is primarily a vehicle for borrowing and lending in an

[5]For additional discussion of the Eurodollar market, see T. Cook and B. Summers, eds., *Instruments of the Money Market,* Fifth Edition (Richmond: Federal Reserve Bank of Richmond, 1981), pp. 123–33.

environment not subject to U.S. banking regulations. Eurobanks are not required to keep noninterest-bearing cash reserves beyond those necessary for their operations, they do not have to pay Federal Deposit Insurance Corporation insurance premiums, and they are not subject to any U.S. interest rate ceilings on deposits and loans.

By avoiding these requirements, which are quite costly to domestic banks, Eurobanks can achieve significant savings. In addition to these regulatory advantages, Eurobanks are often located in areas of low local taxes. Also, the specialization of Eurobanks in large-denomination transactions enables them to achieve lower overheads than domestic financial institutions. Together, the lower costs of regulation, taxation, and operation yield a very favorable result for large investors and borrowers alike; institutions dealing in Eurodollars are often able to both *pay higher interest on dollar deposits and make dollar loans at lower rates than domestic banks.*[6] That is, Eurdollar banks can profitably make transactions on far lower interest rate spreads than can domestic banks.[7]

However, investing in Eurodollar markets entails a bit more risk than does domestic investment. This additional risk stems from political and credit-related factors. From a political standpoint, there is risk that the government in the Eurobank's host country will restrict the movement of dollar-denominated funds out of the country and back to the investor; the government of the Philippines instituted such controls in 1983. Also, any disputes must be settled via the laws of the host country, and these laws may change before the maturity of the deposit.

For several reasons, there may also be additional credit risk in investing via may Eurobanks compared to investing via U.S. banks. First, Eurobanks are not covered by the U.S. government's deposit-insurance program. Second, many Eurobanks are "shell" subsidiaries of other, larger financial institutions. While their parent banking organizations are sound, the Eurobank itself may have a very small capitalization. These additional sources of risk have not deterred many U.S. firms from investing in the Eurodollar market. Instead, the major determinant of a firm's participation in this market is *size*. Required investment amounts are quite large; most Eurodollar deposits are for $500,000 or more.

---

[6]For a more complete discussion regarding why these differentials exist and persist, see D. S. Kidwell, M. W. Marr, and J. L. Trimble, "Domestic versus Eurodollar Bond Sale: A Persistent Borrowing Advantage," paper presented at the 1987 Financial Management Association meeting and available from Trimble at the University of Tennessee.

[7]Further, Eurodollar investments are advantageous in that the interest rate risk on borrowings and lendings in this market can be directly hedged via futures and options traded for this purpose; a cross-hedge is not necessary. See Grabbe, *International Financial Markets*, pp. 250–55.

Prebuy and Presell Foreign Currency in the Spot Market A third strategy for hedging exchange risk in a future foreign currency transaction is to immediately buy or sell the foreign currency in the spot market, then cover the transaction when the foreign currency is required. For example, suppose that a firm is importing goods, with the order denominated in Swiss francs (SF). Required payment in SF will be due in 120 days in the amount of SF 5,000,000. To cover this future cash need, the firm can immediately purchase 5,000,000 in Swiss francs.[8] If the exchange rate is SF 2.0 to the dollar, this currency will cost the firm $2.5 million. The Swiss francs will then be deposited in an account denominated in SF for the 120 days until payment is required. In this way, regardless of fluctuations in the exchange rate, the firm will have the required currency available at a fixed dollar cost.

While this strategy hedges the firm's cash needs, it is often expensive. For the 120-day delay from the initiation of the transaction until the money is due, the firm will have made an investment of $2.5 million (the initial cost of the francs). The return on this investment will be the interest on the invested francs. The interest on such short-term investments is generally less than the return on investments in the firm's operations; this difference in return is a penalty cost of this strategy. Another (and sometimes cheaper) way to hedge exchange risk is the *currency forward*, which is discussed in the following paragraphs.

Currency Forwards One type of contract used to purchase currency for future delivery is called the *forward purchase* of this currency. Forward purchases are negotiated between an international bank and the firm, and are tailored to the firm's specific currency needs. Forwards are not traded by firms on exchanges. Because these contracts cannot be traded, once the firm undertakes a forward exchange contract, it must honor this contract; there is no simple method of making an offsetting transaction or of reselling the contract to another firm. Because of this illiquidity, forwards are generally undertaken to meet specific and known currency needs and are held to maturity.

Representative forward and spot rates are quoted daily in *The Wall Street Journal*; the exchange rates in effect on June 30, 1987 are presented in Table 13-1. These rates are expressed as the number of U.S. dollars required to obtain one unit of the foreign currency. For example, the firm must pay $1.595 dollars for the *current* delivery of each British pound, but need pay only $1.5775 for each pound *to be delivered in 180 days*. Thus, if the firm needs 100,000 pounds to pay for an imported shipment in 180 days, two alternatives are to pay $159,500 on the spot market and invest the 100,000

---

[8]This importing example requires a future *outflow* denominated in a foreign currency. If the transaction instead involved a future *inflow*, the firm would short the currency (borrow it; presell it) in the spot market.

Table 13-1. Spot and Forward Rates for Various Currencies (June 30, 1987).
U. S. Equivalent Dollars

Currency	Spot Rate	30-Day Forward Rate	90-Day Forward Rate	180-Day Forward Rate
Pound	1.595	1.5922	1.5864	1.5775
Yen	.006693	.006712	.006747	.0068
French franc	.1622	.1621	.1618	.1612
Swiss franc	.6508	.6527	.6561	.6618
Mark	.5393	.5407	.5435	.548
Dollars Required to Obtain 100,000 Units of Currency				
Pound	159,500	159,220	158,640	157,750
Yen	669.3	671.2	674.7	680
French franc	16,220	16,210	16,180	16,120
Swiss franc	65,080	65,270	65,610	66,180
Mark	53,930	54,070	54,350	54,800

pounds in an interest-earning pound-denominated account, or purchase a *180-day forward*, which will earn no interest. The optimal strategy in choosing among any forward alternatives thus depends on the interest rates available for dollar- and nondollar-denominated accounts and the available spot and forward exchange rates.[9]

Currency Futures Because the currency forward is a private rather than a traded contract, it is a rather inflexible means of hedging exchange risk. A more flexible approach is the use of *traded futures contracts* in the foreign currency. Like a forward, a currency future is a contract for the purchase of a particular amount of foreign currency at a particular future time. The prices in the future acquisition of currency via forwards and futures have historically been very similar. However, currency futures are different from forwards in three important ways. First, *currency futures are traded on exchanges* and processed through clearinghouses in the same way as are interest rate futures. Currency futures in major currencies, including pounds, yen, marks, Canadian dollars, and Swiss francs, are traded on the International Money Market. The major trading volume is in contracts maturing in March, June, September, and December; volume for contracts maturing in other months is not large enough to provide sufficient liquidity. Delivery of the currency takes place on the third Wednesday of the delivery month. The minimum contract size varies with the currency, as does the margin requirement.

[9]For discussion of the determinants of forward rates, see Grabbe, *International Financial Markets*, pp. 78–89.

Because of the existence of active trading in these currency futures, a firm hedging via this vehicle does not have to hold the contract until maturity. Instead, the firm may offset the contract at any time it deems advantageous by undertaking an opposing transaction (going short in a contract in which it is long, for example). The exchange's clearinghouse will then wipe out the offsetting transactions, and the firm's involvement is ended. Also, no time-consuming negotiations are necessary; the firm deals in standard contracts. In this way, the firm experiences higher liquidity and more rapid execution of currency hedges than by using forwards. Because of the ability to be liquidated before maturity, most futures contracts are reversed. Most forward contracts, on the other hand, are held to maturity.

However, because of the standardization necessary to achieve the economies of scale that make trading economically possible, *the variety of currencies, maturity dates, and amount of futures contracts is limited.* This is the second difference between currency futures and currency forwards. Negotiated *forwards* can be tailored to the firm's particular needs, but the firm is limited to what the *futures* market is trading. For this reason, when hedging in futures markets, it is rare that the hedge exactly matches the future currency transaction. The futures transaction may be different from the hedge in *date* (unless this date happens to be the third Wednesday of March, June, September, or December), *amount* (unless the transaction happens to be a multiple of the standard currency contract), or even *currency* (unless the required currency happens to be one of the traded currencies).

The inevitable mismatch of one or more of these characteristics introduces *basis risk* into hedging with currency futures, just as a parallel mismatch introduces this risk in hedging future financing or investment with interest rate futures. In currency futures, basis risk is the chance that the relationship between the *currency being hedged* (Mexican pesos for delivery in April, for example) and the *currency future being used as a hedge* (Swiss francs for delivery in June, for example), will change over time. If the relationship between the transaction being hedged (the *basis*) and the hedge itself changes, exchange risk will not be completely offset by opposing movements in valuation of the two items.[10]

The third difference between forwards and futures has to do with the patterns of cash flows from the two contracts. In the case of a forward contract, the firm generally will be required to put up only a small cash deposit before the maturity date of the contract (although the amount available for borrowing

---

[10]In hedging the movement of one currency with a contract in another, the amount of basis risk depends on the correlation in the movements of the two currencies. A table of correlation coefficients in price movements between major currencies on which futures and options are available and currencies on which such contracts are not available can be found in J. Madura and T. Veit, "Use of Currency Options in International Cash Management," *Journal of Cash Management* (January/February 1986), page 47.

on its credit line with the bank issuing the forward may also be reduced). The firm pays the balance at the maturity of the contract, and there are no cash flows between the initiation of the contract and its maturity. This is not true for futures contracts. *Futures contracts are usually bought on the margin and are marked to market each day.* In purchasing a future, the firm makes an initial deposit in its margin account, and will be either adding or withdrawing cash from its account based on daily fluctuations in the value of the futures contract. These intermediate cash flows do not occur for forward contracts.

Therefore, neither futures nor forwards dominate as exchange risk hedges. Futures are more liquid and more rapid to execute but introduce basis risk because of their limited variety in amount, maturity, and currency. Also, futures entail cash flows during the period when the contract is being held. If cash inflows are required, the firm will experience opportunity losses on this cash. Forwards do not require cash transactions during these intermediate periods.

Currency Options Another potential exchange risk hedge is the currency option. This contract gives the holder the right to buy (in the case of a call) or sell (in the case of a put) an interest in a specific amount of future currency for a specific amount of time. Option contracts for the acquisition of *currency on the spot market* and for the acquisition of *currency futures* are traded on exchanges. The maturity dates and amounts of these options are similar to those of traded currency futures contracts.

As with futures contracts, the clearinghouse affiliated with the exchange on which options are traded can offset opposing transactions, and the firm can thus liquidate its options position at any time. However, the cash flows related to options contracts are quite dissimilar to those of futures contracts. Options involve a fixed cost of purchase. If the option is not exercised, the firm loses only this fixed cost, and the cost of the options contract does not count toward the purchase or sale of the currency if the firm chooses to exercise the option. Also, there is no daily "marking to market" of margin with an option contract; the only cash flows are the initial fixed cost of the option and the cash flows related to its exercise or reversal.

While they are similar in many respects, one significant difference between some of the available options on foreign exchange and options on interest rate futures (discussed in Chapter 3) concerns the *exercise dates* allowed for the currency options. The options on interest rate futures are all *American-style* options; they can be exercised any time prior to maturity. American-style options are traded on currency in the spot market and on currency futures contracts. However, there are also *European-style* options traded on currency. European-style options can be exercised only on their maturity date and not before.

The use of options on interests in currency has some advantages to firms. Since the option need not be exercised, it offers firms the opportunity to participate in fortuitous movements in exchange rates while being protected from disadvantageous movements. For example, the firm may purchase a call option on a foreign currency in anticipation of a future need for cash in that currency. If the price of that currency rises relative to the dollar, the firm will exercise the option and acquire the currency at the option's exercise price.[11] If the currency falls relative to the dollar, the firm will let the option expire and acquire the currency directly on the spot market.[12]

However, an options strategy also has some disadvantages relative to the use of forwards or futures. The initial cost of the option is paid whether the firm exercises the option or not and does not contribute to the cost of the currency acquired. Also, volumes (and consequently liquidity) in the market for currency options are a good deal less than those on the spot and futures markets for foreign exchange. This smaller volume is probably due in part to the newness of these markets; options on foreign exchange have been traded only since 1982.

In this section, we have briefly described six methods of hedging exchange risk in multicurrency transactions: denominating transactions in dollars, investing in Eurodollars rather than foreign currency, predealing in the nondollar currency, currency forwards, currency futures, and options on currency and currency futures. Each of these approaches has advantages and disadvantages; these and other characteristics are presented in Table 13-2. Other more exotic methods of hedging are also available. Included among these are futures-style options,[13] currency swaps,[14] and the use of futures to hedge exchange risk and interest rate risk simultaneously.[15]

Evaluation Hedges of Exchange Risk To evaluate the effects of these hedges on a particular transaction, the appropriate procedure is to incorporate the cash flows from the hedge within the firm's estimates of the cash flows from the transaction. The cash flows from alternative hedged and unhedged strategies are then discounted at appropriate risk-adjusted discount rates, and the strategy that will result in the highest net present value is chosen.

[11]Note that the same effect could be achieved by selling the option (which would have risen in price) and purchasing the exchange on the spot market.

[12]Good numerical examples in the use of currency options for exchange hedging can be found in Madura and Veit, "Use of Currency Options," pp. 44–46.

[13]For discussion of this instrument, see Grabbe, *International Financial Markets,* pp. 115–16.

[14]See David Watts, "The Structure and Mechanics of Interest Rate and Currency Swaps," in *Inside the Swap Market,* Second Edition (London: IFR Publishing, 1986), pp. 24–32.

[15]This strategy is described in H. Kaufold and M. Smirlock, "Managing Corporate and Interest Rate Exposure," *Financial Management* (Autumn 1986), pp. 64–72.

Let us proceed with an example problem in the pricing and hedging of exchange risk. It is June, 1987, and a firm is considering a transaction that would result in an immediate cash outflow of $50,000 and a cash inflow of 100,000 Swiss francs in six months. The amount (in SF) and timing of the future cash flow is certain, and for simplicity we will ignore any taxes and any transaction costs in currency conversion. The firm is considering three alternatives. First, the firm can go unhedged. However, the SF : dollar exchange rate is volatile, so a risk-adjusted discount rate is required. Based on the firm's cost of capital, assume that the appropriate monthly discount rate is 1.0 percent.

The second alternative is to short the currency in the spot market. That is, the firm would arrange to borrow SF 100,000 from its bank and to repay the loan once the future SF cash inflow is received. The current exchange rate is 0.6508 dollars per SF. In this arrangement, the firm will have to pay interest on the loan at the current rate for SF accounts, but can invest the proceeds of the loan in short-term, SF-denominated investments. Assume that the interest rate on the loan is 0.521 percent per month (paid in SF), and that the interest rate on short-term SF investments is 0.250 percent per month. The firm will formulate an additional hedge against the exchange risk on the future interest expense; this interest expense will then be certain and is appropriately discounted at the risk-free rate for dollar investments, which is 0.542 percent per month.

The final alternative is to engage in a forward exchange contract with the firm's bank. In this arrangement, the firm will short the forward (sell a forward contract) and cover the contract with the future cash inflow; the bank will hold the cash from the selling of the contract. Assume for simplicity that no initial cash will be required to obtain this contract. The current forward rate of 180-day SF forwards is 0.6618 SF per dollar.[16]

The required analysis, in a spreadsheet format, is provided in Table 13-3. The unhedged alternative appears in rows 7 through 14. In this option, there are two cash flows: the initial expense of $50,000 and the future expected inflow of $66,180. The amount of this expected inflow is calculated based on the 180-day forward rate, which is the market's expected exchange rate 180 days hence. At a discount rate of 1.0 percent per month, the present-value interest factor for six months is 0.94205 (cell I12), the contribution to the net present value from the future inflow is $62,345 (in cell I13, which contains "I11*I12"), and the total net present value is $12,345 (in cell I14, which contains "@sum(B13 . . . I13)").

---

[16]Note the relationship between interest rates and forward exchange rates in this example problem. Because the dollar interest rate is higher than the SF interest rate, the SF in the forward market is selling at a premium relative to the spot market (it takes more dollars to buy the future currency than the present currency). This relationship is assured by *interest rate parity*; see Grabbe, *International Financial Markets*, pp. 78–81.

Table 13-2. *Summary of Six Methods of Hedging Exchange Risk.*

Hedge	Application	Where Traded	Currencies Traded	Contract Size
1. Denominate in dollars.	Import and export.	Not traded.	—	—
2. Invest surplus cash in Euro-dollar market.	Investment.	Eurodollar centers throughout the world.	Dollars	Typically over $500,000.
3. Prebuy or presell foreign currency.	All.	Spot currency market is worldwide network of brokers and traders.	All.	Any.
4. Currency forward.	All.	Not traded by firms.	All.	Negotiated.
5. Currency futures.	All.	Intl. Money Market	Pound	25,000 pounds
		Intl. Money Market	Can. Dollar	$100,000 Can.
		Intl. Money Market	Yen	12.5 mil. Yen
		Intl. Money Market	Swiss Francs	125,000 SF
		Intl. Money Market	Marks	125,000 DM
6. Options a. American, on spot.	All.	Phil. & London Stk. Exc.	Pound	12,500 pounds
		Phil. & London Stk. Exc.	Can. Dollar	$50,000 Can.
		Phil. & London Stk. Exc.	Yen	6.25 mil. Yen
		Phil. & London Stk. Exc.	Swiss Francs	62,500 SF
		Phil. & London Stk. Exc.	Marks	62,500 DM
		Phil. & London Stk. Exc.	French Franc	125,000 FF
b. European, on spot.	All.	Chi. Board Options Exc.	Same as futures traded on Intl. Money Market.	
c. American, on futures.	All.	Chi. Mercantile Exchange	Same as futures traded on Intl. Money Market.	

Table 13-2. *Continued.*

Maturity	Advantages	Disadvantages
—	1. Eliminates exchange risk for domestic firm.	1. Shifts exchange risk to foreign trading partner. 2. For exports, subjects firm to political risk of exchange controls.
One-week and six-month maturities are the most common.	1. Interest rates on investments are higher than for domestic investments.	1. Required transaction sizes are large. 2. There is credit and political risk.
Delivery is in two days from order.	1. Entirely eliminates exchange rate risk. 2. Can be arranged for any amount or currency.	1. Requires substantial initial investment.
Negotiated.	1. Entirely eliminates exchange rate risk. 2. Can be arranged for any amount, maturity, or currency.	1. Inflexible and illiquid; cannot be retired before maturity.
Mar./June/Sept./Dec. Mar./June/Sept./Dec. Mar./June/Sept./Dec. Mar./June/Sept./Dec. Mar./June/Sept./Dec.	1. Contact can be liquidated at any time by offsetting transaction. 2. Easy and rapid to execute.	1. Limited currency, maturity, and amount leads to basis risk. 2. Contract marked to market every day; cash may be required for margin calls.
1, 2, 3, 6, 12 mo. 1, 2, 3, 6, 12 mo. 1, 2, 3, 6, 12 mo. 1, 2, 3, 6, 12 mo. 1, 2, 3, 6, 12 mo. 1, 2, 3, 6, 12 mo.	1. Can be executed or sold at any time before maturity. 2. Allows firm to participate in advantageous price movements while protecting on downside.	1. Limited currency, maturity, and amount leads to basis risk. 2. Requires fixed charge that does not reduce eventual cost of currency.
1, 2, 3, 6, 12 mo.	1. Can be sold at any time before maturity. 2. Allows firm to participate in advantageous price movements while protecting on downside.	1. Limited currency, maturity, and amount leads to basis risk. 2. Requires fixed charge that does not reduce eventual cost of currency. 3. Can be executed only at maturity.
	1. Can be executed or sold at any time before maturity. 2. Allows firm to participate in advantageous price movements while protecting on downside.	1. Limited currency, maturity, and amount leads to basis risk. 2. Requires fixed charge that does not reduce eventual cost of currency.

Table 13-3. Analysis of Example Exchange Rate Problem.

	A	B	C	D	E	F	G	H
1	Spot Rate	.6508	Dollars per SF					
2	180-Day Forward Rate	.6618	Dollars per SF					
3	SF required	100000						
4								
5	Month	0	1	2	3	4	5	6
6								
7	Alternative 1 — No Hedge							
8	Monthly Disc. Rate	.01						
9	Initial Expense	-50000						
10	Exp. Future Inflow							66180
11	Total Cash Flows	-50000						66180
12	PVIFs	1	.99010	.98030	.97059	.96098	.95147	.94205
13	Contribution to NPV	-50000	0	0	0	0	0	62345
14	Net Present Value	-50000						12345
15								
16	Alternative 2 — Short the Spot							
17	Monthly Disc. Rate	.00542						
18	Interest Rate on SF	.00521						
19	Int. Income on SF	.0025						
20	Exchange Rates	.6508	.65263	.65447	.65630	.65813	.65997	.66180
21	Net Int. Exp. in SF		271	271	271	271	271	271
22	Net Int. Exp. in $		-177	-177	-178	-178	-179	-179
23	Initial Expense	-50000						
24	Revenues from Loan	65080						
25	Total Cash Flows	15080	-177	-177	-178	-178	-179	-179
26	PVIFs	1	.99461	.98925	.98392	.97862	.97335	.96811
27	Contribution to NPV	15080	-176	-175	-175	-174	-174	-174
28	Net Present Value	15080						14032
29								
30	Alternative 3 — Short the Forward							
31	Monthly Disc. Rate	.00542						
32	Initial Expense	-50000						
33	Future Inflow							66180
34	Total Cash Flows	-50000						66180
35	PVIFs	1	.99461	.98925	.98392	.97862	.97335	.96811
36	Contribution to NPV	-50000	0	0	0	0	0	64069
37	Net Present Value	-50000						14069

Calculations for the alternative of shorting the spot market (borrowing the currency and paying interest) appear in rows 17 through 28. Here, the firm shorts the SF 100,000 and covers this short when the SF is received, so there is no net cash inflow when the SF 100,000 is paid to the firm. However, there are future cash outflows for interest expense and inflows from the investment of the SF 100,000. This interest expense and interest income are based on the rates for these two transactions, which appear in cell B18 and B19. The difference in these rates times the borrowed principal of SF 100,000 gives the net SF outflows in cells C21 through H21 (for example, cell C21 contains "(B18 − B19)*B3"). Projected exchange rates in row 20 are used to calculate the future net interest expenses in dollars, which appear in row 22. The net cash flows in row 25 are discounted by multiplying them by the present-value interest factors in row 26. These present-value interest factors are calculated using the 0.542 percent per month dollar risk-free rate, which appears in cell B17. The net present value of $14,032 from this strategy appears in cell I28.

Analysis of the final strategy (selling a forward contract in SF) appears in rows 30 through 37. Analysis is very similar to the first alternative, except that the shorting of the future exchange rate results in a certain future cash flow, so a discount rate representing only the time value of money (and not risk) is used. The resulting net present value is $14,069. Since this is the highest net present value of the alternative strategies available to the firm, the optimum choice is to sell a forward contract for the 180-day delivery of 100,000 Swiss francs.

Hedging Nonexchange Risks in International Transactions

In the prior section, we discussed the various ways in which the firm can hedge the exchange risks inherent in international dealings. However, the firm also faces other sources of risk in these dealings. First, there are the *normal commercial risks* in any business transaction, domestic or international: the risk of default by customers, the uncertainty of sales and cost level, and so forth. Second, there are the *additional political and economic risks* that accompany international dealings: the risk of nationalization and confiscation, the risk of changing laws and exchange controls, the risks inherent in the structure of the foreign economy, and so forth. In this section, we discuss three strategies that will hedge one or more of these nonexchange risks (and sometimes hedge exchange risk at the same time). These three strategies are: (1) the local financing of investments, (2) the careful structuring of repatriations, and (3) the purchase of insurance on the firm's international investments.

Local Financing of Investments When the firm makes an investment in current assets, whether this investment is in cash, marketable securities, accounts receivable, or inventory, this investment must be financed. By financing foreign investments via the capital markets and the currency of the locale where they reside, the firm can partially hedge both the political risk of expropriation and the exchange risk among currencies.[17] The risk of expropriation is hedged because the net amount of *domestic* investment by the firm is reduced. For example, suppose that a firm makes an inventory investment in a foreign country at a cost of $10 million. If the foreign government expropriates the investment without compensation and the investment has been financed in the firm's host country, the entire $10 million is lost; the foreign government has seized the assets, but the firm must still pay for the financing.

However, assume that the firm has raised $6 million of the required financing in the same foreign country. If the assets are seized, the firm can end its involvment in the country and refuse to repay this debt; its net exposure to possible expropriation is $4 million rather than $10 million. Further, the foreign government may be less likely to undertake such an expropriation since its country has less to gain. While the government can obtain the inventory via expropriation, those providing the financing will lose their investments.

This local financing strategy also provides a partial exchange rate hedge. If the value of the financing as well as of the foreign investment is denominated in the local currency, the effect of disadvantageous swings in exchange rates on asset value will be partially reduced by the parallel effect on financing. Taking our prior example, if the firm's $10 million investment was financed via the capital markets of its home country and the value of the home currency appreciated 10 percent relative to the value of the foreign currency, the investment would be worth only $9 million and the firm would take a $1 million opportunity loss. However, if this investment was partly financed with $6 million in foreign debt, the value of this debt would also fall to $5.4 million; and the firm's loss would be only $0.4 million.

Structuring of Repatriations Another risk faced by firms making foreign investments is that, after the investment is made, the foreign government will change the local laws in an attempt to stop dividend repatriations to the parent firm. To deal with this political risk, the firm may set up business arrangements between the parent and the foreign unit such that these repatriations are in a form other than dividend payments. For example, the firm may require the foreign unit to pay management fees or royalties to the parent. Another strategy is to manipulate the transfer pricing of materials and services

---

[17]The use of local investment to hedge these risks is discussed in E. F. Brigham and L. C. Gapenski, *Intermediate Financial Management* (Chicago: Dryden, 1984), p. 952 and in P. Drucker, "Insulating the Firm from Currency Exposure," *Wall Street Journal* (April 30, 1987), p. 28.

between the firm and the foreign units in such a way that the foreign unit must pay large amounts of cash to the parent.[18]

While these structuring strategies are useful, the firm should realize that they will not go unchallenged by the foreign government. By usurping that government's amended dividend transfer laws, the firm exposes itself to the risk of retaliatory action. In particular, by avoiding regulations intended to restrain repatriations, the firm may expose itself to the risk of expropriation.

Export and Investment Insurance Programs Several agencies offer insurance against political and other risks associated with international dealings. Two of these are the Foreign Credit Insurance Association (FCIA), a unit of the Export-Import Bank, and the Overseas Private Investment Corporation (OPIC). The FCIA offers policies against nonpayment by foreign debtors for political or commercial reasons. Political risks covered include civil disturbances and controls on the amount of available exchange. Commercial risks covered include both economic risks and the default risk of debtors. Policies to cover both commercial and political risk or political risk alone are available. Premiums, deductible loss amounts, and procedures vary among types of policies and among the countries covered by the policy. Policies can cover single-sale transactions or the firm's entire foreign operation. In addition to coverage of default by debtors in paying for exported shipments, coverage is available on inventory residing in a foreign country. Special programs are available for firms whose prior exporting experience has been limited, for service firms, and for firms engaged in foreign leasing. Exports with terms of sale of up to five years may be insured.

OPIC is an agency of the U.S. government, and is primarily concerned with facilitating investments in less-developed foreign countries (where these countries are generally friendly to the United States). Coverage is currently available for investments in many countries all over the world, including such diverse locations as Argentina, Cameroon, China, Fiji, Nepal, and Tonga. OPIC insures against political risks only. Three types of political risk may be covered: (1) restrictions on the amount of exchange, (2) expropriation and nationalization, and (3) violence and civil unrest. Separate premiums are paid to insure against each of these political actions. Coverage of investments is to a maximum of 90 percent of the invested amount. Only new investment (and not existing investment) may be insured. In addition to coverage of exports for a wide range of U.S. products and of working capital investments, coverage is available on loans, leases, and natural resource investments. However, all investments covered must assist in the social or economic development of the country in which the investment is made.

In considering whether to employ these insurance programs, the finan-

---

[18]For a good discussion of these repatriation strategies, see Brigham and Gapenski, *Intermediate Financial Management*, pp. 937–40.

cial analyst needs to estimate their effect on the level, timing, and risk of the expected cash flows from the international transaction. The net present values of the cash flows for the various insured and uninsured strategies should then be compared. For example, in an exporting situation, the net present value of an uninsured sale to a foreign credit applicant may be estimated using the methods outlined in Chapter 6. If the firm can obtain insurance (perhaps from FCIA or OPIC) a new pattern of expected cash flows and risk will result. The risk-adjusted net present value of the uninsured and insured sales are compared, and the strategy with the highest net present value is chosen.

MANAGEMENT OF INTERNATIONAL WORKING CAPITAL ACCOUNTS[19]

Up to this point, the majority of this chapter's discussion has been devoted to the additional political, economic, and exchange risks that occur for the firm in international dealings. These additional risks occur in many situations where the firm is managing international working capital accounts and transactions. For example, keeping an inventory of materials in a foreign country to support sales of an affiliate involves the risk of expropriation of the inventory, the risk of imposition of new taxes on the inventory, the risk that the inventory will not be sold because of local economic conditions, and the risk that the value of the local currency will change before revenues from the sale of the inventory are repatriated.

However, in addition to these *differences in risk* between domestic and international working capital transactions, there are also some differences in the *required techniques for the international management of individual working capital assets and liabilities.* The goal of the firm in the management of these assets and liabilities is still to maximize the wealth of shareholders by maximizing net present value. However, there are additional issues in the achievement of this goal in international settings that do not occur in domestic situations. We discuss some of these issues in this section.

Cash Management As in the management of domestic cash, the firm can maximize net present value by collecting cash as quickly as possible, disbursing it as slowly as possible, and investing temporary surpluses as profitably as possible. However, in the management of international cash, the cash asset is denominated in various currencies and located in various countries. In this context, one set of cash management issues arises in *managing flotation on international cash transfers.*

To understand the importance of the management of flotation of inter-

---

[19]An alternative treatment of the issues discussed in this section can be found in A. C. Shapiro, *International Corporate Finance: Survey and Synthesis* (Tampa, Florida: Financial Management Association, 1986), pp. 32–48.

national cash, consider the relatively simple case of an exporting firm collecting from a foreign importer of its goods. In exporting, the firm has several options in arranging for payment by the foreign customer. Two of these are: (1) the exporting firm may grant credit directly to the customer, or (2) the exporting firm may require that the customer's bank accept drafts for goods before they are delivered to the buyer.[20] In either case, the buyer will eventually wish to pay for the goods, either by paying the firm (in the first option) or paying the drafts (in the second option). Several delays occur between the buyer's instructions to its bank to start payment procedures and the seller's eventual receipt of the funds. Included among these are the delay at the importer's bank in executing these instructions, delay while the funds are moving from the foreign bank to the seller's U.S. bank, and delay between the time the U.S. bank receives the funds and the time they are credited to the seller's account. If the drafts option is used, the processing of these documents can add additional delay.

Together these delays commonly add *eight to ten business days* to the time between the foreign firm's payment and the domestic firm's receipt of this payment. During that time, the domestic firm cannot use the funds. Also, over this substantial time, exchange rates may change and adversely affect the number of dollars received; the funds cannot be exchanged into dollars until received at the seller's bank. It is easy to see that such delays pose a substantial cost to the exporter.

One of the tasks of the manager of international cash is to minimize these delays in the receipt of funds from foreign customers or affiliates.[21] Several tools are available for addressing this task. The ability of foreign and U.S. banks to handle import-export transactions, including document processing and cash transfers, varies substantially from bank to bank, so *proper bank selection* is a major tool for float reduction. The use of *noncheck transfer mechanisms* should be routinely considered.[22] Also, *careful preparation of drafts* and other documents according to the laws of the importing country can avoid substantial delays in cash transfer.

Another technique (called *netting*) can be used to reduce the number of transfers among a firm's own foreign and domestic units, and thus reduce

---

[20]The use of drafts backed by both the firm and its bank in payment results in the creation of bankers' acceptances, a financing and investment instrument discussed in prior chapters.

[21]For an excellent discussion of cash management in exporting, see E. Roberts, "Benefits of Export Cash Management Studies," *Journal of Cash Management* (September/October 1984), pp. 30–34.

[22]If the countries involved are members of the SWIFT transfer network, the out-of-pocket costs of such transfers are very small (less than $1.00); see V. Srinivasan and Y. Kim, "Payments Netting in International Cash Management: A Network Optimization Approach," *Journal of International Business Studies* (Summer 1986), pp. 1–20.

flotation. While there are several versions of this technique, the basic idea is to offset payments among the various units of the firm located in various countries. For example, suppose that the firm's subsidiary in country A needs to make a payment to the parent firm and that the parent firm needs to make a payment in the same amount to another subsidiary in country B. If the funds are transferred from the subsidiary in country A to the firm's head-quarters, and the firm makes a separate transfer from headquarters to the subsidiary in country B, there will be float from two transfers. However, if the transactions are netted, the subsidiary in country A can send the funds to the subsidiary in country B, and only one transfer results. The problem of minimizing float and other transfer costs of funds between the firm's units over multiple periods, given legal and other constraints involved in this transfer, is amenable to sophisticated optimization techniques.[23]

A second set of issues in the management of international cash revolves around the *flotation management for a foreign unit* of the firm. Unfortunately, many of the standard techniques used to shorten float on the incoming domestic checks of U.S. firms are not applicable in other lands. For example, if a firm has made an investment in a foreign subsidiary, and this subsidiary sells and collects within its own country, it would seem that a straightforward application of lockbox location methodologies would minimize the mail float on the subsidiary's incoming checks. However, the financial cultures of many other countries are not oriented toward such lockbox systems, and some are in fact resistant to their application. Although, in the United States, banks have been the largest developers and sellers of these flotation management technologies, banks in other countries (particularly in Europe) have shown no interest in these techniques.[24] To reduce float on incoming checks of foreign affiliates, some firms have gone so far as to set up accounts at the banks of the affiliate's major customers. While such accounts are costly to maintain, they eliminate clearing float completely, since clearing now requires only internal debiting and crediting of the payor's and payee's accounts at the same bank. The advantage and cost of such innovative flotation management strategies will vary from country to country.

Accounts Receivable Management In the management of domestic accounts receivable, the financial manager's basic duties are to make and monitor decisions regarding terms of sale and credit granting. These duties are no different in international situations, but complications occur that are not

[23]Techniques for the analysis of this problem are presented in M. Anvari, "Efficient Scheduling of Cross-Border Cash Transfers," *Financial Management* (Summer 1986), pp. 40–49, A. Shapiro, "Payments Netting in International Cash Management," *Journal of International Business Studies* (Fall 1978), pp. 51–58, and Srinivasan and Kim, "Payments Netting."

[24]See J. Shoch, "Management of U.S. Cash Flows for a Foreign-Based Multinational," *Journal of Cash Management* (May/June 1984), page 44 for discussion.

part of the domestic scene. Several of these complications revolve around the different *levels of information* available regarding foreign markets and credit applicants.

Let us discuss terms-of-sale decisions first. In many countries, terms of sale (particularly for imported goods) are legislated, and there is no decision to be made regarding these terms: the firm complies with the required terms or it does not deal in that country. If the firm is not bound to legislated terms, the optimum terms can then be set for foreign markets just as in domestic markets; the appropriate analysis techniques are discussed in Chapter 5. However, these techniques require an estimate of *the future sales that will result from various terms policies.* Even in an industrialized country where product markets are well-developed, such estimates are quite uncertain. In countries with more fluid product markets, the uncertainty in such estimates is greater. Because of this uncertainty as to future sales volumes and the importance of these sales volumes in terms-of-sale decisions, the appropriate assessment and pricing of risk in these decisions is critical.

As with information on product markets, credit information on foreign customers is often inferior in quantity and quality to that available on domestic customers or is in a form that makes the assessment of default probabilities and recovery rates more uncertain.[25] While the availability of such information and its usefulness varies from country to country, the type of information gathered is similar to that of domestic applicants: histories of trade payments, financial statements, and so forth. There are several organizations, such as Dun and Bradstreet International and FCIB-NACM Corporation, that will assist the firm in obtaining this information. But the information received will often be less than that which the seller would prefer. In fact, international credit managers often use the acronym "LESS" to describe the information available on foreign debtors:

- ☐ *L*imited (not many sources of information)
- ☐ *E*xpensive
- ☐ *S*low (distance/language barrier)
- ☐ *S*uspect (incomplete/neutral information)

One alternative is to price this uncertainty of information by raising the discount rate used to estimate the value of the expected cash flows when credit information is sketchy.[26] Another response is to require that the purchaser use *documentary credit* procedures in order to make purchases. The

---

[25]For discussion of sources of credit information on foreign firms, see G. N. Cristie and A. E. Bracuti, *Credit Management* (Lake Success, N. Y.: Credit Research Foundation, 1981) pp. 644–49.

[26]See Chapter 6 for discussion of the risk introduced in credit-granting decisions as a result of uncertainty regarding estimates of customer-specific parameters.

draft/acceptance procedure that results in a bankers' acceptance is one of these and is one of the safest because the buyer's bank has also agreed to honor the draft, reducing the risk of default. Other documentary credits, such as *export drafts* (which are not guaranteed by a bank), involve a lower default probability than do sales on an open account basis but a higher default probability than do bankers' acceptances.[27]

Inventory Management There are several differences between the management of domestic inventory and the management of inventory in a multinational context. For one thing, any political risk of war and civil disturbance bears heavily on inventory. Unless the civil disturbance results in changed laws, trade creditors within a foreign country will still owe the same amounts to the firm when the disturbance is over. But inventory is a *physical good*; it can be burned or otherwise destroyed in such disturbances.

Another difference between domestic and international inventory management occurs if the firm has set up a local affiliate to sell the firm's exported output. In such cases, the lead times, safety stocks, and order sizes will not be the same as those that would be calculated in domestic inventory management. The mere physical distance between the firm's plant and the sales location raises the lead time from order to delivery and raises the transportation cost in obtaining materials. These differences must be addressed in formulating a strategy for international inventory management.

Short-Term Financing The financial culture and business climate of the foreign country will affect both the optimal level of short-term financing and the available sources of this financing. Firms may finance internationally by using such sources as accounts payable from foreign suppliers, accrued expenses of foreign operations, and so forth. However, the availability and cost of these sources of short-term debt varies substantially among countries based on laws, interest rate levels, local business customs, and so forth.

In choosing among the various sources of short-term financing available in other countries, it is *extremely* important that the firm keep in mind the effects of *different rates of inflation* on the advantage of borrowing in various currencies.[28] A loan from a foreign bank (payable in the bank's home currency) at a lower interest rate may seem a desirable source of financing, but a higher inflation rate in that country may make such borrowing less advantageous than a loan carrying a higher interest rate but denominated in the firm's home currency. To see this, let us assume that a firm has, among its alternative sources of short-term financing, two potential 90-day note ar-

---

[27]See Cristie and Bracuti, *Credit Management*, pp. 659–79 for a discussion of documentary credits.

[28]For discussion of this issue, see Brigham and Gapenski, *Intermediate Financial Management*, p. 929.

rangements. Interest and principal are payable at maturity in both cases. The first of these is from a domestic bank and requires that the firm pay 2 percent interest (over the 90 days) on a principal of $10 million. The second is from a foreign bank and requires the payment of SF 15,634,604 in 90 days based on a principal of SF 15,365,704 (an interest rate of 1.75 percent for the 90 days in SF). If the current spot exchange rate is $0.6508 per SF, this second arrangement also provides $10 million in financing (since 15,634,604 divided by 0.6508 equals $10 million).

On the surface, it would seem that the SF loan is cheaper, since the interest rate is lower. However, the foreign bank's loan must be paid off in SF, and the eventual dollar/SF exchange rate will depend on the relative inflation in the two countries. Let us assume that this differential inflation will result in a rise in the Swiss franc of 0.5 percent relative to the dollar over the 90 days. The analysis appears in Table 13-4. In this case, the anticipated exchange rate at the time the note matures will be $0.654054 per SF (equal to 1.005 times 0.6508), and the firm will have to pay $10,225,875 (equal to 15,463,604 SF divided by $0.654054 per SF). This translates into an interest

Table 13-4. *Effect of Change in Exchange Rate on Interest Cost of Borrowing.*
Dollar Note

Dollar Amount of Financing	*Dollar Interest Rate*	*Dollar Payment in 90 days*	*Dollar Payment/ Dollar Financing*
$10,000,000	$0.02	$10,200,000	$1.02

SF Note

SF Amount of Financing	*SF Interest Rate*	*SF Payment due in 90 days*	
15,365,704	.0175	15,634,604	

Exchange Rate:
Dollars/SF

Current Rate 0.6508		Rate in 90 Days 0.654054	

Dollar Amount of Financing		Dollar Payment in 90 days	
$10,000,000		$10,225,875	1.0225875

rate of about 2.259 percent, which is higher than the interest rate on the dollar-denominated loan.

The point is, that in analyzing nondollar sources of financing, *anticipated changes in exchange rates must be included in the analysis*. Note that in this analysis we are discussing *anticipated* changes in exchange rates (which affect the *expected* levels of cash flows), not *unanticipated* ones (which affect the *risk* of these cash flows). The cash flows in Table 13-4 from the two financing vehicles are the expected flows based on anticipated inflation rates. *Anticipated changes* such as these *will be reflected in the forward and futures market prices* of currencies and are thus observable by the firm.

This concludes our discussion of some of the differences between the management of working capital in a domestic and in an international setting. The following section reviews surveys of practices used by managers in the management of international short-term assets and liabilities.

THE MANAGEMENT OF INTERNATIONAL WORKING CAPITAL IN PRACTICE

Two surveys of large numbers of firms, both conducted in 1983, provide some information on the practice of international working capital management. Collin and Frankle (CF) wanted to assess the international practices of U.S. firms; they surveyed the Fortune 1000.[29] Soenen and Aggarwal (SA) were concerned with contrasting practices among firms in various countries, and surveyed large industrial companies in the Netherlands, in the United Kingdom, and in Belgium.[30]

Of the additional sources of risk in international transactions, exchange risk and political risk (particularly risks of restriction on repatriation and of expropriations) are seen as important by the vast majority of U.S. firms (CF, p. 46). To hedge exchange risk, the majority of U.S. firms use forward exchange contracts; a smaller percentage use futures (CF, pp. 46–47). Forward exchange contracts are also very popular hedging vehicles for firms in the U.K., the Netherlands, and Belgium (SA, p. 64). The denomination of transactions in the currency of the home country is also used as an exchange hedge by a substantial fraction of firms in all three of these countries, but the use of traded market vehicles (such as futures) for hedging is popular only for firms in the U.K. (SA, p. 64). Of these three countries, there is less

---

[29]See J. M. Collins and A. Frankle, "International Cash Management Practices of Large U.S. Firms," *Journal of Cash Management* (July/August 1985), pp. 42–48. The response rate for this survey was 22 percent.

[30]Results are reported in L. Soenen and R. Aggarwal, "Corporate Foreign Exchange and Cash Management Practices," *Journal of Cash Management* (March/April 1987), pp. 62–64. The overall response rate for this survey was 30.5 percent.

hedging of foreign exchange risk by firms in Belgium than in the U.K. or the Netherlands (SA, pp. 63–64).

One method of hedging the risk of controls on dividend repatriation from a foreign affiliate is the careful structuring of the relationship between the companies so that part of the cash flow to the parent firm comes from nondividend sources. While dividends are still the most common form of repatriating cash, this mechanism is by no means dominant. Other mechanisms, which avoid dividends (and thus restrictions on dividend repatriation), are used by many firms. Popular mechanisms include interest payments and principal payments on capital borrowed from the parent, transfer pricing, royalty payments, and management fees (CF, p. 46).

The management of cash and marketable securities on an international basis poses special problems. Although the use of lockbox systems for domestic collections is common among large firms, only a small fraction of large firms use these systems in international dealings (CF, p. 44). In moving cash from one country to another, wire, cable, and mail transfers are used by over half of all firms; netting of payments among foreign units is also common (CF, p. 45). The decision on where and how to invest excess cash depends on the structure of the firm's international operations. Those U.S. firms whose international cash management operations are centralized at their corporate headquarters usually invest in dollar-denominated securities, while firms with decentralized operations usually invest in local, nondollar markets (CF, p. 44).

In domestic credit-granting situations, firms generally either grant credit on an open-account, unsecured, basis or require cash in advance. These two policies are also used in international dealings; many firms sell foreign buyers on open-account terms, and a few cash-in-advance sales are made (CF, page 47). However, letter-of-credit transactions (which are part of the document system that can generate bankers' acceptances) are the most popular credit-granting option in international trade. Other documentary credits (such as drafts) play a lesser role (CF, p. 47).

In addition to investments in short-term international assets, firms may also finance internationally. While several programs are available from domestic and foreign governments, most large U.S. firms obtain international financing from commercial banks in the United States and elsewhere. Only about one-fourth of large firms use United States and foreign government financing programs (CF, pp. 45–46).

SUMMARY

Firms engage in international working capital transactions as part of the process of maximizing shareholder wealth. By trading, investing, or financing in another country, the firm can take advantage of superior conditions in product, labor, or capital markets. However, dealing on an international basis changes both the risk and expected levels of cash flows as compared to parallel dealings done domestically.

Differences in risk between domestic and international transactions stems from currency, political, and economic differences among countries. Differences among currencies used in the denomination of transactions leads to exchange risk. Exchange risk is the uncertainty regarding the future rate of interchange between the currency in which the international transaction is denominated and the currency of the firm's host country. Political risk is of several types, and includes the possibility of civil unrest in the foreign country, changes in the rules under which the firm operates in the foreign country, and controls on the rate or amount of exchange between the foreign country's currency and the currency of the firm's host country. Economic risk stems from the variation in the nature of economic activity among countries.

When considering an international transaction, the risks inherent in that transaction must first be assessed. These risks will encompass the normal business risks in any domestic transaction, plus the additional risks that come from dealing internationally. Once the levels of these risks are assessed, they must be either hedged or priced in evaluating the proposed transaction. Several hedges are available to address the risks associated with international dealings. Exchange risk may be hedged by denominating the transaction in dollars, dealing in the Eurodollar market for investments rather than in nondollar foreign markets, prebuying or preselling required foreign currency, and via currency forwards, futures, or options. Nonexchange risk may be hedged by financing foreign investments within the foreign country, managing relationships between the firm and its foreign affiliates so as to structure cash repatriations in nondividend forms, and insuring the firms' foreign investments. Alternate hedging and pricing strategies for foreign investments and financing are evaluated by their effects on the risk-adjusted net present value of the proposed transaction.

Besides differences in risk, international dealings also entail consideration of other differences, not involved in the management of domestic short-term assets and liabilities. Differences among countries in financial systems, and the cross-border nature of transactions, cause differences in the level and character of cash flows from domestic versus foreign undertakings. In cash management, new problems arise in the international scheduling of cash transfers and in managing flotation of foreign affiliates. Reduced levels of information on foreign markets and credit applicants are challenges in receivables management. In ordering inventory, international lead times and ordering costs are higher than in domestic situations. Finally, the evaluation of current liability financing in nondollar currencies requires the consideration of anticipated changes in exchange rates caused by international differences in inflation.

This chapter, the last in the text, introduces the reader to the management of internationalized working capital investment and financing. However, whether the reader's future involvement with the management of current assets and current liabilities is on a domestic or/and an international basis, it is well to remember that working capital management is a rapidly changing field. New techniques, instruments, and securities for the management of short-term assets and liabilities appear rapidly and increasingly. In a dynamic field such as this, constant study and attention are required to keep one's knowledge current.

Problem

13-1. A firm is trying to decide on a strategy for dealing with the risk of the cash flows from an overseas trade credit applicant. The sale is denominated in wolfgangs, which is the currency of the country in which the sales is to be made. There is no risk of political action in the foreign country, and the terms of sale are 180 days. There is no chance that the debtor will default. The forward exchange rate for 180 days is 5 wolfgangs per dollar, and the invoice amount is 500,000 wolfgangs. One strategy to be evaluated is to make the sale and to purchase a forward currency contract. If this contract is purchased, an immediate deposit of 5 percent of the contract amount (in dollars) will be required; this will be refunded when the contract is executed. The cost of materials necessary for the sale is $75,000, payable immediately, and the discount rate is 1 percent per month. Calculate the net present value of the sale where exchange risk is hedged via the forward contract in wolfgangs. Use a 360-day year for calculation purposes.

Selected Readings

Anvari, M., "Efficient Scheduling of Cross-Border Cash Transfers," *Financial Management* (Summer 1986), pp. 40–49.

Collins, J. M., and A. Frankle, "International Cash Management Practices of Large U.S. Firms," *Journal of Cash Management* (July/August 1985), pp. 42–48.

Cristie, G. N., and A. E. Bracuti, *Credit Management* (Lake Success, N.Y.: Credit Research Foundation, 1981), Chapters 36 and 37.

Grabbe, J. O., *International Financial Markets* (New York: Elsevier, 1986), Chapters 3–6, 8, and 12–15.

Kaufold, H., and M. Smirlock, "Managing Corporate and Interest Rate Exposure," *Financial Management* (Autumn 1986), pp. 64–72.

Madura, J., and T. Veit, "Use of Currency Options in International Cash Management," *Journal of Cash Management* (January/February 1986), page 47.

Roberts, E. G., "Benefits of Export Cash Management Studies," *Journal of Cash Management* (September/October 1984), pp. 30–34.

Roberts, E. G., "Evaluating Country Risk," Occasional Paper of the Credit Research Foundation, 1984.

Shapiro, A. C., *International Corporate Finance: Survey and Synthesis* (Tampa, Florida: Financial Management Association, 1986), Chapter III.

Shapiro, A. C., "Payments Netting in International Cash Management," *Journal of International Business Studies* (Fall 1978), pp. 51–58.

Soenen, L., and R. Aggarwal, "Corporate Foreign Exchange and Cash Management Practices," *Journal of Cash Management* (March/April 1987), pp. 62–64.

Srinivasan, V., and Y. Kim, "Payments Netting in International Cash Management: A Network Optimization Approach," *Journal of International Business Studies* (Summer 1986), pp. 1–20.

Jupiter Machinery[1]
International Cash and Credit Management

Jupiter Machinery was a medium-sized manufacturer of precision machinery; yearly sales were $100 million. The firm was based in the United States and did not advertise internationally. Consequently, the management of Jupiter Manufacturing was quite surprised to be approached by executives from Mechanico General regarding an order. Mechanico General, a firm located in the country of Isla Verde, manufactured parts for the automotive industry in that country. The executives of Mechanico had become familiar with Jupiter's products and service from visits to manufacturers of automotive parts in the United States. Based on this knowledge, they had decided to approach Jupiter regarding the purchase of new machinery.

After considerable discussion between the manufacturing staffs of Mechanico and Jupiter, a list of the required items was compiled. Some of the items were currently available from Jupiter's inventory while others would require manufacturing. It was determined that the order could be ready for shipment in 90 days.

Concurrent with these negotiations, the firm's credit manager, Pamela Vance, had been accumulating a file of credit information on Mechanico General. Ms. Vance was quite experienced with regard to domestic credit investigations and credit-granting decisions, but had no experience in international dealings. Since it was clear from the beginning that the order would be substantial, she decided to collect all possible information on Mechanico General. She first obtained credit reports on the firm from commercial reporting agencies. These indicated that Mechanico General was a large firm with substantial financial strength and a record of satisfactory payments to local suppliers. An inquiry to Mechanico's bank (made through Jupiter's bank) showed the firm to be well-known and respected and to have substantial bank balances. Talks with the international credit departments of other U.S. exporters to Mechanico indicated that sales were being made on an open-account and on a draft basis with terms of 180 days from date of shipment; some of these U.S. firms reported prompt payments, while others showed slowness of up to 30 days beyond terms.

[1]This case was developed with the help of Edward G. Roberts of Union Carbide Corporation.

While this was much less information than could be obtained on a domestic buyer, Ms. Vance recognized that these were all the data she was going to be able to obtain. Based on this limited information, Ms. Vance had estimated that the default probability for Mechanico was relatively low. Her numeric default probability estimate was 0.75 percent, and her estimate of the recovery rate in default was 20 percent. She also estimated that it would take 5 years to make any recovery if the firm defaulted on the debt. Because of the very limited available information, she recognized that these estimates were subject to considerable uncertainty.

Besides the normal commercial risk of default in selling to any applicant, Ms. Vance was also aware of the political risks in selling to a firm in a foreign country. At the time of the proposed sale, Isla Verde was a country with a relatively stable political condition, but there was always the chance that the country's government would respond to domestic political pressures by taking an action that would make the situation more difficult for firms exporting to the country. In particular, she was worried that the government of Isla Verde would institute a freeze on payments to foreign suppliers. If such a political action were undertaken while Jupiter had monies due from Mechanico, collection of the invoice would be substantially delayed. For modeling purposes, Ms. Vance estimated that between the time the shipment was made and the time payment was due, there would be a 5 percent chance that the government would take such an action, and that such an action would result in payments being delayed to foreign suppliers until the end of a two-year period. In addition to these commercial and political factors, there was also currency risk in the sale. The currency in use in Isla Verde was the peseta, and the spot exchange rate at the time of the analysis was 127.30 pesetas per U.S. dollar.

Because of the exchange risk in the proposed sale, it was agreed that Ms. Vance and the firms' cash manager (Jack Roddenberg) would participate in the negotiations between Jupiter's marketing staff and the purchasing agents for Mechanico. These negotiations would determine the price, terms, and currency of the sale. It was made clear rather early in the negotiations that requiring terms shorter than 180 days or requiring that Mechanico purchase on a documentary credit basis would result in the loss of the sale. If the sale were denominated in pesetas, it was agreed that the amount of the invoice would be 82,745,000 pesetas (equivalent to $618,423 at the 270-day forward exchange rate). If the invoice was denominated in dollars, the amount would be $600,000. Jupiter had one week to analyze these two alternatives and decide which of the two would be exercised. In any case, providing the machinery ordered (and replenishing Jupiter's inventory of machinery to desired levels after the order) would cost Jupiter $500,000. For modeling purposes, Ms. Vance assigned this outflow to the day on which the order was to be shipped.

During the one-week period, it was the task of Ms. Vance and Mr. Roddenberg to make hedging and credit-granting decisions regarding the proposed sale. To make such decisions, they had to consider the various risks and the possible hedges available for these risks. To hedge the political and commercial risk of the transaction, the firm could purchase insurance coverage. Since Jupiter did not expect to make any other foreign sales during the upcoming year, it was decided that a single-sale policy (rather than a policy covering multiple sales) was the most economical. The policy Jupiter was considering was a comprehensive one that would partially insure the firm against default by Mechanico for commercial or political reasons. The premium would be $10,000, payable immediately. Under this policy, if Mechanico did not pay for the shipment within 240 days from the date of shipment (180-day terms of sale plus 60 days) for commercial reasons, Jupiter would file a claim for the amount of the invoice with the insurance company, which would pay 90 percent of the invoice value in an additional 60 days. The remaining 10 percent of value constituted Jupiter's deductible; any recoveries in default would go to the insurance company. If the invoice were not paid because of political action, the same timing would apply, but there would be no deductible amount; the insurance would pay for 100 percent of the loss. If both default and political action occurred, the claim would be paid at the commercial loss rate. If the invoice were denominated in dollars, the claim would be paid in dollars. If the invoice were denominated in pesetas, the amount of the payment for the insurance claim would be computed based on the exchange rate in effect at the time the payment was made.

The exchange risk in the sale could be hedged in several ways. One method was to denominate the sale in dollars, which would reduce the amount of the sale from $618,423 (at forward exchange rates) to $600,000. However, Ms. Vance and Mr. Roddenberg also considered hedging of the exchange risk by using currency forwards and futures. They knew that Jupiter would receive the cash in 270 days if Mechanico paid as expected and if no government action occurred: 90 days to assemble the order plus the 180-day terms of sale. Therefore they approached their bank regarding the possibility of selling a forward contract for the receipt of 82,745,000 pesetas in 270 days. The bank quoted a 270-day forward exchange rate of 133.80 pesetas per dollar, and gave Jupiter the option of either paying 5 percent of the current dollar value of the contract in advance or having its credit line reduced by the dollar amount of the contract. In no case were the revenues from the contract's sale available to the company until the contract was fulfilled. Given that Jupiter's

current policy for the management of short-term debt called for substantial reserve credit lines to hedge against cash shortages, Ms. Vance and Mr. Roddenberg knew that the firm would utilize the first of these alternatives, and would present the 5 percent cash advance.

The third alternative for hedging currency risk was the use of futures. While futures on the Isla Verde peseta were not traded, Mr. Roddenberg knew that movements in the German deutsche mark and the peseta were highly (though not perfectly) correlated. In this strategy, futures contracts on deutsche marks with the maturity nearest that of the invoice would be sold and used as a proxy for a contract in the pesetas. The timing and size of the proposed sale was such that Mr. Roddenberg was able to get a close match on the amount and maturity of the contracts, but some basis risk remained because of the use of a proxy currency. Also, Jupiter would have to deposit $19,000 in a noninterest-bearing margin account that would be marked to market each day.

Ms. Vance and Mr. Roddenberg knew that the strategies of using futures and forwards hedged exchange risk on the future cash flow only if Mechanico paid on the 270th day. If Mechanico defaulted or if a government action delayed receipt of the monies from Mechanico, the contracts would be reversed at that time by a transaction in the spot market. That is, if the 82,745,000 pesetas were not received from Mechanico on the 270th day, Jupiter would have to cover the contracts by purchasing pesetas in the spot market. This would subject the firm to two other risks: the risk of currency fluctuations in the spot market when covering the short, and currency risk on other future cash flows, which would not be hedged.

To begin their quantitative analysis, Ms. Vance and Mr. Roddenberg first recognized that there were eight possible strategies: four

Exhibit 1

Jupiter Machinery
Listing of Eight Possible Hedging Strategies

Strategy	Exchange Risk Hedge	Political and Commercial Risk Hedge
A	None	None
B	Denominate in Dollars	None
C	Forward Contract	None
D	Futures Contracts	None
E	None	Insurance
F	Denominate in Dollars	Insurance
G	Forward Contract	Insurance
H	Futures Contracts	Insurance

possible currency hedges (no hedge, denominating in dollars, using a forward, and using futures) and two possible insurance strategies (insure or not insure). These strategies are summarized in Exhibit 1. With regard to the commercial default and political events, they saw that four outcomes were possible. Assuming that these processes were independent, they calculated the probabilities of occurrence of each outcome. The four outcomes and their probabilities are presented in Exhibit 2. They also recognized that, to evaluate the various strategies, they would need expected future

exchange rates for the times of anticipated future events. The projected rates and event dates are presented in Exhibit 3.

Using these data, analysis proceeded as follows. First, the expected cash flows (in the appropriate currencies) were calculated for the various future events for each strategy and converted into dollars. An example of their analysis at this stage for strategy A is presented in Exhibit 4. Risk-adjusted discount rates were then applied to these estimates of expected future cash flows. These risk-adjusted rates were designed to allow for: (1)

Exhibit 2

Jupiter Machinery
Commercial and Political Outcomes with Probabilities

Outcome Number	Commercial Outcome	Political Outcome	Probability
1	No default	No action	0.9429
2	No default	Action	0.0496
3	Default	No action	0.0071
4	Default	Action	0.0004
			1.0000

Exhibit 3

Jupiter Manufacturing

Important Future Dates and Projected Exchange Rates

Time (Days)	Time (Months)	Event (Types of Cash Flows)	Projected Exchange Rate, Pesetas per Dollar
0	0	Insurance, deposit on forwards, initial margin on futures.	127.30
90	3	Initial outflow of $500,000.	129.50
270	9	Inflow from customer payment or reversal of futures or forwards.	133.80
390	13	Insurance payment if there has been default or political action.	136.70
720	24	Payment from customer if sale is uninsured and if there is political action but no default.	144.60
1800	60	Payment if customer defaults and if the sale is uninsured.	170.60

Exhibit 4

Jupiter Machinery
Cash Flows from Strategy A

Monthly Risk-Free Rate .005

	Month						Prob.
	0	3	9	13	24	60	
Proj. Pesetas: $	127.3	129.5	133.8	136.7	144.6	170.6	

Dollar-Denominated Cash Flows

Outcome							Prob.
1		-500000					.9429
2		-500000					.0496
3		-500000					.0071
4		-500000					.0004

Peseta-Denominated Cash Flows

Outcome							Prob.
1			82745000		82745000		.9429
2							.0496
3						16549000	.0071
4						16549000	.0004

Expected Dollar Cash Flows

	0	-500000	583111	0	28383	728	

Hedges of Expected Cash Flows (0 = no hedge, 1 = hedge)

Currency							
Proxy Hedge	0	0	0	0	0	0	
Direct Hedge	0	1	1	0	0	0	
Commercial	0	1	1	0	0	0	
Political	0	1	1	0	0	0	

the commercial risk from the variation in the cash flows due to default or nondefault of Mechanico and the uncertainty in the estimation of the parameters related to the default process, (2) currency risk for nonhedged and partially hedged nondollar flows, and (3) variation in cash flows due to political action and the uncertainty in Ms. Vance's estimate of the probability of this action.

The risk-adjusted rates used in the discounting process were developed based on the firm's cost of capital and the risk-free rate of interest and were compounded monthly. Jupiter's cost of capital was 0.600 percent per month, and the risk-free rate of interest was 0.500 percent per month. In evaluating a domestic credit applicant, the firm's cost of capital would be used as a discount rate for the expected future cash flows from the sale (such a domestic sale would not, of course, involve any exchange or political risk). However, Ms. Vance felt that an additional increment to this risk-adjusted rate was required because of the limited credit information available. It was decided to add an additional 0.100 percent per month to the cost of capital to represent this additional commercial uncertainty. Thus, the adjustment for commercial risk would be 0.200 percent above the risk-free rate rather than the 0.100 percent (equal to 0.600 minus 0.500) used for the evaluation of domestic credit applicants.

Appendixes

Appendix A. Cumulative (Lower Tail) Areas of the Normal Distribution Function

z	.00	.01	.02	.03	.04	.05	.06	.07	.08	.09
−.0	.5000	.4960	.4920	.4880	.4840	.4801	.4761	.4721	.4681	.4641
−.1	.4602	.4562	.4522	.4483	.4443	.4404	.4364	.4325	.4286	.4247
−.2	.4207	.4168	.4129	.4090	.4052	.4013	.3974	.3936	.3897	.3859
−.3	.3821	.3783	.3745	.3707	.3669	.3632	.3594	.3557	.3520	.3483
−.4	.3446	.3409	.3372	.3336	.3300	.3264	.3228	.3192	.3156	.3121
−.5	.3085	.3050	.3015	.2981	.2946	.2912	.2877	.2843	.2810	.2776
−.6	.2743	.2709	.2676	.2643	.2611	.2578	.2546	.2514	.2483	.2451
−.7	.2420	.2389	.2358	.2327	.2297	.2266	.2236	.2206	.2177	.2148
−.8	.2119	.2090	.2061	.2033	.2005	.1977	.1949	.1922	.1894	.1867
−.9	.1841	.1814	.1788	.1762	.1736	.1711	.1685	.1660	.1635	.1611
−1.0	.1587	.1562	.1539	.1515	.1492	.1469	.1446	.1423	.1401	.1379
−1.1	.1357	.1335	.1314	.1292	.1271	.1251	.1230	.1210	.1190	.1170
−1.2	.1151	.1131	.1112	.1093	.1075	.1056	.1038	.1020	.1003	.09853
−1.3	.09680	.09510	.09342	.09176	.09012	.08851	.08691	.08534	.08379	.08226
−1.4	.08076	.07927	.07780	.07636	.07493	.07353	.07215	.07078	.06944	.06811
−1.5	.06681	.06552	.06426	.06301	.06178	.06057	.05938	.05821	.05705	.05592
−1.6	.05480	.05370	.05262	.05155	.05050	.04947	.04846	.04746	.04648	.04551
−1.7	.04457	.04363	.04272	.04182	.04093	.04006	.03920	.03836	.03754	.03673
−1.8	.03593	.03515	.03438	.03362	.03288	.03216	.03144	.03074	.03005	.02938
−1.9	.02872	.02807	.02743	.02680	.02619	.02559	.02500	.02442	.02385	.02330
−2.0	.02275	.02222	.02169	.02118	.02068	.02018	.01970	.01923	.01876	.01831
−2.1	.01786	.01743	.01700	.01659	.01618	.01578	.01539	.01500	.01463	.01426
−2.2	.01390	.01355	.01321	.01287	.01255	.01222	.01191	.01160	.01130	.01101
−2.3	.01072	.01044	.01017	$.0^2 9903$	$.0^2 9642$	$.0^2 9387$	$.0^2 9137$	$.0^2 8894$	$.0^2 8656$	$.0^2 8424$
−2.4	$.0^2 8198$	$.0^2 7976$	$.0^2 7760$	$.0^2 7549$	$.0^2 7344$	$.0^2 7143$	$.0^2 6947$	$.0^2 6756$	$.0^2 6569$	$.0^2 6387$
−2.5	$.0^2 6210$	$.0^2 6037$	$.0^2 5868$	$.0^2 5703$	$.0^2 5543$	$.0^2 5386$	$.0^2 5234$	$.0^2 5085$	$.0^2 4940$	$.0^2 4799$
−2.6	$.0^2 4661$	$.0^2 4527$	$.0^2 4396$	$.0^2 4269$	$.0^2 4145$	$.0^2 4025$	$.0^2 3907$	$.0^2 3793$	$.0^2 3681$	$.0^2 3573$
−2.7	$.0^2 3467$	$.0^2 3364$	$.0^2 3264$	$.0^2 3167$	$.0^2 3072$	$.0^2 2980$	$.0^2 2890$	$.0^2 2803$	$.0^2 2718$	$.0^2 2635$
−2.8	$.0^2 2555$	$.0^2 2477$	$.0^2 2401$	$.0^2 2327$	$.0^2 2256$	$.0^2 2186$	$.0^2 2118$	$.0^2 2052$	$.0^2 1988$	$.0^2 1926$
−2.9	$.0^2 1866$	$.0^2 1807$	$.0^2 1750$	$.0^2 1695$	$.0^2 1641$	$.0^2 1589$	$.0^2 1538$	$.0^2 1489$	$.0^2 1441$	$.0^2 1395$
−3.0	$.0^2 1350$	$.0^2 1306$	$.0^2 1264$	$.0^2 1223$	$.0^2 1183$	$.0^2 1144$	$.0^2 1107$	$.0^2 1070$	$.0^2 1035$	$.0^2 1001$

Source: W. S. Peters and G. W. Summers, *Statistical Analysis for Business Decisions* (Englewood Cliffs, N.J.: Prentice Hall, 1968), pp. 466–69.

(*continued*)

Appendix A (cont.). Cumulative (Lower Tail) Areas of the Normal Distribution Function.

z	.00	.01	.02	.03	.04	.05	.06	.07	.08	.09
−3.1	$.0^3 9676$	$.0^3 9354$	$.0^3 9043$	$.0^3 8740$	$.0^3 8447$	$.0^3 8164$	$.0^3 7888$	$.0^3 7622$	$.0^3 7364$	$.0^3 7114$
−3.2	$.0^3 6871$	$.0^3 6637$	$.0^3 6410$	$.0^3 6190$	$.0^3 5976$	$.0^3 5770$	$.0^3 5571$	$.0^3 5377$	$.0^3 5190$	$.0^3 5009$
−3.3	$.0^3 4834$	$.0^3 4665$	$.0^3 4501$	$.0^3 4342$	$.0^3 4189$	$.0^3 4041$	$.0^3 3897$	$.0^3 3758$	$.0^3 3624$	$.0^3 3495$
−3.4	$.0^3 3369$	$.0^3 3248$	$.0^3 3131$	$.0^3 3018$	$.0^3 2909$	$.0^3 2803$	$.0^3 2701$	$.0^3 2602$	$.0^3 2507$	$.0^3 2415$
−3.5	$.0^3 2326$	$.0^3 2241$	$.0^3 2158$	$.0^3 2078$	$.0^3 2001$	$.0^3 1926$	$.0^3 1854$	$.0^3 1785$	$.0^3 1718$	$.0^3 1653$
−3.6	$.0^3 1591$	$.0^3 1531$	$.0^3 1473$	$.0^3 1417$	$.0^3 1363$	$.0^3 1311$	$.0^3 1261$	$.0^3 1213$	$.0^3 1166$	$.0^3 1121$
−3.7	$.0^3 1078$	$.0^3 1036$	$.0^4 9961$	$.0^4 9574$	$.0^4 9201$	$.0^4 8842$	$.0^4 8496$	$.0^4 8162$	$.0^4 7841$	$.0^4 7532$
−3.8	$.0^4 7235$	$.0^4 6948$	$.0^4 6673$	$.0^4 6407$	$.0^4 6152$	$.0^4 5906$	$.0^4 5669$	$.0^4 5442$	$.0^4 5223$	$.0^4 5012$
−3.9	$.0^4 4810$	$.0^4 4615$	$.0^4 4427$	$.0^4 4247$	$.0^4 4074$	$.0^4 3908$	$.0^4 3747$	$.0^4 3594$	$.0^4 3446$	$.0^4 3304$
−4.0	$.0^4 3167$	$.0^4 3036$	$.0^4 2910$	$.0^4 2789$	$.0^4 2673$	$.0^4 2561$	$.0^4 2454$	$.0^4 2351$	$.0^4 2252$	$.0^4 2157$
−4.1	$.0^4 2066$	$.0^4 1978$	$.0^4 1894$	$.0^4 1814$	$.0^4 1737$	$.0^4 1662$	$.0^4 1591$	$.0^4 1523$	$.0^4 1458$	$.0^4 1395$
−4.2	$.0^4 1335$	$.0^4 1277$	$.0^4 1222$	$.0^4 1168$	$.0^4 1118$	$.0^4 1069$	$.0^4 1022$	$.0^5 9774$	$.0^5 9345$	$.0^5 8934$
−4.3	$.0^5 8540$	$.0^5 8163$	$.0^5 7801$	$.0^5 7455$	$.0^5 7124$	$.0^5 6807$	$.0^5 6503$	$.0^5 6212$	$.0^5 5934$	$.0^5 5668$
−4.4	$.0^5 5413$	$.0^5 5169$	$.0^5 4935$	$.0^5 4712$	$.0^5 4498$	$.0^5 4294$	$.0^5 4098$	$.0^5 3911$	$.0^5 3732$	$.0^5 3561$
−4.5	$.0^5 3398$	$.0^5 3241$	$.0^5 3092$	$.0^5 2949$	$.0^5 2813$	$.0^5 2682$	$.0^5 2558$	$.0^5 2439$	$.0^5 2325$	$.0^5 2216$
−4.6	$.0^5 2112$	$.0^5 2013$	$.0^5 1919$	$.0^5 1828$	$.0^5 1742$	$.0^5 1660$	$.0^5 1581$	$.0^5 1506$	$.0^5 1434$	$.0^5 1366$
−4.7	$.0^5 1301$	$.0^5 1239$	$.0^5 1179$	$.0^5 1123$	$.0^5 1069$	$.0^5 1017$	$.0^6 9680$	$.0^6 9211$	$.0^6 8765$	$.0^6 8339$
−4.8	$.0^6 7933$	$.0^6 7547$	$.0^6 7178$	$.0^6 6827$	$.0^6 6492$	$.0^6 6173$	$.0^6 5869$	$.0^6 5580$	$.0^6 5304$	$.0^6 5042$
−4.9	$.0^6 4792$	$.0^6 4554$	$.0^6 4327$	$.0^6 4111$	$.0^6 3906$	$.0^6 3711$	$.0^6 3525$	$.0^6 3348$	$.0^6 3179$	$.0^6 3019$
.0	.5000	.5040	.5080	.5120	.5160	.5199	.5239	.5279	.5319	.5359
.1	.5398	.5438	.5478	.5517	.5557	.5596	.5636	.5675	.5714	.5753
.2	.5793	.5832	.5871	.5910	.5948	.5987	.6026	.6064	.6103	.6141
.3	.6179	.6217	.6255	.6293	.6331	.6368	.6406	.6443	.6480	.6517
.4	.6554	.6591	.6628	.6664	.6700	.6736	.6772	.6808	.6844	.6879
.5	.6915	.6950	.6985	.7019	.7054	.7088	.7123	.7157	.7190	.7224
.6	.7257	.7291	.7324	.7357	.7389	.7422	.7454	.7486	.7517	.7549
.7	.7580	.7611	.7642	.7673	.7703	.7734	.7764	.7794	.7823	.7852
.8	.7881	.7910	.7939	.7967	.7995	.8023	.8051	.8078	.8106	.8133
.9	.8159	.8186	.8212	.8238	.8264	.8289	.8315	.8340	.8365	.8389
1.0	.8413	.8438	.8461	.8485	.8508	.8531	.8554	.8577	.8599	.8621
1.1	.8643	.8665	.8686	.8708	.8729	.8749	.8770	.8790	.8810	.8830
1.2	.8849	.8869	.8888	.8907	.8925	.8944	.8962	.8980	.8997	.90147
1.3	.90320	.90490	.90658	.90824	.90988	.91149	.91309	.91466	.91621	.91774
1.4	.91924	.92073	.92220	.92364	.92507	.92647	.92785	.92922	.93056	.93189

z	.00	.01	.02	.03	.04	.05	.06	.07	.08	.09
1.5	.93319	.93448	.93574	.93699	.93822	.93943	.94062	.94179	.94295	.94408
1.6	.94520	.94630	.94738	.94845	.94950	.95053	.95154	.95254	.95352	.95449
1.7	.95543	.95637	.95728	.95818	.95907	.95994	.96080	.96164	.96246	.96327
1.8	.96407	.96485	.96562	.96638	.96712	.96784	.96856	.96926	.96995	.97062
1.9	.97128	.97193	.97257	.97320	.97381	.97441	.97500	.97558	.97615	.97670
2.0	.97725	.97778	.97831	.97882	.97932	.97982	.98030	.98077	.98124	.98169
2.1	.98214	.98257	.98300	.98341	.98382	.98422	.98461	.98500	.98537	.98574
2.2	.98610	.98645	.98679	.98713	.98745	.98778	.98809	.98840	.98870	.98899
2.3	.98928	.98956	.98983	$.9^2 0097$	$.9^2 0358$	$.9^2 0613$	$.9^2 0863$	$.9^2 1106$	$.9^2 1344$	$.9^2 1576$
2.4	$.9^2 1802$	$.9^2 2024$	$.9^2 2240$	$.9^2 2451$	$.9^2 2656$	$.9^2 2857$	$.9^2 3053$	$.9^2 3244$	$.9^2 3431$	$.9^2 3613$
2.5	$.9^2 3790$	$.9^2 3963$	$.9^2 4132$	$.9^2 4297$	$.9^2 4457$	$.9^2 4614$	$.9^2 4766$	$.9^2 4915$	$.9^2 5060$	$.9^2 5201$
2.6	$.9^2 5339$	$.9^2 5473$	$.9^2 5604$	$.9^2 5731$	$.9^2 5855$	$.9^2 5975$	$.9^2 6093$	$.9^2 6207$	$.9^2 6319$	$.9^2 6427$
2.7	$.9^2 6533$	$.9^2 6636$	$.9^2 6736$	$.9^2 6833$	$.9^2 6928$	$.9^2 7020$	$.9^2 7110$	$.9^2 7197$	$.9^2 7282$	$.9^2 7365$
2.8	$.9^2 7445$	$.9^2 7523$	$.9^2 7599$	$.9^2 7673$	$.9^2 7744$	$.9^2 7814$	$.9^2 7882$	$.9^2 7948$	$.9^2 8012$	$.9^2 8074$
2.9	$.9^2 8134$	$.9^2 8193$	$.9^2 8250$	$.9^2 8305$	$.9^2 8359$	$.9^2 8411$	$.9^2 8462$	$.9^2 8511$	$.9^2 8559$	$.9^2 8605$
3.0	$.9^2 8650$	$.9^2 8694$	$.9^2 8736$	$.9^2 8777$	$.9^2 8817$	$.9^2 8856$	$.9^2 8893$	$.9^2 8930$	$.9^2 8965$	$.9^2 8999$
3.1	$.9^3 0324$	$.9^3 0646$	$.9^3 0957$	$.9^3 1260$	$.9^3 1553$	$.9^3 1836$	$.9^3 2112$	$.9^3 2378$	$.9^3 2636$	$.9^3 2886$
3.2	$.9^3 3129$	$.9^3 3363$	$.9^3 3590$	$.9^3 3810$	$.9^3 4024$	$.9^3 4230$	$.9^3 4429$	$.9^3 4623$	$.9^3 4810$	$.9^3 4991$
3.3	$.9^3 5166$	$.9^3 5335$	$.9^3 5499$	$.9^3 5658$	$.9^3 5811$	$.9^3 5959$	$.9^3 6103$	$.9^3 6242$	$.9^3 6376$	$.9^3 6505$
3.4	$.9^3 6631$	$.9^3 6752$	$.9^3 6869$	$.9^3 6982$	$.9^3 7091$	$.9^3 7197$	$.9^3 7299$	$.9^3 7398$	$.9^3 7493$	$.9^3 7585$
3.5	$.9^3 7674$	$.9^3 7759$	$.9^3 7842$	$.9^3 7922$	$.9^3 7999$	$.9^3 8074$	$.9^3 8146$	$.9^3 8215$	$.9^3 8282$	$.9^3 8347$
3.6	$.9^3 8409$	$.9^3 8469$	$.9^3 8527$	$.9^3 8583$	$.9^3 8637$	$.9^3 8689$	$.9^3 8739$	$.9^3 8787$	$.9^3 8834$	$.9^3 8879$
3.7	$.9^3 8922$	$.9^3 8964$	$.9^4 0039$	$.9^4 0426$	$.9^4 0799$	$.9^4 1158$	$.9^4 1504$	$.9^4 1838$	$.9^4 2159$	$.9^4 2468$
3.8	$.9^4 2765$	$.9^4 3052$	$.9^4 3327$	$.9^4 3593$	$.9^4 3848$	$.9^4 4094$	$.9^4 4331$	$.9^4 4558$	$.9^4 4777$	$.9^4 4988$
3.9	$.9^4 5190$	$.9^4 5385$	$.9^4 5573$	$.9^4 5753$	$.9^4 5926$	$.9^4 6092$	$.9^4 6253$	$.9^4 6406$	$.9^4 6554$	$.9^4 6696$
4.0	$.9^4 6833$	$.9^4 6964$	$.9^4 7090$	$.9^4 7211$	$.9^4 7327$	$.9^4 7439$	$.9^4 7546$	$.9^4 7649$	$.9^4 7748$	$.9^4 7843$
4.1	$.9^4 7934$	$.9^4 8022$	$.9^4 8106$	$.9^4 8186$	$.9^4 8263$	$.9^4 8338$	$.9^4 8409$	$.9^4 8477$	$.9^4 8542$	$.9^4 8605$
4.2	$.9^4 8665$	$.9^4 8723$	$.9^4 8778$	$.9^4 8832$	$.9^4 8882$	$.9^4 8931$	$.9^4 8978$	$.9^5 0226$	$.9^5 0655$	$.9^5 1066$
4.3	$.9^5 1460$	$.9^5 1837$	$.9^5 2199$	$.9^5 2545$	$.9^5 2876$	$.9^5 3193$	$.9^5 3497$	$.9^5 3788$	$.9^5 4066$	$.9^5 4332$
4.4	$.9^5 4587$	$.9^5 4831$	$.9^5 5065$	$.9^5 5288$	$.9^5 5502$	$.9^5 5706$	$.9^5 5902$	$.9^5 6089$	$.9^5 6268$	$.9^5 6439$
4.5	$.9^5 6602$	$.9^5 6759$	$.9^5 6908$	$.9^5 7051$	$.9^5 7187$	$.9^5 7318$	$.9^5 7442$	$.9^5 7561$	$.9^5 7675$	$.9^5 7784$
4.6	$.9^5 7003$	$.9^5 7987$	$.9^5 8081$	$.9^5 8172$	$.9^5 8258$	$.9^5 8340$	$.9^5 8419$	$.9^5 8494$	$.9^5 8566$	$.9^5 8634$
4.7	$.9^5 8679$	$.9^5 8761$	$.9^5 8821$	$.9^5 8877$	$.9^5 8931$	$.9^5 8983$	$.9^6 0320$	$.9^6 0789$	$.9^6 1235$	$.9^6 1661$
4.8	$.9^6 2067$	$.9^6 2453$	$.9^6 2822$	$.9^6 3173$	$.9^6 3508$	$.9^6 3827$	$.9^6 4131$	$.9^6 4420$	$.9^6 4696$	$.9^6 4958$
4.9	$.9^6 5208$	$.9^6 5446$	$.9^6 5673$	$.9^6 5889$	$.9^6 6094$	$.9^6 6289$	$.9^6 6475$	$.9^6 6652$	$.9^6 6821$	$.9^6 6981$

Source: W. S. Peters and G. W. Summers, *Statistical Analysis for Business Decisions* (Englewood Cliffs, N.J.: Prentice Hall, 1968), pp. 466–69.

Appendix B. *Percentiles of the Chi-Square Distribution.*

| | | | | | Probability in Per Cent | | | | | |
m \ P	0.05	0.1	0.5	1.0	2.5	5.0	10.0	20.0	30.0	40.0
1	$.0^6393$	$.0^5157$	$.0^4393$	$.0^3157$	$.0^3982$	$.0^2393$	.0158	.0642	.148	.275
2	$.0^2100$	$.0^2200$	.0100	.0201	.0506	.103	.211	.446	.713	1.02
3	.0153	.0243	.0717	.115	.216	.352	.584	1.00	1.42	1.87
4	.0639	.0908	.207	.297	.484	.711	1.06	1.65	2.19	2.75
5	.158	.210	.412	.554	.831	1.15	1.61	2.34	3.00	3.66
6	.299	.381	.676	.872	1.24	1.64	2.20	3.07	3.83	4.57
7	.485	.598	.989	1.24	1.69	2.17	2.83	3.82	4.67	5.49
8	.710	.857	1.34	1.65	2.18	2.73	3.49	4.59	5.53	6.42
9	.972	1.15	1.73	2.09	2.70	3.33	4.17	5.38	6.39	7.36
10	1.26	1.48	2.16	2.56	3.25	3.94	4.87	6.18	7.27	8.30
11	1.59	1.83	2.60	3.05	3.82	4.57	5.58	6.99	8.15	9.24
12	1.93	2.21	3.07	3.57	4.40	5.23	6.30	7.81	9.03	10.2
13	2.31	2.62	3.57	4.11	5.01	5.89	7.04	8.63	9.93	11.1
14	2.70	3.04	4.07	4.66	5.63	6.57	7.79	9.47	10.8	12.1
15	3.11	3.48	4.60	5.23	6.26	7.26	8.55	10.3	11.7	13.0
16	3.54	3.94	5.14	5.81	6.91	7.96	9.31	11.2	12.6	14.0
17	3.98	4.42	5.70	6.41	7.56	8.67	10.1	12.0	13.5	14.9
18	4.44	4.90	6.26	7.01	8.23	9.39	10.9	12.9	14.4	15.9

19	4.91	5.41	6.84	7.63	8.91	10.1	11.7	13.7	15.4	16.9
20	5.40	5.92	7.43	8.26	9.59	10.9	12.4	14.6	16.3	17.8
21	5.90	6.45	8.03	8.90	10.3	11.6	13.2	15.4	17.2	18.8
22	6.40	6.98	8.64	9.54	11.0	12.3	14.0	16.3	18.1	19.7
23	6.92	7.53	9.26	10.2	11.7	13.1	14.8	17.2	19.0	20.7
24	7.45	8.08	9.89	10.9	12.4	13.8	15.7	18.1	19.9	21.7
25	7.99	8.65	10.5	11.5	13.1	14.6	16.5	18.9	20.9	22.6
26	8.54	9.22	11.2	12.2	13.8	15.4	17.3	19.8	21.8	23.6
27	9.09	9.80	11.8	12.9	14.6	16.2	18.1	20.7	22.7	24.5
28	9.66	10.4	12.5	13.6	15.3	16.9	18.9	21.6	23.6	25.5
29	10.2	11.0	13.1	14.3	16.0	17.7	19.8	22.5	24.6	26.5
30	10.8	11.6	13.8	15.0	16.8	18.5	20.6	23.4	25.5	27.4
40	16.9	17.9	20.7	22.2	24.4	26.5	29.1	32.3	34.9	37.1
50	23.5	24.7	28.0	29.7	32.4	34.8	37.7	41.4	44.3	46.9
60	30.3	31.7	35.5	37.5	40.5	43.2	46.5	50.6	53.8	56.6
70	37.5	39.0	43.3	45.4	48.8	51.7	55.3	59.9	63.3	66.4
80	44.8	46.5	51.2	53.5	57.2	60.4	64.3	69.2	72.9	76.2
90	52.3	54.2	59.2	61.8	65.6	69.1	73.3	78.6	82.5	86.0
100	59.9	61.9	67.3	70.1	74.2	77.9	82.4	87.1	92.1	95.8

Source: W. S. Peters and G. W. Summers, *Statistical Analysis for Business Decisions* (Englewood Cliffs, N.J.: Prentice Hall, 1968), pp. 470–73.

Appendix B. (cont.) *Percentiles of the Chi-Square Distribution.*

m	\\ P	50.0	60.0	70.0	80.0	Probability in Per Cent 90.0	95.0	97.5	99.0	99.5	99.9	99.95
1		.455	.708	1.07	1.64	2.71	3.84	5.02	6.63	7.88	10.8	12.1
2		1.39	1.83	2.41	3.22	4.61	5.99	7.38	9.21	10.6	13.8	15.2
3		2.37	2.95	3.67	4.64	6.25	7.81	9.35	11.3	12.8	16.3	17.7
4		3.36	4.04	4.88	5.99	7.78	9.49	11.1	13.3	14.9	18.5	20.0
5		4.35	5.13	6.06	7.29	9.24	11.1	12.8	15.1	16.7	20.5	22.1
6		5.35	6.21	7.23	8.56	10.6	12.6	14.4	16.8	18.5	22.5	24.1
7		6.35	7.28	8.38	9.80	12.0	14.1	16.0	18.5	20.3	24.3	26.0
8		7.34	8.35	9.52	11.0	13.4	15.5	17.5	20.1	22.0	26.1	27.9
9		8.34	9.41	10.7	12.2	14.7	16.9	19.0	21.7	23.6	27.9	29.7
10		9.34	10.5	11.8	13.4	16.0	18.3	20.5	23.2	25.2	29.6	31.4
11		10.3	11.5	12.9	14.6	17.3	19.7	21.9	24.7	26.8	31.3	33.1
12		11.3	12.6	14.0	15.8	18.5	21.0	23.3	26.2	28.3	32.9	34.8
13		12.3	13.6	15.1	17.0	19.8	22.4	24.7	27.7	29.8	34.5	36.5
14		13.3	14.7	16.2	18.2	21.1	23.7	26.1	29.1	31.3	36.1	38.1
15		14.3	15.7	17.3	19.3	22.3	25.0	27.5	30.6	32.8	37.7	39.7
16		15.3	16.8	18.4	20.5	23.5	26.3	28.8	32.0	34.3	39.3	41.3
17		16.3	17.8	19.5	21.6	24.8	27.6	30.2	33.4	35.7	40.8	42.9

18	17.3	18.9	20.6	22.8	26.0	28.9	31.5	34.8	37.2	42.3	44.4
19	18.3	19.9	21.7	23.9	27.2	30.1	32.9	36.2	38.6	43.8	46.0
20	19.3	21.0	22.8	25.0	28.4	31.4	34.2	37.6	40.0	45.3	47.5
21	20.3	22.0	23.9	26.2	29.6	32.7	35.5	38.9	41.4	46.8	49.0
22	21.3	23.0	24.9	27.3	30.8	33.9	36.8	40.3	42.8	48.3	50.5
23	22.3	24.1	26.0	28.4	32.0	35.2	38.1	41.6	44.2	49.7	52.0
24	23.3	25.1	27.1	29.6	33.2	36.4	39.4	43.0	45.6	51.2	53.5
25	24.3	26.1	28.2	30.7	34.4	37.7	40.6	44.3	46.9	52.6	54.9
26	25.3	27.2	29.2	31.8	35.6	38.9	41.9	45.6	48.3	54.1	56.4
27	26.3	28.2	30.3	32.9	36.7	40.1	43.2	47.0	49.6	55.5	57.9
28	27.3	29.2	31.4	34.0	37.9	41.3	44.5	48.3	51.0	56.9	59.3
29	28.3	30.3	32.5	35.1	39.1	42.6	45.7	49.6	52.3	58.3	60.7
30	29.3	31.3	33.5	36.3	40.3	43.8	47.0	50.9	53.7	59.7	62.2
40	39.3	41.6	44.2	47.3	51.8	55.8	59.3	63.7	66.8	73.4	76.1
50	49.3	51.9	54.7	58.2	63.2	67.5	71.4	76.2	79.5	86.7	89.6
60	59.3	62.1	65.2	69.0	74.4	79.1	83.3	84.4	92.0	99.6	102.7
70	69.3	72.4	75.7	79.7	85.5	90.5	95.0	100.4	104.2	112.3	115.6
80	79.3	82.6	86.1	90.4	96.6	101.9	106.6	112.3	116.3	124.8	128.3
90	89.3	92.8	96.5	101.1	107.6	113.1	111.1	124.1	128.3	137.2	140.8
100	99.3	102.9	106.9	111.7	118.5	124.3	129.6	135.8	140.2	149.4	153.2

Source: W. S. Peters and G. W. Summers, *Statistical Analysis for Business Decisions* (Englewood Cliffs, N.J.: Prentice Hall, 1968), pp. 470–73.

Appendix C. *Percentiles of the t Distribution.**

m	$t_{.60}$	$t_{.70}$	$t_{.80}$	$t_{.90}$	$t_{.95}$	$t_{.975}$	$t_{.99}$	$t_{.995}$
1	.325	.727	1.376	3.078	6.314	12.706	31.821	63.657
2	.289	.617	1.061	1.886	2.920	4.303	5.965	9.925
3	.277	.584	.978	1.638	2.353	3.182	4.541	5.841
4	.271	.569	.941	1.533	2.132	2.776	3.747	4.604
5	.267	.559	.920	1.476	2.015	2.571	3.365	4.032
6	.265	.553	.906	1.440	1.943	2.447	3.143	3.707
7	.263	.549	.896	1.415	1.895	2.365	2.998	3.499
8	.262	.546	.889	1.397	1.860	2.306	2.896	3.355
9	.261	.543	.883	1.383	1.833	2.262	2.821	3.250
10	.260	.542	.879	1.372	1.812	2.228	2.764	3.169
11	.260	.540	.876	1.363	1.796	2.201	2.718	3.106
12	.259	.539	.873	1.356	1.782	2.179	2.681	3.055
13	.259	.538	.870	1.350	1.771	2.160	2.650	3.012
14	.258	.537	.868	1.345	1.761	2.145	2.624	2.977
15	.258	.536	.866	1.341	1.753	2.131	2.602	2.947
16	.258	.535	.865	1.337	1.746	2.120	2.583	2.921
17	.257	.534	.863	1.333	1.740	2.110	2.567	2.898
18	.257	.534	.862	1.330	1.734	2.101	2.552	2.878

m	$t_{.40}$	$t_{.30}$	$t_{.20}$	$t_{.10}$	$t_{.05}$	$t_{.025}$	$t_{.01}$	$t_{.005}$
19	.257	.533	.861	1.328	1.729	2.093	2.539	2.861
20	.257	.533	.860	1.325	1.725	2.086	2.528	2.845
21	.257	.532	.859	1.323	1.721	2.080	2.518	2.831
22	.256	.532	.858	1.321	1.717	2.074	2.508	2.819
23	.256	.532	.858	1.319	1.714	2.069	2.500	2.807
24	.256	.531	.857	1.318	1.711	2.064	2.492	2.797
25	.256	.531	.856	1.316	1.708	2.060	2.485	2.787
26	.256	.531	.856	1.315	1.706	2.056	2.479	2.779
27	.256	.531	.855	1.314	1.703	2.052	2.473	2.771
28	.256	.530	.855	1.313	1.701	2.048	2.467	2.763
29	.256	.530	.854	1.311	1.699	2.045	2.462	2.756
30	.256	.530	.854	1.310	1.697	2.042	2.457	2.750
40	.255	.529	.851	1.303	1.684	2.021	2.423	2.704
60	.254	.527	.848	1.296	1.671	2.000	2.390	2.660
120	.254	.526	.845	1.289	1.658	1.980	2.358	2.617
∞	.253	.524	.842	1.282	1.645	1.960	2.326	2.576

*When the table is read from the foot, the tabled values are to be prefixed with a negative sign.

Source: W. S. Peters and G. W. Summers, *Statistical Analysis for Business Decisions* (Englewood Cliffs, N.J.: Prentice Hall, 1968), pp. 474–75.

Index